THE BIG BOOK OF SIDES

THE BIG BOOK OF
SIDES

MORE THAN 450 RECIPES FOR THE BEST VEGETABLES,
GRAINS, SALADS, BREADS, SAUCES, AND MORE

Rick Rodgers

BALLANTINE BOOKS
NEW YORK

Published in the United States by Ballantine Books,
an imprint of Random House,
a division of Random House LLC,
a Penguin Random House Company, New York.

BALLANTINE and the HOUSE colophon are registered trademarks of Random House LLC.

Library of Congress Cataloging-in-Publication Data
Rodgers, Rick.
The big book of sides : more than 450 recipes for the best vegetables,
grains, salads, breads, sauces, and more / Rick Rodgers.
pages cm
Includes index.
ISBN 978-0-345-54818-4
eBook ISBN 978-0-345-54819-1
1. Cooking (Vegetables) 2. Side dishes (Cooking) I. Title.
TX801.R68 2014
641.6'5—dc23   2014028382

Photography by Ben Fink

Printed in the United States of America on acid-free paper

www.ballantinebooks.com

9 8 7 6 5 4 3 2 1

First Edition

Book design by Diane Hobbing

CONTENTS

CONTENTS

INTRODUCTION

When a cook decides on a main course, the meal is only half planned. What about the side dishes? After all, what is a burger without fries? Or barbecue without coleslaw, baked beans, or macaroni and cheese (or all three)? Thanksgiving is a parade of side dishes to go with the turkey: sweet potatoes, gravy, cranberry sauce, mashed potatoes, stuffing, and more. But when the cook needs to go beyond these iconic matches, it is easy to draw a blank.

The Big Book of Sides was written to help you choose luscious additions to the main course. This exhaustive cookbook gives the humble side dish its due, elevating it to its proper, important place on the menu. Vegetables of all kinds, pasta dishes, beans, grains, home-baked rolls and savory quick breads, side salads and dressing, sauces, even easy pickles . . . they are here.

I have been collecting side dish recipes for many years. When I was a caterer, I had an international clientele, and I had to be proficient in many different cuisines. For a holiday meal, when the wife was Irish and the husband was Jewish, I had to cook up a meal that satisfied both sides of the family. (I am thinking of my clients, actors Anne Meara and Jerry Stiller, for whom I cooked many meals, and of the holidays where I had to make both colcannon and potato kugel.) Birthday dinners for kids, special meals to impress the boss, backyard cookouts with barbecued ribs, Easter feasts, Passover seders . . . I cooked them all and kept notes.

In addition to my own cookbooks, I often work with chefs to help them create their books. I've worked with celebrity chefs in New York and Chicago, including one of the best-known Chinese restaurants in Manhattan, bakers all over the country, Mexican and Latino restaurants, and more. These excursions into various cuisines and cooking techniques have also informed my cooking, and I have been sure to include a wide variety of ethnic dishes in this collection. And many of my cookbook author colleagues have contributed their recipes.

I come from a family that gives parties at the drop of a hat. It's a large group (my great-grandmother had nine children, and most of them had large families), and it seemed as if there was a birthday party or holiday dinner every weekend. My great-aunts had an unspoken competition for the title of best cook in the family, so I grew up with a never-ending array of side dish classics like potato salads, coleslaws, baked beans, tossed green salads, garlic bread, and more. You didn't need to be a professional chef to figure out that side dishes could make the meal. Many of these beloved family heirloom recipes are included in this book.

All of this experience comes in handy when working with the ever-changing culinary scene. You have to move fast to keep up with the latest ingredients at the market, and many foods that were once esoteric have mainstreamed. This is especially true of produce—some of my favorite recipes were created when an unusual vegetable showed up in my weekly summer CSA delivery. One week, it was kohlrabi, and by the time I had cooked it all, I had a new appreciation for this humble green knob. While I have been sure to offer recipes for classic side dishes, you will find plenty of new favorites, as well.

The Big Book of Sides reflects how I cook at home for my daily meals. My personal cooking style is to produce the most amount of flavor with the least effort. If the main course is complicated, the side dishes should be less so. This isn't just a question of time or expense. In my opinion, a menu can be ruined if there are too many bold flavors on the plate competing for attention. For everyday cooking, when we are all racing against the clock, it is important to have a repertoire of simple, flavorful side dishes. Along with the actual formula for each recipe, I've added appropriate tips to guide you to success every time. But when you need a showstopper for a company meal (say, a caramelized onion tarte Tatin or a luxurious butternut squash and leek gratin), you'll find them here, too.

My main goal with *The Big Book of Sides* is to make the book useful for everyone, whether you are an experienced cook or a beginner. After the title and yield amount, every recipe has basic information to help you decide, at a glance, if this is the one for a specific dish or occasion.

Serve with: This lists the most common main courses that you might want to serve with this side dish. I've matched these according to my experience.

Prep Time: I have estimated the time needed to prepare the ingredients with average kitchen skills. If you are quick with a knife, you will spend less time getting the ingredients ready. I have also included other timing estimates, such as rising times for dough, refrigeration, or marinating.

Cooking Time: In this section, I have added up the minutes required to cook the dish, and rounded them up to the nearest increment of five to allow some leeway. Because of variables (starting with cooking skill levels, which include how fast you can chop an onion or mince herbs), prep and cooking times are never accurate to the minute, and are only provided as an "at-a-glance" general aid.

Make Ahead: Especially when preparing a large menu for entertaining, make-ahead suggestions can be helpful. If the dish or some components can be made ahead, it states so under this heading. More detailed instructions can be found in the recipe. If a recipe is not complicated and best when served right after making, I do not provide the make-ahead tip. That doesn't mean you can't warm up the leftovers for another meal.

Categories: I have designated a wide range of occasions and cooking styles that, in my opinion, apply to the recipe.

Weeknight Suppers: An uncomplicated side dish that usually takes a relatively short time to prepare and cook for a busy weeknight.

Family Favorite: Food that is guaranteed to be a hit with kids.

Holiday Feasts: Recipes that are specific to holidays, including summer cookouts.

Company Fare: These side dishes are sure to impress dinner guests, and usually require a bit more time and effort.

Buffet Dish: Recipes for a buffet menu (taking into consideration if they are easy to serve and eat without a knife), or "covered dishes" that are easy to transport to potlucks and the like.

Retro Recipe: Nostalgic side dish recipes that may be part of the American culinary experience, even if they include a can of condensed soup.

Cooking Classic: An essential recipe that should be in every cook's repertoire.

Vegetarian: These are meatless sides, some of which are hearty enough to serve as main courses. For a complete list of the vegetarian dishes that can double as sides and main courses, see page 13. There are gluten-free and vegan options within this category, but I do not list them separately.

So, whether you are planning a holiday meal for a crowd, or you need to fill out the menu for a weeknight supper from a lone bag of carrots in the refrigerator, you will never be stumped for a side dish again.

Rick Rodgers

THE BIG BOOK OF SIDES

GETTING IT TO THE TABLE

Cooking Methods

The most obvious way to vary your side dishes begins with the choice of ingredients. But choosing one cooking technique over another will also change things up. For example, roasting will add sweet, caramelized notes, while steaming retains the food's natural characteristics, and braising creates an interchange of flavors between the food and the cooking liquid. Most of these techniques refer to vegetables because they are the stars of the side dish menu.

Cooking methods are separated into two large categories: moist heat and dry heat. Moist-heat methods (boiling, simmering, blanching, steaming, braising, and pan-roasting) require liquids, including water and steam, to cook the food. Dry-heat methods (sautéing, stir-frying, roasting, baking, grilling, and deep-frying) do not use water as their cooking element, and the heat source does the work.

Moist-Heat Cooking Methods

Boiling, Simmering, and Blanching

Boiling cooks the food in strongly bubbling hot water (with a temperature of 212ºF at sea level, although you won't need a thermometer!). This technique does a relatively fast job of softening tough vegetables, so it is one of the most common methods for root vegetables, corn, and the like, and boiling also does a great job of brightening the food's color. Its main drawback is that nutrients can be leached into the cooking water.

Simmering uses water heated to a slightly lower temperature than boiling to create smaller bubbles for a more delicate cooking method for tender ingredients.

Blanching is a technique that partially cooks the food by boiling it briefly, and then finishes the cooking later with a second method, usually sautéing.

To cook by boiling, simmering, or blanching, fill a large saucepan or pot from one-half to two-thirds full with cold water. (The jury is out on whether you can use hot tap water to save time, because some experts believe that old hot-water pipes leach lead, so cold water is safer from a health perspective.) The water should be salted—enough that you can taste the salt, but so that the water isn't as salty as seawater. If you require a measurement, use about 2 teaspoons kosher salt (or 1½ teaspoons fine sea or table salt) for every quart of water. The salt isn't just there for flavor; it also helps soften the vegetables for quicker cooking. Cover the saucepan and bring the water to a full boil over high heat.

The vegetables should be cut into uniform pieces that will cook in about 5 minutes. (Potatoes and other very hard vegetables will take longer to cook, but evenly sized pieces are still important.) Cooking in liquid breaks down the cell structure in vegetables, so whether you are boiling, simmering, or blanching, check the food occasionally to avoid overcooking. The best tool for this is the tip of a small, sharp knife.

When the food is cooked to the desired texture, drain the contents of the pot in a large colander. In most cases, the food is now ready to season and serve—rinsing will not "set the color," so it is totally unnecessary at this point.

However, if the vegetables are going to be reheated later, stop the cooking by rinsing them under cold running water. It is not always necessary to transfer them to a bowl of iced water, a step that just uses another bowl and depletes your supply of ice cubes. You can do it if you wish, but be sure to remove any unmelted ice cubes from the water after the vegetables cool. Drain the cooled vegetables well and pat them dry with clean kitchen towels before storing them in plastic zip-tight bags.

Steaming

Steam, the vapor from boiling water, is actually as hot as the water itself, and can cook food on a rack in a closed pot. **Steaming**'s gentle heat retains the vegetable's characteristics (shape, flavor, and texture) and nutrients better than boiling in water, but it can take more time.

Place a collapsible steamer rack in a large saucepan. The saucepan must be large enough to contain the vegetables without crowding so the steam can travel freely around the food. Pour in enough water to come just below the insert. (If you are using a steamer-style saucepan, just add an inch or two of water to the saucepan.) Cover it tightly and bring the water to a full boil over high heat, with a visible head of steam.

Add the food (be careful of the hot vapors) and cover it again. Adjust the heat to maintain the full steam. If you are steaming food (such as artichokes) for more than 15 minutes, check the water level and add more boiling water as needed so it doesn't boil away. Only check when you think it is really necessary, because opening the lid will drop the temperature.

Braising and Pan-Roasting

Sturdy vegetables (such as members of the onion family and other roots) often benefit from **braising**, the technique of slow simmering in a moderate amount of liquid. The gentle cooking tenderizes the vegetable at a relaxed pace, helping it keep its shape. Braising also allows for an exchange of flavors, and the liquid is often turned into a sauce. **Pan-roasting** is similar to braising, but the vegetables are browned first for a bit of rich, caramelized flavor.

Vegetables can be braised in a skillet, but for larger quantities, use a saucepan. Sometimes seasoning vegetables (onions, garlic, and their friends) are cooked in the skillet first as a base flavor. Add the main ingredient with just enough liquid (broth, water, wine, or even milk) to barely cover the vegetables, and bring it to a simmer over medium heat. Thin vegetables, such as asparagus, will use less liquid, but root vegetables will take more. Reduce the heat to medium-low to maintain the simmer, and cover the cooking vessel. Braise the vegetables until they are tender. Often, the lid is removed during the last part of cooking to reduce the liquid and intensify its flavor.

Dry-Heat Cooking Methods

Sautéing

One of the quickest cooking methods, **sautéing** cooks the food in a small amount of fat. *Sauté* comes from the French word "to jump," and the food is tossed or stirred in the pan on a fairly constant basis to keep it from burning.

Oils with high smoke points are best for sautéing. (The smoke point is the temperature where the oil begins to smoke, which detrimentally changes its chemical composition and flavor.) Canola, olive, grapeseed, or peanut oils are equally good.

Choose a heavy-bottomed skillet to protect food from the high heat of the burner. Whether you use a pan with high sides to contain the food or one with sloping sides to facilitate turning the food is a matter of personal choice. Heat the fat (butter or oil) in a skillet over medium-high heat until the oil starts to shimmer or the foam from the melted butter begins to subside. (In some cases, to provide an extra-hot surface for cooking the food, the oil is added to a preheated skillet, as described below for a wok. Don't try this with butter, though, as it will burn when it comes into contact with the hot pan.)

The ingredients should be dry before adding them to the skillet. Add the food and cook, stirring occasionally, until it is cooked through. How much you stir depends on the amount of browning you want.

Stir-Frying

Stir-frying is synonymous with Asian cooking. The food is cooked over very high heat with constant stirring. The curved sides of a wok make turning the food over easier, but I often use a very large skillet with success.

Heat the skillet or wok over high heat for a minute or two—if you hold your hand an inch or two above its surface, you should feel the heat. (Do not preheat a skillet with nonstick coating over high heat as this could decompose the surface.) Add the oil and tilt the skillet to coat the inside. Add the food and cook, stirring almost constantly with a large spoon, until it is cooked through.

(A note on woks: I love my spun-metal wok, but it requires special handling, just like a cast-iron skillet. To build up a natural nonstick patina, cook in it often, even if you aren't making a Chinese recipe. Any cooking technique that uses oil will help "season" the surface. Never wash the wok in soapy water, or you'll remove the seasoning. Just wipe it out with moist paper towels and a large sprinkle of kosher salt, and dry it immediately to prevent rusting.)

Roasting and Baking

This high-temperature technique cooks uncovered food in a hot oven. If the temperature isn't high enough, the vegetables will not develop the delicious browned surface that makes them unique. Solid vegetables, from carrots and potatoes to cauliflower and winter squash, can be **roasted** just as successfully as tender asparagus—it's just a matter of timing.

A large, rimmed baking sheet (also known as a half-sheet pan, measuring about 18 × 13 inches) is a required piece of equipment for roasting. As with the other cooking techniques, to avoid a build-up of steam that would prevent browning, the food should not be crowded on the sheet.

I find that 425°F is a good average temperature for roasting—not too hot and not too cold. Cut the vegetables into uniform pieces as directed in the recipe. Toss them with a tablespoon or two of oil, and spread them on an oiled baking sheet. I do not add salt and pepper at this point because the salt can draw liquid from the vegetables and make more steam to inhibit browning. Roast until a thin, golden brown crust has formed on the undersides of the vegetables. Using a metal spatula, flip the vegetables and continue roasting them until they are tender. If you are adding flavorings, such as garlic or herbs, add them toward the end of roasting so they don't burn.

Also accomplished in an oven, **baking** cooks food at a more moderate temperature, and browning is not necessarily a desired outcome. For example, baked potatoes are cooked at a lower temperature than roasted, and whether or not the skins are browned is immaterial.

Grilling

Grilling is the only cooking method that does not require a vessel to hold the food—it is placed right on the cooking grate. Gas grills make grilling a breeze, and you can control the cooking temperature with the turn of a knob. I am a die-hard charcoal grilling fan because it gives the food a stronger smoke flavor. However, when it comes to side dishes, I turn on my gas grill to save time. Also, it takes about 20 minutes for smoke to really infuse the food, and since most side dishes cook in less time, there is no need to build a charcoal fire for flavor reasons.

If you are cooking with a charcoal grill, build the fire and let it burn until the coals are covered with white ash. Spread the coals out, but leave a border around the edge of the fire. At this point, the coals are very hot, about 550°F. In fact, while it is a good temperature for searing steaks, it is too hot for cooking vegetables. Let the coals burn down, uncovered, until they have reached medium heat: You should be able to hold your palm about an inch away from the grill grate surface for 3 to 4 seconds. If you have a thermometer in the grill lid, it should register 350° to 450°F.

For a gas grill, ignite the heat source and let the grill preheat with the lid closed for at least 15 minutes. Now adjust the heat as needed to the desired temperature, about 400°F. If your grill thermometer doesn't give precise numerical temperatures, go for the "medium" range.

Grilled food is cooked with either direct or indirect heat. Direct cooking, where the food is placed directly over the heat source, is used when the food is thin and delicate and will cook in less than 15 minutes or so. With indirect cooking, only one side of the grill is heated, and the food is placed away from the heat source to be cooked by the radiant heat.

For both charcoal and gas grills, always cook with the lid closed, which traps the heat inside of the grill and reduces the oxygen that feeds the fire and can encourage flare-ups. But do open the top and bottom vents of a charcoal grill to provide some oxygen, or you could extinguish the flame altogether.

Use a wire grill brush to thoroughly clean the grill grate before adding the food. I never oil the grill grates because the oil only burns and leaves ashy marks on the food. It is much better to oil the food itself, or let the oil in a marinade do the lubricating.

Deep-Frying

Deep-frying is only considered a dry-heat method because it does not use water. Instead, the cooking medium is hot oil. Most cooks use deep-frying as an infrequent treat, but it is still important to know how to do it well, as nothing gives food such an irresistibly crisp exterior.

The ideal temperature for deep-frying is 365°F, which allows the outer crust to form while the food cooks through. A deep-frying thermometer is really indispensable. A low-tech alternative is to dip the handle of a wooden spoon or chopstick in the oil. If tiny bubbles form immediately around the wood, the oil is hot enough. I like an instant-read probe thermometer (the kind with a wire cord leading to a digital display unit) because, unlike the standing clip-on model, it can be used to read the temperature in a shallow skillet.

Depending on the size of the food (it needs to float on the oil surface without touching the bottom of the pan), use either a large, heavy skillet or saucepan. I have come to prefer a skillet because it uses less oil. To hold and drain the fried food, place a large wire cooling rack on a large rimmed baking sheet. This works better than draining on paper towels because steam collects and softens the food where it comes in contact with the towels.

The type of oil is immaterial—any neutral-flavored one is fine. Pour in enough oil to come about halfway up the sides of the skillet or saucepan and heat over high heat until the oil reads 365°F on the instant-read thermometer. In batches, add the food to the hot oil without crowding, and cook according to the recipe directions until it is golden brown. Use a wire spider (a very large mesh strainer on a handle) or a slotted spoon to transfer the food to the wire cooling rack. Keep the food warm in a preheated 200°F oven until it has all been cooked, and then serve it immediately.

Never reuse deep-frying oil. It will probably go rancid before you have the chance to use it again, even if stored in the refrigerator. Just let it cool and discard it.

Picking Sides

Perhaps part of the problem of choosing a side dish or two (or more) for a main course is simply that the cook is faced with so many delicious options. Here are some different approaches for zeroing in on the ones that are right for the meal at hand.

Seasonal: Many cooks start the selection process by using produce at the height of its traditional season. We can buy many vegetables and fruits year-round, but that doesn't mean they are at their flavorful best. Pink tomatoes in January, flavorless asparagus in November . . . most of us have eaten these foods, but with little true enjoyment. Serve locally harvested food during its true season and the side dish will sing with flavor.

Ethnic Flavors: Matching dishes from the same cuisine is an obvious method for choosing side dishes. An Italian pasta dinner cries out for focaccia and a crisp salad with Mediterranean flavors. But you can reach beyond a cuisine's boundaries. For example, all Mediterranean foods share some basic flavor profiles—wine, garlic, and herbs are three common ingredients. In Asian cooking, soy sauce and ginger might be a recurring flavor combination. You don't want to be monotonous by repeating too many flavors, but there should be a running thread.

Accenting Flavors: A good meal has balance and can fail when its flavors compete. Often, it is a case of overkill with too many chilies, herbs, or garlic on everything, not giving the palate a chance to refresh itself. Look for ways to accent one dish with another one that may be its culinary opposite. Acidic foods are especially useful in this way—pickles, sauces, and salads all have a sharp edge that balances out blander foods.

Cooking with Umami: In addition to the "big four" tastes of sweet, sour, bitter, and salty, umami is the fifth taste. It is the deep, rounded (but often indefinable) flavor that you find in such ingredients as soy sauce, anchovies, Parmesan cheese, ketchup, canned tomatoes, mushrooms, fermented foods, and others. These foods have a high proportion of naturally occurring glutamates and certain amino acids, receptors that signal deliciousness to the brain. (Monosodium glutamate is specifically processed to be a food additive.) There is a reason why we find bacon so irresistible—it is loaded with umami, and crispy, salty umami at that. Serving a simple main course (say, pan-cooked chicken breast) with a side that is umami rich (roasted broccoli sprinkled with Parmesan) is a sure-fire way to enhance the entire meal.

Color: When choosing a menu, every cook has to face a culinary fact of life: There is a lot of brown food. Look for side dishes to brighten up the plate. Orange carrots, magenta beets, green spinach, and red radishes are appreciated not only for their flavor, but for the color they bring to the table. The old adage, "You eat with your eyes," has never been so true as we are faced with images of food in the media at every turn.

Texture: Our palates respond positively to crispy foods, and their satisfying crunch sets off a "yummy" (a word I use very selectively) alarm in our brains. I often use chopped nuts to add texture and flavor to side dishes for this reason. But we would get tired of a meal where everything had a snap, crackle, or a pop when we bit into it. Use textures to balance the meal, just as you use seasonings. The comforting smoothness of a purée is the perfect match for a firm cut of meat or chicken, yet roasted oven fries might be a better pairing with delicate fish.

Sauce: Is your main course cooked in a sauce? Then you probably want to avoid another sauce in the side dish. They will only run into each other on the plate and fight in your mouth for attention.

Serving It Up

It can be a bit of a challenge to keep side dishes from cooling off before everyone at the table has been served. This is especially an issue at big holiday feasts, where a lot of people are being served. But a home kitchen is a not a restaurant, and it doesn't have the same capabilities. Nonetheless, there are a few tricks that will help you keep your hot food hot for a longer period of time.

The most obvious thing is to serve the food from warm serving vessels. Even at weeknight meals, this isn't as difficult as it seems. Before heating it, be sure that the vessel is heatproof. Most modern tableware can withstand changes in temperature, but delicate china could crack if exposed to very hot water.

- Fill the bowl or platter with hot tap water and let it stand for a few minutes; toss out the water and dry the vessel.
- Fill a microwave-safe bowl with hot water and microwave on High for 30 to 45 seconds; let the vessel stand for up to 5 minutes. Toss out the water and dry the vessel.
- If serving pasta or other boiled foods, put the serving vessel in the sink, then put the colander in the vessel. Drain the food in the colander, letting the hot water fill and warm the vessel. Let the vessel stand while finishing the recipe, then empty and dry it before adding the food.
- Heat the serving vessels in a very low oven (200ºF) for 5 to 10 minutes.
- If you have a warming drawer, put it into action.
- To keep food warm on a buffet, use electric hot plates, fuel-heated chafing dishes, and other appliances or tools. I have used a fondue pot to keep a sauce warm, and a slow cooker to hold mashed potatoes or other vegatables.
- However, a hot serving bowl or platter can be too warm to pass comfortably. Be sure to have clean pot holders or kitchen towels at the table to protect your guests' hands. For a holiday dinner, when I am out shopping, I always pick up an inexpensive pair or two of pot holders at the local dollar store, and set them aside so I don't get them dirty. The pot holders can do double-duty as trivets, too.
- At a large party, check to be sure that you have enough trivets to protect the table from the hot vessels, and spoons (both solid and slotted) for serving.

SPECIAL OCCASION MENUS

I have chosen some of the most common occurrences when you may need some help with selecting side dishes. They are listed in chronological order, starting with New Year's Day in January, and include some year-round menus that I have positioned according to the season in which I serve them most often. I have also provided a list of vegetarian side dishes that can be served as main courses, too.

NEW YEAR'S DAY OPEN HOUSE

This menu goes very well with smoked turkey, ham, or salmon.

- Black-Eyed Peas and Kale Salad with Warm Bacon Vinaigrette
- Potatoes Au Gratin
- Overnight Focaccia
- Deviled Eggs with Horseradish and Bacon
- Stuffed Celery with Liptauer Cheese Spread

SUNDAY ROAST PORK DINNER

Whenever I smell the mouthwatering aroma of roasting pork, it reminds me of Sunday dinners at my grandparents' house. This has become one of my most reliable menus for both casual suppers and holiday dinners.

- Haricots Verts with Shiitakes and Shallots
- Baby Carrots and Apple Sauté with Rosemary
- Celery Root, Potato, and Garlic Gratin

VALENTINE'S DAY STEAK DINNER

Here are some variations on the classic steakhouse sides to complement a sizzling steak. The tomatoes can be made ahead and warmed up with the potatoes.

- "Roasties" (Oven-Fried Potatoes) with Rosemary Salt
- Tomatoes with Mascarpone Spinach
- Sautéed Mushrooms with Garlic and Rosemary

SAINT PATRICK'S DAY CORNED BEEF

The Irish-American celebration calls for corned beef. While many cooks simply boil root vegetables and cabbage in the beef's cooking water, I find that preparing them separately gives much better results.

- Farmhouse Green Cabbage with Root Vegetables and Bacon
- Champ Potato Mash with Buttery Scallions
- Currant and Caraway Soda Bread
- Homemade Sweet and Hot Ale Mustard

EASTER LEG OF LAMB DINNER

Although lamb, asparagus, and peas are available year-round, they symbolize spring and are always on my Easter menu . . . along with eggs, of course.

- Steamed Asparagus with Blender Hollandaise Sauce
- Buttered Fresh Peas with Lettuce
- Celery Root, Potato, and Garlic Gratin
- Buttermilk Cloverleaf Rolls
- Deviled Eggs with Horseradish and Bacon

BAKED HAM BUFFET

A juicy baked ham is one of the most reliable main courses to feed a crowd. I use this menu for Easter and Mother's Day brunch, as well as New Year's open house. These side dishes round out the bill of fare beautifully.

- Smothered Collard Greens
- Butternut Squash and Potato Gratin
- Angel Biscuits
- Bread and Butter Pickles
- Bacon, Onion, and Bourbon Marmalade

PASSOVER

When I was a caterer, I was often hired to cook Passover seders for my clients, so even though I am not Jewish, I gathered some very good recipes as a result.

Asparagus and Pine Nut Sauté

Potato and Leek Kugel

Oranges, Dates, and Shallots on Baby Arugula

Root Vegetable and Fruit Tsimmis

AL FRESCO DINNER

When the weather turns warmer, these sides will go with many grilled meats, chicken, and seafood, especially when they have Mediterranean marinades and herb rubs.

Tomato-Stuffed Bell Peppers

Almost Cobb Salad with Sugar Snap Peas and Corn

Overnight Focaccia

Giardiniera

Italian Salsa Verde

FOURTH OF JULY PICNIC

When hamburgers and hot dogs are on the menu, you can't do better than this menu of delicious versions of old favorites.

Blue Ribbon Potato Salad

Marinated Sweet and Tangy Slaw

Three-Bean Salad with Honey Vinaigrette

Buttermilk Cornbread

Bread and Butter Pickles

BARBECUED RIBS COOKOUT

This is a menu for the dead of summer when smoky, tender ribs are on the menu. If I don't want to deep-fry in the kitchen, I set up an electric skillet outside. And If I don't want to turn on the oven, I "bake" the casserole and beans on the gas grill with indirect medium heat.

Southern-Style Summer Squash Casserole

Sweet and Tangy Beans

Tomato, Grilled Corn, and Basil Salad

Barbecue Shack Chopped Slaw

Scallion and Jalapeño Hush Puppies

OLD-FASHIONED THANKSGIVING

At Thanksgiving, many families demand that nostalgia is served up in heaping portions along with the turkey. Here is a menu that traditionalists will love.

Classic Herb Stuffing

Roasted Brussels Sprouts with Bacon and Maple Syrup

Retro Green Bean Casserole

Make-Ahead Mashed Potato Casserole

Retro Cranberry Gelatin Salad

Old-Fashioned Dinner Rolls

NEW-FASHIONED THANKSGIVING

The flip side of a traditional turkey menu, this spread features old favorites in new guises.

Sourdough and Roasted Root Vegetables Stuffing

Rutabaga, Apple, and Walnut Gratin

Homemade Green Bean and Mushroom Casserole with Crispy Shallots

Lemon Sweet Potatoes with Meringue Topping

Cranberry and Dried Pineapple Mostarda

Brazilian Cheese Rolls

SOUTHERN-STYLE THANKSGIVING

Thanksgiving is a great occasion to cook the satisfying, old-fashioned dishes of the Deep South to accompany a roasted, grilled, or deep-fried turkey.

Ham, Kale, and Cornbread Dressing

Southern Stewed Green Beans with Bacon and Tomatoes

Chipotle Corn Pudding

Buttermilk Mashed Potatoes

Southern Cranberry Sauce

Sweet Potato and Pecan Dinner Rolls

CHRISTMAS EVE BUFFET

The bounty of winter is celebrated in this festive menu that would be great with platters of sliced beef tenderloin or sliced ham.

Mexican Christmas Eve Salad

Annie's Two-Rice "Pizza" Casserole

Carrot Ribbons with Pomegranate Dressing

Pumpernickel Ale Rolls

CHRISTMAS GOOSE

Many families celebrate the holiday season with roast goose, a bird that looks large, but really has enough meat for only about six servings. To stretch the meal, hearty side dishes are in order.

Italian Red Cabbage with Red Wine and Chestnuts

Braised Kohlrabi and Carrots with Lemon and Caraway

German Potato Dumplings

Pumpernickel Ale Rolls

ROAST BEEF CHRISTMAS DINNER

The centuries-old tradition of roast beef for Christmas is still strong. I usually serve a light first course, such as a Celery Rémoulade topped with fresh shrimp.

Brussels Sprouts Chiffonade with Pancetta and Parmesan

Classic Glazed Carrots Vichy

Potato and Fennel Gratin

Herbed Yorkshire Puddings

LABOR DAY IN THE BACKYARD

Smoked brisket, pulled pork, or grilled tri-tip are three main courses that would match up well with this array of all-American sides. You could leave the bacon out of the muffins, and replace the bacon fat with melted butter, but for my guests, there is no such thing as too much bacon.

Dill Pickle Potato Salad

Root Beer Baked Beans

Raw Broccoli Salad with Bacon, Sunflower Seeds, and Raisins

Boiled Corn with BBQ Butter

Jalapeño, Bacon, and Corn Muffins

Pickled Okra

VEGETARIAN MAIN COURSES

Here is a list of hearty dishes that can be served as both sides and main courses.

Whole Roasted Cauliflower with Za'atar Crust

Wild Mushroom and Fontina Tart

Grilled Marinated Portobello Mushrooms

French Chard and Goat Cheese Tian

Poblano and Cheese Casserole

Cajun-Style Stuffed Chayote

Eggplant-Parmesan Gratin

Giambotta

Potato and Fennel Gratin

Tomato-Stuffed Bell Peppers

Butternut Squash and Potato Gratin

Italian Squash Casserole

Zucchini and Scallion Croustade

Onion Tarte Tatin

Potato and Leek Kugel

Annie's Two-Rice "Pizza" Casserole

Macaroni and Cheese with Cheddar and Gruyère

French Macaroni and Cheese with Leeks

Almost-Alfredo Ziti with Creamy Parmesan Sauce

Baked Ziti with Broccoli and Gorgonzola

Stovetop Macaroni and Pimiento Cheese

A NOTE ON BASIC INGREDIENTS

Start with top-notch ingredients, and you're well on your way to cooking a great meal. Salt and cooking oil are two essentials that most cooks use every day, so it is worth taking the time to understand the different kinds.

Salt: I use kosher salt for my everyday cooking, mainly because of its clean, unadulterated taste. Also, its large flakes are easy to see on the food so you have a visual idea of how much you have applied, and they are easy to pick up with your fingertips. There is a difference between the flake size in brands, and I prefer Diamond Crystal (in a red box) to the others. If you use another brand, the amount may have to be adjusted up or down slightly. I like fine table or sea salt for baking because it dissolves more readily in dough and batter.

Oils: Olive oil has become the all-purpose cooking oil of choice for so many cooks for its health prop-erties and flavor. Just as I have at least two kinds of salt in my kitchen, I also use two kinds of olive oil. Extra-virgin olive oil has been minimally processed and has a fuller olive flavor and deep green color. Because it loses its flavor when heated, it is best used uncooked as an ingredient for salad dressings. But it doesn't lose an enormous amount of flavor, so I still will use it for cooking when I want a stronger olive taste. I use less expensive, gold-colored regular olive oil for most of my cooking. (Avoid pomace olive oil, which is cheap and has no flavor at all.)

When you want a neutral flavor, use the vegetable (or seed) oil of your choice. Corn, safflower, or canola are all good choices, or the generic mixed blend vegetable oil. Cooking oils in general have become a slippery slope. Some cooks avoid vegetable and seed oils because of the chemicals used in their extraction, and buy minimally processed expeller-pressed oils. And many of these oils are made from genetically modified ingredients. Because I use these oils in small amounts, I often spend the extra money and buy the all-natural, organic versions.

EAT YOUR VEGETABLES

Vegetables create the most bountiful category of side dishes, if for no other reason than sheer numbers. The produce section at the market is bursting at the seams, and every summer my CSA box and farmer's market offer new surprises. Many classic vegetable sides have become talismans of their seasons—asparagus with hollandaise in the spring, summer corn on the cob slathered with butter, roast squash at an autumn meal, and Brussels sprouts after the first frost.

Listed alphabetically here are the vegetables that grow above the ground, from artichokes to zucchini and other summer squashes, with the root vegetables gathered in the next chapter. Some related vegetables, such as the collards, kale, and mustard in the dark greens section, are grouped together because they share basic information on preparation or cooking procedures. Within each listing, there is a range of side dish recipes using the techniques that show each vegetable at its best.

Artichokes

With a mantle of thorny leaves protecting its tasty heart, it is a wonder that humans ever discovered how to cook and eat the artichoke, the flower bud of a prickly thistle. Cooking the bud yields buttery flesh that is scraped off the leaves with the teeth, eventually revealing the artichoke heart (actually the bottom), which can also be eaten, but avoid the hairy, bitter choke. The most common variety, exclusively grown in California, is the globe artichoke, although you may find Old World purple artichokes at farmer's markets. Artichokes range in size from baby (a little larger than a golf ball) to jumbo (as big as a softball), with an average baseball-sized artichoke as the standard.

Peak Season: Spring and fall.

Purchase: Firm, compact heads that squeak when rubbed. Light brown splotches (caused by cold temperatures and frost) are fine, as long as the artichoke looks moist and fresh.

Storage: Refrigerate unwashed in plastic bags for up to 5 days.

Preparation: Cut off and discard the top inch from the artichoke. The thorny tips from the remaining leaves should be snipped off with kitchen scissors. The stem is usually cut off so the artichoke can sit upright. (The stem can be peeled and cooked along with the artichokes, with slightly reduced cooking time.) Artichoke flesh turns brown when exposed to oxygen, so rub cut areas with cut lemon wedges to discourage discoloring. To prepare baby artichokes or artichoke bottoms, see pages 19 and 21.

BOILED ARTICHOKES WITH ROSEMARY-LEMON BUTTER
MAKES 4 SERVINGS

Serve with veal, pork, and lamb roasts and chops; chicken, seafood, or pasta.
Prep Time: 10 minutes
Cooking Time: 45 minutes to 1 hour
Make Ahead: The artichokes can be refrigerated for up to 2 days.
Family Favorite, Cooking Classic, Vegetarian

If there is one thing I have learned about artichokes (and I grew up eating them, as a farm in our neighborhood sold them for a nickel each), you cannot truly estimate their cooking time. Just be flexible and don't serve them when you are watching the clock—they are equally delicious hot, chilled, or at room temperature. I like this method because the lemon and garlic infuse the artichokes with extra flavor. It is a good idea to squeeze the excess water from the artichokes before serving, a trick I learned years ago working at a California restaurant where I cooked a few cases of artichokes every day.

4 artichokes (about 8 ounces each)

1 lemon, cut in half crosswise

4 garlic cloves, crushed under the flat side of a
    knife and peeled

ROSEMARY-LEMON BUTTER
1 cup (2 sticks) unsalted butter

1 tablespoon finely chopped fresh rosemary

2 garlic cloves, crushed through a garlic press

½ teaspoon hot red pepper flakes

2 tablespoons fresh lemon juice

Kosher salt

1. If necessary, cut the stem from each artichoke so it sits flat; discard the stems. Cut the top inch from each artichoke. Using kitchen scissors, snip off the thorny leaf tips. Rub the artichokes all over with the lemon halves.

2. Squeeze the juice from the lemon halves into a large stockpot. Add the garlic. Half fill the pot with salted water and bring it to a boil over high heat. Add the artichokes and reduce the heat to medium. Partially cover the pot and boil the artichokes until a leaf from the bottom layer can be easily pulled off, 45 minutes to 1 hour. Taste-test the artichoke to be sure that the flesh is tender enough. Drain well.

3. Meanwhile, make the rosemary-lemon butter: Heat the butter, rosemary, garlic, and red pepper flakes in a small saucepan over low heat until the butter melts. Remove them from the heat and stir in the lemon juice. Let the rosemary butter stand to blend the flavors while the artichokes are cooking.

4. Let the artichokes cool until they are easy to handle. One at a time, working over the sink, hold an artichoke upside down and squeeze it gently to remove the excess water. Place it on a platter.

5. Season the rosemary butter with salt and reheat it, if needed. Divide the rosemary butter among four ramekins. Serve the artichokes warm or cooled to room temperature, with the butter for dipping and a bowl to collect the leaves.

Steamed Artichokes: Reserve this method for smallish artichokes, as the big ones take too long to cook through. Place a collapsible metal steamer in a large saucepan. Add enough water to come almost to the underside of the steamer. Cover and bring to a boil over high heat. Stand the artichokes in the steamer. Reduce the heat to medium-low. Simmer, maintaining a strong head of steam and adding more hot water to the pot if the water cooks away, until a leaf from the bottom layer can be easily pulled off, 45 minutes to 1 hour. Taste-test the artichoke to be sure that the flesh is tender enough. Drain, cool slightly, and squeeze out excess water. Serve warm or at room temperature.

STUFFED ARTICHOKES WITH ROMANO AND OREGANO
MAKES 4 SERVINGS

Serve with steaks; veal, pork, or lamb roasts or chops; or roast chicken.
Prep Time: 15 minutes
Cooking Time: 1 hour
Make Ahead: The artichokes can be made up to 1 day ahead.
Family Favorite, Holiday Feasts, Cooking Classic, Vegetarian

These stuffed artichokes really stand out when the main course is on the simple side—marinated and grilled veal chops, for example. Use moderately sized artichokes because the jumbo ones take forever to cook and won't fit in the average home kitchen stockpot.

2½ cups soft bread crumbs, made from slightly stale crusty bread in a blender or food processor	2 garlic cloves, minced
	Kosher salt and freshly ground black pepper
⅔ cup freshly grated Romano cheese (about 3 ounces)	4 artichokes (about 8 ounces each)
	1 lemon, cut in half crosswise
7 tablespoons olive oil	Lemon wedges, for serving
1 teaspoon dried oregano	

1. Mix the bread crumbs, cheese, ¼ cup of the oil, the oregano, and garlic in a medium bowl. Season the stuffing to taste with salt and pepper.

2. If necessary, cut the stem from each artichoke so it sits flat; discard the stems. Cut the top inch from each artichoke. Using kitchen scissors, snip off the thorny leaf tips. Rub the artichokes all over with the lemon halves. Place an artichoke on a plate, top-side up. Work around the artichoke to spread the leaves open—do not bother with the thin leaves that form the core of the artichoke. Force one-quarter of the stuffing between the leaves as well as possible, patting any excess stuffing over the top of the artichoke.

3. Choose a saucepan large enough to hold the artichokes. Pour in enough cold water to come ½ inch up the sides of the pot. Stir in 1 tablespoon of the oil and 2 teaspoons salt. Stand the artichokes, bottoms down, in the pot. Drizzle the remaining 2 tablespoons oil over the tops of the artichokes. Bring them to a boil over high heat.

4. Cover and reduce the heat to medium-low. Simmer, adding hot water as needed to the stockpot if the water cooks away, until a leaf from the bottom layer can be easily pulled off, 45 minutes to 1 hour.

5. Meanwhile, position a rack in the center of the oven and preheat the oven to 400°F. Lightly oil a rimmed baking sheet.

6. Using long tongs, transfer the artichokes to the baking sheet. Bake until the stuffing is lightly browned, 10 to 15 minutes. Serve the artichokes hot or cooled to room temperature, with the lemon wedges and a bowl to collect the leaves.

GRILLED ARTICHOKES WITH PIMENTÓN ALLIOLI

MAKES 4 SERVINGS

Serve with roast lamb and lamb chops; roast chicken; or seafood.
Prep Time: 10 minutes
Cooking Time: 45 minutes
Family Favorite, Company Fare, Vegetarian

I was well into adulthood before I encountered a grilled artichoke. Since then, I've cooked hundreds of them this way, and I've learned a lot about how to do it right. A few pointers: Don't parcook them, don't try to grill them whole, and don't bother to cut out the choke until after cooking. Allioli is the Spanish version of French aïoli. I really like the spicy version on page 196 with these artichokes, as it plays up their smokiness.

1 teaspoon kosher salt	8 tablespoons extra-virgin olive oil, as needed
½ teaspoon hot red pepper flakes	2 garlic cloves, thinly sliced
4 artichokes (about 10 ounces each)	
1 lemon, cut in half crosswise	3 recipes Pimentón Allioli (page 196)

1. Prepare an outdoor grill for direct cooking over medium heat (350° to 450°F). For a charcoal grill, let the coals burn until they are covered with white ash and you can hold your hand about 1 inch above the cooking grate for about 3 seconds. For a gas grill, preheat on high and adjust the thermostat to medium (400°F).

2. Have ready eight 12-inch squares of heavy-duty aluminum foil. In a small bowl, mix the salt and red pepper flakes together. Using a large knife, cut each artichoke in half lengthwise. Rub the artichoke halves all over with the lemon halves. Place an artichoke half in the center of an aluminum foil square. Drizzle it all over with about 1 tablespoon of the oil. Sprinkle it all over with a large pinch of the salt mixture. Squeeze a teaspoon or so of lemon juice on top and add a few garlic slices. Wrap the artichoke half tightly in the foil. Repeat with the remaining artichoke halves, oil, salt mixture, garlic, and lemon juice.

3. Place the foil packets on the cooking grate and cover the grill. Grill, turning occasionally, until the artichoke leaves are golden brown and pull easily from the heart (open a foil packet to check), about 45 minutes.

4. Remove the packets from the grill. Divide the allioli among four ramekins or custard cups. Unwrap the artichokes and transfer them to a serving platter. Serve the artichokes warm or cooled to room temperature, with the allioli for dipping and a bowl to collect the leaves.

ARTICHOKE BOTTOMS WITH MASCARPONE POTATOES DUCHESSE
MAKES 6 SERVINGS

Serve with roast beef, veal, pork, or lamb.

Prep Time: 30 minutes

Cooking Time: 40 minutes

Make Ahead: The bottoms can be prepared up to 1 day ahead. The filled bottoms can be prepared up to 8 hours ahead.

Holiday Feasts, Company Fare

Stuffed artichoke bottoms may sound like something out of Escoffier, but there are usually very good reasons for why certain dishes remain classics, not the least of which is that they taste good. (These can also be made well ahead of serving.) Once you master trimming and cooking the bottoms into solid bowls of artichoke flavor, try other fillings, such as creamed spinach or another vegetable purée.

2 tablespoons cider or red wine vinegar

6 large artichokes (9 to 11 ounces each), stems cut off

1 lemon, cut in half crosswise

1 tablespoon olive oil

1 small yellow onion, thinly sliced

2 garlic cloves, crushed under the flat side of a knife and peeled

½ cup reduced-sodium chicken broth

½ teaspoon kosher salt

Olive oil, for the baking dish

1 recipe Mascarpone Potatoes Duchesse (page 180)

1 tablespoon unsalted butter, melted

2 tablespoons freshly grated Parmesan cheese

1. Stir the vinegar into 2 quarts cold water in a medium bowl. Working with one artichoke at a time, snap off the tough outer leaves to reveal the inner cone of thin, light green leaves. Cut off the top of the cone at the natural indentation where it meets the artichoke bottom. Using the tip of a small, sharp knife, dig out the thistle heart from the center of the bottom. Rub the artichoke all over with a lemon half. Trim away the thick, dark green artichoke skin to reveal the lighter green flesh. Put the artichoke bottom in the vinegar water.

2. Drain the artichoke bottoms and pat them dry with a clean kitchen towel. Heat the oil in a medium skillet over medium heat. Add the artichoke bottoms and cook, turning occasionally, until they are browned on both sides, about 5 minutes. Stir in the onion, garlic, broth, and salt, and pour in enough water, if needed, to come halfway up the sides of the artichokes. Bring them to a boil. Reduce the heat to medium-low and cover the skillet. Simmer until the bottoms are tender when pierced with the tip of a small, sharp knife, about 15 minutes. Drain the artichoke bottoms and let cool. (The artichoke bottoms can be covered and refrigerated for up to 1 day.)

3. Position a rack in the center of the oven and preheat the oven to 400°F. Lightly oil an 8-inch square baking dish.

4. Arrange the artichoke bottoms in the baking dish. Transfer the mashed potato mixture to a pastry bag fitted with a ½-inch-diameter open star tip. Divide the potato mixture equally among the bottoms, piping it into tall swirls. (The filled artichokes can be covered loosely with plastic wrap and refrigerated for up to 8 hours.)

5. Brush the potato swirls with the melted butter and sprinkle them with the Parmesan. Bake until the potato swirls are golden brown, about 20 minutes. Transfer them to a platter and serve.

CHICKEN BROTH

In a perfect world, we would all make our chicken stock from scratch, roll our own homemade pasta, and knit our own sweaters. But the last time I checked, the world wasn't perfect . . . yet. I do have a freezer full of homemade stock, but for my everyday cooking, I am happy to open up a can of broth.

I use chicken broth most often because I find it to be more versatile than the beef or vegetable versions. And I have developed a preference for reduced-sodium broth for its fuller flavor. There is a big difference between brands, and some are too salty or have an artificial or off taste.

One 13¾-ounce can equals 1¾ cups. When a recipe calls for 2 cups of broth, don't bother opening up another can to supply the missing quarter-cup—just make up the difference with water.

For the record, I do make homemade stock on a regular basis. Because I always buy a whole chicken and cut it up as I need for a recipe, I have a regular supply of chicken giblets. I can't bear to throw them away, so I make a stock with them, the back of the cut-up chicken, and some seasoning vegetables. In an hour or so, I have a quart of homemade chicken stock. And when I see meat bones at a reasonable price, I make a large pot of beef or veal stock as a weekend afternoon project.

BRAISED BABY ARTICHOKES, CARROTS, AND ROSEMARY

MAKES 4 TO 6 SERVINGS

Serve with steak; veal, pork, and lamb chops; or roast chicken.

Prep Time: 15 minutes

Cooking Time: 30 minutes

Make Ahead: The braise can be prepared up to one day ahead.

Weeknight Suppers, Family Favorite, Holiday Feasts, Company Fare, Buffet Dish, Retro Recipe, Cooking Classic

Tender baby artichokes pick up sweet notes from carrots and onions, with rosemary chiming in as another unifying flavor.

2 tablespoons cider or red wine vinegar

9 baby artichokes, trimmed and cut in half lengthwise

2 tablespoons extra-virgin olive oil

1 yellow onion, chopped

2 carrots, cut into ½-inch dice

2 garlic cloves, minced

½ cup dry white wine

½ cup reduced-sodium chicken broth

One 2-inch fresh rosemary sprig

Kosher salt and freshly ground black pepper

3 tablespoons freshly grated Parmesan cheese, for serving (optional)

1. Stir the vinegar into 2 quarts cold water in a medium bowl. Working with one artichoke at a time, snap off the tough outer leaves to expose the tender cone of thin, light green leaves. Cut the artichoke in half lengthwise. If the fuzzy choke is visible, dig it out of the artichoke half with the tip of a small, sharp knife, leaving the artichoke half intact. Add the artichoke to the vinegar water.

2. Drain the artichokes and pat them dry with a clean kitchen towel. Heat the oil in a large skillet over medium-high heat until hot but not smoking. Add the artichokes, flat-sides down, and cook until they are beginning to turn golden brown, about 3 minutes. Stir the artichokes and add the onion, carrots, and garlic. Cook, stirring occasionally, until the onion softens, about 3 minutes more.

3. Add the wine, broth, ½ cup water, and the rosemary and bring them to a boil. Reduce the heat to medium-low and cover with the lid ajar. Simmer, stirring occasionally, until the artichokes and carrots are tender and the liquid is almost completely evaporated (add a few tablespoons of water if the artichokes are not tender by the time the liquid evaporates), about 25 minutes. Discard the rosemary. Season to taste with salt and pepper. (The braise can be cooled, covered, and refrigerated for up to 1 day. Reheat in the skillet.) Transfer the braise to a serving dish, sprinkle it with the Parmesan, if using, and serve.

Asparagus

While we can buy asparagus throughout the year, it is better to wait until your area's traditional spring harvest for the best flavor. The window of opportunity will be small (only a couple of weeks), but you will be well rewarded for your patience. There are three distinct parts to the asparagus spear: the woody bottom (which is discarded), the tender stalk, and the delicate tip. To keep the flavor fresh and the color bright, it is important to avoid overcooking asparagus. **White asparagus,** an imported product, has been covered with dirt during its growing season to cut off the light that triggers chlorophyll production. In my opinion, it doesn't travel well, but if you find local white asparagus, give it a try.

Peak Season: March to June.

Purchase: Plump, moist spears with tightly compacted tips. Avoid spears with splayed tips and limp or wrinkled stalks. The thickness of the stalk is not an indication of quality, and is just a matter of personal taste.

Storage: Asparagus keeps best if the ends are standing in water to keep the stalks hydrated. Cut 1 inch from the end of the bunch, stand the bunch in a container with about 1 inch of water, cover it loosely with a plastic bag, and refrigerate for up to 3 days.

Preparation: Bend the stalk to find the point where the natural break occurs, and snap off and discard the woody bottom. At this point, you can peel the stalk with a vegetable peeler, but honestly . . . I never do this except on very thick spears where the skin might be especially tough. White asparagus has a tough skin that must be peeled before cooking.

ASPARAGUS WITH GREMOLATA BUTTER
MAKES 6 TO 8 SERVINGS

Serve with roast and grilled beef, veal, pork, and lamb; roast and grilled chicken; or grilled seafood.
Prep Time: 10 minutes
Cooking Time: 5 minutes
Make Ahead: The gremolata butter can be made up to 2 days ahead.
Weeknight Suppers, Family Favorite, Holiday Feasts, Company Fare, Buffet Dish, Vegetarian

Gremolata, a seasoning blend of citrus zest, parsley, and garlic, is traditionally used to accent the flavor of hearty Italian stews (especially osso buco). I use the mixture to make a lovely compound butter that goes beautifully with boiled asparagus.

GREMOLATA BUTTER

¼ cup (½ stick) unsalted butter, at room
  temperature

Finely grated zest of ½ orange

Finely grated zest of ½ lemon

2 teaspoons finely chopped fresh flat-leaf parsley

1 garlic clove, minced

2 pounds asparagus, woody ends snapped off

Kosher salt and freshly ground black pepper

1. To make the butter: In a small bowl, using a silicone spatula, mash and smear the butter, orange and lemon zest, parsley, and garlic together until combined. (The gremolata butter can be covered and refrigerated for up to 2 days. Bring it to room temperature before using.)

2. Bring a large saucepan of salted water to a boil over high heat. Add the asparagus and boil until it is barely tender, 4 to 6 minutes, depending on the thickness of the asparagus. Scoop out and reserve about ¼ cup of the cooking water. Drain the asparagus.

3. Return the asparagus to the saucepan. Off heat, add the gremolata butter and 2 tablespoons of the cooking liquid. Using kitchen tongs, gently toss the asparagus in the saucepan until the butter has melted and melded with the cooking water and the asparagus is coated with the sauce. Season to taste with salt and pepper. Transfer the asparagus to a serving dish and serve hot.

STEAMED ASPARAGUS WITH BLENDER HOLLANDAISE SAUCE

MAKES 6 SERVINGS

Serve with beef, steak, pork, and lamb roasts and chops; roast chicken; fish fillets or sautéed shrimp.

Prep Time: 10 minutes

Cooking Time: 10 minutes

Make Ahead: The hollandaise can be stored at room temperature for up to 30 minutes.

Family Favorite, Holiday Feasts, Company Fare, Cooking Classic, Vegetarian

The Fred and Ginger of the culinary world, this perfect pair can turn any meal into a special occasion. The timing can be a bit tricky, so I strongly suggest (make that insist) that the sauce be made before cooking the asparagus. Hollandaise is not supposed to be piping hot, and it will warm up when it comes into contact with the steamed asparagus. The blender version of the sauce is virtually foolproof. If you want a stronger lemon flavor, add finely grated lemon zest. Of course, this sauce is wonderful with artichokes, broccoli, and other green vegetables. If you have qualms about making hollandaise sauce because of the raw egg yolks, simply substitute Beurre Blanc (page 433), which has a very similar texture and flavor, or use pasteurized eggs.

HOLLANDAISE SAUCE

¾ cup (1½ sticks) unsalted butter

4 large egg yolks (see headnote above)

1 tablespoon fresh lemon juice

Kosher salt and freshly ground black pepper

Cayenne pepper

2 pounds asparagus, woody ends snapped off

1. To make the sauce: Melt the butter in a small saucepan over medium heat until it is foaming. Pour it into a glass liquid measuring cup and let it stand for 1 minute. Skim off the foam from the surface.

2. Pulse the egg yolks and lemon juice in a blender to combine. With the machine running, slowly pour in all of the melted butter (including the whey at the bottom of the cup) through the hole in the lid—this should take about 1 minute—to make a thick, smooth sauce. If the sauce separates, add 1 tablespoon of cold water to emulsify it. Season to taste with salt and a pinch of cayenne. Transfer the sauce to a bowl, cover with plastic wrap, and let it stand at room temperature for up to 30 minutes.

3. Place a collapsible steamer in a large saucepan and add enough water to almost reach the bottom of the steamer. (If you have another kind of steamer, just set it up as needed.) Bring the water to a boil over high heat. Add the asparagus to the steamer and tightly cover the saucepan. Cook until the asparagus is just tender, 3 to 5 minutes.

4. Transfer the asparagus to a warm serving platter. Sprinkle the asparagus lightly with salt and pepper. Spoon the sauce over the asparagus and serve.

ASPARAGUS AND PINE NUT SAUTÉ

MAKES 4 SERVINGS

Serve with roasted and grilled meats; poultry; or seafood.

Prep Time: 5 minutes

Cooking Time: 5 minutes

Weeknight Suppers, Family Favorite, Holiday Feasts, Company Fare, Vegetarian

During the spring asparagus season, I have to stop myself from making this for dinner every night. It is made in a flash in a single skillet. Cook up a large batch for a big party, or just a pound for a family supper. The broth adds another layer of flavor, but you can just use water if you don't want to open an entire can for only 2 tablespoons.

¼ cup pine nuts

1 tablespoon extra-virgin olive oil

1 pound asparagus, woody ends snapped off, spears cut into 1½-inch lengths

2 tablespoons dry white wine or dry vermouth

2 tablespoons reduced-sodium chicken broth or water

Kosher salt and freshly ground black pepper

1. Heat a large skillet over medium heat. Add the pine nuts and cook, stirring occasionally, until they are toasted, 2 to 3 minutes. Transfer them to a plate.

2. Add the oil to the skillet over medium-high heat until it is very hot but not smoking. Add the asparagus and cook, stirring almost constantly, until it turns a brighter shade of green, about 1 minute. Stir in the wine, broth, and ⅓ cup water. Reduce the heat to medium and cook, stirring occasionally, until the liquid is evaporated and the asparagus is crisp-tender, 2 to 3 minutes more. Season to taste with salt and pepper. Sprinkle with the toasted pine nuts and serve.

WARM SHAVED ASPARAGUS WITH PARMESAN, PINE NUTS, AND BASIL
MAKES 4 SERVINGS

Serve with delicate main courses, such as chicken breast or seafood.

Prep Time: 10 minutes

Cooking Time: 2 minutes

Weeknight Suppers, Holiday Feasts, Company Fare, Vegetarian

This elegant side dish with asparagus in an unfamiliar guise is sure to surprise and delight your dinner guests. I only make this warm salad when my local market has thick, super-fresh spears for shaving into thin ribbons. A Y-shaped peeler works best for this job.

1 pound thick asparagus, woody ends snapped off	2 tablespoons fresh lemon juice
¼ cup pine nuts	2 tablespoons thinly sliced fresh basil
2 tablespoons extra-virgin olive oil	1 chunk Parmesan cheese (at least 4 ounces)
2 garlic cloves, minced	Kosher salt and freshly ground black pepper

1. Working with one asparagus spear at a time, place the spear on a work surface. Using a Y-shaped vegetable peeler, and holding the asparagus stationary, shave it from bottom to tip into long, thin ribbons. Transfer the ribbons to a bowl.

2. Heat a small skillet over medium heat. Add the pine nuts and cook, stirring occasionally, until they are toasted, 2 to 3 minutes. Add the pine nuts to the asparagus.

3. Off heat, add the oil and garlic to the skillet (the skillet will be hot enough that it does not need to be returned to the heat) and let them stand just until the garlic is fragrant and softened, but not browned, about 1 minute. Pour the garlic mixture over the asparagus.

4. Add the lemon juice and basil to the asparagus mixture and toss gently. Using the vegetable peeler, shave about 1 ounce of Parmesan curls into the bowl. Toss again, seasoning to taste with salt and pepper. Top with another ounce of Parmesan curls and serve.

ASPARAGUS AND SPRING VEGETABLE RAGOUT WITH TARRAGON CREAM
MAKES 6 SERVINGS

Serve with roast lamb or pork, roast chicken, or fish fillets.

Prep Time: 10 minutes

Cooking Time: 20 minutes

Make Ahead: The various components can be prepared up to 4 hours ahead.

Holiday Feasts, Company Fare, Buffet Dish

Hardly an Easter dinner goes by when I don't serve this side dish. Depending on how late the holiday arrives and what is in the market, I make substitutions as opportunities present themselves. For example, I have used a handful of fresh ramps instead of scallions, shiitake caps if morels weren't available, and fiddleheads in addition to asparagus.

1½ pounds asparagus, woody ends snapped off, cut into 1-inch pieces, stalks and tips separated

1 cup fresh or frozen peas

2 tablespoons (¼ stick) unsalted butter

6 ounces morels, cut in half lengthwise, thinly sliced

Kosher salt and freshly ground black pepper

1 large scallion (white and green parts), finely chopped

¼ cup reduced-sodium chicken broth

¼ cup heavy cream

2 teaspoons finely chopped fresh tarragon

1. Prepare a large bowl of iced water. Bring 1 inch of salted water to a boil in a large saucepan over high heat. Add the asparagus stalks and cook for 1 minute. Add the asparagus tips and cook until the asparagus is crisp-tender, 2 to 3 minutes more. Using a wire spider or slotted spoon, transfer the asparagus to the iced water, leaving the pan water boiling.

2. Add the peas to the pan and cook until tender, about 5 minutes for fresh peas and 3 minutes for frozen peas. Drain and add the peas to the bowl with the asparagus. Drain well. Pat the vegetables dry with paper towels. (The vegetable mixture can be prepared up to 4 hours ahead, covered and refrigerated.)

3. Melt the butter in a large skillet over medium heat. Add the morels and season lightly with salt and pepper. Cook, stirring occasionally, until they are tender, about 4 minutes. Add the scallion and cook until it softens, about 1 minute. (The morels can be prepared up to 4 hours ahead, stored in the skillet at room temperature. Reheat over low heat.)

4. Add the broth and increase the heat to high. Boil the broth until it is reduced to a glaze, about 2 minutes. Add the reserved vegetables and cream and bring them to a boil. Cook until the cream is reduced by half, about 2 minutes. Stir in the tarragon and season with salt and pepper. Serve hot.

ASPARAGUS AND CREMINI WITH BALSAMIC SAUCE
MAKES 4 TO 6 SERVINGS

Serve with roasts, steaks, and chops; grilled or roast poultry; or seafood.

Prep Time: 10 minutes

Cooking Time: 12 minutes

Weeknight Suppers, Family Favorite, Company Fare, Buffet Dish, Vegetarian

Balsamic vinegar is often paired with olive oil, but in this versatile recipe, I use butter to smooth the vinegar's sharpness and make a smooth sauce. For the best results, use aged balsamic vinegar, although the cheaper industrial version is fine.

1 pound asparagus, woody ends snapped off, cut
   into 1½-inch lengths, stalks and tips separated
3 tablespoons unsalted butter, 2 tablespoons cold
   and cubed
10 ounces cremini mushrooms, thinly sliced

2 tablespoons finely chopped shallots
1 garlic clove, minced
2 tablespoons balsamic vinegar, preferably aged
Kosher salt and freshly ground black pepper

1. Bring 1 inch of salted water to a boil in a large skillet over high heat. Add the asparagus stalks and cook for 1 minute. Add the asparagus tips and cook until the asparagus is crisp-tender, 2 to 3 minutes more, depending on its thickness. Drain the asparagus, but do not rinse it.

2. Wipe out the skillet. Add the 1 tablespoon uncubed butter to the skillet and melt it over medium-high heat. Add the mushrooms and cook, stirring occasionally, until they give off their juices and begin to brown, about 5 minutes. Stir in the shallots and garlic and cook until the garlic is fragrant, about 30 seconds.

3. Return the asparagus to the skillet and cook, stirring often, just until it is reheated, about 1 minute. Reduce the heat to very low. Add the vinegar and cubed butter and stir until the butter has melded with the vinegar into a smooth sauce. Do not overheat the sauce, or it will separate. Remove the skillet from the heat and season the sauce to taste with salt and pepper. Serve hot.

BALSAMIC VINEGAR

Traditional balsamic vinegar is an artisan product, made by hand with wine from the sweet Trebbiano grape. Over the many years of aging (at least twelve), the vinegar is occasionally transferred to casks from various woods, picking up different flavors in the process. And as the liquid evaporates, it acquires a thick, almost viscous consistency. In Italy, true balsamic vinegar (labeled "*aceto balsamico tradizionale*") is reserved for very special occasions, and drizzled sparingly over food. No Italian cook I know would dream of making balsamic vinaigrette with "real" *balsamico*. This vinegar, sold at the best specialty markets, is always pricey. If you want to splurge, look for the key word "tradizionale" on the label.

Most of the balsamic vinegar sold in supermarkets is actually a factory product made from artificially flavored wine vinegar. This is the one to use for salads and everyday cooking. But for holiday dinners and other special meals, where you are likely to treat yourself and your guests, you might want to do better than the supermarket brands, which are just labeled "*aceto balsamico.*"

Between the supermarket brands and the *tradizionale* is the *condimento* grade. This excellent balsamic vinegar is aged for eight years, and is pretty close to the high-quality version, with a heavy body and complex flavor. For my money, this is the way to go. You'll find it online and at many specialty markets and gourmet shops.

ROASTED ASPARAGUS WITH PROSCIUTTO–RED PEPPER CONFETTI

MAKES 4 TO 6 SERVINGS

Serve with roast beef, steak, pork or lamb roasts; pork or lamb chops; roast chicken, chicken sautés; fish fillets or sautéed shrimp.

Prep Time: 10 minutes

Cooking Time: 10 minutes

Weeknight Suppers, Holiday Feasts, Company Fare, Buffet Dish

Roasting has become the favorite cooking method for asparagus, as the dry heat deepens its flavor. This topping of diced prosciutto and sweet red pepper gives the dish a green-and-red palette that makes it perfect for serving along with a Christmas roast, but it is just as compatible with a springtime leg of lamb. Season the asparagus and the topping lightly, as the prosciutto can be salty.

1½ pounds asparagus, woody ends snapped off

2 tablespoons extra-virgin olive oil

CONFETTI

1 tablespoon extra-virgin olive oil

½ cup seeded and diced red bell pepper

⅓ cup (¼-inch) diced prosciutto

Kosher salt and freshly ground black pepper

Lemon wedges, for serving

1. Position a rack in the center of the oven and preheat the oven to 425°F.

2. Toss the asparagus on a large rimmed baking sheet with the oil. Spread the spears in a single layer. Bake until the spears are crisp-tender, 10 to 15 minutes.

3. Just before serving, make the confetti: Heat the oil in medium skillet over medium-high heat. Add the red pepper and cook, stirring occasionally, until it is tender and lightly browned, about 3 minutes. Stir in the prosciutto and cook until heated through, about 1 minute. Season lightly to taste with salt and pepper. Reduce the heat to very low to keep the confetti warm.

4. Season the asparagus lightly with salt and pepper. Heap the asparagus on a serving platter. Top it with the confetti and serve it with the lemon wedges.

Roasted Asparagus with Parmesan Curls: Omit the prosciutto and red pepper topping. Using a Y-shaped vegetable peeler, shave an ounce or two of curls from a block of Parmesan cheese over the seasoned asparagus. Serve it immediately, with lemon wedges.

ROASTING VEGETABLES

Cooks have discovered the many pleasures of roasting vegetables. Not only is the technique ridiculously simple; the sweet, toasty results are irresistible. Just toss prepared vegetables with some oil, spread them on a rimmed baking sheet, and roast them in a hot oven until they are tender and browned. Even on a busy weeknight, if you preheat the oven when you walk in the door, you can have roasted vegetables for your dinner.

For proper browning, the vegetables must not be crowded together on the baking sheet. A half-sheet pan, measuring about 18 × 13 inches, is your best bet because it easily holds about 2 pounds of vegetables. Oil the baking sheet before adding the ingredients, or line it with parchment paper.

Before roasting, toss the vegetables with olive oil or vegetable oil, allowing about 1 tablespoon for every pound of vegetables. You can do this right on the oiled or lined baking sheet, or in a large bowl.

I do not season the vegetables until after roasting, as the salt can draw moisture from the vegetables to create excess steam and slow browning. This could be my imagination, but it's a habit that I have developed. I also usually hold off on spice rubs, herb sprinkles, and other flavorings until the end of the roasting period because the high oven temperature can scorch some of these additions. Because a wet marinade would inhibit browning, for me, marinades are out of the question for roasted vegetables.

Various vegetables have different roasting times, so I rarely cook two kinds together. However, there are ways around this. First, you can put the different vegetables on separate pans and oven racks, and roast them for their corresponding times. (I love my quarter-sheet pans, measuring 9 × 13, for this purpose.) Or you can put two different vegetables at opposite ends of a large half-sheet pan. Sometimes, I'll use a little guesswork and cut the softer vegetables a bit larger (carrots) so they are done at the same time as the larger ones (potatoes). But usually, I just keep it simple with a single vegetable.

The best average temperature for roasting vegetables is 425°F. Higher ones encourage scorching and require careful watching, and lower ones discourage browning. Using a wide metal spatula, flip the vegetables over about halfway through roasting for even cooking. (This is not always necessary with thin vegetables, such as asparagus.) Season the vegetables with salt, pepper, spice rubs, or fresh or dried herbs during the last few minutes of roasting, or even when they are removed from the oven.

ESTIMATED ROASTING TIMES FOR VEGETABLES (AT 425°F)

Toss with 1 tablespoon olive or vegetable oil for every pound of vegetables

VEGETABLE	PREPARATION	ROASTING TIME
Asparagus	Woody ends discarded, spears unpeeled	10 to 15 minutes
Beets	Left whole, scrubbed, wrapped in aluminum foil	1¼ to 2 hours
Broccoli	Cut into bite-sized florets, stems peeled and cut into ½-inch rounds	15 to 20 minutes
Brussels sprouts	Blanched in boiling water for 3 minutes; large sprouts cut in half	15 to 20 minutes
Butternut squash	Peeled, seeded, cut into 1½-inch chunks	30 minutes
Carrots	Cut into 1-inch lengths	30 to 40 minutes
Cauliflower	Cut into bite-sized florets	25 to 35 minutes
Eggplant	Cut into ½-inch rounds	20 to 30 minutes
Fennel	Cut lengthwise into ½-inch slices	20 to 30 minutes
Green Beans	Trimmed, left whole	20 to 30 minutes
Onions, Yellow	Cut into 6 wedges	20 to 30 minutes
Potatoes	Peeled or unpeeled, cut into 1½- to 2-inch chunks	40 to 50 minutes
Sweet Bell Peppers	Stemmed, cored, and seeded; cut into 1-inch strips; peel after roasting	30 minutes
Sweet potatoes	Peeled, pointed tips cut off, cut into ½-inch wedges	35 to 45 minutes
Turnips	Leave young, small turnips unpeeled; cut into ½-inch wedges	45 to 55 minutes
Zucchini	Cut lengthwise, then into 2-inch lengths	15 to 20 minutes

Grilled Asparagus with Seared Lemon and Tarragon

MAKES 4 TO 6 SERVINGS

Serve with grilled meats, poultry, and seafood.
Prep Time: 5 minutes
Cooking Time: 10 minutes
Weeknight Suppers, Family Favorite, Company Fare, Vegetarian

Because grilling asparagus is such a simple procedure, it is best to keep the dish unfussy. Grilling the lemon halves, with their cut sides down to caramelize the natural sugars, gives the juice a hint of sweetness. It is also a nice touch to use a flaky finishing salt.

1½ pounds asparagus, woody ends snapped off
2 to 3 small lemons, halved crosswise
2 tablespoons extra-virgin olive oil

Flaky sea salt (such as Maldon) or kosher salt and
  freshly ground black pepper
2 teaspoons finely chopped fresh tarragon

1. Prepare an outdoor grill for direct cooking over medium heat (350° to 450°F). For a charcoal grill, let the coals burn until they are covered with white ash and you can hold your hand about 1 inch above the cooking grate for about 3 seconds. For a gas grill, preheat on high and adjust the thermostat to medium (400°F).
2. In a large bowl, toss the asparagus and lemon halves with the oil.
3. Brush the cooking grate clean. Spread the asparagus on the cooking grate, perpendicular to the grid. Cook, with the lid closed, occasionally rolling the asparagus on the grate to turn the spears, until the asparagus is seared with grill marks and crisp-tender, 5 to 7 minutes. After 5 minutes, put the lemons, cut-sides down, on the grill, to sear and brown the cut surfaces with grill marks.
4. Transfer the asparagus and lemon halves to a serving platter. Season them to taste with salt and pepper. Sprinkle them with the tarragon and serve.

FINISHING SALTS

In just a few seconds, a sprinkle of finishing salt can elevate a simple side dish to a higher level. These salts have characteristics that separate them from cooking salts like kosher or table salt. The first distinction is visual—finishing salts usually are flaky and often naturally colored. Red or black Hawaiian, pink Himalayan, and gray fleur de sel are some options. Finishing salts also have richer, stronger flavors than cooking salts. Reserve finishing salts to use on uncomplicated dishes where their texture, color, and flavor will stand out.

Beans, Green and Wax

The bean formerly known as string has had its string bred out, so the correct name is now green bean. As for the other beans in the family, not all of them are green (consider the yellow wax bean and the purple bean). There are slender **haricots verts,** flat **Romano beans,** and the **common snap beans** (so called because of the noise that they make when broken during preparation). The green bean is the main ingredient for two of the most essential side dishes: green bean casserole (I offer versions with or without the canned soup and onions) and green bean amandine (choose between the classic and another with spicy nuts). Purple beans lose their color when cooked, so if you are buying them for their hue, it is best to thinly slice the raw beans and use them as a crunchy garnish.

Peak Season: Late summer and early fall, but available year-round.

Purchase: Moist, firm beans without any shriveling.

Storage: Refrigerate unwashed in a plastic bag for 3 to 5 days.

Preparation: Most varieties do not have strings, but pull them lengthwise from the pods, if necessary. Trim off the stem ends; leave the pointed tips as they are or trim, if you prefer.

GREEN BEANS WITH HOT-AND-SWEET ALMONDS
MAKES 4 TO 6 SERVINGS

Serve with beef, pork, and lamb chops or roasts; roast chicken; baked fish fillets; or sautéed shrimp.
Prep Time: 5 minutes
Cooking Time: 8 minutes
Make Ahead: The green beans can be blanched and refrigerated for up to 1 day, and the nuts stored at room temperature for up to 8 hours.
Weeknight Suppers, Family Favorite, Holiday Feasts, Company Fare, Buffet Dish, Vegetarian

Green beans amandine is an enduring side dish, but recently I've been giving them a twist with these easy-to-make zesty nuts. Whether you serve them at a holiday meal or for a simple weeknight supper, they rarely disappoint. I especially like to make them with a combination of yellow wax and green beans. For the comforting classic version, see the variation.

ALMONDS
1 teaspoon sugar
1 teaspoon chili powder
½ teaspoon ground cumin
½ teaspoon kosher salt
Pinch of cayenne pepper

2 teaspoons unsalted butter
⅔ cup slivered almonds

12 ounces green beans, cut into 1½-inch lengths
1 tablespoon unsalted butter or olive oil
Kosher salt and freshly ground black pepper

1. To make the almonds: In a small bowl, combine the sugar, chili powder, cumin, salt, and cayenne. Melt the butter in a medium nonstick skillet over medium heat. Add the almonds and cook, stirring occasionally, until they are beginning to brown, about 2 minutes. Sprinkle them with the sugar mixture and stir almost constantly until the spices are fragrant, about 30 seconds more. Transfer the almonds to a plate. (The almonds can be cooled, covered, and stored at room temperature for up to 8 hours.)

2. Meanwhile, bring a medium saucepan of salted water to a boil over high heat. Add the green beans and cook until crisp-tender, about 4 minutes. Drain well. (If serving immediately, there is no need to rinse the beans. To prepare the green beans ahead, drain and rinse them well under cold running water after cooking. Pat the beans dry with a clean kitchen towels. Wrap them in paper towels, transfer to a 1-gallon plastic zip-tight bag, and refrigerate for up to 1 day.)

3. Add the butter to the saucepan and melt it over medium heat. Add the green beans and toss well. (If the green beans have been refrigerated, cook, stirring often, until they are heated through, about 2 minutes.) Season to taste with salt and pepper. Transfer the green beans to a serving dish. Top them with the almonds and serve.

Classic Green Beans Amandine: Substitute ⅔ cup sliced or slivered almonds, toasted (see below) for the spiced almonds.

TOASTING NUTS

In just a few minutes, nuts can be toasted to give them a deeper flavor. While some people do this in a skillet (which does not require preheating the oven and trims some time from the operation), you get much better coloring in the oven. (Pine nuts and pumpkin seeds can be successfully toasted in a skillet.) If you have to toast only a small amount of nuts, you can even use a toaster oven, spreading the nuts on the toaster tray.

To toast almonds, pecans, and walnuts, position a rack in the center of the oven and preheat the oven to 350°F. Spread the nuts on a rimmed baking sheet. Bake, stirring occasionally, being sure to mix the nuts around the edges into the center, until the nuts are lightly browned and smell toasted, about 10 minutes. Immediately transfer the nuts to a plate to cool completely.

To toast hazelnuts, bake the nuts in a preheated 350°F oven, stirring occasionally, until the skins are cracked and the flesh underneath the skins looks lightly browned, 10 to 12 minutes. Wrap the hazelnuts in a clean kitchen towel and let them cool for 10 minutes. Use the towel to rub the nuts together and remove as much skin as possible. Do not worry if not every bit of skin comes off, as the skin will add a bit of color and character to the dish.

To toast pine nuts and shelled pumpkin seeds, heat a medium skillet over medium heat. Add the pine nuts and cook, stirring often, until they are lightly toasted on all sides, about 2 minutes. Transfer them to a plate and let cool.

HARICOTS VERTS WITH SHIITAKES AND SHALLOTS

MAKES 8 SERVINGS

Serve with roast beef, pork, and veal; roast chicken; roast turkey; or fish fillets.
Prep Time: 10 minutes
Cooking Time: 15 minutes
Make Ahead: The haricots verts can be blanched and refrigerated up to 1 day ahead.
Holiday Feasts, Company Fare, Buffet Dish

*T*hin haricots verts are a delicacy that I save for holidays and other special occasions. This dish is indispensable for a big roast, and I hardly ever serve roast beef or turkey without it alongside. These are light, but not austere, and full of flavor. Use the appropriate broth (beef, chicken, or turkey) to match your main course.

• If you wish, add a teaspoon or two of finely chopped fresh tarragon or rosemary, but I often leave them out if the other side dishes are highly seasoned with herbs.

12 ounces haricots verts

2 tablespoons (¼ stick) unsalted butter

10 ounces shiitake mushrooms, stems removed, caps cut into ½-inch strips

¼ cup finely chopped shallots

½ cup reduced-sodium chicken or beef broth or Giblet Turkey Stock (page 401)

Kosher salt and freshly ground black pepper

1. Bring a large saucepan of salted water to a boil over high heat. Add the haricots verts and cook until they're crisp-tender, about 2 minutes. Drain, rinse under cold running water, and drain again. Pat the haricots verts dry with a clean kitchen towel. (To prepare the haricots verts ahead, wrap them in paper towels, transfer to a 1-gallon plastic zip-tight bag, and refrigerate for up to 1 day.)

2. Melt the butter in a large skillet over medium-high heat. Add the mushrooms and cook, stirring occasionally, until they begin to brown, 8 to 10 minutes. Stir in the shallots and cook until they soften, about 1 minute.

3. Add the haricots verts and the broth and cook over medium-high heat, stirring occasionally, until the haricots verts are heated through and the broth is almost completely evaporated, about 2 minutes. Season to taste with salt and pepper. Transfer the vegetables to a serving dish and serve.

SOUTHERN STEWED GREEN BEANS WITH BACON AND TOMATOES

MAKES 4 TO 6 SERVINGS

Serve with roasts, chops, ham, sausages; barbecued meats and poultry; fried chicken; or fried seafood.
Prep Time: 10 minutes

Cooking Time: 35 minutes

Make Ahead: The green beans can be made up to 2 days ahead.

Weeknight Suppers, Family Favorite, Buffet Dish, Cooking Classic

There is no rule that says green beans must be cooked crisp-tender, and this way of serving them—braised until tender in a simple tomato-bacon sauce—is an old favorite. The beans should not be cooked to a mush, but just long enough to lose their snap and soak up some of the tasty sauce. I also like the Italian variation on page 38, but when the menu features good old-fashioned American food, this is a beloved favorite.

2 slices bacon, coarsely chopped

1 tablespoon vegetable oil

1 yellow onion, chopped

1 garlic clove, minced

One 14½-ounce can plum tomatoes in juice,

drained, with juices reserved, and coarsely chopped

1 tablespoon finely chopped fresh flat-leaf parsley, plus more for garnish

1 pound green beans, cut into 1½-inch lengths

Kosher salt and freshly ground black pepper

1. Cook the bacon and oil together in a medium saucepan over medium heat, stirring occasionally, until the bacon is crisp and browned, about 5 minutes. Add the onion and cook, stirring often, until it softens, about 3 minutes. Stir in the garlic and cook until it is fragrant, about 1 minute. Stir in the tomatoes and their juices with ⅓ cup water and the parsley. Bring to a simmer. Reduce the heat to medium-low and simmer until the liquid is reduced by about one-third, 7 to 10 minutes.

2. Stir in the green beans and bring them to a boil over medium heat. Return the heat to medium-low and cover. Cook at a brisk simmer, stirring often, until the beans are tender and the tomato juices have thickened, adding more water if the sauce gets too thick, 10 to 15 minutes. Season to taste with salt and pepper. (The beans can be cooled, covered, and refrigerated for up to 2 days. Reheat in a skillet over medium heat.)

3. Transfer the beans to a serving bowl, sprinkle with parsley, and serve.

CANNED TOMATOES

Canned tomatoes are an umami-packed ingredient, and I like to have a full variety of canned plum tomatoes, tomato sauce, and tomato paste in a tube. Italian plum tomatoes from the region of San Marzano, near Naples, are famous for their intense flavor and meaty texture, but there are excellent domestic brands, too, and for my money, the San Marzano are not always worth the extra cash.

To chop canned tomatoes, just dump them (with or without their juices, as the recipe requires) into a food processor and pulse a few times to cut them into coarse pieces. Or use the low-tech method: Watching out for any sharp edges on the can, reach into the can and squeeze the tomatoes between your fingers to crush them. You can do this over a bowl or right over the saucepan of food.

HOMEMADE GREEN BEAN AND MUSHROOM CASSEROLE WITH CRISPY SHALLOTS

MAKES 8 SERVINGS

Serve with holiday meals of roast turkey or baked ham.

Prep Time: 15 minutes

Cooking Time: 40 minutes

Make Ahead: The green beans and mushroom sauce can be prepared

and refrigerated separately up to 1 day ahead.

Weeknight Suppers, Family Favorite, Holiday Feasts, Company Fare, Buffet Dish

A fresh alternative to the traditional green bean casserole, this one also has just-fried shallot rings for a topping. This last-minute job can be best accomplished at a big meal if you designate a person to be the "fry master," because you may not want to do this job while dealing with the other dishes.

CASSEROLE

1 pound green beans, cut into 1-inch lengths

3 tablespoons unsalted butter

10 ounces cremini mushrooms, sliced

½ cup finely chopped shallots

3 tablespoons all-purpose flour

1 cup whole milk

1 cup reduced-sodium chicken broth

1 teaspoon Maggi Seasoning or soy sauce (see Note)

Freshly ground black pepper

SHALLOTS

Vegetable oil, for deep-frying

¾ cup (90 g) all-purpose flour

½ teaspoon kosher salt

¼ teaspoon freshly ground black pepper

2 large shallots, cut into ¼-inch rings, rings
   separated

¾ cup buttermilk

1. Position a rack in the center of the oven and preheat the oven to 350°F. Lightly butter a 13 × 9 × 2-inch baking dish.

2. To prepare the casserole: Bring a large saucepan of salted water to a boil over high heat. Add the green beans and cook just until they turn a brighter shade of green, about 2 minutes. Drain, rinse under cold running water, and drain well. Pat them dry with a clean kitchen towel. (To prepare the green beans ahead, wrap them in paper towels after drying, transfer to a 1-gallon plastic zip-tight bag, and refrigerate for up to 1 day.)

3. Melt the butter in large skillet over medium-high heat. Add the mushrooms and cook, stirring occasionally, until they begin to brown, about 10 minutes. Stir in the shallots and cook, stirring often, until they soften, about 2 minutes. Sprinkle with the flour and stir well. Stir in the milk, broth, and Maggi and bring them to a boil, stirring often. (The mushroom sauce can be cooled, covered, and refrigerated for 1 day. Reheat in a large skillet over low heat.)

4. Stir the green beans into the mushroom sauce. Transfer them to the baking dish. Season with pepper. Bake until the sauce is bubbling, about 20 minutes. Remove the casserole from the oven and tent with aluminum foil to keep warm. Reduce the oven temperature to 200ºF.

5. To deep-fry the shallots: Meanwhile, pour enough of the oil into a large, deep skillet to come halfway up the sides and heat until the oil is shimmering and reads 365ºF on an instant-read thermometer. Place a wire cake rack in a rimmed baking sheet.

6. Mix the flour, salt, and pepper together in a brown paper bag. Mix the shallot rings and buttermilk in a medium bowl. In batches, remove the shallots from the buttermilk, letting the excess buttermilk drain back into the bowl. Add the shallots to the flour mixture and shake to coat. Transfer them to the oil and deep-fry until golden brown, about 1½ minutes. Using a wire spider or a slotted spoon, transfer the onion rings to the cake rack to drain and place them in the oven to keep warm. Top the casserole with the fried shallots and serve.

Note: Maggi is a soy-based seasoning sold in the condiments section of most supermarkets. A splash of it amps up food with a burst of umami—the quality of enhancing the food without supplying a strong taste of its own. It is the secret ingredient of many cooks (my mom always has a bottle of it in her kitchen cupboard) and is especially popular in Mexican cuisine. Soy sauce is similar and a good substitute.

RETRO GREEN BEAN CASSEROLE
MAKES 6 TO 8 SERVINGS

Serve with roast turkey, baked ham, and fried chicken.
Prep Time: 5 minutes
Cooking Time: 30 minutes
Make Ahead: The casserole can be prepared (without the onion topping) up to 1 day ahead.
Weeknight Suppers, Family Favorite, Holiday Feasts, Buffet Dish, Retro Recipe, Vegetarian

It has been almost sixty years since a Campbell's Soup home economist, Dorcas Reilly, invented this dish that rapidly (and, it seems, irrevocably) became one of America's favorite side dishes. I include it here because it is fascinating to me that while cooking has changed, it has also stayed the same. Note that the recipe includes a teaspoon of soy sauce, because even then Mrs. Reilly (who recently had a scholarship named after her at Drexel, her alma mater) knew about umami. There are recipes for this casserole that call for canned beans, but to say that I do not recommend using them is an understatement.

One 10¾-ounce can cream of mushroom soup
½ cup whole milk
1 teaspoon soy sauce

Dash of freshly ground black pepper
One 20-ounce bag frozen cut green beans, thawed
One 2.8-ounce can French-fried onions

1. Preheat the oven to 350°F. In a 1½-quart casserole, combine the soup, milk, soy sauce, and pepper. Stir in the green beans and half of the onions. (The casserole can be prepared up to 1 day ahead, covered and refrigerated.)

2. Bake until bubbling, about 25 minutes. Top with the remaining onions and bake for 5 minutes more. Serve hot.

ROMANO GREEN BEANS WITH TOMATO, PANCETTA, AND ROSEMARY SAUCE

MAKES 4 TO 6 SERVINGS

Serve with Italian-seasoned pork roasts and chops, sausages, grilled chicken, or fish fillets.

Prep Time: 10 minutes

Cooking Time: 35 minutes

Make Ahead: The green beans can be made up to 2 days ahead.

Weeknight Suppers, Family Favorite, Buffet Dish

The flat green bean variety called Romano has a meatier texture than standard green beans, and when I come across them during the summer at the market, I prepare them in a manner harmonious with their Italian origin. I have never had these in Italy unless they have been simmered to full tenderness, so that's what I've done here, with fine results. You may omit the pancetta and increase the olive oil to 2 tablespoons.

¼ cup (¼-inch) diced pancetta

1 tablespoon olive oil

½ cup chopped red onion

1 garlic clove, minced

One 14½-ounce can plum tomatoes in juice,

drained, with juices reserved, and coarsely chopped

1 teaspoon finely chopped fresh rosemary

1 pound Romano beans, cut into 1½-inch lengths

Kosher salt and freshly ground black pepper

3 tablespoons freshly grated Parmesan cheese

1. Heat the pancetta and oil together in a medium saucepan over medium heat, stirring occasionally, until the pancetta is lightly browned, about 5 minutes. Add the onion and cook, stirring often, until the onion softens, about 3 minutes. Stir in the garlic and cook until fragrant, about 1 minute. Stir in the tomatoes and their juices with ½ cup water and the rosemary. Bring them to a simmer. Reduce the heat to medium-low and simmer until the liquid is reduced by about one-third, 7 to 10 minutes.

2. Stir in the beans and bring them to a boil over medium heat. Return the heat to medium-low and cover. Cook at a brisk simmer, stirring often, until the beans are tender and the tomato juices have thickened, adding more water if the sauce gets too thick, about 15 minutes. Season to taste with salt and pepper. (The beans can be cooled, covered, and refrigerated for up to 2 days. Reheat in a skillet over medium heat.)

3. Transfer the beans to a serving bowl, sprinkle with the Parmesan, and serve.

GRILLED GREEN BEANS WITH SOY-GINGER

MAKES 6 SERVINGS

Serve with grilled red meats and poultry, especially recipes with Asian flavors.

Prep Time: 5 minutes

Cooking Time: 5 minutes

Weeknight Supper Company Fare, Vegetarian

Special Equipment: Perforated grill grate

Grilling gives green beans a smoky sear that heightens their flavor, and here they are served with a quick sauce prepared on the stove (or your grill's side burner). If you don't have Sichuan peppercorns, use a pinch of hot red pepper. A perforated grill grate will keep the beans from falling into the flames.

12 ounces green beans

2 tablespoons vegetable oil

1 tablespoon peeled and minced fresh ginger

1 garlic clove, minced

⅛ teaspoon ground Sichuan peppercorns

1 tablespoon soy sauce

Kosher salt and freshly ground black pepper

1. Prepare an outdoor grill for direct cooking over medium heat (350° to 450°F). For a charcoal grill, let the coals burn until they are covered with white ash and you can hold your hand about 1 inch above the cooking grate for about 3 seconds. For a gas grill, preheat on high and adjust the thermostat to medium (400°F). Heat a perforated grill grate on the grill.

2. In a large bowl, toss the whole green beans with 1 tablespoon of the oil to coat the beans. Place them on the perforated grill grate and cook, occasionally rolling the beans on the grate, until they are lightly seared with dark brown marks, about 5 minutes. Transfer them to a serving bowl.

3. Heat a small skillet over high heat. Add the remaining 1 tablespoon oil to the skillet and swirl it to coat the bottom. Add the ginger, garlic, and Sichuan peppercorns and stir just until fragrant, about 10 seconds. Remove from the heat. Let cool slightly. Stir in the soy sauce.

4. Pour the soy mixture over the green beans and stir well. Season to taste with salt and black pepper and serve.

Beans, Shell

Shell beans have outer pods (consisting of two halves, similar to hinged seashells) that protect the edible inner beans. Most often, the beans are removed from the pods and dried, but during the summer season, they are sold whole for the cook to discard the shells and cook the fresh beans. **Black-eyed peas, cranberry beans, fava beans** (sometimes called **broad beans**), **lima beans**, and **edamame** (fresh soy beans) are all members of this family. In general, 1 pound of beans in the shell yields 1 cup shelled beans.

Peak Season: Late spring and summer.

Purchase: Firm pods that feel like they contain plump beans. Fava bean pods are naturally soft, so look for evenly green pods.

Storage: Refrigerate for up to 5 days.

Preparation: Split the pods open, remove the beans, and discard the pods. Fava beans are peeled before cooking: Cook the fava beans in boiling water for about 30 seconds to loosen the skins; drain, rinse under cold running water, and pinch off the thin skins.

MINESTRONE SECCO WITH FRESH BEANS, ZUCCHINI, AND PROSCIUTTO

MAKES 4 SERVINGS

Serve with steaks, pork and lamb chops, sausages, or chicken.
Prep Time: 10 minutes
Cooking Time: 20 minutes
Weeknight Suppers, Company Fare

This appealing dish has the components of minestrone soup, but without a copious amount of broth, to make it "dry" (secco in Italian). My local ethnic supermarket, which caters to a Portuguese clientele, imports fresh cranberry beans all year, so I can make this outside of the usual summer season, often in a bowl with grilled sausages on top. If you can't find the beans, substitute a 15-ounce can of pink beans, rinsed and drained, and add them with the zucchini and tomato.

¼ cup (¼-inch) diced prosciutto

1 tablespoon olive oil

¼ cup chopped red onion

1 garlic clove, finely chopped

1½ cups fresh shell beans, preferably cranberry (from 1½ pounds beans in the pod)

1½ cups reduced-sodium chicken broth or water

1 zucchini, cut into ½-inch dice

1 ripe plum (Roma) tomato, seeded and cut into ½-inch dice

2 teaspoons finely chopped fresh sage or ½ teaspoon dried

⅛ teaspoon hot red pepper flakes

Kosher salt

Freshly grated Parmesan cheese, for serving

1. Heat the prosciutto and oil together in a medium skillet over medium heat, stirring occasionally, until the prosciutto begins to brown, about 3 minutes. Stir in the onion and garlic. Cook, stirring occasionally, until the onion softens, about 3 minutes more.

2. Stir in the beans and broth. Bring them to a simmer and reduce the heat to medium-low. Simmer until the beans are beginning to soften, about 5 minutes, depending on their age and tenderness.

3. Stir in the zucchini, tomato, sage, and red pepper flakes. Increase the heat to medium and cook, stirring occasionally, until the zucchini and beans are tender and the broth has reduced to a few table-spoons, about 10 minutes. Season to taste with salt.

4. Transfer the vegetables to a serving bowl, top with the Parmesan, and serve.

SUMMER SUCCOTASH
MAKES 6 SERVINGS

Serve with barbecued meats and poultry, steaks, chops, fried chicken, and seafood.

Prep Time: 15 minutes

Cooking Time: 15 minutes

Make Ahead: The succotash can be made up to 1 day ahead.

Weeknight Suppers, Family Favorite, Holiday Feasts, Company Fare, Buffet Dish,

Cooking Classic, Vegetarian

In my travels in the Southern states, I have seen many different kinds of succotash, and the only constants seem to be lima beans and corn. My favorite versions use those and other vegetables in season, with a big tomato and a little thyme in the mix. If fresh lima beans aren't available (look for them at farmer's markets), use any shell bean (cranberry beans are good) or even frozen lima beans.

1½ cups fresh lima beans (from 2 pounds beans in
   the pod; see Note page 42)

Kosher salt

3 tablespoons unsalted butter

1 large yellow onion, chopped

1 red bell pepper, cored, seeded, and cut into
   ½-inch dice

1 garlic clove, minced

1 zucchini, cut into ½-inch dice

1 yellow squash, cut into ½-inch dice

1 cup fresh corn kernels, cut from about 2 ears

1 ripe beefsteak tomato, seeded and cut into
   ½-inch dice

1 teaspoon finely chopped fresh thyme or
   ½ teaspoon dried

Freshly ground black pepper

1. Bring 2 cups water to a boil in a medium saucepan over high heat. Add the lima beans and ½ tea-spoon salt. Return to the boil and partially cover the saucepan. Reduce the heat to medium and cook at a brisk simmer until the beans are barely tender, about 15 minutes. (Do not cook the thawed frozen beans.) Drain and rinse under cold running water.

2. Melt the butter in a large skillet over medium heat. Add the onion, bell pepper, and garlic and cook, stirring occasionally, until tender, about 5 minutes.

3. Add the zucchini and yellow squash and cook, stirring often, until the squash is beginning to soften, about 3 minutes. Add the corn, tomato, lima beans, and thyme and cook, stirring occasionally, until the squash is tender and the mixture is hot, about 3 minutes more. Season to taste with salt and pepper. Transfer the succotash to a serving bowl and serve.

Note: If you wish, substitute one 10-ounce package thawed frozen lima beans for the fresh beans. Do not cook the beans; instead add them to the skillet with the corn.

FAVA BEAN AND SWISS CHARD SFAGATA
MAKES 4 SERVINGS

Serve with pork or veal roasts and chops; roast chicken and chicken sautés; baked or grilled fish fillets.
Prep Time: 10 minutes
Cooking Time: 15 minutes
Weeknight Suppers, Company Fare, Buffet Dish, Vegetarian

In Umbria, sfagata *is a light vegetable stew with fava beans as the main ingredient. They can be mixed with fennel, baby artichokes, asparagus, tomatoes, or, in this case, chard. There are no herbs here, just lots of vegetable flavor. You can substitute thawed frozen fava or lima beans or peas for the fresh beans, if you wish, adding them to the skillet with the Swiss chard stems. You will find frozen fava beans at Latino and Italian grocers.*

1 cup fresh fava beans (from 1 pound beans in the pod)	1 pound Swiss chard, well washed, shaken to remove excess water, but not dried
2 tablespoons extra-virgin olive oil	1 tablespoon fresh lemon juice
1 yellow onion, chopped	Kosher salt and freshly ground black pepper
1 carrot, cut into ½-inch dice	

1. Bring a medium saucepan of water to a boil over high heat. Add the beans and cook until the skins loosen, about 1 minute. Drain and rinse under cold running water. Peel the beans.
2. Heat the oil in a large saucepan over medium heat. Add the onion and carrot and cover. Cook, stirring occasionally, until the onion softens, about 3 minutes.
3. Meanwhile, remove the thick stems from the chard leaves. Cut the stems crosswise into ½-inch strips. Set the stems aside. Coarsely chop the chard leaves and set them aside, separated from the stems.
4. Add the sliced stems, beans, and ½ cup water to the onion mixture. Cover and cook until the stems soften, about 3 minutes. In batches, stir in the chopped chard leaves, letting the first batch wilt before adding more. Cook until the leaves and stems are tender, about 5 minutes more. Remove from the heat and stir in the lemon juice. Season to taste with salt and pepper. Transfer the *sfagata* to a serving dish and serve hot.

Belgian Endive

Ground and roasted chicory roots have long been an addition to brewed coffee to augment the expensive beans. In the 1830s, a Belgian farmer accidentally let some chicory roots sprout in a dark cellar, and he found their sunlight-deprived, white leaves to be delicious. In addition to the pale variety, there is also red endive with burgundy coloration. Both kinds are good for cooking as well as in salads.

Peak Season: Available all year.

Purchase: Firm heads without any browning.

Storage: Refrigerate, wrapped in paper towels in a plastic bag, for up to 2 weeks.

Preparation: Trim the base and discard any damaged leaves. Rinse under cold water just before using.

SIMPLE BRAISED BELGIAN ENDIVE
MAKES 4 TO 6 SERVINGS

Serve with roast beef, steak, pork roast and chops, or roast chicken.
Prep Time: 5 minutes
Cooking Time: 20 minutes
Make Ahead: The endive can be made up to 1 day ahead.
Weeknight Suppers, Holiday Feasts, Company Fare, Buffet Dish, Vegetarian

This is a simple way to take a few heads of Belgian endive and turn them into a truly succulent side dish that beautifully complements the deeper flavors of roasted meats and poultry.

1 tablespoon unsalted butter	½ teaspoon sugar
4 heads Belgian endive, each halved lengthwise	½ teaspoon kosher salt
½ cup reduced-sodium chicken broth	¼ teaspoon freshly ground black pepper
¼ cup dry white wine or dry vermouth	Finely chopped fresh flat-leaf parsley, for serving

1. Melt the butter in a large skillet over medium-high heat. Place the endive in the skillet, cut-sides down. Cook until the undersides are browned, about 3 minutes.
2. Turn the endive over. Add the broth and wine or vermouth and sprinkle in the sugar, salt, and pepper. Bring them to a boil. Reduce the heat to medium-low and cover tightly. Simmer until the endive cores are tender when pierced with the tip of a small, sharp knife, about 15 minutes.
3. Using a slotted spoon, transfer the endive to a serving bowl. Return the skillet to high heat and boil the cooking liquid until reduced to a few tablespoons, 3 to 5 minutes. Pour it over the endive. Sprinkle with the parsley and serve.

BELGIAN ENDIVE WITH CRISP GRUYÈRE TOPPING

MAKES 4 TO 8 SERVINGS

Serve with pork roasts and chops, baked ham, roast lamb and chops, or firm-fleshed fish.

Prep Time: 5 minutes

Cooking Time: 25 minutes

Weeknight Suppers, Holiday Feasts, Company Fare, Buffet Dish, Vegetarian

The endive is first braised in broth and lemon juice until it is tender, and then topped with Gruyère and bread crumbs for a crisp finish. Be sure to use a skillet with an ovenproof handle, or wrap it well in aluminum foil to protect it from the broiler heat.

3 tablespoons unsalted butter

4 heads Belgian endive, each halved lengthwise

½ cup reduced-sodium chicken broth

1 tablespoon fresh lemon juice

½ teaspoon sugar

½ teaspoon kosher salt

¼ teaspoon freshly ground black pepper

¾ cup shredded Gruyère or Swiss cheese (3 ounces)

⅓ cup soft bread crumbs, made in a food processor or blender from slightly stale crusty bread

1. Position the broiler rack about 6 inches from the source of heat and preheat the broiler.

2. Melt 2 tablespoons of the butter in a large skillet with a flameproof handle over medium heat. Place the endive in the skillet, cut-sides down. Cook until the undersides are browned, about 3 minutes.

3. Turn the endive over. Add the broth and lemon juice, sprinkle in the sugar, and then season with the salt and pepper. Bring them to a boil. Reduce the heat to medium-low and cover tightly. Simmer until the endive cores are tender when pierced with the tip of a small, sharp knife, about 15 minutes. Uncover, increase the heat to high, and cook until the liquid has reduced by half, about 3 minutes. Remove from the heat.

4. Sprinkle the Gruyère, then the bread crumbs, over the endive, and dot them with the remaining 1 tablespoon butter. Broil until the cheese is melted and the crumbs are browned, 1 to 2 minutes. Serve hot.

Bok Choy

Related to cabbage and other cruciferous vegetables, bok choy (also called **pak choy**) has a sweet, mild flavor when cooked. Large bok choy has succulent white stems with leafy dark green tops. **Baby bok choy** (the correct botanical name is **Shanghai bok choy**) are only a few inches long and have an even pale green color.

Peak Season: Available all year.

Purchase: Firm heads without wilted or browned leaves.

Storage: Refrigerate unwashed in a plastic bag for up to 3 days.

Preparation: Cut large bok choy leaves crosswise into 1- to 2-inch strips, trimming away the tough core. Rinse well in a sink or large bowl of cold water to remove any grit.

BOK CHOY WITH JALAPEÑO AND CHARRED ONIONS
MAKES 4 TO 6 SERVINGS

Serve with Asian-seasoned steaks, chops, poultry, and seafood.
Prep Time: 5 minutes
Cooking Time: 10 minutes
Weeknight Suppers, Vegetarian

Bok choy has a neutral flavor that can take strong seasonings. Here deeply browned onions add a smoky flavor to the dish. You will be surprised how much the bok choy cooks down, so don't be alarmed when it is crowded into your skillet. When I was working with the fine New York Chinese restaurant Shun Lee on their cookbook, I learned how a drizzle of sesame oil can quickly transform a simple dish with its nutty flavor. For a one-bowl meal, serve this over rice and top it with cooked chicken or shrimp.

3 tablespoons vegetable oil
1 yellow onion, cut into ¼-inch half-moons
1 jalapeño, seeded and minced
1 garlic clove, minced
1 head bok choy (1½ pounds), tough core
discarded, stems and leaves cut
    into 1- to 2-inch pieces
3 tablespoons soy sauce
½ teaspoon sugar
Dark sesame oil, for serving

1. Heat a large skillet or wok over medium-high heat. Add 1 tablespoon of the vegetable oil and swirl to coat the bottom of the skillet. Add the onion and cook until crisp-tender and deeply browned around the edges, about 3 minutes. Transfer it to a plate.
2. Add the remaining 2 tablespoons vegetable oil, swirl to coat the bottom of the skillet, and heat over medium-high heat. Add the jalapeño and garlic and stir just until fragrant, about 10 seconds. In batches, stir in the bok choy, letting the first batch wilt before adding more. Cook until crisp-tender, 3 to 5 minutes. Stir in the reserved onion.
3. Stir in the soy sauce and sugar. Transfer the bok choy to a serving bowl, drizzle with the sesame oil, and serve hot.

BABY BOK CHOY WITH OYSTER SAUCE

MAKES 4 TO 6 SERVINGS

Serve with Asian-seasoned steaks, pork or lamb chops, poultry, or seafood.
Prep Time: 5 minutes
Cooking Time: 5 minutes
Weeknight Suppers, Cooking Classic

Baby bok choy cooks quickly and looks great on the plate. Here it is dressed up with a Chinese-style sauce that is sweet, salty, and earthy—keep it in mind whenever you want to add a bit of Asian flair to simple steamed vegetables like asparagus, broccoli, or summer squash. Oyster sauce is a thick, umami-packed condiment made from oyster concentrate, but it doesn't taste particularly fishy any more than Worcestershire sauce does. This recipe provides enough sauce to serve with the main protein and rice, and is great with grilled foods prepared with Asian marinades.

12 heads baby bok choy, halved lengthwise	2 tablespoons Chinese rice wine or dry sherry
1 tablespoon vegetable oil	2 tablespoons reduced-sodium chicken broth
1 garlic clove, minced	Pinch of sugar
1 teaspoon peeled and minced fresh ginger	2 tablespoons coarsely chopped roasted unsalted
2 tablespoons oyster sauce	cashews or peanuts (optional)

1. Bring a large saucepan of salted water to a boil over high heat. Add the bok choy. Cook until they are barely tender when pierced with the tip of a small, sharp knife, about 3 minutes, depending on their size.

2. Meanwhile, heat the oil, garlic, and ginger together in a small saucepan over medium-high heat, stirring often, until the garlic mixture is softened and fragrant, about 1 minute. In a small bowl, whisk the oyster sauce, rice wine, broth, and sugar together. Stir them into the garlic mixture, bring to a boil, and cook until lightly thickened, about 1 minute.

3. Drain the bok choy well and arrange it on a platter. Pour the sauce over the bok choy. Sprinkle with the cashews, if using, and serve hot.

Broccoli and Broccolini

Broccoli has been a part of Italian cuisine for centuries. But for all of its ubiquity, it was not cultivated in America until Italian farmers started planting it in California during the 1920s. It is usually sold as an entire head, including the thick stems. But broccoli crowns alone, with the largest stems removed, are a recent innovation, and, at least in my market, are more economical than the heads. **Broccolini** looks like baby broccoli, but it is actually a Japanese hybrid with thinner stems.

Peak Season: October to May, but available all year.

Purchase: Heads should have tightly closed buds without any yellowing. Stems should not show any signs of cracking.

Storage: Refrigerate for up to 3 days.

Preparation: The thick stems are tougher than the top part of the stalk, so cut them off at the point where the skin is visibly thinner. Peel the stems with a vegetable peeler for quicker cooking, and cut as directed. Cut florets into bite-sized pieces. Broccolini is simply cut into the desired lengths.

BROCCOLI WITH EASY LEMON-BUTTER SAUCE
MAKES 4 SERVINGS

Serve with roast meats and poultry, steaks, chops, or seafood.
Prep Time: 5 minutes
Cooking Time: 5 minutes
Weeknight Suppers, Family Favorite, Cooking Classic, Vegetarian

This is one of my favorite vegetable side dishes, and so easy, melding the cooking water, butter, and lemon juice to create a light sauce. Cook the broccoli in a skillet to cut back on the time needed to bring a larger container of water to a boil. If you wish, finish the broccoli with a sprinkle of toasted sliced almonds.

1 pound broccoli crowns, stems peeled and cut into ½-inch rounds, tops cut into bite-sized florets	Finely grated zest of 1 lemon
	2 tablespoons fresh lemon juice
	Kosher salt and freshly ground black pepper
2 tablespoons (¼ stick) unsalted butter	

1. Half-fill a large skillet with salted water and bring it to a boil over high heat. Add the stem rounds and cook for 1 minute. Add the broccoli tops and cover the skillet. Cook until the broccoli is crisp-tender, about 3 minutes.

2. Drain the broccoli, reserving 2 tablespoons of the cooking water. Return the broccoli to the skillet and add the cooking water, butter, and the lemon zest and juice. Cook over low heat, shaking the pan until the butter softens and thickens the liquid to make a light sauce, about 1 minute. Season to taste with salt and pepper. Transfer the broccoli to a serving bowl and serve.

EASY BUTTER SAUCE

It is very simple to make a light butter sauce for boiled green vegetables. Once you master this technique, you'll probably use it as often as I do.

Before draining the vegetables, scoop out and reserve a few tablespoons of the cooking water. After draining, return the vegetables to the cooking vessel. Add 2 tablespoons unsalted butter with 2 tablespoons of the reserved water (or more of each, depending on the amount of vegetables and desired quantity of sauce). Toss gently over very low heat until the butter is melted and combined with the water, about 1 minute. Season to taste with salt and pepper, and add chopped fresh herbs if you wish. That's it. Unless you want to add a squeeze of fresh lemon juice.

PAN-STEAMED BROCCOLI WITH HUNAN SAUCE
MAKES 4 SERVINGS

Serve with Asian-seasoned steaks, pork chops, chicken, or salmon.
Prep Time: 10 minutes
Cooking Time: 5 minutes
Weeknight Suppers, Holiday Feasts, Company Fare, Buffet Dish, Retro Recipe, Cooking Classic

Hunan cooking is known for its spiciness, and this zingy sauce lives up to the reputation. Its forthright taste goes well with broccoli, and I also like it with asparagus and cauliflower, which can be pan-steamed in a skillet in the same manner. This is a generous amount of sauce, all the better to spread on the plate to act as a condiment for the meal's chosen protein and rice.

½ cup reduced-sodium chicken broth
2 tablespoons soy sauce
2 tablespoons rice vinegar
2 tablespoons chili-bean sauce (*toban jan*)
1½ teaspoons oyster sauce
1 teaspoon sugar
1½ teaspoons cornstarch

1 pound broccoli crowns, stems peeled and cut
  into ½-inch rounds, tops cut into bite-sized
  florets
1 tablespoon vegetable oil
2 teaspoons peeled and minced fresh ginger
2 garlic cloves, minced
1 teaspoon sesame seeds, toasted (see page 33)

1. In a small bowl, whisk the broth, soy sauce, rice vinegar, chili-bean sauce, oyster sauce, and sugar together to dissolve the sugar. Sprinkle the cornstarch over the mixture and whisk to dissolve the cornstarch.

2. Half fill a large skillet with salted water and bring it to a boil over high heat. Add the stem rounds and cook for 1 minute. Add the broccoli tops and cover the skillet. Cook until the broccoli is crisp-tender, about 3 minutes. Drain the broccoli.

3. Wipe out the skillet. Add the oil, ginger, and garlic to the skillet and cook over high heat, stirring often, until the mixture is sizzling, about 1 minute. Whisk the broth mixture to incorporate any cornstarch on the bottom of the bowl, and pour it into the skillet. Stir until the mixture comes to a boil and thickens. Return the broccoli to the skillet and stir until the broccoli is coated with the sauce. Sprinkle it with the sesame seeds and serve.

BROCCOLI AND CHEDDAR CASSEROLE
MAKES 12 SERVINGS

Serve with ham, barbecued meats and poultry, and seafood.
Prep Time: 10 minutes
Cooking Time: 1 hour
Family Favorite, Holiday Feasts, Company Fare, Buffet Dish, Retro Recipe, Vegetarian

My friend Michael Tyrrell told me about the wonderful old-fashioned casserole he enjoyed from the family recipe collection of his colleague Julie Miltenberger. Michael and Julie are food editors at Family Circle *magazine, so it is their job to know crowd-pleasing side dishes. This "retro recipe" is no less tasty just because it is easy to make from convenience foods. Serve this at a big family gathering, be it a summer barbecue or a holiday meal.*

Nonstick vegetable oil spray, for the baking dish
4 large eggs
Two 10¾-ounce cans cream of mushroom soup
1 cup mayonnaise
1 large yellow onion, shredded on the large holes of a box shredder

Two 20-ounce bags thawed frozen chopped broccoli, well drained
2 cups shredded sharp Cheddar cheese (8 ounces)
2 cups crushed square cheese crackers (such as Cheez-Its)

1. Position a rack in the center of the oven and preheat the oven to 350ºF. Spray the inside of a 15 × 10 × 2-inch baking dish with oil.

2. In a large bowl, whisk the eggs together. Add the soup, mayonnaise, and onion and whisk to combine. Stir in the broccoli, Cheddar, and ¾ cup of the crackers. Spread everything in the baking dish. Top it with the remaining 1¼ cups cracker crumbs.

3. Bake until the top is golden brown and all but the very center is set when the dish is shaken, about 1 hour. (The casserole can be cooled, covered with aluminum foil, and refrigerated for up to 1 day. Reheat, covered, in a 350ºF oven until heated through, about 20 minutes.) Let stand 10 minutes. Serve hot.

ROASTED BROCCOLINI WITH EAST-WEST BUTTER SAUCE

MAKES 4 TO 6 SERVINGS

Serve with steaks, pork or veal chops, roast chicken, and seafood.

Prep Time: 5 minutes

Cooking Time: 10 minutes

Weeknight Suppers, Family Favorite, Company Fare, Buffet Dish, Vegetarian

My friend and colleague David Bonom gave me this recipe for an interesting sauce for broccolini that intermingles three flavor powerhouses: butter, soy sauce, and balsamic vinegar.

1 pound broccolini, cut into 2- to 3-inch lengths

2 teaspoons vegetable oil

2 tablespoons (¼ stick) unsalted butter

1 tablespoon soy sauce

1 tablespoon balsamic vinegar

⅛ teaspoon freshly ground black pepper

1. Position a rack in the center of the oven and preheat the oven to 425ºF. Lightly oil a large, rimmed baking sheet.

2. Toss the broccolini with the oil in the baking sheet. Roast, flipping the broccolini halfway through cooking, until it is just tender, about 10 minutes.

3. Meanwhile, melt the butter in a small saucepan over medium heat, stirring occasionally, until it is lightly browned, about 3 minutes. Remove from the heat and stir in the soy sauce, vinegar, and pepper. Pour the sauce over the broccolini, mix gently, and serve.

Broccoli Rabe

Also called rapini, this green has a sharp flavor that can be paired with blander foods to tone it down. Many of my Italian friends blanch it first in boiling water to remove some of the bitterness, yet others prepare it without precooking because they like the peppery taste. It is a cool-weather vegetable (it bolts too easily in hot weather), and to me, it represents autumn cooking.

Peak Season: Available all year, but best in fall and spring.

Purchase: Sprightly bunches without signs of yellowing.

Storage: Refrigerate for up to 3 days.

Preparation: Trim off stem ends. Rinse heads well in cold water to remove any grit.

BROCCOLI RABE AND GARBANZO BEANS

MAKES 4 SERVINGS

Serve with pork roasts and chops, sausages, or roast chicken.
Prep Time: 10 minutes
Cooking Time: 30 minutes
Weeknight Suppers, Vegetarian

At my house, this is a popular way to serve broccoli rabe, and few sides go better with Italian sausage. The beans and onion cushion the greens' aggressive flavor. And we like our broccoli rabe cooked until it is very tender, but you can adjust the cooking time to suit your taste.

2 tablespoons olive oil
1 yellow onion, chopped
2 garlic cloves, minced
1 pound broccoli rabe, stems cut into 1-inch
  pieces, and tops coarsely chopped

One 15-ounce can garbanzo beans (chickpeas),
  drained and rinsed
Kosher salt and hot red pepper flakes

1. Heat the oil in a large skillet over medium heat. Add the onion and cook, stirring occasionally, until it is softened, about 3 minutes. Stir in the garlic and cook until it is fragrant, about 1 minute.
2. Wash the broccoli rabe well in a large bowl or sink filled with cold water. Lift out the broccoli rabe (leaving any grit behind in the bowl) and transfer it, with any clinging water, to the skillet. Stir well and cover the skillet. Reduce the heat to medium-low. Cook, stirring occasionally, until the broccoli rabe is tender, about 20 minutes.
3. Stir in the beans. Season to taste with salt and red pepper flakes. Cover again and cook, stirring often, until the beans are heated through and the broccoli rabe is very tender, about 5 minutes. Serve hot.

BROCCOLI RABE AND FARRO GRATIN

MAKES 6 SERVINGS

Serve with Italian-style roasts, chops, sausages, roast chicken, or chicken sautés.
Prep Time: 20 minutes
Cooking Time: 1 hour
Make Ahead: The gratin can be made up to 1 day ahead.
Holiday Feasts, Company Fare, Buffet Dish, Vegetarian

This Italian-inspired gratin has farro and broccoli rabe, not common ingredients for this kind of dish, bound together with ricotta cheese. The broccoli rabe is so flavorful that the dish does not need herbs.

½ cup farro

2 tablespoons olive oil, plus more for the baking dish

1 red onion, chopped

2 garlic cloves, finely chopped

1 pound broccoli rabe, stems cut into 1-inch pieces, and tops coarsely chopped, washed well, but not dried

3 large eggs

One 16-ounce container ricotta cheese

½ cup whole milk

1 teaspoon kosher salt

½ teaspoon freshly ground black pepper

3 tablespoons freshly grated Parmesan cheese

1. Position a rack in the center of the oven and preheat the oven to 325ºF. Lightly oil an 11½ × 8 × 2-inch baking dish.

2. Bring a medium saucepan of salted water to a boil over high heat. Add the farro and cook (just like pasta) until it is tender, about 20 minutes. Drain well.

3. Meanwhile, heat the oil in a large skillet over medium heat. Add the onion and cook, stirring occasionally, until it softens, about 3 minutes. Stir in the garlic and cook until it is fragrant, about 1 minute. Add the broccoli rabe with any clinging water and stir well. Reduce the heat to medium-low and cover. Cook, stirring occasionally, until the broccoli rabe stems are tender, about 15 minutes. Drain in a colander, pressing on the mixture with a heatproof spatula to extrude excess moisture. Transfer to a cutting board and coarsely chop the mixture.

4. Whisk the eggs together in a medium bowl. Add the ricotta, milk, salt, and pepper and whisk again. Stir in the farro and broccoli rabe. Spread the mixture in the baking dish. Sprinkle the Parmesan over the top.

5. Bake until the top of the gratin is lightly puffed and a knife inserted in the center comes out clean, about 40 minutes. (The gratin can be cooled, covered with aluminum foil, and refrigerated for up to 1 day. Reheat, covered, in a preheated 350ºF oven for about 20 minutes.) Let cool for 5 minutes and serve.

Brussels Sprouts

These tiny cabbages have a high tolerance for cold temperatures, so they are often featured on winter menus. They are sweeter if exposed to frost before harvesting. First cultivated in quantity in Belgium, they didn't really take off in this country until they were grown to supply the frozen food industry in the 1950s, which meant that many people grew up never tasting fresh sprouts. Now, roasted Brussels sprouts are one of the most beloved of all side dishes.

Peak Season: October to March, but available all year.

Purchase: Compact heads without any signs of yellowing.

Storage: Refrigerate for up to 1 week.

Preparation: Trim off the stem ends and any wilted leaves.

BRUSSELS SPROUTS CHIFFONADE WITH PANCETTA AND PARMESAN

MAKES 4 SERVINGS

Serve with roast pork and chops, roast chicken or turkey, or grilled halibut or salmon.

Prep Time: 10 minutes

Cooking Time: 12 minutes

Weeknight Suppers, Holiday Feasts, Company Fare, Buffet Dish

Shredded Brussels sprouts cook quickly and have a wonderfully fresh flavor. A food processor with the slicing disk is the quickest way to slice the sprouts, but you certainly can use a knife. Leftovers are wonderful heated up and tossed with pasta.

1 pound Brussels sprouts

⅓ cup diced (¼-inch) pancetta

1 tablespoon olive oil

Kosher salt and freshly ground black pepper

¼ cup freshly grated Parmesan cheese

1. Fit a food processor with the slicing disk. With the motor running, drop the sprouts through the feed tube. Don't worry if they slice randomly, and only use the plunger to push the last couple of sprouts through the blade. (Or use a large knife to cut the sprouts crosswise into ⅛-inch slices.)

2. Cook the pancetta and oil together in a large skillet over medium heat, stirring occasionally, until the pancetta is lightly browned, about 5 minutes. Add the shredded Brussels sprouts and increase the heat to medium-high. Cook the sprouts, uncovered, stirring occasionally, until they are crisp-tender and heated through, 5 to 7 minutes. Season to taste with salt and pepper.

3. Transfer the Brussels sprouts to a serving dish, sprinkle with the Parmesan, and serve.

BRUSSELS SPROUTS WITH POMEGRANATE AND BALSAMIC VINEGAR

MAKES 4 TO 6 SERVINGS

Serve with roast pork or chops, roast lamb or chops, roast chicken, or turkey.

Prep Time: 10 minutes

Cooking Time: 20 minutes

Weeknight Suppers, Company Fare, Buffet Dish

Puckery pomegranate juice brightens the flavor of pan-roasted Brussels sprouts. I give instructions for removing the arils from the fruit on page 54 in the sidebar, but many supermarkets now carry packaged pomegranate arils year-round. While I love pomegranate-balsamic vinegar, the unflavored variety works well, too.

1 tablespoon extra-virgin olive oil

1 pound Brussels sprouts, halved lengthwise if larger than a walnut

½ cup reduced-sodium chicken broth

Kosher salt and freshly ground black pepper

½ cup pomegranate arils (also called seeds; see sidebar below)

2 tablespoons pomegranate-flavored or standard balsamic vinegar

1. Heat the oil in a large skillet over medium heat. Add the sprouts and cook, stirring occasionally, until they are lightly browned in spots, about 5 minutes.

2. Add the broth and ½ cup water and bring them to a brisk skimmer. Season the sprouts with salt and pepper. Partially cover the skillet and cook at a brisk simmer, stirring occasionally, until the sprouts are almost tender when pierced with the tip of a small, sharp knife, about 12 minutes. Uncover, increase the heat to high, and cook until the liquid is evaporated and the sprouts are sizzling, about 3 minutes. Remove from the heat.

3. Stir in the pomegranate arils and vinegar. Season to taste with salt and pepper. Transfer the Brussels sprouts to a serving dish and serve hot.

POMEGRANATES

When I was growing up in the multiethnic San Francisco Bay Area, pomegranates (also called Chinese apples at that period in time) were an annual autumn treat. I loved the effort it took to get to the reward of the tart juice. (The seeds are actually enveloped inside the juice-filled, capsule-like arils.) Removed from the fruit, pomegranate arils can be used as a beautiful and delicious garnish for many side dishes.

There is a very easy way to remove the arils that I wish I had learned earlier in my life. It will take you less than a minute to separate them from the bitter pale yellow flesh. Using a paring knife, cut around the equator of the pomegranate, reaching about ⅛ inch into the flesh, but not cutting into the arils. Wedge the knife into the cut, and twist the knife to open the pomegranate, and then pull the two halves apart with your hands. Turn a pomegranate half over a medium bowl. Using a wooden spoon, bang the pomegranate skin hard, and the arils will drop into the bowl. Don't be gentle—really whack the pomegranate. Pick out any stray bits of membrane and flesh from the bowl. The arils can be covered and refrigerated for up to 3 days.

ROASTED BRUSSELS SPROUTS WITH BACON AND MAPLE SYRUP

MAKES 6 SERVINGS

Serve with roast turkey, pork roast or chops, or grilled salmon.

Prep Time: 5 minutes

Cooking Time: 35 minutes

Make Ahead: The bacon and Brussels sprouts can be prepared up to 1 day ahead, and the dish cooked just before serving.

Weeknight Suppers, Family Favorite, Holiday Feasts, Company Fare, Buffet Dish

Maybe I am being a little hyperbolic, but the sweet-salty-crisp combination of bacon and maple syrup can almost induce euphoria, at least according to unscientific evidence gathered from my dinner guests. I supply detailed make-ahead instructions because you really should think about adding this to a holiday dinner menu. When I serve this at Thanksgiving, the turkey gets jealous.

3 slices bacon, preferably thick cut

1¼ pounds Brussels sprouts, halved lengthwise if larger than a walnut

3 tablespoons pure maple syrup, preferably Grade A Dark (see Note page 56)

Kosher salt and freshly ground black pepper

1. Cook the bacon in a large skillet over medium heat, turning once, until it is crisp and browned, 7 to 8 minutes. Using a slotted spatula, transfer it to paper towels to drain and cool. Pour the rendered bacon fat into a small bowl and set aside. (The bacon and bacon fat can be cooled, covered separately, and refrigerated for up to 1 day. Reheat the bacon fat in a microwave oven or in a skillet just until melted.)

2. Meanwhile, bring a large pot of salted water to a boil over high heat. Add the sprouts and cook until they turn a brighter shade of green, about 3 minutes. Drain, rinse well under cold running water, and drain again. Pat the sprouts dry with paper towels. (The sprouts can be wrapped in dry paper towels, stored in plastic zip-tight bags, and refrigerated for up to 1 day.)

3. Position a rack in the center of the oven and preheat the oven to 400°F. Line a half-sheet pan with parchment paper.

4. Toss the sprouts and bacon fat in a large bowl until coated. Spread the sprouts on the prepared pan. Bake the sprouts, turning them occasionally, until they are beginning to brown, about 20 minutes. Remove the pan from the oven. Drizzle the sprouts with the syrup and stir to coat them evenly. Return the sprouts to the oven and continue baking, stirring once or twice, until the syrup has reduced to a glaze, about 5 minutes more.

5. Season the sprouts to taste with salt and pepper. Transfer them to a serving dish. Coarsely chop the bacon, sprinkle it over the sprouts, and serve.

Note: American maple syrup is graded according to its color and depth of flavor. Recently, the names of the grades have changed. Grade A Dark (formerly called Grade B), which has a robust flavor and mahogany hue, is my choice for all-purpose syrup for both cooking and pouring over pancakes. In Canada, which supplies about 80 percent of the world's maple syrup, this syrup is graded Number 2. If I use the lighter, more delicate Amber, I add a few drops of pure maple extract to boost the flavor.

Cabbage, Chinese (Napa)

This elongated, pale green cabbage with white stalks is great in stir-fries and slaws. It is sometimes called celery cabbage because its mild flavor is a cross between the two vegetables. There are two distinct shapes, oblong and barrel, but they taste the same.

Peak Season: Available all year.

Purchase: Compact heads without any tiny brown or black spots.

Storage: Refrigerate for up to 1 week.

Preparation: Cut in half and cut out the hard core.

STIR-FRIED CHINESE CABBAGE WITH RAMEN TOPPING
MAKES 6 SERVINGS

Serve with Asian-flavored grilled steaks, chops, and poultry.
Prep Time: 10 minutes
Cooking Time: 5 minutes
Weeknight Suppers, Family Favorite

This stir-fry gets lots of spice to steer the cabbage away from blandness, and gets crushed ramen noodles on top for crunch. The ramen will soften as the dish stands, which only means that the noodles acquire a different texture as time elapses, and the soft noodles are as good as the crisp ones. A head of chopped napa cabbage may look like a mountain of greens, but don't be deterred, as it shrinks quite a bit when cooked.

2 tablespoons soy sauce

2 tablespoons oyster sauce

1 tablespoon rice vinegar

½ teaspoon Chinese chili-garlic sauce or Sriracha

½ teaspoon sugar

2 tablespoons vegetable oil

2 scallions (white and green parts), sliced

1 tablespoon peeled and minced fresh ginger

4 garlic cloves, minced

1 small head Chinese (napa) cabbage, cored and cut into pieces about 2 inches square

Kosher salt

One 3-ounce package instant ramen, without its seasoning packet, coarsely crushed

1. In a small bowl, stir the soy sauce, oyster sauce, vinegar, chili-garlic sauce, and sugar together.

2. Heat a large skillet or wok over high heat. Add the oil and swirl the skillet to distribute the oil. Add the scallions, ginger, and garlic and stir until fragrant, about 15 seconds.

3. In two or three batches, add the cabbage and cook, stirring almost constantly, until the first batch is wilted, 2 to 3 minutes, before adding another. Pour in the soy sauce mixture and stir until boiling. Season to taste with salt.

4. Transfer the cabbage to a serving bowl, top with the ramen, and serve.

Cabbage, Green, and Sauerkraut

As a side dish, cabbage is forever paired with corned beef, but it is also indispensable for a summer picnic slaw, or made into chow-chow to go with a hot dog. Varieties include the familiar green (also called white) and curly Savoy types. And even though it isn't fresh, I am including store-bought **sauerkraut**, naturally fermented cabbage, here. The refrigerated kind, sold in plastic bags or glass containers, is much better than canned sauerkraut, and it is the only kind I cook with.

Peak Season: Available all year.

Purchase: Unblemished heads that are heavy for their size.

Storage: Refrigerate whole heads for up to 2 weeks; cut heads should be wrapped in plastic and used within 2 days.

Preparation: Discard the wilted outer leaves, cut the head into quarters, and cut out the core.

STEAMED CABBAGE WITH BACON AND OLD BAY
MAKES 4 SERVINGS

Serve with corned beef, brisket, roast pork, pork chops, ham, sausages, fried chicken, or shrimp.
Prep Time: 5 minutes
Cooking Time: 30 minutes
Weeknight Suppers, Buffet Dish

The commercial spice mixture of Old Bay Seasoning, with over a dozen herbs and spices listed on the label, is beloved on the Eastern Seaboard, where it is usually sprinkled in liberal amounts over steamed crab and other seafood. But it can also be used to spice up other dishes, such as this green cabbage. Steaming gives the cabbage a firmer texture and fresher flavor than the boiling method, and the Old Bay adds zing. And I can't resist adding bacon, as it is a time-tested complement to cabbage, but you could make the Old Bay Butter variation. You probably will not need to season the cabbage with salt and pepper because Old Bay is both salty and spicy.

½ head green cabbage (about 1 pound), cored and quartered lengthwise

3 slices bacon, coarsely chopped

2 scallions (white and green parts), chopped

1½ teaspoons Old Bay Seasoning

1. Place a collapsible steamer in a large saucepan and add enough water to almost reach the bottom of the steamer. (If you have another kind of steamer, just set it up as needed.) Bring the water to a boil over high heat.

2. Add the cabbage wedges to the steamer and cover tightly. Cook until the cabbage is just tender when pierced with the tip of a small, sharp knife, about 25 minutes.

3. About 10 minutes before the cabbage is done, cook the bacon in a medium skillet over medium heat, stirring occasionally, until crisp and browned, about 8 minutes. Add the scallions to the fat in the skillet and cook, stirring often, until softened, about 2 minutes. Remove from the heat and stir in the Old Bay Seasoning.

4. Transfer the cabbage to a serving bowl. Using a heatproof spatula, scrape the bacon mixture over the cabbage, mix gently, and serve.

Steamed Cabbage with Old Bay Butter: Omit the bacon. Melt 2 tablespoons unsalted butter in a medium skillet over medium heat. Add the scallions and cook until softened, about 2 minutes. Remove from the heat and stir in the Old Bay Seasoning.

FARMHOUSE GREEN CABBAGE WITH ROOT VEGETABLES AND BACON

MAKES 6 TO 8 SERVINGS

Serve with corned beef, pork roast, pork chops, ham, barbecued meats, roast duck, roast goose, or salmon fillets.

Prep Time: 5 minutes

Cooking Time: 1 hour

Make Ahead: The cabbage can be refrigerated for up to 2 days.

Buffet Dish

In country cooking, cabbage, carrots, and onions are workhorses in the kitchen. Simmered together for an hour, they share flavors and become a truly comforting side dish that can be served with a wide range of main courses. One of my favorite pairings for this is grilled salmon.

2 slices bacon, cut crosswise into 1-inch lengths

2 tablespoons vegetable oil

1 yellow onion, chopped

2 carrots, cut into ½-inch pieces

1 small head green cabbage (about 2 pounds), cored and cut into 8 to 10 wedges

½ cup reduced-sodium beef broth
Kosher salt and freshly ground black pepper

Cider vinegar, for serving

1. Cook the bacon and oil together in a large skillet over medium heat, stirring occasionally, until the bacon is crisp and brown, about 5 minutes. Using a slotted spoon, transfer the bacon to paper towels to drain, leaving the fat in the pan.

2. Add the onion and carrots and cook, stirring occasionally, until the onion softens, about 3 minutes. Arrange the cabbage wedges, overlapping as needed, in the skillet. Pour in the broth, season with 1 teaspoon salt and ¼ teaspoon pepper, and bring to a boil. Reduce the heat to medium-low and cover tightly. Simmer until the cabbage is very tender, 50 minutes to 1 hour.

3. Uncover and increase the heat to high. Boil until the cooking liquid is reduced to a few tablespoons, about 3 minutes. Season to taste with salt and pepper. Sprinkle with the bacon. Serve hot, with the vinegar passed on the side for sprinkling.

ROASTED CABBAGE WITH SOUR CREAM AND MUSTARD GLAZE

MAKES 4 TO 6 SERVINGS

Serve with pork roast and chops, baked ham, sausages, roast chicken, chicken sautés, or roast duck.
Prep Time: 5 minutes
Cooking Time: 30 minutes
Weeknight Suppers, Vegetarian

A side that you could probably make with your eyes closed (although I don't recommend it), roasted cabbage sports sweet toasted edges, and the creamy mustard finish brings the dish home. This is now one of the most popular winter sides in our house.

2 tablespoons olive oil, plus more for the baking
  sheet
1 small head green cabbage (about 2 pounds),
  cored and cut into 6 to 8 wedges

1 teaspoon kosher salt
¼ teaspoon freshly ground black pepper
2 tablespoons sour cream
2 tablespoons stone-ground or Dijon mustard

1. Position a rack in the center of the oven and preheat the oven to 450ºF. Lightly oil a large rimmed baking sheet.

2. Place the cabbage wedges on the baking sheet. Brush them on all sides with the oil and season with the salt and pepper. Roast for 15 minutes. Flip the cabbage over and continue roasting until it is deeply browned around the edges and just tender, about 15 minutes more. Remove from the oven.

3. In a small bowl, mix the sour cream and mustard together. Spread it over the flat sides of the cabbage and return to the oven. Continue roasting until the glaze is set, about 5 minutes. Transfer the cabbage to a serving platter and serve hot.

Sauerkraut

FRENCH SAUERKRAUT WITH CIDER AND APPLES
MAKES 6 TO 8 SERVINGS

Serve with sausages, smoked pork chops, ham, roast duck, or roast goose.
Prep Time: 5 minutes
Cooking Time: 1 ¼ hours
Make Ahead: The sauerkraut can be refrigerated for up to 3 days.
Holiday Feasts, Cooking Classic

Slowly simmered with cider and apples, this resembles French choucroute, the sauerkraut dish that is served with an array of sausages and smoked meats as a nigh-perfect cold-weather meal. Although choucroute is made with wine, I like the additional apple flavor provided by cider. This recipe is easy to reduce by half for four servings, and it is really good with crisp crumbled bacon on top . . . but then, what cabbage dish isn't?

2 pounds refrigerated sauerkraut	1 cup hard cider or ½ cup dry white wine and
2 tablespoons vegetable oil	½ cup apple juice
1 yellow onion, cut into thin half-moons	½ teaspoon dried thyme
2 tart apples, such as Granny Smith, cored and	6 juniper berries
thinly sliced (no need to peel)	¼ teaspoon freshly ground black pepper
1 cup reduced-sodium chicken broth	1 bay leaf

1. Drain the sauerkraut in a colander and rinse under cold running water. Squeeze the excess liquid from the sauerkraut.

2. Heat the oil in a large saucepan over medium heat. Add the onion and cook, stirring occasionally, until it is softened, about 3 minutes. Add the apples and cook, stirring occasionally, until the onions are golden, about 2 minutes more. Add the sauerkraut, broth, cider, thyme, juniper berries, pepper, and bay leaf. Bring them to a boil.

3. Reduce the heat to medium-low and cover tightly. Cook, stirring occasionally, until the sauerkraut is very tender, about 1 hour. Uncover, increase the heat to medium, and cook, stirring occasionally, until most of the liquid has been absorbed, about 10 minutes. Discard the bay leaf and serve.

SAUERKRAUT WITH BEER, BACON, AND MUSTARD SEEDS

MAKES 6 TO 8 SERVINGS

Serve with sausages, smoked pork chops, ham, roast duck, or roast goose.

Prep Time: 5 minutes

Cooking Time: 1 ¼ hours

Make Ahead: The sauerkraut can be refrigerated for up to 3 days.

Holiday Feasts, Cooking Classic

When trying to decide between this version of sauerkraut with crunchy mustard seeds or the cider-based recipe (page 60), it usually boils down to whether I am going to serve beer or wine with the meal. This goes well with coarse-textured sausages, such as bratwurst.

2 pounds refrigerated sauerkraut

4 slices bacon, cut crosswise into 1-inch pieces

1 large onion, cut into thin half-moons

2 large carrots, cut into ½-inch dice

2 tablespoons yellow mustard seeds

2 garlic cloves, minced

One 12-ounce bottle dark beer (not stout or porter)

1 cup reduced-sodium chicken broth

Freshly ground black pepper

1. Drain the sauerkraut in a colander and rinse under cold running water. Squeeze the excess liquid from the sauerkraut.

2. Cook the bacon in a large saucepan over medium heat, stirring occasionally, until it is crisp and browned, about 8 minutes. Using a slotted spoon, transfer the bacon to paper towels to drain, leaving the fat in the saucepan.

3. Add the onion and carrots to the saucepan and cook, stirring occasionally, until they're softened, about 3 minutes. Stir in the mustard seeds and garlic and cook until the garlic is fragrant, about 1 minute. Add the sauerkraut, beer, and broth and bring them to a boil.

4. Reduce the heat to medium-low and cover tightly. Cook, stirring occasionally, until the sauerkraut is very tender, about 1 hour. Uncover, increase the heat to medium, and cook, stirring occasionally, until most of the liquid has been absorbed, about 10 minutes more. Season to taste with pepper. Stir in the drained bacon and serve.

Cabbage, Red

Red cabbage actually has reddish purple outer leaves, with the inner leaves lightening to magenta. Braised, it is the ultimate German side dish for main courses from sausage to sauerbraten. Red cabbage can also be very thinly sliced and used sparsely in slaw, but I find that it tends to discolor the slaw and remains too tough for my taste.

Peak Season: Available all year.

Purchase: Unblemished heads that are heavy for their size.

Storage: Refrigerate whole heads for up to 2 weeks; cut heads should be wrapped in plastic and used within 2 days.

Preparation: Discard the wilted outer leaves, cut the head into quarters, and cut out the core.

SWEET AND SOUR RED CABBAGE WITH APPLES
MAKES 4 TO 6 SERVINGS

Serve with sausages, sauerbraten, pork roasts and chops, roast duck, or roast goose.
Prep Time: 10 minutes
Cooking Time: 1¼ hours
Make Ahead: The red cabbage can be made up to 2 days ahead.
Family Favorite, Holiday Feasts, Company Fare, Buffet Dish, Cooking Classic

Red cabbage, cooked to tender shreds and infused with tangy-sweet flavor, was a staple in our house when I was growing up, and I still cook it often. Mom always made it with the bacon fat collected from morning meals. In this recipe, as few cooks still save bacon fat for cooking, I start from scratch with bacon strips. If you wish, substitute 2 tablespoons of butter for the bacon fat, or use the rendered fat from roast goose or duck. (Roast duck is our annual New Year's Eve dinner.) Don't try to rush the cabbage, as it takes about an hour to tenderize and meld the flavors. It is even better if made a day or two ahead and reheated.

2 slices bacon, cut into 1-inch pieces

1 tablespoon vegetable oil

2 Granny Smith apples, unpeeled, cored and cut into ¾-inch pieces

1 yellow onion, chopped

1 head red cabbage (about 2 pounds), cored and cut into ¼-inch strips

⅓ cup cider vinegar or red wine vinegar

⅓ cup (packed) light brown sugar

½ teaspoon dried thyme

Kosher salt and freshly ground black pepper

1 bay leaf

1. Cook the bacon and oil in a large saucepan over medium heat, stirring occasionally, until the bacon is crisp and brown, about 5 minutes. Using a slotted spoon, transfer the bacon to paper towels to drain, leaving the fat in the saucepan.

2. Add the apples and cook, stirring once or twice, until they're beginning to soften and brown, about 3 minutes. Stir in the onion and cook, stirring occasionally, until softened and golden, about 4 minutes. Add the cabbage, vinegar, and brown sugar and stir well to coat the cabbage. Stir in ⅓ cup water, the thyme, ½ teaspoon salt, ¼ teaspoon pepper, and the bay leaf.

3. Cover tightly and reduce the heat to medium-low. Cook, stirring occasionally, and adding more water if the cabbage threatens to scorch, until the cabbage is very tender, about 1 hour. If necessary, increase the heat to medium-high and cook, stirring often, until the liquid reduces to a few tablespoons. Discard the bay leaf and stir in the reserved bacon. Season to taste with salt and pepper and serve hot.

ITALIAN RED CABBAGE WITH RED WINE AND CHESTNUTS
MAKES 6 TO 8 SERVINGS

Serve with grilled sausages, pork roast, pork chops, ham, roast duck, or roast goose.
Prep Time: 10 minutes
Cooking Time: 1½ hours
Make Ahead: The cabbage can be refrigerated for up to 3 days.
Holiday Feasts, Buffet Dish

Germany isn't the only country with great red cabbage recipes, as this northern Italian recipe with chunks of chestnuts and bits of pancetta shows. The wine heightens the cabbage's color and flavor. I cook it for an especially long time to marry the flavors.

⅓ cup (¼-inch) diced pancetta

2 tablespoons vegetable oil

1 yellow onion, chopped

2 carrots, cut into ¼-inch dice

1 cup hearty red wine, such as Shiraz

½ cup balsamic vinegar

¼ cup sugar

1 teaspoon dried marjoram

1 head red cabbage (about 2 pounds), cored and cut into ¼-inch strips

Kosher salt and freshly ground black pepper

1 bay leaf

1 cup coarsely chopped Basic Roasted Chestnuts (page 401) or vacuum-packed chestnuts

1. Heat the pancetta and oil together in a large saucepan over medium heat, stirring occasionally, until the pancetta is lightly browned, about 5 minutes. Add the onion and carrots and cook, stirring often, until the onion is golden, about 5 minutes more.

2. Add the wine, vinegar, sugar, and marjoram. Gradually stir in the cabbage, coating it with the wine mixture. Season with ½ teaspoon salt and ½ teaspoon pepper and add the bay leaf. Bring everything to a simmer. Reduce the heat to medium-low and cook, stirring occasionally, for 1 hour. Uncover and continue cooking, stirring occasionally, until the cabbage is very tender, about 30 minutes more. During the last 10 minutes, stir in the chestnuts. Season to taste with salt and pepper. Discard the bay leaf and serve.

Cauliflower and Broccoflower

Big heads of white cauliflower are a common sight in fall and winter produce stands. But more vibrant colors are showing up with regularity at supermarkets and farmer's markets, including purple, orange, and green. **Broccoflower** is similar to green cauliflower, but the **Romanesco** variety (with fractal buds that look like neon-green pine cones) is a separate type. These varieties can be used interchangeably with the old favorite, and they are sure to be conversation starters. However, their bright colors fade when cooked, so don't expect them to retain the exact same hue.

Peak Season: September to November, but available all year.

Purchase: Creamy white heads without bruised buds. The leaves should be bright green.

Storage: Refrigerate whole heads for up to 5 days; use cut florets within 2 days.

Preparation: Remove the green leaves. Cut out the stem, and cut the buds into bite-sized florets.

PAN-COOKED CAULIFLOWER WITH BROWN BUTTER AND LEMON
MAKES 6 SERVINGS

Serve with roast meats, steaks, chops, roast chicken, and salmon.
Prep Time: 5 minutes
Cooking Time: 15 minutes
Weeknight Suppers, Family Favorite, Vegetarian

Browning butter deepens its flavor and gives it a nutty quality. It is just the thing to keep plain cauliflower from being . . . well, plain. And because I am too impatient to wait for a pot of water to come to a boil, I cook the florets in a skillet to slash the cooking time.

1 head cauliflower (about 2¼ pounds), cut into bite-sized florets	2 tablespoons fresh lemon juice
3 tablespoons unsalted butter	Kosher salt and freshly ground black pepper
Finely grated zest of 1 lemon	1 tablespoon finely chopped fresh chives or flat-leaf parsley, for garnish (optional)

1. Pour about 1 inch of salted water into a large skillet, cover, and bring it to a boil over high heat. Add the cauliflower florets in a single layer and cover. Cook, stirring occasionally, just until the cauliflower is crisp-tender, about 5 minutes. Drain well.

2. Meanwhile, melt the butter in a small saucepan over medium heat until it is boiling and the milk solids begin to turn brown. Remove it from the heat and immediately add the lemon zest and juice to keep the butter from cooking further. Set aside.

3. Toss the drained cauliflower and butter mixture together in a serving bowl. Season to taste with salt and pepper. Sprinkle with the chives, if using, and serve.

BASIC MASHED CAULIFLOWER
MAKES 4 SERVINGS

Serve with meat and poultry stews and other sauced main courses.
Prep Time: 5 minutes
Cooking Time: 15 minutes
Make-Ahead: The purée can be made up to 1 day ahead.
Weeknight Suppers, Family Favorite, Holiday Feasts, Company Fare, Buffet Dish,
Cooking Classic, Vegetarian

Some people discover mashed cauliflower when eliminating starchy food from their diets, but you don't need to be counting carbs to make it. Absolutely delicious, this purée is actually easier to make than mashed potatoes, and can also be flavored with herbs, cheese, horseradish, or other additions. The secret is to steam the cauliflower instead of boiling it, a simple method that saves it from mushiness.

1 head cauliflower (2¼ pounds), cut into bite-sized florets	2 tablespoons milk or heavy cream
2 tablespoons (¼ stick) unsalted butter	Kosher salt and freshly ground white or black pepper

1. Place a collapsible steamer in a large saucepan and add enough water to almost reach the bottom of the steamer. (If you have another kind of steamer, just set it up as needed.) Bring the water to a boil over high heat.

2. Add the cauliflower florets and tightly cover the saucepan. Reduce the heat to medium and cook until the cauliflower is tender when pierced with the tip of a small, sharp knife, 12 to 15 minutes. Remove the cauliflower and steamer from the saucepan and pour out the water. Return the cauliflower to the empty saucepan.

3. Using an immersion blender, a handheld electric mixer, or a potato masher, mash the cauliflower into a coarse purée. Add the butter and milk and mash them in until the butter melts. (For a smooth purée, process the cauliflower with the butter and milk in a food processor, but the mash stays hotter from the residual heat in the saucepan.) Season to taste with salt and pepper. (The purée can be cooled, transferred to a bowl, covered, and refrigerated for up to 1 day. Reheat in a skillet over medium heat, stirring often.) Transfer the purée to a serving bowl and serve hot.

ROASTED CAULIFLOWER MIMOSA

MAKES 4 TO 6 SERVINGS

Serve with roasts, steaks, and chops.
Prep Time: 10 minutes
Cooking Time: 30 minutes
Weeknight Suppers, Holiday Feasts, Company Fare, Buffet Dish

The pretty combination of finely chopped hard-boiled egg and parsley is said to resemble mimosas, the tiny yellow and white flowers of the Provençal countryside. While roasted cauliflower is delicious with no more than salt and pepper, the "mimosa" topping can turn it into a great-looking dish that can be served to company. If you already have a hard-boiled egg in the refrigerator, most of the work is done. Otherwise, start cooking the egg while the oven preheats, and it will be ready for chopping by the time the cauliflower is done.

1 head cauliflower (about 2¼ pounds), cut into
  bite-sized florets
2 tablespoons olive oil, plus more for the baking
  sheet

1 hard-boiled egg (see sidebar below)
2 tablespoons finely chopped fresh flat-leaf parsley
Kosher salt and freshly ground black pepper

1. Position a rack in the center of the oven and preheat the oven to 425°F. Lightly oil a large rimmed baking sheet.

2. Spread the cauliflower florets on the baking sheet. Drizzle them with the oil and toss to coat. Roast for 15 minutes. Flip the cauliflower over and continue roasting until the florets are golden brown and tender, about 15 minutes more. Season to taste with salt and pepper.

3. Finely chop the hard-boiled egg and mix it with the parsley in a small bowl. Transfer the cauliflower to a serving dish. Sprinkle it with the egg and parsley mixture and serve.

HARD-BOILED EGGS

This is my preferred method for hard-cooking eggs, which uses only an initial short boiling period to discourage cracked shells and overcooked, gray-green yolks. Put the egg in a small saucepan and add enough cold water to cover it by ½ inch. Bring it just to a boil over high heat. Remove the pan from the heat, cover it, and set aside for 20 minutes. Using a slotted spoon, transfer the egg to a bowl of iced water. Let stand for 5 to 10 minutes to chill the egg. Drain, crack, and shell the egg.

SAUTÉED CAULIFLOWER WITH PANCETTA, SAGE, AND GRAPE TOMATOES

MAKES 4 SERVINGS

Serve with roast meats, steaks, chops, roast chicken, and salmon.
Prep Time: 5 minutes
Cooking Time: 8 minutes
Weeknight Suppers, Company Fare

As a member of the cabbage family, cauliflower has an affinity for bacon (or, in this case, its Italian cousin, pancetta). Sautéing cauliflower gives it a crisp-tender quality that is wonderful. And the tomatoes give the dish a touch of acidity. In other words . . . make it.

3 tablespoons olive oil

1 head (about 2 pounds) cauliflower, broken into large florets, and cut into ½-inch slices

⅓ cup diced (¼-inch) pancetta

1 cup halved grape tomatoes

2 tablespoons finely chopped fresh sage

Kosher salt and freshly ground black pepper

1. Heat a large skillet over medium-high heat until hot. Add the oil and swirl to coat the bottom of the pan with oil. Add the cauliflower and cook, without stirring, until the undersides are lightly browned, about 1 minute. Flip the cauliflower over and brown the other sides. Add 1 cup water and bring it to a boil. Reduce the heat to medium and tightly cover the skillet. Boil until the cauliflower is crisp-tender, about 3 minutes. Using a slotted spoon, transfer the cauliflower to a serving bowl and set aside. Pour out the water.

2. Wipe out the skillet and return it to medium heat. Add the pancetta and cook, stirring often, until it begins to brown, about 2 minutes. (The skillet is already hot, so the pancetta won't take long to brown.) Stir in the tomatoes. Cook, stirring occasionally, until the tomatoes are hot, about 1 minute. Return the cauliflower to the skillet and sprinkle it with the sage. Stir and cook until the tomato juices begin to thicken, about 1 minute. Season to taste with salt and pepper. Return the cauliflower and sauce to the serving bowl and serve.

WHOLE ROASTED CAULIFLOWER WITH ZA'ATAR CRUST

MAKES 8 SERVINGS

Serve with leg of lamb, lamb chops, poultry, or salmon.
Prep Time: 10 minutes
Cooking Time: 1 hour
Holiday Feasts, Company Fare, Buffet Dish, Vegetarian

This is a showstopper—an entire head of cauliflower roasted with a yogurt topping to a golden brown turn. For such a simple dish, it gets points for its dramatic appearance and complex flavors. Za'atar is both the name of a specific herb family and a spice mixture in Middle Eastern cooking, and although you can buy it, I use a homemade mix here. The sumac (the red-purple berry of the shrub, dried and ground to use as a tart seasoning) is entirely optional. Za'atar is also delicious sprinkled on green salads.

¾ cup low-fat plain yogurt

1 teaspoon dried oregano

1 teaspoon dried thyme

1 teaspoon sesame seeds

1 teaspoon ground sumac (optional)

2 garlic cloves, crushed through a press

1 teaspoon kosher salt

½ teaspoon freshly ground black pepper

1 head (about 2 pounds) cauliflower, green leaves
   trimmed

1. Position a rack in the center of the oven and preheat the oven to 400ºF. Line a large rimmed baking sheet with parchment paper or nonstick aluminum foil.

2. In a medium bowl, whisk the yogurt, oregano, thyme, sesame seeds, and sumac, if using, until smooth; add the garlic, salt, and pepper and mix again. Stand the cauliflower on the baking sheet and spread the yogurt mixture all over the top and sides.

3. Roast until the topping is deep golden brown and the cauliflower is tender when pierced with a long, thin knife, 50 minutes to 1 hour. Cut the cauliflower into wedges and serve.

Celery

Most of us keep a head of celery in the refrigerator crisper drawer for salads and sandwich fillings, but it can be braised or stir-fried for an easy side dish. In combination with onion and carrots, the trio is extremely useful as a classic seasoning mixture, and it is a main ingredient in turkey stuffing.

Peak Season: Available all year.

Purchase: Crisp, bright green heads; avoid any that are limp or yellowing.

Storage: Refrigerate in a plastic bag for up to 2 weeks.

Preparation: Break the ribs away from the head and rinse well to remove any dirt. In some cooked dishes, the strings are first removed from the ribs with a vegetable peeler.

CANTONESE CELERY AND ALMONDS

MAKES 4 SERVINGS

Serve with Asian-flavored dishes, especially grilled meats, poultry, and seafood.

Prep Time: 10 minutes

Cooking Time: 5 minutes

Weeknight Suppers, Family Favorite, Cooking Classic

*W*hen the main course has Asian flavors (say, soy-marinated flank steak), try this classic vegetable stir-fry. It's a dish that shows off the pleasant crunchiness of the celery, which is played up by the almonds.

2 tablespoons soy sauce

2 tablespoons Asian rice wine or dry sherry

2 tablespoons reduced-sodium chicken broth

1 teaspoon cornstarch

Pinch of sugar

⅓ cup slivered blanched almonds

2 tablespoons vegetable oil

1 large scallion (white and pale green bottom, minced; green top, thinly sliced)

1 tablespoon peeled and minced fresh ginger

1 garlic clove, minced

6 large celery ribs, cut crosswise into ½-inch pieces

1. In a small bowl, stir the soy sauce, rice wine, broth, cornstarch, and sugar together to dissolve the cornstarch.

2. Heat a large skillet or wok over medium-high heat. Add the almonds and cook, stirring occasionally, until the almonds are toasted, 2 to 3 minutes. Transfer them to a plate.

3. Add the oil to the skillet and swirl to coat the bottom. Add the minced scallion bottom, ginger, and garlic and stir until fragrant, about 10 seconds. Add the celery and ¼ cup water. Cook, stirring almost constantly, until the water has evaporated and the celery is crisp-tender, about 1 minute.

4. Stir the soy sauce mixture again to mix in the cornstarch on the bottom of the bowl. Pour it into the skillet and cook until boiling and thickened. Stir in the reserved almonds. Sprinkle with the scallion tops and serve.

CELERY WITH TARRAGON AND LEMON SAUCE

MAKES 4 SERVINGS

Serve with pork roast, pork chops, roast chicken, or chicken sautés.

Prep Time: 10 minutes

Cooking Time: 15 minutes

Make Ahead: The celery can be refrigerated for up to 1 day and served chilled or reheated.

Weeknight Suppers, Holiday Feasts, Buffet Dish, Cooking Classic

This flavor combination is based on an old San Francisco favorite, celery Victor, which was still on restaurant menus when I was a kid growing up in that city.

6 large celery ribs, strings removed lengthwise with a vegetable peeler, ribs cut crosswise into 3-inch pieces

1¾ cups reduced-sodium chicken broth

3 sprigs fresh tarragon

½ teaspoon kosher salt

¼ teaspoon freshly ground black pepper

SAUCE

Finely grated zest of 1 lemon

1 tablespoon fresh lemon juice

2 teaspoons finely chopped fresh tarragon

½ teaspoon anchovy paste

2 tablespoons extra-virgin olive oil

Kosher salt and freshly ground black pepper

1. Arrange the celery in a single layer in a medium skillet. Add the broth, tarragon sprigs, salt, and pepper. Pour in enough water to barely cover the celery. Bring it to a boil over high heat. Reduce the heat to medium-low and tightly cover. Simmer until the celery is tender, 10 to 15 minutes.

2. To make the sauce: In a small bowl, whisk the lemon zest and juice, tarragon, and anchovy paste together. Gradually whisk in the oil. Season to taste with salt and pepper.

3. Using a slotted spoon, transfer the celery to a serving bowl. (The cooking liquid can be reserved to use as a broth.) Drizzle the sauce over the celery. Serve it hot, at room temperature, or chilled.

Chard, Swiss (Green, Red, and Rainbow)

Swiss chard is from the Mediterranean, although it was a Swiss botanist who gave it its scientific name, thus the confusion. Green chard, with the wide white ribs, is the most common, with red chard following right behind. (The red shows chard's kinship to beets.) Rainbow chard has thinner stems in red, yellow, and orange. Because the stems are tougher than the leafy greens, they are often cooked first to give them a head start.

Peak Season: June to August, but available all year.

Purchase: Sprightly, unwilted leaves with crisp stalks.

Storage: Refrigerate in a plastic bag in the crisper for up to 3 days.

Preparation: Swiss chard is very sandy, so wash it well in a sink or bowl of cold water, lifting out the leaves so the grit sinks to the bottom of the water. Tear the leaves from the stems.

SICILIAN SWISS CHARD WITH CURRANTS AND PINE NUTS
MAKES 4 TO 6 SERVINGS

Serve with roast pork and lamb, sausages, roast chicken, or fish fillets.

Prep Time: 10 minutes

Cooking Time: 15 minutes

Weeknight Suppers, Holiday Feasts, Company Fare, Buffet Dish, Retro Recipe, Cooking Classic,
Vegetarian

Sicilian cooks often add a sweet touch to their cooking with dried grapes in the form of currants or raisins. Here I've soaked currants briefly in Marsala to plump them up and add another layer of flavor to this Swiss chard.

3 tablespoons dry Marsala (see Note)

¼ cup dried currants or coarsely chopped seedless
  or golden raisins

2 bunches green, red, or rainbow Swiss chard
  (about 1½ pounds)

2 tablespoons extra-virgin olive oil

1 garlic clove, thinly sliced

¼ cup pine nuts, toasted (see page 33)

Kosher salt and freshly ground black pepper

1. Bring the Marsala to a simmer in a small saucepan over low heat. Add the currants and remove the pan from the heat. Let it stand while cooking the chard.

2. Wash the chard well in a large bowl or sink filled with cold water. Lift the wet chard from the water, shake off the excess water, and transfer it to a cutting board, but do not dry the chard. Stack the chard with the stems running horizontally. Trim the stem ends and discard. Cut the chard crosswise into ½-inch strips, separating the leaves from the thick stems.

3. Heat the oil and garlic together in a large skillet over medium-low heat, stirring often, just until the garlic turns golden, 1 to 2 minutes. Add the chard stems with any clinging water, stir well, and cover. Cook, stirring occasionally, until the stems are beginning to soften, about 3 minutes. In two or three batches, stir in the chard leaves with their water and cover, letting each batch wilt before adding more. Cover and cook, stirring occasionally, just until the chard leaves are tender, about 3 minutes.

4. Stir in the currants with the Marsala and pine nuts. Season to taste with salt and pepper and serve.

Note: Marsala is a fortified wine that originated in Sicily, but it is also produced in California. While there are a few classifications of Italian Marsala, in this country you are likely to find only the sweet or dry varieties. I prefer to use the sweet version for desserts (such as tiramisù or zabaglione), and the dry for savory dishes, such as the one here. The domestic version tends to be on the sweet side, but it can be used in this dish.

CHARD PUTTANESCA

MAKES 4 SERVINGS

Serve with steaks and chops, sausages, roast chicken, or salmon.
Prep Time: 10 minutes
Cooking Time: 10 minutes
Weeknight Suppers, Buffet Dish

Chard matches well with the muscular anchovy, garlic, olive, and tomato flavors that you find in pasta puttanesca. I prefer green chard with the wide stems for this Old World treatment. And don't worry about leftovers, as they are excellent tossed with pasta and Parmesan for a quick lunch.

1 pound green Swiss chard	¼ teaspoon hot red pepper flakes
2 tablespoons extra-virgin olive oil	One 14½-ounce can diced tomatoes in juice,
2 garlic cloves, minced	drained
4 anchovy fillets packed in oil, finely chopped, or	⅓ cup coarsely chopped pitted kalamata olives
1 teaspoon anchovy paste	Kosher salt

1. Wash the chard well in a large bowl or sink filled with cold water. Lift the wet chard from the water, shake off the excess water, and transfer it to a cutting board, but do not dry the chard. Stack the chard with the stems running horizontally. Trim the stem ends and discard. Cut the chard crosswise into ½-inch strips, separating the leaves from the thick stems.

2. Heat the oil and garlic together in a large skillet over medium heat, stirring often, just until the garlic softens, about 1 minute. Add the anchovies and red pepper flakes and let them sizzle for a few seconds. Stir in the chard stems with any clinging water, reduce the heat to medium-low, and cover. Cook, stirring occasionally, until the stems are beginning to soften, about 3 minutes. In two or three batches, stir in the chard leaves and cover, letting each batch wilt before adding more. Stir in the tomatoes and olives. Cover and cook, stirring occasionally, just until the chard leaves are tender, about 3 minutes. Season with salt and serve hot.

FRENCH CHARD AND GOAT CHEESE TIAN

MAKES 8 SERVINGS

Serve with roast beef or lamb, steaks and chops, sausages, chicken, or seafood.
Prep Time: 20 minutes
Cooking Time: 1 hour, 10 minutes
Make Ahead: The tian can be made up to 1 day ahead.
Holiday Feasts, Company Fare, Buffet Dish, Cooking Classic, Vegetarian

*F*resh out of culinary school, I headed to Provence to follow in the footsteps of M. F. K. Fisher, James Beard, and my other favorite food writers. At an inn in the South of France, I noticed how the proprietor took the leftover vegetables from the previous night's dinner menu and mixed them with eggs, milk, and cheese to bake into a custardy tian to serve on the lunch menu. I have used this truc *(French for a culinary trick)* ever since, although this recipe uses a freshly prepared mélange of vegetables. Try it at an alfresco dinner with grilled lamb.

3 tablespoons extra-virgin olive oil, plus more for the baking dish

4 tablespoons plain dry bread crumbs

1 pound green, rainbow, or red Swiss chard

1 large red bell pepper, cored, seeded, and chopped

1 yellow onion, chopped

2 large garlic cloves, finely chopped

½ cup drained and chopped (½-inch pieces) sun-dried tomatoes in oil

2 teaspoons finely chopped fresh rosemary or 1 teaspoon dried

¾ cup (3 ounces) crumbled soft goat cheese

5 large eggs

2 cups whole milk

1 teaspoon kosher salt

½ teaspoon freshly ground black pepper

2 tablespoons freshly grated Parmesan cheese

1. Position an oven rack in the center of the oven and preheat the oven to 350°F. Lightly oil a 13 × 9 × 2-inch baking dish. Sprinkle it with 2 tablespoons of the bread crumbs, tilt to coat the dish with the crumbs, and tap out the excess crumbs.

2. Wash the chard well in a large bowl or sink filled with cold water. Lift the wet chard from the water, shake off the excess water, and transfer it to a cutting board, but do not dry the chard. Pull off the thick stems and cut them into ½-inch pieces. Stack the leaves and coarsely chop them.

3. Heat 2 tablespoons of the oil in a large saucepan over medium-low heat. Stir in the chard stems and cover. Cook, stirring occasionally, until the stems are beginning to soften, about 3 minutes. In two or three batches, stir in the chard leaves and cover, letting each batch wilt before adding more. Cover and cook until the chard leaves are very tender, about 5 minutes. Drain and let cool. A handful at a time, squeeze the excess liquid from the chard. Coarsely chop the chard stems and leaves again.

4. Heat the remaining 1 tablespoon oil in a large skillet over medium heat. Add the bell pepper, onion, and garlic and cook, stirring often, until the onion is golden, about 4 minutes. Stir in the chard, sun-dried tomatoes, and rosemary. Cook, stirring occasionally, until the mixture is hot, about 2 minutes. Spoon it evenly into the prepared baking dish and let cool slightly.

5. Scatter the goat cheese over the vegetables. In a medium bowl, whisk the eggs together. Whisk in the milk, salt, and pepper, and pour them evenly over the vegetable mixture. Sprinkle the top with the remaining 2 tablespoons bread crumbs and the Parmesan. Bake until the top of the tian is golden brown and puffed, about 45 minutes. Let the tian cool for 5 minutes. (It can be covered with aluminum foil and refrigerated for 1 day; reheat, covered, in a 350°F oven until heated through, about 30 minutes.) Serve slices warm or at room temperature.

Chayote

My local Latino market always has a mountain of reasonably priced green or white chayotes for sale, so I have added them to my regular vegetable lineup for sides. Because of the interest in ethnic foods, chayote (also called mirliton) is showing up more often on restaurant menus, too. A member of the squash family, chayote is mild and picks up the flavors of the ingredients cooked with it.

Peak Season: October to March, but available all year.

Purchase: Unblemished, evenly colored squash.

Storage: Refrigerate for up to 2 weeks.

Preparation: Smaller chayote can be left unpeeled. Peeled chayote gives off a sticky juice that should be rinsed off. Cut the chayote in half lengthwise and dig out the large central seed with the tip of a dessert spoon.

CHAYOTE AND MUSHROOMS WITH JALAPEÑO AND COTIJA

MAKES 4 TO 6 SERVINGS

Serve with Latino-flavored roasts, steaks, and chops, poultry, or seafood.
Prep Time: 10 minutes
Cooking Time: 15 minutes
Weeknight Suppers, Company Fare, Vegetarian

If you have never tried chayote, this recipe will make you a fan of the squash. Try it with spice-rubbed steaks, chops, and chicken parts for both family suppers and company dinners. Cotija is a Mexican cheese that is crumbly when fresh, but hardens enough to be grated when aged. Romano is a good substitute.

2 tablespoons extra-virgin olive oil

10 ounces white button or cremini mushrooms, sliced

1 garlic clove, minced

1 chayote, peeled, hard center seed discarded, cut into ½-inch sticks

1 jalapeño, seeded and minced

2 tablespoons fresh lemon juice

Kosher salt and freshly ground black pepper

2 tablespoons freshly grated aged cotija or Romano cheese

1. Heat 1 tablespoon of the oil in a large skillet over medium-high heat. Add the mushrooms and cook, stirring occasionally, until they begin to brown, about 8 minutes. Stir in the garlic and cook until it is fragrant, about 1 minute. Transfer the vegetables to a plate.

2. Heat the remaining 1 tablespoon oil in the skillet over medium-high heat. Add the chayote and cook, stirring occasionally, until it is lightly browned, about 5 minutes. During the last minute, stir in the jalapeño. Stir in the mushroom mixture and cook, stirring occasionally, until the chayote is just tender. Stir in the lemon juice. Season to taste with salt and pepper.

3. Transfer the chayote mixture to a serving bowl and sprinkle it with the cheese. Serve it hot.

CAJUN-STYLE STUFFED CHAYOTE
MAKES 6 SERVINGS

Serve with fish fillets, shrimp, or chicken.
Prep Time: 15 minutes
Cooking Time: 50 minutes
Make Ahead: The stuffed chayote can be refrigerated for up to 6 hours before baking.
Holiday Feasts, Company Fare, Vegetarian

In the South, chayote is known as mirliton, and it has a long and happy connection to Cajun cooking. The squash is often stuffed with sausage as a main course, but I prefer to fill it with vegetables to serve with snapper, shrimp, or other light main courses.

6 chayote, cut in half lengthwise

4 tablespoons unsalted butter, plus more for the baking dish

½ cup diced (¼-inch) red bell pepper

1 celery rib, cut into ¼-inch dice

1 garlic clove, minced

2 scallions (white and green parts), chopped

1½ cups soft bread crumbs, made from slightly stale crusty bread in a blender or food processor

½ cup shredded Cheddar cheese (2 ounces)

½ teaspoon dried oregano

½ teaspoon kosher salt

¼ teaspoon freshly ground black pepper

1 large egg, beaten to blend

Two 10-ounce cans diced tomatoes with green chilies

2 teaspoons no-salt Cajun seasoning

1. Place a collapsible steamer in a large saucepan and add enough water to almost reach the bottom of the steamer. (If you have another kind of steamer, just set it up as needed.) Bring the water to a boil over high heat.

2. Place the chayote halves in the steamer and tightly cover the saucepan. Steam until the chayote are just tender, 12 to 15 minutes. Remove the chayote from the steamer and let them cool until easy to handle. Discard the hard central seed from each half. Using a melon baller or a dessert spoon, scoop out and reserve the chayote flesh from each half to create a ½-inch-thick shell. Coarsely chop the chayote flesh and set it aside.

3. Melt 2 tablespoons of the butter in a medium skillet. Add the reserved chayote flesh with the bell pepper, celery, and garlic. Cook, stirring occasionally, until the bell pepper is tender, about 3 minutes.

Stir in the scallions and cook until they soften, about 1 minute more. Transfer the vegetable mixture to a medium bowl. Stir in the bread crumbs, Cheddar, oregano, salt, and pepper, followed by the egg.

4. Position a rack in the center of the oven and preheat the oven to 350°F. Lightly butter a 13 × 9 × 2-inch baking dish.

5. Divide the stuffing evenly among the chayote shells, pressing each firmly to shape the stuffing into a mound. Place the chayote in the baking dish. In a medium bowl, stir the diced tomatoes, their juices, and Cajun seasoning together. Pour the tomato mixture around the chayote. Melt the remaining 2 tablespoons butter and drizzle over the stuffing.

6. Bake until the topping is browned and the tomato mixture is bubbling, about 30 minutes. Serve the chayote from the baking dish.

Chilies, Fresh

Chilies are separated from sweet bell peppers by their size and their spiciness, which is supplied by the compound capsaicin. In general, the smaller chilies (jalapeño, habanero, and serrano) are chopped and used sparingly as seasoning, but some of the larger ones (Anaheim and poblano) are mild enough to eat whole.

Peak Season: Summer, but available all year.

Purchase: Glossy, firm, and unwrinkled chilies.

Storage: Refrigerate for up to 1 week.

Preparation: The heat is contained in the chile seeds and ribs. If your skin is sensitive, wear rubber gloves when preparing chilies. After handling the chilies, be sure to keep your hands away from your eyes and any other delicate areas of your body. For small chilies, cut the chile in half and discard the stem. Use the tip of a small, sharp knife to cut out the ribs and seeds. (They can be set aside and added to the dish later for hotter seasoning.) Large chilies have tough skins that should be removed according to the instructions for roasting bell peppers on page 77.

POBLANO AND CHEESE CASSEROLE
MAKES 6 TO 8 SERVINGS

Serve with Mexican-flavored grilled steak, pork chops, or chicken; or grilled sausages.
Prep Time: 20 minutes
Cooking Time: 45 minutes
Make Ahead: The casserole can be made up to 1 day ahead.
Company Fare, Buffet Dish, Vegetarian

For a meaty main course with Tex-Mex flavors, consider serving this puffy, cheesy, and spicy casserole on the side. It is also a fine dish for a brunch buffet. Note that poblano chilies are sometimes mislabeled as ancho chilies, especially in California. Technically, ancho refers to the dried version of the poblano. You want the fresh dark green poblano chile for this recipe.

1 tablespoon olive oil, plus more for the baking dish

1 yellow onion, chopped

2 garlic cloves, minced

8 large poblano or fresh ancho chilies, roasted (see sidebar below), seeds and skins removed

2 cups shredded sharp Cheddar cheese (8 ounces)

5 large eggs, at room temperature

1¼ cups whole milk

3 tablespoons unbleached all-purpose flour

1¾ teaspoons baking powder

¼ teaspoon kosher salt

One 8-ounce can tomato sauce

2 teaspoons chili powder

1. Position the rack in the center of the oven and preheat the oven to 350°F. (If you have broiled the chilies, adjust the stove controls to the oven setting and set it to 350°F.) Lightly oil a 13 × 9 × 2-inch baking dish

2. Heat the oil in a medium skillet over medium heat. Add the onion and garlic and cook, stirring occasionally, until the onion is tender, about 4 minutes. Remove the skillet from the heat.

3. Arrange half of the chilies, cut to fit the dish as needed, in the baking dish. Top them with the onion mixture, 1 cup of the cheese, and the remaining chilies. In a medium bowl, whisk the eggs. Gradually whisk in the milk, followed by the flour, baking powder, and salt. Pour them evenly into the baking dish.

4. Bake until the casserole is puffed and lightly browned, about 30 minutes. Remove the baking dish from the oven. Mix the tomato sauce and chili powder together in a medium bowl. Spread them over the casserole and top it with the remaining 1 cup Cheddar. Return the dish to the oven and bake until the tomato sauce has thickened to a glaze and the cheese has melted slightly, about 7 minutes. Remove from the oven and let stand for 5 minutes. (The casserole can be cooled, covered with aluminum foil, and refrigerated for up to 1 day. Reheat, covered, in a preheated 350°F oven until heated through, about 30 minutes.) Serve warm.

ROASTING BELL PEPPERS AND CHILIES

Colored bell peppers and large chilies have thick skins that are usually removed before eating. (Green bell peppers and small chilies have thinner skins that do not need peeling.) While you can use a swivel-style vegetable peeler (I've seen it done), it is less tedious to roast or grill the peppers, a process that blackens the skins for easier removal.

Position a broiler rack about 6 inches from the source of heat and preheat the broiler on high. Place the peppers on the rack—you do not have to oil them. Broil, turning them occasionally, until the skins are blackened and blistered (take care not to burn the flesh under the skin), about 12 minutes.

You can also blacken the bell peppers over direct high heat (about 500°F) on a grill, with the lid closed as much as possible. This method is especially nice when you want an extra measure of smoky flavor.

Let the peppers cool until easy to handle. (Some cooks cool the peppers in a covered bowl to further loosen the skins, but this is unnecessary, and the collected steam in the bowl will overcook the peppers.) Using a small, sharp knife, remove and discard the skins, ribs, and seeds from the peppers. Try not to rinse the peppers under cold water, as this removes the flavor.

Corn and Hominy

Late summer is the time to celebrate fresh corn, and I am lucky enough to live near a farm where I can get it freshly picked. That's important, because the sugars in the corn start to turn to starch and lose sweetness very soon after picking. I also keep a bag of corn kernels in the freezer to use in some sides when the real McCoy isn't available. Yellow corn is around most often, but white corn (when you can find it) is prized for its small kernels and sweet flavor. **Hominy** is dried corn that has been treated with the mineral lime, to give the kernels a firmer texture. Canned hominy is another item that I always have on hand to make a quick side dish.

Peak Season: May to September.

Purchase: Ears with clean, green husks; moist, bright yellow silks; and tightly packed, plump kernels with no sign of drying.

Storage: Cook as soon as possible after purchase, or refrigerate for up to 2 days.

Preparation: Do not husk the corn until just before cooking! (Some markets make the mistake of providing a garbage pail near the corn so customers can shuck the corn before leaving the store. This is entirely incorrect, as husked corn spoils more quickly.) Pull off and discard the husks and silks.

To remove the kernels from the cob, cut the stem from the end of the ear. Stand the the cut end on a work surface. (If you wish, stand the ear in the center of a large bowl to catch the kernels as they are cut from the ear.) Using a large, sharp knife, cut down where the kernels meet the cob. After all of the kernels have been cut off, scrape the knife along the corn, from the bottom up, to remove the corn milk (actually the small germs from the kernels left behind in the cob).

BOILED CORN WITH BBQ BUTTER
MAKES 8 SERVINGS

Serve with meat, chicken, and shrimp.
Prep Time: 10 minutes
Cooking Time: 10 minutes
Make Ahead: The butter can be made up to 3 days ahead.
Weeknight Suppers, Family Favorite, Holiday Feasts, Company Fare, Vegetarian

I think it is safe to say that everyone loves corn on the cob with butter. Boiling is the most familiar cooking method. Instead of taking the time to bring a big pot of water to a boil before adding the corn, I heat the corn and water together just to the boiling point. That way, the corn is heated through without overcooking and in the minimum amount of time. (I've provided a steamed variation, another great way to cook corn on the cob.) I have gotten out of the habit of salting the water for corn because the corn will certainly be salted at the table. Serve the corn on the cob with this sweet, salty, and spicy butter to turn a humble side dish into a standout.

BUTTER
8 tablespoons (1 stick) unsalted butter, at room
   temperature
4 teaspoons chili powder
2 tablespoons clover or orange blossom honey
½ teaspoon dried oregano

½ teaspoon kosher salt
¼ teaspoon granulated garlic
¼ teaspoon granulated onion

8 ears corn, husks and silks removed
Kosher salt, for serving

1. To make the butter: Melt 2 tablespoons of the butter in a small skillet over medium-low heat. Add the chili powder and stir for 10 seconds. (This heats the chili powder for better flavor.) Remove from the heat and stir in the honey. Transfer the mixture to a small bowl and freeze until cooled, about 10 minutes.

2. Add the oregano, salt, granulated garlic, and granulated onion to the honey mixture. Add the remaining 6 tablespoons butter and mash it with a flexible spatula until the mixture is smooth. (The butter can be covered and refrigerated for up to 3 days. Let stand at room temperature for 1 hour before serving.)

3. Meanwhile, put the corn in a large saucepan and add enough cold water to cover by 1 inch. Cover the saucepan and bring to a boil over high heat. Drain well.

4. Serve the corn immediately, with the butter and salt passed on the side.

Steamed Corn: Place a collapsible steamer in a large saucepan and add enough water to almost reach the bottom of the steamer. If the steamer has a removable central stem, remove it to make more room for the corn. (If you have another kind of steamer, just set it up as needed.) Bring the water to a boil over high heat. Add the corn and cover the saucepan tightly. Steam until the corn is heated through, about 10 minutes. If the corn is stacked, occasionally move the corn from top to bottom for even cooking.

PAN-TOASTED CORN WITH BACON AND MISO
MAKES 4 TO 6 SERVINGS

Serve with roasted chicken, grilled pork chops, grilled salmon, or grilled shrimp.
Prep Time: 5 minutes
Cooking Time: 15 minutes
Weeknight Suppers, Family Favorite, Holiday Feasts, Company Fare, Buffet Dish

Chef David Chang first popularized this combination that has become a modern classic. Corn's sweetness is a natural for playing off the saltiness of the bacon and miso, and these last two bring powerful umami to the dish.

3 slices bacon

3 cups fresh corn kernels (cut from about 4 large ears)

2 scallions (white and pale green bottoms, finely chopped; green tops, thinly sliced)

1 tablespoon unsalted butter

1 tablespoon white miso (see Note)

Freshly ground black pepper

1. Cook the bacon in a large skillet over medium heat, stirring occasionally, until the bacon is crisp and browned, about 8 minutes. Using a slotted spoon, transfer the bacon to paper towels to drain and cool.
2. Pour off and discard all but 1 tablespoon of the bacon fat from the skillet. Return to medium heat. Add the corn and cook, stirring once or twice, until the corn is beginning to brown, about 5 minutes. Stir in the scallion bottoms and cook until softened, about 1 minute.
3. Stir in the butter, miso, and ½ cup water and bring to a simmer, stirring to dissolve the miso. Season to taste with pepper. Coarsely chop the bacon. Sprinkle the bacon and scallion tops over the corn mixture and serve.

Note: Miso is an umami-rich paste of fermented grains and legumes, and it is often sold according to its color. White (also called shiro) miso, made from soybeans and rice, is actually beige to light brown and has a mild, sweet-and-salty flavor.

SUMMER SAUTÉ OF CORN, HEIRLOOM CHERRY TOMATOES, AND BASIL

MAKES 4 SERVINGS

Serve with grilled and barbecued meats, poultry, and seafood.

Prep Time: 5 minutes

Cooking Time: 5 minutes

Weeknight Suppers, Family Favorite, Buffet Dish, Vegetarian

There are other foods that could make their way into this dish (for example, minced fresh chile, a topping of chopped bacon, or cooked black beans), but I like this mixture because it is so versatile with warm-weather main courses. For the most attractive visual effect, use multicolored cherry tomatoes.

1 tablespoon extra-virgin olive oil

2 tablespoons chopped shallots

2 cups fresh corn kernels (cut from about 3 large ears)

1 cup heirloom cherry tomatoes, preferably multi-colored, cut in half

2 tablespoons finely chopped fresh basil

Kosher salt and freshly ground black pepper

2 tablespoon freshly grated Parmesan cheese

1. Heat the oil in a large skillet over medium heat. Add the shallots and cook, stirring occasionally, until softened, about 2 minutes. Add the corn and cook, stirring occasionally, until heated through, about 2 minutes.

2. Add the cherry tomatoes and cook, stirring occasionally, until they are heated through, about 2 minutes. Stir in the basil. Season to taste with salt and pepper. Transfer the mixture to a serving dish, sprinkle with the Parmesan, and serve.

REAL CREAMED CORN

MAKES 4 TO 6 SERVINGS

Serve with pork roasts and chops, baked ham, barbecued meats and poultry, fried chicken, and fried seafood.

Prep Time: 10 minutes

Cooking Time: 10 minutes

Make Ahead: The creamed corn can be made up to 1 day ahead.

Weeknight Suppers, Family Favorite, Buffet Dish, Cooking Classic, Vegetarian

Banish any bad memories that you may have of canned creamed corn and try this fresh version. It is as rich as Hades, I grant you, but its comforting smoothness and sweet creaminess is just the thing for

a Southern-style meal. Creamed corn isn't especially pretty, so use minced fresh herbs (or shredded Cheddar cheese) to accent its monochromatic color.

2 tablespoons (¼ stick) unsalted butter

½ cup finely chopped yellow onion

3 cups fresh corn kernels (cut from about 4 large ears)

2 tablespoons all-purpose flour

2 cups half-and-half or whole milk

Kosher salt and freshly ground black pepper

Chopped fresh chives, flat-leaf parsley, or thyme, for garnish

1. Melt the butter in a large skillet over medium heat. Add the onion and cook, stirring often, until softened, about 3 minutes. Stir in the corn and cook, stirring often, until it is heated through, about 2 minutes.

2. Sprinkle the flour over the corn and mix well. Stir in the half-and-half and bring to a simmer, stirring often. Reduce the heat to medium-low and simmer, stirring often, until the liquid has thickened slightly, about 5 minutes. Season with salt and pepper to taste.

3. Purée about half of the corn mixture in a blender or food processor. Stir the purée back into the corn mixture. Transfer it to a bowl and sprinkle with the chives. Serve hot.

SOUTHWESTERN HOMINY WITH MONTEREY JACK AND CILANTRO

MAKES 4 TO 6 SERVINGS

Serve with grilled steaks, pork roast and chops, or grilled chicken.

Prep Time: 10 minutes

Cooking Time: 10 minutes

Weeknight Suppers, Family Favorite, Buffet Dish, Cooking Classic, Vegetarian

This sauté has a down-home quality that I find irresistible, especially when it's made with both white and yellow hominy. If you aren't a cilantro fan, substitute ½ teaspoon dried oregano and add it with the scallion and garlic.

1 tablespoon olive oil

⅓ cup diced (¼-inch) red or green bell pepper

1 jalapeño, seeded and minced

1 scallion (white and pale green bottoms, chopped; green tops, thinly sliced)

1 garlic clove, minced

Two 15-ounce cans white or yellow hominy (or a combination), drained and rinsed

1 tablespoon unsalted butter

2 tablespoons finely chopped fresh cilantro

Kosher salt and freshly ground black pepper

½ cup shredded Monterey Jack cheese (2 ounces)

1. Heat the oil in a large skillet over medium heat. Add the bell pepper and jalapeño and cook, stirring occasionally, until the pepper softens, about 3 minutes. Stir in the scallion bottoms and garlic and cook, stirring occasionally, until the scallion is wilted, about 1 minute.

2. Stir in the hominy with ¼ cup water. Cover the skillet and cook, stirring occasionally, until the hominy is heated through, about 5 minutes. Remove from the heat and stir in the scallion tops with the butter and cilantro. Season to taste with salt and pepper. Transfer the hominy to a serving dish and sprinkle with the Monterey Jack. Serve hot.

MEXICAN GRILLED CORN ON THE COB

MAKES 6 SERVINGS

Serve with grilled and barbecued meat and poultry, especially with Mexican flavors.

Prep Time: 10 minutes

Cooking Time: 20 minutes

Weeknight Suppers, Vegetarian

Grilled corn on the cob, slathered with mayonnaise, then sprinkled with grated cheese, ground chilies, and a squeeze of lime, is a favorite—if messy—street food in Mexico. To reduce the hands-on work at the table, I combined the topping ingredients to make a glaze for the grilled corn, which makes it a bit easier to eat. For a milder level of spiciness, substitute ½ teaspoon smoked or standard paprika (mild), chili powder, or pure ground ancho chile for the cayenne.

6 ears corn, husked

2 tablespoons (¼ stick) unsalted butter, melted

½ cup freshly grated cotija or Romano cheese
  (about 2 ounces)

⅓ cup Mayonnaise (page 436), store-bought
  mayonnaise, or sour cream

1 tablespoon fresh lime juice

¼ teaspoon cayenne pepper or pure ground
  chipotle chile

1. Prepare an outdoor grill for direct cooking over medium heat (350° to 450°F). For a charcoal grill, let the coals burn until they are covered with white ash and you can hold your hand about 1 inch above the cooking grate for about 3 seconds. For a gas grill, preheat on high and adjust the thermostat to medium (400°F).

2. Place the corn on the grill grate, brush all over with the butter, and cover the grill. Grill, turning occasionally, until the corn is hot and a few kernels are toasted dark brown, 12 to 15 minutes.

3. In a small bowl, mix the cheese, mayonnaise, lime juice, and cayenne together.

4. Using a heatproof spatula, spread the tops of the corn ears with some of the mayonnaise mixture. Cover the cooker again and grill until the mayonnaise is partially melted and set, about 30 seconds.

Give the corn a quarter turn and spread the exposed top with more mayonnaise. Cover and continue grilling, turning, and spreading the mayonnaise on the corn, until the corn is coated and the mayonnaise mixture is half-melted, about 2 minutes more. Transfer the corn to a platter and serve hot.

Mexican Broiled Corn on the Cob: Position a broiler rack about 6 inches from the source of heat and preheat the broiler on high. Broil the corn, turning occasionally, until browned in spots. Slather it with the mayonnaise mixture and continue broiling until glazed, about 3 minutes.

Grilled Corn with Thyme Aïoli and Parmesan: I serve this variation at summer cookouts when the main course has Mediterranean flavors. Substitute Parmesan cheese for the cojita. Omit the lime juice and cayenne. Stir 2 teaspoons finely chopped fresh thyme and 2 garlic cloves, crushed through a press, into the mayonnaise. Season to taste with freshly ground pepper. Cook as for the Mexican Grilled Corn on the Cob, and serve with lemon wedges.

CHIPOTLE CORN PUDDING
MAKES 6 SERVINGS

Serve with ham, barbecued meats and poultry, fried chicken, and seafood.
Prep Time: 10 minutes
Cooking Time: 30 minutes
Make Ahead: The pudding can be made up to 1 day ahead.
Weeknight Suppers, Family Favorite, Holiday Feasts, Company Fare, Buffet Dish, Vegetarian

This has become one of my most requested side dishes, and I serve it all summer long at family gatherings. I have also made it with frozen corn for a Thanksgiving side, and it is still excellent.

Softened butter, for the baking dish	2 canned chipotle chilies in adobo, minced
3 cups fresh corn kernels (cut from about 4 large ears) or thawed frozen corn kernels	1 teaspoon kosher salt
	¼ teaspoon freshly ground pepper
1½ cups whole milk	½ cup shredded sharp Cheddar cheese (2 ounces)
3 large eggs	1 scallion (white and green parts), finely chopped
2 tablespoons all-purpose flour	2 tablespoons freshly grated Parmesan cheese

1. Position a rack in the center of the oven and preheat the oven to 350°F. Heavily butter an 11½ × 8 × 2-inch baking dish.

2. Purée 2 cups of the corn in a food processor (or in batches in a blender). Transfer the corn mixture to a bowl. Add the milk, eggs, flour, chilies, salt, and pepper and whisk until smooth. Add the remaining 1 cup corn kernels with the Cheddar and scallion, and whisk until combined. Pour into the baking dish and sprinkle the Parmesan on top.

3. Bake until a knife inserted in the center comes out almost clean, about 30 minutes. Let stand 5 minutes. Serve hot.

Eggplant

White, purple, or streaked (not to mention elongated, small and round, or egg-shaped and plump), eggplant comes in a wide variety of choices. Salting eggplant before cooking is now a matter of personal preference. It was originally done to remove excess bitterness from the eggplant, but that was mainly necessary because eggplant was not as popular as it is now, and the vegetables used tended to be old. Also, the most common way to cook eggplant was frying, and salting broke down the cellulose to reduce the absorption of the oil. (Eggplant can soak up oil like a sponge.) Now that we grill, broil, roast, and bake eggplant more often than we fry it, salting it is usually pointless. Note that eggplant is never eaten raw.

Peak Season: July to October, available all year.

Purchase: Firm eggplant without any spongy areas or brown spots.

Storage: Refrigerate for up to 3 days.

Preparation: Cut off the cap and cut as needed. Only white eggplant should be peeled; otherwise, leave unpeeled.

ROASTED EGGPLANT AND TOMATOES WITH TAHINI-YOGURT SAUCE
MAKES 4 TO 6 SERVINGS

Serve with lamb roasts, chops, and sausages; or roast chicken.
Prep Time: 15 minutes
Cooking Time: 35 minutes
Weeknight Suppers, Holiday Feasts, Company Fare, Buffet Dish, Vegetarian

For many cooks, roasting has become the method of choice for cooking eggplant, as the oven heat creates a delicious crust. The garlicky sauce and acidic tomatoes bring this dish together. Spreading the thick sauce on the platter allows for much better distribution than dolloping it on top of the vegetables. I recently served this as a side for grilled lamb with Greek Greens (page 99) and pita bread, and everyone at the table was very pleased.

3 tablespoons olive oil, plus more for the baking dish

SAUCE
½ cup whole milk or low-fat yogurt
2 tablespoons tahini
2 tablespoons fresh lemon juice
1 garlic clove, crushed through a press
⅛ teaspoon crushed hot red pepper flakes

1 globe eggplant (1½ pounds), cut into 1-inch cubes
½ pint cherry or grape tomatoes, cut in half lengthwise
Kosher salt and freshly ground black pepper
2 tablespoons coarsely chopped fresh flat-leaf parsley or cilantro

1. Position a rack in the center of the oven and preheat the oven to 425°F. Lightly oil a large rimmed baking sheet.

2. To make the sauce: Prepare it first and let it stand while roasting the vegetables so it can lose its chill. In a small bowl, whisk the yogurt, tahini, lemon juice, garlic, and red pepper flakes together. Cover and let stand at room temperature for up to 2 hours.

3. Spread the eggplant on the baking sheet, drizzle it with 2 tablespoons of the oil, and toss with your hands to coat the eggplant with the oil. Roast for 15 minutes. Flip the eggplant cubes and roast until the eggplant is tender and golden brown, about 15 minutes more.

4. Toss the tomatoes with the remaining 1 tablespoon oil in a medium bowl. Move the eggplant to one side of the baking sheet. Spread the tomatoes on the empty side of the baking sheet and roast until they are hot and beginning to shrink, about 5 minutes. Season the vegetables to taste with salt and pepper.

5. Spread the sauce on a serving platter. Top with the vegetable mixture. Sprinkle with the parsley and serve.

GIAMBOTTA
MAKES 8 TO 12 SERVINGS

Serve with grilled sausages, pork roast, lamb chops, roast chicken and chicken sautés.
Prep Time: 20 minutes
Cooking Time: 45 minutes
Make Ahead: The giambotta can be refrigerated for up to 5 days; serve warm or at room temperature.
Holiday Feasts, Company Fare, Buffet Dish, Cooking Classic, Vegetarian

You will be glad to have a big pot of giambotta (always pronounced according to Southern Italian dialect as "jyam-bot") on the stove. This wonderful vegetable stew is so packed with produce that it can't really be made in a small batch, anyway. It keeps for a few days, and gets even better as it ages. Be sure to boil the potatoes separately because they take too long to cook in the tomato sauce.

½ cup olive oil, or as needed

1 small globe eggplant (about 1¼ pounds), trimmed and cut into 1-inch pieces

2 zucchini, cut into ½-inch dice

1 red onion, chopped

1 red bell pepper, cored, seeded, and cut into ½-inch dice

4 garlic cloves, minced

One 28-ounce can plum tomatoes in juice, coarsely chopped, with juices

Kosher salt

Hot red pepper flakes

1 pound small, thin-skinned boiling potatoes, cut into quarters

½ cup chopped pitted kalamata olives

½ cup toasted pine nuts

¼ cup chopped fresh basil

1. Heat ¼ cup of the oil in a large skillet over medium-high heat until it is shimmering but not smoking. In batches without crowding, add the eggplant. Cook, stirring occasionally, until it is lightly browned, about 8 minutes. Using a slotted spoon, gently press the eggplant to squeeze out some of the oil, and transfer it to a bowl.

2. Add more oil to the skillet, if needed. Add the zucchini and cook, stirring occasionally, until it is golden brown, about 8 minutes. Transfer it to the bowl with the eggplant.

3. Meanwhile, heat the remaining ¼ cup oil in a large saucepan over medium heat. Add the onion and bell pepper and cook, stirring occasionally, until the onion softens, about 3 minutes. Stir in the garlic and cook until fragrant, about 1 minute. Add the tomatoes and their juices, 1 cup water, and season with salt and red pepper flakes. Stir in the eggplant and zucchini. Bring everything to a simmer over medium heat. Reduce the heat to medium-low and cook, stirring occasionally, until the juices thicken, about 30 minutes.

4. Meanwhile, put the potatoes in a medium saucepan and add salted water to cover. Bring them to a boil over high heat. Reduce the heat to medium and cook until the potatoes are tender, about 20 minutes. Drain well, reserving about 2 cups of the potato cooking water.

5. Stir the drained potatoes into the vegetable mixture. Stir in 1 cup of the potato water and return the pot to the simmer. Cook until the potatoes have absorbed some of the sauce, adding more potato water, if desired, to adjust the thickness of the sauce. Stir in the olives and pine nuts. Season again to taste with salt and red pepper flakes. Transfer the giambotta to a serving bowl, sprinkle with the basil, and serve.

COOKING POTATOES WITH TOMATOES

Have you ever noticed that potatoes take an extraordinarily long time to cook in tomato sauce? A thick tomato sauce is too dense to penetrate the hard potato as well as water does. Also, tomato sauce will burn if cooked more than a few degrees above boiling, so the potato will cook at a much slower rate than it does in a pot of rapidly boiling water. All of these caveats apply to rice, too, which is why it is better to make Spanish rice, for example, with tomato juice.

EGGPLANT-PARMESAN GRATIN

Serve with pork roast or chops, lamb roasts and chops, or sausages.

Prep Time: 20 minutes

Cooking Time: 30 minutes

Make Ahead: The gratin can be cooked up to 1 day ahead.

Family Favorite, Holiday Feasts, Company Fare, Buffet Dish, Cooking Classic, Vegetarian

My version of eggplant Parmesan uses broiled, not fried, eggplant, for a quicker and lighter end result that still has a lot of traditional flavor. This is another ample side dish that I like to serve when I have both meat-eaters and vegetarians at the same table. It has really only a few steps and a tight ingredients list.

2 globe eggplants (about 2¾ pounds total), cut crosswise into ½-inch rounds

2 tablespoons extra-virgin olive oil, plus more for brushing the eggplant

1 yellow onion, chopped

2 garlic cloves, minced

2 teaspoons dried oregano

⅛ teaspoon hot red pepper flakes

One 28-ounce can crushed tomatoes

1 cup shredded mozzarella cheese (4 ounces)

½ cup freshly grated Parmesan cheese (2 ounces)

1. Position the broiler rack about 6 inches from the source of heat and preheat the broiler. In batches, lightly brush the eggplant with oil and place them on the rack. Broil until the eggplant is lightly browned, about 5 minutes. Turn the eggplant (no need to brush with oil again) and continue broiling to brown the other side, about 5 minutes more. Transfer the eggplant to a platter.

2. Meanwhile, heat the 2 tablespoons oil in a medium saucepan over medium heat. Add the onion and cook, stirring often, until golden, about 6 minutes. Add the garlic and cook until it gives off its aroma, about 1 minute. Stir in the oregano and red pepper flakes. Stir in the tomatoes and bring them to a boil. Reduce the heat to low. Simmer, uncovered, stirring often, until the sauce has lightly thickened, about 20 minutes. Remove the sauce from the heat and cover to keep warm.

3. Position a rack in the center of the oven and preheat the oven to 350ºF. Lightly oil an 11½ × 8 × 2-inch baking dish.

4. Spread about ½ cup of the tomato sauce in the baking dish. Arrange half of the eggplant in the dish, overlapping the slices. Spread half of the remaining sauce on top and sprinkle with half of the mozzarella. Repeat with the remaining eggplant, sauce, and mozzarella. Sprinkle the top with the Parmesan.

5. Bake until the sauce is bubbling, about 30 minutes. Let stand for 5 minutes, then serve hot.

ROASTED RATATOUILLE

MAKES 6 SERVINGS

Serve with grilled or roasted meats, poultry, or seafood.
Prep Time: 20 minutes
Cooking Time: 50 minutes
Make Ahead: The ratatouille can be made up to 2 days ahead.
Family Favorite, Company Fare, Buffet Dish, Retro Recipe, Cooking Classic, Vegetarian

One reason why ratatouille is so beloved is probably its versatility. Not only does it go well with just about any main course (well, those that aren't sauced, anyway), but it is equally delicious served hot or cool. It is usually simmered on the stove, but lately I have been roasting the vegetables, and it makes a firmer ratatouille with deeper flavors.

3 tablespoons extra-virgin olive oil, plus more for the baking sheets

1 globe eggplant (about 1¼ pounds), cut into 1-inch cubes

3 plum tomatoes, halved lengthwise, seeded

1 yellow onion, cut into sixths

1 large red bell pepper, cored, seeded, and cut into 1-inch pieces

1 large zucchini, trimmed and cut into ½-inch rounds

4 garlic cloves, minced

½ teaspoon hot red pepper flakes

Kosher salt

3 tablespoons coarsely chopped fresh basil

1. Position racks in the top third and center of the oven and preheat the oven to 400ºF. Lightly oil two large rimmed baking sheets.

2. Divide the eggplant, tomatoes, onion, bell pepper, and zucchini among the baking sheets. Drizzle them with the oil. Roast until the eggplant has softened, about 30 minutes. Stir and roast until the vegetables are tender, about 15 minutes more.

3. Sprinkle the garlic and red pepper flakes over the vegetables and roast until the garlic is fragrant and tender, about 5 minutes. Transfer the vegetables to a large bowl and season to taste with salt. Using the side of a large metal spoon, coarsely chop the tomatoes into bite-sized pieces. Stir in the basil. Serve hot or cooled to room temperature.

MISO-GLAZED EGGPLANT WITH GINGER AND GARLIC

MAKES 4 TO 6 SERVINGS

Serve with Asian-flavored grilled meats, poultry, and seafood.
Prep Time: 10 minutes

Cooking Time: 10 minutes

Weeknight Suppers, Buffet Dish, Cooking Classic, Vegetarian

In just a few years, this Japanese recipe, with sweet and salty glaze topping tender eggplant, has become a staple with grilling fans. It shows how the availability of such foods as miso, mirin, and Japanese eggplants has affected the way we eat daily. You can also use other Asian (white or green) or dark purple globe eggplants, cut into ¾-inch rounds, instead of the Japanese variety. And you can broil the eggplant if you don't have a grill. But one thing to remember if you are grilling the eggplant is that the grill heat should only be medium-high, or the eggplant will burn before it is cooked through.

2 tablespoons mirin (see Note)

2 tablespoons white miso (see Note page 80)

1 tablespoon sugar

2 teaspoons peeled and minced fresh ginger

1 garlic clove, crushed through a press

3 elongated Japanese eggplants, trimmed and
  halved lengthwise

Vegetable oil, for brushing the eggplant

1 scallion (white and green parts), thinly sliced on
  the diagonal

Toasted sesame oil, for serving

1. Prepare an outdoor grill for direct cooking over medium heat (350º to 450ºF). For a charcoal grill, let the coals burn until they are covered with white ash and you can hold your hand about 1 inch above the cooking grate for about 3 seconds. For a gas grill, preheat on high and adjust the thermostat to medium (400ºF).

2. In a small bowl, whisk the mirin, miso, sugar, ginger, and garlic together.

3. Lightly brush the eggplants on both sides with the oil. Place them on the grill, cut-sides down. Cook, with the lid closed, until the eggplants are seared with grill marks, about 5 minutes. Turn the eggplants and brush them generously with the miso mixture. Cover again and cook until the eggplants are tender and the miso mixture has reduced to a glaze, about 5 minutes.

4. Transfer the eggplants to a serving platter. Let them cool for a few minutes, then cut them crosswise on the diagonal into 2-inch chunks. Sprinkle with the scallion, followed by a drizzle of sesame oil, and serve.

Note: Mirin is Japanese sweetened rice wine. It used to be available only at Asian markets, but it is now carried by many supermarkets. Sweet sherry, such as amontillado, is an acceptable substitute.

Broiled Miso-Glazed Eggplant: Position a broiler rack about 6 inches from the source of heat and preheat the broiler on high. Place the oiled eggplant on a broiler pan, flat-side down. Broil until the eggplant skin is lightly browned, about 4 minutes. Flip the eggplant and cook until the cut side is beginning to brown, about 3 minutes. Brush with the miso mixture and broil until the mixture has thickened into a glaze and the eggplant is tender, about 1 minute more. If the glaze threatens to burn before the eggplant is tender, turn off the broiler and let the eggplant cook in the hot oven for a few more minutes, until it is tender.

Fennel

A treasured vegetable in Italian cooking, fennel has a reputation for its anise/licorice flavor, and it seems some people don't like this particular taste. However, when fennel is cooked, the anise flavor mellows, and I have served it to many people who have since changed their opinion. (By the way, fennel is sometimes incorrectly labeled as anise, which is a seed used as a spice, and not a vegetable.) If you purchase fennel with the fronds still attached, cut them off and reserve them, and then sprinkle the finished dish with the chopped fronds for their stronger licorice (or anise, if you will) flavor.

Peak Season: Available all year, but best during the winter months.

Purchase: Firm, unblemished bulbs with bright white and green color; sprig, if attached, should be sprightly.

Storage: Refrigerate, wrapped in paper towels, for up to 5 days, as it tends to lose flavor with long storage.

Preparation: Trim off the fronds, if attached, and reserve, if desired to use as a garnish. Cut the bulb in half vertically, and trim out the thick triangular core. Cut the bulb and stalks as directed.

BRAISED FENNEL WITH ORANGE-BUTTER SAUCE
MAKES 6 SERVINGS

Serve with pork roast and chops, roast chicken, baked fish fillets, or sautéed shrimp.
Prep Time: 5 minutes
Cooking Time: 40 minutes
Make Ahead: The fennel can be made up to 1 day ahead.
Holiday Feasts, Company Fare, Vegetarian

When I served this the first time, everyone at the table agreed that it changed their preconceptions about the licorice flavor of fennel. The cooking juices are lightly thickened at the end with a bit of butter for a smooth sauce. I serve it at Thanksgiving, for supper with roast chicken, and as a bed for pork chops, and it always gets compliments. Use your largest skillet (my 6-quart skillet is 14 inches in diameter) so the two heads of fennel will fit in a relatively single layer.

2 heads fennel (about 1 pound each)

2 navel oranges

3 tablespoons olive oil, as needed

3 tablespoons chopped shallots

¾ cup dry white wine or dry vermouth

Kosher salt and freshly grated black pepper

1 tablespoon cold unsalted butter

1. Cut off the stems of the fennel where they meet the bulbs. Finely chop about 1 tablespoon of the fronds and reserve them for the garnish. If desired, save the stems for another use (thinly sliced, they can be added to a salad like celery). Cut each fennel vertically into ½-inch slices. Trim out the thick triangular core from each slice.

2. Finely grate the zest from 1 orange and reserve. Juice both oranges; you should have ¾ cup orange juice.

3. Heat 2 tablespoons of the oil in a very large skillet over medium-high heat. Add the fennel in batches, flat-side down, and cook, turning once, adding more oil if needed, until browned on both sides, about 4 minutes. Transfer to a platter.

4. Add the remaining 1 tablespoon oil to the skillet with the shallots. Cook over medium heat, stirring often, until the shallots are tender, about 2 minutes. Stir in the orange juice and wine. Return the fennel to the skillet, overlapping as necessary. Add enough water to barely cover the fennel. Season with ½ teaspoon salt and ¼ teaspoon pepper. Bring everything to a boil over high heat.

5. Reduce the heat to medium-low and cover tightly. Simmer, occasionally flipping the fennel for even cooking, until it is tender when pierced with the tip of a knife, 25 to 30 minutes. Using a slotted spoon, transfer the fennel to a serving bowl and tent it with aluminum foil to keep warm.

6. Return the skillet to high heat. Boil the cooking liquid until it is reduced to about 3 tablespoons, about 3 minutes. Remove from the heat. Whisk in the butter until it thickens the cooking liquid. Season to taste with salt and pepper. Pour the sauce over the fennel, sprinkle with the orange zest and fennel fronds, and serve.

ROASTED FENNEL WITH PARMESAN CRUST AND LEMON

MAKES 4 TO 6 SERVINGS

Serve with pork, lamb, and veal roasts and chops; sausages; fish fillets; salmon fillets; or shrimp.

Prep Time: 5 minutes

Cooking Time: 30 minutes

Make Ahead: The fennel, without the Parmesan topping, can be roasted up to 2 hours ahead.

Weeknight Suppers, Holiday Feasts, Company Fare, Buffet Dish, Vegetarian

This wonderful dish is now one of my go-to sides, as it is very versatile, especially with salmon or shrimp. I came up with it when I needed an easy side dish for a Christmas Eve seafood dinner feast and it was so popular that I could have doubled the batch. The sweet roasted fennel with the umami-rich Parmesan and a squeeze of lemon is a simple combination that will win you over.

Olive oil, for the baking sheet and for brushing

2 heads fennel (about 1 pound each)

Kosher salt and freshly ground black pepper

⅓ cup freshly grated Parmesan cheese (about 1½ ounces)

Lemon wedges, for serving

1. Position a rack in the center of the oven and preheat the oven to 425ºF. Lightly oil a large rimmed baking sheet.

2. If your fennel has the stalks and fronds attached, cut them off about 1 inch from the bulb. If you wish, save the stalks for another use (cut into thin slices and add to salads), and finely chop the fronds for garnishing the roasted fennel. Cut the fennel bulbs lengthwise into ½-inch slices. Arrange the fennel on the baking sheet and brush it on both sides with oil.

3. Roast the fennel for 15 minutes. Flip the fennel over and continue roasting until it is tinged golden brown and just tender when pierced with the tip of a small, sharp knife, about 10 minutes. Remove from the oven.

4. Move the fennel together on the baking sheet. Season to taste with salt and pepper and sprinkle with the Parmesan. Return it to the oven and roast until the Parmesan is melted and lightly browned, about 5 minutes. Transfer the fennel to a serving platter and sprinkle it with the fennel fronds, if using. Add the lemon wedges and serve.

Greens, Dark

I have collected all of the cruciferous leafy greens (curly and Tuscan kale, escarole, and curly endive, as well as collard, mustard, and turnip greens) here because they share so many characteristics. (Dandelion greens are not cruciferous, but their flavor and cooking methods put them in this category.) They all have a somewhat bitter flavor that can be retained with quick cooking or toned down with long simmering. I admit that I mainly restrict Tuscan (aka lacinato or dinosaur) kale to Italian-inspired recipes, but otherwise I use these greens interchangeably. (But not Swiss chard, which is sweeter and more tender, and has its own section on page 70). You can now purchase bags of washed and cut collard greens and kale, which I recommend as time savers, or buy bunches of greens and prep them yourself.

Peak Season: December to April, but available all year.

Purchase: Evenly colored, springy leaves without holes or brown spots.

Storage: Refrigerate in a plastic bag for up to 3 days.

Preparation: Dark greens are very sandy, so wash them well in a sink or bowl of cold water, lifting out the leaves so the grit sinks to the bottom of the water. Tear the leaves from the stems. If you are using prewashed bags of kale or collards, any harmful bacteria will be killed during cooking. However, if you are using bagged raw kale for salad, you should rinse it first as a precaution. In some cases, dark greens are rinsed and cooked with their clinging water to avoid adding extra liquid during cooking.

SKILLET KALE AND GARLIC

MAKES 4 SERVINGS

Serve with pork chops, baked ham or ham steaks, sausages, barbecued meats and poultry, or fried chicken.

Prep Time: 10 minutes

Cooking Time: 10 minutes

Weeknight Suppers, Holiday Feasts

While I profess a love for long-cooked greens, I also appreciate this method for cooking them in a flash. If you wish, brown a chopped slice of bacon in the skillet with only 1 tablespoon oil, then cook the greens in the resulting fat. If you buy a bag of washed and chopped kale, the side is likely to be done before the main course!

One 1-pound bag chopped curly kale (or
   1¼ pounds kale, tough stems discarded and
   leaves coarsely chopped)

2 tablespoons extra-virgin olive oil

2 garlic cloves, thinly sliced

¼ teaspoon hot red pepper flakes

½ cup reduced-sodium chicken broth

Kosher salt

Cider vinegar, for serving

1. Rinse the chopped kale in a colander under cold running water. (If using freshly chopped kale, wash it well in a sink of cold running water.) Lift the kale out of the water and transfer it to a bowl. Do not dry the kale.

2. Heat the oil, garlic, and red pepper flakes in a large skillet over medium heat, stirring occasionally, until the garlic softens, about 2 minutes. A handful at a time, stir in the wet kale, letting the first batch wilt before adding the next. Add the broth and bring it to a boil. Reduce the heat to medium-low and simmer, stirring occasionally, just until the greens are tender, 10 to 12 minutes. Season to taste with salt. Serve hot, with the vinegar passed on the side for sprinkling.

SWEET AND SPICY GREENS WITH SWEET POTATOES

MAKES 6 SERVINGS

Serve with pork roast, pork chops, ham, sausages, or poultry.

Prep Time: 10 minutes

Cooking Time: 15 minutes

Make Ahead: This dish can be made up to 1 day ahead.

Weeknight Suppers, Buffet Dish

You often see greens and sweet potatoes on the same menu, but prepared separately. They obviously go well together, so why not pair them in the same side dish? Unless you are willing to roast the sweet potatoes for about an hour, you'll need a microwave to make this dish. Experiment with other greens (such as turnip or mustard), as the sweet flavor of the potatoes offsets the tang of the leaves.

2 slices bacon, cut into 1-inch pieces

1 tablespoon vegetable oil

1 yellow onion, chopped

2 garlic cloves, chopped

½ Fresno or jalapeño chile, seeded and minced

One 16-ounce bag chopped curly kale or collard greens (see Note), rinsed but not dried

Kosher salt and freshly ground black pepper

1 tablespoon cider vinegar, plus more for serving

2 sweet potatoes (also called yams; 8 to 9 ounces each), scrubbed and pierced a few times with a fork

1. Cook the bacon and oil together in a large saucepan over medium heat, stirring occasionally, until the bacon is crisp and browned, about 8 minutes. Add the onion, garlic, and chile and cook, stirring occasionally, until the onion is softened, about 3 minutes. In batches, stir in the kale with any clinging water, letting the first batch wilt before adding the next. Cover and simmer until the kale is just tender, about 15 minutes. Season to taste with salt and pepper. Stir in the vinegar.

2. Meanwhile, cook the sweet potatoes in a microwave oven on high until they're just tender when pierced with the tip of a small, sharp knife, about 8 minutes. Let them stand for 5 minutes.

3. Using a kitchen towel to protect your hands, peel the sweet potatoes and cut the flesh into 1-inch chunks. Season the sweet potatoes to taste with salt and pepper. Transfer the kale to a serving dish and top it with the sweet potatoes. Serve hot, with vinegar passed on the side.

Note: If you wish, substitute 1 bunch curly kale or collard greens (about 1¼ pounds) for the bagged greens. Discard the tough stems. Stack the leaves and cut them crosswise into ½-inch strips. Wash the leaves well in cold water and shake off the excess water, but do not dry the leaves.

PORTUGUESE KALE WITH LINGUIÇA

MAKES 4 TO 6 SERVINGS

Serve with grilled or roast pork or chops, sausages, or chicken.

Prep Time: 10 minutes

Cooking Time: 55 minutes

Make Ahead: The kale can be made up to 2 days ahead.

Holiday Feasts, Company Fare, Buffet Dish, Retro Recipe, Cooking Classic

In this national dish of Portugal, the flavors of the kale and sausage meld as they simmer together. It's a great side dish, and I always make a big batch to ensure leftovers. Although my Portuguese heritage gives me a fondness for linguiça, any spicy smoked sausage (even kielbasa) will do.

1 tablespoon extra-virgin olive oil	2 garlic cloves, minced
4 ounces linguiça or other spicy smoked sausage, such as chorizo, cut into ¼-inch pieces	2 pounds curly kale
	¼ teaspoon hot red pepper flakes
1 yellow onion, chopped	Kosher salt

1. Heat the oil in a large saucepan over medium heat. Add the linguiça and cook, stirring often, until it is lightly browned, about 5 minutes. Stir in the onion and cook, stirring often, until softened, about 3 minutes. Stir in the garlic and cook until fragrant, about 1 minute.

2. Meanwhile, wash the kale well in a large bowl or sink filled with cold water. Lift the wet kale from the water, shake off the excess water, but do not dry the kale. Strip the leaves from the stems. Chop the stems crosswise into ½-inch pieces. In batches, stack the leaves and cut them crosswise into ¼-inch strips.

3. Stir the kale leaves and stems with any clinging water into the saucepan. Add ½ cup water and bring it to a boil. Reduce the heat to medium-low and cover. Simmer, stirring occasionally, until the kale is very tender, about 45 minutes. Season with the red pepper flakes and salt to taste. (The kale can be cooled, covered, and refrigerated for up to 2 days. Reheat in a large saucepan over medium-low heat for about 10 minutes.) Serve hot.

LINGUIÇA

Both of my grandfathers were of Portuguese heritage, so I grew up with the richly seasoned food of that country. A chunky sausage seasoned with red pepper and vinegar, linguiça is distinctly spicy and tangy, and similar to Mexican smoked chorizo links (not the unsmoked fresh chorizo). It is a coincidence that my current home in New Jersey is also near a Portuguese community, and I still have easy access to linguiça. With all of the culinary interest in things porcine, more and more butchers are making it. When you find linguiça, buy a couple of pounds and freeze it for up to six months.

In my relatively small hometown in the San Francisco Bay Area, there were *three* flourishing Portuguese sausage factories. A few years ago, one of the factories was closed after the demented owner staged a murderous attack on three government agents coming to inspect the facility in an unbelievable sequence of events right out of a television drama. Yet my family still compares the three different brands as if you could buy them all.

GARBANZO BEANS WITH TUSCAN KALE

MAKES 4 SERVINGS

Serve with roasts, grilled chops, sausages, roast chicken, or grilled salmon.
Prep Time: 5 minutes

Cooking Time: 15 minutes

Make Ahead: The kale can be made up to 1 day ahead.

Weeknight Suppers, Buffet Dish, Family Favorite

*O*ne *of our favorites to serve with chops and sausages, this Italian dish can be made in minutes on the stove while the main course is in the broiler or on the grill. Tuscan kale is a little sweeter than curly kale, and the leaves hold less grit, so it is very easy to work with. And yes, you can skip the pork.*

¼ cup diced (¼-inch) pancetta or prosciutto

1 tablespoon olive oil

2 garlic cloves, thinly sliced

1 cup reduced-sodium chicken broth

8 ounces Tuscan (lacinato) kale, thick stems
   discarded, well rinsed and coarsely chopped

One 15-ounce can garbanzo beans (chickpeas),
   rinsed and drained

Kosher salt and freshly ground black pepper

1. Cook the pancetta and oil together in a medium saucepan over medium heat, stirring occasionally, until the pancetta is lightly browned, about 3 minutes. Stir in the garlic and cook until it is fragrant, about 1 minute.

2. Stir in the broth and bring it to a boil over high heat. Cook until reduced by half, about 1 minute. In two or three additions, stir in the kale, letting the first addition wilt before adding the next. Stir in the garbanzo beans. Reduce the heat to medium-low and cover. Cook, stirring occasionally, just until the kale is tender, about 5 minutes. Season to taste with salt and pepper and serve.

STEAMED COLLARD GREENS WITH SPICY TOFU

MAKES 4 SERVINGS

Serve with other vegetable dishes for a meatless meal.

Prep Time: 20 minutes, plus 30 minutes pressing time

Cooking Time: 25 minutes

Weeknight Suppers, Buffet Dish, Vegetarian

I *turn to my old buddy and cookbook author Dana Jacobi when I need a sure-fire vegetarian recipe. As her contribution to this book, she sent over this vegan recipe for steamed greens with a genius crispy tofu topping, which can also be used with other greens, or to top baked potatoes or salads. I think that you'll love the fresh, clean flavor of the steamed collards. Dana serves this with other vegetarian dishes, but I can report that it goes very well with pork chops and ham, as you would expect of collard greens. You will have leftover plain tofu for another meal.*

TOFU

One 14- to 18-ounce package firm tofu

½ teaspoon kosher salt

½ teaspoon garlic powder

½ teaspoon dried oregano

½ teaspoon dried thyme

¼ teaspoon chili powder

¼ teaspoon ground cumin

¼ teaspoon sweet paprika

⅛ teaspoon freshly ground black pepper

Pinch of cayenne pepper

1½ pounds collard greens, tough stems removed, leaves stacked and cut into ½-inch strips (see Note)

1 tablespoon vegetable oil

Kosher salt

1. Cut the tofu in half vertically, and wrap and refrigerate one half for another use. Cut the remaining tofu in half vertically. Place the cut halves side by side on a plate and cover them loosely with plastic wrap. Cover with a second plate and top with a heavy can to weight the tofu. Let it stand for 30 minutes.

2. Mix the salt, garlic powder, oregano, thyme, chili powder, cumin, paprika, pepper, and cayenne together in a medium bowl; set aside.

3. Place a collapsible steamer in a large saucepan and add enough water to almost reach the bottom of the steamer. (If you have another kind of steamer, just set it up as needed.) Bring the water to a boil over high heat.

4. Wash the collard greens well in a large bowl or sink filled with cold water. Add them to the steamer and cover the saucepan. Steam the greens until they are cooked to your desired texture, about 11 minutes for chewy and 15 minutes for tender.

5. Meanwhile, discard the liquid pressed from the tofu. Crumble the pressed tofu into the bowl (it should look like scrambled eggs) and mix to coat it with the spice mixture.

6. Heat the oil in a medium skillet over medium-high heat. Add the spiced tofu and cook, stirring occasionally, until the small bits of tofu are crisp and browned and the larger pieces are golden, about 8 minutes.

7. Transfer the greens to a serving bowl and season to taste with salt. Top with the tofu mixture and serve.

Note: Substitute a 1-pound bag of chopped and prewashed collard greens for the bunched greens, if you wish. Rinse the bagged collard greens before using.

SMOTHERED COLLARD GREENS WITH POT LIKKER

MAKES 6 TO 8 SERVINGS

Serve with baked ham, grilled and pan-cooked pork chops, barbecued ribs, or fried chicken.

Prep Time: 10 minutes

Cooking Time: 2¼ hours

Weeknight Suppers, Family Favorite, Holiday Feasts, Company Fare, Buffet Dish, Retro Recipe, Cooking Classic

In spite of the fashion for quickly sautéed greens, there is a flavor exchange that can only occur when greens are slowly simmered with vegetables and smoked pork. The cooking liquid is called "pot likker" and should be so tasty that you'll want to sop it up with cornbread. My method adds the greens to a simmering ham hock for lots of deep flavor.

2 tablespoons canola oil

1 large yellow onion, chopped

1 carrot, chopped

6 garlic cloves, smashed under the flat side of a knife and peeled

2 ham hocks (about 1½ pounds), preferably sawed into thick slices by the butcher

2 pounds collard greens

2 tablespoons cider vinegar

1 teaspoon hot red pepper sauce

Kosher salt

1. Heat the oil in a large pot over medium heat. Add the onion and carrot and cook, stirring occasionally, until the onion is softened, about 3 minutes. Stir in the garlic and cook until it is fragrant, about 1 minute. Add the ham hocks and pour in 1 quart water. Bring it to a boil over high heat. Reduce the heat to medium-low and simmer until the liquid has reduced by about one-quarter, about 1 hour, 10 minutes.

2. Strip the collard leaves from the stems. Chop the stems crosswise into ½-inch pieces. In batches, stack the leaves, roll them into a thick cylinder, and cut them crosswise into ½-inch strips. Coarsely chop the strips. Wash the collard greens well in a large bowl or sink filled with cold water. Lift the wet greens from the water, leaving any grit in the bottom of the bowl, and shake off the excess water.

3. Stir the collard leaves and stems into the ham hock stock. Increase the heat to high and return the stock to a simmer. Return the heat to medium-low and simmer until the stems are tender, about 1 hour.

4. Using tongs, remove the ham hocks from the pot, transfer them to a chopping board, and let cool until easy to handle. Remove the meat from the hocks, discarding the rind and bones. Chop the ham meat and return it to the collards. Stir in the vinegar and hot sauce and season with salt to taste. Transfer the greens to a serving bowl with as much of the pot likker as you like. Serve hot.

GREEK GREENS (HORTA)
MAKES 6 TO 8 SERVINGS

Serve with grilled meats, especially lamb, beef, or swordfish kebabs; as part of a Mediterranean-flavored meal; with leg of lamb, roast chicken, or sautéed shrimp.

Prep Time: 15 minutes

Cooking Time: 20 minutes, plus 1 hour cooling time

Make Ahead: The horta can be refrigerated for 3 days; serve at room temperature.

Weeknight Suppers, Buffet Dish, Vegetarian

One of the national dishes of Greece, horta is an unpretentious tangle of foraged wild greens. We make due with the usual suspects in the American lexicon of bitter greens, and what delicious substitutes they are. Truthfully, just about any leafy green can be prepared this way, but I like this mixture of curly endive, escarole, and dandelion because it is a good balance of bitterness levels. The secret is to cook the horta just until the greens are tender and to avoid overcooking. Horta is best served at room temperature.

1 pound curly endive, cored and coarsely chopped	¼ cup extra-virgin olive oil
1 pound escarole, cored and coarsely chopped	2 tablespoons fresh lemon juice
1 pound dandelion greens, coarsely chopped	Kosher salt and freshly ground black pepper

1. Bring a large pot of salted water to a boil over high heat.

2. In batches, wash the endive, escarole, and dandelion greens well in a sink of cold water. Lift the greens from the water, leaving any grit at the bottom of the sink, and transfer them to the boiling water. Cover and return to the boil. Uncover and reduce the heat to medium. Cook, uncovered, until the greens are bright dark green and just tender, 15 to 20 minutes.

3. Drain the horta in a large colander and rinse under cold running water. Using your hands or a large rubber spatula, press on the greens to extrude excess liquid. Let them cool to room temperature, at least 1 hour. (The horta can be transferred to a bowl, covered, and refrigerated for up to 3 days. Return the greens to room temperature before serving.)

4. Transfer the greens to a serving platter. Drizzle them with the oil and lemon juice, season to taste with salt and pepper, and serve.

Greens, Tender (see Chard, Swiss and Spinach)

Kohlrabi

One week, I received a dozen kohlrabi in a CSA box. Until then, I hadn't cooked with it very much. Now it is one of my favorite vegetables, especially at dinner parties when I want to serve something out of the ordinary. Its name means "cabbage turnip" in German, and that is a fair assessment of its flavor and crisp, apple-like texture. Braised or roasted, or raw in a salad, kohlrabi gets a workout in my kitchen.

Peak Season: Summer to early autumn.

Purchase: Firm, shiny bulbs without any bruises.

Storage: Refrigerate for up to 1 week.

Preparation: Use a paring knife to trim off the rough edges, and peel with a vegetable peeler.

BRAISED KOHLRABI AND CARROTS WITH LEMON AND CARAWAY

MAKES 4 TO 6 SERVINGS

Serve with pork roasts and chops, sausages, or poultry sautés.

Prep Time: 10 minutes

Cooking Time: 25 minutes

Make Ahead: The braise can be prepared up to 1 day ahead.

Weeknight Suppers, Vegetarian

Caraway seed has become an essential spice in my kitchen for the flavor it brings to members of the cabbage family (like kohlrabi) and carrots. Take a minute or two to toast the caraway first and bring its flavor to the fore.

1 teaspoon caraway seed

1 tablespoon unsalted butter

8 carrots, cut into ½-inch rounds

1 kohlrabi (about 9 ounces), peeled and cut into
  ½-inch pieces

1 yellow onion, chopped

1 tablespoon fresh lemon juice

Kosher salt and freshly ground black pepper

1. Cook the caraway seed in a medium skillet over medium heat, stirring occasionally, until it is toasted and fragrant (you may see a wisp of smoke), about 2 minutes. Transfer it to a plate to cool.
2. Add the butter to the skillet and let it melt. Add the carrots, kohlrabi, and onion and cook, stirring occasionally, until the onion is tender, about 5 minutes. Add ½ cup water and bring it to a boil. Reduce the heat to medium-low and cover. Simmer until the vegetables are tender, about 15 minutes. Uncover, increase the heat to high, and boil until the liquid has reduced to a few tablespoons, 2 to 3 minutes.
3. Meanwhile, coarsely crush the caraway seed in a mortar or electric spice grinder. Stir the lemon juice and crushed caraway seed into the vegetable mixture, season with salt and pepper, and serve.

ROASTED KOHLRABI WITH DIJON AND GARLIC

MAKES 6 SERVINGS

Serve with pork roast, pork chops, ham, sausages, roast chicken, or chicken sautés.

Prep Time: 5 minutes

Cooking Time: 35 minutes

Weeknight Suppers, Vegetarian

Roasting gives kohlrabi a sweet touch, so you can match it with strong flavors like Dijon mustard and garlic.

3 kohlrabi (about 9 ounces each), peeled and cut into ½-inch wedges

2 tablespoons olive oil

2 tablespoons Dijon mustard

2 garlic cloves, minced

Kosher salt

1. Position a rack in the center of the oven and preheat the oven to 425°F.

2. On a large rimmed baking sheet, toss the kohlrabi wedges with the oil and spread them out in a single layer. Roast until the undersides are crisp and browned, about 15 minutes. Flip the kohlrabi and continue roasting until golden brown and tender, about 15 minutes more.

3. Move the kohlrabi close together. In a small bowl, mix the mustard and garlic together and spread the mixture all over the kohlrabi. Continue roasting just until the mustard mixture has reduced to a glaze, 3 to 5 minutes. Season to taste with salt and serve.

Mushrooms

These days, mushrooms are usually cultivated and not foraged, making for a huge selection. Over the course of a year, my local produce market must offer at least a dozen different kinds. White button mushrooms are still the standard-bearers, but I often get brown cremini (baby bella) or shiitake mushrooms for their richer flavors. Orange-colored chanterelles and honeycombed morels make their respective appearances in the spring and fall. If I am shopping at an Asian market, I have these options along with floppy oyster, tall king, matsutake, and more.

Peak Season: Available all year.

Purchase: Evenly colored mushrooms without any sign of decay, such as slime or brown spots.

Storage: Store in a paper bag in the refrigerator for up to 5 days (or 3 days for wild mushrooms, such as morel and chanterelle).

Preparation: While some cooks recommend brushing fresh mushrooms clean with a brush, this is very tedious work. After all, in their natural setting, mushrooms are waterproof, so I don't see any reason why they can't be cleaned in water, as long as they aren't soaked. Add the mushrooms to a bowl of cold water and agitate them briefly to loosen grit. Lift the mushrooms out of the water and pat them dry with towels. With the exception of shiitake (whose inedible stems should be cut off and discarded), use the entire mushroom, with the tough stem ends trimmed, if necessary.

SAUTÉED MUSHROOMS WITH GARLIC AND ROSEMARY

MAKES 4 SERVINGS

Serve with grilled or sautéed meat, poultry, and seafood main courses.
Prep Time: 5 minutes
Cooking Time: 10 minutes
Weeknight Suppers, Company Fare, Vegetarian

I should have a plaque hanging in my kitchen that reads "When in Doubt, Sauté Mushrooms." If I am being indecisive about a side dish, this recipe often comes to the rescue. Quick and chameleon-like, it works with main courses from pork chops to chicken breasts, steaks to salmon. I prefer the wine or vermouth option, but I have used broth and even water. The variation is a nice treat when you want a creamier dish. The brown mushrooms benefit from the fresh green color of the rosemary, so if you are using dried rosemary, garnish the finished mushrooms with a sprinkle of chopped parsley.

2 tablespoons extra-virgin olive oil

1 pound assorted mushrooms, such as cremini, button, and stemmed shiitake, cut into quarters

2 garlic cloves, minced

⅓ cup dry white wine, dry vermouth, or reduced-sodium chicken broth

1 teaspoon finely chopped fresh rosemary or ½ teaspoon dried

Kosher salt and freshly ground black pepper

1 tablespoon cold unsalted butter (optional)

1. Heat the oil in a large skillet over medium-high heat. Add the mushrooms and cook, stirring occasionally, until they have given off their juices and are beginning to brown, about 8 minutes. Add the garlic and cook until it is fragrant, about 1 minute.

2. Stir in the wine and rosemary and bring them to a boil. Cook until the mixture has reduced to about 2 tablespoons, about 2 minutes. Remove from the heat. Season to taste with salt and pepper. Add the butter, if using, and stir until it has melted and lightly thickened the sauce. Serve hot.

Creamed Mushrooms with Shallots and Rosemary: Substitute 2 tablespoons minced shallots for the garlic. Reduce the wine to ¼ cup. Add ½ cup heavy cream to the skillet with the wine and boil it over high heat until the liquid is reduced to about 2 tablespoons, about 4 minutes. Omit the butter.

MUSHROOMS BOURGUIGNON

MAKES 4 SERVINGS

Serve with steak, roast beef, pork chops, lamb chops, salmon or striped bass fillets.
Prep Time: 10 minutes

Cooking Time: 20 minutes
Weeknight Suppers, Holiday Feasts, Company Fare

There is a fairly long list of side dishes that are considered ideal with grilled steak—baked potatoes, creamed spinach, and asparagus hollandaise appear on steakhouse menus with regularity. But this one has to join the group, a combination of mushrooms, shallots, and bacon in a red wine sauce.

2 slices bacon, cut crosswise into 1-inch pieces	1 teaspoon finely chopped fresh thyme or
1 pound cremini mushrooms, cut into quarters	½ teaspoon dried
2 tablespoons minced shallots	1 tablespoon cold unsalted butter
⅓ cup hearty red wine, such as Shiraz	Kosher salt and freshly ground black pepper
⅓ cup reduced-sodium beef or chicken broth	1 tablespoon finely chopped fresh flat-leaf parsley

1. Cook the bacon in a large skillet over medium heat, stirring occasionally, until it is crisp and browned, about 5 minutes. Using a slotted spoon, transfer the bacon to paper towels to drain, leaving the fat in the skillet.

2. Increase the heat to medium-high. Add the mushrooms and cook, stirring occasionally, until they have given off their juices and are beginning to brown, about 8 minutes. Add the shallots and cook until they soften, about 2 minutes.

3. Stir in the wine, broth, and thyme and bring them to a boil. Cook until the mixture has reduced to ¼ cup, about 3 minutes. Remove from the heat. Add the butter and stir until it has melted and lightly thickened the sauce. Season to taste with salt and pepper. Stir in the parsley and reserved bacon. Serve hot.

CANTONESE BRAISED SHIITAKE MUSHROOMS WITH BABY BOK CHOY
MAKES 4 SERVINGS

Serve with Asian-flavored steaks and chops, poultry dishes, or seafood.
Prep Time: 20 minutes
Cooking Time: 10 minutes
Weeknight Suppers, Company Fare, Buffet Dish, Cooking Classic

Growing up near San Francisco, I remember when Chinese restaurants—the vast majority of which featured Cantonese food—irreversibly changed with the arrival of spicy Sichuan and Hunan cuisine. For me, the mellow flavors of this dish make it comfort food, with the mushrooms simmered in a soy-and-ginger sauce and the bok choy on top steaming to tenderness. I serve this most often with grilled salmon, but it is also perfect with sliced soy-marinated flank steak.

2 tablespoons soy sauce

2 tablespoons reduced-sodium chicken broth

2 tablespoons Chinese rice wine or dry sherry

½ teaspoon sugar

1 tablespoon vegetable oil

1 scallion (white and pale green bottoms, finely chopped; green tops, thinly sliced)

1 tablespoon peeled and minced fresh ginger

1 garlic clove, minced

8 ounces shiitake mushrooms, stemmed, caps intact

4 baby bok choy (about 5 ounces total), halved lengthwise

Freshly ground black pepper

Toasted sesame oil, for serving

1. In a small bowl, mix the soy sauce, broth, rice wine, sugar, and 2 tablespoons water together.

2. Heat a medium skillet over medium heat. Add the oil and swirl to coat the bottom of the skillet. Add the scallion bottoms, ginger, and garlic and cook until they are fragrant, about 10 seconds. Add the mushrooms and stir well. Stir in the soy sauce mixture. Reduce the heat to low. Place the bok choy over the mushrooms.

3. Tightly cover the skillet and simmer, adding a tablespoon or so of water if the liquid reduces too quickly, until the bok choy is just tender when pierced with the tip of a small, sharp knife, about 10 minutes. Season to taste with the pepper. Transfer to a serving bowl, drizzle with sesame oil, and serve.

PORTOBELLO MUSHROOMS "FONDUE"

MAKES 4 SERVINGS

Serve with chicken, steaks, chops, or fish fillets.

Prep Time: 10 minutes

Cooking Time: 15 minutes

Weeknight Suppers, Family Favorite, Holiday Feasts, Company Fare, Vegetarian

Whenever I make fondue, I always include raw mushrooms as a dipping ingredient alongside the expected bread cubes. One frigid winter night, I took the combination of mushrooms and Gruyère cheese a step further to make a side dish for sautéed chicken breasts. The results were such a success that I now serve this dish with steaks, chops, and fish, too.

4 large portobello mushroom caps, well cleaned

3 tablespoons olive oil

Kosher salt and freshly ground black pepper

1 garlic clove, minced

1 teaspoon finely chopped fresh thyme or

½ teaspoon dried

¾ cup shredded Gruyère or Swiss cheese (about 3 ounces)

½ cup dry white wine

1. Position a rack in the center of the oven and preheat the oven to 425°F.

2. Cut off the mushroom stems from the caps. Coarsely chop the stems and set them aside.

3. Place the caps on a large rimmed baking sheet and drizzle them on both sides with 2 tablespoons of the oil. Season them all over with 1 teaspoon salt and ½ teaspoon pepper. Roast until the caps are giving off their juices, about 10 minutes.

4. Meanwhile, heat the remaining 1 tablespoon oil in a medium skillet over medium-high heat. Add the mushroom stems and cook, stirring occasionally, until they are beginning to brown, about 5 minutes. Stir in the garlic and thyme and cook, stirring occasionally, until the garlic is fragrant, about 1 minute. Remove them from the heat and lightly season the stems to taste with salt and pepper.

5. Remove the baking sheet with the caps from the oven. Fill each cap with an equal amount of the chopped stem mixture, and then top them with the cheese. Continue roasting until the cheese melts and the mushrooms are tender, about 5 minutes more.

6. Transfer the mushrooms to a serving platter. Heat the baking sheet over high heat on the stove. Add the wine and let it boil, stirring up any browned bits on the sheet with a wooden spoon, until the wine has reduced to about 3 tablespoons, 2 to 3 minutes. Pour the wine reduction over the mushrooms and serve.

WILD MUSHROOM AND FONTINA TART

MAKES 8 SERVINGS

Serve with roast beef, veal, or pork; roast chicken; or salmon fillets.

Prep Time: 30 minutes, plus 30 minutes refrigeration time

Cooking Time: 45 minutes

Make Ahead: The tart can be stored at room temperature for up to 8 hours; reheat it in a 350°F oven until warm, about 10 minutes.

Holiday Feasts, Company Fare, Buffet Dish, Vegetarian

When buying the mushrooms for this lovely still life of a side dish, I usually head to my Asian market to choose a variety of shapes, sizes, and colors. The offerings may include long and plump king oysters, narrow beech, earth-colored matsutake, clustered hen of woods, and the familiar shiitake and white button. When cutting them up, keep the mushroom's general shape so you can appreciate the range of varieties in the crust.

TART DOUGH

1 cup (130 g) unbleached all-purpose flour, plus
   more for rolling out the dough

1 teaspoon sugar

¼ teaspoon fine sea or table salt

6 tablespoons (¾ stick) cold unsalted butter, cut
   into ½-inch pieces

4 tablespoons iced water, as needed

MUSHROOMS

2 tablespoons (¼ stick) unsalted butter

1½ pounds assorted wild mushrooms, such as king oyster, beech, and stemmed shiitakes, trimmed and cut as needed into ½-inch slices or small clusters

Kosher salt and freshly ground black pepper

⅔ cup coarsely chopped shallots

1 teaspoon finely chopped fresh thyme or ½ teaspoon dried

3 tablespoons Cognac or brandy

½ cup heavy cream

1 cup shredded Fontina cheese (about 4 ounces)

Fresh thyme sprigs, for serving (optional)

1. To make the dough: Pulse the flour, sugar, and salt together in a food processor to combine. Add the butter and pulse about ten times, until the mixture resembles coarse crumbs with some pea-sized pieces of butter. Do not overprocess, as the larger pieces of butter will give the dough its flakiness. Transfer the mixture to a bowl. (To make by hand, stir the flour, sugar, and salt together in a medium bowl. Add the butter. Using a pastry blender or two knives, cut in the butter until the mixture resembles coarse crumbs with some pea-sized pieces of butter.) One tablespoon at a time, stir in the water until the mixture begins to clump together. You may not need all of the water. Gather the dough into a thick disk and wrap it in plastic wrap. Refrigerate it for 30 minutes to 1 hour. The dough is easiest to work with when it is cold, but not chilled until hard.

2. On a lightly floured work surface, roll out the dough into a 12- to 13-inch round about ⅛ inch thick. You should see thin flakes of butter in the dough. Fit the dough into a 9-inch tart pan with a removable bottom, taking care not the stretch the dough, and being sure that it fits snugly into the corners of the pan. Trim the dough flush with the pan edge. Freeze the dough-lined pan for 30 minutes to 1 hour.

3. Position a rack in the bottom third of the oven and preheat the oven to 375°F.

4. Place the tart pan on a large rimmed baking sheet. Line the tart pan with aluminum foil and fill it with pie weights or dried beans. Bake until the visible edge of the dough looks dry and set, about 15 minutes. Remove the foil and weights. Quickly pierce the dough all over with a fork. Continue baking until the dough is lightly browned, about 15 minutes more.

5. Meanwhile, prepare the mushrooms: Melt the butter in a large skillet over medium-high heat. Add the mushrooms and season with ½ teaspoon salt and ¼ teaspoon pepper. Cook, stirring occasionally, until the mushrooms are beginning to brown, about 10 minutes. (Be flexible with the timing here, because some mushrooms give off more juices than others and take longer to get to the browning stage.) Stir in the shallots and thyme and cook, stirring occasionally, until the shallots soften, about 2 minutes. Add the Cognac and cook until it has reduced completely, about 1 minute. Stir in the cream, bring it to a boil, and cook until it has reduced to about 3 tablespoons, about 2 minutes. Season to taste with salt and pepper. Set the mushrooms aside.

6. Remove the tart pan on its baking sheet from the oven. Sprinkle half of the Fontina over the bottom of the crust. Top it with the mushroom mixture and sprinkle that with the remaining Fontina. Return the tart to the oven and bake until the cheese is melted, 15 to 20 minutes.

7. Let the tart cool in the pan for 10 minutes. Remove the sides of the pan. Scatter a few thyme sprigs on top of the tart. Serve warm.

GRILLED MARINATED PORTOBELLO MUSHROOMS

MAKES 6 SERVINGS

Serve with grilled steaks and chops, poultry, or grilled salmon.
Prep Time: 10 minutes, plus 30 minutes marinating time
Cooking Time: 6 minutes
Weeknight Suppers, Company Fare, Vegetarian

As good as grilled steak is, the sides always get equal billing. These mushroom caps are soaked in a wine-and-herb marinade and can match any steak for flavor.

MARINADE
½ cup hearty red wine, such as Shiraz
2 tablespoons balsamic vinegar
½ teaspoon dried oregano
½ teaspoon dried thyme
1 garlic clove, finely chopped

¼ teaspoon kosher salt
¼ teaspoon hot red pepper flakes
¼ cup extra-virgin olive oil

6 large portobello mushroom caps
Kosher salt and freshly ground black pepper

1. To make the marinade: Whisk the wine, vinegar, oregano, thyme, garlic, salt, and red pepper flakes together in a medium bowl. Gradually whisk in the oil.

2. Arrange the mushrooms in a large glass or ceramic baking dish. Pour the marinade over the mushrooms and let them stand, flipping the mushrooms occasionally, for 15 to 30 minutes.

3. Prepare an outdoor grill for direct cooking over medium heat (350º to 450ºF). For a charcoal grill, let the coals burn until they are covered with white ash and you can hold your hand about 1 inch above the cooking grate for about 3 seconds. For a gas grill, preheat on high and adjust the thermostat to medium (400ºF).

4. Remove the mushrooms from the marinade. Place them, gill-sides up, on the grill. Cook, with the lid closed, until the undersides are seared with grill marks, about 3 minutes. Flip the mushrooms over and continue grilling, with the lid closed, until the mushrooms are tender, about 3 minutes more. Remove them from the grill. Season to taste with salt and pepper and serve.

Okra

As an edible seed pod, okra is related to the legume family. The flavor reminds me of green beans, but it is the mucilaginous juice that makes problems for many cooks. There are a few tricks to modify the juice's consistency; I use a couple of them in the recipes that follow. Okra is at its best when very fresh, so use it within a day or so of purchasing.

Peak Season: Summer, but available all year.

Purchase: Crisp, firm pods without any bruises.

Storage: Refrigerate for only 1 or 2 days.

Preparation: Slice off the tough cap and tip. Cut into pieces as needed.

SEARING SAUTÉ OF OKRA, TOMATOES, GINGER, AND LIME
MAKES 4 SERVINGS

Serve with Asian and Indian foods, as well as pork chops, lamb chops, fish fillets, and sautéed shrimp.
Prep Time: 10 minutes
Cooking Time: 5 minutes
Weeknight Suppers, Vegetarian

Two techniques (searing in a hot skillet and lime juice) are used here to set the okra juices and keep them from getting gooey. With tomatoes and ginger adding bright flavors, try this fast side dish with rice as accompaniments for sautéed or grilled fish.

1 large lime	½ fresh Thai or Fresno chile, seeded and minced,
2 tablespoons vegetable oil	or ¼ teaspoon hot red pepper flakes
12 ounces fresh okra, top and tail trimmed, cut	2 garlic cloves, minced
into ½-inch slices	½ teaspoon sugar
1 tablespoon peeled and minced fresh ginger	Kosher salt and freshly ground black pepper

1. Finely grate the zest of the lime and set it aside. Juice the lime; you should have 2 to 3 tablespoons.
2. Heat a very large skillet over high heat. Add the oil, swirl to coat the bottom of the pan, and heat it until the oil is very hot but not smoking. Add the okra and spread it out in a single layer. Sprinkle it with the lime juice. Cook, stirring almost constantly, until the okra is lightly browned and crisp-tender, about 2½ minutes.
3. Stir in the lime zest, ginger, chile, garlic, and sugar and stir constantly until these seasonings are fragrant, about 1 minute. Season to taste with salt and pepper. Serve hot.

BRUNSWICK STEW
MAKES 6 TO 8 SERVINGS

Serve with barbecued meats and poultry or baked ham.
Prep Time: 15 minutes

Cooking Time: 50 minutes

Make Ahead: The stew can be made up to 1 day ahead.

Buffet Dish, Cooking Classic

During a barbecue joint crawl in and around Atlanta with my friend and meat expert Bruce Aidells, we noticed that just about every place had this flavorful okra and vegetable mixture on their menus. Here's my version, which borrows from the array we tasted that day, seasoned with Cajun spices. The okra juices serve to thicken the stew. But if someone has their mind set against okra, this is not a dish that will make them change their mind.

3 slices bacon, cut into 1-inch pieces	One 28-ounce can tomatoes in thick purée,
1 tablespoon canola oil	coarsely chopped
1 yellow onion, chopped	1 cup reduced-sodium chicken broth
1 green bell pepper, cored, seeded, and cut into	1 tablespoon Worcestershire sauce
½-inch dice	8 ounces fresh okra, topped and tailed, cut into
2 garlic cloves, minced	½-inch rounds
1 teaspoon sweet paprika	1 cup fresh or thawed frozen corn kernels
½ teaspoon dried oregano	1 cup fresh or thawed frozen lima beans
½ teaspoon dried thyme	Kosher salt
⅛ teaspoon cayenne pepper	

1. Heat the bacon and oil together in a large saucepan over medium heat, stirring occasionally, until the bacon is crisp and browned, about 5 minutes. Using a slotted spoon, transfer the bacon to paper towels to drain, leaving the fat in the pan.

2. Add the onion and green pepper to the saucepan and cook, stirring occasionally, until the vegetables are tender, about 4 minutes. Stir in the garlic and cook until it is fragrant, about 1 minute. Add the paprika, oregano, thyme, and cayenne and stir well. Mix in the tomatoes with their purée, the broth, and Worcestershire sauce, and bring them to a simmer. Reduce the heat to medium-low and simmer, stirring occasionally, until the sauce is slightly reduced, about 10 minutes.

3. Add the okra, corn, and lima beans. Simmer, stirring occasionally, until the sauce has thickened, about 30 minutes. Season to taste with salt. Transfer the stew to a serving bowl. Coarsely chop the bacon and sprinkle it over the stew. Serve hot.

Peas, Green

Peas appear at my local farmer's markets for only a few weeks, and their fresh flavor is one of the true signs of early summer. And, because their sugars turn to starch soon after picking, you have to cook them very soon after purchase. The rest of the year, I will happily make do with frozen peas because they are an excellent product. It is another food that I always have in the freezer to combine with fresh vegetables (say, carrots) for an easy side dish. Petit pois are a dwarf variety of the larger peas, and you can use them, if you prefer.

Peak Season: Late spring and early summer.

Purchase: Crisp-looking pods.

Storage: Use as soon after purchasing as possible, or refrigerate in a plastic bag for up to 3 days.

Preparation: Shell peas just before using; snap the pod at the stem end, then pull down to split the pod. Remove the peas from the pod.

BUTTERED FRESH PEAS WITH LETTUCE
MAKES 4 SERVINGS

Serve with roasts and seafood, especially poached salmon.
Prep Time: 10 minutes (or less if not shelling the peas)
Cooking Time: 12 minutes
Weeknight Suppers, Holiday Feasts, Company Fare, Cooking Classic

This is the French way of gently cooking fresh peas in lettuce leaves, with the sweet flavors of the two vegetables mixing together. Made with fresh local peas in season, this is one of the very best early summer side dishes, but you can use the same recipe to dress up frozen peas, too. You won't need herbs if the peas are top-notch, although a sprinkle of fresh tarragon would be nice. This is the recipe to use as the beginnings of peas and baby onions, a side dish classic.

2 tablespoons (¼ stick) unsalted butter
1 head Bibb or Boston lettuce, separated into
   individual leaves

2 cups shelled fresh peas (11 ounces; from
   2 pounds peas in the pod)
Kosher salt and freshly ground black pepper
½ cup reduced-sodium chicken broth

1. Melt 1 tablespoon of the butter in a medium saucepan over low heat. Place half of the lettuce leaves in the saucepan. Add the peas and season with a light sprinkle of salt and pepper. Top with the remaining lettuce leaves, pour in the broth, and season with another sprinkle of salt and pepper. Cut the remaining 1 tablespoon of butter into small cubes and scatter them over the lettuce.
2. Bring the liquid to a simmer over medium heat. Reduce the heat to medium-low and cover. Simmer until the peas are tender, 10 to 12 minutes.
3. Using a slotted spoon, transfer the peas and lettuce to a serving bowl and tent with aluminum foil to keep warm. Bring the liquid in the pan to a boil over high heat and boil until reduced by half, about 2 minutes. Pour the broth over the peas and lettuce. Season to taste with salt and pepper and serve.

Peas and Lettuce with Baby Onions: For a very special occasion, I make this with 1 cup braised fresh baby or pearl onions (see steps 1 and 2 of Classic Creamed Onions on page 167), and freeze any remaining onions for another use. But I have to admit that the convenience of the frozen baby onions is hard to beat. After reducing the broth in step 3, add 1 cup thawed frozen baby onions and 2 tablespoons water. Cover and cook just until the onions are heated through, about 3 minutes. Pour the onions and the broth over the peas and lettuce. Makes 6 servings.

PISELLI E PROSCIUTTO
MAKES 4 SERVINGS

Serve with beef and lamb roasts, steaks, chops, sausages, chicken sautés, fish fillets, or shrimp.
Prep Time: 10 minutes (or less if not shelling the peas)
Cooking Time: 15 minutes
Weeknight Suppers, Family Favorite, Holiday Feasts, Company Fare, Buffet Dish, Cooking Classic

In this Italian dish, fresh peas and prosciutto exchange flavors to make a fine dish to serve with roasts and chops. You can easily substitute thawed frozen peas, but cook them with the prosciutto for only 5 minutes.

¼ cup diced (¼-inch) prosciutto
2 teaspoons olive oil
⅓ cup finely chopped white or yellow onion

1½ cups shelled fresh peas (7 ½ ounces; from about 1½ pounds peas in the pod)
½ cup reduced-sodium chicken broth
Kosher salt and freshly ground black pepper

1. Cook the prosciutto and oil together in a medium skillet over medium heat, stirring occasionally, until the prosciutto begins to brown, about 3 minutes. Stir in the onion and cook, stirring occasionally, until it softens, about 2 minutes.

2. Add the peas and broth and bring them to a simmer. Reduce the heat to medium-low and cover tightly. Simmer, stirring occasionally, until the peas are tender and most of the broth has reduced, 7 to 10 minutes. Season to taste with salt and pepper. Transfer them to a serving bowl and serve.

Peas and Bacon: Substitute 2 strips bacon, coarsely chopped, for the prosciutto, and cook, stirring occasionally, until crisp and browned, about 8 minutes. Using a slotted spoon, transfer the bacon to paper towels to drain. Add the peas to the bacon fat in the skillet and cook as directed. Stir the bacon into the cooked peas.

Peas, Snow and Sugar Snap

In French, snow peas are called *mangetout*, which literally means "eat all." That is just what you do with these sweet green treats, as well as their very close cousins, sugar snap peas. Snow peas have been feeding humans for centuries and have long been a staple in Asian cooking. Sugar snap peas, however, are relatively new to the market and were developed in the late 1960s as a cross between snow peas and green peas, to create an entirely edible pod.

Peak Season: Late spring and summer, but available all year.

Purchase: Crisp pods without any yellowing or soft spots.

Storage: Use as soon after purchase as possible, or refrigerate for up to 2 days.

Preparation: For snow peas, trim off both ends with a paring knife or kitchen scissors. For sugar snap peas, snap off the stem, then pull down to remove the string.

SNOW PEAS AND GRAPE TOMATOES WITH VIETNAMESE SAUCE
MAKES 4 TO 6 SERVINGS

Serve with Asian-style grilled meats, poultry, and seafood.
Prep Time: 10 minutes
Cooking Time: 5 minutes
Weeknight Suppers

The complex flavors of Vietnamese food are used in this stir-fry with crisp-tender snow peas and juicy grape tomatoes. Fish sauce is a key ingredient in this cuisine, and, like soy sauce, a little goes a long way.

3 tablespoons Thai or Vietnamese fish sauce

2 tablespoons fresh lime juice

2 teaspoons light brown sugar

½ small hot red chile, such as Thai, thinly sliced, or ¼ teaspoon hot red pepper flakes

1 tablespoon vegetable oil

9 ounces snow peas, cut on the diagonal into 2-inch lengths

1 large shallot, thinly sliced and separated into rings (⅓ cup)

2 teaspoons peeled and minced fresh ginger

2 garlic cloves, minced

1 cup halved grape or cherry tomatoes

1. In a small bowl, stir the fish sauce, lime juice, brown sugar, and chile together to dissolve the sugar. Set aside.

2. Heat a large skillet over high heat. Add the oil, swirl to coat the bottom of the skillet, and heat until the oil is very hot but not smoking. Add the peas and cook, stirring often, until they turn a brighter shade of green, about 1 minute.

3. Add the shallot, ginger, and garlic and stir until they are fragrant, about 15 seconds. Add the tomatoes and cook, stirring often, until they begin to give off some juices, about 1 minute. Add the fish sauce mixture and stir until it reduces by half, about 30 seconds. Transfer the vegetables to a serving bowl and serve.

PAN-CHARRED SUGAR SNAP PEAS WITH MINT CHUTNEY
MAKES 4 TO 6 SERVINGS

Serve with steaks, chops, chicken, and seafood.
Prep Time: 5 minutes
Cooking Time: 5 minutes
Weeknight Suppers, Company Fare, Buffet Dish, Vegetarian

By searing tender snap peas on a ridged grill pan, their sweetness is accented by the slightly bitter char. Tossed with a quick fresh mint chutney, this beautiful green side dish is both attractive and delicious. The chutney recipe makes about ½ cup, so you can use it as a condiment for the main course, too.

CHUTNEY
½ cup packed fresh mint leaves
1 tablespoon fresh lemon juice
1 tablespoon vegetable oil
½ jalapeño, seeded and minced, or ¼ teaspoon hot red pepper flakes

1 small garlic clove, crushed under a knife and peeled
Kosher salt

12 ounces sugar snap peas
1 tablespoon vegetable oil

1. To make the chutney: Pulse the mint leaves, lemon juice, oil, jalapeño, and garlic in a blender to combine. Add ¼ cup water, adding more as needed, to make a moderately thin sauce. Season to taste with salt. Set aside.

2. Heat a large ridged grill pan over high heat. Toss the sugar snap peas with the oil in a large bowl. Spread them in the grill pan and cook until the peas are charred on the undersides, about 2 minutes. Turn the peas and cook just until they're crisp-tender, about 1 minute more. Transfer them to a serving bowl.

3. Add 2 tablespoons of the chutney to the peas, stir to combine, and serve, with the remaining chutney on the side.

Peppers, Sweet Bell

Bell peppers do look a bit like bells, but they have nothing to do with pepper (as in peppercorns) except for their mild heat. They are members of the same botanical family, Capsicum, as chilies, but they don't contain the capsaicin that makes the latter so spicy. Green peppers are picked when they are fully formed but not completely ripe—their color changes to red as they stay on the vine. Or they can be specifically cultivated for their color—red, orange, yellow, purple, or chocolate brown. These cultivars have a sweeter, fruitier flavor than green peppers.

Peak Season: Summer, but available all year.

Purchase: Shiny, firm, unblemished peppers with bright green stems.

Storage: Store in the refrigerator for up to 1 week.

Preparation: Cut ½ inch off the top and bottom of the pepper to resemble "lids." Discard the stem. Cut down the length of the pepper, and open the pepper up so it lies flat. Remove the ribs and seeds. Cut the peppers as needed.

MINI-PEPPERS AGRODOLCE
MAKES 4 TO 6 SERVINGS

Serve with steak, pork chops, lamb chops, roast chicken, salmon fillets, or sautéed shrimp.
Prep Time: 10 minutes
Cooking Time: 30 minutes
Make Ahead: The peppers can be made up to 3 days ahead.
Holiday Feasts, Company Fare, Vegetarian

Agrodolce is the Italian version of sweet-and-sour sauce. This recipe makes good use of the miniature sweet peppers now available in every supermarket. I prefer to serve these warm or at room temperature, not hot from the skillet, so plan ahead. Also be sure to use white balsamic vinegar or red wine vinegar, as standard balsamic will turn the peppers dark brown. For a special meal, I make the Sicilian variation, with added olives and capers.

3 tablespoons olive oil

1 yellow onion, chopped

Kosher salt

1 pound miniature sweet peppers, cut lengthwise into quarters, stems, ribs, and seeds discarded (see Note)

1 garlic clove, thinly sliced

⅔ cup warm water

2 tablespoons white balsamic vinegar or red wine vinegar

1 tablespoon sugar

1 tablespoon tomato paste

| 1 teaspoon dried oregano | ½ cup seedless raisins |
| ¼ teaspoon hot red pepper flakes | Chopped fresh flat-leaf parsley, for garnish |

1. Heat 1 tablespoon of the oil in a large skillet over medium heat. Stir in the onion and ¼ teaspoon salt. Cover and cook, stirring occasionally, until the onion is golden, about 5 minutes. Uncover and reduce the heat to medium-low. Cook, stirring often, until the onion is golden brown, about 10 minutes more. Transfer it to a bowl. Wipe out the skillet.

2. Heat the remaining 2 tablespoons oil in the skillet over medium-high heat. Add the peppers and cook, stirring occasionally, until they are softened and lightly browned, about 10 minutes. Stir in the garlic and cook until it is fragrant, about 1 minute.

3. In a small bowl, whisk together the warm water, vinegar, sugar, and tomato paste to dissolve the tomato paste. Stir them into the skillet along with the onion, add the oregano and red pepper flakes. Bring everything to a simmer and reduce the heat to medium-low. Simmer until the liquid has reduced to a few tablespoons, about 5 minutes. Season with salt. Stir in the raisins.

4. Transfer the agrodolce to a serving bowl and let it cool. Sprinkle it with the parsley. Serve warm or at room temperature. (The peppers can be covered and refrigerated for up to 5 days. Let stand at room temperature for 1 hour before serving.)

Note: If you wish, substitute 1 sweet red bell pepper and 1 green bell pepper, cored, seeded, and cut into ½-inch strips, for the mini peppers.

Sicilian Mini-Peppers Agrodolce: Add ⅓ cup chopped pitted kalamata olives and ⅓ cup rinsed and drained capers to the peppers with the raisins.

TOMATO-STUFFED BELL PEPPERS
MAKES 4 SERVINGS

Serve with grilled meats, poultry, or seafood.
Prep Time: 5 minutes
Cooking Time: 50 minutes
Make Ahead: The bell peppers can be stored at room temperature for up to 8 hours.
Weeknight Suppers, Family Favorite, Holiday Feasts, Company Fare, Buffet Dish,
Retro Recipe, Cooking Classic, Vegetarian

Before Julia Child, the British food writer Elizabeth David promoted Mediterranean cuisine to the masses with her books. In one, peppers are stuffed with tomatoes and anchovies, and while I like that idea, I much prefer this version with olives, which is more versatile. It is amazingly simple, a kind of Russian doll of a side dish with ingredients tucked inside each other, and it can be served warm or at room temperature.

2 red bell peppers

2 small plum tomatoes

½ teaspoon kosher salt

¼ teaspoon freshly ground black pepper

¼ cup coarsely chopped pitted kalamata olives

2 tablespoons extra-virgin olive oil, plus more for
 the baking dish

1 garlic clove, minced

2 tablespoons finely chopped fresh basil or
 2 teaspoons finely chopped rosemary or thyme

1. Position a rack in the center of the oven and preheat the oven to 400°F. Generously oil a shallow baking dish (preferably earthenware) just large enough to hold the pepper halves.

2. Cut each pepper in half through the stem and use a paring knife to cut out the ribs and seeds. Cut each tomato in half through the stem and poke out the gel and seeds with your fingertip. Season the pepper and tomato halves with the salt and pepper.

3. Divide the olives among the pepper halves. Insert a tomato half into each bell pepper half. Place the stuffed peppers in the baking dish. Mix the oil and garlic together in a small bowl. Drizzle the oil mixture over the peppers.

4. Bake until the peppers are tender, about 50 minutes. Let them stand for 5 minutes or cool to room temperature. Sprinkle with the basil and serve.

CRUMBED AND ROASTED RED PEPPERS

MAKES 6 TO 8 SERVINGS

Serve with steaks, pork chops, sausages, lamb chops, roast chicken, fish fillets, or sautéed shrimp.

Prep Time: 10 minutes

Cooking Time: 30 minutes

Make Ahead: The peppers can be made a few hours ahead and served at room temperature.

Weeknight Suppers, Family Favorite, Buffet Dish, Vegetarian

Whole stuffed peppers are delicious, but usually too big for a side dish. These strips of red pepper are lighter but no less flavorful with their coating of cheese and oregano–flavored crumbs.

Extra-virgin olive oil, for the baking sheet

2 large red bell peppers

SEASONED CRUMBS

2 tablespoons extra-virgin olive oil, plus more for
 drizzling

1 yellow onion, finely chopped

2 garlic cloves, minced

1 cup soft bread crumbs, made in a food processor
 or blender from slightly stale crusty bread

⅓ cup freshly grated Romano cheese (about
 1⅓ ounces)

1 tablespoon finely chopped fresh flat-leaf parsley

¼ teaspoon hot red pepper flakes

Kosher salt

1. Position a rack in the center of the oven and preheat the oven to 400ºF. Lightly oil a large rimmed baking sheet.

2. Working with one pepper at a time, cut the top and bottom inch or so from the bell pepper. (Save the trimmings for another use.) Make a vertical cut down the side of the pepper, open it up, and cut out the ribs and seeds. Cut the pepper vertically into four equal pieces to make eight pieces total.

3. To prepare the crumbs: Heat 1 tablespoon of the oil in a medium skillet over medium heat. Add the onion and cook, stirring occasionally, until it is softened, about 3 minutes. Add the garlic and cook until it is fragrant, about 1 minute more. Transfer them to a medium bowl and let cool slightly. Stir in the bread crumbs, followed by the Romano, parsley, and red pepper flakes. Stir in the remaining 1 tablespoon oil. Season to taste with salt.

4. Divide the crumb mixture among the pepper pieces, pressing the mixture firmly onto the cut sides of the peppers. Place them on the baking sheet, crumbed-sides up, and drizzle with oil.

5. Bake until the crumbs are browned and the peppers are tender, about 30 minutes. Serve hot or cooled to room temperature.

Radicchio

This Italian vegetable, which looks like red cabbage but is closely related to endive, has gained popularity as a salad ingredient. And, like its relative, it can also be cooked. Radicchio rosso di Chioggia is the round, most-common variety, but you might also find the elongated radicchio di Treviso.

Peak Season: Winter to early spring, but available all year.

Purchase: Heads with crisp leaves and no brown spots.

Storage: Refrigerate for up to 3 days.

Preparation: Cut out the core from the head, and cut as needed.

RADICCHIO AND GARBANZO BEAN BRAISE
MAKES 4 TO 6 SERVINGS

Serve with pork and veal roasts, pork and veal chops, roast chicken, and chicken sautés.
Prep Time: 10 minutes
Cooking Time: 15 minutes
Make Ahead: The braise can be refrigerated for up to 1 day; reheat gently before serving.
Weeknight Suppers, Holiday Feasts, Company Fare

Radicchio can be braised like other bitter greens. It does turn an odd shade of reddish-brown, so it needs the yellow-beige of the garbanzo beans as a color contrast. What it doesn't have in looks, it makes up for in flavor.

2 tablespoons olive oil

1 small red onion, chopped

2 garlic cloves, minced

One 15-ounce can garbanzo beans (chickpeas), drained and rinsed

½ cup reduced-sodium chicken broth

1 teaspoon finely chopped fresh thyme

1 head radicchio, cored and cut into ½-inch strips

¼ cup freshly grated Parmesan cheese (about 1 ounce)

Kosher salt and freshly ground black pepper

Chopped fresh flat-leaf parsley, for serving (optional)

1. Heat the oil in a large skillet over medium heat. Add the onion and cook, stirring occasionally, until it is softened, about 3 minutes. Stir in the garlic and cook until it is fragrant, about 1 minute. Add the garbanzo beans, broth, and thyme. Bring them to a simmer and cook over medium heat until the liquid is reduced by half, about 5 minutes.

2. Stir in the radicchio. Cook, stirring often, until the radicchio is tender and the liquid has reduced to a few tablespoons, about 5 minutes. Stir in the Parmesan. Season to taste with salt and pepper. Sprinkle with the parsley, if using, and serve.

Spinach

Spinach can be depended upon to bring a splash of bright green color to the menu. And it tastes good, too. Advances in how spinach is sold have cut down on its preparation time, so we can enjoy fresh spinach more often. Keep in mind that spinach does shrink a lot when it is cooked, so allow 6 to 8 ounces per person or fortify it with other vegetables or sauce. There are two main commercial varieties. Curly spinach grows very close to the ground, so take extra care when washing it to remove any dirt lurking in its creases. Flat-leaf spinach has a milder flavor and thinner stems—baby spinach is the immature leaves of this variety.

Peak Season: Available all year.

Purchase: Bright green leaves without any wilting or yellowing.

Storage: Refrigerate in a plastic bag for up to 3 days.

Preparation: Pull off the tough stems and discard them from curly or leaf spinach. Wash the leaves well in a sink or bowl of cold water, lifting them out so the grit sinks to the bottom of the water. The jury is out on rinsing bagged "prewashed" spinach. As a rule of thumb, if the spinach is going to be cooked, heating will kill the bacteria, so you could skip rinsing. For salad greens, it could be a smart precaution.

SPINACH WITH GARLIC CHIPS

MAKES 4 SERVINGS

Serve with beef, pork, veal, poultry, and seafood.

Prep Time: 5 minutes

Cooking Time: 10 minutes

Weeknight Suppers, Family Favorite, Holiday Feasts, Company Fare, Buffet Dish,

Cooking Classic, Vegetarian

Spinach and garlic is one of the great culinary combinations. The trick is to have browned, but not burned, garlic, which can be accomplished if the garlic is added to the oil at the beginning of the heating process. Also, slice the garlic lengthwise to make long, wide chips, as these will cook more evenly than chopped garlic. If you wish, top the spinach with crumbled ricotta salata or feta cheese before serving.

2 tablespoons olive oil

2 garlic cloves, thinly sliced lengthwise

Two 9-ounce bags baby spinach (see Note), rinsed
  but not dried

Kosher salt and freshly ground black pepper

1. Heat the oil and garlic together in a large nonreactive saucepan over medium heat until the garlic chips are lightly browned, about 2 minutes. Using a slotted spoon, transfer the garlic chips to a paper towel to drain, keeping the oil in the saucepan.

2. A handful at a time, stir the spinach with any clinging water into the saucepan, letting the first addition wilt before adding another. When all of the spinach has been added, reduce the heat to medium-low and cook, stirring often, until the spinach is tender and heated through, 2 to 3 minutes. Season to taste with salt and pepper.

3. Using a slotted spoon, transfer the spinach to a serving bowl. Top with the garlic chips and serve.

Note: If you wish, substitute 1½ pounds leaf spinach, tough stems removed, washed well (but not dried), and coarsely chopped.

CLASSIC CREAMED SPINACH

MAKES 6 SERVINGS

Serve with roast beef and lamb, steaks, and chops.

Prep Time: 10 minutes

Cooking Time: 10 minutes

Make Ahead: The spinach can be made up to 1 day ahead.

Family Favorite, Holiday Feasts, Company Fare, Buffet Dish

Most Americans know creamed spinach as a staple at steakhouses—just the thing to set off a juicy grilled steak. That's true, but it is terrific with just about any roast meat. Here's how to make it from scratch, with fresh spinach. I developed this recipe, which utilizes the cooking liquid from the spinach, for a deeper vegetable flavor than the standard version.

Three 9-ounce bags baby spinach, rinsed but not dried

1 cup reduced-sodium chicken broth

¾ cup heavy cream

5 tablespoons unsalted butter

1 garlic clove, crushed through a press

⅓ cup (43 grams) all-purpose flour

A few gratings of fresh nutmeg

Kosher salt and freshly ground pepper

1. Bring 1 cup lightly salted water to a boil in a large saucepan over high heat. In batches, add the spinach, stirring until the first batch is wilted before adding the next. Cover tightly and reduce the heat to medium. Cook until the spinach is tender, about 3 minutes.

2. Drain the spinach over a bowl, reserving 1¼ cups of the cooking liquid. Rinse the spinach under cold water. A handful at a time, squeeze the spinach between your fingers to remove excess water and to "chop" the leaves. Transfer them to a bowl.

3. In a small saucepan over medium heat, or in a microwave in a heatproof glass measuring cup, heat the reserved cooking liquid, broth, and heavy cream until simmering. Heat the butter and garlic in a medium saucepan over medium-low heat, just until the butter melts. Whisk in the flour and let it bubble without browning for 2 minutes. Whisk in the hot cream mixture and bring it to a simmer. Cook, whisking often, until the sauce is thickened and no raw flour taste remains, about 5 minutes. Stir in the spinach. Add the nutmeg and season to taste with salt and pepper. (The spinach can be cooled, covered, and refrigerated for up to 1 day. Reheat in a nonstick skillet over medium heat. If the spinach is too thick, thin it with additional cream.)

4. Transfer the spinach to a serving bowl and serve hot.

Creamed Spinach with Parmesan: Just before serving, stir ½ cup (2 ounces) freshly grated Parmesan cheese into the spinach.

Creamed Spinach with Blue Cheese: Just before serving, stir ½ cup (2 ounces) crumbled blue cheese into the spinach. Domestic or Danish blue, as well as Roquefort or Gorgonzola, all work well, so it is just a matter of budgeting or what you have on hand. If you use Italian Gorgonzola, use the sharp *picante* (also called *montagna*) variety, which crumbles better than the creamy *dolce* Gorgonzola.

Creamed Spinach with Gorgonzola and Garlic: Substitute ½ cup (2 ounces) crumbled domestic or Gorgonzola *picante* or *montagna* for the Parmesan. Increase the garlic to 2 cloves.

SPINACH AND SHALLOT TIMBALES

MAKES 6 SERVINGS

Serve with roast beef and lamb, steaks, and chops.
Prep Time: 15 minutes
Cooking Time: 40 minutes
Make Ahead: The timbales can be made up to 1 day ahead.
Holiday Feasts, Company Fare, Cooking Classic, Vegetarian

These elegant custards, verdant green with an undertone of garlic, are like creamed spinach taken up a notch. If you wish, substitute ¾ cup thawed frozen chopped spinach (squeezed to remove excess water before measuring) for the fresh spinach to save a bit of time.

1 tablespoon unsalted butter, plus softened butter
   for the ramekins
2 tablespoons finely chopped shallots
1 garlic clove, minced
1½ pounds fresh flat-leaf spinach, stems removed,
   well washed but not dried
1 cup half-and-half
3 large eggs
2 large egg yolks

¼ cup freshly grated Parmesan cheese (about
   1 ounce)
¾ teaspoon kosher salt
¼ teaspoon freshly ground white pepper
A few gratings of fresh nutmeg

Special Equipment: Six ½- to ¾-cup ramekins or
   custard cups

1. Position a rack in the center of the oven and preheat the oven to 325°F. Lightly butter six ½-cup ramekins. Have ready a roasting pan or baking dish large enough to hold the ramekins.

2. Melt the butter in a large saucepan over medium heat. Add the shallots and garlic and cook, stirring often, until they are softened, about 2 minutes. Add the spinach and cover tightly. Cook over medium heat, stirring occasionally, until the spinach is completely wilted and tender, about 4 minutes. Drain it in a wire sieve and rinse briefly under cold running water. Let it stand until cool enough to handle. A handful at a time, squeeze the spinach mixture to remove as much water as possible. You should have about ¾ cup.

3. Transfer the spinach mixture to a blender or food processor. Add the half-and-half, whole eggs, yolks, Parmesan, salt, white pepper, and nutmeg. Process until the spinach is puréed. (Or finely chop the spinach mixture on a chopping board, transfer it to a bowl, and whisk in the other ingredients.) Ladle or pour the mixture evenly among the ramekins.

4. Place the ramekins in the roasting pan. Pour in enough hot tap water around the ramekins to come about ½ inch up the sides. (The hot water is meant to insulate the ramekins and keep the custard from cooking too quickly, so the water does not have to be boiling or be more than ½ inch up the sides of the ramekins.) Tent the roasting pan with aluminum foil.

5. Bake until a knife inserted into the center of a custard comes out clean, 35 to 40 minutes. Remove the pan with the ramekins from the oven and uncover. Let the ramekins stand for 5 minutes in the water. Protecting your hands with a kitchen towel, remove the ramekins from the water and dry them. (The timbales can be cooled, covered with plastic wrap, and refrigerated for up to 1 day. Reheat in a microwave oven at 50 percent power for about 5 minutes.)

6. To unmold, working with one timbale at a time, run a dinner knife around the inside of the ramekin. Place a small plate on top of the ramekin. Hold the ramekin and plate together and invert. Give them a couple of sharp shakes to unmold the timbale. Using a spatula, transfer the timbale to a dinner plate. Serve warm.

Squash, Winter

Winter squash is typically grown in the late summer and fall, but its thick, inedible skin protects the lush, golden flesh so it can be stored throughout the cold season. There are many kinds of winter squash, but I find myself turning to butternut, acorn, and kabocha most often because of their moderate size. And buying a box of peeled, cubed winter squash can be a real timesaver and worth the extra expense. You can certainly use other varieties if you have plans for cooking the entire squash, as with a huge Hubbard squash.

Peak Season: Available all year.

Purchase: Squash that is heavy for its size, without any dings or bruises.

Store: Keep winter squash in a cool, dark place for up to 1 month; refrigeration encourages the development of mold.

Preparation: Scrub the squash under cold running water. To cut, use a large, heavy knife and a lot of upper body strength. Scrape out the seeds and fibers with a soup spoon. To peel butternut squash, use a sturdy vegetable peeler.

PAN-ROASTED BUTTERNUT SQUASH WITH GARLIC AND ROSEMARY
MAKES 4 TO 6 SERVINGS

Serve with roast pork, pork chops, or roast chicken.
Prep Time: 10 minutes
Cooking Time: 20 minutes
Weeknight Suppers, Company Fare, Buffet Dish, Vegetarian

This is a quick way of preparing winter squash and does not require turning on the oven. It is also a good method for using the precut butternut squash cubes at the market. I really like using this herb-scented dish as a bed for broiled or grilled pork chops. Sage works just as well as rosemary here.

2 tablespoons extra-virgin olive oil

1½ pounds peeled and (½- to ¾-inch) cubed
  butternut squash

2 teaspoons finely chopped fresh rosemary or sage

1 garlic clove, minced

Kosher salt and freshly ground black pepper

1. Heat the oil in a large skillet over medium-high heat. Add the squash and cook, stirring occasionally, until it is lightly browned, about 10 minutes.

2. Add ⅓ cup water and reduce the heat to medium-low. Cover and cook until the squash is just tender, about 5 minutes more. Uncover, increase the heat to high, and cook until the water is completely evaporated, about 1 minute.

3. Remove the pan from the heat and stir in the rosemary and garlic. Season to taste with salt and pepper. Transfer the squash to a dish and serve hot.

BUTTERNUT SQUASH AND POTATO GRATIN
MAKES 8 SERVINGS

Serve with pork roast, pork chops, ham, sausages, roast chicken, or roast turkey.

Prep Time: 20 minutes

Cooking Time: 1½ hours

Make Ahead: The gratin can be cooled, covered, and stored at room temperature for up to 8 hours.

Family Favorite, Holiday Feasts, Company Fare, Buffet Dish, Vegetarian

I first had this truly incredible side dish at chef Mary Cleaver's The Green Table in the Chelsea Market in New York City. I did not leave until I had the recipe in hand. It has since become one of my most reliable dishes for a dinner party, and now I have to give out the recipe myself. You will use only the top part of the butternut squash, so reserve the remainder for another meal.

2 tablespoons (¼ stick) unsalted butter, plus more
  for the baking dish

2 leeks (white and pale green parts), chopped

Kosher salt and freshly ground black pepper

1 teaspoon finely chopped fresh thyme

2 cups heavy cream, as needed

½ teaspoon sweet paprika

⅛ teaspoon freshly grated nutmeg

1 butternut squash (2 pounds)

1 pound Yukon Gold potatoes, peeled

¼ cup freshly grated Parmesan cheese (about
  1 ounce)

1. Position a rack in the center of the oven and preheat the oven to 400°F. Generously butter an 11½ × 8 × 2-inch baking dish.

2. Melt the butter in a large skillet over medium heat. Add the leeks and season with ¼ teaspoon salt and a few grinds of pepper. Cook, stirring occasionally, until the leeks are tender but not browned, about 8 minutes. Stir in the thyme. Remove from the heat.

3. Bring the cream, paprika, and nutmeg to a simmer in a medium saucepan over medium heat. Stir in 1 teaspoon salt and ½ teaspoon pepper. Remove from the heat.

4. Cut the top "neck" from the butternut squash where it meets the bulbous bottom. Peel the squash. (Reserve the bottom part of the squash for another use.) Using a mandoline, a plastic V-slicer, or a large, sharp knife, cut the squash and potatoes into ⅛-inch slices. Mix the potatoes and squash together in a large bowl.

5. Spread one-third of the potato mixture in the baking dish and top it with one-half of the leeks. Pour one-third of the warm cream mixture evenly over the vegetables. Repeat with another third of the potato mixture, the remaining leeks, and another third of the cream mixture. Finish with the remaining potato mixture. Slowly pour the remaining cream mixture evenly over the vegetable mixture, moving the vegetables with a fork to spread them into an even layer, until they are barely covered with the cream mixture, adding more cream, if needed. Cover the baking dish with aluminum foil and place it on a large rimmed baking sheet.

6. Bake for 45 minutes. Remove the gratin from the oven and remove the foil. Sprinkle the Parmesan over the gratin. Return it to the oven and reduce the heat to 350°F. Continue baking until the gratin is golden brown and tender when pierced in the center with the tip of a small, sharp knife and the cream has thickened, about 45 additional minutes. If the top becomes too brown before the vegetables are tender, tent the gratin with foil. Let stand for 10 minutes before serving.

SPAGHETTI SQUASH WITH BASIL, WALNUTS, AND PARMESAN

MAKES 6 SERVINGS

Serve with veal, lamb, or pork chops; grilled Italian sausages; roast chicken; or breaded fish fillets.

Prep Time: 10 minutes

Cooking Time: 45 minutes

Weeknight Suppers, Vegetarian

The flesh of roasted spaghetti squash can be shredded with a fork and tossed with other ingredients for an intriguing side dish. I like this deconstructed pesto, which has crunchy, aromatic, and garlicky notes.

2 tablespoons extra-virgin olive oil, plus more for the baking sheet

1 spaghetti squash (about 2⅓ pounds), halved lengthwise, seeds scooped out and discarded

1 garlic clove, finely chopped

½ cup toasted and chopped walnuts (see page 33)

¼ cup freshly grated Parmesan cheese (about 1 ounce), plus more for serving

3 tablespoons finely chopped fresh basil

Kosher salt and freshly ground black pepper

1. Position a rack in the center of the oven and preheat the oven to 400°F. Lightly oil a large rimmed baking sheet or line it with parchment paper.

2. Place the squash, cut-sides down, on the baking sheet. Bake until the squash is tender when pierced with a meat fork, about 45 minutes. Let the squash cool for 5 minutes.

3. Heat the oil and garlic together in a small saucepan over medium heat until small bubbles appear around the garlic, about 3 minutes. Do not brown the garlic. Remove the saucepan from the heat.

4. Protecting your hand with a clean kitchen towel (the squash will be very hot), use a fork to scrape the flesh from each squash half into a medium bowl; discard the squash skin. Add the walnuts, Parmesan, and basil and toss to combine. Drizzle the squash with the garlic oil and toss again. Season to taste with salt and pepper. Transfer the squash to a serving bowl. Serve with more Parmesan passed on the side.

SWEET AND SMOKY ACORN SQUASH

MAKES 4 SERVINGS

Serve with pork roast or chops, or roast chicken.

Prep Time: 5 minutes

Cooking Time: 50 minutes

Weeknight Suppers, Family Favorite, Holiday Feasts, Company Fare, Buffet Dish, Vegetarian

Smoked paprika works its magic to give old-fashioned baked acorn squash an update. Be careful when cutting the squash. Here's the best way: Trim a thin slice from the side of the squash to stabilize it and keep it from rolling. If you need extra strength to split the squash, position the knife in place, and hit the top of the knife with a mallet.

1 acorn squash (1¼ pounds), cut into quarters,
   seeds removed

1 tablespoon unsalted butter, melted

1 tablespoon pure maple syrup, preferably
   Grade A Dark

½ teaspoon smoked paprika (see Note)

Salt and freshly ground black pepper

1. Position a rack in the center of the oven and preheat the oven to 400°F.

2. Place the squash, cut-sides up, in a roasting pan. Add enough water to come ¼ inch up the sides of the squash. Cover the pan tightly with aluminum foil. Bake for 15 minutes. Uncover the pan and bake until the squash is almost tender when pierced with a knife, 25 to 30 minutes more. Do not worry if the water evaporates.

3. Remove the roasting pan with the squash from the oven. In a small bowl, mix the butter, maple syrup, and paprika together. Brush the butter mixture over the squash and season it with salt and pepper. Return it to the oven and bake until the squash is glazed, about 10 minutes. Serve hot.

Note: This paprika, often labeled *Pimentón de La Vera* for the region that produces it, gets its smokiness from red peppers that have been slowly smoked over oak logs. The *dulce* (sweet) version is more common and has more versatility than the *picante* (hot) kind. It is available at specialty markets, many supermarkets, and online.

Chipotle-Glazed Acorn Squash: This is quite spicy, but the heat plays nicely off the inherent sweetness of the squash. Substitute pure ground chipotle chilies for the smoked paprika.

ROASTED BUTTERNUT SQUASH WITH CRISPY GARBANZO BEANS

MAKES 6 SERVINGS

Serve with pork or lamb chops, roast chicken, or salmon fillets.

Prep Time: 10 minutes

Cooking Time: 40 minutes

Weeknight Suppers, Company Fare, Buffet Dish, Vegetarian

One morning, my friend and cookbook author Barbara Scott Goodman called me to say that she had made a great side dish for dinner the night before. I made it myself, and she was right, as it takes a handful of ingredients and combines them in just the right proportions to make a simple dish.

1 butternut squash (about 2 pounds), peeled, seeded, and cut into 1-inch cubes

One 15-ounce can garbanzo beans (chickpeas), drained and rinsed

2 tablespoons olive oil

Kosher salt and freshly ground black pepper

1 tablespoon balsamic vinegar

¼ cup freshly grated Parmesan cheese (about 1 ounce)

1. Position a rack in the center of the oven and preheat the oven to 425°F.

2. On a large rimmed baking sheet, toss the butternut squash, garbanzo beans, and oil together. Bake for 15 minutes. Using a metal spatula, turn the squash over and stir the garbanzo beans. Continue baking until the squash is tender and browned and the garbanzo beans are crisp, about 15 minutes more. Season to taste with salt and pepper. Drizzle with the vinegar. Sprinkle with 2 tablespoons of the Parmesan.

3. Transfer the vegetables to a serving bowl, sprinkle with the remaining 2 tablespoons Parmesan, and serve.

MASHED KABOCHA SQUASH WITH MAPLE SYRUP

MAKES 4 SERVINGS

Serve with pork and veal chops, ham, sausages, roast chicken, and roast duck.
Prep Time: 10 minutes
Cooking Time: 1¼ hours
Make Ahead: The purée can be made up to 1 day ahead.
Family Favorite, Holiday Feasts, Company Fare, Buffet Dish, Vegetarian

Mottled kabocha squash is a firm winter squash that does not submit to the knife without a fight. Its shell is not quite as hard as a rock, but it is pretty darned tough, so use caution when cutting it open. After roasting, its flesh has a nice balance of sweet and savory, and when it comes to flavoring, it can go in either direction. I provide a maple and butter version for the basic recipe, with a Parmesan and herb variation.

Vegetable oil, for the roasting pan

1 kabocha squash (about 4¼ pounds), scrubbed (see Note)

3 tablespoons maple syrup, preferably Grade A Dark

2 tablespoons (¼ stick) unsalted butter

Kosher salt and freshly ground black pepper

1. Position a rack in the center of the oven and preheat the oven to 400°F. Line a large roasting pan with aluminum foil and oil the foil.

2. Place the squash on a chopping board. Using substantial upper body strength and an extra measure of caution, cut the squash in half on either side of the stem. (If the squash is too hard to cut into, rap on the spine of the knife with the flat side of a meat pounder mallet to force the knife through the shell.) Scoop out the seeds and fibers. Place the squash halves, cut-sides down, in the roasting pan. Cover the pan with aluminum foil.

3. Roast for 45 minutes. Remove the foil and continue roasting until the squash is tender when pierced with a meat fork, about 30 minutes more.

4. Using a pot holder to protect your hand, scoop out the squash flesh with a slotted spoon into a medium bowl. Discard the squash skin. Add the maple syrup and butter and mash them into the squash with a spoon. (If you want a smooth purée, process the mixture in a food processor.) Season to taste with salt and pepper. Transfer the purée to a serving bowl and serve hot.

Note: You can substitute a sugar (also called cheese or pie) pumpkin for the kabocha squash, if you wish. The Cinderella variety (which looks like the heroine's coach in the classic French story) is also a good choice. Do not use a large jack-o'-lantern pumpkin, as they are too watery after cooking.

Kabocha Squash with Parmesan Cheese: Omit the maple syrup. Stir ⅓ cup freshly grated Parmesan cheese (about 1⅓ ounces) into the purée. If you wish, stir in 1 teaspoon finely chopped fresh rosemary or thyme, or a combination.

ROASTING SQUASH SEEDS

Whenever I roast winter squash, I sometimes wonder if the seeds are my favorite part. I never throw them away and instead roast them until crunchy. Season them simply with salt and pepper, or use a spice blend like curry or chili powder or Old Bay Seasoning.

Seeds from l large winter squash
1 tablespoon olive oil, as needed

Kosher salt and freshly ground black
   pepper

1. Remove any large clumps of flesh and fibers from the seeds. Transfer the seeds to a medium bowl and add enough cold water to cover well. Rub the seeds with your fingertips to remove as much of the squash flesh as possible. Lift the seeds from the water and drain them well in a wire sieve. Pat the seeds dry in a clean kitchen towel. Spread them on a large rimmed baking sheet and let them dry, uncovered, at room temperature for at least 8 and up to 24 hours.

2. Position a rack in the center of the oven and preheat the oven to 350°F.

3. Drizzle the oil over the seeds and toss well to coat. Bake, stirring occasionally, until the seeds are toasted, 10 to 15 minutes. Season to taste with salt and pepper. Serve them warm or cool to room temperature.

Tomatoes

The iconic image of a big, round red tomato is changing. We have learned that a tomato does not necessarily have to be either of these things to be delicious. Tomatoes come in an array of sizes, shapes, and colors. I always have a container of grape tomatoes on my kitchen counter, not just for salads, but to add to vegetable sautés for a bit of extra color and acidity. And I also like the individual serving size provided by a tomato half, ready to stuff with creamy spinach or top with crumbs. Tomatoes are always best during their summer season, but my market is carrying some pretty good Florida tomatoes year-round that ripen very nicely at room temperature.

Peak Season: Summer for local varieties; commercial varieties available all year.

Purchase: Plump, smooth tomatoes without any bruises.

Store: Out of direct sunlight at room temperature for up to 2 days; cherry and grape tomatoes last for about 1 week.

Preparation: Rinse the tomatoes and cut out the stem end of large varieties with the tip of a paring knife.

SLOW-ROASTED TOMATOES WITH ROSEMARY AND GARLIC
MAKES 4 TO 8 SERVINGS

Serve with steaks, chops, poultry, or grilled fish fillets.
Prep Time: 5 minutes
Cooking Time: 2 hours
Make Ahead: The tomatoes can be cooked up to 2 hours ahead.
Family Favorite, Holiday Feasts, Company Fare, Vegetarian

These utterly simple, slowly roasted tomatoes bring their concentrated flavor to simple meals. Serve them warm or cooled to room temperature; they work well with hearty grilled meats and delicate fish or poultry. Of course, this recipe is best with seasonal tomatoes, but I have also used this recipe to improve lackluster supermarket winter tomatoes.

2 tablespoons extra-virgin olive oil, plus more for the baking dish

4 ripe plum (Roma) tomatoes, halved lengthwise

1 garlic clove, thinly sliced into slivers

1 teaspoon fresh rosemary or ½ teaspoon dried

1 teaspoon kosher salt

½ teaspoon freshly ground black pepper

1. Position a rack in the center of the oven and preheat the oven to 300°F. Lightly oil an 11½ × 8 × 2-inch baking dish.

2. Place the tomato halves, cut-sides up, in the baking dish. Sprinkle the tomato halves with the garlic and rosemary, and use your fingertip to poke them into the tomato seed pockets. Sprinkle with the salt and pepper. Drizzle with the oil.

3. Bake until the tomatoes have shrunk slightly and the edges are lightly browned, about 1½ hours. Serve them warm or let cool completely to room temperature.

RISI E BISI TOMATOES

MAKES 6 SERVINGS

Serve with grilled firm white fish, such as halibut or mahi-mahi; or grilled meats and poultry with Italian seasonings.

Prep Time: 10 minutes

Cooking Time: 50 minutes

Make Ahead: The tomatoes can be stored at room temperature for up to 8 hours.

Weeknight Suppers, Family Favorite, Holiday Feasts, Company Fare, Buffet Dish, Vegetarian

Rise e bisi *is a Venetian dish that resembles a pea risotto. It can be used to stuff ripe tomatoes for a side dish that pairs with many main courses, but I really like it with grilled fish.*

2 tablespoons extra-virgin olive oil, plus more for the baking dish

½ cup rice for risotto, such as Arborio

3 large beefsteak tomatoes (about 9 ounces each)

Kosher salt and freshly ground black pepper

½ cup thawed frozen petite peas

⅓ cup plus 2 tablespoons freshly grated Parmesan cheese (about 2 ounces)

1 scallion (white and green parts), finely chopped

1 teaspoon finely chopped fresh thyme or ½ teaspoon dried

1 garlic clove, minced

1. Position a rack in the center of the oven and preheat the oven to 375ºF. Lightly oil a 13 × 9 × 2-inch baking dish.

2. Bring a medium saucepan of salted water to a boil over high heat. Add the rice and boil (like pasta) until tender, about 18 minutes.

3. Meanwhile, cut each tomato in half crosswise. Using your fingertip, poke out the gel and seeds from the tomato halves. Using a dessert spoon, scoop out and reserve the tomato flesh to make tomato shells. Coarsely chop the flesh and set aside. If necessary, cut a small slice from the rounded bottom of each shell to keep the shell from rolling. Season the shells lightly with salt and pepper.

4. Drain the rice in a wire sieve, rinse it under cold running water, and drain again. Transfer it to a bowl. Stir in the chopped tomato flesh, peas, ⅓ cup of the Parmesan, the scallion, thyme, and garlic. Season to taste with salt and pepper. Spoon the rice mixture into the tomato halves and place them in the baking dish. Sprinkle with the remaining 2 tablespoons Parmesan, and drizzle with the oil.

5. Bake until the tomatoes are heated through and tender, about 30 minutes. Serve them warm or cool to room temperature.

TOMATOES WITH MASCARPONE SPINACH

MAKES 4 SERVINGS

Serve with roast beef or steak.

Prep Time: 15 minutes

Cooking Time: 35 minutes

Make Ahead: The tomatoes can be stuffed 4 hours before baking.

Weeknight Suppers, Family Favorite, Holiday Feasts, Company Fare, Vegetarian

Serve these plump tomatoes next to a sizzling steak and you will have a pitch-perfect pair. Because they are so easy to prepare, you could probably fit them into a weeknight cooking schedule. Mascarpone makes a very good version of creamed spinach without a separately prepared sauce.

Olive oil, for the pan and drizzling

2 beefsteak tomatoes (about 9 ounces each)

1 tablespoon unsalted butter

2 tablespoons finely chopped shallots

18 ounces fresh flat-leaf spinach, tough stems
   removed, well washed and drained, but not dried

¼ cup mascarpone cheese

3 tablespoons freshly grated Parmesan cheese
   (about ¾ ounce)

Kosher salt and freshly ground black pepper

2 tablespoons panko bread crumbs

1. Position a rack in the center of the oven and preheat the oven to 350°F. Lightly oil an 8-inch square baking dish (or one large enough to hold the tomato halves).

2. Cut each tomato in half crosswise. Using your finger, poke out the seeds and gel in each tomato. Place the tomato halves, cut-sides down, on paper towels to drain while preparing the filling.

3. Melt the butter in a large nonstick skillet over medium heat. Add the shallots and cook, stirring often, until they are softened, about 2 minutes. In three or four additions, stir in the wet spinach, letting the first addition wilt before adding the next. Reduce the heat to medium-low and cook, stirring often, until the spinach is tender, about 5 minutes. Drain the spinach mixture in a wire sieve. Use a heatproof spatula and press gently on the mixture to extrude moisture. Transfer the spinach to a bowl and stir in the mascarpone and 2 tablespoons of the Parmesan. Season to taste with salt and pepper.

4. Stuff the tomato halves with the spinach mixture. Place the tomato halves in the baking dish. Sprinkle them with the panko and the remaining 1 tablespoon Parmesan and drizzle with oil. (The tomatoes can be stored at room temperature for up to 4 hours.)

5. Bake until the tomato halves are heated through and the topping is golden brown, about 30 minutes. Let them cool in the dish for 5 minutes and serve.

SCALLOPED TOMATOES WITH GORGONZOLA CRUMBS

MAKES 6 SERVINGS

Serve with roasts, steaks, chops, and roast chicken.

Prep Time: 10 minutes

Cooking Time: 20 minutes

Make-Ahead: The tomatoes can be made up to 4 hours ahead.

Holiday Feasts, Company Fare, Buffet Dish, Vegetarian

*T*hese stuffed tomatoes are especially worthwhile to make during the summer, but they also do wonders for out-of-season tomatoes that aren't so stellar. They are equally good served hot or at room temperature.

3 tablespoons extra-virgin olive oil, plus more for the baking dish

3 large beefsteak tomatoes (about 9 ounces each)

2 garlic cloves, minced

1 teaspoon finely chopped fresh thyme

½ teaspoon kosher salt

½ teaspoon freshly ground black pepper

½ cup soft bread crumbs, made in a food processor or blender from slightly stale crusty bread

½ cup crumbled Gorgonzola or blue cheese (about 2 ounces)

1. Position a rack in the center of the oven and preheat the oven to 400ºF. Lightly oil a 13 × 9 × 2-inch baking dish.

2. Cut each tomato in half crosswise. Using your fingertip, poke out most of the seeds and gel from each half. Place the tomatoes in the baking dish, cut-side up. In a small bowl, mix 2 tablespoons of the oil with the garlic, thyme, salt, and pepper. Spoon the oil mixture over the tomatoes.

3. Bake until the tomatoes are beginning to soften, about 15 minutes. Remove the pan of tomatoes from the oven. Toss together the bread crumbs, Gorgonzola, and remaining 1 tablespoon oil in another small bowl. Divide the crumb mixture equally over the tomatoes. Return them to the oven and bake until the crumb topping is golden brown, about 15 minutes more. Serve them hot or cooled to room temperature.

GRILLED TOMATOES WITH PESTO AND BURRATA

MAKES 6 SERVINGS

Serve with grilled meats, poultry, and seafood, especially on Italian-inspired menus.

Prep Time: 5 minutes

Cooking Time: 45 minutes

Holiday Feasts, Company Fare, Buffet Dish, Vegetarian

Burrata is an especially soft fresh mozzarella cheese with a moist center that runs when cut. It adds a creamy quality to dishes, and it is wonderful in this side dish with tomatoes and basil. The tomatoes are cooked in a baking dish to catch the melting Burrata.

Extra-virgin olive oil, for the dish and drizzling

3 ripe beefsteak tomatoes (about 9 ounces each), cut in half crosswise

½ teaspoon kosher salt

¼ teaspoon freshly ground black pepper

2 tablespoons Pesto (page 425)

One 4-ounce ball Burrata cheese

1. Prepare an outdoor grill for indirect cooking over medium-high heat (400° to 450°F). For a charcoal grill, let the coals burn until they are covered with white ash and you can hold your hand about 1 inch above the cooking grate for about 3 seconds. For a gas grill, preheat on high and adjust the thermostat to medium-high (425°F).

2. Lightly oil a baking dish to hold the tomato halves. Place the tomatoes in the dish, cut-sides up. Drizzle the tomatoes with oil and season with the salt and pepper.

3. Place the dish on the empty area of the grill and close the grill. Grill with the lid closed, until the tomatoes are beginning to brown around the edges, about 40 minutes. Remove the baking dish from the grill.

4. Spread the pesto over the tomato halves. Working over the baking dish, cut the Burrata into six pieces, and divide the cheese and its cream among the tomato halves. Return them to the grill and close the lid. Grill until the cheese is melted, about 5 minutes. Serve immediately.

FRIED GREEN TOMATOES WITH SAUCE RAVIGOTE
MAKES 6 TO 8 SERVINGS

Serve with pork chops, ham, sausages, barbecued meats and poultry, fried chicken, or shrimp.

Prep Time: 10 minutes

Cooking Time: 10 minutes

Weeknight Suppers, Family Favorite, Cooking Classic, Vegetarian

We are talking about unripened vine tomatoes here—not a specific variety that is grown to be green. Fried green tomatoes hold a place in the Southern cooking pantheon. I was taught to make these with a cornmeal crust and a squeeze of lemon, but lately I've bucked tradition by adding seasoned bread crumbs to the coating and serving them with a spicy sauce. I serve them most often with steamed shrimp as the ravigote is great with seafood.

¾ cup (98 grams) all-purpose flour

2 teaspoons kosher salt

¼ teaspoon freshly ground black pepper

1 cup whole milk

2 large eggs

1 teaspoon hot red pepper sauce

½ cup (65 grams) yellow cornmeal, preferably stone-ground

½ cup Italian-seasoned dry bread crumbs (without cheese)

3 green (unripened) tomatoes, cored and cut into ¼-inch rounds

Vegetable oil, for frying

Sauce Ravigote (page 437), for serving

1. Mix the flour, salt, and pepper in a shallow dish. Whisk together the milk, eggs, and hot sauce in another shallow dish. Mix the cornmeal and bread crumbs in a third dish.

2. One at a time, dip the tomato slices in the flour to coat, shaking off the excess flour. Dip them in the egg mixture, then in the cornmeal, gently patting on the cornmeal to help it adhere. Transfer the slices to a baking sheet.

3. Pour enough oil into a large, deep skillet to come 1 inch up the sides and heat it over high heat until the oil is shimmering (350°F on an instant-read thermometer).

4. Position a rack in the center of the oven and preheat the oven to 200°F. Line a large rimmed baking sheet with a wire cooling rack.

5. In batches, without crowding, add the tomato slices to the hot oil and cook until the undersides are golden brown, about 2 minutes. Turn and cook to brown the other sides, about 2 minutes more. Using a slotted spatula, transfer the tomatoes to the wire rack and keep warm in the oven while cooking the remaining tomatoes. Serve them hot, adding a dollop of the sauce to each serving.

Zucchini and Other Summer Squash

Some summer squash, such as pattypan, is traditionally a warm-weather crop, but we can get zucchini and yellow squash all year long. With a thin, edible skin and seeds, it is very simple to prepare—just give it a scrub and you are good to go. Don't skip this step because rinsing is not enough to loosen tiny bits of grit that could be hiding in the peel. From there, it can be sautéed in a few minutes for a super-quick side dish, grilled for a salad, or used as a component in a more complicated casserole or flaky filo pie. Yellow squash, for all of its bright color, can be bland, so use it in combination with zucchini and other more flavorful ingredients.

Peak Season: Available all year.

Purchase: Firm squash without any bruises, cuts, or soft spots.

Store: Refrigerate for up to 5 days.

Preparation: Scrub under cold water and trim the stem end.

ZUCCHINI SAUTÉ WITH LEMON AND DILL

MAKES 4 TO 6 SERVINGS

Serve with beef, lamb, pork, chicken, or salmon.

Prep Time: 5 minutes

Cooking Time: 10 minutes

Weeknight Suppers, Family Favorite, Buffet Dish, Vegetarian

Lemon and dill have an affinity, and they work together here to give a Mediterranean touch to sautéed zucchini. Stir the zucchini infrequently to allow the slices to brown—that golden surface carries a lot of flavor. For a creamy side dish, stir in ¼ cup plain Greek yogurt after the scallions have wilted, and cook just until the yogurt comes to a simmer.

2 tablespoons olive oil	Finely grated zest of 1 lemon
3 medium zucchini, cut in half lengthwise, and cut into ½-inch slices	2 tablespoons fresh lemon juice
	2 tablespoons finely chopped fresh dill
2 scallions (white and green parts), thinly sliced	Kosher salt and freshly ground black pepper

1. Heat the oil in a large skillet over medium-high heat. Add the zucchini and cook, stirring occasionally, until it is browned, 6 to 8 minutes. Stir in the scallions and cook just until they are wilted, about 1 minute.

2. Stir in the lemon zest and juice and the dill. Season to taste with salt and pepper. Transfer the zucchini to a serving bowl and serve.

Zucchini Sauté with Feta: Just before serving, sprinkle the vegetables with ⅓ cup crumbled feta cheese (about 1½ ounces).

ROASTED SUMMER SQUASH WITH PEPITAS AND CILANTRO

MAKES 4 TO 6 SERVINGS

Serve with steaks, pork or lamb chops, or seafood.

Prep Time: 5 minutes

Cooking Time: 20 minutes

Weeknight Suppers, Buffet Dish, Vegetarian

This side dish is inspired by Mexican cuisine, but I have left out the chilies so it can complement a wider range of main courses. If you like it spicy, add a sprinkle of pure ground ancho chilies or chili powder just before serving.

3 medium zucchini, cut into ½-inch rounds

2 medium yellow squash, cut into ½-inch rounds

2 tablespoons extra-virgin olive oil

1 garlic clove, finely chopped

⅓ cup shelled pumpkin seeds (pepitas), roasted
  (see page 129)

2 tablespoons fresh lime juice

2 tablespoons finely chopped fresh cilantro or
  oregano

Kosher salt and freshly ground black pepper

1. Position a rack in the center of the oven and preheat the oven to 450°F.

2. On a large rimmed baking sheet, toss the zucchini, yellow squash, and olive oil together to coat the squash. Roast them, occasionally flipping the squash with a metal spatula, until they're golden brown, about 20 minutes. During the last 3 minutes, stir in the garlic. Sprinkle the squash with the pumpkin seeds, stir in the lime juice and cilantro, and season to taste with salt and pepper. Transfer the squash to a bowl and serve hot.

Roasted Summer Squash with Feta Cheese: Just before serving, sprinkle ½ cup crumbled feta cheese (about 2 ounces) over the squash mixture.

ZUCCHINI AND SCALLION CROUSTADE
MAKES 8 SERVINGS

Serve with leg of lamb, lamb chops, or roast pork.

Prep Time: 20 minutes, plus 1 hour draining and 30 minutes cooling times

Cooking Time: 45 minutes

Make Ahead: The croustade can be baked up to 4 hours ahead.

Family Favorite, Holiday Feasts, Company Fare, Buffet Dish, Vegetarian

A croustade is a beautiful, impressive-looking French tart made with paper-thin layers of flaky dough. This zucchini version has Greek overtones, with crumbled feta and fresh dill. I serve it most often as a rich side dish to grilled lamb, and it can also be a vegetarian main course. Allow time for the filling to cool completely before making the croustade.

4 large zucchini (2 pounds total), shredded on the
  large holes of a box grater

Kosher salt

2 tablespoons extra-virgin olive oil

4 large scallions (white and green parts), sliced
  (1 cup)

2 garlic cloves, minced

2 tablespoons finely chopped fresh dill

¼ teaspoon freshly ground black pepper

6 tablespoons (¾ stick) unsalted butter, melted

½ cup crumbled feta cheese (2 ounces)

2 large eggs, beaten to blend

10 sheets thawed frozen filo dough (half of a
  1-pound package, see the sidebar on page 138)

1. Toss the zucchini in a colander with 1 tablespoon salt. Let it drain in the sink for 1 hour. Do not rinse. A handful at a time, squeeze the excess liquid from the zucchini.

2. Heat the oil in a large nonstick skillet over medium heat. Add the zucchini, scallions, and garlic and cook, stirring often, until the vegetables are tender, about 5 minutes. Stir in the dill and pepper. Spread the vegetables in a shallow baking dish and refrigerate, stirring occasionally, until they're cooled, at least 30 minutes.

3. Position a rack in the center of the oven and preheat the oven to 350°F. Brush the inside of a 9-inch pie plate with some of the melted butter.

4. Transfer the zucchini mixture to a large bowl. Stir in the feta and eggs. Place a filo sheet in the pie plate, letting the excess dough hang over the side. Lightly brush the filo with butter, taking care not to tear the dough. Repeat with seven more sheets of dough, arranging the points of the filo sheets around the plate like the spokes on a wheel. Spread the filling in the plate. Fold one of the remaining filo sheets in half, place it on the filling, and lightly brush it with butter; repeat with the last sheet. Fold the overhanging edges of the dough toward the center of the plate and brush the unbuttered dough with melted butter.

5. Place the pie plate on a rimmed baking sheet. Bake until the croustade is golden brown, 45 to 50 minutes. Let it cool for 5 to 10 minutes. (The croustade can be made up to 4 hours ahead and stored at room temperature. Reheat in a preheated 350°F oven for about 15 minutes. The croustade is also good served at room temperature.) Slide the croustade onto a round serving platter. Cut it into wedges and serve hot or cool to room temperature.

Provençal Croustade with Rosemary and Chèvre: Substitute 2 teaspoons chopped fresh rosemary and ½ cup crumbled goat cheese for the dill and feta.

FILO DOUGH

Ultra-thin filo dough has a reputation for being temperamental, which is really more the fault of the baker than the dough. I have baked with tons of filo over the years (this is not an exaggeration, as any caterer can tell you), so I have a number of tips, learned by trial and error.

- Unless you live near a Greek bakery that makes fresh filo, it is almost always sold frozen. Perhaps the most important pointer I can provide is this: Thaw the filo overnight in the refrigerator. If it's thawed at room temperature, the sheets tend to stick together.
- When working with the filo, cover the stack of sheets with a sheet of plastic wrap, topped with a damp kitchen towel. This keeps the sheets from drying out. Don't let the damp towel touch the dough or it could make it soggy.
- Use a soft natural-bristle brush to apply the melted butter to keep from tearing the dough. Some bakers prefer a pastry brush made from large feathers tied together to ensure delicate brushing.

ZUCCHINI PIE WITH POLENTA CRUST

MAKES 4 TO 6 SERVINGS

Serve with roast pork or lamb, pork or lamb chops, sausages, roast chicken, or seafood.

Prep Time: 30 minutes

Cooking Time: 25 minutes

Weeknight Suppers, Family Favorite, Holiday Feasts, Company Fare, Buffet Dish, Retro Recipe, Cooking Classic, Vegetarian

A vegetarian member of the deep-dish pie family, this version has a cheesy polenta layer for its top crust. If you want a spicier version with a Southwestern accent, substitute cilantro for the fresh basil, and add one seeded and chopped jalapeño with the onion mixture.

2 tablespoons extra-virgin olive oil, plus more for the pie plate

2 pounds zucchini, trimmed and cut into ½-inch dice

1 large yellow onion, chopped

1 medium red bell pepper, seeded and cut into ½-inch dice

2 garlic cloves, minced

2 tablespoons chopped fresh basil or 2 teaspoons dried

One 14½-ounce can diced tomatoes in juice

Kosher salt and freshly ground pepper

POLENTA CRUST

1 cup (125 grams) yellow cornmeal

¾ teaspoon Kosher salt

¼ teaspoon freshly ground pepper

1½ cups shredded Fontina Val d'Aosta or Swiss cheese (6 ounces)

1. Position a rack in the center of the oven and preheat the oven to 350°F. Lightly oil a 9½-inch deep-dish pie plate.

2. Heat the oil in a 12-inch skillet over medium-high heat. Add the zucchini, onion, bell pepper, and garlic. Cook, stirring occasionally, until the zucchini is tender and lightly browned, about 15 minutes. Stir in the basil. Add the tomatoes and their juices and bring them to a boil. Reduce the heat to medium-low and simmer until the tomato juices thicken, about 5 minutes. Season to taste with salt and pepper. Spread the mixture evenly in the pie plate.

3. Meanwhile, to make the polenta crust: Whisk the cornmeal with 1 cup cold water in a medium bowl. Bring another 1 cup water and the salt and pepper to a boil in a medium, heavy-bottomed saucepan over high heat. Whisk in the cornmeal mixture and bring it to a boil. Reduce the heat to medium-low and let it bubble for 2 minutes. Stir in 1 cup of the cheese. Spread the polenta over the zucchini to within 1 inch of the edge of the plate. Sprinkle the remaining ½ cup cheese on top. Place the pie plate on a baking sheet.

4. Bake until the edges of the crust are lightly browned, about 25 minutes. Let the pie stand for 5 minutes, then serve it hot.

SOUTHERN-STYLE SUMMER SQUASH CASSEROLE

MAKES 8 SERVINGS

Serve with barbecued meats and poultry, fried chicken, or fried fish fillets.

Prep Time: 40 minutes

Cooking Time: 30 minutes

Make Ahead: The casserole can be made up to 1 day ahead.

Family Favorite, Holiday Feasts, Company Fare, Buffet Dish, Cooking Classic, Vegetarian

Whenever I am in the South, I try to eat at a "meat and threes" restaurant—a buffet that gets its name because you get to choose three sides to go with your single choice of meat. You'll usually find a version of this casserole on every menu, but my recipe has extra touches to be sure that it is worthy of your best barbecue. For example, the squash must be precooked to remove excess moisture (many recipes use raw squash), and while most Southern cooks do not put basil in their casserole, I recommend it. I often add 1 cup cooked corn kernels to the squash mixture and top it with a sliced beefsteak tomato before adding the crumbs.

7 tablespoons unsalted butter, plus softened butter for the baking dish

1 large yellow onion, chopped

4 garlic cloves, minced

1¾ pounds zucchini, cut into ½-inch rounds

1¾ pounds yellow squash, cut into ½-inch rounds

2 cups shredded sharp Cheddar cheese (about 8 ounces)

2 cups coarsely crushed buttery, flaky crackers, such as Ritz

3 large eggs

1 cup whole milk

½ cup heavy cream

3 tablespoons chopped fresh basil

1 teaspoon kosher salt

½ teaspoon hot red pepper sauce

1. Position a rack in the center of the oven and preheat the oven to 350°F. Lightly butter a 13 × 9 × 2-inch baking dish.

2. Melt 2 tablespoons of the butter in a large skillet over medium-high heat. Add the onion and garlic and cook, stirring occasionally, until they are tender, about 10 minutes. Transfer them to a medium bowl.

3. Melt 2 more tablespoons of the butter in the skillet over medium-high heat. Add the zucchini and cook, stirring occasionally, until it is browned and tender, about 10 minutes. Transfer it to a colander and let it drain over a plate. Wash and dry the skillet. Melt 2 more tablespoons of the butter and add the yellow squash, cooking it for about 10 minutes. Add it to the zucchini in the colander. Using a rubber spatula, press gently on the squash mixture to remove excess moisture. Stir into the onion mixture and add 1 cup of the Cheddar.

4. Sprinkle 1 cup of the crackers in the baking dish. Top them with the squash mixture. Whisk the eggs in a medium bowl. Add the milk, cream, basil, salt, and hot sauce and whisk until combined. Pour the mixture evenly over the squash. Sprinkle the remaining 1 cup each of the crackers and the Cheddar over the casserole. Melt the remaining 1 tablespoon butter in the skillet over medium heat; drizzle it over the cracker topping.

5. Bake until the casserole feels set when pressed gently in the center, about 30 minutes. Let it stand for 5 minutes and serve.

ITALIAN SQUASH CASSEROLE
MAKES 6 SERVINGS

Serve with roasts, sausages, roast chicken, chicken sautés, fish fillets, or sautéed shrimp.
Prep Time: 25 minutes
Cooking Time: 30 minutes
Make Ahead: The casserole can be made up to 1 day ahead.
Family Favorite, Holiday Feasts, Company Fare, Buffet Dish, Cooking Classic, Vegetarian

I have a feeling that the Southern-style squash casserole that is served at so many barbecues (see opposite) is based on this Italian version. It mixes zucchini and other vegetables with Parmesan and bread crumbs for a dish that you can serve with everything from grilled fish to sausages.

CRUMBS
2 tablespoons olive oil
1½ cups soft bread crumbs, made from slightly stale crusty bread in a food processor or blender
½ cup freshly grated Parmesan cheese (2 ounces)
2 teaspoons dried oregano

4 tablespoons olive oil, plus more for the baking dish

1 red onion, chopped
1 red bell pepper, seeded and chopped
2 celery ribs, cut into ½-inch dice
2 garlic cloves
2½ pounds zucchini, cut into ½-inch rounds
1¼ teaspoons kosher salt
½ teaspoon freshly ground black pepper
3 large eggs, beaten to blend

1. To make the crumbs: Heat the oil in a large skillet over medium heat. Add the bread crumbs and cook, stirring occasionally, until they're golden brown, about 3 minutes. Transfer them to a medium bowl and let cool. Stir in the Parmesan and oregano.

2. Heat 2 tablespoons of the oil in a large skillet over medium-high heat. Add the onion, bell pepper, and celery and cook, stirring occasionally, until the vegetables are tender, about 5 minutes. During the last minute, stir in the garlic. Transfer the onion mixture to a large bowl.

3. Wash and dry the skillet. Return it to medium-high heat. Add the remaining 2 tablespoons oil and heat until it is hot but not smoking. Add the zucchini and cook until the undersides are golden brown, about 3 minutes. Turn the zucchini and cook, stirring occasionally, until it is tender and browned, about 6 minutes more. Transfer it to the onion mixture and let it cool until tepid, about 15 minutes. (The casserole can be prepared to this point and stored at room temperature for up to 2 hours.)

4. Position a rack in the center of the oven and preheat the oven to 350°F. Lightly oil an 8-inch-square baking dish.

5. Season the vegetable mixture with the salt and pepper. Stir in half of the crumb mixture and the eggs. Spread the mixture in the baking dish. Sprinkle it with the remaining crumb mixture.

6. Bake until the casserole feels set when gently pressed in the center, about 30 minutes. Let it stand for 5 minutes. Serve warm.

ZUCCHINI WITH SUN-DRIED TOMATO AND RICOTTA STUFFING

MAKES 4 SERVINGS

Serve with beef roasts and steaks; pork and lamb roasts and chops; sausages; chicken; or seafood.

Prep Time: 20 minutes

Cooking Time: 40 minutes

Family Favorite, Holiday Feasts, Company Fare, Buffet Dish, Vegetarian

Here's my most-requested recipe for stuffed zucchini. Sun-dried tomatoes add bursts of concentrated flavor to the ricotta filling. If you wish, substitute 1 tablespoon finely chopped fresh basil for the dried oregano.

2 tablespoons extra-virgin olive oil, plus more for the baking dish

1 yellow onion, chopped

1 garlic clove, crushed through a press

1 cup ricotta cheese

⅓ cup plus 2 tablespoons freshly grated Parmesan cheese (about 2 ounces)

1 large egg, beaten

2 tablespoons drained and finely chopped sun-dried tomatoes

2 tablespoons plain dry bread crumbs

1 teaspoon dry oregano

¼ teaspoon kosher salt

⅛ teaspoon freshly ground black pepper

2 large zucchini (about 1½ pounds total)

1. Position a rack in the upper third of the oven and preheat the oven to 350°F. Lightly oil a 13 × 9 × 2-inch baking dish.

2. Heat 1 tablespoon of the oil in a medium skillet over medium heat. Add the onion and cook, stirring often, until it is tender, about 4 minutes. Add the garlic and cook until it is fragrant, about 1 minute. Transfer the mixture to a medium bowl and let it cool slightly. Stir in the ricotta, ⅓ cup of the

Parmesan, the egg, sun-dried tomatoes, 1 tablespoon of the bread crumbs, the oregano, salt, and pepper.

3. Cut each zucchini in half lengthwise. Using a dessert spoon, scrape out the flesh to make ½-inch-thick shells. Place the zucchini shells in the baking dish, and fill them with the ricotta mixture. In a small bowl, mix the remaining 2 tablespoons Parmesan and 1 tablespoon bread crumbs together and sprinkle them over the filling. Drizzle the zucchini with the remaining 1 tablespoon oil. Cover the dish tightly with aluminum foil.

4. Bake for 15 minutes. Uncover and bake until the tops are lightly browned, about 20 minutes. Let the zucchini stand for 5 minutes, and serve.

GRILLED SUMMER SQUASH WITH MINT AND GOAT CHEESE

MAKES 4 TO 6 SERVINGS

Serve with grilled lamb and pork chops.
Prep Time: 5 minutes
Cooking Time: 8 minutes
Make Ahead: The squash can be marinated for up to 4 hours.
Weeknight Suppers, Company Fare, Buffet Dish, Vegetarian

One of the simple pleasures of this room-temperature side dish is that it should be marinated for a couple of hours before serving. It is a good way to use squash in the summer when it is everywhere you turn.

2 medium zucchini

2 medium yellow squash

⅓ cup extra-virgin olive oil, plus more for brushing

1½ tablespoons red wine vinegar

1 garlic clove, crushed through a press

Kosher salt

⅛ teaspoon hot red pepper flakes

2 tablespoons finely chopped fresh mint

⅓ cup crumbled goat cheese (about 1½ ounces)

1. Prepare an outdoor grill for direct cooking over medium heat (350º to 450ºF). For a charcoal grill, let the coals burn until they are covered with white ash and you can hold your hand about 1 inch above the cooking grate for about 3 seconds. For a gas grill, preheat on high and adjust the thermostat to medium (400ºF).

2. Using a sharp knife, trim the ends of the zucchini and squash. Slice each lengthwise into strips about ½ inch wide. Place the strips on a rimmed baking sheet and brush them on both sides with oil.

3. Put the zucchini and squash on the grill, running perpendicular to the cooking grate. Cook, with the lid closed, until the undersides are seared with grill marks, about 3 minutes. Flip the zucchini and squash and continue cooking until the other sides are seared but still hold their shape, about 3 minutes more. Remove the zucchini and squash from the grill.

4. In a small bowl, whisk the vinegar, garlic, ½ teaspoon salt, and red pepper flakes together to dissolve the salt. Gradually whisk in the ⅓ cup oil.

5. Arrange the zucchini and squash strips side-by-side, overlapping as needed, on a serving platter. Pour the vinaigrette on top and sprinkle with the mint. Let the squash marinate at room temperature, turning occasionally, for at least 30 minutes and up to 4 hours. Just before serving, sprinkle it with the goat cheese. Serve at room temperature.

FROM THE ROOT CELLAR

From time eternal, humans have relied on root vegetables for sustenance. These plants, whose edible portions grow below the ground, keep well long after harvest and fill the pot when summer crops are long gone. Now we eat root vegetables year-round because of their taste and nutritional value. Some of the most iconic side dishes, especially those from the potato family, come from this valuable group. In this chapter, creamy mashed potatoes, golden gratins, and glazed carrots are joined by less common, but no less delicious, contributions to the side dish lexicon from parsnips, rutabagas, and even radishes.

Beets

Many cooks associate beets with their deep magenta color, but there are also orange, yellow, and striped Chioggia beets. They may be as big as a grapefruit or as small as a walnut. While roasting has become the most popular way to cook this dense root vegetable, don't neglect other methods—shredded raw beets are great in salads.

Peak Season: June to October, but available all year.

Purchase: Hard beets without any cracks; if the greens are attached, they should be sprightly.

Storage: Refrigerate, with leaves trimmed off, for up to 3 weeks.

Prep: Scrub under cold water, but do not trim the pointed end.

ROASTED BEETS WITH BALSAMIC-ORANGE GLAZE

MAKES 4 TO 6 SERVINGS

Serve with pork roast, pork chops, baked ham, roast duck, or salmon.

Prep Time: 10 minutes

Cooking Time: about 2¼ hours

Make Ahead: The beets can be cooled, covered, and refrigerated for up to 3 days.

Family Favorite, Holiday Feasts, Company Fare, Buffet Dish, Vegetarian

In the summer, I'll serve these beets, dressed with orange zest and juice with balsamic vinegar, at room temperature; when it's cold outside, they're great warm with roasts or baked salmon. Be sure to allow time for roasting the beets, or use the precooked beets available in the produce section of some supermarkets. Once that's done, the final glaze only takes a few minutes.

6 beets (1½ pounds), green tops removed, beets scrubbed

2 tablespoons (¼ stick) unsalted butter

2 tablespoons finely chopped shallots

Freshly grated zest of 1 large navel orange

⅓ cup fresh orange juice (from 1 large navel orange)

1 tablespoon balsamic vinegar

½ teaspoon light brown sugar

Kosher salt and freshly ground black pepper

1. Position a rack in the center of the oven and preheat the oven to 400°F.

2. Wrap each beet in aluminum foil. Place them on a rimmed baking sheet. Bake until the beets are tender when pierced with a meat fork, 1½ to 2 hours, depending on the size and age of the beets. Let them cool in the foil for about 15 minutes. Slip the skins from the warm beets. Cut the beets into bite-sized pieces.

3. Melt the butter in a large skillet over medium heat. Add the shallots and cook, stirring often, until they're tender, about 2 minutes. Add the beets and stir well. Add the orange zest and juice, vinegar, and brown sugar. Bring them to a boil over high heat, stirring gently to dissolve the brown sugar. Boil, stirring occasionally, until the liquid has reduced to a glaze, about 3 minutes. Season to taste with salt and pepper. Serve them warm, or cool to room temperature.

SHREDDED BEETS WITH SCALLIONS AND WALNUTS

MAKES 4 TO 6 SERVINGS

Serve with corned beef, pork chops, ham, sausages, or roast duck.

Prep Time: 10 minutes

Cooking Time: 6 minutes

Weeknight Suppers, Holiday Feasts, Company Fare, Buffet Dish, Vegetarian

If you are a beet fan but don't have the time to commit to roasting, here is a way to enjoy them that takes only a few minutes. A quick sauté retains the beets' earthy flavor and firm texture. I have served this dish with everything from a holiday ham to a weeknight platter of pork chops, and it is always popular. Note that walnut oil is always used as a flavoring and not for sautéing.

1 pound beets, green tops removed, peeled
1 tablespoon vegetable oil
2 scallions (white and green parts), chopped
¼ cup toasted and coarsely chopped walnuts (see page 33)

1 tablespoon walnut oil or more olive oil
1 tablespoon sherry or white wine vinegar
Kosher salt and freshly ground black pepper
2 teaspoons chopped fresh flat-leaf parsley (optional)

1. Shred the beets in a food processor with the large-hole shredding disk. (Or use the large holes on a box shredder.)

2. Heat the vegetable oil in a very large skillet over medium-high heat. Add the scallions and cook, stirring occasionally, until they're softened, about 1 minute. Add the shredded beets and cook, stirring occasionally, until they're hot, about 5 minutes. Remove them from the heat and stir in the walnuts, walnut oil, and vinegar. Season to taste with salt and pepper.

3. Transfer the beets to a serving bowl and sprinkle them with the parsley. Serve hot.

CIDER-BRAISED BEETS

MAKES 6 SERVINGS

Serve with chops, sausages, roast duck, or roast goose.
Prep Time: 5 minutes
Cooking Time: 20 minutes
Make Ahead: The beets can be made up to 2 days ahead.
Weeknight Suppers, Holiday Feasts, Vegetarian

It wasn't so long ago that beets were always cooked in liquid, but that method fell out of favor when roasted beets appeared on the scene. I admit that beets boiled in water are usually nothing to write home about, but these beets, cooked in apple juice, topped with fresh tarragon (or toasted caraway), make a terrific side dish without turning on the oven.

1 cup fresh apple cider
2 tablespoons (¼ stick) unsalted butter
10 beets (2 pounds), green tops removed, peeled, and cut into ½-inch rounds

Kosher salt and freshly ground black pepper
2 teaspoons finely chopped fresh tarragon

1. Combine 1½ cups water, the cider, and butter in a large, deep, nonreactive skillet. Add the beets and enough water, if needed, to barely cover them. Bring them to a boil over high heat.

2. Reduce the heat to medium and cover the skillet with the lid ajar. Cook at a brisk simmer until the beets are just tender when pierced with the tip of a small, sharp knife, about 20 minutes. Season the beets to taste with salt and pepper.

3. Using a slotted spoon, transfer the beets to a serving bowl. Sprinkle them with the tarragon and serve.

Cider-Braised Beets with Toasted Caraway: Omit the tarragon. Cook 1½ teaspoons caraway seed in a small skillet over medium heat, stirring occasionally, until they are toasted and fragrant, 2 to 3 minutes. Immediately transfer them to a plate and let cool. Coarsely crush the seeds with a mortar and pestle (or pulse in an electric spice grinder). Just before serving, sprinkle the caraway seed over the beets.

Carrots

Traditionally, carrots are cold-weather vegetables, stored in the root cellar with the other crops that would feed the family throughout the winter. Now they are available all year, and thin summer carrots are a real treat. "Baby" carrots are not miniature carrots (although you can sometimes find these at specialty grocers with their tops still attached), but large carrots cut down to size. Large, small, or "baby"—carrots can create a wide range of side dishes, especially if you're on a budget.

Peak Season: Available all year.

Purchase: Hard, evenly shaped roots with tops (if attached) that are bright green and succulent; avoid rubbery or sprouting carrots.

Store: Refrigerate for up to 2 weeks.

Preparation: Scrub the carrots under cold running water; peel, if desired. "Baby" carrots don't need peeling.

CARROTS WITH POMEGRANATE GLAZE
MAKES 4 SERVINGS

Serve with roast beef, steak, pork chops, leg of lamb, lamb chops, roast chicken, salmon fillets, or sautéed shrimp.
Prep Time: 5 minutes
Cooking Time: 15 minutes
Make Ahead: The carrots can be made up to 1 day ahead.
Weeknight Supper, Holiday Feasts, Company Fare, Vegetarian

In this recipe clearly based on Classic Glazed Carrots Vichy (below), the vegetables are cooked in pomegranate juice to make a sweet-and-sour glaze. You can also apply this method to whole, miniature, or baby (cut) carrots. While these carrots are utterly delicious, they could use a green accent of fresh green herbs. Mint is my favorite, but you can try parsley, thyme, or rosemary.

2 tablespoons (¼ stick) unsalted butter

1 pound carrots, cut into ½-inch rounds

1 cup pomegranate juice, as needed (see Note)

1 tablespoon light brown sugar

Kosher salt and freshly ground black pepper

Finely chopped fresh mint, for garnish

Pomegranate arils (seeds), for garnish (optional)

1. Melt the butter in a medium skillet over medium heat. Add the carrots and spread them in a single layer. Pour in enough pomegranate juice to barely cover the carrots. Sprinkle the brown sugar on top and season with ¼ teaspoon salt and a few grinds of pepper. Bring them to a boil over high heat, occasionally stirring to dissolve the sugar.

2. Cover and reduce the heat to medium-low. Cook at a brisk simmer for 10 minutes. Uncover and increase the heat to high. Boil until the carrots are tender and the juice has reduced to a glaze, about 5 minutes more. Season to taste with salt and pepper.

3. Transfer the carrots to a serving bowl and sprinkle them with the mint and pomegranate arils, if using. Serve hot.

Note: Domestic pomegranate juice is sold at every supermarket. It is also worth searching out the very reasonably priced imported brands sold at Mediterranean grocers and specialty shops.

Carrots with Apple Glaze: Substitute fresh apple juice for the pomegranate juice and omit the brown sugar.

CLASSIC GLAZED CARROTS VICHY

MAKES 4 SERVINGS

Serve with roast beef, roast pork and lamb, roast chicken, and fish fillets.

Prep Time: 10 minutes

Cooking Time: 25 minutes

Weeknight Suppers, Family Favorite, Holiday Feasts, Company Fare, Buffet Dish,

Cooking Classic, Vegetarian

Carrots Vichy is named for the French resort town famous for its alkaline and mineral-rich carbonated spring water, and in the original recipe, only Vichy water was used. While you can add a pinch of baking soda to club soda to simulate the "real thing," this simple dish is just as good with tap water. It is one of the most revered side dishes. In my version, I let the carrots provide their own natural sweetness and keep the added sugar to a minimum. (I have seen recipes that substitute soda pop for the carbonated water. Mon Dieu!)

2 tablespoons (¼ stick) unsalted butter	Kosher salt and freshly ground black pepper
1½ pounds slender carrots, cut into ½-inch rounds	1 tablespoon finely chopped fresh flat-leaf parsley
2 teaspoons sugar	

1. Melt the butter in a large skillet over medium heat. Add the carrots and toss well to coat them with the butter. Add enough cold water to come halfway up the carrots and stir in the sugar, ½ teaspoon salt, and ¼ teaspoon pepper. Bring them to a boil over high heat.

2. Reduce the heat to medium-low and cover the carrots. Cook until the carrots are almost tender, about 4 minutes. Uncover and return the heat to high. Cook, stirring often, until the liquid has reduced to about 2 tablespoons and the carrots are glazed and tender, about 5 minutes. Season to taste with salt and pepper. Transfer the carrots to a serving dish, sprinkle them with the parsley, and serve.

BABY CARROTS AND APPLE SAUTÉ WITH ROSEMARY
MAKES 4 TO 6 SERVINGS

Serve with pork, lamb and veal chops, sausages, roast chicken, or sautéed chicken.
Prep Time: 10 minutes
Cooking Time: 10 minutes
Weeknight Suppers, Family Favorite, Holiday Feasts, Company Fare, Buffet Dish, Vegetarian

Here's a wonderful side dish for autumn, when it seems like the seasonal pickings are slim. Carrots and apples go beautifully with rosemary (or sage or thyme, for that matter), but if you don't have fresh herbs, just leave them out.

12 ounces "baby" carrots	2 tablespoons finely chopped shallots
2 tablespoons (¼ stick) unsalted butter	2 teaspoons minced fresh rosemary
2 tart apples, such as Granny Smith, peeled, cored, and cut into ½-inch wedges	Kosher salt and freshly ground black pepper

1. Put the carrots in a skillet and add just enough salted water to cover. Cover and bring them to a boil over high heat. Reduce the heat to medium-low and simmer just until the carrots are crisp-tender, 4 to 5 minutes. Drain the carrots and set them aside. (There is no need to rinse the carrots.)

2. Dry the skillet and return it to the stove. Add 1 tablespoon of the butter and melt it over medium-high heat. Add the apples and cook, stirring occasionally, until they are lightly browned, about 3 minutes. Stir in the shallots and cook, stirring occasionally, until they soften, about 1 minute.

3. Add the carrots with the remaining 1 tablespoon butter and the rosemary. Cook, stirring occasionally, until they are well combined and the carrots are hot, about 1 minute. Season to taste with salt and pepper and serve.

CARROTS WITH CREAMY THAI SAUCE

MAKES 4 TO 6 SERVINGS

Serve with rice and Asian-style grilled meats, poultry, or seafood.
Prep Time: 10 minutes
Cooking Time: 15 minutes
Weeknight Suppers, Company Fare

I always have a bag of carrots in the refrigerator, so even when I don't think that I have anything in the house for a side dish, they can be pulled into play with other odds and ends in the refrigerator and pantry. This is how I prepared them recently to go with sautéed shrimp. Dinner was ready in about fifteen minutes.

1 tablespoon vegetable oil	2 tablespoons Thai or Vietnamese fish sauce
1½ pounds carrots, cut on the diagonal into ½-inch ovals	2 tablespoons fresh lime juice
	1 tablespoon soy sauce
2 tablespoons finely chopped shallots	1 tablespoon brown sugar
1 tablespoon peeled and minced fresh ginger	¼ teaspoon hot red pepper flakes
2 garlic cloves, minced	Kosher salt
¾ cup unsweetened coconut milk	2 tablespoons coarsely chopped fresh cilantro

1. Heat a large skillet over medium-high heat. Add the oil and swirl to coat the bottom of the skillet with the oil. Heat until the oil is very hot but not smoking. Add the carrots and cook, stirring occasionally, until they begin to brown, about 3 minutes. Stir in the shallots, ginger, and garlic and cook until they are fragrant, about 30 seconds.

2. Add the coconut milk, fish sauce, lime juice, soy sauce, brown sugar, and red pepper flakes and stir well. Bring them to a boil and reduce the heat to medium-low. Cook at a brisk simmer, stirring often, until the carrots are tender and the sauce has reduced by half, about 5 minutes. Season to taste with salt. Transfer the carrots to a serving bowl, sprinkle them with the cilantro, and serve.

CARROT AND SWEET POTATO PURÉE

MAKES 4 TO 6 SERVINGS

Serve with pork roast and chops, baked ham, fried chicken, roast turkey, or roast duck.
Prep Time: 5 minutes

Cooking Time: 30 minutes

Make Ahead: The purée can be prepared up to 1 day ahead.

Weeknight Suppers, Family Favorite, Holiday Feasts, Company Fare, Buffet Dish, Vegetarian

Two appetizingly orange root vegetables combine to make this a purée that scores points for looks, flavor, and ease of preparation. While it is a simple dish for a weeknight supper, try it alongside a holiday ham. I prefer its natural sweetness, but you could add a tablespoon or two of maple syrup, or give it an herbaceous note with a tablespoon of finely chopped fresh chives or tarragon.

8 medium carrots (1 pound), cut into ½-inch rounds

1 large orange-fleshed sweet potato (yam), peeled and cut into 1-inch chunks

3 tablespoons unsalted butter, cut into tablespoons

Kosher salt and freshly ground black pepper

1. Combine the carrots and sweet potato in a medium saucepan. Add enough cold salted water to cover the vegetables by 1 inch. Bring it to a boil over high heat. Reduce the heat to medium-low and cook at a brisk simmer until the vegetables are very tender, about 25 minutes.

2. Drain the vegetables and return them to the saucepan. Cook over medium heat, stirring almost constantly, to evaporate excess moisture, about 2 minutes. Transfer the mixture to a food processor. With the processor running, drop the butter, 1 tablespoon at a time, through the feed tube and process until the mixture is smooth. (The vegetables and butter can also be mixed together in a bowl with a handheld electric mixer set on high speed, although the purée will be chunky.) Season to taste with salt and pepper. (The purée can be cooled, covered, and refrigerated for up to 1 day. Reheat in a nonstick skillet over medium-low heat for about 5 minutes.) Transfer the purée to a serving bowl and serve.

CARROT AND CHIVE TIMBALES

MAKES 6 TIMBALES

Serve with delicate fish dishes; roast rack of lamb; or veal roast.

Prep Time: 15 minutes

Cooking Time: 35 minutes

Make Ahead: The timbales can be made up to 1 day ahead.

Holiday Feasts, Company Fare, Buffet Dish, Cooking Classic, Vegetarian

Timbales are unmolded savory custards, and they do much to add a splash of color to a formal menu with a wonderful (but brown-colored) roast as the main course. These creamy carrot timbales are a sophisticated side dish that will instantly upgrade any roasted meat. If you have other onion flavors in the menu, substitute 2 teaspoons finely chopped rosemary, tarragon, or thyme for the chives.

Softened butter, for the ramekins

1 pound carrots, peeled and cut into 1-inch chunks

1 cup half-and-half

3 large eggs plus 2 large egg yolks

¾ teaspoon kosher salt

¼ teaspoon freshly ground white pepper

Pinch of freshly grated nutmeg

2 tablespoons finely chopped fresh chives, plus more for serving

Special Equipment: Six ½- to ¾-cup ramekins or custard cups

1. Position a rack in the center of the oven and preheat the oven to 325°F. Lightly butter six ½- to ¾-cup ramekins.

2. Put the carrots in a medium saucepan and add enough cold salted water to cover the carrots by ½ inch. Bring it to a boil over high heat. Reduce the heat to medium and simmer the carrots until they are very tender, about 20 minutes. Drain well.

3. Transfer the carrots to a blender. Add ½ cup of the half-and-half and process until puréed. Pour the purée into a medium bowl. Add the remaining ½ cup half-and-half with the eggs, yolks, salt, pepper, and nutmeg and whisk just until combined. Whisk in the chives. Pour or ladle equal amounts of the custard mixture into the ramekins.

4. Place the ramekins in a roasting pan. Pour in enough hot tap water around the ramekins to come ¼ to ½ inch up the sides. (The hot water insulates the ramekins to keep the timbales from cooking too quickly, so it does not have to be boiling or deeper than ½ inch.) Tightly cover the pan with aluminum foil.

5. Bake until a knife inserted into the center of a timbale comes out clean, 30 to 40 minutes. The timbales will be puffed but will deflate upon cooling. Remove the pan with the ramekins from the oven and uncover. Let the ramekins stand for 5 minutes in the water. Protecting your hands with a kitchen towel, remove the ramekins from the water and dry the ramekins. (The timbales can be cooled, covered with plastic wrap, and refrigerated for up to 1 day. Reheat them in a microwave oven at 50 percent power for 3 to 5 minutes.)

6. To unmold, run a dinner knife around the inside of a ramekin. Place a small plate on top of the ramekin. Hold the ramekin and plate together. Invert them and give a couple of sharp shakes to unmold the timbale. Using a metal spatula, transfer the timbale to a dinner plate. Sprinkle the timbales with additional chives and serve.

CARROT AND SHALLOT GRATIN

MAKES 8 SERVINGS

Serve with roast meats and poultry, or grilled salmon.

Prep Time: 10 minutes

Cooking Time: 50 minutes

Make Ahead: The gratin can be made up to 1 day ahead.

Family Favorite, Holiday Feasts, Company Fare, Buffet, Vegetarian

Carrots and shallots are roasted together, and then bound with mustard-flavored crème fraîche for a gratin that will have guests asking for seconds. This dish is strikingly pretty when made with rainbow carrots, although regular carrots will do just fine.

1½ pounds slender carrots, cut in half lengthwise, then into 2-inch pieces

2 tablespoons vegetable oil

8 shallots, cut in half lengthwise (or separated, if they break naturally into lobes)

½ teaspoon kosher salt

¼ teaspoon freshly ground black pepper

2 tablespoons (¼ stick) unsalted butter, melted, plus softened butter for the baking dish

1 cup crème fraîche (see below)

2 teaspoons Dijon mustard

½ cup soft bread crumbs, made from slightly stale crusty bread in a food processor or blender

1 tablespoon finely chopped fresh flat-leaf parsley

1. Position a rack in the center of the oven and preheat the oven to 400°F.

2. On a rimmed baking sheet, toss the carrots and oil together. Spread the carrots in a single layer. Roast until the carrots are beginning to brown on the undersides, about 15 minutes. Add the shallots and toss to coat them with the oil. Continue roasting until the shallots are beginning to brown and soften, about 15 minutes more. Season the vegetables with the salt and pepper.

3. Lightly butter a 13 × 9 × 2-inch baking pan with the softened butter. Spread the carrot mixture in the baking pan. In a small bowl, whisk the crème fraîche and mustard together and spread them over the carrot mixture. In a medium bowl, mix the bread crumbs, melted butter, and parsley together and sprinkle the mixture evenly over the carrots.

4. Bake until the topping is golden brown and the crème fraîche mixture has thickened, about 20 minutes. Let cool for 5 minutes and serve.

CRÈME FRAÎCHE

Crème fraîche looks a lot like sour cream. However, it is more buttery than tangy, and, unlike sour cream, will not curdle when heated. So do not substitute sour cream in this recipe. Crème fraîche is sold in the cheese section of many supermarkets and at specialty markets.

You can also make crème fraîche at home, although it takes a couple of days to ferment and chill. Whisk 2 tablespoons buttermilk into 1 cup heavy cream (not ultra-pasteurized) in a medium bowl. Cover it with plastic wrap, but leave in an area vented slightly to allow some air into the bowl. Let it stand in a warm place (such as near the stove in a kitchen) until the mixture thickens, 24 to 36 hours. Transfer it to a covered container and refrigerate until the crème fraîche has thickened more and is chilled, at least 1 day. The crème fraîche can be refrigerated for up to 2 weeks.

ROOT VEGETABLE AND FRUIT TSIMMIS

MAKES 10 SERVINGS

Prep Time: 15 minutes

Cooking Time: 1 hour, 5 minutes

Make Ahead: The tsimmis can be made 1 day ahead.

Family Favorite, Holiday Feasts, Company Fare, Buffet Dish, Vegetarian

One of the traditional foods at a Passover Seder, in Yiddish, a tsimmis means "much ado about nothing." So it follows that a fruit and vegetable stew of the same name should have a little of this and a little of that. This recipe, redolent of sweet and spice, was adapted from my friend Norene Gilletz, a terrific writer who specializes in kosher cooking.

¾ cup pitted prunes

¾ cup dried apricots

½ cup seedless raisins

3 cups boiling water

2 pounds carrots, peeled and cut into ¼-inch rounds

1 elongated medium orange-fleshed sweet potato (yam), peeled, quartered lengthwise, and cut into ¼-inch slices

One 15½-ounce can pineapple chunks in juice

½ cup fresh orange juice

½ cup honey

2 tablespoons nondairy margarine, melted, or olive oil

1 teaspoon ground cinnamon

Nonstick cooking oil spray

Kosher salt and freshly ground black pepper

1. Combine the prunes, apricots, and raisins in a medium heatproof bowl. Add the boiling water and let them stand until plumped, about 30 minutes.

2. Meanwhile, bring a large saucepan of salted water to a boil over high heat. Add the carrots and sweet potatoes and cook until they are crisp-tender, about 5 minutes. Drain well.

3. Drain the pineapple chunks well in a wire sieve over a bowl; reserve ½ cup of the juice. In a medium bowl, whisk the pineapple juice, orange juice, honey, margarine, and cinnamon together. Set the pineapple chunks aside.

4. Position a rack in the center of the oven and preheat the oven to 350°F. Spray a 13 × 9 × 2-inch baking dish with the oil.

5. Drain the dried fruit well. Transfer it to the baking dish with the carrots and sweet potatoes and mix them gently to combine. Pour the juice mixture evenly over the vegetables and fruits. Season to taste with salt and pepper. Cover the baking dish with aluminum foil.

6. Bake for 35 minutes. Remove the foil and stir in the reserved pineapple chunks. Bake, uncovered, basting occasionally, until the juice mixture is syrupy, about 15 minutes. (The tsimmis can be cooled, covered with aluminum foil, and refrigerated for a day. Reheat in a preheated 350°F oven for 15 minutes, then uncover and bake until heated through, about 10 minutes more.) Let it stand for 5 minutes and serve.

Celery Root

It is easy to pass over bulbous celery root at the supermarket . . . but don't. After peeling away its gnarly exterior, you'll find a creamy white flesh with a flavor slightly reminiscent of celery (the two are not related at all). Although French cooks can't get enough of celery root (also known as celeriac), Americans have been slow to come around. One of the recipes below, or the celery root rémoulade on page 328, is bound to make you a fan, if you aren't already.

Peak Season: October to March, available all year.

Purchase: Hard roots that are heavy for their size without cracks or soft spots.

Store: Refrigerate for up to 2 weeks.

Preparation: Do not wash the celery root until after you peel it because the dirt hiding in the gnarls could turn to mud. Pare the celery root with a sharp knife or use a sturdy vegetable peeler.

CELERY ROOT PURÉE
MAKES 8 SERVINGS

Serve with roast beef, pork, or lamb; steaks and chops; roast chicken; or roast salmon.
Prep Time: 10 minutes
Cooking Time: 30 minutes
Weeknight Suppers, Family Favorite, Holiday Feasts, Company Fare, Buffet Dish,
Cooking Classic, Vegetarian

Celery root purée may look like mashed potatoes, but when my guests take their first bite, their faces light up with surprise. (I do include potatoes in this purée to give it a more substantial texture than celery root alone.) Unlike mashed potatoes, this can be puréed in a food processor. The size of celery root varies, so you could need anywhere from two large roots to four smaller ones for this dish.

3 pounds celery roots
1 pound baking potatoes, peeled and cut into
  1-inch chunks
¼ cup (½ stick) unsalted butter, at room
  temperature

½ cup whole milk, heated to steaming
Salt and freshly ground pepper, preferably white
  pepper

1. Using a sharp knife, pare off the skin and gnarly roots from the celery roots. Rinse well. Cut the celery roots into 1-inch cubes, paring away any soft woody spots.
2. Put the celery roots and potatoes in a large saucepan and add enough lightly salted cold water to

cover the vegetables by 1 inch. Cover and bring them to a boil over high heat. Reduce the heat to medium-low and set the lid ajar. Cook until both vegetables are tender when pierced with the tip of a sharp knife, about 25 minutes.

3. Drain the vegetables well and return them to the pot. Stir them over medium-low heat until they begin to film the bottom of the pot, about 2 minutes. Remove the pot from the heat.

4. Add the butter to the vegetables. Using a potato masher or a handheld electric mixer, mash the vegetables, adding enough of the hot milk to reach the desired consistency. (The celery root mixture can also be puréed with the butter and milk in a food processor.) Season the purée to taste with salt and pepper. Transfer it to a bowl and serve.

CELERY ROOT, POTATO, AND GARLIC GRATIN
MAKES 6 TO 8 SERVINGS

Serve with roast beef, pork, or lamb; steaks and chops; or roast chicken.

Prep Time: 15 minutes

Cooking Time: 1¾ hours

Make Ahead: The gratin can be baked up to 4 hours ahead.

Family Favorite, Holiday Feasts, Company Fare, Buffet Dish, Cooking Classic, Vegetarian

There has hardly been an occasion when I have served this outrageously lush gratin that a guest hasn't remarked, "I could eat this for dinner!" With just the right amount of garlic, it is as addictive as any controlled substance.

Softened butter, for the baking dish and foil

3 cups heavy cream, as needed

2 garlic cloves, coarsely chopped

½ teaspoon finely chopped fresh thyme or ¼ teaspoon dried

1¼ teaspoons kosher salt

½ teaspoon freshly ground black pepper

1½ pounds baking potatoes, peeled and cut into ⅛-inch slices

1½ pounds celery roots, pared and cut into ⅛-inch slices

1 cup shredded Gruyère cheese (4 ounces)

1. Position a rack in the center of the oven and preheat the oven to 400°F. Generously butter an 11½ × 8 × 2-inch baking dish

2. Bring the cream, garlic, and thyme to a simmer in a medium saucepan over medium-low heat. Remove the pan from the heat and let the garlic steep to flavor the cream for about 10 minutes.

3. In a small bowl, mix the salt and pepper together. Spread half of the potatoes and celery root in the prepared baking dish and sprinkle them with half of the salt mixture. Sprinkle them with the Gruyère. Using a slotted spoon, scatter all of the chopped garlic over the cheese, then pour half of the cream mixture on top. Spread the remaining vegetables in the dish. Carefully and evenly pour the remaining cream mixture over the vegetables. (If necessary, add more heavy cream to barely cover the vegetables.) Sprinkle the top with the remaining salt mixture. Tightly cover the baking dish with aluminum foil (preferably nonstick foil), tenting the foil so it does not touch the vegetables.

4. Place the baking dish on a large, rimmed baking sheet. Bake it for 1 hour. Remove the foil and continue baking until the gratin is golden brown and tender when pierced with a knife, about 45 minutes more. (The gratin can be cooled, covered, and stored at room temperature for up to 4 hours. Reheat in a preheated 350ºF oven for 20 to 30 minutes.) Let it stand 5 to 10 minutes before cutting. Serve hot.

ROAST GARLIC

Once America learned how to roast garlic, there was no turning back. Roasting gives garlic an entirely different flavor, mellower and sweeter, but still distinctive. Here are two methods: one for entire heads to serve next to roast lamb, and one for individual cloves to store in the refrigerator to add to salad dressings, mashed potatoes, and the like.

ROAST GARLIC HEADS
MAKES ABOUT 4 SERVINGS OR ½ CUP MASHED GARLIC

Serve with roast beef or lamb, steaks, and chops.
Prep Time: 5 minutes
Cooking Time: 45 minutes
Make Ahead: The mashed garlic can be made up to 5 days ahead.
Holiday Feasts, Company Fare, Vegetarian

This is the classic way to roast garlic heads for squeezing the soft flesh from the hulls, especially when it is going to be mashed and used as a flavoring for mashed potatoes and the like. I have also served roast garlic halves alongside roast beef and leg of lamb as a condiment, but only with good friends and family who don't mind getting a little garlic on their hands.

2 large, plump heads garlic   Kosher salt and freshly ground black
2 teaspoons olive oil   pepper

1. Position a rack in the center of the oven and preheat the oven to 400ºF.
2. Cut each head of garlic in half crosswise, trying to keep the two halves intact. Drizzle 1 teaspoon of the oil over the cut surfaces of each head of garlic, and season them lightly with salt and pepper. Put the two halves back together into their original shape, and wrap the garlic in aluminum foil. Place the wrapped garlic on a baking sheet.

3. Bake until the garlic is very tender and golden brown, 45 minutes to 1 hour, depending on the size of the heads. Unwrap the garlic heads and let them cool until easy to handle, about 10 minutes. Serve warm, allowing each guest to squeeze the tender flesh from the hulls.

4. To mash the garlic to use as a flavoring, squeeze the flesh from the hulls into a small bowl. Using a fork, mash the flesh. Cover and refrigerate it for up to 5 days.

SIMPLE ROASTED GARLIC CLOVES
MAKES ABOUT 1 CUP ROASTED GARLIC CLOVES

Serve with beef, pork, and lamb roasts, steaks, and chops; or roast chicken.

Prep Time: 5 minutes (if using store-bought peeled garlic cloves)

Cooking Time: 1 hour

Make Ahead: The garlic can be cooked up to 5 days ahead.

Holiday Feasts, Company Fare, Vegetarian

Most supermarkets now carry peeled garlic cloves. I never use them for everyday cooking (after all, it doesn't take long to chop a garlic clove, and I can never use all of the store-bought garlic before it goes bad), but when I want intact roasted garlic cloves, I'll buy a container. Strew the tender roasted cloves over steaks or chops for an instant flavor-rouser. Thanks to my friend Michael Northern, executive chef of Nordstrom, for teaching me this method.

1½ cups peeled garlic cloves (see Note)   1 teaspoon finely chopped fresh thyme
2 tablespoons olive oil   (optional)
Kosher salt and freshly ground black pepper

1. Position a rack in the center of the oven and preheat the oven to 375ºF.

2. Toss the garlic cloves and oil together in an 8-inch-square baking dish. Season the garlic with a couple of pinches of salt and a few grinds of pepper. Add ½ cup water and cover the dish tightly with aluminum foil.

3. Bake for 35 minutes. Remove the foil (be careful of the hot steam) and continue baking, stirring occasionally, until the water has almost completely evaporated and the garlic is golden and tender, about 20 minutes more. Drain well. (The garlic can be cooled, covered, and refrigerated for up to 5 days.)

4. To serve it as a side dish, transfer the garlic to a serving bowl. Sprinkle it with the thyme, season to taste with salt and pepper, and mix gently. Serve hot.

Note: If you wish, substitute the cloves from 2 large, plump heads of garlic for the store-bought garlic. Use a small, sharp knife to individually peel each clove without crushing it; the cloves must be intact.

Leeks

This long, tall member of the Lilium family has a mild onion flavor. (And because it is handled differently than its round cousins, I give it a separate entry.) The white and pale green bottom is often used as a seasoning ingredient in tandem with carrots and celery, although the leek can also star as the main ingredient in a side dish. Unfortunately, its dark green top doesn't have much culinary use, so you may as well discard it.

Peak Season: October to May, available all year.

Purchase: Straight leeks with fresh-looking green tops without any yellowing.

Store: Refrigerate for up to 1 week.

Preparation: Trim off the root end. Cut off and discard the dark green tops, just above the light green portion of each leek. Leeks harbor dirt and must be washed well. For chopped leeks, it is best to cut them before washing. Submerge the leeks in a bowl of cold water, agitate them to loosen the dirt, then lift the leeks out of the water, leaving the grit to sink to the bottom of the bowl. For whole leeks, split them lengthwise into quarters, stopping about ¼ inch from the root end, and rinse them well under cold running water, opening the layers underneath the stream of water to remove any grit.

MELTED LEEKS WITH CRÈME FRAÎCHE AND CHIVES
MAKES 4 SERVINGS

Serve with sautéed chicken breast or fish fillets.
Prep Time: 10 minutes
Cooking Time: 20 minutes
Make Ahead: The leeks can be made up to 1 day ahead.
Weeknight Suppers, Family Favorite, Holiday Feasts, Company Fare

Thin rounds of leeks, cooked until they are meltingly tender and mixed with delectable crème fraîche, make for a pretty rich side dish, so I serve it with light fare like sautéed chicken breast, salmon, or halibut. And, if no one at the table is on a diet, I make the bacon variation.

2 tablespoons (¼ stick) unsalted butter

6 leeks (white and pale green parts only), cut into ¼-inch rounds, washed well, and separated into rings (about 6 cups)

Kosher salt and freshly ground black pepper

½ cup reduced-sodium chicken broth

½ cup crème fraîche or heavy cream

1 tablespoon finely chopped fresh chives

1. Melt the butter in a large skillet over medium-high heat. Add the leeks and season with ¼ teaspoon salt and ¼ teaspoon pepper. Cook, stirring occasionally, until the liquid evaporates and they are lightly browned, 5 to 7 minutes.

2. Stir in the broth and ¼ cup water and bring them to a boil, stirring up the browned juices in the skillet with a wooden spoon. Reduce the heat to medium-low and cover the skillet. Simmer until the leeks are very tender, about 15 minutes. Increase the heat to high and uncover the skillet. Boil, stirring often, until the liquid is almost completely evaporated, 2 to 3 minutes. Stir in the crème fraîche and bring it to a boil. (If using heavy cream, continue boiling until it is lightly reduced, about 1 minute.) Season to taste with salt and pepper. (The leeks can be prepared up to 1 day ahead. Reheat in a skillet over low heat, adding a few tablespoons of water.)

3. Transfer the leeks to a serving bowl. Sprinkle them with the chives and serve.

Melted Leeks with Bacon: Sprinkle 2 slices cooked and crumbled bacon over the leeks before serving.

LEEK AND CHÈVRE TART
MAKES 8 SERVINGS

Serve with leg of lamb, lamb chops, or as part of a brunch buffet with baked ham or sausages.

Prep Time: 30 minutes, plus 30 minutes to 2 hours refrigeration time for the dough.

Cooking Time: 45 minutes

Make Ahead: The tart can be made up to 2 hours ahead.

Holiday Feasts, Company Fare, Buffet Dish, Vegetarian

This tart is a member of the quiche family, but with heaps of tender leeks and sharp goat cheese, I prefer to serve it as an elegant partner to roast lamb at a holiday dinner when such indulgences are expected and encouraged. Or serve as part of a brunch menu with baked ham or a selection of sausages. It's also useful because it can be served either warm or at room temperature.

1 recipe Tart Dough (page 106), chilled for at least
   30 minutes

FILLING

2 tablespoons (¼ stick) unsalted butter

3 leeks (white and pale green parts), cut into thin
   rounds, washed well and drained

Kosher salt and freshly ground black pepper

2 large eggs

½ cup heavy cream

½ cup whole milk

2 teaspoons finely chopped fresh rosemary

¾ cup crumbled goat cheese (3 ounces)

1. On a lightly floured work surface, roll out the dough into a 12- to 13-inch round about ⅛ inch thick. Fit the dough into a 9-inch tart pan with a removable bottom, taking care not to stretch the dough, and being sure that the dough fits snugly into the corners of the pan. Trim the dough flush with the edge of the pan. Freeze the dough-lined pan for 30 minutes to 1 hour.

2. Position a rack in the bottom third of the oven and preheat the oven to 375ºF.

3. Place the tart pan on a large rimmed baking sheet. Line the pan with aluminum foil and fill it with pie weights or dried beans. Bake until the visible edge of the dough looks dry and set, about 15 minutes. Remove the foil and weights. Quickly pierce the dough all over with a fork. Continue baking until the dough is lightly browned, about 15 minutes more.

4. Meanwhile, make the filling: Melt the butter in a large skillet over medium heat. Add the leeks, ½ teaspoon salt, and ¼ teaspoon pepper. Cook, stirring often, until the leeks are tender, about 10 minutes. Remove from the heat and set aside.

5. In a medium bowl, whisk the eggs together. Whisk in the cream, milk, and rosemary with ½ teaspoon salt and a grind or two of pepper. Scatter the leeks and goat cheese in the tart shell (the tart does not have to be cool), and pour in the cream mixture.

6. Return the pan on the baking sheet to the oven and reduce the temperature to 350ºF. Bake until the filling is puffed and lightly browned, and a knife inserted in the center of the filling comes out clean, about 25 minutes. Remove it from the oven and let the tart cool in the pan for 10 minutes. Remove the sides of the pan. Serve it warm or cooled to room temperature.

Onions

There are two branches to the onion family. **Seasoning onions,** usually cooked as a flavoring in recipes and not served alone as the main ingredient, are often categorized by their color: yellow, white (popular in Latino cuisines), and red (a common salad ingredient). They are also called globe, storage, or dry onions in the trade, but they are hardly ever labeled this way at markets. Spanish onions are extra-large yellow onions. **Shallots,** smaller seasoning onions essential to French cooking, look like a cross between a head of garlic and a red onion. **Sweet onions** (including Vidalia, Maui, and others named for their place of harvest) are often served raw in salads, but, like the seasoning onions, they can also be cooked and served as side dishes. The second branch, **boiling onions**, are always served cooked. The common walnut-sized white boiling onion is also available in red and yellow varieties; the smallest ones are labeled **pearl onions**. An Italian boiling onion, **cipollini,** is sold at specialty markets and many supermarkets.

Peak Season: Available all year.

Purchase: Choose heavy, firm onions with dry skins and without sprouts, cuts, or signs of mold.

Store: Uncovered in a cool, dark, and dry place; do not store with potatoes (as they give off gases that encourage each other's decay). Cut onions can be wrapped tightly in plastic and refrigerated for up to 3 days.

Preparation: Peel before use. To loosen the skins of small boiling onions, shallots, and cipollini before cooking, drop them into boiling water and cook just until the skin loosens, about 1 minute. Drain, rinse under cold running water, and peel with a small, sharp knife.

ROASTED VIDALIA ONION WEDGES WITH GRUYÈRE CRUMBS
MAKES 4 TO 6 SERVINGS

Serve with roast beef, steaks, or roast chicken.

Prep Time: 10 minutes

Cooking Time: 1 hour

Weeknight Suppers, Family Favorite, Holiday Feasts, Company Fare, Buffet Dish,

Retro Recipe, Cooking Classic

The fabulous flavors of French onion soup show up in this side dish for grilled steaks or even roast chicken. Keep an eye on the liquid as it reduces in the oven; if it cooks down too quickly, add a few tablespoons of additional stock or water to the baking dish. On the other hand, if any stock remains after the onions are done, transfer the liquid to a small saucepan and boil it over high heat until thickened.

2 tablespoons (¼ stick) unsalted butter, at room temperature

3 sweet onions, such as Vidalia (about 10 ounces each), cut into quarters

½ cup reduced-sodium beef or chicken stock

¼ cup dry white wine or dry vermouth

1 teaspoon finely chopped fresh thyme or ½ teaspoon dried

Kosher salt and freshly ground black pepper

½ cup shredded Gruyère or Swiss cheese (about 2 ounces)

¼ cup panko bread crumbs

1. Position a rack in the center of the oven and preheat the oven to 400°F. Generously butter an 11½ × 8 × 2-inch baking dish with 1 tablespoon of the butter.

2. Place the onions, cut-sides up, in the baking dish. Pour the stock and wine over the onions. Season the onions with the thyme, salt, and pepper, keeping the seasonings on the onions as best as you can. Dot the onions with the remaining 1 tablespoon butter. Cover the dish tightly with aluminum foil.

3. Bake the onions for 30 minutes. Uncover and continue baking, basting occasionally with the stock mixture in the baking dish, until the onions are tender when pierced with the tip of a knife and the stock mixture has reduced by about two-thirds, adding more stock or water if needed to keep the mixture from evaporating completely, about 20 minutes.

4. In a small bowl, combine the Gruyère cheese and panko. Sprinkle them evenly over the onions and continue baking until the topping is browned and the stock is reduced to a few tablespoons, about 10 minutes more. Remove the dish from the oven and let it stand for 5 minutes. Serve hot.

ONION TARTE TATIN

Serve with beef and pork roasts, chops, and steaks; or roast chicken.

Prep Time: 30 minutes, plus 30 minutes refrigeration time for the dough

Cooking Time: 45 minutes

Make Ahead: The tart can be made up to 2 hours ahead.

Buffet Dish, Cooking Classic, Holiday Feast, Vegetarian

A savory tart inspired by the famous French upside-down apple dessert, this is a luscious side dish for a special meal. The first time I made this, news of its invention spread among my friends like wildfire (with its photo on Facebook fanning the flames). That holiday season, it was requested time and again. You will need a 9-inch nonstick skillet so the onions don't stick.

2 yellow onions (about 6 ounces each)	Kosher salt and freshly ground black pepper
1 red onion (about 6 ounces)	½ teaspoon sugar
2 tablespoons (¼ stick) unsalted butter	1 recipe Tart Dough (page 106)
1 teaspoon finely chopped fresh thyme, plus extra for serving	Flour, for rolling out the dough

1. Position a rack in the center of the oven and preheat the oven to 375°F.

2. Cut each yellow and red onion lengthwise into 8 wedges, keeping the wedges as intact as possible. Set aside 1 yellow onion. Melt the butter in a 9-inch nonstick skillet with an ovenproof handle (or wrap the handle in aluminum foil as protection) over medium heat. Remove from the heat. Alternating the remaining red and yellow wedges, arrange them in a circle, flat-sides down, in the skillet, placing the wedges close together and filling in the center with a couple of wedges. Break the reserved onion into layers and scatter them on top. In a small bowl, mix the chopped thyme, 1 teaspoon salt, ½ teaspoon pepper, and the sugar together and sprinkle them over the onions.

3. Return the skillet to medium heat. Cover it and cook, occasionally giving the skillet a gentle shake to move the onions as a unit and keep them from sticking, until the onions soften, 8 to 10 minutes. Uncover, increase the heat to medium-high, and cook until the juices reduce and the onions are sizzling in the butter, 3 to 5 minutes. Remove them from the heat.

4. On a lightly floured work surface, roll out the dough into a round about ⅛ inch thick. Using the skillet's lid (be sure it is cool) as a template, cut out a 9-inch round. Place it over the onion mixture in the pan, tucking the edges of the round into the skillet.

5. Bake until the pastry is crisp and a rich golden brown, about 30 minutes. Do not underbake it or the crust could be soggy when served. Remove the skillet from the oven. Slip a heatproof spatula around the inside of the skillet and shake the pan with a sharp side-to-side motion to be sure that the onions aren't sticking. Place a serving plate over the skillet. Using a pot holder for the skillet handle, hold the plate and skillet together and flip them over to unmold the tarte onto the plate. Let it cool for 10 minutes.

6. Season the onions with salt and pepper and sprinkle them with extra thyme leaves. Cut the tarte into wedges and serve it warm or cooled to room temperature.

BUTTERMILK ONION RINGS

MAKES 4 TO 6 SERVINGS

Serve with hamburgers, hot dogs, and other sandwiches; barbecued meats; and poultry.
Prep Time: 10 minutes
Cooking Time: 10 minutes
Weeknight Suppers, Family Favorite, Company Fare, Buffet Dish, Cooking Classic, Vegetarian

You may be surprised to discover how easy great onions rings are to make. I used to make them with a batter, but one day, in a lazy mood, I just dipped them in buttermilk and flour, and the results were great. There is nothing like onion rings right from the pot, so I suggest serving them in batches, as they are fried.

Vegetable oil, for deep-frying

2 large sweet onions, such as Vidalia, or yellow Spanish onions, sliced ¼ to ½ inch thick and separated into rings

1 cup buttermilk

1 teaspoon hot red pepper sauce

1½ cups (195 grams) unbleached all-purpose flour

Kosher salt

½ teaspoon freshly ground black pepper

1. Position a rack in the center of the oven and preheat the oven to 200ºF. Place a large wire cooling rack over a large rimmed baking sheet.

2. Pour enough oil into a large, deep skillet to come halfway up the sides and heat it over high heat to 365ºF on an instant-read thermometer.

3. Use only the outer rings of the onions, saving the smaller rings for another use. In a large bowl, toss the onion rings, buttermilk, and hot pepper sauce together to coat the onions. In another large bowl, whisk the flour, 1½ teaspoons salt, and the pepper together.

4. In batches, remove the onion rings from the buttermilk mixture, shaking off the excess buttermilk, and transfer them to the flour mixture. Toss to coat them with the flour. Add the onion rings to the hot oil and deep-fry until they are golden brown, about 3 minutes. Using a wire spider or slotted spoon, transfer the onion rings to the wire rack and keep them warm in the oven while frying the rest. Season the rings to taste with salt, and serve immediately.

BABY ONIONS MONEGASQUE

MAKES 6 SERVINGS

Serve with pork or lamb roasts and chops; baked ham; grilled sausages; or roast chicken.

Prep Time: 15 minutes

Cooking Time: 30 minutes

Make Ahead: The onions can be made up to 5 days ahead.

Holiday Feasts, Company Fare, Buffet Dish, Cooking Classic, Vegetarian

A spoonful of these sweet-and-sour onions complements meats and poultry. The cuisine of Monaco, the tiny Mediterranean principality, has influences from Provence to North Africa that are discernible in this dish. Make them a few hours (or even a few days) ahead so the flavors can mingle. It is especially good-looking when made with a trio of red, yellow, and white pearl onions, which often show up bagged at specialty grocers.

⅓ cup dried currants	2 teaspoons sugar
½ cup boiling water	½ teaspoon herbes de Provence, or ¼ teaspoon
1 pound pearl or other baby onions	each dried rosemary and thyme
1 tablespoon olive oil	Pinch of crumbled saffron
¾ cup dry white wine, such as Pinot Grigio	1 bay leaf
2 tablespoons white wine vinegar	Kosher salt and freshly ground black pepper
1 tablespoon tomato paste	

1. In a small bowl, soak the currants in the boiling water until the currants are plumped and softened, about 30 minutes.

2. Bring a medium saucepan of water to a boil over high heat. Add the onions and cook just until the skins loosen, about 1 minute. Drain and rinse them under cold running water. Using a paring knife, trim the tops and bottoms from the onions and peel them.

3. Meanwhile, heat the oil in a skillet large enough to hold the onions in a single layer. Add the onions and cook, turning occasionally, until lightly browned, 3 to 5 minutes. In a medium bowl, whisk the wine, ½ cup water, vinegar, and tomato paste together to dissolve the tomato paste. Pour the wine mixture into the skillet and add the sugar, herbes de Provence, saffron, and bay leaf. Stir well and bring everything to a boil over high heat.

4. Reduce the heat to medium-low and cover the skillet. Simmer until the onions are almost tender, about 20 minutes. Uncover and increase the heat to medium-high. Boil until the sauce has reduced to a few tablespoons, about 5 minutes. Drain the currants and stir them into the onions. Discard the bay leaf. Season to taste with salt and pepper. Transfer the onions to a bowl and let them cool. Cover and refrigerate them to blend the flavors, at least 4 hours. (The onions can be refrigerated for up to 5 days. Bring them to room temperature before serving.)

CIPOLLINI WITH BALSAMIC-HONEY GLAZE

MAKES 6 SERVINGS

Serve with Italian sausages; roast pork, veal, and chicken; baked ham; pork and veal chops; roast duck or roast goose.

Prep Time: 15 minutes

Cooking Time: 15 minutes

Make Ahead: The cipollini can be made up to 5 days ahead.

Holiday Feasts, Company Fare, Buffet Dish

Cipollini are boiling onions, but their unique shape gives them an Italian sense of style. Here, they are glazed as a variation on the sweet-and-sour theme, and can be used in both plain (grilled Italian sausages) and fancy (roast pork or even turkey) menus. Choose cipollini of equal size so they cook at the same time. At my market recently, some onions were twice as large as others.

18 cipollini (about 1 pound)	2 tablespoons balsamic vinegar
2 tablespoons (¼ stick) unsalted butter	1 tablespoon honey
½ cup reduced-sodium chicken broth	Kosher salt and freshly ground black pepper
3 sprigs fresh rosemary or ¼ teaspoon crumbled dried	

1. Bring a medium saucepan of water to a boil over high heat. Add the cipollini and cook just until the skins loosen, about 1 minute. Drain and rinse them under cold running water. Using a paring knife, trim the tops and bottoms from the onions and peel them. Pierce a deep slash in the top of each onion. (The slash will help the onions keep their shape during cooking.)

2. Melt the butter in a large skillet over medium-high heat. Add the onions and spread them in a single layer. Cook, turning occasionally, until they are lightly browned on both flat sides, about 3 minutes. Add ½ cup water with the broth and rosemary and bring them to a boil. Reduce the heat to medium-low and cover tightly. Simmer, flipping the onions after 5 minutes, until they are tender when pierced with the tip of the knife, about 10 minutes. Discard the rosemary sprigs.

3. Uncover the skillet and increase the heat to high. Boil until the liquid has reduced to about 1 tablespoon. Reduce the heat to medium-low. Drizzle in the vinegar and honey. Gently stir the mixture until the liquid forms a thick glaze to coat the onions. Season to taste with salt and pepper.

CLASSIC CREAMED ONIONS

MAKES 4 TO 6 SERVINGS

Serve with roast turkey, roast pork and chops, or baked ham.

Prep Time: 15 minutes

Cooking Time: 45 minutes

Make Ahead: The creamed onions can be prepared up to 1 day ahead.

Family Favorite, Holiday Feasts, Company Fare, Buffet Dish, Retro Recipe, Cooking Classic

This is another classic American side dish that is on countless Thanksgiving tables every year. My version uses a few tricks to be sure that the onions have plenty of flavor and are more than just plain onions in dull white sauce. I usually make this with fresh onions, as befits a holiday dish for company. However, frozen onions are a very good option and do not need the extra preparation of peeling and cooking. And for a large holiday dinner, when you may have to make a double or triple batch, frozen onions could be the ticket.

1 pound white boiling or red, yellow, or white baby (pearl) onions

1 bay leaf

2 cups reduced-sodium chicken broth, as needed

2 tablespoons (¼ stick) unsalted butter (plus 1 tablespoon butter, cut into cubes, if making the sauce ahead)

2 tablespoons all-purpose flour

½ cup half-and-half, or more as needed

Kosher salt and freshly ground black pepper

Pinch of freshly grated nutmeg

1 tablespoon finely chopped fresh flat-leaf parsley

1. Bring a medium saucepan of water to a boil over high heat. Add the onions and cook just until the skins loosen, about 1 minute. Drain and rinse them under cold water. Using a paring knife, trim the tops and bottoms from the onions and peel them. Pierce the side of each onion with the tip of the knife. (The slash will help the onions keep their shape during cooking.)

2. Spread the onions in a single layer in a medium skillet. Add the bay leaf and enough broth to barely cover the onions and bring it to a boil over high heat. Reduce the heat to medium-low and cover the skillet. Simmer until the onions are tender, 12 to 15 minutes for the boiling onions and 8 to 10 minutes for the baby onions. Using a slotted spoon, transfer the onions to a bowl. Measure and reserve ½ cup of the cooking liquid; discard the bay leaf and remaining liquid. (The onions can be cooled, stored in a plastic zip-tight bag, and refrigerated for up to 1 day.)

3. Melt the butter in a medium saucepan over medium-low heat. Whisk in the flour and let it bubble without browning for 1 minute. Whisk in the reserved cooking liquid and half-and-half and bring them to a simmer over medium heat. Reduce the heat to low and simmer, whisking often, until the sauce has no raw flour taste, about 5 minutes. Season to taste with salt, pepper, and nutmeg. (The sauce can be made up to 2 hours ahead. Dot the top of the sauce with the additional 1 tablespoon cubed butter and store in the saucepan at room temperature. Reheat it over low heat, whisking often, until hot, about 5 minutes. If the sauce is too thick, thin it to the desired consistency with half-and-half.)

4. Add the onions and cook, stirring often, until they are heated through, about 3 minutes. Transfer the creamed onions to a serving dish, sprinkle them with the parsley, and serve.

WINE-GLAZED SHALLOTS WITH THYME

MAKES 6 TO 8 SERVINGS

Serve with red meat roasts and chops.
Prep Time: 10 minutes
Cooking Time: 25 minutes
Make Ahead: The shallots can be refrigerated for up to 1 day.
Holiday Feasts, Company Fare

*W*hole shallots, braised until tender with a glaze made from the cooking juices, are a wonderful side dish to red meats and roast chicken. Since they are as rich as they are delicious, allow only a couple of shallots per serving, and serve them with lighter fare, such as steamed spinach or asparagus.

16 whole large shallots, peeled

1 tablespoon unsalted butter

½ cup hearty red wine, such as Shiraz

½ cup reduced-sodium beef or chicken broth

¼ teaspoon kosher salt

⅛ teaspoon freshly ground black pepper

One 3-inch sprig fresh thyme, plus 1 teaspoon finely chopped

Pinch of sugar

1. If the shallots consist of two lobes, separate the lobes. Otherwise, cut each shallot in half vertically, from the stem end to the bottom, keeping the halves intact.

2. Melt the butter in a large skillet over medium heat. Add the shallots, flat-side down, and cook until the undersides are lightly browned, 3 to 4 minutes. Flip the shallots and brown the other sides, about 3 minutes more.

3. Add the wine, broth, salt, pepper, thyme sprig, and sugar and stir gently to combine. Bring them to a boil. Reduce the heat to medium-low and cover. Simmer until the shallots are almost tender when pierced with the tip of a small, sharp knife, about 10 minutes. Uncover and increase the heat to medium-high. Boil until the liquid has reduced to about 2 tablespoons, about 5 minutes. (The shallots can be cooled, covered, and refrigerated for up to 1 day. Reheat in a covered microwave-safe bowl in a microwave oven at Medium-High power for 3 to 5 minutes.) Discard the thyme sprig.

4. Transfer the glazed shallots to a serving dish and sprinkle them with the chopped thyme. Serve hot.

Parsley Root

Celery root is not related to celery, but real honest-to-goodness parsley does sprout from parsley root. In fact, parsley root is usually sold with its tops, which is one way to tell it from a parsnip, which it closely resembles. Parsley root can be used as an alternative to (or in tandem with) parsnips or carrots in recipes, so you really have quite a lot of ways to use this uncommon vegetable.

Peak Season: October to March, available all year.

Purchase: Pale beige roots with fresh-looking green tops (if attached).

Store: Refrigerate tops for up to 3 days, and roots for up to 2 weeks.

Preparation: Cut off the tops, if attached. Scrub the parsley roots well before using; they do not need to be peeled, although I usually do for a smoother appearance.

PARSLEY ROOT AND CARROTS WITH HONEY WALNUTS
MAKES 4 SERVINGS

Serve with roast pork, pork chops, roast chicken, roast turkey, or roast duck.
Prep Time: 10 minutes
Cooking Time: 8 minutes
Weeknight Suppers, Family Favorite, Holiday Feasts, Buffet Dish, Vegetarian

This recipe is an excellent way to make the acquaintance of parsley root. The color contrast of the beige parsley roots and orange carrots makes a very attractive dish. Tart lemons and slightly bitter walnuts balance the vegetable's sweetness.

6 parsley roots (about 10 ounces total), cut into
   ½-inch rounds
2 carrots, cut into ½-inch rounds
1 tablespoon unsalted butter
1 tablespoon fresh lemon juice

1 tablespoon honey
1 tablespoon finely chopped fresh flat-leaf parsley
Kosher salt and freshly ground black pepper
⅓ cup toasted and chopped walnuts (see page 33)

1. Bring a medium saucepan of salted water to a boil over high heat. Add the parsley roots and carrots and cook until just tender, about 5 minutes. Drain the vegetables, rinse them under cold running water, and drain again. (The vegetables can be patted dry with paper towels, stored in a plastic zip-tight bag, and refrigerated for up to 1 day.)
2. Melt the butter in a large skillet over medium-high heat. Add the vegetables and cook, stirring often, until heated through, about 2 minutes. Add the lemon juice, honey, and parsley and stir well. Season to taste with salt and pepper. Stir in the walnuts. Serve hot.

Parsnips

The parsnip is actually sweeter after it has been exposed to a hard frost before harvest, making it a true winter vegetable. It looks and tastes like a big, pale carrot, but its tough skin is always peeled. You can use oversized parsnips (often the only ones available at the market) if the tough bitter core is trimmed out before cooking. Balance its sweet flavor by combining it with other root vegetables, or play up the sugar by using it with autumn fruits.

Peak Season: October to March; available all year.

Purchase: Narrow, evenly shaped parsnips without any nicks, soft spots, or tiny roots growing from the sides.

Store: Refrigerate for up to 2 weeks.

Preparation: Peel before use. If the taproot is very thin, cut it off and discard it. Cut very large and wide parsnips in half lengthwise, then trim out the tough core. Parsnip flesh discolors when exposed to oxygen, so use it immediately or store in a bowl of acidulated water (with 1 tablespoon vinegar or lemon juice to every quart of water).

PARSNIP, APPLE, AND BACON HASH

MAKES 4 TO 6 SERVINGS

Serve with roast pork, pork chops, roast chicken, or sautéed chicken breasts.
Prep Time: 10 minutes
Cooking Time: 25 minutes
Weeknight Suppers, Family Favorite, Holiday Feasts, Company Fare, Buffet Dish,
Retro Recipe, Cooking Classic, Vegetarian

Two harbingers of fall, parsnips and apples, are paired for a hash that goes beautifully with dishes that have deep, caramelized flavors. I first served this recipe with pan-cooked chicken finished with a cider sauce, but it also is a winner with pork roast and gravy.

4 medium parsnips (about 1 pound), peeled and
  cut into ½-inch dice
3 bacon slices, coarsely chopped
1 Granny Smith apple, peeled, cored, and cut into
  ½-inch dice

1 tablespoon finely chopped shallot
1 teaspoon finely chopped fresh rosemary or sage
Kosher salt and freshly ground black pepper

1. Bring a medium saucepan of lightly salted water to a boil over high heat. Add the parsnips and cook just until they're barely tender, about 10 minutes. Drain, rinse them under cold running water, and pat dry.

2. Meanwhile, cook the bacon in a large skillet over medium heat, stirring occasionally, until it is crisp and browned, about 8 minutes. Using a slotted spoon, transfer the bacon to paper towels to drain.

3. Pour off all but 1 tablespoon of the bacon fat from the skillet and return it to medium heat. Add the apple and cook, stirring occasionally, until it is beginning to brown, about 3 minutes. Add the parsnips and cook, turning occasionally, until they are lightly browned, 5 to 7 minutes. Stir in the shallot and rosemary and cook until the shallot softens, about 2 minutes more. Season to taste with salt and pepper. Transfer the hash to a serving dish and serve.

PARSNIP OVEN FRIES WITH LEMON-PEPPER SALT

MAKES 4 TO 6 SERVINGS

Serve with roasted red meats and poultry, sausages, or salmon fillets.
Prep Time: 10 minutes
Cooking Time: 40 minutes
Weeknight Suppers, Holiday Feasts, Vegetarian

Thick sticks of parsnips roasted into "fries" are so tasty that they give the standard potato version a run for their money. Parsnips are naturally sweet, so I often add tart or spicy as a counterpoint—here, I use both lemon and pepper with coarse salt. Look for large, wide parsnips, as they are easiest to cut into fries.

2 pounds large, wide parsnips, peeled
2 tablespoons olive oil
Finely grated zest of 1 lemon

1 teaspoon kosher salt
½ teaspoon freshly ground black pepper

1. Position a rack in the center of the oven and preheat the oven to 425°F.
2. Cut the parsnips into thick sticks about 3 inches long and ¾ inch square. Spread the parsnips on a large, rimmed baking sheet. Drizzle and toss them with the oil to coat.
3. Roast until the parsnips can be easily released from the baking sheet with a metal spatula, about 20 minutes. Flip them over and continue roasting until they are golden brown and tender, 15 to 20 minutes longer.
4. In a small bowl, use your fingertips to rub the lemon zest, salt, and pepper together until well combined. Sprinkle the lemon salt over the parsnips and serve hot.

ROASTED PARSNIP AND PEAR PURÉE

MAKES 4 SERVINGS

Serve with venison roast or chops, or roast duck.
Prep Time: 10 minutes
Cooking Time: 30 minutes
Make Ahead: The purée can be made up to 2 days ahead.
Weeknight Suppers, Holiday Feasts, Company Fare, Buffet Dish, Vegetarian

Game has rich, deep flavors that need to be matched with equally intense sides. This mash, which is sweet and starchy at the same time, was a big success when I offered it alongside grilled venison with a red wine sauce. It is also a boon at a complicated meal (as game dinners tend to be because of accompanying sauces) because it can be made ahead and reheated just before serving. Finding ripe pears to use the day of purchase is an iffy proposition; buy them a few days ahead and let them ripen at room temperature.

1½ pounds parsnips, peeled and cut into 1-inch chunks

1 tablespoon vegetable oil

2 ripe, juicy pears, such as Comice or Anjou, peeled, cored, and cut into ½-inch wedges

2 tablespoons unsalted butter, at room temperature

1 tablespoon sherry vinegar

Kosher salt and freshly ground black pepper

1. Position a rack in the center of the oven and preheat the oven to 400ºF.

2. Toss the parsnips and oil on a large rimmed baking sheet and spread them in a single layer. Roast, stirring occasionally, until the parsnips are browned and almost tender, about 20 minutes. Add the pears to the baking sheet and stir to combine them with the parsnips and the oil. Continue roasting until the parsnips are tender and the pears are beginning to brown, about 10 minutes more.

3. Transfer the parsnips and pears to a food processor. Add the butter and vinegar and process them into a chunky purée. (The mixture can also be mashed by hand in a medium bowl with a potato masher.) Season to taste with salt and pepper. (The purée can be cooled, covered, and refrigerated for up to 2 days. Reheat in a nonstick skillet over medium-low heat, stirring often.) Serve hot.

Potatoes

The superstars of the side dish world, potatoes are transformed into some of the most delicious and iconic accompaniments in the canon: mashed potatoes, hash browns, and French fries are but a few. Choosing the right potato for the recipe is the first step. **Baking potatoes** are especially starchy and have a dry, fluffy texture and therefore are ideal for baking. The most common examples are russets, although you may see such similar brown-skinned varieties named for where they were grown: Maine, Eastern, Idaho, or Long Island are a few. **Boiling potatoes** hold their shape well after cooking in water and are often named for the color of their skins: white, red, and red bliss are examples. Their cooked interiors are waxy, firm, and shiny. **New potatoes** are immature boiling potatoes, picked while they are about the size of a Ping-Pong ball. **Yukon Golds** have characteristics of both varieties and can be used for both baking and boiling. Some heirloom or unusual varieties, such as fingerlings and blue potatoes, are also multipurpose.

Peak Season: Available all year.

Purchase: Smooth, dry potatoes without any eyes or soft spots.

Store: Uncovered in a cool, dark place (but not the refrigerator), away from onions (which give off gases that speed the spoilage of both vegetables).

Preparation: Potatoes can be peeled or not, according to taste and the recipe. If you don't peel them, scrub the potatoes well under cold running water. Green areas occur when the potato is exposed to too much sunlight; as this is toxic, be sure to remove the green parts before cooking.

Baked Potatoes

CLASSIC BAKED POTATOES
MAKES 4 SERVINGS

Serve with roast beef and steak.
Prep Time: 10 minutes
Cooking Time: 50 minutes
Weeknight Suppers, Family Favorite, Holiday Feasts, Company Fare, Buffet Dish, Cooking Classic, Vegetarian

Everyone knows how to bake potatoes—or do they? The perfect specimen has an appealing dry skin and a fluffy interior, but that perfection can be elusive, and there are a few tricks. For the times when you need a side dish in a hurry, use the microwave variation (although the dry heat of the oven makes the best potato skins.) Here are some tips to give you great results every time.

• While you can bake a huge baked potato as a main course, for a side dish, a more reasonably sized spud (6 to 8 ounces) is in order. For larger potatoes, increase the baking time accordingly. It can take a full hour or more to bake a 12-ounce potato.
• Never wrap the potato in aluminum foil before baking. This creates steam that softens the skins, and you want the skins exposed to the heat of the oven to dry out a bit.
• For the classic steakhouse flavor, use starchy baking potatoes (such as russets). Yukon Golds are also good, but they have a more waxy interior.
• Oil the outside of the potato lightly with vegetable or olive oil to attract the oven heat to the surface and help crisp the skin.
• The potato skin will probably get eaten, so season it well with salt before baking. Also, the salt will help dry the potato surface for a crispier skin.
• Baked potatoes can be kept warm in a warm, turned-off oven for up to 1 hour. After that, they lose their pillowy texture.
• See the sidebar opposite for some ideas for baked potato toppings.

4 baking potatoes, such as russets (about 7 ounces each)

Vegetable oil, for coating the potatoes

Kosher salt

Unsalted butter, for serving

Freshly ground black pepper

1. Position a rack in the center of the oven and preheat the oven to 400°F.

2. Scrub the potatoes under cold running water. Deeply pierce each potato a couple of times with a meat fork. Place them on a large rimmed baking sheet. Coat the potatoes with a drizzle of oil, rubbing them all over with your hands. Season them all over with salt.

3. Bake them for 30 minutes. Flip the potatoes over and continue baking until they are tender when pierced with the tip of a small, sharp knife, about 15 minutes more.

4. Protecting your hand with a clean kitchen towel, hold a potato at both ends with one hand. Cut a long, lengthwise slit into the potato. Squeeze from both ends at the same time, and the potato will pop open. Transfer it to a dinner plate and top with butter. Serve with salt and pepper for seasoning.

Microwaved Potatoes: Microwave the potatoes on High for 4 minutes. Flip them over and continue baking until they are tender when pierced with the tip of a small, sharp knife, about 4 minutes more. Let them stand for 5 minutes before serving. If microwaving more than four potatoes at once, increase the microwave time by 1 minute for each additional potato.

BAKED POTATO TOPPINGS

The toppings for a side dish of baked potatoes should be simple, with a minimum of meat. Remember that this is not the main course. A little bacon is OK, but chili would be too filling. On the other hand, when I am offered a choice of toppings at a steakhouse, I usually go "all the way" with a little bit of everything. (Reminding me of the quote from Oscar Wilde: "Everything in moderation, including moderation.")

- Sour cream or crème fraîche
- Cooked and crumbled bacon or pancetta
- Finely chopped fresh chives or scallions
- Mojo with olive oil and minced garlic (page 221)
- Plain Greek yogurt with feta cheese, minced garlic, and fresh dill
- Roast garlic cloves (see page 159) mashed with softened butter
- Caramelized onions, cooked bacon, and smoked Gouda cheese
- Crumbled blue cheese (such as Gorgonzola or Roquefort) and crème fraîche
- Crumbled goat cheese with chopped pitted kalamata olives
- Cooked, chopped broccoli florets with Cheddar cheese
- Freshly grated Parmesan cheese with chopped fresh basil

- Buttered Fresh Peas with Lettuce (page 111)
- Romesco (page 431)
- The Best Ranch Dressing (page 344)
- Pesto, Kale Pesto, or Ramp Pesto (pages 425–426), with or without sour cream or crème fraîche

DOUBLE-BAKED POTATOES WITH GOAT CHEESE AND CREMINI MUSHROOMS

MAKES 6 SERVINGS

Serve with roast beef or lamb, steaks, or chops.

Prep Time: 10 minutes

Cooking Time: 1 hour, 35 minutes

Make Ahead: The potatoes can be prepared up to 8 hours ahead.

Family Favorite, Holiday Feasts, Company Fare, Vegetarian

Baked potatoes are tempting enough, but when they are stuffed with cheese and vegetables, they move into the higher echelon of indulgence. Feel free to substitute your favorite blue cheese (Roquefort or Gorgonzola, for example) for the goat cheese.

3 large baking potatoes, such as russets (about 12 ounces each), scrubbed

Vegetable oil, for coating the potatoes

Kosher salt

2 tablespoons (¼ stick) unsalted butter (1 tablespoon cut into small cubes)

12 ounces coarsely chopped cremini or white button mushrooms

2 scallions (white and green parts), finely chopped

1 cup crumbled goat cheese (4 ounces)

⅓ cup heavy cream

Freshly ground black pepper

3 tablespoons freshly grated Parmesan cheese

1. Position a rack in the center of the oven and preheat the oven to 400°F.

2. Pierce each potato a few times with a fork. Coat the potatoes with a drizzle of oil, rubbing them all over with your hands. Season the skins with salt. Bake the potatoes directly on the oven rack until tender, about 1 hour. Reduce the oven temperature to 350°F.

3. Meanwhile, melt 1 tablespoon of the butter in a large nonstick skillet over medium heat. Add the mushrooms and cook, stirring often, until the juices evaporate and the mushrooms are beginning to brown, about 8 minutes. Stir in the scallions and cook, stirring occasionally, until they soften, about 2 minutes.

4. Protecting your hand with a clean kitchen towel, hold a potato at both ends with one hand. Cut a long, lengthwise slit into the potato and scoop the cooked potato flesh into a large bowl, leaving the skin intact. Repeat with the remaining potatoes. Add the goat cheese and heavy cream to the potato flesh and mash with a handheld masher or electric mixer. Stir in the mushroom mixture and season with salt and pepper. Mound the mashed potatoes into the potato skins. Place the potatoes on a baking sheet. Sprinkle the tops with the Parmesan, and dot with the remaining 1 tablespoon cubed butter. (The potatoes can be loosely covered with plastic wrap and refrigerated for up to 8 hours. Let stand at room temperature for 1 hour before the final baking.)

5. Bake the potatoes until they are heated through and the tops are browned, about 25 minutes. Serve hot.

Whipped, Mashed, and Smashed Potatoes

PERFECT WHIPPED POTATOES

MAKES 6 SERVINGS

Serve with roast beef; grilled and pan-cooked steaks; braised beef dishes; roast pork; grilled and pan-cooked pork chops; roast chicken; fried chicken; or grilled and pan-cooked salmon.

Prep Time: 10 minutes

Cooking Time: 25 minutes

Weeknight Suppers, Family Favorite, Holiday Feasts, Company Fare, Buffet Dish, Cooking Classic, Vegetarian

Mashed potatoes are an old-fashioned comfort food that never goes out of style. Over the years, I've learned many little tricks that will ensure the very best mashed potatoes you've ever had. And there are lots of quick ways to add ingredients and gussy up a bowl of plain spuds; see the variations after the basic recipe. Here's a rundown of my tips:

• The peeled, chunked potatoes can be prepared and stored in cold unsalted water to cover, for up to 8 hours at cool room temperature or refrigerated.

• For fluffy mashed potatoes, use floury, brown-skinned baking potatoes, such as russets. Yukon Golds are another option. Waxy thin-skinned boiling potatoes absorb too much water and retain their shape too well to make smooth mashed potatoes.

• Start cooking the potatoes in cold water to gradually soften their exteriors. If the potatoes are added to boiling water, the outsides will fall apart and get mushy by the time the interiors are cooked.

• I am usually not fussy about warming serving bowls, but mashed potatoes cool off quickly, so they are an exception. It's an easy matter to drain the hot cooking water from the potatoes into a heatproof serving bowl in the sink. The water will heat the bowl as you finish the potatoes. Empty out the water, give the bowl a quick wipe, and you are good to go.

• After draining, return the potatoes to the cooking pot and cook them over medium heat, stirring almost constantly, until they start to leave a thin film on the bottom of the pot. This extra cooking drives excess moisture from the potatoes to give them a lighter, drier texture.

• My favorite implement for mashing is a handheld mixer. However, as my friend the food stylist Marie Haycox often reminds me, a mixer makes whipped, not mashed, potatoes. I also like using a mixer because, unlike a ricer or masher, it can be used for many other jobs.

• A potato ricer is another popular tool for mashing potatoes. After drying the potatoes in the pot, transfer the potatoes to a bowl, then rice them back into the warm pot to help keep them from cooling too quickly.

• If you prefer a chunkier mash, use a handheld potato masher.

• Never use a handheld stick blender or a food processor for mashing potatoes. These super-choppers release too much of the potatoes' cellulose and make them sticky.

• Use softened butter and warm milk when mashing the potatoes. If cold, these ingredients can cause lumps.

3 pounds baking potatoes, such as russets, peeled
  and cut into 2-inch chunks
4 tablespoons (½ stick) unsalted butter, at room
  temperature, plus more for serving

½ cup whole milk, warmed
Kosher salt and freshly ground white or black
  pepper

1. Put the potatoes in a large saucepan and add enough cold salted water to cover them by 1 inch. Cover the saucepan and bring it to a boil over high heat. Reduce the heat to medium-low and set the lid ajar. Cook the potatoes at a steady simmer until they are tender when pierced with the tip of a small, sharp knife, 20 to 25 minutes.

2. Place a heatproof serving bowl in the sink. Drain the potatoes into it, letting the hot water fill the bowl. Return the drained potatoes to the saucepan. Cook them over low heat, stirring almost constantly, until the potatoes begin to film the bottom of the saucepan, about 2 minutes. Remove from the heat.

3. Add the butter to the potatoes. Using a handheld electric mixer on medium speed, whip the potatoes until smooth. Gradually mix in the milk. Season to taste with salt and pepper.

4. Empty the hot water from the bowl and wipe out the bowl. Transfer the potatoes to the bowl, top them with additional butter, if using, and serve hot.

Buttermilk Mashed Potatoes: Substitute ½ cup buttermilk, heated just to remove its chill, for the milk and butter.

Herbed Mashed Potatoes: Mix 2 tablespoons finely chopped fresh chives, dill, oregano, or tarragon into the mashed potatoes.

Horseradish Mashed Potatoes: These are fantastic with grilled steaks. Add 2 tablespoons drained prepared horseradish to the mashed potatoes.

Italian Mascarpone Mashed Potatoes: Substitute ½ cup mascarpone cheese, at room temperature, for the butter and milk.

Parmesan Mashed Potatoes: Stir ½ cup freshly grated Parmesan cheese (2 ounces) into the mashed potatoes.

Roquefort Mashed Potatoes: Stir ½ cup well-crumbled Roquefort or Gorgonzola cheese (2 ounces) into the mashed potatoes.

Smoked Gouda Mashed Potatoes: Stir ¾ cup shredded smoked Gouda (3 ounces) into the mashed potatoes.

Sour Cream and Chive Mashed Potatoes: Substitute ½ cup sour cream, at room temperature, for the milk. Stir in 3 tablespoons minced fresh chives.

MAKE-AHEAD MASHED POTATO CASSEROLE
MAKES 10 TO 12 SERVINGS

Serve with roast beef, pork, chicken, or turkey.
Prep Time: 20 minutes
Cooking Time: 1 hour
Make Ahead: The casserole can be made up to 1 day ahead.
Family Favorite, Holiday Feasts, Company Fare, Buffet Dish, Cooking Classic, Vegetarian

Anyone who has had to make a mountain of mashed potatoes for a big holiday dinner knows that it can be quite a mad dash to get the potatoes on the table in a timely manner. When faced with a crowd, I prepare this casserole the day before and bake it with the other side dishes. Thanks, Katy Keck, for this recipe, which is now part of my family's culinary heritage.

5 pounds baking potatoes, such as russets, peeled and cut into 2-inch chunks

8 ounces cream cheese, cut into chunks, at room temperature

1 cup sour cream

½ cup whole milk

8 tablespoons (1 stick) unsalted butter (6 tablespoons at room temperature, 2 tablespoons cut into small cubes), plus softened butter for the baking dish

Kosher salt and freshly ground black or white pepper

1. Put the potatoes in a large pot and add enough cold salted water to cover them by 1 inch. Cover the pot and bring it to a boil over high heat. Set the lid ajar and reduce the heat to medium-low. Cook the potatoes at a steady simmer until they are barely tender when pierced with the tip of a small, sharp knife, 20 to 25 minutes. Drain the potatoes well.

2. Return the potatoes to the pot. Cook them over medium-low heat, stirring almost constantly, until the potatoes begin to film the bottom of the pot, about 3 minutes. Add the cream cheese. Using a handheld electric mixer, whip the potatoes until the cream cheese melts. Add the sour cream, milk, and the 6 tablespoons room-temperature butter, and mix well. Season to taste with salt and pepper.

3. Lightly butter a 13 × 9 × 2-inch baking dish. Transfer the potato mixture to the dish and smooth the top. Dot the top of the casserole with the 2 tablespoons of cubed butter. Let cool completely. Cover with plastic wrap and refrigerate for up to 1 day. Remove from the refrigerator 1 hour before the final baking.

4. Meanwhile, position a rack in the center of the oven and preheat the oven to 375ºF.

5. Uncover the casserole. Bake it until the top is lightly browned and the casserole is heated through, about 30 minutes. Serve hot.

MASCARPONE POTATOES DUCHESSE
MAKES 6 TO 8 SERVINGS

Serve with roast beef, veal, pork, or lamb.

Prep Time: 15 minutes

Cooking Time: 40 minutes

Make Ahead: The potatoes can be prepared up to 8 hours ahead.

Family Favorite, Holiday Feasts, Company Fare, Buffet Dish, Cooking Classic, Vegetarian

This is the original make-ahead mashed potato dish—if you were a trained chef, you had to be able to make this with your eyes closed. Some cooks bake the swirls and reheat them just before serving, and I admit that it is convenient. But for the best flavor, I prefer to bake them right before serving. And while you can simply spoon the potato mixture into mounds, a pastry bag and tip give them a professional look. The recipe is easy to expand for more servings. I also use the potatoes to stuff artichoke bottoms (page 19) for a very elegant side dish for extra-special roasts.

POTATOES DUCHESSE

1½ pounds baking potatoes, such as russets, peeled and cut into 1½-inch chunks

¼ cup mascarpone cheese or sour cream

2 large egg yolks

1 teaspoon kosher salt

¼ teaspoon freshly ground white or black pepper

1 tablespoon unsalted butter, melted

2 tablespoons freshly grated Parmesan cheese

1. To prepare the potatoes duchesse: Put the potatoes in a medium saucepan and add enough cold salted water to cover them by 1 inch. Cover the saucepan and bring it to a boil over high heat. Reduce the heat to medium-low and set the lid ajar. Cook the potatoes at a steady simmer until they are tender when pierced with the tip of a small, sharp knife, 20 to 25 minutes.

2. Drain the potatoes and return them to the saucepan. Cook them over low heat, stirring almost constantly, until the potatoes begin to film the bottom of the saucepan, about 2 minutes. Remove them from the heat and let cool for 5 minutes.

3. Add the mascarpone to the saucepan. Using a potato masher or a handheld electric mixer on low speed, beat the potatoes until smooth. Beat in the yolks, salt, and pepper. (The mashed potato mixture can be covered and refrigerated for up to 8 hours.)

4. Position a rack in the center of the oven and preheat the oven to 400ºF. Line a large rimmed baking sheet with parchment paper.

5. Fit a pastry bag with a ½-inch-diameter open star tip. Fill the bag with the mashed potato mixture. Pipe 8 swirls of the mashed potato mixture onto the lined baking sheet, making each swirl about 2 inches wide and 2½ inches tall. Or make 6 swirls of a slightly larger size. (The potato swirls can be loosely covered with plastic wrap and refrigerated for up to 8 hours.) Brush the swirls with the melted butter and sprinkle them with the Parmesan.

6. Bake until the swirls are golden brown, about 20 minutes. Transfer them to a serving platter and serve at once.

CHAMP POTATO MASH WITH BUTTERY SCALLIONS
MAKES 6 SERVINGS

Serve with meat and poultry roasts, steaks, chops, or stews.
Prep Time: 10 minutes
Cooking Time: 30 minutes
Weeknight Suppers, Family Favorite, Holiday Feasts, Company Fare, Buffet Dish,
Cooking Classic, Vegetarian

Potatoes and Ireland are forever linked, and along with colcannon, champ is synonymous with the country's cuisine. This specific dish of mashed potatoes and scallions with lots of butter got its name from the old Irish word champ, *which means "to bruise" (and because they are pounded, they are sometimes called "poundies"). For a real treat or for a dinner with company, I make champ with Irish butter, made from pasture-raised cows, and the flavor difference is astonishing.*

3 pounds baking potatoes, such as russets, peeled and cut into 2-inch chunks

6 tablespoons (¾ stick) unsalted butter, preferably Irish, such as Kerrygold

6 large scallions (white and green parts), finely chopped

½ cup whole milk, warmed

Kosher salt and freshly ground white or black pepper

1. Put the potatoes in a large saucepan and add enough cold salted water to cover the potatoes by 1 inch. Cover the saucepan and bring it to a boil over high heat. Reduce the heat to medium-low and set the lid ajar. Cook the potatoes at a steady simmer until they are tender when pierced with the tip of a small, sharp knife, 20 to 25 minutes.

2. Place a heatproof serving bowl in the sink. Drain the potatoes into it, letting the hot water fill the bowl. Return the drained potatoes to the saucepan. Cook them over low heat, stirring almost constantly, until the potatoes begin to film the bottom of the saucepan, about 2 minutes. Remove them from the heat. Cover the saucepan with a clean kitchen towel and set the pan aside while cooking the scallions. (The kitchen towel will absorb even more of the steam while keeping the potatoes warm.)

3. Melt the butter in a medium skillet over medium heat. Pour half of the butter into a small bowl and set it aside. Add the scallions to the skillet and cook, stirring often, until they're softened, about 2 minutes. Remove from the heat.

4. Using a potato masher, mash the potatoes with the milk until smooth. Beat in the scallion butter. Season to taste with salt and pepper.

5. Empty the hot water from the bowl and wipe out the bowl. Transfer the potatoes to the bowl and make a well in the center. Pour the reserved melted butter into the well, and serve.

GARLICKY SMASHED POTATOES

MAKES 6 SERVINGS.

Serve with meat and poultry roasts, steaks, chops, or stews.
Prep Time: 10 minutes
Cooking Time: 25 minutes
Weeknight Suppers, Family Favorite, Buffet Dish, Retro Recipe, Vegetarian

Smashed potatoes have a comforting texture similar to mashed potatoes, but, because no peeling is required, they are perfect for weeknight meals when time is of the essence. In this version, garlic-flavored olive oil replaces the butter and milk of standard-issue mashed potatoes. Use a thin-skinned potato, such as Yukon Gold or an heirloom variety, such as fingerlings or blue potatoes. I also like to make this when I want to showcase the flavor of the potatoes.

3 pounds boiling potatoes, such as Yukon Gold, scrubbed
⅓ cup extra-virgin olive oil

2 garlic cloves, thinly sliced
Kosher salt and freshly ground black pepper

1. Put the potatoes in a large saucepan and add enough cold salted water to cover by 1 inch. Cover the saucepan and bring it to a boil over high heat. Reduce the heat to medium-low and remove the lid. Simmer until the potatoes are tender when pierced with the tip of a small, sharp knife, about 25 minutes. Drain the potatoes and return them to the pot.

2. Heat the oil and garlic together in a small skillet over medium heat, stirring often, until the garlic is bubbling in the oil but not browned, about 1 minute. Remove it from the heat.

3. Using a large slotted spoon, smash the potatoes into a chunky texture. Add the garlic and its oil and fold them into the potatoes. Season to taste with salt and pepper. Transfer the potatoes to a serving bowl and serve.

SMOKED AND SMASHED BBQ POTATOES

MAKES 6 SERVINGS

Serve with barbecued meats and poultry.
Prep Time: 10 minutes
Cooking Time: 1 hour
Company Fare, Buffet Dish, Vegetarian

And now for an entirely different way to make mashed potatoes—smoked on the grill. Sweet fruit-wood, such as apple or cherry, works best, as some of the most assertive woods (mesquite and hickory) are a bit too strong for this. The spiced butter at the end adds a fillip, but I have served them with just a dollop of plain butter and a sprinkle of chopped scallions, too. I usually grill boneless chicken breasts or pork chops directly over the heat source while the potatoes cook with indirect heat on the opposite ("empty") side of the grill.

2 large handfuls of apple, cherry, or pecan wood chips, soaked in water for at least 30 minutes

2 pounds small new potatoes, scrubbed

1 tablespoon olive oil

2 tablespoons (¼ stick) unsalted butter, at room temperature

2 teaspoons chili powder

½ teaspoon smoked paprika (Pimentón de la Vera)

¼ teaspoon garlic powder

Kosher salt

1. Prepare an outdoor grill for indirect cooking over medium-low heat (350º to 400ºF). For a charcoal grill, let the coals burn until they are covered with white ash and you can hold your hand about 1 inch above the cooking grate for about 3 seconds. For a gas grill, preheat on high and adjust the thermostat to medium-low (350ºF). Set up a smoker box in the gas grill according to the manufacturer's instructions.

2. Scatter a handful of the drained chips over the coals or into the smoker box and let them build up a head of smoke. Spread the potatoes in a single layer in a metal baking dish and toss them with the oil. Place them in the dish on the unheated side of the grill (not over the heat source).

3. Cook, with the lid closed, until the potatoes are tender, about 1 hour, adding the remaining drained chips to the coals or smoker box after 20 minutes. For a charcoal grill, after 40 minutes of cooking, add 12 briquets (or small chunks of hardwood charcoal) to the coals to maintain the heat.

4. Meanwhile, in a small bowl, mash the butter, chili powder, smoked paprika, and garlic powder together to combine. Set them aside at room temperature.

5. Transfer the smoked potatoes to a large serving bowl. Using a potato masher or wooden spoon, coarsely smash the potatoes. Add the spiced butter and toss until the butter has melted and coated the potatoes. Season to taste with salt. Serve hot.

Potato Gratins and Casseroles

This rib-sticking category includes French gratins, American scalloped potatoes, and even Passover potato kugels.

- These dishes are often made from sliced potatoes, which cook best if they are cut into uniform rounds with a mandoline, plastic V-slicer, food processor, or a large knife and a steady hand. If you wish, cut the potatoes lengthwise into wide slabs, which doesn't seem to affect the cooking one way or another, but makes the gratin look a little more elegant than the standard version.

- A mandoline is a very efficient tool, but, in my opinion, its size, cost, and learning curve have always made it more useful for chefs than for home cooks. There are many light and sturdy plastic V-slicers on the market that do the same job for a smaller investment of cash and practice time. However, V-slicers still have very sharp blades and must be handled with caution. Always use the guard, and trim the food as necessary to give it a flat edge before cutting. If you wish, wear a cut-resistant glove made specifically for protection when operating a mandoline or slicer.

- The baking dish is an important factor. Earthenware is my first choice, as it holds the oven heat and transfers it directly to the cream for even cooking. Ceramic or enameled cast iron are also good choices, and I have made good gratins in a Pyrex dish. You serve the gratin directly from the dish, so it must be attractive, which is one reason why most cooks don't use metal. (The crust tends to scorch around the edges in a metal dish, too.) Rubbing the dish with garlic imparts a gentle flavor.

- Most gratins use starchy potatoes, such as russets, to give off their starch and help thicken the cream during baking. Yukon Golds are fine, but skip waxy, thin-skinned potatoes. You might find some varieties worth experimenting with at your farmer's market, but be sure that the farmer assures you that the potatoes are starchy.

- The potatoes in these dishes must be cooked to tenderness. To help them cook in a reasonable length of time, heat the cream (or milk) in a saucepan or the microwave until it is steaming. In either case, take care that the cream doesn't boil over. Also, it is important to cover the dish with buttered aluminum foil to create steam to cook the vegetables more quickly. The foil is removed toward the end of baking to expose the top and allow browning.

- Baked potato dishes have the best flavor if served right after baking. This can be impractical if the potatoes are sharing the oven with a main course. The best solution is to make the gratin early in the day and to store it in a cool place (but preferably not the refrigerator) a few hours before reheating. Covered with foil, it should take about 30 minutes at 350ºF to reheat. Remove the foil during the last few minutes of baking.

POTATOES AU GRATIN
MAKES 10 TO 12 SERVINGS

Serve with roast beef, steak, meat loaf, or ham.
Prep Time: 15 minutes
Cooking Time: 1 hour, 40 minutes

Make Ahead: The potatoes can be made up to 1 day ahead.

Family Favorite, Holiday Feasts, Company Fare, Buffet Dish, Cooking Classic, Vegetarian

An enduring classic on American steakhouse menus, potatoes au gratin is related to the French *family of gratins. The difference is that the vegetables are baked in a cheese sauce, and not just layered with cream, infusing every slice with cheese flavor.*

3 pounds baking potatoes, such as russets, peeled and cut into ⅛-inch rounds

¼ cup (½ stick) unsalted butter, plus more for the baking dish

¼ cup (33 grams) all-purpose flour

2½ cups whole milk, heated to steaming

1 cup shredded sharp Cheddar cheese (4 ounces)

1 cup shredded Gruyère or Swiss cheese (4 ounces)

Kosher salt and freshly ground black pepper

½ cup chopped yellow onion

1. Position a rack in the center of the oven and preheat the oven to 350°F. Lightly butter a 13 × 9 × 2-inch baking dish

2. Bring a large pot of salted water to a boil over high heat. Add the potatoes and cook until they are beginning to soften, about 5 minutes. Drain.

3. Melt the butter in a medium saucepan over medium-low heat. Whisk in the flour. Let it bubble without browning for 1 minute. Whisk in the milk. Cook, whisking often, until the sauce is simmering and thickened. Remove the pan from the heat. Mix the Cheddar and Gruyère together. Add 1½ cups of the cheese mixture to the sauce and stir until the cheeses melt. Season to taste with salt and pepper.

4. Spread half of the parcooked potatoes in the baking dish. Pour in half of the sauce, spread it evenly, and sprinkle with the onion. Repeat with the remaining potatoes and sauce.

5. Bake until the potatoes are just tender, about 1½ hours. Sprinkle the top with the remaining ½ cup cheese mixture. Increase the heat to 450°F and bake until the top of the gratin begins to brown, about 10 minutes. (The gratin can be cooled, covered with aluminum foil, and refrigerated for up to 1 day. Reheat, covered, in a preheated 350°F oven, until heated through, about 30 minutes.) Let it stand for 10 minutes, then serve hot.

CLASSIC SCALLOPED POTATOES
MAKES 10 TO 12 SERVINGS

Serve with roast beef, meat loaf, pork, and veal chops.

Prep Time: 15 minutes

Cooking Time: 2 hours

Make Ahead: The scalloped potatoes can be made up to 1 day ahead.

Family Favorite, Holiday Feasts, Company Fare, Buffet Dish, Cooking Classic, Vegetarian

Scalloped potatoes and potatoes au gratin share the same ingredients, but the former doesn't require a separately prepared sauce. This is another old-fashioned dish that gets high marks whenever I serve it.

4 tablespoons (½ stick) unsalted butter, cut into small pieces, plus softened butter for the baking dish and foil

1½ teaspoons kosher salt

½ teaspoon freshly ground black pepper

3½ pounds baking potatoes, such as russets, peeled and cut into ⅛-inch rounds

2 cups shredded sharp Cheddar cheese (8 ounces)

⅓ cup minced onion

3 tablespoons all-purpose flour

3 cups whole milk, heated to steaming

1. Position a rack in the center of the oven and preheat the oven to 400°F. Lightly butter a 13 × 9 × 2-inch baking dish. Butter the dull side of a sheet of aluminum foil to cover the dish.

2. Mix the salt and pepper together. Layer half of the potatoes in the prepared dish. Season the potatoes with half of the salt mixture and dot with 2 tablespoons of the butter. Sprinkle with 1 cup of the cheese, the onions, and the flour. Spread the remaining potatoes on top. Sprinkle with the remaining salt mixture and dot with the remaining 2 tablespoons butter. Pour the hot milk over it all. Cover the dish tightly with the foil, buttered-side down, and place the dish on a baking sheet.

3. Bake for 1½ hours. Uncover and sprinkle with the remaining 1 cup of the cheese. Continue baking, uncovered, until the potatoes are tender when pierced with the tip of a small, sharp knife, about 30 minutes. Let them stand for 10 minutes, then serve hot.

GRATIN DAUPHINOIS

MAKES 6 TO 8 SERVINGS

Serve with roast beef, pork, lamb steaks or chops, or roast chicken.

Prep Time: 15 minutes

Cooking Time: 1¾ hours

Make Ahead: The baked gratin can be cooled, covered, and refrigerated up to 4 hours ahead.

Family Favorite, Holiday Feasts, Company Fare, Buffet Dish, Cooking Classic, Vegetarian

A golden brown potato gratin, held together with cream and cheese, is one of the glories of French cuisine. It originated in the old Dauphiné province of southeast France, where rural households would turn two farm staples, cream and potatoes, into this filling and indescribably delicious casserole. Cheese is a later addition to the traditional recipe, but now it is considered de rigueur. This is one dish where you have to resist the temptation to cut the cream's calories with milk or broth. Not only is the flavor diminished, but the reduced fat will make the gratin curdle.

1 garlic clove, peeled

Softened butter, for the baking dish and foil

1½ teaspoons kosher salt

½ teaspoon freshly ground black pepper

A few fresh gratings of nutmeg

2½ pounds russet potatoes, peeled, cut on a mandoline or V-slicer into ¹⁄₁₆-inch rounds

1 cup shredded Gruyère cheese (about 4 ounces)

3 cups heavy cream, heated to steaming, as needed

1. Position a rack in the upper third of the oven and preheat the oven to 400°F. Rub the inside of an 11½ × 8 × 2-inch baking dish with the garlic clove, discarding any unused garlic. Butter the inside of the dish.

2. In a small bowl, mix the salt, pepper, and nutmeg together. Spread half of the potatoes evenly in the baking dish and season with half of the salt mixture. Sprinkle the Gruyère evenly over the potatoes. Top with an evenly spread layer of the remaining potatoes, seasoned with the remaining salt mixture. Carefully pour the hot cream over the potatoes to just cover them; add more heated cream, if needed. Butter a sheet of aluminum foil. Cover the dish with the foil, buttered-side down. Place the dish on a rimmed baking sheet.

3. Bake for 1 hour. Remove the foil and use a bulb baster to baste the potatoes with the cream. Continue baking until the top is golden brown and the potatoes are tender when pierced with the tip of a small, sharp knife, 30 to 45 minutes more. (The gratin can be cooled, covered with aluminum foil, and stored at room temperature for up to 4 hours. Reheat in a preheated 350°F oven, covered, for about 30 minutes.) Let it stand at room temperature for 10 minutes. Serve hot.

POTATO AND FENNEL GRATIN

MAKES 9 SERVINGS

Serve with roast beef, leg of lamb, or lamb chops.

Prep Time: 20 minutes

Cooking Time: 2 hours

Make Ahead: The baked gratin can be cooled, covered, and refrigerated for up to 1 day.

Family Favorite, Holiday Feasts, Company Fare, Buffet Dish, Vegetarian

Cookbook author Beth Hensperger and I have swapped recipes for years. She has been touting this gratin, her family's favorite, to me for a couple of decades, and I am just now getting around to promoting it here. When I make it, everyone asks about the "secret ingredient," which, of course, is fennel.

2 tablespoons (¼ stick) unsalted butter, plus softened butter for the baking dish

1 medium red onion, cut into thin half-moons

1 large fennel bulb (about 1 pound)

2 tablespoons olive oil

3 cups heavy cream, plus more as needed

1 cup crumbled blue cheese, such as Roquefort or Danish blue (4 ounces)

2 teaspoons kosher salt

½ teaspoon freshly ground black pepper

2 pounds baking potatoes, such as russet or Burbank, peeled and cut into ⅛-inch slices

1. Position a rack in the center of the oven and preheat the oven to 400°F. Butter the inside of an 11½ × 8 × 2-inch baking dish. Butter a sheet of aluminum foil to cover the dish.

2. Melt the butter in a large skillet over medium heat. Add the red onion and cook, stirring occasionally, until it is tender, about 5 minutes. Transfer it to a medium bowl.

3. If necessary, trim off the fennel stalks and fronds. Cut the fennel bulb vertically into ¼-inch slices and trim out the thick core from each slice. Heat the oil in the skillet over medium heat. Add the fennel and cover. Cook, stirring occasionally, until the fennel is softened and lightly browned, about 10 minutes. Transfer it to the bowl with the red onion.

4. Heat the cream in a medium saucepan over medium heat until steaming. Remove it from the heat and stir in the blue cheese. The cheese does not have to melt.

5. In a small bowl, mix the salt and pepper together. Spread one-third of the potatoes in the baking dish. Top them with half of the fennel and ½ cup of the cream mixture, then season with one-third of the salt mixture; repeat. Top with the remaining potatoes, cream mixture, and salt mixture. The vegetables should fit snugly in the dish and be barely covered with the cream mixture; add more hot cream as needed. Cover the dish with the aluminum foil, buttered-side down. (The gratin can be stored at room temperature for up to 4 hours.) Place the dish on a rimmed baking sheet.

6. Bake for 1¼ hours. Remove the foil and use a bulb baster to baste the potatoes with the cream mixture. Reduce the temperature to 350°F. Continue baking, uncovered, until the top is golden brown and the potatoes are tender when pierced with the tip of a small, sharp knife, about 30 minutes more. If the top browns too quickly, tent it with the foil. Let the gratin stand at room temperature for 10 minutes. (The gratin can be cooled, covered with aluminum foil, and refrigerated for up to 1 day. Reheat, covered, in a preheated 350°F oven for about 30 minutes, removing the foil during the last 10 minutes.) Serve hot.

POTATO, BACON, AND ONION TARTIFLETTE
MAKES 6 SERVINGS

Serve with roast beef, roast pork, pork or veal chops, or roast chicken.
Prep Time: 10 minutes
Cooking Time: 1 hour, 10 minutes
Family Favorite, Holiday Feasts, Company Fare, Buffet Dish

If French women don't get fat, then they have never eaten tartiflette, *this outrageous gratin of potatoes, cheese, and bacon. (Well, at least the onions aren't fattening.) It is usually made with Reblochon cheese, but it is pricey and not easy to find, so I use Brie with excellent results.*

2 tablespoons (¼ stick) unsalted butter, plus more for the dish

2 pounds thin-skinned boiling potatoes, scrubbed and cut into ¼-inch rounds

½ cup dry white wine, such as Pinot Grigio

6 slices bacon, cut into 1-inch pieces

1 large yellow onion, chopped

1½ teaspoons kosher salt

½ teaspoon freshly ground black pepper

8 ounces Brie, cut into ½-inch pieces, including
the rind

1. Position a rack in the center of the oven and preheat the oven to 350°F. Lightly butter an 11½ × 8 × 2-inch baking dish.

2. Melt the butter in a large skillet over medium-high heat. Add the potatoes and cook, stirring occasionally, until they are partially cooked and do not look raw in the center, about 15 minutes. Add the wine and cook until it has reduced to a few tablespoons, about 2 minutes. Transfer the potato mixture to a large bowl.

3. Wipe out the skillet with paper towels. Add the bacon and cook it over medium heat, stirring occasionally, until it is crisp and browned, about 8 minutes. Using a slotted spoon, transfer the bacon to paper towels to drain, leaving the bacon fat in the pan.

4. Add the onion to the fat in the skillet and cook, stirring occasionally, until the onion softens, about 3 minutes. Add it to the potatoes with the bacon. Season with the salt and pepper and mix well. Spread the mixture in the baking dish and top it with the Brie.

5. Bake until the potatoes are tender and the cheese is melted and lightly browned, about 30 minutes. Let the tartiflette stand for 5 minutes, then serve hot.

POTATO GRATIN SQUARES WITH ROQUEFORT AND HERBS

MAKES 9 SERVINGS

Serve with beef, veal, or lamb roasts; steaks; or chops.

Prep Time: 20 minutes

Cooking Time: 1½ hours initial cooking, plus 20 minutes before serving

Refrigerating Time: 2 to 24 hours

Make Ahead: The gratin can be made up to 1 day ahead.

Holiday Feasts, Company Fare, Buffet Dish

The main attraction of this robust potato dish is its flavor, but I also love that it can be made ahead. It is a mash-up between three French potato classics: pommes boulangère *(sliced potatoes baked with broth),* pommes Anna *(a compact savory potato cake), and* pommes gratin *(layered with cheese). You will need two 8-inch baking pans to make this dish, as the baked gratin needs to be covered and weighted before serving. Also use some kind of cutting tool (a food processor, mandoline, or V-slicer) to evenly slice the potatoes.*

1 tablespoon unsalted butter, plus softened butter
for the baking pan

1 yellow onion, cut into thin half-moons

2 garlic cloves, minced

1 teaspoon chopped fresh rosemary or ½ teaspoon
dried

1 teaspoon chopped fresh thyme or ½ teaspoon dried	½ cup crumbled Roquefort or Danish blue cheese (2 ounces)
2 pounds baking potatoes, such as russets, peeled	2 cups reduced-sodium chicken broth, heated to boiling
1½ teaspoons kosher salt	Oil for the baking sheet
½ teaspoon freshly ground black pepper	

1. At least 6 hours before serving, position a rack in the center of the oven and preheat the oven to 400ºF. Butter the inside of an 8-inch square baking pan with the softened butter. Line the bottom of the pan with parchment paper and butter it as well.

2. Melt the butter in a large skillet over medium heat. Add the onion and cook, stirring occasionally, until it is tender and golden, about 5 minutes. Stir in the garlic and cook until it is fragrant, about 1 minute. Transfer them to a bowl and stir in the rosemary and thyme.

3. Using a food processor, mandoline, or plastic V-slicer, cut the potatoes into ¹⁄₁₆-inch rounds. Do not rinse the potatoes. Transfer them to a bowl and season with the salt and pepper.

4. Spread one-third of the potatoes in the baking dish. Top with half of the onion mixture and half of the Roquefort. Repeat with another third of the potatoes and the remaining onion mixture and Roquefort. Top with the remaining potatoes, spreading them as evenly as possible and being sure to cover the Roquefort. Pour in the boiling broth. Cover the dish tightly with aluminum foil and put it on a baking sheet.

5. Bake for 30 minutes. Uncover the pan and continue baking until the top is golden brown and the potatoes are tender when pierced with the tip of a small, sharp knife, about 1 hour.

6. Let the gratin cool on a wire cake rack for 30 minutes. Cover the top of the gratin with a square of parchment paper. Place a second 8-inch square baking pan on the gratin and weigh it down with heavy canned goods. Let it cool at room temperature for 1½ hours. Refrigerate the gratin, still covered, but without the cans, until chilled, at least 2 hours and up to 24 hours.

7. When ready to serve, position a rack in the center of the oven and preheat the oven to 400ºF. Lightly oil a large rimmed baking sheet.

8. Remove the top sheet of parchment paper. Unmold the gratin onto a carving board and discard the paper. Cut the gratin into 9 equal squares and arrange them on the baking sheet. Bake until the squares are lightly browned and heated through, about 25 minutes. Serve hot.

POTATOES ANNA

MAKES 6 SERVINGS

Serve with steak, pork, and lamb chops; roast chicken; or salmon fillets.

Prep Time: 10 minutes

Cooking Time: 1 ½ hours

Family Favorite, Holiday Feasts, Company Fare, Cooking Classic, Vegetarian

Nobody is quite sure who Anna was, but she must have been quite a lady to have such a glorious dish named after her. It is a cake constructed of potato slices and lots of butter, then baked to give it a golden shell. The potatoes are cooked with clarified butter, an easy technique that removes the milk solids in the butter that would burn and discolor the cake.

½ cup (1 stick) unsalted butter, thinly sliced

2 pounds baking potatoes, such as russets, peeled

1½ teaspoons kosher salt

1 teaspoon finely chopped fresh rosemary or thyme, for serving (optional)

¼ teaspoon freshly ground black pepper

Special Equipment: A mandoline or V-slicer; a heatproof flat lid or plate to fit inside the skillet.

1. Position a rack in the center of the oven and preheat the oven to 350°F.

2. Melt the butter in a small saucepan over medium heat, and let it come to a full boil. Remove the pan from the heat. Let it stand for 5 minutes. Skim off the foam from the top of the butter. Pour the clear yellow melted butter (now called clarified butter) into a 1-cup liquid measure, leaving the milky sediment behind in the saucepan.

3. Using a mandoline or a V-slicer, cut the potatoes into ⅛-inch rounds. Do not rinse the potatoes.

4. Add 2 tablespoons of the clarified butter to a 9-inch nonstick skillet (measured at the top) with an ovenproof handle over medium heat. In a small bowl, mix the salt, rosemary, and pepper together. Add a layer of potatoes to the skillet, overlapping the rounds by about ½ inch. Season the potatoes with some of the salt mixture and drizzle them with about 1 tablespoon of the clarified butter. Make another layer of the potatoes, salt mixture, and butter in the skillet, finishing with a layer of potatoes and a drizzle of butter. Top the potatoes with a round of parchment paper cut to fit inside the pan. Place a heatproof flat lid or plate that fits inside the skillet on top, pressing directly on the parchment. Adjust the heat to medium-low. Cook until the underside of the potato cake is beginning to brown, about 5 minutes. Give the skillet a gentle shake by the handle; the cake should move in the pan as a unit.

5. Bake, with the potatoes still covered by the smaller lid, until the potatoes are almost tender when pierced with the tip of a small, sharp knife, about 40 minutes. Remove the lid with the parchment paper and continue baking until the potatoes are fully browned, about 20 minutes more.

6. Hold a serving plate over the skillet. Using pot holders, hold the skillet and plate together and invert them to turn the cake over onto the plate. Serve immediately.

BOULANGÈRE POTATOES
MAKES 8 SERVINGS

Serve with roast meats, steaks, or chops.

Prep Time: 15 minutes

Cooking Time: 1¼ hours

Family Favorite, Holiday Feasts, Company Fare, Buffet Dish

Before every home had its own oven, French cooks would take their holiday meal of meat and potatoes to the town baker to roast. So potatoes baked in broth became known as pommes boulangère *("baker's wife" in French). Much leaner than cream-based gratins, but just as good with its layers of onions and herbs, this useful dish deserves to be better known.*

3 tablespoons unsalted butter, plus softened butter
    for the baking dish
1 large yellow onion, thinly sliced
2 teaspoons finely chopped fresh rosemary, sage,
    or thyme
1 teaspoon kosher salt

½ teaspoon freshly ground black pepper
3 pounds baking potatoes, such as russets, peeled
    and cut into ⅛-inch rounds (a mandoline or
    plastic V-slicer works best)
2½ cups reduced-sodium beef broth, heated to
    boiling

1. Position a rack in the center of the oven and preheat the oven to 400°F. Lightly butter a 13 × 9 × 2-inch baking dish.

2. Melt 2 tablespoons of the butter in a large skillet over medium heat. Add the onion and cover. Cook, stirring occasionally, until the onion softens, about 5 minutes. Uncover and cook, stirring occasionally, until the onion is golden brown but not caramelized, about 10 minutes more. Stir in the rosemary.

3. In a small bowl, mix the salt and pepper together. Beginning and ending with the potatoes, alternate three layers of potatoes with two layers of the onion mixture in the baking dish, seasoning the layers with the salt mixture. Pour in the boiling broth. Dot the top with the remaining 1 tablespoon of butter. Cover the dish with aluminum foil and put it on a baking sheet.

4. Bake for 1 hour. Uncover and continue baking until the top is lightly browned and the potatoes are tender when pierced with the tip of a small, sharp knife, about 30 minutes more. Let the gratin stand for 5 minutes. Serve hot.

POTATO AND LEEK KUGEL

MAKES 12 SERVINGS

Prep Time: 15 minutes
Cooking Time: 1 hour, 10 minutes
Make Ahead: The kugel can be made up to 1 day ahead.
Family Favorite, Holiday Feasts, Company Fare, Buffet Dish, Cooking Classic, Vegetarian

This potato kugel doesn't stray too far from familiar territory, but it has all of the qualities that make a great example of the genre. The outside is crisp and golden brown, and in addition to the expected onion, it has a lush leek filling. It can be made ahead and reheated, but I have to admit that I prefer my kugel served fresh out of the oven. And for those of you who aren't Jewish, this dairy-free recipe will come in handy when you want a potato gratin without cream or cheese.

½ cup plus 3 tablespoons olive oil

2 large leeks (white and pale green parts), chopped (2 cups)

Kosher salt and freshly ground black pepper

3 pounds baking potatoes, such as russets, peeled

1 large yellow onion

4 large eggs, beaten to blend

¼ cup matzo meal (see Note)

1. Position a rack in the center of the oven and preheat the oven to 400°F.

2. Heat 2 tablespoons of the oil in a large skillet over medium heat. Add the leeks, ½ teaspoon salt, and ¼ teaspoon pepper. Cook, stirring often, until the leeks are very tender, 8 to 10 minutes. Remove them from the heat.

3. Using a food processor fitted with the shredding disk, or the large holes of a box shredder, shred the potatoes and the onion. A handful at a time, working over a medium bowl, squeeze the potato mixture in your hands to remove excess moisture, and transfer the squeezed mixture to a large bowl. Add the eggs, matzo meal, ½ cup of the remaining oil, 2½ teaspoons salt, and ½ teaspoon pepper. Carefully pour off the liquid from the mixture in the medium bowl, revealing the potato starch, and scrape the starch into the potato mixture. Mix well.

4. Pour the remaining 1 tablespoon oil into a 13 × 9 × 2-inch baking dish and tilt the dish to coat the bottom with the oil. Place it in the oven and heat until the oil is hot but not smoking, about 3½ minutes. Remove the dish from the oven. Spread half of the potato mixture evenly into the baking dish. Top with the leeks, then add the remaining potato mixture.

5. Bake for 15 minutes. Reduce the heat to 350°F and continue baking until the top is golden brown and the potatoes are tender, about 45 minutes more. Let the kugel stand for 10 minutes. (The kugel can be cooled, covered with aluminum foil, and refrigerated for 1 day. Reheat in a preheated 350°F oven for 15 minutes. Remove the foil and continue baking until the top is crisp and the kugel is heated through, about 15 minutes more.) Cut it into squares and serve.

Note: Substitute plain dry bread crumbs for the matzo meal, if desired.

Roasted Potatoes

CRISP OVEN STEAK FRIES WITH GARLIC AND PARSLEY
MAKES 4 SERVINGS

Serve with hamburgers and sandwiches, steaks, or chops.

Prep Time: 5 minutes

Cooking Time: 45 minutes

Weeknight Suppers, Family Favorite, Cooking Classic, Vegetarian

Traditional French fries are in a class by themselves, but I don't always have the time for the deep-frying setup. With this method, I can have excellent fries from the oven with a minimum of effort. For golden fries, be sure to use a baking sheet large enough to hold the potatoes without crowding. Lately, I have been serving the Buffalo Steak Fries variation as a special treat.

2 tablespoons vegetable or olive oil, plus more for
    the baking sheet
4 large baking potatoes (about 9 ounces each),
    such as russets, peeled and cut lengthwise into
    6 wedges

2 garlic cloves, finely chopped
2 tablespoons finely chopped fresh flat-leaf parsley
Kosher salt and freshly ground black pepper

1. Position a rack in the top third of the oven and preheat the oven to 425°F. Lightly oil a large rimmed baking sheet.

2. Put the potato wedges on the baking sheet, drizzle them with the oil, and mix with your hands until coated. Spread out the wedges on the baking sheet so they are not touching.

3. Bake until the undersides are golden brown, 15 to 20 minutes. Using a metal spatula, flip the potatoes over and continue baking until the fries are golden brown, 15 to 20 minutes more. During the last 2 minutes or so, stir in the garlic and parsley. Season the fries to taste with salt and pepper. Transfer them to a serving bowl and serve.

Buffalo Steak Fries: Instead of the garlic and parsley, sprinkle the fries with your favorite Cajun seasoning, and serve them with Steakhouse Blue Cheese Dressing (page 343) for dipping.

ROASTED LEMON POTATOES AND ARTICHOKES
MAKES 4 SERVINGS

Serve with roast lamb, lamb chops, beef stew, veal chops, roast chicken, or seafood.
Prep Time: 10 minutes
Cooking Time: 40 minutes
Holiday Feasts, Company Fare, Buffet Dish, Retro Recipe, Cooking Classic, Vegetarian

Lemon potatoes are a classic of Greek cuisine. With the addition of artichoke hearts, they become a dish fit for company, especially with roast lamb. If you wish, sprinkle the mixture with feta cheese just before serving.

2 large baking potatoes (about 9 ounces each),
    such as russets, peeled and cut lengthwise into
    6 wedges

2 tablespoons extra-virgin olive oil, plus more for
    the baking sheet
One 9-ounce package thawed frozen artichoke
    hearts

Finely grated zest of 1 lemon

2 tablespoons fresh lemon juice

2 tablespoons chopped fresh flat-leaf parsley

Kosher salt and freshly ground black pepper

1. Position a rack in the lower third of the oven and preheat the oven to 425°F. Lightly oil a large rimmed baking sheet or 15 × 10 × 2-inch baking dish.

2. Toss the potatoes with the oil on the baking sheet to coat the potatoes. Spread the potatoes on the baking sheet. Bake until the undersides are golden brown, about 20 minutes. Flip the potatoes over with a metal spatula. Continue baking for 10 minutes more. Scatter the artichokes into the dish and continue baking until the potatoes are golden brown, about 10 minutes more.

3. Remove the baking sheet from the oven. Sprinkle the vegetables with the lemon zest, lemon juice, and parsley. Season to taste with salt and pepper. Transfer the potatoes to a serving bowl and serve.

"ROASTIES" (OVEN-FRIED POTATOES) WITH ROSEMARY SALT

MAKES 6 TO 8 SERVINGS

Serve with roast beef, veal, or pork; steaks and chops; roasted or grilled whole fish.

Prep Time: 5 minutes

Cooking Time: 1 hour, 10 minutes

Family Favorite, Holiday Feasts, Company Fare, Buffet Dish, Cooking Classic, Vegetarian

If you don't know British "roasties" already, be prepared to meet a new favorite—crisp and golden potato chunks with fluffy interiors, made in the oven without deep-frying. They do require an easy three-step process, and they are worth every second of prep. First, they are parboiled, then tossed about in the cooking pot to dry out, and only then are they roasted in a pool of hot oil. A fragrant, flaky salt is the perfect finish. Make these once, and you will be hooked.

3 pounds baking potatoes, such as russets, peeled, halved lengthwise, and cut into 2-inch chunks

½ cup canola or vegetable oil, as needed

1 tablespoon finely chopped fresh rosemary or thyme

2 teaspoons flaky sea salt, such as Maldon or fleur de sel

Freshly ground black pepper

1. Put the potato chunks in a large pot of salted water and bring them to a boil over high heat. Reduce the heat to medium and boil until the outsides of the potatoes begin to soften, about 5 minutes. Drain well.

2. Return the potatoes to the empty cooking pot over medium heat. Cook, stirring occasionally, until the outsides of the potatoes are scuffed and look drier, about 2 minutes. (The rough surface will cook into a crisp crust.) Remove the pot from the heat.

3. Meanwhile, position a rack in the center of the oven and preheat the oven to 400ºF. Choose a metal roasting pan large enough to hold the potatoes in a single layer.

4. Pour enough oil into the pan to create a shallow pool of oil about ¹⁄₁₆ inch deep. Place the pan in the oven and heat until the oil is very hot but not smoking, about 5 minutes. Remove the pan from the oven. Carefully arrange the potatoes, flat-sides down, in the hot oil. Return the pan with the potatoes to the oven and roast until the potato undersides are golden and can be easily released from the pan with a metal spatula, about 30 minutes. Using the spatula, flip the potatoes. Continue roasting until the potatoes are crisp and golden all over, about 30 minutes more. Using a slotted spoon, transfer the potatoes to a serving dish.

5. In a small bowl, use your fingertips to rub the rosemary and salt together to release the rosemary's flavor and scent into the salt. Sprinkle the rosemary salt over the potatoes and season with the pepper. Serve hot.

CRISPY ROAST POTATOES WITH PIMENTÓN ALLIOLI
MAKES 4 TO 6 SERVINGS

Serve with grilled or roast beef, pork, lamb, or chicken; meaty fish like halibut; or shrimp.
Prep Time: 10 minutes
Cooking Time: 30 minutes
Weeknight Suppers, Company Fare, Vegetarian

Patatas bravas *("bold potatoes" in Spanish) are deep-fried potatoes topped with a spicy sauce that is typically in the tapas family. But, with a few tweaks, they can be an excellent side dish. This is one of my favorite sides to serve with grilled or steamed shrimp, in which case I may make extra allioli for dipping the seafood.*

2 pounds thin-skinned boiling potatoes, quartered

2 tablespoons olive oil

PIMENTÓN ALLIOLI

1 teaspoon sherry vinegar

1 teaspoon tomato paste

⅓ cup mayonnaise

1 teaspoon smoked paprika (Pimentón de la Vera)

2 garlic cloves, crushed through a garlic press

½ teaspoon hot red pepper sauce

Kosher salt

2 tablespoons finely chopped fresh cilantro, for serving (optional)

1. Position a rack in the center of the oven and preheat the oven to 425ºF.

2. Toss the potato quarters and oil together on a large, rimmed baking sheet. Roast them for 15 minutes. Flip the potatoes with a metal spatula and continue roasting until they are golden brown and tender, 15 to 20 minutes more.

3. Meanwhile, to make the allioli: In a small bowl, whisk the vinegar and tomato paste together to loosen the tomato paste. Add the mayonnaise, paprika, garlic, and hot pepper sauce and whisk to combine. Set the allioli aside at room temperature while the potatoes are roasting.

4. Season the potatoes to taste with salt. Transfer them to a serving bowl and top with the aïoli. Mix them gently, sprinkle with the cilantro, if using, and serve immediately.

Boiled and Steamed Potatoes

BOILED BABY POTATOES WITH GREEN BEANS AND PESTO

MAKES 6 SERVINGS

Serve with pork and lamb roasts and chops, or roast chicken.

Prep Time: 10 minutes

Cooking Time: 25 minutes

Weeknight Suppers, Family Favorite, Holiday Feasts, Company Fare, Vegetarian

In Liguria, the birthplace of pesto, the trio of potatoes, green beans, and pesto is served as a pasta sauce. With all due respect to the pasta, the mixture is perfectly delicious on its own. This recipe is a good excuse to have pesto in the refrigerator, ready to be put into action.

8 ounces green beans, cut into 2-inch lengths

1½ pounds small potatoes, such as baby Yukon
   Golds, scrubbed

2 tablespoons Pesto (page 425)

Kosher salt and freshly ground black pepper

2 tablespoons freshly grated Parmesan cheese

1. Bring a large saucepan of salted water to a boil over high heat. Add the green beans and cook just until they are crisp-tender, about 3 minutes. Using a wire spider or sieve, transfer the green beans to a bowl of cold water. Drain the green beans well and set them aside.

2. Add the potatoes to the water and return it to a boil. Reduce the heat to medium-low and cook the potatoes at a brisk simmer until they are barely tender when pierced with the tip of a small, sharp knife, about 20 minutes. During the last minute or so, return the green beans to the saucepan to reheat. Scoop out and reserve about ¼ cup of the cooking water. Drain the potatoes and green beans.

3. Return the potatoes and green beans to the saucepan. Add the pesto and mix, adding enough of the reserved cooking water to make a light sauce. Season to taste with salt and pepper. Transfer the vegetables to a serving bowl, sprinkle with the Parmesan, and serve.

STEAMED POTATOES WITH KALE PESTO

MAKES 4 TO 6 SERVINGS

Serve with pork or lamb chops; sausages; roast chicken; halibut and other firm, white fish; or shrimp.

Prep Time: 10 minutes

Cooking Time: 30 minutes

Weeknight Suppers, Holiday Feasts, Company Fare, Buffet Dish, Vegetarian

When I have small potatoes with better-than-average taste—such as heritage varieties from the farmer's market—I steam them, knowing that no flavor will be left behind in the cooking liquid. While this recipe is similar to the preceding recipe, the kale pesto makes it unique.

1½ pounds small, thin-skinned potatoes, such as fingerlings or baby Yukon Golds, scrubbed

⅓ cup Kale Pesto (page 426)

Kosher salt

1. Place a collapsible steamer in a large saucepan and add enough water to almost reach the bottom of the steamer. (If you have another kind of steamer, just set it up as needed.) Bring the water to a boil over high heat.

2. Put the potatoes in the steamer and tightly cover the saucepan. Reduce the heat to medium. Steam the potatoes, adding more hot water to the saucepan if needed, until the potatoes are tender when pierced with the tip of a small, sharp knife, 20 to 25 minutes.

3. Transfer the potatoes to a serving bowl, reserving ½ cup of the steaming water. Coarsely crush the potatoes with a fork. Top the potatoes with the pesto and mix, adding enough of the reserved water to make a creamy sauce. Season to taste with salt and serve.

Braised Potatoes

BRAISED POTATOES WITH SHALLOTS AND THYME

MAKES 4 TO 6 SERVINGS

Serve with roasted or grilled meats and poultry, fish fillets; or sautéed shrimp.

Prep Time: 5 minutes

Cooking Time: 25 minutes

Make Ahead: The potatoes can be made up to 1 day ahead.

Weeknight Suppers, Family Favorite, Holiday Feasts, Company Fare, Buffet Dish

This is another simple French classic that I learned to make while I was studying cooking in Paris, and that has been part of my life ever since. It takes utilitarian potatoes and infuses them with the flavors of broth, wine, and herbs. While plain buttered potatoes have their place, so do these.

2 tablespoons (¼ stick) unsalted butter

2 tablespoons minced shallots

1½ pounds small thin-skinned boiling potatoes, scrubbed and quartered

¾ cup reduced-sodium chicken broth

¼ cup dry white wine or dry vermouth

Four 3-inch sprigs fresh thyme

¼ teaspoon kosher salt

⅛ teaspoon freshly ground black pepper

1. Melt the butter in a medium, deep skillet over medium heat. Add the shallots and cook, stirring occasionally, until they are tender, about 2 minutes. Spread the potatoes in the skillet in a single layer. Add the broth and wine, top with the thyme, and season with the salt and pepper. Bring the liquid to a boil over high heat.

2. Reduce the heat to medium-low and cover the skillet. Simmer, stirring occasionally, until the potatoes are tender when pierced with the tip of a small, sharp knife, about 20 minutes. Uncover, increase the heat to high, and boil until the liquid has reduced to about 2 tablespoons, 4 to 6 minutes more. Discard the thyme stems and serve immediately.

Potato Pancakes

POTATO PANCAKES (LATKES) WITH CHIVE SOUR CREAM

MAKES 4 TO 6 SERVINGS

Serve with braised beef, especially braised brisket and pot roast; or egg dishes.

Prep Time: 10 minutes

Cooking Time: 10 minutes

Weeknight Suppers, Family Favorite, Holiday Feasts, Company Fare, Cooking Classic, Vegetarian

The perfect potato pancake is crisp on the outside and creamy within. There are a few tricks to reaching this goal, including squeezing starchy potatoes of excess liquid and reserving the potato starch to act as glue, and using plenty of oil for frying. They can be held briefly on a cake rack in the oven, but don't let them languish or they'll lose their crunch. (The pancakes also get soggy if drained on paper towels for longer than a few minutes.) The chive sour cream is optional . . . or is it?

CHIVE SOUR CREAM

1 cup sour cream

3 tablespoons finely chopped fresh chives

Freshly ground black pepper

LATKES

2 pounds baking potatoes, such as russets, peeled

1 yellow onion

2 large eggs, beaten

2 tablespoons matzo meal or dry bread crumbs

1½ teaspoons kosher salt

½ teaspoon freshly ground black pepper

Vegetable oil, for frying

1. Position a rack in the center of the oven and preheat the oven to 200°F. Line a baking sheet with a wire cake rack. Line a second baking sheet with paper towels.

2. To make the chive sour cream: In a small bowl, mix the sour cream and chives together. Season to taste with pepper. Let it stand at room temperature while making the pancakes.

3. To make the latkes: Shred the potatoes on the large holes of a box shredder into a large bowl. Grate the onion into the bowl. (Or use a food processor to grate the potatoes and onion.) A handful at a time, squeeze the potato mixture over a medium bowl to extract and reserve the excess liquid. Transfer the potato mixture to a large bowl. The mixture may turn a strange shade of red, from the oxidation of the potatoes, but don't be concerned.

4. Pour off the thin reserved liquid to reveal the potato starch that has settled to the bottom of the bowl. Scrape it into the potato mixture. Add the eggs, matzo meal, salt, and pepper and mix well.

5. Pour enough oil into a large skillet to come about ⅛ inch up the sides and heat it over medium-high heat until the oil shimmers. Using about ⅓ cup of the potato mixture for each pancake, drain away the excess liquid, transfer the mixture to the hot oil, and spread it into a 3-inch pancake. Add another pancake or two to the pan, but do not crowd the pancakes in the skillet. Cook until the underside is golden brown, about 2½ minutes. Turn and cook until the other side is brown, about 2½ minutes more. Transfer it to the rack to keep warm in the oven while making the remaining latkes.

6. Just before serving, transfer the latkes to paper towels to drain briefly. Serve them immediately, with the chive sour cream passed on the side.

ITALIAN MASHED POTATO PANCAKES

MAKES 6 PANCAKES

Serve with steaks, chops, roast chicken, or salmon.

Prep Time: 10 minutes

Cooking Time: 6 minutes

Weeknight Suppers, Family Favorite, Holiday Feasts, Company Fare, Buffet Dish, Retro Recipe, Cooking Classic, Vegetarian

Beyond the obvious reason of flavor, there are other motivations for making these potato pancakes. They use up leftover mashed potatoes, don't require shredding the potatoes, and partner well with Italian-

flavored dishes. The pancakes hold their shape best if the mashed potatoes are used cold from the refrigerator.

2 cups cold Perfect Whipped Potatoes (page 177; see Note)

½ yellow onion, shredded on the large holes of a box grater

¼ cup freshly grated Parmesan cheese (about 1 ounce)

1 tablespoon potato starch or cornstarch

1 tablespoon finely chopped fresh oregano or flat-leaf parsley or 1 teaspoon dried oregano

Kosher salt and freshly ground black pepper

1 large egg yolk

½ cup panko bread crumbs

¼ cup olive oil

1. Position a rack in the center of the oven and preheat the oven to 200°F. Line a baking sheet with paper towels.

2. In a medium bowl, mix the mashed potatoes, onion, Parmesan, potato starch, and oregano together. Season to taste with salt and pepper. Stir in the egg yolk.

3. Using hands rinsed under cold water, shape the potato mixture into six 3-inch cakes about ½ inch thick and transfer the cakes to a baking sheet. Spread the panko on a plate. Coat each cake with the panko and return it to the baking sheet.

4. Heat the oil in a very large skillet over medium heat until the oil is shimmering. Carefully transfer the patties to the skillet without crowding them (work in batches, if necessary). Cook until the undersides are golden brown, about 3 minutes. Turn the pancakes and cook until the other sides are golden brown, about 3 minutes more. Transfer them to the paper towels to drain briefly. Serve hot.

Note: If you don't have leftover mashed potatoes, you can make just enough for the pancakes. Following the instructions for Perfect Whipped Potatoes (page 177), use 1½ pounds baking potatoes, 2 tablespoons softened unsalted butter, and 2 tablespoons warm whole milk. Season to taste with salt and pepper. Let them cool to room temperature. Cover and refrigerate until chilled, about 1 hour. Measure 2 cups of mashed potatoes to use in the pancakes.

SWISS POTATO CAKE (RÖSTI)

MAKES 6 SERVINGS

Serve with steaks, chops, roast chicken, or salmon.
Prep Time: 5 minutes, plus cooling time for the potatoes
Cooking Time: 12 minutes to cook the potatoes plus 15 minutes for the rösti
Weeknight Suppers, Family Favorite, Cooking Classic, Vegetarian

I once took an intensive training course at a chocolate factory in Zurich. (Hey, someone has to do it!) While in Switzerland, I became enamored of rösti, a big potato pancake (with some hash-brown

DNA) served with almost every meal. They require chilled potatoes, so put that timing into the game plan.

4 large potatoes, such as russets (about 2 pounds), scrubbed, each pierced a few times with a fork

2 tablespoons canola oil

2 tablespoon unsalted butter

1 teaspoon kosher salt

¼ teaspoon freshly ground black pepper

1. Microwave the potatoes, uncovered, on the tray of a microwave oven on High power for 4 minutes. Turn the potatoes over and continue microwaving until they are tender, 8 to 10 minutes, depending on the wattage of your oven. Remove them from the oven and let cool slightly. Put the potatoes in a 1-gallon plastic zip-tight bag. Place the bag, with the top open, in a large bowl of iced water. Let stand until the potatoes are chilled, about 30 minutes. (Or, at least 4 hours before serving, put the potatoes in a large saucepan and add enough salted water to cover. Cover the saucepan and bring it to a boil over high heat. Reduce the heat to medium-low and set the lid ajar. Cook the potatoes at a brisk simmer until they can be pierced with the tip of a small sharp knife, about 30 minutes. Drain and rinse the potatoes well under cold running water. Drain again. Transfer the potatoes to a bowl and refrigerate them until chilled, at least 3 hours or up to 1 day.)

2. Peel the potatoes. Coarsely shred them on the large holes of a box grater (discard the remaining skin from the side where you held the potato). Transfer the shredded potatoes to a bowl and toss with the salt and pepper.

3. Heat 1 tablespoon of the oil and 1 tablespoon of the butter together in a large nonstick skillet over medium-high heat until the foam subsides. Scatter the shredded potato mixture in a shallow single layer into the skillet. Reduce the heat to medium. Cook until the edges are golden brown, about 7 minutes. Slide the rösti out of the skillet onto a plate. Place a second place on top and invert them together to turn the rösti over.

4. Add the remaining oil and butter to the skillet and heat until the foam subsides. Slide the rösti, browned side up, back into the skillet. Cook until the underside is golden brown, about 7 minutes more. Slide the rösti out of the skillet on a serving platter. Cut into wedges and serve hot.

CLASSIC HASH BROWNS
MAKES 4 SERVINGS

Serve with steaks, chops, sausages, or chicken.
Prep Time: 5 minutes, plus 30 minutes cooling time for the potatoes
Cooking Time: 12 minutes to cook the whole potatoes, plus 15 minutes for the hash browns
Weeknight Suppers, Family Favorite, Cooking Classic, Vegetarian

Of course, there are many ways to make hash browns—crispy, golden shreds of potatoes that signify the best of "country cooking." Some people shred raw potatoes, but I get the best results with cooked ones. Also, I shred the cooked potato with its skin for extra flavor, but remove the skin if you wish. All this used to mean thinking ahead to have boiled or baked potatoes ready. Now, I just microwave them and cool them down in ice water, which considerably reduces the cooking and cooling times. I serve these most often with sausages or steak at dinner, although they sure are good at breakfast with eggs.

3 baking potatoes, such as russets (about 1¼ pounds), scrubbed, each pierced a few times with a fork	½ teaspoon kosher salt ¼ teaspoon freshly ground black pepper 3 tablespoons vegetable oil

1. Microwave the potatoes, uncovered, on the tray of a microwave oven on high for 4 minutes. Turn the potatoes over and continue microwaving until they are tender, 8 to 10 minutes, depending on the wattage of your oven. Remove them from the oven and let cool slightly. Put the potatoes in a 1-gallon plastic zip-tight bag. Place the bag, with the top open, in a large bowl of iced water. Let stand until the potatoes are chilled, about 30 minutes. (Or, at least 4 hours before serving, put the potatoes in a large saucepan and add enough salted water to cover. Cover the saucepan and bring it to a boil over high heat. Reduce the heat to medium-low and set the lid ajar. Cook the potatoes at a brisk simmer until they can be pierced with the tip of a small, sharp knife, about 30 minutes. Drain and rinse the potatoes well under cold running water. Drain again. Transfer the potatoes to a bowl and refrigerate them until chilled, at least 3 hours or up to 1 day.)

2. Coarsely shred the unpeeled potatoes on the large holes of a box grater (discard the remaining skin from the side where you held the potato). Transfer the shredded potatoes to a bowl and toss with the salt and pepper.

3. Add the oil to a large nonstick skillet over medium-high heat and warm it until the oil is hot but not smoking. Scatter the shredded potato mixture in a shallow single layer into the skillet. Cook until the edges are golden brown, about 5 minutes. In sections, flip the hash browns over and cook until the underside is golden brown, about 5 minutes. Flip the hash browns again and continue cooking until they are very crisp and browned, 3 to 5 minutes. Serve hot.

SAN FRANCISCO HOME FRIES WITH SOUR CREAM AND SCALLIONS

MAKES 6 SERVINGS

Serve with pork chops or sausages.

Prep Time: 10 minutes, plus 3 hours cooling time for the potatoes

Cooking Time: 25 minutes

Make Ahead: The potatoes can be cooked and cooled up to 1 day ahead.
Weeknight Suppers, Family Favorite, Cooking Classic, Vegetarian

I once worked in a very popular San Francisco restaurant that specialized in Sunday brunch. It was there that I learned how to make golden, crispy home fries from precooked potatoes, as raw potatoes burn before they can cook through. (If you wish, microwave and cool the potatoes as for classic Hash Browns on page 202.) Bay Area restaurants still compete for who can serve the most over-the-top home fries; we finished ours with sour cream and scallions. Other options include shredded Cheddar or Monterey Jack cheese and chives, tomato salsa and Mexican crema, or caramelized onions and crème fraîche. I've seen (and ordered) them all.

3 large baking potatoes, such as russets (about 1½ pounds), scrubbed

1 tablespoon unsalted butter

1 medium yellow onion, chopped

1 medium green or red bell pepper, cored, seeded, and cut into ½-inch dice

2 tablespoons olive oil (not extra-virgin), as needed

Kosher salt and freshly ground black pepper

⅔ cup sour cream, preferably at room temperature

1 scallion (white and green parts), thinly sliced

1. At least 3 hours before cooking the home fries, prepare the potatoes: Put the potatoes in a large saucepan and add enough salted water to cover. Cover the saucepan and bring it to a boil over high heat. Reduce the heat to medium-low and set the lid ajar. Cook the potatoes at a brisk simmer until they can be pierced with the tip of a small sharp knife, about 30 minutes. Drain and rinse the potatoes well under cold running water. Drain again. Transfer the potatoes to a bowl and refrigerate them until chilled, at least 3 hours or overnight.

2. Melt the butter in a large nonstick skillet over medium heat. Add the onion and bell pepper and cook, stirring often, until the vegetables are tender, about 5 minutes. Transfer them to a plate.

3. Peel the potatoes, or leave them unpeeled, according to your preference, and cut them into ¾-inch cubes. Heat the oil in the skillet over medium-high heat. Add the potatoes and cook, turning them occasionally, adding more oil if the skillet gets dry, until they are golden brown, about 15 minutes. Stir in the reserved vegetables and cook until they are reheated, about 1 minute. Season to taste with salt and pepper.

4. Transfer the potato mixture to a bowl and top it with dollops of the sour cream. Sprinkle with the scallions and serve hot.

O'Brien Potatoes: Leave off the sour cream and scallions, and you have O'Brien potatoes, the classic diner home fries with onions and peppers.

Fried Potatoes

CLASSIC FRENCH FRIES

Serve with sandwiches and burgers, hot dogs, steaks, or steamed mussels.
Prep Time: 10 minutes, plus 1 to 4 hours cooling time
Cooking Time: 10 minutes
Make Ahead: The initial frying can be done up to 4 hours ahead of the final frying.
Family Favorite, Company Fare, Cooking Classic, Vegetarian

Homemade French fries are a special treat, served crisp and piping hot, fresh from the oil. I remember my mom making them at our family dinners, and I like to keep up the tradition now. If you want to serve the French fries in the European manner, dip them in Mayonnaise (page 436)

• The best method uses two frying periods: the first in low-temperature oil to create a thin wall of potato starch on the fries, and, after a cooling period, a second to crisp the potatoes at a higher oil temperature.
• Be sure to use large, mature, and floury potatoes with brown skins for French fries. Depending on where you live, these could be labeled as Eastern, Idaho, or russet potatoes. Don't use Yukon Golds or any of the waxy thin-skinned varieties.
• The quickest way to cut the potatoes into strips is to use a French-fry cutter (crisscrossed wires on a metal frame).

3 large baking potatoes, such as russets (about
  2 pounds), peeled
Vegetable oil, for deep-frying

Fine sea salt
Tomato ketchup, for serving

1. Starting at least 2 hours before serving, use a French fry cutter or large, sharp knife to cut the potatoes into strips about ¼-inch square. Transfer the potatoes to a large bowl of iced water and let them stand for 5 minutes. In batches, spin the potatoes in a salad spinner. Pat the potatoes completely dry with kitchen or paper towels. Wrap the potatoes in the towels to keep them from discoloring.
2. Place a wire cooling rack on a large, rimmed baking sheet. Pour enough oil into a large saucepan to come halfway up the sides and heat until the oil is shimmering and reads 325°F on a deep-frying thermometer. In batches, without crowding, add the potatoes to the oil and deep-fry until they are tender and just beginning to color, about 3 minutes. Using a wire spider or slotted spoon, transfer the potatoes to the wire rack. Let them cool completely, at least 1 hour and up to 4 hours.
3. Position a rack in the center of the oven and preheat the oven to 200°F. Transfer the potatoes to paper towels and pat them dry to remove the excess oil. Reheat the oil over high heat to 365°F.
4. In batches, without crowding, add the potatoes to the oil and deep-fry until they are crisp and

golden brown, 1 to 2 minutes. Using a wire spider or slotted spoon, transfer the fries to the wire rack to keep warm in the oven while frying the remainder. Season with salt and serve immediately, with the ketchup for dipping.

Radishes

When it comes to the radish, most cooks don't think outside of the salad bowl. However, this cousin of the turnip can also be braised to make a pastel pink dish with green accents whose gentle coloring belies its slightly spicy flavor. Beyond the familiar red radish, look for oval radishes, elongated French radishes, and radishes in a rainbow of colors.

Peak Season: May to July, available all year.

Purchase: Firm radishes without cracks; green tops should be crisp and not wilted.

Store: Refrigerate, unwashed, without tops for up to 2 weeks.

Preparation: Trim off tops and taproot.

BRAISED RADISHES WITH SCALLIONS
MAKES 4 SERVINGS

Serve with roast pork and chops; roast chicken; or grilled seafood.
Prep Time: 5 minutes
Cooking Time: 15 minutes
Weeknight Suppers, Holiday Feasts, Company Fare, Buffet Dish, Vegetarian

Like many cooks, I only ate radishes raw, sometimes with a little butter and salt as a nibble with drinks. But when I realized that they were similar to turnips, I tried cooking them and discovered a new way to serve them. A little sugar helps balance their bite.

2 tablespoons (¼ stick) unsalted butter
2 scallions (white and pale green bottoms, finely
   chopped; green tops, thinly sliced)

1 pound (about 25) radishes, trimmed and
   scrubbed
1 teaspoon sugar
Kosher salt and freshly ground black pepper

1. In a medium skillet large enough to hold the radishes in a single layer, melt the butter over medium-low heat. Add the white and pale green parts of the scallions and cook, stirring often, until they are softened, about 2 minutes.

2. Add the radishes, sprinkle with the sugar, and mix well. Pour in enough water to come halfway up the sides of the radishes. Bring it to a boil over high heat. Return the heat to medium-low and cover the skillet with the lid ajar. Simmer, stirring occasionally, for 10 minutes. Increase the heat to medium-high and uncover the skillet. Cook, stirring often, until the radishes are tender and the water has evaporated, about 5 minutes more. Season to taste with salt and pepper. Remove from the heat and stir in the dark green scallion tops. Serve hot.

Braised Radishes with Shallots and Herbs: Substitute 2 tablespoons finely chopped shallot for the white and pale green parts of the scallions. Substitute 1 tablespoon finely chopped fresh chives, dill, flat-leaf parsley, or tarragon for the dark green scallion tops.

Rutabaga

Often called a Swede, rutabaga has a vibrant yellow flesh that can really brighten up a winter table—mashed rutabagas are as popular as mashed potatoes at my house. When harvested young, rutabagas look somewhat like large turnips with white and purple skins. In my opinion, it is worth waiting until later in the autumn when the very large older rutabagas come into season. These are often labeled "waxed turnips" because they are coated to keep out moisture and discourage spoilage.

Peak Season: October to March; available all year.

Purchase: Heavy rutabagas without any soft areas.

Store: Refrigerate for up to 3 weeks.

Preparation: Use a sturdy vegetable peeler to remove the outer wax coating and peel.

RUTABAGA AND YUKON GOLD MASH WITH CARAMELIZED ONIONS
MAKES 4 TO 6 SERVINGS

Serve with roast pork, grilled pork chops, roast chicken, or roast turkey.
Prep Time: 10 minutes
Cooking Time: 1 hour
Make Ahead: The mash and the onion topping can be made up to 4 hours ahead.
Holiday Feasts, Company Fare, Buffet Dish, Vegetarian

To most of my friends who were raised in New England, mashed rutabaga is integral to holiday meals, and as unthinkable to omit from the menu as cranberry sauce. Raised in California, I never had rutabaga until I moved to the East Coast, and I thought, "What have I been missing?" In this version, Yukon Gold potatoes enhance the already golden rutabagas and give the mash a smoother texture.

CARAMELIZED ONIONS
2 tablespoons (¼ stick) unsalted butter
1 large yellow onion, cut into ⅛-inch half-moons
Kosher salt and freshly ground black pepper

1 large waxed yellow rutabaga (1¾ pounds), peeled and cut into 2-inch chunks
3 Yukon Gold potatoes (12 ounces total), peeled and cut into 1-inch chunks
3 tablespoons unsalted butter, plus more for serving

1. To make the caramelized onions: Melt the butter in a large skillet over medium heat. Stir in the onion and cover the skillet. Cook, stirring occasionally, until the onion softens, about 5 minutes. Uncover the skillet and reduce the heat to medium-low. Cook, stirring often, until the onion is very tender and deep golden brown, about 25 minutes more. Season to taste with salt and pepper. (The onion can be stored at room temperature for up to 4 hours. Reheat in the skillet over medium-low heat for about 5 minutes before serving.)

2. Put the rutabaga chunks in a large saucepan and add enough cold salted water to cover by 1 inch. Cover and bring to a boil over high heat. Reduce the heat to medium-low. Uncover and simmer for 15 minutes. Add the potatoes to the saucepan, increase the heat to high, and return the cooking liquid to a boil. Reduce the heat to medium-low and simmer until the rutabaga and potatoes are tender, 20 to 25 minutes more. Drain well.

3. Return the drained vegetables to the saucepan. Cook them over low heat, stirring often, until the vegetables begin to leave a film on the bottom of the saucepan, about 2 minutes. Remove the pan from the heat.

4. Using a handheld electric mixer on high speed, add the butter and beat the vegetables until mashed. (Or use a handheld potato masher.) Season to taste with salt and pepper. Transfer the mash to a serving bowl, top with the onions, and serve.

RUTABAGA, APPLE, AND WALNUT GRATIN
MAKES 8 TO 12 SERVINGS

Serve with Thanksgiving turkey, pork roast, pork chops, ham, sausages, or roast chicken.
Prep Time: 15 minutes
Cooking Time: 1¼ hours
Make Ahead: The gratin can be cooled, covered, and refrigerated for up to 1 day.
Holiday Feasts, Company Fare, Buffet Dish, Retro Recipe, Vegetarian

In this sumptuous gratin, golden slices of rutabaga alternate with apple wedges and peek through the cream that binds all of the ingredients together. Flavorful onions are found in every bite because their skillet juices are deglazed with the cream, a little touch that makes the difference in this recipe. Instead of the typical bread crumbs, this gratin has a crunchy topping of chopped walnuts.

1 large waxed yellow rutabaga (2½ pounds), peeled

2 tablespoons (¼ stick) unsalted butter, plus more for the baking dish

1 large yellow onion, chopped

Kosher salt and freshly ground black pepper

2½ cups heavy cream

2 Granny Smith apples, peeled, cored, and cut into ¼-inch wedges

½ cup coarsely chopped walnuts

1. Bring a large pot of salted water to a boil over high heat. Trim the top and bottom of the rutabaga so it stands securely on the work surface. Cut the rutabaga in half from top to bottom. Place a rutabaga half, flat-side down, on the work surface and cut it crosswise into half-moon slices about ½ inch thick. Add them to the boiling water and cook until the rutabaga slices are softened but not tender, about 10 minutes. Drain well.

2. Meanwhile, melt the butter in a large skillet over medium heat. Add the onions and season with ¼ teaspoon salt and a few grinds of pepper. Cover the skillet and cook, stirring the onions occasionally, until they soften, about 5 minutes. Uncover and reduce the heat to medium-low. Cook, stirring occasionally, until the onions are golden brown, about 15 minutes more. Transfer the onions to a bowl.

3. Return the skillet to medium heat. Add the cream and bring it to a boil, scraping up the caramelized onion juices in the skillet. Remove the pan from the heat.

4. Position a rack in the center of the oven and preheat the oven to 375ºF. Lightly butter a 13 × 9 × 2-inch baking dish.

5. Spread the onions in the bottom of the baking dish. Layer overlapping rutabaga slices in two rows over the onions. Tuck the apple wedges between the rutabaga slices; don't worry if you have more or less apples than rutabagas. Season them all over with 1 teaspoon salt and ¼ teaspoon pepper. Pour the cream mixture evenly over the vegetables in the baking dish, and press them down so they are almost submerged in the cream.

6. Bake, occasionally using a bulb baster to baste the rutabagas with the cream mixture and pressing the ingredients down with the back of a large spoon, until the rutabagas are tender, the top is golden brown, and the cream has thickened and reduced by about half, about 1 hour. Sprinkle the top with the walnuts and bake until they are lightly toasted, about 10 minutes. Let the gratin stand at room temperature for 5 to 10 minutes. Serve hot. (The gratin can be cooled, covered, and refrigerated for up to 1 day. Reheat in a preheated 350ºF oven, covered, until heated through, 30 to 40 minutes.)

Scallions

At a glance, you can tell that scallions (also called green onions) and leeks are closely related members of the onion family, with size being their main difference. But scallions are much more tender and require very little cooking . . . when they are cooked at all. Some recipes use just the more strongly flavored white and pale green parts, but that doesn't mean that the dark green tops are inedible. In fact, when a dowdy-looking dish needs a little fresh green color, a sprinkle of chopped scallion tops can come to the rescue.

Peak Season: Available all year.

Purchase: Brightly colored scallions without wilted tops.

Store: Refrigerate in a plastic bag for 3 days.

Preparation: Rinse well under cold running water and trim off the root end.

KOREAN SCALLION PANCAKE
MAKES 4 SERVINGS

Serve with Asian-style meats, poultry, or seafood.
Prep Time: 10 minutes
Cooking Time: 6 minutes
Weeknight Suppers, Family Favorite, Vegetarian

When I was on a teaching tour of Korea, showing Korean culinary students how to cook with American ingredients, I was able to sample a wide variety of the country's fare firsthand. This is one of the recipes I brought back with me, and I serve it a lot with grilled chicken or shrimp. The dipping sauce works for both the main course and the pancake, so I often double the amount of sauce.

DIPPING SAUCE

3 tablespoons soy sauce

3 tablespoons rice vinegar

3 teaspoons toasted sesame oil

1½ teaspoons sugar

1 small hot red chile, such as Thai, cut into very
   thin rounds, or ½ teaspoon hot red pepper flakes

1 garlic clove, minced

PANCAKE

½ cup (65 g) unbleached all-purpose flour

1 large egg, beaten to blend

½ teaspoon salt

1 tablespoon vegetable oil

8 scallions (white and green parts), cut into thin
   rounds

1. To make the dipping sauce: In a small bowl, whisk together the soy sauce, vinegar, sesame oil, sugar, chile, and garlic to dissolve the sugar. Divide the sauce among four ramekins.

2. To make the pancake: In a medium bowl, whisk together the flour, egg, ¼ cup water, and the salt just until the ingredients are combined; do not overmix. Heat the oil in a medium nonstick skillet over medium heat. Add the scallions and cook, stirring often, until they are softened, about 2 minutes. Pour in the batter and cover the skillet. Cook until the underside is golden brown and the top is set, about 3 minutes. Slide the pancake out of the skillet onto a plate. Top the pancake with another plate, invert the two plates, and slide the pancake, browned-side up, back into the skillet. Cook until the other side is golden brown, about 3 minutes more.

3. Slide the pancake onto a serving plate. Cut it into 4 wedges and serve it with the ramekins of sauce for dipping.

Sweet Potatoes

While sweet potatoes are a must-have on the Thanksgiving menu, more and more cooks are using them year-round. There are two things to know about sweet potatoes: They are not always sweet, and they are not yams, although many Americans call them by that name. The true yam (also called *name*, pronounced *nyah-meh*) is native to Africa and Asia, and has white flesh and scaly skin. The most **common sweet potato** in supermarkets has orange flesh and orange-brown, or sometimes purple, skin. Louisiana, garnet, and jewel sweet potatoes are examples of the type. At Latino markets and many supermarkets, you'll also find a **Latino sweet potato** called *boniato* or *batata* (the word that became "potato" in English). This kind sports creamy white or pale yellow flesh and skin that ranges from light beige to purple. Cooked, its interior is drier and blander than the orange-fleshed sweet potato. There are also **Japanese sweet potatoes** related to the Latino kind. I mention all this because there are markets, particularly in California, where you can choose from six or seven sweet potato types.

Peak Season: Early fall; available all year.

Purchase: Unblemished, hard tubers of a similar size for even cooking.

Store: In a cool, dark place (but not the refrigerator), for up to 1 week.

Preparation: For cooking whole, scrub the sweet potatoes under cold running water. Be sure to prick whole sweet potatoes with a fork before cooking. Otherwise peel them.

BAKED SWEET POTATOES WITH GINGER-LIME BUTTER
MAKES 4 SERVINGS

Serve with roast pork, pork chops, sausages, roast chicken, or fried chicken.
Prep Time: 10 minutes
Cooking Time: 50 minutes
Weeknight Suppers, Family Favorite, Holiday Feasts, Company Fare, Vegetarian

Here's a way to make roasted sweet potatoes a bit more special with an easy fresh ginger butter. This recipe gives directions for oven-roasted yams, but of course it works for the microwaved ones as well.

4 orange-fleshed sweet potatoes scrubbed and pierced with a fork (about 8 ounces each)

BUTTER
5 tablespoons unsalted butter, at room temperature

1 tablespoon peeled and finely chopped fresh ginger
Finely grated zest of 1 lime
Kosher salt and freshly ground black pepper

1. Position a rack in the center of the oven and preheat the oven to 400°F.

2. Put the sweet potatoes on a large, rimmed baking sheet. Roast until they are tender when pierced with the tip of a small sharp knife, about 50 minutes.

3. To make the ginger butter: Melt 1 tablespoon of the butter in a small skillet over medium heat. Add the ginger and cook, stirring occasionally, until it softens, about 3 minutes. Transfer the ginger and butter to a medium bowl and refrigerate until cooled, about 10 minutes. Add the remaining 4 tablespoons butter and the lime zest to the ginger mixture and whisk well. Set it aside at room temperature.

4. Remove the sweet potatoes from the oven. Protecting your hand with a kitchen towel, make a deep lengthwise cut into each sweet potato. Press both ends of the sweet potato at the same time to open the cut and place the sweet potato on a dinner plate. Top with a dollop of the ginger butter and serve, allowing each guest to season the sweet potato to taste with salt and pepper.

MASHED SWEET POTATOES WITH HONEY BUTTER
MAKES 4 TO 6 SERVINGS

Serve with roast turkey, roast pork, pork chops, sausages, or fried chicken.
Prep Time: 15 minutes
Cooking Time: 40 minutes
Weeknight Suppers, Family Favorite, Holiday Feasts, Company Fare, Buffet Dish, Retro Recipe, Cooking Classic, Vegetarian

This is my basic, no-fuss mashed sweet potato recipe. As there aren't a lot of additional seasonings here, I prefer to roast peeled potatoes to get some browning on the flesh for more flavor. But frankly, speed is on the side of the microwaved variation. So make your choice according to the amount of time you have.

5 large, elongated orange-fleshed sweet potatoes, peeled and cut into 1-inch chunks
2 tablespoons vegetable oil

3 tablespoons unsalted butter, at room temperature
2 tablespoons honey
Kosher salt and freshly ground black pepper

1. Position a rack in the center of the oven and preheat the oven to 425°F.

2. In a large bowl, toss the sweet potatoes with the oil. Spread them in a single layer on a large rimmed baking sheet. Roast, flipping the sweet potatoes over after 20 minutes, until they are browned and tender, about 20 minutes.

3. Meanwhile, in a small bowl, whisk the butter and honey together until combined. Set the mixture aside at room temperature.

4. Transfer the sweet potatoes to a large bowl. Using a handheld electric mixer set on low speed or a potato masher, mash the sweet potatoes. Season to taste with salt and pepper. Transfer the sweet potatoes to a serving bowl, top them with the honey butter, and serve.

Microwave Sweet Potatoes with Honey Butter: Pierce each sweet potato a few times with a fork. Microwave them on high, turning them over after 4 minutes, until they are barely tender when pierced with the tip of a small, sharp knife, about 8 minutes. Let stand for 5 minutes. Protecting your hands with a kitchen towel, peel the sweet potatoes and transfer the flesh to a large bowl. Mash as directed, top with the honey butter, and serve.

BRAISED SWEET POTATOES WITH RED CURRY SAUCE
MAKES 4 SERVINGS

Serve with rice and Asian-flavored grilled meats, poultry, or seafood.
Prep Time: 5 minutes
Cooking Time: 15 minutes
Make Ahead: The sweet potatoes can be made up to 1 day ahead.
Weeknight Suppers, Vegetarian

Thai red curry paste is one of the most incredible seasonings in the world; it contains about ten natural ingredients blended to deliver a jolt of flavor in every spoonful. Buy the paste in inexpensive small cans at an Asian market, and it is a bargain, too. The combination of browned sweet potatoes and spicy sauce is fantastic, and sometimes I purée the mixture for a mashed version. I can't say that it is too sophisticated for kids, because I was surprised when a neighbor's child ate more than his share at a dinner party.

2 tablespoons vegetable oil

2 large orange-fleshed sweet potatoes (1 pound), peeled, halved lengthwise, and cut into ½-inch slices

1 to 2 tablespoons Thai red curry paste (see page 214)

1 cup unsweetened coconut milk

Kosher salt

2 tablespoons coarsely chopped fresh cilantro

1. Heat a large skillet over medium-high heat. Add the oil, swirl to coat the bottom of the skillet, and heat until the oil is hot but not smoking. Spread the sweet potatoes in the skillet, flat-sides down. Cook, without turning, until the undersides of the sweet potatoes are browned, adjusting the heat as needed so they don't brown too quickly, about 3 minutes. Flip the sweet potatoes over and cook until the other sides are browned, about 3 minutes more.

2. Move the sweet potatoes to one side of the skillet. Add the curry paste to the skillet and cook until the paste leaves a browned film in the skillet, about 1 minute. (Don't breathe in the fumes from the browning curry paste, as they can be irritating.) Pour the coconut milk over the paste and stir until the paste dissolves. Spread the sweet potatoes in the skillet and stir them into the coconut milk mixture. Bring it to a simmer.

3. Reduce the heat to medium-low and cook until the sauce has thickened and the sweet potatoes are tender, 7 to 10 minutes. Season to taste with salt. Transfer the potatoes to a serving bowl, sprinkle with the cilantro, and serve.

Note: Thai curry paste comes in three main types: red (which gets its color from red chilies), green (made with green ingredients such as fresh chilies, cilantro, and kaffir lime leaf), and yellow (with Indian spices). It is sold in very reasonably priced cans at Asian grocers and in larger jars in the ethnic aisle of most supermarkets. Leftover curry paste can be refrigerated in a covered container for up to 2 weeks.

SWEET POTATO OVEN FRIES WITH JERK SEASONING
MAKES 4 SERVINGS

Serve with steak, meat loaf, hamburgers and other sandwiches; pork chops, ham, sausages, roast chicken, or fried chicken.

Prep Time: 10 minutes
Cooking Time: 40 minutes
Weeknight Suppers, Family Favorite, Vegetarian

Sweet potato fries taste great, but because of their sugar content, they have a tendency to go soggy after cooking, and the thin tips tend to burn. For crisp fries, be sure to trim off the pointed tips before cutting the potatoes into thin wedges, no more than ¼ inch across on the wide side. A spicy sprinkle of Caribbean jerk seasonings is a tasty way to wake up plain fries.

2 tablespoons olive oil, plus more for the baking sheet

2 large orange-fleshed sweet potatoes (1 pound), peeled

SEASONING
¾ teaspoon kosher salt

½ teaspoon granulated onion
¼ teaspoon granulated garlic
¼ teaspoon ground allspice
¼ teaspoon dried thyme
⅛ teaspoon cayenne pepper

1. Position a rack in the center of the oven and preheat the oven to 425°F. Lightly oil a large, rimmed baking sheet.
2. Using a large, sharp knife, cut off 1 inch at the pointed ends of each sweet potato. Cut the sweet potatoes lengthwise into wedges about ¼ inch wide at the widest part. In a large bowl, toss the sweet potato wedges with the oil.
3. Heat the oiled baking sheet in the oven until the oil is hot but not smoking, about 3 minutes. Remove it from the oven. Spread the sweet potatoes on the baking sheet, being sure that they do not touch each other. Return the baking sheet to the oven and roast the sweet potatoes until the undersides are golden brown, 20 to 25 minutes. Using a wide metal spatula, flip the sweet potatoes and continue roasting them until they are tender, 10 to 15 minutes more.

4. Meanwhile, make the seasoning: In a small bowl, whisk together the salt, granulated onion, granulated garlic, allspice, thyme, and cayenne.

5. Sprinkle the sweet potatoes with the seasoning and serve immediately.

LEMON SWEET POTATOES WITH MERINGUE TOPPING
MAKES 8 SERVINGS

Serve with roast turkey or baked ham.

Prep Time: 10 minutes

Cooking Time: 2 hours, 5 minutes

Make-ahead: The sweet potato base can be cooled, covered, and refrigerated for up to 1 day.

Holiday Feasts, Company Fare, Vegetarian

If you like the theory of traditional sweet potatoes with marshmallow topping, but not the actual execution, I heartily recommend this updated version with homemade meringue taking the place of the store-bought candy. Lemon in the mixture plays very well with the meringue. The turkey will get jealous if you serve this for Thanksgiving.

PURÉE

2 tablespoons (¼ stick) unsalted butter, at room temperature, plus more for the baking dish

4 large, elongated orange-fleshed sweet potatoes (about 3 pounds), scrubbed, pierced all over with a fork

¼ cup heavy cream

2 tablespoons light brown sugar

Finely grated zest of 1 lemon

2 tablespoons fresh lemon juice

½ teaspoon freshly grated nutmeg

4 large egg yolks (reserve the whites for the meringue)

MERINGUE

4 large egg whites, at room temperature

½ cup granulated sugar

1. To make the purée: Position a rack in the center of the oven and preheat the oven to 400°F. Lightly butter a 9-inch ceramic quiche dish or glass pie plate.

2. Put the sweet potatoes on a large, rimmed baking sheet. Roast until they are tender when pierced with the tip of a small, sharp knife, about 50 minutes. Let them cool until easy to handle, about 15 minutes.

3. Peel the sweet potatoes and put the flesh in a medium bowl. Add the heavy cream, brown sugar, butter, lemon zest and juice, and nutmeg. Using a handheld electric mixer on medium speed, whip the mixture until smooth. Beat in the yolks. Spread the purée in the baking dish.

4. Reduce the oven temperature to 350°F. Bake the purée until it is set and barely beginning to brown, about 30 minutes. (The sweet potato base can be cooled, covered with aluminum foil, and refrigerated for up to 1 day. Reheat, covered, in a preheated 350ºF oven until heated through, about 20 minutes. Uncover the purée.)

5. To make the meringue: Using the mixer with clean beaters, beat the egg whites in a medium bowl until soft peaks form (see Note). Gradually beat in the granulated sugar until the mixture forms stiff, shiny peaks. Using a spoon, spread and swirl the meringue over the purée.

6. Bake until the meringue is touched with golden brown, 7 to 10 minutes. Serve immediately.

Note: This dish is easiest to make with an electric handheld mixer. I love my standing mixer, but it is too large for some jobs. For example, the amount of egg whites for the meringue is too small to beat efficiently in the mixer's large bowl, and a hand mixer works much better.

Orange Sweet Potatoes with Meringue Topping: Substitute orange zest and juice for the lemon zest and juice.

SWEET POTATO AND PEAR CASSEROLE WITH BOURBON, BACON, AND MAPLE SYRUP

MAKES 8 SERVINGS

Serve with roast turkey or ham at a holiday meal.

Prep Time: 15 minutes

Cooking Time: 30 minutes

Make Ahead: The sweet potatoes can be prepared, without the topping, up to 1 day ahead.

Family Favorite, Holiday Feasts, Company Fare, Buffet Dish,

Add this to your list of sweet potato dishes to try, because the title says it all. If you have a crowd with equal amounts of adults and kids, make two batches: one with bourbon and the other with apple juice. The topping of bacon and pecans puts this over the top in a good way.

2 pounds orange-fleshed sweet potatoes, peeled and cut into ½-inch rounds

4 slices bacon

2 tablespoons (¼ stick) unsalted butter

½ teaspoon cornstarch

2 tablespoons bourbon, such as Four Roses, or apple juice

¼ cup pure maple syrup, preferably Grade A Dark

2 Bosc pears, peeled, cored, and cut crosswise into ¼-inch slices

kosher salt and freshly ground black pepper

⅓ cup toasted and coarsely chopped pecans (see page 33)

1. Position a rack in the center of the oven and preheat the oven to 400ºF.

2. Bring a large saucepan of salted water to a boil over high heat. Add the sweet potatoes and cook until they are beginning to soften, about 3 minutes. Drain, rinse, drain again, and pat them dry with paper towels.

3. Cook the bacon in a large skillet over medium heat, turning occasionally, until it is crisp and brown, about 8 minutes. Transfer the bacon to paper towels to drain and cool. Pour about 2 tablespoons of the bacon fat into a 13 × 9 × 2-inch baking dish, and brush the fat in the pan to coat the inside. Discard the remaining bacon fat.

4. Melt the butter in a small saucepan. While the butter is melting, sprinkle the cornstarch over the bourbon in a ramekin or custard cup and mix with a fork to dissolve the cornstarch. Add the bourbon mixture and maple syrup to the saucepan. Cook, stirring constantly, just until they are simmering and thickened, about 1 minute.

5. Arrange the sweet potatoes in two slightly overlapping rows in the baking dish. Randomly tuck the pear slices between the sweet potatoes. Pour the syrup mixture evenly over the sweet potatoes and pears and season them with ½ teaspoon salt and ¼ teaspoon pepper.

6. Bake, occasionally using a bulb baster to baste the sweet potatoes and pears with the syrup mixture in the baking dish, until the top is beginning to brown and the sweet potatoes are tender, about 30 minutes. (The casserole can be cooled, covered, and refrigerated for up to 1 day. Reheat, covered, in a preheated 350ºF oven for about 20 minutes.) Coarsely chop the bacon. Sprinkle the bacon and pecans over the top of the casserole and bake to heat the topping for 5 minutes more. Serve hot.

STEAMED BONIATO WITH ORANGE MOJO
MAKES 4 TO 6 SERVINGS

Serve with pork roast, pork chops, ham, or roast chicken.
Prep Time: 15 minutes
Cooking Time: 30 minutes
Weeknight Suppers, Holiday Feasts, Buffet Dish, Vegetarian

The yellow-fleshed boniato (also called batata) is a staple of Latino cooking. It is less sweet than the common American orange-fleshed "yam," and this recipe is more savory than you might think, with a garlic and citrus mojo (a twist on the classic garlic sauce of Puerto Rico) and a topping of fresh cilantro. To be sure that the boniato doesn't get waterlogged, I prefer steaming to boiling.

2 pounds white-fleshed boniatos, batatas, or
   Japanese sweet potatoes, peeled and cut into
   1-inch chunks (see Note page 218)

MOJO
¼ cup extra-virgin olive oil
2 garlic cloves, finely chopped
Finely grated zest of ½ orange
1 tablespoon fresh orange juice

1 tablespoon fresh lime juice
Kosher salt and freshly ground black
   pepper

2 tablespoons chopped fresh cilantro,
   for garnish

1. Place a collapsible steamer in a large saucepan and add enough water to almost reach the bottom of the steamer. (If you have another kind of steamer, just set it up as needed.) Bring the water to a boil over high heat.

2. Put the boniatos in the steamer and cover tightly. Cook until they are tender when pierced with the tip of a small, sharp knife, about 25 minutes.

3. To make the mojo: Heat the oil and garlic in a small skillet over medium heat just until the garlic begins to turn golden, 2 to 3 minutes. Remove the skillet from the heat. Add the orange zest, orange and lime juices, ¼ teaspoon salt, and ¼ teaspoon pepper and stir to dissolve the salt.

4. Transfer the boniatos to a serving dish. Season lightly to taste with salt and pepper. Spoon about 2 tablespoons of the mojo over them and sprinkle with the cilantro. Serve, with the remaining mojo passed on the side.

Note: White-fleshed sweet potatoes discolor more quickly than orange-fleshed ones, so if you won't be cooking them immediately, transfer the cut pieces to a bowl and cover with cold water and store them for up to 2 hours at room temperature.

Turnips

The no-nonsense, peppery flavor of turnip reminds me of the loudmouthed person in the office who needs to work on their social skills. Turnip can be a bit aggressive for some palates, but when I cook it with other ingredients to quiet it down, the results are very palatable. Turnips develop a stronger flavor as they age, and the smallest ones are the mildest. Turnips are members of the Brassica family, and their tops can be cooked like any other dark greens, such as collards or kale.

Peak Season: October to March; available all year.

Purchase: Firm, hard turnips without any dents or bruises; avoid large ones, which can be very spicy and tough.

Store: Refrigerate for up to 1 week.

Preparation: Trim off the top and bottom. Unless the turnips are small with tender skins, peel them.

MASHED TURNIPS WITH GARLIC
MAKES 4 TO 6 SERVINGS

Serve with roast pork, sausage, or roast chicken.
Prep Time: 10 minutes
Cooking Time: 25 minutes
Weeknight Suppers, Buffet Dish, Retro Recipe

This is a full-flavored alternative to mashed potatoes, and it is especially good with pork roast or roast chicken with gravy. Chicken broth boosts the flavor, but you can use water alone, if you wish.

1½ pounds turnips, peeled and cut into 1-inch chunks

1 pound baking potatoes, such as russets, peeled and cut into 1-inch chunks

8 garlic cloves, crushed under a knife and peeled

1¾ cups reduced-sodium chicken broth

3 tablespoons heavy cream or milk

2 tablespoons (¼ stick) unsalted butter, at room temperature

Kosher salt and freshly ground black pepper

Chopped fresh flat-leaf parsley or dill, for serving

1. Place the turnips, potatoes, and garlic in a medium saucepan. Pour in the broth and add just enough cold water to barely cover the vegetables. Bring them to a boil over high heat. Reduce the heat to medium and cover. Cook at a brisk simmer until the vegetables are tender, about 25 minutes. Drain the vegetables, reserving ¼ cup of the cooking liquid.

2. Return the vegetables to the saucepan. Using a handheld mixer at high speed, beat the vegetables, cream, and butter into a smooth purée, adding some of the reserved cooking liquid, if needed. (Or mash the ingredients together with a handheld potato masher.) Season to taste with salt and pepper. Transfer the mash to a serving bowl, sprinkle with the parsley, and serve.

PAN-ROASTED TURNIPS AND APPLES

MAKES 4 TO 6 SERVINGS

Serve with roast pork, pork chops, baked ham, roast chicken, or roast duck.

Prep Time: 5 minutes

Cooking Time: 25 minutes

Weeknight Suppers, Holiday Feasts, Buffet Dish

In a recipe that shows how opposites attract, spicy turnips and sweet apples play well together here. Enjoy this side dish during the cold weather, when the main ingredients are at the peak of their seasons. I usually make this without any herbs, but a sprinkle of chopped fresh chives, mint, or sage would be a nice addition.

2 tablespoons (¼ stick) unsalted butter

2 Granny Smith apples, peeled, cored, and cut into eighths

1 teaspoon sugar

2 medium turnips (about 11 ounces), peeled and cut into eighths

1 cup reduced-sodium chicken broth

Kosher salt and freshly ground black pepper

1. Melt 1 tablespoon of the butter in a large nonstick skillet over medium-high heat. Add the apples and cook, stirring occasionally, until they are lightly browned and hold their shape, about 5 minutes.

Sprinkle them with the sugar and cook, stirring occasionally, until the sugar caramelizes, about 1 minute. Transfer the apple mixture to a serving bowl.

2. Heat the remaining 1 tablespoon butter in the skillet over medium-high heat. Add the turnips and cook, stirring occasionally, until they are lightly browned, about 4 minutes. Add the broth and bring it to a boil. Cover the skillet tightly and reduce the heat to medium-low. Simmer the turnips until they are crisp-tender, about 8 minutes. Uncover the skillet and increase the heat to high. Cook, stirring often, until the turnips are tender and the broth has evaporated, about 5 minutes.

3. Return the apples to the skillet and cook, stirring occasionally, until they are reheated, about 1 minute. Season to taste with salt and pepper. Transfer the mixture to the serving bowl and serve hot.

Yuca

When the main course has Latino roots (*pernil*, marinated Puerto Rican roast pork shoulder, is one of my go-to main courses for a big dinner party), consider yuca for the side dish. This starchy tuber has mainstreamed to the point that even my supermarket carries it. Also called cassava or manioc, and the source of tapioca, it is no relation to yucca, the desert plant. The flesh is similar to potatoes, but a bit smoother and sweeter. Yuca's brown bark is always coated with wax to keep it from dehydrating during shipping and storage, and it is easily removed with a special method described below. Raw yuca is toxic, so be sure to cook the tuber before eating.

Peak Season: Available all year.

Purchase: Firm, evenly shaped yuca without any mold or dents.

Store: Store in a cool, dark place for up to 3 days.

Preparation: Cut off the pointed ends, and cut the yuca crosswise into 3- to 4-inch chunks. Cut a lengthwise slit down the side of each piece, cutting just into the skin. Slip a knife under the skin, and peel the skin away from the flesh. Using a vegetable peeler, remove the purple outer layer to expose the white flesh. The yuca contains a tough central string that must be removed, and it is easier to do this before cooking. Quarter the yuca lengthwise. Stand each quarter on its end, cut down to trim away the pointed center section that contains the (barely visible) tough cord. If not cooking immediately, avoid discoloration by transferring the cut yuca to a bowl of cold water, and store for up to 2 hours.

CLASSIC YUCA WITH GARLICKY MOJO
MAKES 4 TO 6 SERVINGS

Serve with Latino-style main courses, especially roast pork or pork chops, and chicken.
Prep Time: 10 minutes

Weeknight Suppers, Holiday Feasts, Vegetarian

My friend and neighbor Yvonne Ortiz was the food editor of our local newspaper, and she inspired me to try new things at the Latino diners in our neighborhood. I learned that when it comes to Puerto Rican cooking (she has written a book on the subject and has another in the works), Yvonne has few peers. This is how she would make yuca fresh from the farmer's market for dinner with her grandparents. This mojo is the classic version with just olive oil and garlic.

¼ cup extra-virgin olive oil

2 garlic cloves, minced

2 pounds yuca, peeled, quartered, central string removed, and flesh cut into steak-fry shapes about 3 × ¾ inches

Kosher salt

1. Bring 2 quarts of salted water to a boil in a large saucepan. (To avoid overcooking, yuca should be boiled in just enough water to cover it.)

2. In a small bowl, mix the oil and garlic together. Let them stand at room temperature while cooking the yuca.

3. Add the yuca to the boiling water and reduce the heat to medium. Partially cover the saucepan. Cook the yuca at a brisk simmer until it is barely tender when pierced with the tip of a small, sharp knife, about 15 minutes. Drain well.

4. Transfer the yuca to a serving dish and season to taste with salt. Stir the mojo well to distribute the garlic, and pour it over the yucca. Serve hot.

A HILL OF BEANS

Beans are a summer crop, and while we eat some of them fresh (see the pea and shell beans entries in the vegetable chapter), most of them are dried and cooked much later, after harvesting. Because dried beans require a soaking and cooking time of at least three hours, as much as I love them, I save them as a special treat when I have extra time. Canned beans are versatile, nutritious, and tasty, and can help you get a great side dish on the table in no time. The recipes in this chapter are divided into three categories, separated by their basic flavors and types: American-style beans are the ones you find at outdoor cookouts, perfect with barbecued meats, and usually glazed with some kind of sweet sauce. Latino-style beans, most often black and pinto, get their seasoning from aromatic peppers, onions, and chilies, and can be served in their traditional manner over a bed of rice. Mediterranean-style beans, including Italian cannellini and French flageolets, are simmered in broth to infuse them with herbaceous flavor.

COOKING DRIED BEANS

For sheer convenience, I cook most often with canned beans. I have a cupboard full of different varieties, from white to black, to use at a moment's notice. However, when time is not a factor, I also cook dried beans to store in the refrigerator or freezer. There are a lot of disagreements on how to cook beans: soaking vs. not soaking, when to add the salt, and more. This is how I cook beans, so feel free to experiment with other methods.

Freshness: Dried beans have a shelf life of about six months after purchase. They will lose flavor and become drier (and more difficult to estimate cooking times) as they age. Buy beans from a reliable source with a fast turnover. After opening the bag, store any leftover dried beans at room temperature in an airtight container, such as a jar.

Soaking: I always soak dried beans in water before cooking. Soaking breaks down some of the water-soluble complex sugars in the beans that cause digestion problems and softens the beans to speed up the cooking time. Yes, you can cook unsoaked beans, but the cooking time will be dramatically increased and you'll have to take the consequences in the digestion department. Small beans, such as black beans and adzuki, require less soaking time, and larger beans (white kidney and lima) take the maximum; thin lentils do not need any soaking at all.

Before soaking, spread the beans on a large, rimmed baking sheet and sort through them, discarding any foreign material like little clods of dirt and pebbles. Transfer the beans to a colander and rinse them well under cold running water. I forgot to do the sort-and-rinse recently, and ended up with a pot of dirty beans that I had to throw away.

The traditional soaking method is the "overnight" soak for 8 to 24 hours. But it has been shown that the beans are sufficiently hydrated and ready for cooking after 4 hours. Don't soak for longer than 8 hours, as the beans can absorb too much water and lose their shape during cooking. Place the rinsed beans in a large bowl (at least triple the volume of the beans) and add enough cold water to cover by at least 2 inches. (The dried beans are thirsty and will drink more water than you might imagine.) Discard any beans that float to the top of the water. Let the beans stand in a cool place for 4 to 8 hours; refrigerate during hot weather. Drain the beans and rinse again. (I do not drain black beans; instead I cook them in their soaking water because some of their pigment leaches into the water, and cooking the beans in new water will lighten their color.) Some bean experts argue against draining the beans, saying that you are tossing out nutrients.

The quick-soak method can be accomplished in about 1 hour. Put the rinsed beans in a saucepan and add enough cold water to cover by 2 inches, discarding any "floaters." Cover the pot and bring it to a full boil over high heat; boil for 1 minute. Remove from the heat and let stand, covered, for 1 hour. (Some cooks recommend 2 hours, but I find that that can be too long and can lead to overcooked beans.) Drain and rinse.

Timing: Whether the beans are cooked in a saucepan or with a pressure cooker (a great time-saver), there is a large range of cooking times for the various beans, due to variables in their age and relative dryness, the amount of hydration after soaking, and the mineral content of the cooking water. Beans cook best in soft water, so if your water is very hard, use distilled water. Use the chart on the facing page as a guide, but taste the beans occasionally during cooking to check their progress.

Salting Beans: When to add the salt to the cooking water for beans is a long-standing controversy. Some find that if salt is added at the beginning, it softens the beans too much and they break up during cooking. Others find the opposite, and that the salt hardens the beans. Yet there are cooks who even recommend soaking the beans in salt water. Personally, I add the salt about halfway through the cooking time, usually around my first "taste test" for texture. With a pressure cooker, the only option is to salt the beans at the beginning—unsalted beans taste bland. For both methods, I use about ½ teaspoon of kosher salt per cup of dried beans. If you wish, add a halved yellow onion and a couple of peeled garlic cloves to the beans for a bit of additional flavor.

Cooking Methods: To cook the beans on the stove, put the soaked beans in a saucepan and add enough cold water to cover by 1 inch. Bring them to a boil over high heat and simmer according to the estimated cooking times in the chart on the facing page, adding salt to taste about halfway through cooking.

To cook the beans in a pressure cooker, it is a good idea to read the manufacturer's recommendations. Today's pressure cookers are much more efficient than the old "toggle top" models; they have safety valves that allow for cooking beans and legumes. Formerly, many of these, especially split peas, could not be pressure-cooked because the foam released during cooking clogged the valves of the old models.

When cooking beans in a pressure cooker, for 1 cup beans, use 3 cups water or broth; for 1½ cups dried beans, use 4 cups; and for 2 cups beans, use 6 cups. Add 1 tablespoon of vegetable or olive oil to discourage foaming. Bring the cooker to high pressure over high heat, and cook according to the timings on the chart. Beans cook to about twice their dried volume, so be sure to use a pressure cooker of the appropriate size, allowing at least 2 inches of headroom. After pressure-cooking, quick-release the steam by running cold tap water over the lid of the cooker. Open the lid, tilting it away from you to block any escaping steam. If the beans are not quite done, just simmer them, uncovered, in the pressure cooker bottom on top of the stove until they are tender, or return to pressure for 1 minute.

Try to let the beans cool in their cooking liquid before using. Store the beans in a covered container, adding enough of the cooking liquid to cover. Refrigerate for up to 5 days, or freeze for up to 3 months.

One 15-ounce can of canned beans, drained, equals about 2 cups of cooked beans. For that reason, it is convenient to store home-cooked beans in 1-pint containers for easy substitution in recipes.

ESTIMATED TIMES FOR COOKING BEANS (IN MINUTES)

TYPE	STOVE TOP	PRESSURE COOKER
Black (Turtle)	60 to 90	8
Black-Eyed Peas	45 to 60	5
Cranberry	45 to 60	5
Garbanzos (Chickpeas)	60 to 75	7
Great Northern	45 to 60	5
Kidney, Red	60 to 75	7
Kidney, White (Cannellini)	45 to 60	5
Lentils (do not soak)	30 to 45	3
Lima, Baby	45 to 60	not recommended
Navy	45 to 60	5
Pink	45 to 60	5
Pinto	60 to 75	7
Red	60 to 75	7

American-Style Beans

A brimming pot of glazed beans is an essential item at backyard cookouts, not just because they are delicious, but because they are a sure-fire (and inexpensive) way to feed a crowd. Most of these recipes feature sweet and salty flavors, a combination that has proven irresistible for centuries.

SLOW-BAKED BOSTON BEANS

MAKES 8 SERVINGS

Serve with barbecued meats, baked ham, hamburgers, or hot dogs.
Prep Time: 15 minutes, plus 1 to 8 hours for soaking the beans
Cooking Time: 3 hours, 50 minutes
Make Ahead: The beans can be made up to 1 day ahead.
Family Favorite, Holiday Feasts, Company Fare, Buffet Dish, Retro Recipe, Cooking Classic

During the Colonial period, Boston was the major port for sugar and its by-products, such as molasses and rum, so molasses became an essential ingredient in the town's famous slow-baked beans. Baked beans remains one of the best sides for smoked or barbecued foods—sweet and salty in just the right balance, with some meaty notes from the pork. The rum amps up the flavor even more, but it is optional.

1 pound dried Great Northern beans, picked over for stones, rinsed, and drained

12 ounces salt pork

1 large yellow onion, chopped

½ cup molasses (not blackstrap)

2 tablespoons light brown sugar

1 teaspoon dry mustard powder

2 teaspoons kosher salt

½ teaspoon freshly ground black pepper

Pinch of ground cloves

½ cup dark rum (optional)

1. Put the beans in a large bowl and add enough cold water to cover by 2 inches. Let stand in a cool place for at least 4 and up to 8 hours. (Or put the beans in a large saucepan and add enough cold water to cover by 2 inches. Bring them to a boil over high heat. Cook for 1 minute. Remove from the heat and cover tightly. Let stand for 1 hour.) Drain, rinse under cold running water, and drain again.

2. Position a rack in the center of the oven and preheat the oven to 300°F.

3. Cut the rind off the salt pork in one piece and set the rind aside. Cut the salt pork vertically into ½-inch slices. Cut the slices into ½-inch strips (each strip will have fatty and meaty layers). Cook the pork strips in a Dutch oven or flameproof casserole over medium-high heat, stirring often, until they are swimming in fat and are golden brown, 5 to 7 minutes. Using a slotted spoon, transfer the pork to a plate.

4. Pour off and discard all but 2 tablespoons of the fat from the Dutch oven. Add the onion. Cook over medium heat, stirring often, until the onion is golden, about 5 minutes. Stir in the beans, browned pork, molasses, brown sugar, dry mustard, salt, pepper, and cloves. Add enough water to cover the beans by ½ inch and bring them to a boil over high heat. Place the reserved pork rind on the beans (it will enrich the cooking liquid) and tightly cover the Dutch oven.

5. Bake, stirring every 30 minutes or so, adding hot water if needed to keep the beans barely covered, until they are tender and the liquid has reduced by about half, about 3 hours. During the last hour of cooking, stir in the rum, if using. Remove the pot from the oven and let stand for 10 minutes. Discard the pork rind. (The beans can be cooled, covered, and refrigerated for up to 1 day. Stir ½ cup hot water into the beans. Reheat, covered, in a preheated 350ºF oven, stirring occasionally, until they are heated through, about 40 minutes.) Serve the beans from the Dutch oven.

SWEET AND TANGY BEANS
MAKES 6 TO 8 SERVINGS

Serve with barbecued meats, hamburgers, and hot dogs.
Prep Time: 10 minutes
Cooking Time: 1 hour, 10 minutes
Make Ahead: The beans can be made up to 1 day ahead.
Family Favorite, Buffet Dish

One of my easiest bean recipes just happens to also be one of my most popular, perhaps proof of the American sweet tooth. Surprisingly, the apple and raisins don't make these beans too sweet at all, and people love the bacon slices on top of the glazed beans. I recommend a hickory-flavored barbecue sauce to play up the smokiness of the bacon.

3 slices thick-sliced bacon, cut into 1-inch pieces

1 yellow onion, chopped

1 Granny Smith apple, peeled, cored, and cut into ½-inch pieces

1 cup barbecue sauce

1 cup seedless raisins

½ cup packed light brown sugar

One 15-ounce can pinto beans, drained and rinsed

One 15-ounce can white kidney (cannellini) beans, drained and rinsed

One 15-ounce can black beans, drained and rinsed

1. Position a rack in the center of the oven and preheat the oven to 350°F.

2. Cook 1 slice of the bacon in a Dutch oven or large flameproof casserole over medium heat, stirring occasionally, until the bacon is partially cooked and has rendered some of its fat, about 4 minutes.

3. Stir in the onion and apple. Cook, stirring often, until the onion is tender, about 4 minutes. Add the barbecue sauce, raisins, and brown sugar, mix well, and bring them to a simmer. Stir in the beans and bring them to a simmer. Top with the remaining bacon pieces and cover.

4. Bake for 30 minutes. Uncover and continue baking until the bacon pieces are browned and the beans are glazed, about 30 minutes more. (The beans can be cooled, covered, and refrigerated for up to 1 day. Stir ½ cup hot water into the beans. Reheat, covered, in a preheated 350ºF oven, stirring occasionally, until they are heated through, about 40 minutes.) Serve the beans from the Dutch oven.

BEER AND MAPLE BEANS
MAKES 10 TO 12 SERVINGS

Serve with barbecued meats, hamburgers, or hot dogs.
Prep Time: 15 minutes
Cooking Time: 1¾ hours
Make Ahead: The beans can be made up to 1 day ahead.
Family Favorite, Company Fare, Buffet Dish

There are many reasons to like these beans. The recipe uses canned beans to save some time, and the beans get plenty of flavor from the beer and maple syrup. This makes a large batch for a big cookout.

5 slices bacon, cut into 1-inch pieces

2 yellow onions, chopped

4 garlic cloves, chopped

One 12-ounce bottle dark beer (not stout)

½ cup tomato ketchup

½ cup pure maple syrup, preferably Grade A Dark

¼ cup spicy brown mustard

Five 15-ounce cans white kidney (cannellini) beans, drained and rinsed

1. Position a rack in the center of the oven and preheat the oven to 350°F.

2. Cook the bacon in a Dutch oven or large flameproof casserole over medium heat, stirring occasionally, until the bacon is browned, about 5 minutes. Using a slotted spoon, transfer the bacon to paper towels, leaving the fat in the pan.

3. Add the onions to the fat in the Dutch oven and cook, stirring occasionally, until they are golden brown, about 5 minutes. Stir in the garlic and cook until it is fragrant, about 1 minute. Stir in the beer, ketchup, maple syrup, and mustard. Cook, stirring occasionally, until slightly thickened, 8 to 10 minutes. Stir in the beans and reserved bacon. Bring them to a simmer. Cover the Dutch oven.

4. Bake for 1 hour. Uncover and continue baking until the beans have absorbed most of the liquid and look glazed, about 30 minutes. (The beans can be cooled, covered, and refrigerated for up to 1 day. Stir ½ cup water into the beans. Reheat, covered, in a preheated 350ºF oven, stirring occasionally, until they are heated through, about 40 minutes.) Serve the beans from the Dutch oven.

TEXAN POT OF PINTOS

MAKES 10 TO 12 SERVINGS

Serve with barbecued or grilled meats; hamburgers or hot dogs.

Prep Time: 15 minutes, plus 1 to 8 hours soaking time for the beans

Cooking Time: 1¼ hours

Make Ahead: The beans can be made up to 2 days ahead.

Family Favorite, Company Fare, Buffet Dish, Retro Recipe, Cooking Classic

In Texas, It's not a barbecue without a pot of chile-spiced beans. These are full of flavor, but not so hot that they will overpower the main dish. I am happy when there are leftovers, because these freeze beautifully and can be spooned into warmed tortillas with a few strips of grilled meat to make burritos for another meal. The thickness of the cooking liquid can be adjusted by the amount of beans that you mash in the pot. Some cooks prefer to leave them whole, giving the beans a soupy consistency. I like them on the thick side, so they don't run all over the plate.

1 pound dried pinto beans, picked over for stones, rinsed, and drained

4 slices bacon, cut into 1-inch pieces

1 yellow onion, chopped

1 red bell pepper, cored, seeded, and chopped

1 jalapeño chile, seeded and minced

2 garlic cloves, chopped

1¾ cups reduced-sodium beef broth

3 tablespoons tomato paste

1 teaspoon dried oregano

1 teaspoon ground cumin

1 teaspoon kosher salt

1. Put the beans in a large bowl and add enough cold water to cover by 2 inches. Let stand in a cool place for at least 4 and up to 8 hours. (Or put the beans in a large saucepan and add enough cold water to cover by 1 inch. Bring them to a boil over high heat. Cook for 1 minute. Remove from the heat and cover tightly. Let stand for 1 hour.) Drain, rinse under cold running water, and drain again.

2. Cook the bacon in a Dutch oven over medium heat, stirring occasionally, until the bacon is crisp and browned, about 5 minutes. Using a slotted spoon, transfer the bacon to paper towels, leaving the fat in the pan.

3. Add the onion, bell pepper, jalapeño, and garlic to the Dutch oven. Cook over medium heat, stirring often, until the onion is golden, about 5 minutes. Add the drained beans and the broth. Add enough cold water to cover the beans by 1 inch and bring them to a boil over high heat.

4. Reduce the heat to medium-low and cover, leaving the lid askew. Simmer, stirring occasionally, until the beans are almost tender, about 45 minutes. Stir in the reserved bacon, tomato paste, oregano, cumin, and salt. Simmer until the beans are tender, about 10 minutes more. (The beans can be cooled, covered, and refrigerated for up to 2 days. Reheat over low heat, stirring occasionally, for about 15 minutes.)

5. Using a large spoon, crush enough beans against the side of the pot to thicken the cooking liquid to the desired consistency. Serve the beans from the Dutch oven.

ROOT BEER BAKED BEANS

MAKES 8 SERVINGS

Serve with barbecued or grilled meats; hamburgers or hot dogs
Prep Time: 10 minutes
Cooking Time: 1 hour, 20 minutes
Make Ahead: The beans can be made up to 1 day ahead.
Family Favorite, Company Fare, Buffet Dish

A few years ago, I started experimenting with using soda pop as the sweet ingredient in my baked beans. Root beer, with its wide range of herbs and spices, is especially good. (Sometimes I use cola or ginger ale—all equally tasty.) Use a full-flavored brand—the small-batch ones seem to be the best—and skip the diet versions.

4 slices thick-sliced bacon, cut into 1-inch pieces

1 large yellow onion, chopped

2 garlic cloves, minced

Four 15-ounce cans small white beans, drained and rinsed

2 tablespoons tomato paste

2 tablespoons cider vinegar

1 tablespoon spicy yellow mustard

1 tablespoon molasses (not blackstrap)

1 teaspoon kosher salt

½ teaspoon freshly ground black pepper

Two 12-ounce bottles root beer, preferably a small-batch brand

1. Position a rack in the center of the oven and preheat the oven to 350°F.

2. Cook the bacon in a Dutch oven, stirring occasionally, until it is crisp and browned, about 8 minutes. Using a slotted spoon, transfer the bacon to paper towels to drain.

3. Pour off all but 3 tablespoons of the fat from the Dutch oven. Add the onion and cook, stirring occasionally, until it is golden and beginning to brown around the edges, about 7 minutes. Stir in the garlic and cook for about 1 minute. Stir in the reserved bacon, beans, tomato paste, vinegar, mustard, molasses, salt, and pepper. Pour in enough root beer to just cover the beans. Bring them to a simmer, stirring to dissolve the tomato paste.

4. Bake, uncovered, until the beans are glazed, about 1 hour. (The beans can be cooled, covered, and refrigerated for up to 1 day. Stir in ½ cup water. Reheat, covered, in a 350°F oven, stirring occasionally, until they are heated through, about 40 minutes.) Let stand 5 minutes and serve the beans from the Dutch oven.

HOPPIN' JOHN

MAKES 10 TO 12 SERVINGS

Serve as the centerpiece of a New Year's celebration with baked ham or grilled sausages.

Prep Time: 30 minutes

Cooking Time: About 3¼ hours, including standing time

Make Ahead: The broth and its meat can be cooled, covered, and refrigerated for 3 days,

but Hoppin' John is best made right before serving.

Holiday Feasts, Company Fare, Buffet Dish, Cooking Classic

In the South, there are many people who would not dream of starting the New Year without a mess of greens and a bowl of Hoppin' John, a stew of black-eyed peas and rice. The greens and beans represent currency in the form of paper bills and coins. I have made many versions over the years, and this one borrows from them all to make a hearty, full-flavored dish that will warm you on the coldest January day. (When my friend Jessica Harris, cookbook author and food historian, saw this recipe, she raised her eyebrows at the tomatoes . . . but she admitted that their acidity would be a good, if nontraditional, addition to the stew.) Hoppin' John is not very meaty, so serve ham or sausages as the main course.

HAM BROTH

1 tablespoon vegetable oil

1 small yellow onion, chopped

1 small carrot, chopped

1 small celery rib with leaves, chopped

6 garlic cloves, coarsely chopped

2 pounds smoked ham hocks, cut crosswise in half
  by the butcher

One 13¾-ounce can reduced-sodium chicken
  broth

HOPPIN' JOHN

1⅓ cups (8 ounces) dried black-eyed peas, picked
  over for stones, rinsed, and drained

1 tablespoon vegetable oil

4 slices bacon, cut into 1-inch pieces

1 large yellow onion, cut into ½-inch dice

2 large celery ribs with leaves, cut into ½-inch dice

1 red bell pepper, cored, seeded and cut into
  ½-inch dice

6 garlic cloves, minced

One 14½-ounce can diced tomatoes, drained

2 teaspoons kosher salt

½ teaspoon hot red pepper sauce, such as Tabasco,
  plus more for serving

2 cups long-grain rice

6 scallions (white and green parts), finely chopped,
  for serving

1. To make the ham broth: Heat the oil in a large pot over medium-high heat. Add the onion, carrot, and celery and cook, stirring occasionally, until they are softened, about 3 minutes. Add the garlic and cook until it is fragrant, about 1 minute. Add the ham hocks, broth, and 1½ quarts cold water. Bring them to a boil over high heat, skimming off the foam that rises to the surface. Reduce the heat to low and simmer until the meat on the hocks is tender enough to be cut from the bones, about 1½ hours.

2. Strain the broth into a large bowl, reserving the ham hocks but discarding the other solids. Cut the meat from the hocks, discarding the bones, and chop it into ¼-inch pieces. Measure the broth; you should have about 1¾ quarts. (The broth and meat can be separately cooled, covered, and refrigerated for up to 3 days. Bring the broth to a boil over high heat before proceeding.)

3. To make the Hoppin' John: Put the black-eyed peas in a large saucepan and add enough cold water to cover by 1 inch. Bring them to a boil over high heat. Cook for 1 minute. Remove from the heat and cover tightly. Let them stand for 1 hour. Drain well.

4. Heat the oil in a large pot over medium heat. Add the bacon and cook, stirring occasionally, until it is crisp and browned, about 8 minutes. Using a slotted spoon, transfer the bacon to paper towels to drain, leaving the fat in the pot.

5. Add the onion, celery, and bell pepper to the pot. Cook, stirring occasionally, until they are softened, about 3 minutes. Stir in the garlic and cook until it is fragrant, about 1 minute. Add the drained peas and 6 cups of the ham broth and bring them to a boil over high heat. (Set the remaining broth aside at room temperature.) Reduce the heat to medium-low and simmer, stirring occasionally, until the peas are barely tender, 30 to 45 minutes.

6. Stir in the drained tomatoes, diced ham, salt, and hot sauce and return the pot to a boil over high heat. Stir in the rice. Reduce the heat to medium and cook at a steady simmer, stirring occasionally, until the rice is tender and has absorbed almost all of the cooking liquid, about 20 minutes. If the rice has absorbed the liquid before it is done, add some of the reserved broth. (Leftover broth can be covered and frozen for up to 2 months; use it for soups, especially split pea soup.)

7. Remove the pot from the heat and cover it. Let it stand for 5 to 10 minutes to finish cooking and soaking up the liquid. Transfer the contents to a huge bowl, fluffing the rice as you do so. Sprinkle with the scallions and reserved bacon and serve hot, with hot sauce passed on the side.

Latino-Style Beans

Fresh chilies (also ground as chili powder or paprika, or canned chipotles) flavor these beans with their warm spiciness to serve with Mexican main courses or foods with Spanish flavors.

ENCHILADA BEANS
MAKES 6 SERVINGS

Serve with grilled tri-tip, Mexican-style main courses, roast pork, or sausages.
Prep Time: 10 minutes
Cooking Time: 20 minutes
Make Ahead: The beans can be made up to 1 day ahead.
Weeknight Suppers, Buffet Dish

The Central Coast region of California is famous for grilled tri-trip, a part of the bottom sirloin that for decades was processed only by that state's butchers and is now being found elsewhere. The area's road-

side barbecues sell tri-tip dinners with sliced meat accompanied by these spicy beans, green salad, and garlic bread. The beans are usually made with the local dried pinquito beans, a kind of small pinto, but this quick version with canned beans is excellent. The sauce is perfect for sopping up with garlic bread. Serve this any time you want a chile-seasoned bean dish, whether tri-tip is on the menu or not.

¼ cup olive oil

1 yellow onion, chopped

2 garlic cloves, minced

2 tablespoons unbleached all-purpose flour

2 tablespoons chili powder

½ teaspoon ground cumin

1¼ cups reduced-sodium chicken broth or water

One 8-ounce can tomato sauce

Three 15-ounce cans small red beans, drained and
 rinsed

Kosher salt

1. Heat the oil in a medium saucepan over medium heat. Add the onion and cook, stirring occasionally, until it is softened, about 3 minutes. Stir in the garlic and cook until it is fragrant, about 1 minute. Sprinkle with the flour, chili powder, and cumin and stir well. Stir in the broth and tomato sauce. Bring to a boil over high heat. Reduce the heat to medium-low and simmer, stirring often, until no raw flour taste remains, about 5 minutes.

2. Stir in the beans and season to taste with salt. Return the beans to a simmer and cook, stirring often, until the sauce has thickened and reduced by about one-quarter, 15 to 20 minutes. (The beans can be cooled, covered, and refrigerated for up to 1 day. Reheat them in a skillet over medium-low heat, adding more broth or water, if needed.) Transfer the beans to a serving bowl and serve.

MEXICAN BLACK BEANS WITH CHORIZO
MAKES 6 SERVINGS

Serve with grilled steaks, chops, and poultry, or with a tortilla-based Mexican main course.

Prep Time: 10 minutes

Cooking Time: 20 minutes

Make Ahead: The beans can be made up to 1 day ahead.

Weeknight Suppers, Buffet Dish, Cooking Classic

This recipe is why I always have beans in the pantry and chorizo links in the freezer. When a side dish is as flavorful and substantial as this one, the main course can be very casual. Recently, I served these beans with roasted chicken legs, rubbed with olive oil and seasoned with chili powder, salt, and pepper, for a very simple supper.

2 to 3 ounces smoked chorizo, cut into ½-inch dice

1 tablespoon olive oil

1 small yellow onion, chopped

½ red bell pepper, cored, seeded, and cut into
 ½-inch dice

½ jalapeño, seeded and minced

2 garlic cloves, minced

Two 15-ounce cans black beans, drained and
  rinsed

½ cup reduced-sodium chicken broth or water

½ teaspoon ground cumin

1 bay leaf

Kosher salt

Crumbled cotija or feta cheese, for serving
  (optional)

Chopped fresh cilantro, for serving (optional)

1. Cook the chorizo and oil together in a medium saucepan over medium heat, stirring occasionally, until the chorizo begins to brown, about 2 minutes. Add the onion, bell pepper, and jalapeño and cook, stirring occasionally, until the onion softens, about 3 minutes. Stir in the garlic and cook until it is fragrant, about 1 minute.

2. Stir in the beans, broth, cumin, and bay leaf and bring them to a simmer over high heat. Reduce the heat to medium-low and simmer, stirring occasionally, until the broth has reduced by about half, about 10 minutes. Season to taste with salt. Discard the bay leaf. (The beans can be cooled, covered, and refrigerated for up to 1 day. Reheat them in a skillet over medium-low heat, adding more broth or water, if needed.)

3. Transfer the beans to a serving bowl and top with the cotija and cilantro. Serve hot.

CARIBBEAN BLACK BEANS

MAKES 6 SERVINGS

Serve with steaks, roast pork and chops, chicken, or shrimp.

Prep Time: 10 minutes

Cooking Time: 20 minutes

Make Ahead: The beans can be made up to 1 day ahead.

Weeknight Suppers, Holiday Feasts, Company Fare, Buffet Dish, Cooking Classic

Both Cuban and Puerto Rican cooks serve these savory black beans with a hint of vinegar. I first had them at a Christmas party with roast pork and white rice, a triple-match that is made in heaven. When the rice is cooked with the beans in the same pot, the dish is called congrí *(or sometimes* moros y cristianos, *after the Negro Moors and Caucasian Christian occupants of the islands). I find it much tastier with the rice on the side.*

2 slices bacon, frozen for about 30 minutes to firm
  slightly, and cut into ½-inch dice

½ red bell pepper, cored, seeded, and chopped

½ yellow onion, chopped

2 garlic cloves, finely chopped

2 tablespoons olive oil

½ teaspoon ground cumin

½ teaspoon dried oregano

¼ teaspoon hot red pepper flakes

Two 15-ounce cans black beans, drained and
  rinsed

One 14½-ounce can diced tomatoes, with juice

1 tablespoon red wine vinegar

Kosher salt

1 recipe Perfect Steamed Rice (page 247), for serving

1. Using a large, heavy knife, chop the bacon, bell pepper, onion, and garlic together on a chopping board to blend the flavors and mince the ingredients more finely. (Do not use a food processor; it tends to pulverize the ingredients and release too many juices.) This mixture is called *sofrito*.

2. Heat the oil in a medium saucepan over medium heat. Add the *sofrito* and cook, stirring occasionally, until it softens, about 3 minutes. Stir in the cumin, oregano, and red pepper flakes. Stir in the beans, tomatoes with their juices, and vinegar. Bring them to a boil over high heat. Reduce the heat to medium-low and simmer, stirring occasionally, until the tomato juices have reduced by half, about 15 minutes.

3. Season to taste with salt. (The beans can be cooled, covered, and refrigerated for up to 1 day. Reheat them in a skillet over medium-low heat, adding more broth or water, if needed.) Serve hot, with the rice.

CHIPOTLE BLACK BEAN CAKES

MAKES 6 CAKES

Serve with roasts, steaks, chops, or sausages.

Prep Time: 10 minutes, plus 30 minutes refrigeration time

Cooking Time: 6 minutes

Make Ahead: The cakes can be refrigerated for up to 2 hours before cooking.

Weeknight Suppers, Vegetarian

I like to serve these smoky bean cakes with marinated meats for dinner, but they are also excellent with fried eggs and tortillas for a hearty breakfast. After making many versions of bean cakes over the years, I have learned one very important tip: Refrigerate the cakes well before cooking so they hold together when flipped over.

Two 15-ounce cans black beans, drained, rinsed, and patted dry on paper towels

3 scallions (white and green parts), coarsely chopped

2 tablespoons coarsely chopped fresh cilantro

2 canned chipotle chilies in adobo

8 tablespoons (65 grams) yellow cornmeal, preferably stone-ground

1 tablespoon red wine vinegar

1 teaspoon adobo sauce from canned chilies

1 teaspoon ground cumin

2 garlic cloves, crushed through a garlic press

½ teaspoon salt

2 tablespoons olive oil, as needed

Sour cream, for serving

Lime wedges, for serving

1. In a food processor, pulse the black beans, scallions, cilantro, chipotles, 2 tablespoons of the cornmeal, the vinegar, adobo, cumin, garlic, and salt together until the mixture forms a thick purée. (To make it by hand, finely chop the scallions, cilantro, and chipotles. Combine them with the remaining ingredients in a large bowl and mash them together with a potato masher or slotted spoon to purée the beans.)

2. Line a baking sheet with parchment or waxed paper. Shape the purée into 6 equal cakes. Place the cakes on the baking sheet. Cover them with plastic wrap and refrigerate for at least 30 minutes and up to 2 hours.

3. Heat the oil in a large nonstick skillet over medium heat until it is hot but not smoking. Sprinkle the remaining 6 tablespoons cornmeal on both sides of the cakes. In batches, if necessary, add the cakes to the skillet and cook until the cornmeal on the underside of the cakes is golden brown, about 3 minutes. Turn the cakes and brown the other sides, about 3 minutes more. (If cooking in batches, wipe out the skillet and add more oil before cooking the remaining cakes.) Transfer the cakes to plates and serve, with the sour cream and lime wedges passed on the side.

REFRIED BEANS

MAKES 4 TO 6 SERVINGS

Serve with Mexican-style main courses, especially tortilla-based dishes.
Prep Time: 5 minutes
Cooking Time: 15 minutes
Make Ahead: The beans can be made up to 1 day ahead.
Weeknight Suppers, Family Favorite, Buffet Dish, Cooking Classic

Once I learned how easy it was to make first-class refried beans at home, I stopped buying the canned version. The flavor is pumped up with a couple of strips of bacon, but if you don't have bacon, use 2 tablespoons olive oil to cook the onions and garlic. Top each serving with crumbled cotija cheese and chopped fresh cilantro, if you wish.

Two 15-ounce cans pinto beans
2 slices bacon, cut into 1-inch pieces
½ cup finely chopped white or yellow onion
2 garlic cloves, minced

½ teaspoon chili powder
½ teaspoon ground cumin
Kosher salt and freshly ground black pepper

1. Drain the beans in a colander, reserving ½ cup of the liquid. Rinse the beans under cold running water, and drain them again. Purée the beans and reserved liquid in a food processor (or in batches in a blender).

2. Cook the bacon in a medium nonstick skillet over medium heat, stirring occasionally, until the bacon is crisp and browned, about 5 minutes. Using a slotted spoon, transfer the bacon to paper towels to drain, leaving the fat in the skillet.

3. Add the onion to the skillet and cook, stirring occasionally, until it is softened, about 3 minutes. Stir in the garlic and cook until it is fragrant, about 1 minute. Stir in the chili powder and cumin, followed by the bean purée. Reduce the heat to medium-low and cook, stirring often with a heatproof spatula to scrape up any purée clinging to the skillet, until the beans have reduced into a thick mass, 12 to 15 minutes. Season to taste with salt and pepper. (The beans can be made up to 1 day ahead. Reheat in a nonstick skillet, adding water as needed to thin to the desired consistency.) Transfer the refried beans to a bowl.

4. Coarsely chop the bacon. Sprinkle the bacon over the beans and serve.

Refried Black Beans: Substitute black beans and ½ cup of their liquid for the pinto beans.

SPANISH GARBANZOS WITH HAM
MAKES 4 TO 6 SERVINGS

Serve with pork roast, pork chops, sausages, roast chicken, fish fillets, or sautéed shrimp.
Prep Time: 10 minutes
Cooking Time: 15 minutes
Make Ahead: The beans can be made up to 1 day ahead.
Weeknight Suppers, Buffet Dish

While a Spanish cook would make this with diced Serrano ham, it is usually sold in this country packaged in very thin slices that are too delicate to slice. Prosciutto is a highly acceptable substitute that can be used for this recipe. The air-cured ham will infuse the beans with its distinctive taste, along with the Spanish flavors of red pepper, sherry, and smoked paprika.

⅓ cup (¼-inch) diced Serrano ham or prosciutto
1 tablespoon olive oil
1 small red onion, chopped
½ red bell pepper, cored, seeded, and cut into ½-inch dice
2 garlic cloves, minced
½ teaspoon sweet smoked paprika (Pimentón de la Vera)

⅛ teaspoon hot red pepper flakes
¼ cup dry sherry
Two 15-ounce cans garbanzo beans (chickpeas), drained and rinsed
½ cup reduced-sodium chicken broth
Kosher salt
1 tablespoon chopped fresh flat-leaf parsley (optional)

1. Cook the Serrano ham and oil together in a medium saucepan over medium heat, stirring occasionally, until the Serrano ham begins to brown, about 3 minutes. Add the red onion and bell pepper and cook, stirring occasionally, until the onion softens, about 3 minutes. Stir in the garlic and cook until it is fragrant, about 1 minute. Stir in the paprika and red pepper flakes.

2. Add the sherry and cook until it has reduced by half, about 2 minutes. Stir in the beans and broth and bring them to a simmer over high heat. Reduce the heat to medium-low and simmer, stirring occasionally, until the broth has reduced by about half, about 10 minutes. Season to taste with salt. (The beans can be cooled, covered, and refrigerated for up to 1 day. Reheat in a skillet over medium-low heat, adding more broth or water, if needed.)

3. Transfer the beans to a serving bowl, sprinkle with the parsley, if using, and serve.

PROSCIUTTO, SERRANO HAM, AND PANCETTA

There was a time when prosciutto and pancetta were esoteric products in the United States—now they are available at most grocery stores. Serrano ham, the national ham of Spain, is mainstreaming in the same way. There are similarities and differences among the three.

Prosciutto and Serrano hams are both cured from the back leg of a pig. Italian prosciutto, the best of which hails from the region around Parma, is salted for two to four weeks and then goes through two separate aging processes for six months each. While there are domestic brands of prosciutto, imported prosciutto has a more delicate flavor and moister texture than the American versions. However, the Italian ham is too costly for everyday cooking.

Serrano means "highlands" in Spanish, and the ham is cultivated in the mountain communities. It is salted for two weeks, and then air-dried for six to eighteen months, depending on the size of the cut, elevation, and ambient temperature. Serrano ham made from the Ibérico breed of pig is superior, so ham labeled as such is more expensive. You will have to search for freshly sliced Serrano ham, although presliced packages are showing up at markets.

Pancetta is made from pork belly, so it is really bacon and not ham. It is salted and cured in a way similar to prosciutto, but rolled into a cylinder with some herbs and spices. (The amount of these changes from brand to brand, as does the saltiness.) The high fat-to-meat ratio of pancetta makes it a great seasoning meat.

Many supermarkets now carry packages of diced prosciutto and pancetta that are perfect for cooking. Refrigerated, these keep for a few weeks. Or ask the delicatessen to cut ¼-inch slices of the cured meat and then dice them at home. All three meats can also be frozen in airtight containers for up to a few months, and thawed as needed.

Because their flavors change if they are browned too deeply, prosciutto, pancetta, and Serrano ham should be cooked gently. For this reason, instead of the usual practice of heating the oil separately in the cooking utensil until it is hot, I often heat the oil with the cured meat for better control of the browning process.

PINTO AND CORN SAUTÉ

MAKES 4 SERVINGS

Serve with grilled steaks or chops.
Prep Time: 10 minutes
Cooking Time: 10 minutes
Weeknight Suppers, Family Favorite, Buffet Dish, Vegetarian

Corn and beans have been culinary partners for eons. When I want a "dry" side dish to go with a sauced main course, this appetizingly colorful sauté is the way to go. With the addition of a couple of ingredients, it can be expanded into an excellent vegetarian chili. Either way, you can't lose. Of course, you can change this up with your favorite beans—black beans are a nice alternative to the pintos.

1 tablespoon olive oil

½ red onion, chopped

½ red bell pepper, cored, seeded, and chopped

1 jalapeño, seeded and finely chopped

1 garlic clove, finely chopped

½ teaspoon ground cumin

½ teaspoon dried oregano

One 15-ounce can pinto beans, drained and rinsed

1 cup fresh or thawed frozen corn kernels

Kosher salt and freshly ground black pepper

2 tablespoons chopped fresh cilantro

1. Heat the oil in a large skillet over medium heat. Add the onion, bell pepper, and jalapeño and cook, stirring occasionally, until the onion softens, about 3 minutes. Stir in the garlic and cook until it is fragrant, about 1 minute. Stir in the cumin and oregano.

2. Add the pinto beans and corn with ¼ cup water. Cook, stirring occasionally, until the beans and corn are hot and the water has evaporated, about 5 minutes. Season to taste with salt and pepper. Transfer the mixture to a serving bowl, sprinkle with the cilantro, and serve.

Quick Vegetarian Chili: Stir 1 tablespoon chili powder into the sautéed vegetables with the cumin and oregano. Add one 15½-ounce can plum tomatoes in juice (coarsely chopped, including juices) with the beans and corn. Bring the pot to a simmer and reduce the heat to medium-low. Simmer, stirring occasionally, until the tomato juices have reduced by half, about 10 minutes. Makes 4 to 6 servings.

Mediterranean-Style Beans

In many countries around the Mediterranean, beans are simply cooked with seasoning vegetables, herbs, or spices as a side dish to roasted meats. Often the beans are topped with a spoonful of the roast's pan juices for a final fillip.

WHITE BEANS WITH WINE AND HERBS

MAKES 4 SERVINGS

Serve with roast lamb or pork roast; lamb or pork chops; grilled Italian sausage; or grilled salmon.

Prep Time: 5 minutes

Cooking Time: 15 minutes

Make Ahead: The beans can be made up to 1 day ahead.

Weeknight Suppers, Company Fare

*T*he combination of white beans and lamb is beloved throughout the Mediterranean, and I serve these beans often alongside slices of my own roast leg of lamb. These aromatic beans also make a fine bed for a platter of grilled fresh Italian sausages.

1 tablespoon olive oil	Two 3-inch sprigs fresh thyme
2 tablespoons minced shallots	1 bay leaf
1 garlic clove, minced	Two 15-ounce cans white kidney (cannellini)
¾ cup reduced-sodium chicken broth	beans, drained and rinsed
¼ cup dry vermouth or dry white wine	Kosher salt and freshly ground black pepper

1. Heat the oil in a medium saucepan over medium heat. Add the shallots and garlic and cook, stirring occasionally, until they are softened, about 2 minutes. Add the broth, vermouth, thyme, and bay leaf and bring them to a boil. Reduce the heat to medium and simmer until the liquid is slightly reduced, about 5 minutes.

2. Add the beans and cover the saucepan with the lid ajar. Cook, stirring occasionally, until the beans are heated through and the liquid has reduced a bit more, about 5 minutes. Discard the bay leaf and thyme stems. Season to taste with salt and pepper. (The beans can be cooled, covered, and reheated for up to 1 day. Reheat in a covered medium saucepan over medium heat, adding water if the beans have absorbed the liquid, about 10 minutes.) Serve warm.

WHITE BEAN PURÉE WITH THYME-GARLIC CRUMBS

MAKES 6 SERVINGS

Serve with pork or lamb roasts or chops; grilled chicken; or seafood.

Prep Time: 10 minutes, plus 1 to 8 hours soaking time

Cooking Time: 50 minutes

Make Ahead: The bean purée can be made up to 1 day ahead.

Holiday Feasts, Company Fare, Buffet Dish

The next time you serve a pork or lamb roast, forgo the mashed potatoes and make this wonderful bean purée. Topped with the meaty pan juices, it is a side dish that you will return to again and again. The crumbs make a nice textural contrast, but I often skip them and simply drizzle a tablespoon or so of extra-virgin olive oil over the purée.

PURÉE

1 pound dried white kidney (cannellini) beans, picked over for stones, rinsed, and drained

3 cups reduced-sodium chicken broth

1 small yellow onion, coarsely chopped

8 garlic cloves, crushed under a knife and peeled

Kosher salt

2 sprigs fresh thyme

3 tablespoons extra-virgin olive oil

Freshly ground black pepper

BREAD CRUMBS

2 tablespoons extra-virgin olive oil

1 garlic clove, finely chopped

1 cup soft bread crumbs, made in a food processor or blender from slightly stale crusty bread

1 teaspoon finely chopped fresh thyme

1. To make the beans: Put the beans in a large bowl and add enough cold water to cover by 2 inches. Let them stand in a cool place (or the refrigerator in hot weather) for at least 4 and up to 8 hours. (Or put the beans in a large saucepan and add enough cold water to cover by 1 inch. Bring them to a boil over high heat. Cook for 1 minute. Remove from the heat and cover tightly. Let stand for 1 hour.) Drain, rinse under cold running water, and drain again.

2. Transfer the beans to a large saucepan. Add the broth, onion, garlic, 1½ teaspoons salt, and the thyme. Pour in enough fresh water to cover the beans by 1 inch. Cover the saucepan and bring it to a boil over high heat. Set the lid ajar and reduce the heat to medium-low. Cook at a brisk simmer, adding hot water to keep the beans covered, until the beans are tender, about 45 minutes.

3. Meanwhile, make the bread crumbs: Heat the oil and garlic together in a medium skillet over medium heat, stirring occasionally, just until the garlic softens without browning, about 2 minutes. Add the bread crumbs and cook, stirring occasionally, until they are toasted and golden brown, 3 to 5 minutes. Stir in the thyme. Transfer them to a plate and set aside.

4. Drain the beans, reserving the liquid. Discard the thyme stems. Transfer the beans, with the onion and garlic cloves, to a food processor. Add the oil and process, adding enough of the reserved liquid as needed (about ⅓ cup) to make a smooth purée. (Or, for a coarser purée, process the bean mixture and oil in the cooking pot with a stick blender, adding the reserved cooking liquid as needed.) Season to taste with salt and pepper. (The purée can be cooled, covered, and refrigerated for up to 1 day. Reheat in a medium nonstick skillet over medium-low heat, adding water as needed to reach the desired consistency, about 10 minutes.) Transfer the purée to a serving dish, top with the crumbs, and serve.

FRENCH FLAGEOLETS WITH TOMATOES AND THYME

MAKES 6 SERVINGS

Serve with lamb and pork roasts or chops, leg of lamb, grilled or braised sausages, or grilled salmon.

Prep Time: 10 minutes, plus 1 to 8 hours to soak the beans

Cooking Time: 40 minutes

Make Ahead: The beans can be made up to 2 days ahead.

Holiday Feasts, Company Fare, Buffet Dish, Cooking Classic, Vegetarian

Flageolets are a cherished comfort food in France. Somewhat small, these white to pale green beans are always sold dried. They have an especially creamy texture, hold their shape well after cooking, and are commonly served alongside roast lamb or pork sausage. In fact, I often add smoked sausages (kielbasa, garlic sausage, or even franks) to the pot during the last twenty minutes of cooking to heat along with the beans. Sometimes, I purée the drained beans (adding enough of the cooking liquid as needed) for a nice alternative to mashed potatoes. You can substitute dried small white beans, if you wish.

1¼ cups dried flageolet beans, picked over for stones, rinsed, and drained

2 tablespoons olive oil

1 yellow onion, chopped

1 carrot, cut into ½-inch dice

1 celery rib, cut into ½-inch dice

2 garlic cloves, chopped

Four 3-inch sprigs fresh thyme

2 ripe plum (Roma) tomatoes, seeded and cut into ½-inch dice

1 teaspoon kosher salt

¼ teaspoon freshly ground black pepper

1. Soak the flageolets by either the traditional or quick-soak method according to the directions on page 224 for at least 1 and up to 8 hours. Drain well.

2. Heat the oil in a large saucepan over medium heat. Add the onion, carrot, and celery and cook, stirring occasionally, until they are softened, about 3 minutes. Stir in the garlic and thyme sprigs and cook until it is fragrant, about 1 minute. Add the flageolets and enough fresh water to cover the beans by ¼ inch. Bring them to a boil over high heat. Reduce the heat to medium-low and simmer, stirring occasionally, for 20 minutes.

3. Add the tomatoes, salt, and pepper and cook, stirring occasionally, adding boiling water to the saucepan, if needed, to keep the flageolets barely covered with liquid, until they are tender, about 20 to 30 minutes more. Discard the thyme stems and serve. (The beans can be cooled, covered, and refrigerated for up to 2 days. Reheat in a saucepan over medium-low heat, stirring occasionally, for about 10 minutes.)

ITALIAN LENTILS AND PANCETTA

MAKES 8 SERVINGS

Serve with pork and lamb roasts and chops; sausages; or grilled salmon.

Prep Time: 10 minutes

Cooking Time: 50 minutes

Make Ahead: The lentils can be made up to 1 day ahead.

Weeknight Suppers, Holiday Feasts, Company Fare, Buffet Dish

Lentils cook more quickly than other dried beans, so you can feasibly serve these on a weeknight. Or serve them Italian-style, for a New Year's meal (the beans represent coins for prosperity). This is a bean stew on its way to becoming a soup. In fact, I purposely use the entire bag of lentils for a large batch so any leftovers can be transformed into a soup with the addition of more broth. I really like these lentils with grilled salmon on top.

½ cup (¼-inch) diced pancetta or prosciutto

1 tablespoon olive oil

1 small yellow onion, chopped

1 small carrot, cut into ¼-inch dice

1 small celery rib, cut into ¼-inch dice

3 garlic cloves, finely chopped

1 pound dried brown lentils, picked over for stones, rinsed, and drained

2 cups reduced-sodium chicken broth

3 large sprigs fresh thyme or ½ teaspoon dried

1 bay leaf

Kosher salt

½ teaspoon hot red pepper flakes

One 14½-ounce can diced tomatoes

1. Heat the pancetta and oil together in a medium saucepan over medium heat, stirring occasionally, until the pancetta begins to brown, about 3 minutes. Stir in the onion, carrot, celery, and garlic and cook, stirring occasionally, until the onion softens, about 3 minutes.

2. Add the lentils, broth, thyme, bay leaf, 1½ teaspoons salt, and red pepper flakes. Pour in enough water to cover the lentils by 1 inch. Bring them to a boil over high heat. Reduce the heat to medium-low and cover the saucepan with the lid askew. Simmer, stirring occasionally, until the lentils are almost tender, adding more hot water as necessary to keep the lentils covered, about 30 minutes. Stir in the tomatoes with their juices and increase the heat to medium. Cook at a brisker simmer until the lentils are tender and the liquid level is below the surface of the lentils, about 20 minutes more. Using a large spoon, mash some of the lentils into the liquid to thicken.

3. Discard the thyme stems and bay leaf. (The lentils can be cooled, covered, and refrigerated for up to 1 day. Reheat in a medium saucepan over medium heat, adding water as needed to reach the desired consistency.) Season to taste with salt and serve.

LENTIL AND BROWN RICE PILAF

MAKES 4 TO 6 SERVINGS

Serve with lamb chops; sausages, especially lamb; chicken; salmon; or grilled or roasted vegetables.

Prep Time: 10 minutes

Cooking Time: 45 minutes

Buffet Dish, Cooking Classic, Vegetarian

Mjeddrah *(also spelled many other ways) is a Lebanese pilaf that is often served as a vegetarian meal with a heap of mixed green salad on top. I think that it is also a perfect side dish for smoky grilled food, especially lamb chops or sausages. Don't let the long ingredient list discourage you, as it really takes very little effort to cook the pilaf and its crowning touch of caramelized onions.*

PILAF

2 tablespoons olive oil

1 small yellow onion, chopped

1 small carrot, chopped

1 small celery rib, chopped

2 garlic cloves, minced

1½ teaspoons kosher salt

1 teaspoon ground cumin

¼ teaspoon hot red pepper flakes

1 bay leaf

¾ cup uncooked brown rice

¾ cup dried brown lentils, picked over for stones, rinsed, and drained

CARAMELIZED ONIONS

2 tablespoons olive oil

2 yellow onions, cut into ¼-inch half moons

Kosher salt and freshly ground black pepper

Chopped fresh flat-leaf parsley or mint, for garnish

1. To make the pilaf: Heat the oil in a medium saucepan over medium heat. Add the onion, carrot, and celery and cook, stirring until the onion is softened, about 3 minutes. Stir in the garlic and cook until it is fragrant, about 1 minute. Stir in the salt, cumin, red pepper flakes, and bay leaf. Add the brown rice and lentils.

2. Pour in enough water to cover the mixture by ½ inch. Bring the pot to a boil over high heat. Reduce the heat to low and cover tightly. Simmer, checking and adding more hot water if needed, until the rice and lentils are tender, about 45 minutes. Remove the pilaf from the heat and let it stand, covered, for 5 minutes.

3. Meanwhile, make the caramelized onions: Heat the oil in a large nonstick skillet over medium heat. Add the onions, season with salt and pepper, and cover. Cook, stirring often, until the onions soften, about 5 minutes. Reduce the heat to low. Cook uncovered, stirring often, until the onions are very tender and deep golden brown, 20 to 30 minutes. Remove them from the heat and cover to keep warm.

4. Drain the pilaf in a wire sieve, if necessary. Discard the bay leaf. Transfer the pilaf to a serving bowl and fluff it with a fork. Top with the onions and sprinkle with the parsley. Serve hot.

GARBANZO FLOUR FRIES WITH AÏOLI

MAKES 4 TO 6 SERVINGS

Serve with sandwiches and burgers, roast lamb, lamb chops, roast chicken, or salmon fillets.

Prep Time: 10 minutes, plus 1 hour cooling time

Cooking Time: 10 minutes

Make Ahead: The garbanzo bean mixture can be made up to 1 day ahead.

Family Favorite, Company Fare

While these fries are made with garbanzo bean flour, and not whole beans, they are so marvelous that I am including them here. Cooks in the South of France know them as panisses. *(*Panisse *is also the name of a character in Marcel Pagnol's* Fanny *film trilogy, and the namesake of Alice Waters's seminal restaurant, Chez Panisse.)*

2 cups garbanzo bean (chickpea) flour (see Note)

2 teaspoons kosher salt

½ teaspoon freshly ground black pepper

¼ cup olive oil, as needed, plus extra for the baking dish

Aïoli (page 437)

1. In a medium, heavy-bottomed saucepan, whisk together 4 cups water with the garbanzo bean flour, salt, and pepper. Bring them to a simmer, whisking constantly, over medium heat. Reduce the heat to medium-low and cook, whisking often to discourage scorching on the bottom, until the mixture is very thick, about 5 minutes.

2. Oil an 11½ × 8 × 2-inch baking dish. Spread the garbanzo bean mixture in the baking dish and smooth the top with an oiled spatula. Cover loosely with plastic wrap and refrigerate until cooled and set, at least 2 hours and up to 1 day.

3. Hold a baking sheet over the dish and invert them together to unmold the cooled garbanzo bean mixture. Using an oiled sharp knife, cut the mixture lengthwise in half, and then crosswise to make ½-inch sticks (*panisses*).

4. Position a rack in the center of the oven and preheat the oven to 200ºF. Place a large wire cooling rack over a large, rimmed baking sheet.

5. Heat the oil in a large nonstick skillet over medium-high heat. In batches, without crowding, add the *panisses* and cook, turning occasionally, until they are crisp and golden brown on all sides, about 6 minutes. Add more oil to the skillet as needed. Using a slotted spatula, transfer them to the rack to keep warm in the oven while frying the rest. Serve hot with the aïoli for dipping.

Note: Garbanzo bean flour used to be sold only at Mediterranean markets (where it may be labeled chickpea flour) or Indian grocers (where it is called *besan*). However, with the advent of gluten-free cooking, you can now find the Bob's Red Mill brand of garbanzo bean flour (labeled as such) at most supermarkets.

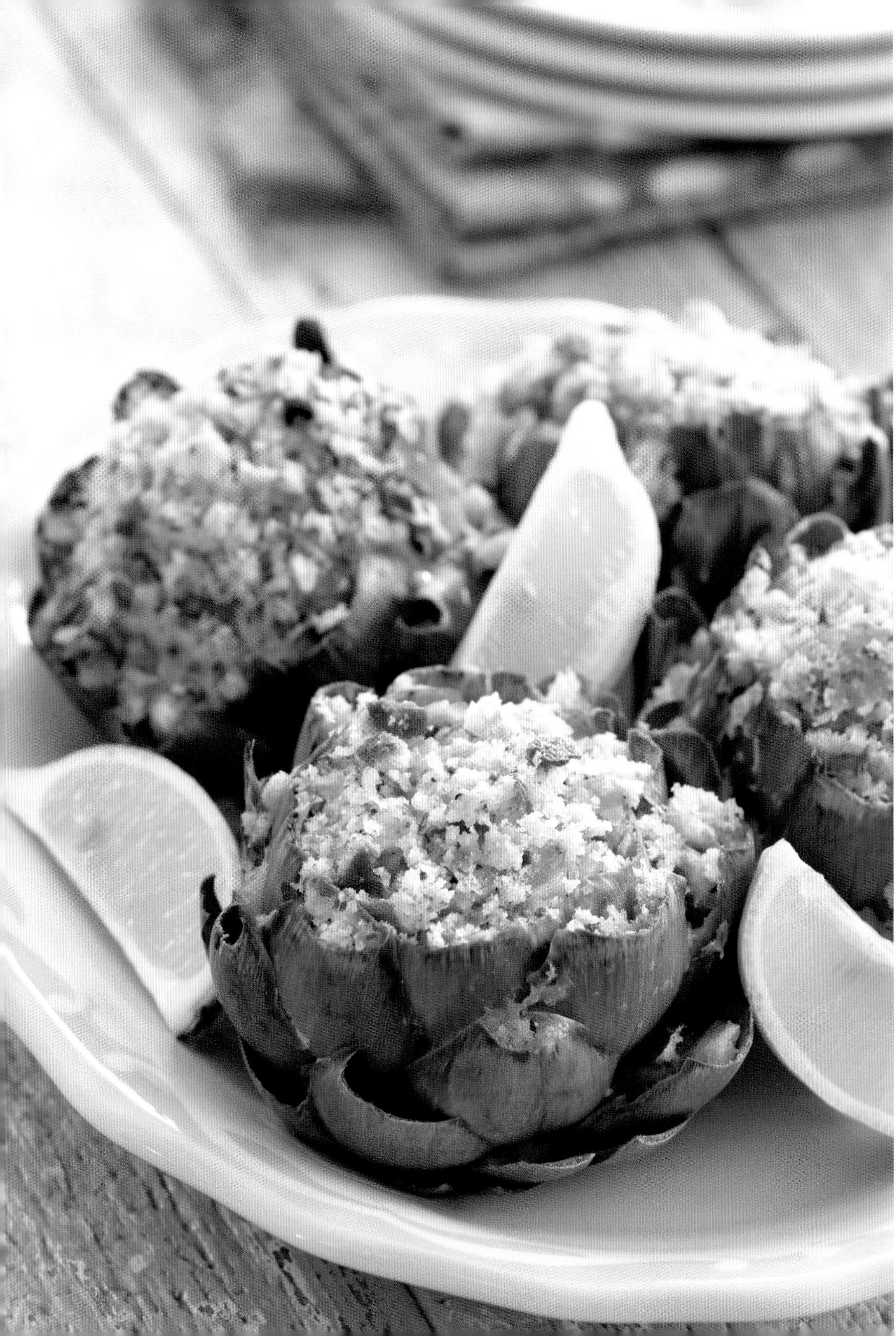

Stuffed Artichokes with Romano and Oregano (page 17)

Asparagus and Spring Vegetable Ragout with Tarragon Cream (page 25)

Roasted Brussels Sprouts with Bacon and Maple Syrup (page 55)

French Chard and Goat Cheese Tian (page 72)

Grilled Corn with Thyme Aïoli and Parmesan (page 84)

Risi e Bisi Tomatoes (page 131)

Zucchini and Scallion Croustade (page 137)

Roasted Beets with Balsamic-Orange Glaze (page 146)

Onion Tarte Tatin (page 164)

Potato and Fennel Gratin (page 187)

Lemon Sweet Potatoes with Meringue Topping (page 215)

Lentil and Brown Rice Pilaf (page 244)

Jasmine Rice with Green Tea, Edamame, and Ginger (page 253)

RIGHTEOUS RICE AND GREAT GRAINS

Rice and other grains, from millet to quinoa, are indispensable as side dishes. (In many countries, they are the main source of food.) These little guys are extremely versatile and able to take on other flavors while retaining their own character. For cultural and traditional reasons, white rice is prized in Asian countries, while more and more Americans are cooking with unprocessed grains. I have given recipes for the entire palette of rice colors, including red, brown, and black, and a wide range of international varieties (Japanese short grain and Italian risotto). Here, too, are side dishes running the gamut of the most useful grains for everyday cooking, from quinoa to millet, concentrating on the ones that can be cooked in less than 45 minutes.

PERFECT STEAMED RICE
MAKES 4 TO 6 SERVINGS

Serve with meat, chicken, or seafood dishes with sauces.
Prep Time: 5 minutes
Cooking Time: 20 minutes
Weeknight Suppers, Family Favorite, Buffet Dish, Cooking Classic, Vegetarian

A pot of rice, ready to soak up the sauce from your main course, is a beautiful thing. However, a little knowledge is powerful, so I am adding some words of advice below to ensure perfect results every time. You can use this method for any variety of rice except brown and wild. Use your discretion with the variations, as most of them are best made with white or brown rice.

• For decades, the only rice you could find at the supermarket was long-grain white rice. My local store now sells black Thai, Bhutanese red, Japanese-style short grain for sushi, medium-grain for risotto or paella, brown, and mixed blends. Processing has removed a lot of the nutrients in white rice along with the bran, so many cooks are turning to the ethnic rice varieties (which retain their outer bran).

• When cooking rice, the pot is probably the most important factor. Raw rice triples in volume when cooked, so if you have a pot that is too small, the rice will boil over. A heavy-bottomed saucepan discourages scorching, and a tight-fitting lid is a must. If the pot is too large or wide, the water evaporates before the rice has the time to cook until tender. Look at the pot you have chosen and imagine how the cooked rice will fill it. You want the raw rice and water to fill the pot by no more than half to allow for expansion.

• It is unnecessary (in fact, not recommended) to rinse rice. Domestic white rice is processed to remove the bran, which unfortunately removes vitamins, so replacement vitamins are sprayed on (that's why the labels say "enriched"). If you wash the rice, these vitamins go down the drain. When the rice is from a foreign country with different harvesting practices, you can rinse the rice well in a wire sieve under cold water. Some ethnic cookbooks recommend soaking the rice to hydrate it, but adopting that as a regular practice can wreak havoc with standard cooking times. But if you are using a recipe that recommends soaking or rinsing, then do it.

• Rice is divided into three categories according to length: long-, medium-, and short-grain. The shorter the grain, the more starch in the rice, and this translates into the degree of stickiness. In some cultures, stickiness in cooked rice is considered an attribute. For example, sticky short-grain rice is used for sushi so it will hold its shape when molded, and the starch in medium-grain Italian rice gives risotto its creaminess. For fluffy rice, use long-grain. I do not recommend converted rice. While it virtually guarantees fluffy rice with individual grains, it has been overprocessed to a taste-free state.

• Cook the rice at a gentle simmer so it can absorb the liquid at a leisurely pace. If the flame is too high, the water will evaporate before the rice is tender and you could end up with scorched rice. Too low, and you will have soggy rice that requires draining. Never stir rice while it is cooking, as this disrupts the cooking process. When the rice is done, remove the saucepan and let it stand, covered, for at least 5 minutes before serving. This allows the rice to "settle" and soak up any remaining moisture. Cooked rice will stay hot in its covered pot for 15 to 20 minutes.

• In my kitchen, I do not use a rice cooker on a regular basis. I have nothing against them, but we just don't eat enough rice as a couple to warrant losing the space on the kitchen counter. When I do use my rice cooker, I use it to cook the entire meal, and add a piece of salmon or halibut on top of the rice so it can cook at the same time. If you prefer to use a rice cooker, follow the manufacturer's instructions because the proportions can change from brand to brand. I also do not find any huge advantages to cooking rice in the microwave. It takes trial and error to find the correct cooking vessel to hold the rice without bubbling over.

• If you have leftover rice, it can be cooled and refrigerated in a zip-tight plastic bag for up to 3 days. Cold rice is great to have on hand to make fried rice. Otherwise, the best way to reheat rice is in a microwave on high in a covered microwave-safe bowl for 2 to 3 minutes, stirring occasionally. The exact timing will depend on the amount of rice.

• Boiling is an alternative to steaming. Simply add the rice to a saucepan of boiling salted water, just as you do with pasta, and boil until tender about 20 minutes. Drain in a wire mesh sieve. Some people don't like this method because the rice flavor can be diluted by the extra water. But there is no denying that it is very convenient, especially for a crowd, and useful if you are going to be adding butter, herbs, and other seasonings.

• The basic proportions for cooking rice are 2 parts liquid to 1 part rice.

1½ cups long-grain white rice	**1 teaspoon kosher salt**

1. Combine 3 cups cold water with the rice and salt in a medium, heavy-bottomed saucepan. (The level of water should not be any higher than halfway up the sides of the pan.) Bring the pot to a boil over high heat. Reduce the heat to medium-low and tightly cover the saucepan.

2. Cook at a low simmer, without stirring, until the rice is tender and has absorbed the water, about 20 minutes. Remove the saucepan from the heat and let it stand, covered, for 5 minutes. (The rice will stay hot in the pot for up to 20 minutes.) Fluff it with a fork and serve hot.

Basic Brown Rice: Substitute brown rice for the long-grain rice and increase the cooking time to 40 to 45 minutes.

Pesto Rice: Stir 2 tablespoons Pesto (page 425) into the finished rice.

Jalapeño Jack Rice: Stir ⅓ cup shredded jalapeño Jack cheese (about 1⅓ ounces) into the finished rice.

Parmesan Rice: Stir ¼ cup freshly grated Parmesan cheese (about 1 ounce) into the finished rice.

Saffron Rice: Add ⅛ teaspoon crumbled saffron threads to the rice with the water.

Lemon Rice: Stir the finely grated zest of 1 lemon into the finished rice.

BASIC BAKED RICE
MAKES 6 SERVINGS

Serve with sauce-based main courses, from meat to seafood.

Prep Time: 5 minutes

Cooking Time: 23 minutes

Weeknight Suppers, Family Favorite, Buffet Dish, Cooking Classic, Vegetarian

(with water or vegetable broth)

I know people who swear by this method because it is slightly more forgiving than the stovetop method. If you have been cursed with scorched rice in the past (due to a too-thin saucepan bottom and a too-hot flame), then try baking it. Just like any plain rice, you can embellish it with herbs, more butter, or Parmesan cheese (see the variations above).

3 cups water or reduced-sodium chicken broth
1½ cups long-grain rice
1 tablespoon olive oil

1½ teaspoons kosher salt (1 teaspoon if using broth)

1. Position a rack in the center of the oven and preheat the oven to 350°F.

2. Bring the water, rice, oil, and salt to a boil in a medium ovenproof saucepan over high heat. Tightly cover the saucepan. Transfer it to the oven and bake until the rice is tender and has absorbed the liquid, about 20 minutes.

3. Remove the pot from the oven and let it stand, covered, for 5 minutes. (The rice will stay hot in the pot for about 20 minutes.) Fluff the rice with a fork, transfer it to a serving bowl, and serve.

Baked Brown Rice: Baking is an especially good method for brown rice because the heat cooks the tough grains from all sides, and not just the bottom. Substitute brown rice for the long-grain rice, and increase the cooking time to 40 to 45 minutes.

COOKING RICE WITHOUT MEASURING CUPS

The classic Chinese method for cooking rice does not require measuring cups and works on the principle that rice takes twice its volume of water to cook. This technique can be used for virtually any amount of raw rice. You need rice, water, salt, a saucepan, and your finger.

The rice will triple in volume after cooking, so choose a heavy saucepan that will give you the desired amount of cooked rice with about 2 inches of headroom. Pour in the amount of raw rice needed (that is, one-third the amount of cooked rice). Add enough cold water to cover the rice by about 1 inch. You can use your finger to measure this amount. Just put your fingertip on the rice surface and if the water reaches the first joint crease on your finger, that's it. Add a couple of pinches of salt, if you wish. (Asian cooks don't salt their rice.) Bring the mixture to a boil over high heat. Reduce the heat to medium-low and tightly cover the saucepan. Simmer until the rice is tender and has absorbed the water, about 20 minutes. Remove it from the heat and let it stand covered for 5 minutes before fluffing and serving.

COCONUT-LIME RICE
MAKES 4 SERVINGS

Serve with Indian or Asian main courses.
Prep Time: 5 minutes

Cooking Time: 20 minutes

Weeknight Suppers, Company Fare, Buffet Dish, Retro Recipe, Vegetarian

Rice cooked in coconut milk has a creamy quality that goes well with many Far Eastern dishes. We are used to thinking of coconut as a dessert ingredient, but it is really fairly savory, and isn't sweet until it gets a sugar coating. This rice shines with Asian or Indian main courses that don't have sauce of their own, such as tandoori chicken or shrimp. If you wish, toast a few tablespoons of desiccated coconut in a skillet and sprinkle it over the rice before serving.

1 tablespoon vegetable oil	1 cup unsweetened coconut milk
1 large scallion (white and green parts), chopped	¾ teaspoon kosher salt
1 cup jasmine, basmati, or long-grain rice	Finely grated zest of 1 lime

1. Heat the oil in a medium, heavy-bottomed saucepan over medium heat. Add the scallion and cook, stirring often, until it is softened, about 1 minute. Add the rice and stir well. Add the coconut milk, 1 cup water, and the salt.

2. Bring the pot to a boil over high heat. Reduce the heat to medium-low and tightly cover the saucepan. Cook at a low simmer, without stirring, until the rice is tender and has absorbed the water, about 20 minutes. Remove the saucepan from the heat and let it stand, covered, for 5 minutes. (The rice will stay hot in the pot for up to 20 minutes.)

3. Add the lime zest and stir it in with a fork, fluffing the rice at the same time. Transfer the rice to a bowl and serve hot.

Coconut-Lime Rice with Cilantro: Stir 2 tablespoons finely chopped fresh cilantro into the rice with the lime zest.

FRENCH RICE WITH SHALLOTS
MAKES 4 SERVINGS

Serve with meat, poultry, or seafood stews and other sauced main courses.

Prep Time: 5 minutes

Cooking Time: 20 minutes

Weeknight Suppers, Family Favorite, Holiday Feasts, Company Fare, Buffet Dish, Cooking Classic

At our house, we call this "restaurant rice," because it is how I learned to make rice during a stint in a hotel restaurant kitchen. The shallots, broth, and wine definitely give it a fancier flavor profile that matches up with French ragouts like coq au vin.

1 tablespoon unsalted butter

2 tablespoons finely chopped shallots

1 cup long-grain rice

1¾ cups reduced-sodium chicken broth

¼ cup dry white wine or dry vermouth

½ teaspoon kosher salt

1 tablespoon finely chopped fresh flat-leaf parsley

1. Melt the butter in a small, heavy-bottomed saucepan over medium heat. Add the shallots and cook, stirring often, until they are softened, about 1½ minutes. Stir in the rice and mix well. Add the broth, wine, and salt.

2. Bring the pot to a boil over high heat. Reduce the heat to medium-low and tightly cover the saucepan. Cook at a low simmer, without stirring, until the rice is tender and has absorbed the liquid, about 20 minutes. Remove the saucepan from the heat and let it stand for 5 minutes. (The rice will stay hot in the pot for up to 20 minutes.)

3. Add the parsley and stir it in with a fork, fluffing the rice at the same time. Transfer the rice to a serving bowl and serve hot.

Brown Rice with Shallots: Substitute brown rice for the long-grain rice and increase the cooking time to about 45 minutes.

SPICED BASMATI RICE

MAKES 4 SERVINGS

Serve with sauce-based lamb, chicken, and seafood main courses, especially curries; or grilled chicken and lamb chops.

Prep Time: 10 minutes

Cooking Time: 25 minutes

Weeknight Suppers, Company Fare, Buffet Dish, Vegetarian

The aromas that come from this rice are almost intoxicating. If you like to cook Indian food, then you will have these spices in your kitchen, but you can subtract any that you don't have (say, the cardamom or brown mustard seeds) and still have a fine dish to serve with sauced main courses, especially curries. Don't bother to discard the spices before serving the cooked rice, but do warn your guests to remove the ones they find in their portion. I also like it with tandoori chicken. If you wish, add 1 cup cooked fresh or thawed frozen peas to the saucepan (but do not stir them in) during the five-minute rest period.

2 tablespoons (¼ stick) unsalted butter

1 small yellow onion, finely chopped

2 teaspoons peeled and minced fresh ginger

2 garlic cloves, minced

One 3-inch cinnamon stick

½ teaspoon brown mustard seeds

½ teaspoon cumin seeds

2 cardamom pods, crushed

2 whole cloves

1 bay leaf

⅛ teaspoon hot red pepper flakes

1 cup basmati or long-grain rice

½ teaspoon kosher salt

1. Melt the butter in a small, heavy-bottomed saucepan over medium heat. Add the onion, ginger, and garlic and cook, stirring occasionally, until the onion softens, about 3 minutes.

2. Add the cinnamon stick, mustard seeds, cumin, cardamom, cloves, bay leaf, and red pepper flakes and stir well. Add the rice and stir again. Add 2 cups water and the salt and bring the pot to a boil over high heat. Reduce the heat to medium-low and tightly cover the saucepan. Cook at a low simmer, without stirring, until the rice is tender and has absorbed the water, about 20 minutes. Remove the saucepan from the heat and let it stand, covered, for 5 minutes. (The rice will stay hot in the pot for up to 20 minutes.)

3. Fluff the rice with a fork and serve, asking the guests not to eat the spices.

Spiced Brown Basmati Rice: Substitute brown basmati rice for the white basmati rice and increase the cooking time to 45 minutes.

JASMINE RICE WITH GREEN TEA, EDAMAME, AND GINGER

MAKES 4 SERVINGS

Serve with Japanese dishes with sauce, such as teriyaki chicken or pork.

Prep Time: 10 minutes

Cooking Time: 25 minutes

Weeknight Suppers, Company Fare, Buffet Dish, Vegetarian

*P*lay up rice's Asian heritage with an unexpected ingredient—green tea. Whole-leaf tea (not the finely crushed kind in a teabag) works best here. The dish is particularly fragrant with jasmine rice, but this is also a good way to jazz up plain long-grain rice. If you like slightly sticky rice (which is much easier to eat with chopsticks), try the short-grain variation. (By the way, none of my Asian friends ever salt their rice, so it is entirely optional.)

1½ cups jasmine or other long-grain rice

3 quarter-sized slices peeled fresh ginger

2 teaspoons whole-leaf green tea, preferably gunpowder

1 teaspoon salt (optional)

½ cup thawed frozen shelled edamame

1. Combine 3 cups water with the rice, ginger, tea, and salt, if using, in a medium, heavy-bottomed saucepan. Bring the pot to a boil over high heat. Reduce the heat to medium-low and tightly cover the saucepan.

2. Cook at a low simmer, without stirring, until the rice is tender and has absorbed the water, about 20 minutes. Remove the saucepan from the heat.

3. Add the edamame but do not stir it in. Cover the saucepan again and let the rice stand for 5 minutes. (The rice will stay hot in the pot for up to 20 minutes.) Fluff it with a fork and serve hot.

Short-Grain Rice with Green Tea, Edamame, and Ginger: Substitute short-grain rice for the jasmine rice.

RED RICE WITH SESAME BROCCOLINI
MAKES 4 TO 6 SERVINGS

Serve with Asian-style main courses.
Prep Time: 10 minutes
Cooking Time: 30 minutes
Weeknight Suppers, Company Fare, Buffet Dish, Vegetarian

Thai or Bhutanese red rice is similar to brown rice, except that its outer coating is red and the rice takes less time to cook. It has a chewy texture and nutty flavor that is a good base for vegetables, such as this broccolini stir-fry. I do not add salt to the red rice and let the soy sauce in the broccolini do the seasoning.

1 cup red rice

1½ teaspoons sesame seeds

1 tablespoon vegetable oil

2 scallions (white and green parts), chopped

1 tablespoon peeled and minced fresh ginger

1 garlic clove, chopped

⅛ teaspoon hot red pepper flakes

1 bunch broccolini (8 to 10 ounces), cut into
    1-inch pieces

2 tablespoons soy sauce

2 tablespoon Chinese rice wine or dry sherry

1. Bring the rice and 2 cups water to a boil in a small, heavy-bottomed saucepan over high heat. Reduce the heat to medium-low and tightly cover the saucepan.

2. Cook at a low simmer, without stirring, until the rice is tender and has absorbed the water, 20 to 25 minutes. Remove the saucepan from the heat and let it stand, covered, for 5 minutes. (The rice will stay hot in the pot for up to 20 minutes.)

3. Meanwhile, heat a large skillet over medium heat. Add the sesame seeds and cook, stirring often, until they are toasted, about 2 minutes. Transfer them to a plate and set aside.

4. Return the skillet to high heat. Add the oil and swirl to coat the bottom of the skillet. Stir in the scallions, ginger, garlic, and red pepper flakes. Add the broccolini and ¼ cup water. Cook, stirring often, until the broccolini is crisp-tender and the water has evaporated, 2 to 3 minutes. Stir in the soy sauce and rice wine and immediately remove the skillet from the heat.

5. Fluff the rice with a fork and transfer it to a serving bowl. Top it with the broccolini mixture, sprinkle with the sesame seeds, and serve.

RICE AND VERMICELLI PILAF WITH PINE NUTS
MAKES 6 SERVINGS

Serve with veal, pork, or lamb chops, sausages, leg of lamb, grilled chicken, fish fillets, or sautéed shrimp.
Prep Time: 5 minutes
Cooking Time: 25 minutes
Make Ahead: The pilaf can be made up to 1 day ahead.
Weeknight Suppers, Family Favorite, Buffet Dish, Retro Recipe

Don't tell anyone, but I could eat this every night. Although it is an old Armenian recipe, it was popularized commercially in California (and then elsewhere) as "the San Francisco treat." My cousin was a strolling violinist who worked for many years at an Armenian restaurant in the City by the Bay, and this recipe, with aromatic rice and strands of toasted pasta set off by buttery pine nuts, has been kicking around my family for a few decades. Make it with beef or chicken broth according to the main dish. I can make this pilaf with my eyes closed, and everyone loves it. I always make this largish batch because it reheats beautifully in the microwave.

1 tablespoon unsalted butter
½ small yellow onion, finely chopped
½ cup vermicelli or angel hair pasta, broken into
   1-inch lengths to fit the cup
1 cup basmati or other long-grain rice
1¾ cups reduced-sodium chicken or beef broth

½ teaspoon kosher salt
1 bay leaf
½ cup pine nuts, toasted (see page 33)
2 tablespoons finely chopped fresh flat-leaf parsley,
   dill, or mint, or a combination

1. Melt the butter in a small, heavy-bottomed saucepan over medium heat. Add the onion and cook until it is softened, about 3 minutes. Stir in the vermicelli and cook, stirring occasionally, until it looks toasty, about 1 minute. Stir in the rice. Add the broth, ½ cup water, the salt, and bay leaf and bring them to a boil over high heat.
2. Reduce the heat to medium-low and tightly cover the saucepan. Cook at a low simmer until the rice is tender and has absorbed the liquid, about 20 minutes. Remove the saucepan from the heat. Add the pine nuts, but do not stir them into the rice. Cover again and let the rice stand for 5 minutes. (The pilaf can be cooled, covered, and refrigerated for up to 1 day. To reheat, melt 1 tablespoon unsalted butter in a large nonstick skillet. Add the pilaf and cook, stirring often, until hot, about 5 minutes. Or reheat in a covered microwave-safe bowl in a microwave on high for about 5 minutes.)
3. Discard the bay leaf. Transfer the pilaf to a serving dish, fluffing the rice as you do so. Sprinkle it with the parsley and serve hot.

GOLDEN-CRUSTED PERSIAN RICE

MAKES 6 SERVINGS

Serve with lamb and beef stews, roast lamb or lamb chops; poultry stew, or seafood stews.

Prep Time: 5 minutes

Cooking Time: 30 minutes, plus 5 minutes cooling

Weeknight Suppers, Family Favorite, Company Fare, Buffet Dish, Vegetarian

In this Iranian dish, rice is parboiled, then finished with butter in a unique method that creates crusty golden bits. Once you learn this technique, you will find yourself craving it every time you make rice. It's that good.

2 cups basmati or other long-grain rice	**1 teaspoon kosher salt**
3 tablespoons unsalted butter	**⅛ teaspoon crumbled saffron threads (optional)**

1. Bring a medium, heavy-bottomed saucepan of salted water to a boil over high heat. Add the rice and cook, stirring occasionally, until the rice is partially cooked (it should have a chalky center when you bite into a grain), about 10 minutes. Drain it in a wire sieve.

2. Rinse and dry the saucepan. Add the butter to the saucepan and melt it over medium heat. Add the rice to the saucepan. In a small bowl, stir together 2 tablespoons water with the salt and the saffron, if using. Gently stir the water mixture into the rice, taking care not to disturb the rice touching the bottom of the saucepan.

3. Dampen a clean kitchen towel (with a thin weave, not terry cloth) under cold water and wring it out. Place the towel over the top of the saucepan and cover it with the lid, bringing the towel edges up to keep them away from the burner's heat. Reduce the heat to low and cook for 15 minutes.

4. Increase the heat to medium and cook, covered, until the rice is tender and a light golden crust has formed on the bottom (use a fork to check), about 5 minutes. Remove the saucepan from the heat and let it stand, covered, for 5 minutes. Using a wooden spoon, scrape up the crust, mix it with the rice, and transfer everything to a bowl. Serve immediately.

CLASSIC SPANISH RICE

MAKES 4 TO 6 SERVINGS

Serve with Mexican food, chili, pork chops, sausages, barbecued meats and poultry, or sautéed shrimp.

Prep Time: 5 minutes

Cooking Time: 20 minutes

Weeknight Suppers, Family Favorite, Buffet Dish, Cooking Classic

Here is one of the most popular of all rice side dishes, gently flavored with tomato and spices. Don't make the mistake of adding more tomato paste, because too much will keep the rice from cooking. If you wish, stir in a couple of tablespoons of chopped fresh cilantro before serving.

1 tablespoon olive oil

1 small yellow onion, chopped

1 garlic clove, chopped

¼ cup hot water

1 tablespoon tomato paste

1¾ cups reduced-sodium chicken broth

1 cup long-grain rice

1 teaspoon chili powder

1 teaspoon kosher salt

1. Heat the oil in a small saucepan over medium heat. Add the onion and cook, stirring occasionally, until it is golden, about 4 minutes. Stir in the garlic and cook until it is fragrant, about 1 minute.

2. Meanwhile, in a 2-cup liquid measure, whisk the hot water and tomato paste together to dissolve the paste. Add the broth and set aside.

3. Add the rice to the saucepan and stir well. Stir in the chili powder and salt. Add the broth mixture and bring it to a boil over high heat. Reduce the heat to medium-low and tightly cover the saucepan. Cook at a low simmer, without stirring, until the rice is tender and has absorbed the liquid, about 20 minutes. Remove the saucepan from the heat and let it stand, covered, for 5 minutes. (The rice will stay hot in the pot for up to 20 minutes.)

4. Fluff the rice with a fork and serve hot.

Spanish Rice with Peas: Remove the cooked rice in the saucepan from the heat. Add ½ cup thawed frozen petit peas to the rice, but do not stir. Cover the saucepan and let it stand for 5 minutes to heat the peas. Fluff the rice, stirring in the peas, and serve.

Spanish Brown Rice: Preheat the oven to 350ºF. Make the rice mixture in a medium ovenproof saucepan. Cover tightly and bake until the rice is tender and has absorbed the liquid, about 45 minutes.

ARROZ CON GANDULES

MAKES 6 SERVINGS

Serve with Latino dishes, especially pork (roast, chops, sausages, or spareribs); sautéed chicken, fish fillets, or sautéed shrimp.

Prep Time: 10 minutes

Cooking Time: 25 minutes

Weeknight Suppers, Family Favorite, Holiday Feasts, Company Fare, Buffet Dish, Cooking Classic

Rice with pigeon peas (gandules) *is Puerto Rican comfort food of the highest order. With the addition of more ham, it can be substantial enough for a main course, but I prefer serving it as a side dish for*

roast pork, especially the garlic-infused Puerto Rican lechón. *Try to make it with slightly sticky medium-grain rice. The not-so-secret ingredient of arroz con gandules is the ubiquitous Caribbean seasoning mixture* sazón, *which gives the rice a yellow color. You'll find it, and medium-grain rice and pigeon peas, in the Latino aisle of the supermarket.*

½ cup chopped yellow onion

½ cup chopped green bell pepper

⅓ cup (¼-inch) diced prosciutto or smoked ham
   or 1 slice bacon, coarsely chopped

1 garlic clove, coarsely chopped

2 tablespoons olive oil

1½ cups medium-grain rice

1 tablespoon tomato paste

1¼ cups boiling water

1¾ cups reduced-sodium chicken broth

1 package (1¼ teaspoons) Latino-style seasoning
   with *culantro* and annatto, such as Sazón (see
   Note)

½ teaspoon ground cumin

½ teaspoon kosher salt

2 tablespoons finely chopped fresh cilantro

One 15-ounce can *gandules* (pigeon peas), or about
   1 cup thawed frozen green pigeon peas or green
   peas

1. Using a large, heavy knife, chop the onion, bell pepper, prosciutto, and garlic together on a chopping board to blend the flavors and mince the ingredients more finely. (Do not use a food processor; it tends to pulverize the ingredients and release too many juices.) This mixture is called *sofrito*.

2. Heat the oil in a medium, heavy-bottomed saucepan over medium heat. Add the *sofrito* and cook, stirring occasionally, until it softens, about 3 minutes. Add the rice and stir well.

3. Dissolve the tomato paste in the boiling water. Add it to the saucepan along with the broth, seasoning, cumin, and salt. Bring to a boil over high heat. Reduce the heat to low and tightly cover the saucepan. Cook at a low simmer, without stirring, until the rice is tender and has absorbed the liquid, about 20 minutes.

4. Reduce the heat to its lowest setting. Sprinkle the cilantro into the saucepan and add the *gandules,* but do not stir them in. Let the saucepan stand, with the lid ajar, for 5 minutes. This step will help a golden crust (*pegao*) form on the bottom of the saucepan.

5. Transfer the rice mixture to a serving bowl, fluffing the rice and stirring in the *gandules* as you do so, being sure to scrape up the crust from the bottom of the saucepan. Serve hot.

Note: Sazón is the name of the seasoning mixture as well as a branded version of the seasoning. If you wish, substitute ½ teaspoon salt, ¼ teaspoon garlic powder, ¼ teaspoon onion powder, ¼ teaspoon freshly ground black pepper, and a pinch of crumbled saffron. *Culantro*, an ingredient in many commercial sazón blends, is a broad-leaf variety of cilantro used in Caribbean cooking. It is not available dried, but the fresh cilantro in the recipe is sufficient for flavoring.

Fried Rice

I usually make fried rice according to what happens to be in the refrigerator at the time. On the other hand, it is so good that I sometimes think ahead and buy ingredients to create a specific recipe, as the fried rice principle can be applied to other flavor combinations outside of the Chinese tradition.

- Fried rice must be made with cold rice, preferably rice that has chilled in the refrigerator for at least 12 hours. It will not work with hot-from-the-pot rice. Try it and you will have a sticky mess. Get in the habit of making extra white rice so you'll have leftovers ready to cook for another meal.
- To prepare the cold rice for frying, just break up any lumps with your fingertips.

CHINESE FRIED RICE WITH SHIITAKES, SNAP PEAS, AND EGGS
MAKES 4 TO 6 SERVINGS

Serve with Chinese-seasoned meats, poultry, or seafood.

Prep Time: 10 minutes

Cooking Time: 6 minutes

Weeknight Suppers, Family Favorite, Cooking Classic, Vegetarian

Here is my basic formula for Chinese-style fried rice with soy sauce and Asian vegetables. The vegetables should be crisp-tender, so add them to the skillet according to their texture, and give the harder ingredients a head start. Prosciutto stands in for Chinese sausage or ham, but it is totally optional. Note that the soy sauce and oyster sauce, while very tasty, will give the fried rice a brown color—I sometimes leave them out and just serve soy sauce on the side. This fried rice is a huge hit served with marinated grilled chicken or flank steak.

2 tablespoons soy sauce

1 tablespoon oyster sauce

2 tablespoons vegetable oil

1 carrot, cut into thin strips

¼ cup (¼-inch) diced prosciutto or smoked ham (optional)

1 yellow onion, chopped

4 ounces stemmed shiitake caps, cut into ½-inch strips

4 ounces sugar snap peas, cut crosswise into ½-inch pieces

3 cups cold Perfect Steamed Rice (page 247), clumps broken up with your fingertips

2 large eggs, beaten to blend

Kosher salt and freshly ground black pepper

1. In a small bowl, whisk the soy sauce and oyster sauce together; set aside.

2. Heat the oil in a large nonstick skillet over medium-high heat until it is hot but not smoking. Add

the carrot and prosciutto, if using, and cook, stirring often, until the carrot is beginning to soften, about 30 seconds. Add the onion, shiitakes, and snap peas and cook, stirring often, until the onions soften, about 1½ minutes.

3. Add the rice to the skillet and cook, stirring almost constantly, until the rice is heated, about 1½ minutes. Add the soy sauce mixture and mix well. Move the fried rice mixture to one side of the skillet. Pour the beaten eggs into the empty side of the skillet and let them cook until the edges are set, about 30 seconds. Stir the eggs until they scramble into soft curds, about 20 seconds, and then mix them into the fried rice. Season to taste with salt and pepper and serve.

Fried Brown Rice with Shiitakes, Snap Peas, and Eggs: Substitute cold cooked brown rice for the white rice.

KIMCHI FRIED RICE WITH CELERY AND SCALLIONS
MAKES 6 SERVINGS

Serve with grilled flank steak or chicken marinated with Asian flavors.
Prep Time: 10 minutes
Cooking Time: 12 minutes
Weeknight Suppers, Vegetarian

One of the many reasons I make my own kimchi (page 411) is to have it on hand for this easy Korean side dish, one that I have been making since my first trip to Korea many years ago. It is sometimes cooked with bits of meat (ham, bacon, or even Spam, which I had in Hawaii) to create a light lunch or supper. But I serve this lighter vegetarian version as a spicy side dish for Asian main courses.

2 teaspoons sesame seeds

2 tablespoons vegetable oil

4 large celery ribs, cut into ¼-inch slices

4 scallions (white and green parts), thinly sliced

1½ cups coarsely chopped Napa Cabbage Kimchi
  (page 411) with juices, or store-bought kimchi

3 cups cold cooked long-grain rice, clumps broken
  up with your fingertips

2 teaspoons toasted sesame oil

Soy sauce, for serving

1. Cook the sesame seeds in a large nonstick skillet over medium heat, stirring often, until they are toasted, about 3 minutes. Transfer them to a small plate.

2. Return the skillet to high heat. Add the vegetable oil and swirl to coat the bottom and inside of the skillet. Add the celery and stir almost constantly until it begins to soften, about 1 minute. Add the scallions and stir until they are wilted, about 1 minute. Add the kimchi and its juices and cook, stirring often, until it is hot, about 2 minutes. Add the rice and cook, breaking up the rice with the spoon, stirring often, until the rice is hot and the ingredients are well combined, about 5 minutes. Drizzle with the sesame oil.

3. Transfer the fried rice to a serving bowl. Top it with the toasted sesame seeds and serve hot, with the soy sauce passed on the side.

SPICY FRIED RICE WITH CORN AND CILANTRO

MAKES 6 SERVINGS

Serve with chili, steaks, pork or lamb chops, roast chicken, or seafood.

Prep Time: 15 minutes

Cooking Time: 12 minutes

Weeknight Suppers, Family Favorite, Buffet Dish, Vegetarian

When I'm serving an uncomplicated main dish, such as roast chicken or pork chops, I like to balance the plate with a slightly more complicated side dish. Fried rice, prepared from leftover cold rice with vegetables, does the trick.

2 tablespoons extra-virgin olive oil

1 red bell pepper, cored, seeded, and cut into ½-inch dice

4 scallions (white and green parts), chopped

1 jalapeño, seeded and minced

1 garlic clove, crushed through a garlic press

1 cup fresh or thawed frozen corn kernels

½ cup reduced-sodium chicken broth

3½ cups cold cooked long-grain rice, clumps broken up with your fingertips

2 tablespoons chopped fresh cilantro

Kosher salt and freshly ground black pepper

3 tablespoons freshly grated Romano or Parmesan cheese

Lime wedges, for serving

1. Heat the oil in a large skillet over medium-high heat. Add the bell pepper and cook, stirring occasionally, until it is crisp-tender, about 3 minutes. Add the scallions, jalapeño, and garlic and stir until the scallions are wilted, about 1 minute. Add the corn and broth and boil until the broth is reduced to 2 tablespoons, about 3 minutes.

2. Add the rice and cook, breaking up the rice with a spoon, stirring often, until it is hot, about 3 minutes. Stir in the cilantro. Season to taste with salt and pepper.

3. Transfer the fried rice to a serving bowl. Sprinkle it with the Romano and serve with the lime wedges.

Risotto

In its birthplace, Italy, risotto is usually a first course before the main course. (The exception is the saffron risotto made with beef marrow that accompanies osso buco.) But risotto is very useful as a side dish to serve with a simply prepared protein. Very often, dinner at our house is a vegetable risotto topped with sautéed shrimp or a roasted fish fillet.

- Risotto gets its creamy texture from the natural starches in the rice. It is essential to use imported Italian rice grown specifically for risotto. Arborio is the most common variety, but it isn't the only one. Look for carnaroli or vialone nano, both of which make excellent risotto. They are more expensive than Arborio, but worth it.

- The risotto should be stirred almost constantly during cooking, but that doesn't mean you can't occasionally walk away from the stove. Stirring helps release the starches and, of course, discourages the rice from sticking to the bottom of the pot.

- The broth mixture (which is purposely diluted because risotto made with full-strength broth is too rich) must be kept steaming hot so the risotto keeps a steady temperature throughout the cooking process. You will need at least 6 cups of the broth mixture for every 1½ cups of rice. If you run out of broth toward the end of the cooking process, use hot water.

- For me, one of the pleasures of making risotto is stirring up a pot while chatting with my friends in the kitchen. But it can be partially made ahead, which may be more convenient. Cook the risotto for about 15 minutes, or until it is about three-quarters done. Spread the risotto on a large, rimmed baking sheet and cover it with parchment paper. The risotto can stand at room temperature for up to 2 hours. When ready to finish the cooking, return the risotto to the cooking pot, add a ladle of hot broth, and pick up where you left off, cooking the rice until it is barely tender.

SAFFRON AND SPRING VEGETABLE RISOTTO
MAKES 6 SERVINGS

Serve with chicken breast, fish fillets, or sautéed shrimp.

Prep Time: 10 minutes

Cooking Time: 30 minutes

Make Ahead: See the instructions above.

Weeknight Suppers, Family Favorite, Company Fare, Buffet Dish, Cooking Classic

This is the basic risotto recipe, and you can omit the saffron, if you wish. Improvise with other vegetables—cooked asparagus spears or sautéed mushrooms are also excellent. If you wish, substitute vegetable broth for the chicken to make a vegetarian dish.

1 cup fresh or thawed frozen peas

4 ounces sugar snap peas, trimmed

½ teaspoon crushed saffron threads

4 cups reduced-sodium chicken broth, plus more as needed

2 tablespoons (¼ stick) unsalted butter

1 yellow onion, chopped

1 garlic clove, minced

1½ cups rice for risotto, such as Arborio, carnaroli, or vialone nano

1 cup dry white wine, such as Pinot Grigio

½ cup freshly grated Parmesan cheese (2 ounces)

Kosher salt and freshly ground black pepper

1. Bring a medium saucepan of lightly salted water to a boil over high heat. Add the fresh peas and cook until they are tender, about 5 minutes. During the last minute or so, add the sugar snap peas. Drain, rinse under cold running water, and set aside. (Thawed frozen peas do not need to be cooked.)

2. Heat a medium saucepan over medium heat. Add the saffron and stir until it is slightly brittle, about 15 seconds. Add the broth and 2 cups water and bring to a boil over high heat. Turn the heat to very low to keep the liquid hot.

3. Melt the butter in a large, heavy-bottomed saucepan over medium heat. Add the onion and cook, stirring occasionally, until it is softened, about 3 minutes. Add the garlic and cook until it is fragrant, about 1 minute. Add the rice and cook, stirring often, until it turns from translucent to opaque (do not brown it), and it feels somewhat heavier in the spoon, about 2 minutes. Add the wine and cook until it is reduced to a few tablespoons, about 2 minutes.

4. Stir about ¾ cup of the hot broth into the rice. Cook, stirring almost constantly, until the rice absorbs almost all of the broth, about 3 minutes. Stir in another ¾ cup of the broth, and stir until it is almost absorbed. Repeat, keeping the risotto at a steady simmer and adding more broth as it is absorbed, until you use all of the broth and the rice is barely tender, about 20 minutes total. If you run out of broth and the rice isn't tender, use hot water. During the last 5 minutes of cooking, stir in the reserved pea mixture.

5. Remove the risotto from the heat and stir in the Parmesan. Season to taste with salt and pepper. Serve hot.

Saffron Risotto alla Milanese: Omit the peas and sugar snap peas. Substitute beef broth for the chicken broth. (The risotto is usually made with poached beef marrow added at the end, but I prefer this version, which is less rich.)

RISOTTO WITH RADICCHIO AND PANCETTA
MAKES 4 TO 6 SERVINGS

Serve with pork or veal chops, sausage, or salmon.

Prep Time: 10 minutes

Cooking Time: 30 minutes

Make Ahead: See the instructions on page 262.

Weeknight Suppers, Holiday Feasts, Company Fare

I make this risotto to serve with grilled sausages or boneless pork chops. The risotto takes on a brown-red hue from the wine, but the topping of shredded fresh radicchio adds a splash of color.

4 cups reduced-sodium chicken broth

¼ cup (¼-inch) diced pancetta

1 tablespoon olive oil

1 yellow onion, chopped

2 garlic cloves, minced

1½ cups rice for risotto, such as Arborio, carnaroli, or vialone nano

1 cup hearty red wine, such as Chianti

1 head radicchio, cored, cut crosswise into very thin shreds, and coarsely chopped

½ cup freshly grated Parmesan cheese (2 ounces)

Kosher salt and freshly ground black pepper

1. Bring the broth and 2 cups water to a boil in a medium saucepan over high heat. Turn the heat to very low to keep the liquid hot.

2. Cook the pancetta with the oil in a large, heavy-bottomed saucepan over medium heat, stirring occasionally, until the pancetta is beginning to brown, about 3 minutes. Add the onion and garlic and cook, stirring occasionally, until the onion softens, about 3 minutes.

3. Add the rice and cook, stirring often, until it turns from translucent to opaque (do not brown it) and it feels somewhat heavier in the spoon, about 2 minutes. Add the wine and cook until it is reduced to a few tablespoons, about 2 minutes.

4. Stir about ¾ cup of the hot broth into the rice. Cook, stirring almost constantly, until the rice absorbs almost all of the broth, about 3 minutes. Stir in another ¾ cup of broth, and stir until it is almost absorbed. Repeat, keeping the risotto at a steady simmer and adding more broth as it is absorbed, until you use all of the broth and the rice is barely tender, about 20 minutes total. During the last 5 minutes, stir in two-thirds of the radicchio. If you run out of broth and the rice isn't tender, use hot water.

5. Remove the risotto from the heat and stir in the Parmesan. Season to taste with salt and pepper. Spoon the risotto into individual serving bowls. Top each with the reserved radicchio and serve.

Wild Rice

Long, dark wild rice has a nutty flavor and chewy texture. Actually a grass, and not a grain, it takes longer to cook than true rice and may not soak up all of its cooking liquid. You can still purchase hand-harvested wild rice (at a premium), but most of the product on the market is machine-harvested rice. Wild rice should be rinsed before cooking because some of the minimally processed varieties could retain a little grit.

- The cooking proportions for wild rice are 1 part wild rice to 3 parts liquid (water, broth, or a combination).

WILD RICE WITH SHALLOTS AND THYME

MAKES 6 SERVINGS

Serve with pork, chicken, turkey, duck, goose, or salmon.

Prep Time: 5 minutes

Cooking Time: 45 minutes to 1 hour

Family Favorite, Holiday Feasts, Company Fare, Buffet Dish, Cooking Classic

Wild rice is a perfect side dish for main courses, especially at special holiday meals when you are already spending a bit of extra money. More so than white rice, wild rice needs a bit of extra seasoning to enhance its flavor, which I usually accomplish with shallots and herbs. For perfect results, be flexible with your cooking time. Remember that wild rice is its own animal, and it does not conform to the same cooking methods as white (or even brown) rice.

• The cooking time will fluctuate depending on how the rice is harvested (by hand or machine), which may or may not be listed on the packaging. For chewy, intact grains, cook the rice for the minimum time. For puffed, tender kernels, cook it longer. Add more hot water if it cooks away, or drain any leftover liquid.

1½ cups wild rice

2 tablespoons (¼ stick) unsalted butter

3 tablespoons finely chopped shallots

4½ cups reduced-sodium chicken broth or water

1 teaspoon finely chopped fresh thyme, rosemary, or sage

1 teaspoon kosher salt

1. Rinse the rice well in a wire sieve under cold running water. Melt the butter in a medium, heavy-bottomed saucepan and add the shallots. Cook, stirring often, until the shallots soften, about 2 minutes.

2. Add the rice, broth, thyme, and salt and bring them to a boil over high heat. Tightly cover the saucepan and reduce the heat to medium-low. Simmer until the rice has reached the desired consistency, 45 minutes to 1 hour.

3. Drain the rice in a wire sieve. Transfer it to a serving bowl and serve.

Wild Rice with Dried Cherries and Pistachios: Add ½ cup coarsely chopped dried cherries and ½ cup coarsely chopped pistachios to the wild rice in the saucepan and let it stand for 5 minutes before serving.

ANNIE'S TWO-RICE "PIZZA" CASSEROLE

MAKES 8 TO 12 SERVINGS

Serve as a buffet dish, with roast pork, baked ham, grilled meats or poultry, or poached salmon.

Prep Time: 30 minutes

Cooking Time: 1¾ hours

Make Ahead: The casserole can be made up to 1 day ahead.

Family Favorite, Holiday Feasts, Company Fare, Buffet Dish, Retro Recipe, Cooking Classic, Vegetarian

My late friend Dick Kniss really only had two employers in his long, amazing career as a professional bassist: John Denver (with whom, along with Mike Taylor, he co-wrote "Sunshine on My Shoulders") and Peter, Paul, and Mary. This beloved recipe, directly from Denver's first wife, Annie, has long been a must-have at our extended family's feasts. Its tomato-and-cheese flavor profile reminds me of a wild rice lasagna, if such a thing should exist. Note that the casserole takes a long time to bake while the rice slowly absorbs the tomato juices. Thank you Joan Authenrieth for reconstructing this recipe for me.

2 tablespoons plus ¼ cup extra-virgin olive oil, plus more for the baking dish

1 yellow onion, chopped

2 celery ribs, cut into ½-inch dice

8 ounces cremini or white button mushrooms, thinly sliced

½ green bell pepper, cored, seeded, and cut into ½-inch dice

½ red bell pepper, cored, seeded, and cut into ½-inch dice

2 garlic cloves, minced

One 28-ounce can crushed tomatoes

1½ cups shredded sharp Cheddar cheese (about 6 ounces)

1½ cups shredded Monterey Jack cheese (about 6 ounces)

⅔ cup wild rice, rinsed and drained

⅔ cup basmati rice

½ cup chopped pitted kalamata olives

7 tablespoons unsalted butter, cut into small cubes

2 teaspoons kosher salt

1 teaspoon freshly ground black pepper

1½ cups boiling water

1. Position a rack in the center of the oven and preheat the oven to 350°F. Lightly oil a 13 × 9 × 2-inch baking dish and a large sheet of aluminum foil to cover the dish.

2. Heat 2 tablespoons of the oil in a very large skillet over medium-high heat. Add the onion, celery, mushrooms, and the green and red bell peppers and cook, stirring occasionally, until the vegetables are tender and beginning to brown, 8 to 10 minutes. During the last minute, stir in the garlic. Transfer the vegetables to a very large bowl.

3. Stir in the tomatoes and let the mixture cool slightly. Add the Cheddar and Jack cheeses, wild and basmati rices, olives, 6 tablespoons of the butter, and the salt and pepper and mix well. Add the boiling water and the remaining ¼ cup oil and mix again. Spread the mixture in the baking dish. Dot it with the remaining 1 tablespoon butter. Cover tightly with the foil, oiled-side down. Place the baking dish on a large, rimmed baking sheet.

4. Bake until all of the liquid is absorbed and the rice is tender, about 1¾ hours. Let it stand, uncovered, for 15 minutes. (The casserole can be cooled, covered, and refrigerated for up to 1 day. Reheat, covered, in a preheated 350ºF oven for about 30 minutes.) Serve hot.

Polenta and Grits

Polenta and grits are both coarsely ground dried corn, and they have mainstreamed beyond their rustic roots to become darlings of the culinary world. In both cases, the corn is cooked in liquid into a thick mush. While polenta and grits are essentially the same, there are differences.

Polenta, originally from Italy, is made from the yellow dent corn variety (the domestic version is labeled corn grits). Some cooks resort to stone-ground cornmeal to make polenta, and while it will do in a pinch (reduce the cooking time by half), unless it is labeled coarsely ground, it is too fine. True polenta should be tender but still have some texture after cooking.

Grits are an essential food of the Deep South and can be ground from either yellow or white flint corn. The type of corn affects the cooked consistency. Polenta is very thick and can feel bumpy on the tongue, while grits are smoother and almost mushy.

Whenever possible, buy stone-ground polenta and grits because their flavor and texture are superior to the highly processed supermarket brands. While stone-ground cornmeal and old-fashioned grits (which are ground more finely to cook more quickly than coarse grits) can be used for these recipes, nothing beats the authentic versions. Quick-cooking grits and instant polenta have also been par-cooked for very fast cooking. They will do in a pinch and should be cooked according to the package directions.

- The cooking proportions for polenta or grits are 1 part of the grains to 4 parts liquid (water, broth, milk, or a combination).
- It is important to cover the saucepan while cooking to create the steam that keeps the polenta moist for a longer period of time. If the polenta is undercooked, the corn will taste bitter.
- The mixture will not truly boil or simmer, but "plop" with only a few bubbles breaking the surface. Whisk often to avoid scorching on the bottom of the saucepan.

BASIC SOFT AND CREAMY POLENTA
MAKES 4 TO 6 SERVINGS

Serve with stews and other sauce-based main courses.
Prep Time: 5 minutes
Cooking Time: 1 hour
Family Favorite, Cooking Classic, Vegetarian

For some stews, especially those with Italian flavors, polenta is the perfect bed to hold the saucy food. Milk helps give this polenta a creamy texture and even more substantial flavor. Use one of the variations as your mood (or the main course) dictates.

2 cups whole milk   **Kosher salt**

1 cup polenta (corn grits or coarse-grind cornmeal)

1. Whisk together the milk, 2 cups water, polenta, and 1½ teaspoons salt in a medium, heavy-bottomed saucepan. Bring them to a simmer over medium heat, whisking often.

2. Cook (the mixture will not boil), whisking often, until the polenta is stiff and has no bitter taste, about 1 hour. Season to taste with salt (be careful, as the polenta is very hot). Serve hot.

Hearty Polenta: Substitute 2 cups reduced-sodium chicken broth for the water.

Gorgonzola Polenta: Stir ½ cup (2 ounces) crumbled Gorgonzola into the finished polenta, and sprinkle additional Gorgonzola on top before serving.

Mascarpone and Thyme Polenta: Stir ½ cup (2 ounces) mascarpone and 1 teaspoon finely chopped fresh thyme into the finished polenta.

Parmesan Polenta: Stir ½ cup (2 ounces) freshly grated Parmesan cheese into the finished polenta, and sprinkle additional Parmesan on top before serving.

Roasted Garlic Polenta: Add 2 tablespoons mashed Roasted Garlic Heads (page 158) into the finished polenta.

Rosemary Polenta: Stir 2 teaspoons finely chopped fresh rosemary into the finished polenta.

CREAMY GRITS WITH GARLIC BUTTER

MAKES 4 SERVINGS

Serve with beef stew, chili, smoked pork chops, ham, sausages, fried chicken, or sautéed shrimp.

Prep Time: 5 minutes

Cooking Time: 25 minutes

Weeknight Suppers, Family Favorite, Cooking Classic, Vegetarian

Not having grown up in the South, I came late to the grits party. Can we please build a statue to the first cook who put garlic in grits? Some people eat grits for breakfast, but I like them with saucy food like chili and stew. Be sure to use a heavy-bottomed saucepan to keep the grits from scorching on the bottom.

• The basic proportions for cooking grits is 1 part grits to 4 parts liquid (milk, water, broth, or a combination).

1 cup whole milk

¾ cup white corn grits, preferably stone-ground (see Note)

Kosher salt

3 tablespoons unsalted butter

2 garlic cloves, finely chopped

1. Whisk together 2 cups water with the milk, grits, and 1 teaspoon salt in a medium heavy-bottomed saucepan. Bring them to a simmer over medium heat, whisking often. Reduce the heat to medium-low.

2. Cook (bubbles will only occasionally break the surface), whisking occasionally, until the grits are very thick and tender, about 20 minutes. If the grits become too thick before they are tender, whisk in ½ cup hot water. Season to taste with salt (be careful, as the grits are very hot).

3. A few minutes before serving, melt the butter in a small saucepan over medium heat. Add the garlic and cook, stirring often, just until it is softened but not browned, about 2 minutes. Remove the pan from the heat.

4. Transfer the grits to a serving bowl. Pour the butter and garlic on top and serve.

Note: If you use supermarket "old-fashioned grits," reduce the cooking time to about 12 minutes.

Smoky Grits with Garlic Butter: Stir ¾ cup shredded smoked Cheddar cheese (about 3 ounces) into the cooked grits. Transfer the grits to the serving bowl and top with the garlic butter.

CHEESE AND GRITS SOUFFLÉ
MAKES 4 TO 6 SERVINGS

Serve with grilled or pan-cooked sausages, fried chicken, egg dishes, or vegetarian meals.

Prep Time: 15 minutes

Cooking Time: 40 minutes

Family Favorite, Holiday Feasts, Company Fare, Buffet Dish, Vegetarian

Everyone loves the warming comfort of a good grits casserole. Here's my version, with a few twists to make it fit for a company brunch or barbecue. I made this recently for friends in California who had never had grits before, and they ran immediately to their laptop to mail order some.

3 tablespoons unsalted butter (1 tablespoon softened)

3 tablespoons freshly grated Parmesan cheese

2 garlic cloves, minced

1 jalapeño, seeded and minced

2 cups whole milk

1¼ teaspoons kosher salt

1 cup grits, preferably stone ground (see Note)

3 large eggs, at room temperature, separated

1 cup shredded sharp Cheddar cheese (4 ounces)

¼ teaspoon hot red pepper sauce

1. Position a rack in the center of the oven and preheat the oven to 400°F. Butter the inside of a 1½-quart soufflé dish with 1 tablespoon of the softened butter. Sprinkle the inside of the dish with the Parmesan, tilt to coat it completely with the cheese, and leave any excess cheese in the bottom of the dish.

2. Heat the remaining 2 tablespoons butter in a medium, heavy-bottomed saucepan over medium heat. Add the garlic and jalapeño and cook, stirring often, until they are softened but not browned, about 1 minute. Add 2 cups water with the milk and salt and bring to a boil over high heat, being careful that the mixture does not boil over. Gradually whisk in the grits. Reduce the heat to medium-low and simmer, whisking often to avoid sticking, until the grits are very thick and smooth, about 20 minutes. (The grits will be cooked more during baking, so they are not simmered for as long here as in other recipes.) Remove from the heat.

3. Using a whisk or a handheld electric mixer on high speed, whip the egg whites until they form stiff, but not dry, peaks; set them aside. Immediately add the Cheddar and hot sauce to the grits mixture, and stir to melt the cheese. Whisk the egg yolks in a small bowl. Whisk in about ½ cup of the grits mixture, and quickly whisk the yolk mixture back into the saucepan. Stir about one-fourth of the whites into the grits mixture to lighten it, then fold in the remaining whites. Transfer the mixture to the prepared dish and smooth the top.

4. Place the dish on a baking sheet. Bake until the top is evenly golden brown and puffed, about 35 minutes. Serve immediately.

Note: If using supermarket "old-fashioned grits," reduce the cooking time to about 12 minutes.

Bulgur

Parboiled, dried, and cracked wheat berries—bulgur cooks in just a few minutes and is a great alternative to rice on a busy weeknight. It is processed into four grinds: fine, medium, coarse, and extra-coarse. Most supermarkets and natural food stores carry only the medium variety, and you have to make a special effort to find the other grinds at a Middle Eastern grocer.

- The cooking proportions for bulgur are 1 part bulgur to 2 parts liquid (water, broth, or a combination).
- If you want plain bulgur (not cooked in broth), there is an alternative method. Put the bulgur in a heatproof bowl and add enough boiling water to cover. Stir the mixture and let stand until the bulgur is softened and has absorbed most of the water, about 20 minutes. Drain the bulgur in a wire mesh sieve.

BULGUR WITH DRIED APRICOTS AND PISTACHIOS

MAKES 4 SERVINGS

Serve with roast lamb, chops, or kebabs; lamb stew; or roast chicken.

Prep Time: 10 minutes

Cooking Time: 25 minutes

Weeknight Suppers, Family Favorite, Holiday Feasts, Company Fare, Vegetarian

As a Middle Eastern ingredient, bulgur is a natural with such grilled lamb dishes as chops and kebabs. The sweet fruit in this dish plays off the nutty flavor of the cracked wheat. Dried fruits are sometimes plumped in hot water, but here they are simply steamed during the bulgur's resting period, for the same effect without diluting any flavor.

1 tablespoon olive oil

2 scallions (white and pale green bottoms, finely chopped; green tops, thinly sliced)

1 cup medium-grind bulgur

2 cups reduced-sodium chicken broth or water

¾ teaspoon kosher salt

6 dried apricots, cut into ½-inch dice (about ½ cup)

3 tablespoons toasted and coarsely chopped pistachios (see page 33)

1. Heat the oil in a small saucepan over medium heat. Add the scallion bottoms and cook, stirring often, until they are softened, about 2 minutes. Stir in the bulgur. Add the broth and salt and bring to a boil over high heat. Reduce the heat to medium-low and cover tightly. Simmer until the liquid is absorbed and the bulgur is just tender, 12 to 15 minutes. Remove the pan from the heat.

2. Sprinkle the apricots over the bulgur, but do not stir. Let the pan stand, covered, until the apricots are heated and softened, about 5 minutes more. Fluff the bulgur with a fork. Stir in the scallion tops and pistachios. Serve hot.

Bulgur with Dried Cherries and Mint: Omit the scallions. Substitute ½ cup dried sour cherries for the diced apricots. Stir 2 tablespoons chopped fresh mint into the cooked bulgur with the pistachios.

Farro

In the Old World, farro has been eaten for centuries, but it has been available here for only the last few years. Farro can be one of three wheat varieties: small (eikhorn), medium (emmer), or large (spelt). Most of the farro sold in our markets is emmer that has been semi-pearled (that is, with some of its tough bran removed), but it may not always be labeled that way. If the recommended cooking time is about 20 minutes, it is semi-pearled. Otherwise, allow about 45 minutes to cook the farro to chewy tenderness.

- The cooking proportions for farro are 1 part farro to about 3 parts liquid (water, broth, or a combination).

FARRO, BUTTERNUT SQUASH, AND WILTED ARUGULA
MAKES 6 SERVINGS

Serve with grilled meats, sausages, or poultry, especially those with
Mediterranean seasonings; or grilled fish and shrimp.
Prep Time: 10 minutes
Cooking Time: 30 minutes
Weeknight Suppers, Holiday Feasts, Company Fare, Buffet Dish

With a package of precut butternut squash to reduce the prep time, this filling and tasty dish is a very simple way to use Old World ingredients in a contemporary way. Peppery arugula is usually served as a salad green, but here I use it as a savory green with steamed farro and roasted squash. For a vegetarian dish, substitute vegetable broth for the chicken broth. Often, I roast bone-in chicken breasts with their skin on the same baking sheet as the squash, starting the chicken about 15 minutes ahead.

One 20-ounce container butternut squash cubes (about 4 cups, see Note)
1 tablespoon olive oil
1 cup semi-pearled farro
2 cups reduced-sodium chicken broth

Kosher salt
2 ounces baby arugula, coarsely chopped (about 1 cup packed)
Freshly ground black pepper

1. Position a rack in the center of the oven and preheat the oven to 425°F.

2. Toss the squash with the oil on a large, rimmed baking sheet. Spread the squash in a singer layer on the sheet. Roast until the undersides are golden brown, about 15 minutes. Using a metal spatula, flip the squash over and continue roasting until the squash is golden brown and tender, about 15 minutes.

3. Meanwhile, bring the farro, broth, 1¼ cups water, and ½ teaspoon salt to a boil in a medium saucepan over high heat. Reduce the heat to low and cover. Simmer until the farro is tender and has absorbed most of the liquid, about 20 minutes. Remove it from the heat and add the arugula but do not stir it into the farro. Cover again and let it stand for 5 minutes. If necessary, drain the farro mixture in a wire sieve. Season to taste with salt and pepper.

4. Remove the squash from the oven and season to taste with salt and pepper. Transfer the farro and arugula to a serving dish, fluffing the farro as you do so, and top it with the squash. Mix them together gently, and serve hot.

Note: If you wish, substitute one 2-pound butternut squash, peeled, seeded, and cut into 1-inch cubes. Roast all of the squash, and save any leftovers for another meal.

Freekeh

Also a dried wheat with roots in Middle Eastern cuisine, freekeh is similar to bulgur. The grains are harvested while still yellowish-green, young, and tender, and then roasted and sun-dried to give them a toasted flavor. For the shortest cooking time (20 minutes), buy the cracked version instead of the whole grain (45 minutes).

- The cooking proportions for freekeh are 1 part freekeh to about 2½ parts liquid (water, broth, or a combination).

FREEKEH WITH ZUCCHINI, YOGURT, AND DILL
MAKES 4 SERVINGS

Serve with lamb roasts or chops; roast chicken; or salmon fillets.
Prep Time: 5 minutes
Cooking Time: 25 minutes
Holiday Feasts, Company Fare, Buffet Dish

2 tablespoons olive oil

1 zucchini, cut into ¼-inch dice

1 small yellow onion, finely chopped

1 garlic clove, minced

¾ cup whole-grain freekeh (see Note page 274)

2 cups reduced-sodium chicken broth, vegetable broth, or water

¾ teaspoon kosher salt

¼ cup toasted pine nuts (see page 33)

1 tablespoon finely chopped fresh dill

⅓ cup plain low-fat or whole-milk Greek yogurt

1. Heat 1 tablespoon of the oil in a small saucepan over medium-high heat. Add the zucchini and cook, stirring often, until it is lightly browned, about 4 minutes. Using a slotted spoon, transfer the zucchini to a bowl and set aside.

2. Add the remaining 1 tablespoon oil to the saucepan and heat. Add the onion and garlic and cook, stirring occasionally, until the onion is softened, about 3 minutes. Stir in the freekeh. Add the broth and salt and bring to a boil over high heat. Reduce the heat to medium-low and tightly cover the saucepan. Simmer until the freekeh is tender and has absorbed the broth, about 45 minutes. Do not worry if there is some liquid left. Remove the pan from the heat and let stand, covered, for 5 minutes. Drain the freekeh in a wire sieve, if necessary.

3. Transfer the freekeh mixture to a serving bowl. Add the zucchini, pine nuts, and dill and combine. Dollop the yogurt on the pilaf and serve.

Note: If using cracked freekeh, reduce the cooking time to about 20 minutes.

Kasha (Buckwheat Groats)

A staple of Eastern European cooking, kasha is toasted buckwheat groats. They are reddish-brown, with a distinct roasted aroma, so don't confuse them with untoasted buckwheat groats. This is another quick-cooking grain that could become a regular side dish, as it has in my house.

- The cooking portions for kasha are 1 part kasha to about 2 parts liquid (water, broth, or a combination).

KASHA WITH BOW-TIE PASTA AND CARAMELIZED ONIONS
MAKES 6 TO 8 SERVINGS

Serve with roast lamb or chicken.
Prep Time: 10 minutes
Cooking Time: 35 minutes
Weeknight Suppers, Family Favorite, Holiday Feasts, Company Fare, Buffet Dish, Retro Recipe, Cooking Classic

Nutty, toasty, and sweet flavors mingle in this iconic dish of Jewish cuisine. The kasha is coated with beaten egg and cooked before adding the liquid, a step that helps keep the grains separate. You will need the parsley to spruce up the color of the brown ingredients. Because this takes up two burners to cook, serve it with an oven-roasted main course to avoid a traffic jam on the stovetop.

2 tablespoons canola oil	1 large egg
2 yellow onions, chopped	1 cup kasha
Kosher salt and freshly ground black pepper	1¾ cups reduced-sodium chicken broth
2 cups bow-tie pasta	2 tablespoons finely chopped fresh flat-leaf parsley

1. Heat the oil in a medium skillet over medium heat. Add the onions and cover the skillet. Cook, stirring occasionally, until the onions are well softened, about 5 minutes. Reduce the heat to medium-low and uncover. Cook, stirring occasionally, until the onions are deep golden brown and very tender, about 25 minutes more. Season to taste with salt and pepper. Transfer the caramelized onions to a bowl and cover to keep warm.

2. Meanwhile, bring a medium saucepan of salted water to a boil over high heat. Add the bow-tie pasta and cook according to the package directions until the pasta is tender.

3. Meanwhile, cook the kasha. Beat the egg in a medium bowl, add the kasha, and stir well to coat the kasha. Heat a nonstick medium skillet over medium heat. Add the coated kasha and cook, stirring almost constantly with a wooden spoon to break up the clumps of kasha, until the mixture looks dry, 2 to 3 minutes. Add the broth, ½ cup water, ½ teaspoon salt, and ¼ teaspoon pepper to the kasha and bring it to a boil. Reduce the heat to low and cover tightly. Simmer until the kasha is tender, 8 to 10 minutes. Remove it from the heat and let it stand, covered, to keep warm.

4. Drain the pasta well and return it to its cooking pot. Fluff the kasha with a fork and stir it into the pasta. Add half of the onions and the parsley and mix well. Transfer the mixture to a serving bowl and top it with the remaining onions. Serve hot.

Kasha with Bow-Tie Pasta and Walnuts: The walnuts play up the nutty flavor of the kasha. Stir ⅓ cup toasted coarsely chopped walnuts into the kasha mixture with the caramelized onions.

KASHA WITH PORTOBELLOS AND THYME
MAKES 4 TO 6 SERVINGS

Serve with roast chicken, roast duck, or roast lamb or chops.
Prep Time: 10 minutes
Cooking Time: 15 minutes
Weeknight Suppers, Family Favorite, Cooking Classic

Mushrooms and kasha are a combination that many mid-European cooks know and love. In this recipe, they are cooked separately and combined just before serving. Portobello mushrooms are my first choice because they give off dark juices to flavor the kasha, but you can substitute other mushrooms as long as you cook them just to the point where they give off their liquid.

2 cups reduced-sodium chicken broth
Kosher salt
1 cup kasha
2 tablespoons (¼ stick) unsalted butter
2 portobello mushrooms, caps and stems cut into
 ½-inch dice

Freshly ground black pepper
2 tablespoons finely chopped shallots
1 teaspoon minced fresh thyme or ½ teaspoon
 dried

1. Bring the broth and ¾ teaspoon salt to a boil in a medium saucepan over high heat. Stir in the kasha and return it to a boil. Reduce the heat to very low and cover tightly. Simmer until the liquid is absorbed and the kasha is just tender, 8 to 10 minutes. Remove the pan from the heat and let it stand, covered, for 5 minutes.

2. Meanwhile, melt the butter in a large nonstick skillet over medium-high heat. Add the mushrooms and season with salt and pepper. Cook, stirring occasionally, until the mushrooms give off their juices, about 5 minutes. Stir in the shallots and thyme. Cook, stirring often, until the shallots soften, about 1 minute. Remove them from the heat.

3. Fluff the kasha with a fork. Stir in half of the mushroom mixture. Transfer the kasha to a serving bowl and top it with the remaining mushrooms. Serve hot.

Millet

I can't help but make the obvious connection between millet and bird seed, because they are one and the same. Maybe that is one of the reasons why millet gets little respect from the average cook. I know that my attitude changed once I started cooking it. This tiny yellow grain is the main food for millions, so it deserves to be a staple in my kitchen (and maybe yours, too, if you are coming late to the millet party).

- The cooking proportions for millet are 1 part millet to 2 parts liquid (water, broth, or a combination).

TOASTED MILLET PILAF WITH CURRANTS

MAKES 4 SERVINGS

Serve with roasted vegetables, roast chicken, or seafood.
Prep Time: 5 minutes
Cooking Time: 25 minutes
Weeknight Suppers, Company Fare

Toasting brings out millet's nutty flavor, and the sweet currants balance its earthy notes. For vegetarians, make this with vegetable broth for a side dish, or top it with your favorite roasted vegetables to turn it into a main course.

1 tablespoon unsalted butter	2 cups reduced-sodium chicken broth or water
1 cup millet	Kosher salt
1 small yellow onion, finely chopped	½ cup dried currants or seedless raisins

1. Melt the butter in a small saucepan over medium heat. Add the millet and cook, stirring occasionally, until the seeds start to pop and they smell toasted, about 3 minutes. Add the onion and stir well.

2. Add the broth and ½ teaspoon salt and bring them to a boil over high heat. Reduce the heat to medium-low and tightly cover the saucepan. Simmer until the millet is tender and has absorbed the broth, about 20 minutes. Remove it from the heat. Add the currants but do not stir them in. Cover the saucepan again and let it stand for 5 minutes. Season to taste with salt.

3. Transfer the millet to a serving dish, fluffing it and mixing in the currants with a fork as you do so, and serve.

Quinoa

In addition to its nutty flavor and fluffy texture, quinoa has many other attractive qualities. It is a complete protein (meaning it contains all nine of the essential amino acids, which combine to create a protein), something that is not found in any other edible plants. For example, beans and rice must be eaten together to complement each other's missing amino acids. Although quinoa has been grown and consumed in the Andes for centuries, it has only recently been found in American kitchens, and it has taken off like wildfire. The four varieties sold in this country, which are interchangeable as far as cooking goes, are yellow (the most common), red (with a bit more flavor), black (with a firmer texture), and a rainbow combination of all three. Choose a color that will complement your main course.

- A very important caveat: Quinoa must be rinsed before cooking to remove the saponin, its natural and bitter coating. Just put the seeds in a fine-mesh wire sieve and rinse well under cold running water. (The sieve must be fine enough to hold the tiny quinoa without letting them fall through the mesh.)

- The cooking proportions for quinoa are 1 part quinoa to 1½ parts liquid (water, broth, or a combination).

QUINOA WITH CARROT AND MINT
MAKES 4 SERVINGS

Serve with meat, chicken, or seafood dishes, especially those with sauces.
Prep Time: 5 minutes
Cooking Time: 20 minutes
Weeknight Suppers, Company Fare, Buffet Dish

Quinoa can be slightly bitter, even after you rinse off the saponin coating that causes the flavor. Carrot and mint balance this quality with their sweetness and perk up the quinoa's neutral color, too.

1 tablespoon unsalted butter or extra-virgin olive oil

1 small yellow onion, finely chopped

1 carrot, cut into ½-inch dice

1 cup quinoa, rinsed well under cold water in a fine wire sieve, and drained

1½ cups reduced-sodium chicken broth

½ teaspoon kosher salt

2 tablespoons finely chopped fresh mint

1. Melt the butter in a medium saucepan over medium heat. Add the onion and carrot and cover the saucepan. Cook, stirring occasionally, until the vegetables soften, about 3 minutes.

2. Add the quinoa and stir well. Add the broth and salt and bring to a boil over high heat. Reduce the heat to medium-low and cover the saucepan again. Simmer until the quinoa is tender and has absorbed the liquid, 20 to 25 minutes. (Don't worry if the quinoa is tender and some liquid remains.) Remove it from the heat and let it stand, covered, for 5 minutes. Drain the quinoa in a wire sieve, if necessary.

3. Add the mint and fluff the quinoa with a fork. Serve hot.

RAINBOW QUINOA WITH SPINACH AND WALNUTS

MAKES 4 TO 6 SERVINGS

Serve with meat, chicken, and seafood dishes, especially those with sauces.

Prep Time: 10 minutes

Cooking Time: 20 minutes

Weeknight Suppers, Company Fare, Buffet Dish

I often make a side dish that includes the meal's starch and green vegetable together, cutting down on pans and cleanup. The walnuts are an important part of this recipe to bring the flavors together, but the walnut oil is optional. When I have such a small amount of nuts to toast, I do the job in the toaster oven.

2 tablespoon olive oil

2 garlic cloves, finely chopped

1 cup rainbow quinoa, rinsed well under cold
 water in a fine wire sieve, and drained

1½ cups reduced-sodium chicken broth

½ teaspoon kosher salt

One 5-ounce bag spinach, coarsely chopped

⅓ cup toasted and coarsely chopped walnuts (see
 page 33)

1 tablespoon toasted walnut oil (optional)

1. Heat the olive oil and garlic together in a medium saucepan, stirring occasionally, until the garlic softens, about 2 minutes. Add the quinoa and stir well. Add the broth and salt and bring them to a boil over high heat. Reduce the heat to medium-low and cover the saucepan. Simmer until the quinoa is tender and has absorbed the liquid, 20 to 25 minutes. (Don't worry if the quinoa is tender and some liquid remains.) Remove it from the heat. Add the spinach to the saucepan but do not stir. Cover again and let it stand for 5 minutes.

2. Stir well to wilt the spinach more. Stir in the walnuts. Transfer the quinoa to a serving dish. Drizzle it with the walnut oil, if using, and serve.

CRISP QUINOA CAKES

MAKES 4 CAKES

Serve with sliced flank steak or London broil, chops, sausages, chicken, fish fillets, or shrimp.

Prep Time: 10 minutes, plus 15 minutes refrigeration time

Cooking Time: 6 minutes

Weeknight Suppers, Company Fare, Vegetarian

I try to cook extra quinoa to be sure to have leftovers so I can make these crisp cakes. This works with plain quinoa, but the Rainbow Quinoa with Spinach and Walnuts (opposite) is especially good. If you are using plain quinoa, add a tablespoon of chopped fresh parsley or basil to the mixture. Very often, if I have fish fillets cooking in the oven, these quinoa cakes are frying in a skillet on the stove. (Use gluten-free bread crumbs, if you wish.)

1½ cups cooked quinoa

¼ cup freshly grated Parmesan cheese (1 ounce)

¼ cup plain dry bread crumbs

1 scallion (white and green parts), finely chopped

1 large egg, beaten to blend

½ teaspoon kosher salt

¼ teaspoon freshly ground black pepper

2 tablespoons olive oil

1. Line a plate with waxed paper. In a medium bowl, mix the quinoa, Parmesan, bread crumbs, scallion, egg, salt, and pepper together. Shape the mixture into four 3-inch cakes and transfer them to the plate. Refrigerate them for 10 to 15 minutes.

2. Heat the oil in a large nonstick skillet over medium heat. Add the quinoa cakes and cook until the undersides are golden brown and crisp, about 2½ minutes. Flip the cakes over and continue cooking until the other sides are crisp, about 2½ minutes more. Transfer them to dinner plates and serve.

THE SIDE SALAD BOWL

This chapter has a profusion of salads for all occasions and seasons. Most often, a side salad is fresh greens tossed with vinaigrette for a weeknight supper. No fuss, no muss. But it can also be the hearty potato salad at a backyard cookout, or the colorful fruit salad on a holiday buffet. Side salads can be made from a tangle of shredded vegetables or a heap of grains. With a few exceptions, where bacon or shrimp add a bit of flavor, they do not include any meat, as the protein will be provided from other courses. (However, some salads are certainly substantial enough to become a full meal with the addition of meat, poultry, or seafood.) And they have been designed to be served directly from a bowl or platter, and not individually presented like a first-course salad at a restaurant, although for a formal dinner, you could do so. I have also included a collection of my favorite salad dressings.

Potato Salad

At my family's get-togethers, it is simply not a party without potato salad. An all-American classic, it can be made in many international variations. Baking potatoes make a crumbly salad, and waxy potatoes yield firm slices, and the dressing can be based on mayonnaise, vinaigrette, or yogurt. It really doesn't matter. It seems that I've never met a potato salad I didn't like.

- The quickest way to ruin potato salad is with undercooked potatoes. To keep them from getting waterlogged, it is best to boil the potatoes whole until they still hold their shape but are tender enough to be pierced with a small, sharp knife. The time will vary according to the size of the potatoes.

BLUE RIBBON POTATO SALAD
MAKES 8 TO 12 SERVINGS

Serve with sandwiches or burgers; steaks, sausages, grilled or fried chicken; or poached or grilled salmon.
Prep Time: 15 minutes, plus 2 hours of refrigeration time

Cooking Time: 30 minutes

Make Ahead: The salad can be made up to 2 days ahead.

Family Favorite, Buffet Dish, Cooking Classic, Vegetarian

Every cook has a unique recipe for potato salad—baking or boiling potatoes, with pickles or without, with or without hard-boiled eggs, with mayonnaise or creamy salad dressing, with onions or scallions. For me, this is the gold standard for potato salad, the version that my family has made for decades. The secret is a combination of mayonnaise and sour cream. The marinated artichoke version gets a lot of play at our parties, too.

3 pounds baking potatoes, such as russets, scrubbed

2 tablespoons cider vinegar, as needed

½ cup mayonnaise

½ cup sour cream

1 tablespoon prepared yellow or Dijon mustard

4 hard-boiled eggs (see page 66), sliced

3 medium celery ribs with leaves, cut into ¼-inch dice

3 scallions (white and green parts), finely chopped

2 tablespoons finely chopped fresh flat-leaf parsley

Kosher salt and freshly ground black pepper

1. Put the potatoes in a large saucepan and add enough cold salted water to cover them by 1 inch. Cover the saucepan and bring it to a boil over high heat. Reduce the heat to medium and set the lid ajar. Cook the potatoes at a steady simmer until they are tender when pierced with the tip of a small, sharp knife, 20 to 30 minutes. Drain and rinse them under cold running water. Let them cool slightly.

2. Slice the potatoes into ½-inch rounds, peeling them if you wish, and place them in a large bowl. Sprinkle and toss them with the vinegar. Let them stand until the potatoes have cooled, about 30 minutes.

3. In a medium bowl, whisk together the mayonnaise, sour cream, and mustard. Stir this mixture into the potatoes. Add the eggs, celery, scallions, and parsley and mix gently. Season to taste with salt and pepper. Cover and refrigerate until the salad is chilled, at least 2 hours or up to 2 days. Just before serving, reseason the salad with vinegar, salt, and pepper. Serve chilled.

Artichoke and Potato Salad: Add two 7-ounce jars marinated artichoke hearts, drained and chopped, to the salad.

SEASONING SALADS

Starch-based salads—potato, pasta, and grain—taste different after a few hours' refrigeration, as the ingredients soak up the dressing. Be prepared to reseason the salad with salt, pepper, and vinegar before serving. If you have transported the salad to a picnic, bring these ingredients along with you.

NEW POTATO AND PEA SALAD WITH GREEN GARLIC AÏOLI

MAKES 4 TO 6 SERVINGS

Serve as a buffet or picnic salad with beef, pork, chicken, or seafood.

Prep Time: 15 minutes, plus 2 hours refrigeration time

Cooking Time: 30 minutes

Make Ahead: The salad can be made (without the peas) up to 8 hours ahead.

Buffet Dish, Vegetarian

Late spring is the time to make this delicate potato salad. That's when small new potatoes, green garlic, and peas show up at the farmer's market and you want to showcase their fresh-from-the-garden flavors. If you can't find green garlic (although I see it at just about every farmer's market in major cities, if not quite at the supermarket produce section yet), substitute 4 scallions. And you can also substitute thawed frozen peas for the fresh, if you wish. This salad is terrific with grilled salmon.

1½ cups shelled fresh peas (from about 1½ pounds peas in the pod)

2 pounds small thin-skinned boiling or new potatoes, scrubbed

1 tablespoon white wine or cider vinegar, as needed

⅔ cup mayonnaise

2 teaspoons Dijon mustard

Pinch of cayenne pepper

2 bulbs green garlic (white and tender pale green parts), finely chopped

3 celery ribs, cut into ⅛-inch slices

Kosher salt and freshly ground black pepper

1 tablespoon finely sliced fresh chives, for garnish

1. Bring a large saucepan of salted water to a boil over high heat. Add the peas and cook until they are tender, about 5 minutes. Using a wire sieve, transfer the peas to a bowl of ice water, keeping the water in the saucepan boiling. Set the peas aside.

2. Add the potatoes to the boiling water and return it to a boil. Reduce the heat to medium and cover it, with the lid ajar. Cook until the potatoes are tender when pierced with the tip of a small, sharp knife, 20 to 25 minutes. Drain and rinse them under cold running water. Let them cool slightly.

3. Slice the potatoes into ½-inch rounds and place them in a large bowl. Sprinkle and toss them with the vinegar. Let the potatoes stand until they have cooled, about 30 minutes. (You can speed this up by spreading the potatoes on a large, rimmed baking sheet.)

4. In a small bowl, whisk together the mayonnaise, mustard, and cayenne. Add them to the potatoes with the green garlic and celery and mix. Season to taste with salt and pepper. Cover and refrigerate until the salad is chilled, at least 2 hours and up to 8 hours.

5. Just before serving, add the peas and mix gently. Reseason the salad with vinegar, salt, and pepper. Sprinkle it with the chives and serve chilled.

HERBED FRENCH POTATO SALAD

MAKES 8 SERVINGS

Serve at picnics with beef, pork, lamb, poultry, or seafood.
Prep Time: 15 minutes, plus 2 hours refrigeration time
Cooking Time: 30 minutes
Make Ahead: The salad can be made up to 1 day ahead.
Holiday Feasts, Company Fare, Buffet Dish, Vegetarian

Creamy potato salad is a must-have at American picnics. In France, this mayonnaise-free version is also de rigueur at outdoor meals. Dry white wine (or vermouth) is another distinctive touch that sets this salad apart from its cousins.

3 pounds thin-skinned boiling potatoes, scrubbed	⅔ cup extra-virgin olive oil
3 tablespoons dry white wine or dry vermouth	4 celery ribs, thinly sliced
3 tablespoons white or red wine vinegar, as needed	3 tablespoons finely sliced fresh chives
1 tablespoon Dijon mustard	1 tablespoon finely chopped fresh tarragon
Kosher salt and freshly ground black pepper	1 tablespoon finely chopped fresh flat-leaf parsley

1. Put the potatoes in a large saucepan and add enough cold salted water to cover them by 1 inch. Cover the saucepan and bring it to a boil over high heat. Reduce the heat to medium and set the lid ajar. Cook the potatoes at a steady simmer until they are tender when pierced with the tip of a small, sharp knife, 25 to 30 minutes. Drain and rinse them under cold running water. Let them cool slightly.
2. Slice the potatoes into ½-inch rounds and place them in a large bowl. Sprinkle and toss them with the wine. Let them stand until the potatoes have cooled, about 30 minutes. (You can speed this up by spreading the potatoes on a large, rimmed baking sheet.)
3. In a medium bowl, whisk together the vinegar, mustard, ½ teaspoon salt, and ½ teaspoon pepper to dissolve the salt. Gradually whisk in the oil. Pour the mixture over the potatoes and toss gently. Add the celery, chives, tarragon, and parsley and toss again. Cover and refrigerate until the salad is chilled, at least 2 hours and up to 1 day.
4. Let the salad stand at room temperature for 30 minutes. Reseason the salad with vinegar, salt, and pepper, and serve.

DILL PICKLE POTATO SALAD

MAKES 8 SERVINGS

Serve as a buffet salad with baked ham, grilled meats, poultry, or seafood.
Prep Time: 20 minutes, plus 2 hours refrigeration time
Cooking Time: 30 minutes

Make Ahead: The salad can be made up to 1 day ahead.

Family Favorite, Holiday Feasts, Company Fare, Buffet Dish, Cooking Classic, Vegetarian

The flavor power of pickle juice has recently been discovered by the young folks who drink it as a chaser to bourbon at modern speakeasy cocktail lounges. Seasoned cooks know it as a terrific flavoring for potato salad. (And I have to say, I prefer my pickle juice in a salad instead of on the rocks.) Of course, the better the pickles, the better the salad, so if your market carries top-quality refrigerated pickles, give them a try. I sometimes make this salad with sweet gherkins and their juice. If you are a Miracle Whip fan, this is a good recipe in which to use it.

3 pounds baking potatoes, such as russets, scrubbed

¼ cup dill pickle juice, as needed

1 cup mayonnaise or prepared salad dressing, such as Miracle Whip

2 tablespoons spicy brown mustard

1 small yellow onion, shredded on the large holes of a box shredder

½ cup (¼-inch) diced dill pickles

2 celery ribs, thinly sliced

3 tablespoons finely chopped fresh dill, plus more for garnish

Kosher salt and freshly ground black pepper

2 hard-boiled eggs (see page 66), cut into ¼-inch rounds

1. Put the potatoes in a large saucepan and add enough cold salted water to cover them by 1 inch. Cover the saucepan and bring it to a boil over high heat. Reduce the heat to medium and set the lid ajar. Cook the potatoes at a steady simmer until they are tender when pierced with the tip of a small, sharp knife, 25 to 30 minutes.

2. Drain the potatoes and rinse them under cold running water. Let them cool slightly. Slice the potatoes into ½-inch rounds and transfer them to a large bowl. Sprinkle the rounds with the pickle juice and let them cool.

3. In a small bowl, whisk together the mayonnaise, mustard, and shredded onion. Add them to the potatoes along with the dill pickles, celery, and dill. Mix gently. Season to taste with salt and pepper. Cover and refrigerate until the salad is chilled, at least 2 hours and up to 1 day.

4. Reseason the salad with pickle juice, salt, and pepper. Top it with the hard-boiled eggs and sprinkle it with the dill. Serve chilled.

LOADED POTATO SALAD WITH SOUR CREAM, BACON, AND CHEDDAR

MAKES 8 SERVINGS

Serve with sandwiches or burgers, steak or ham.

Prep Time: 15 minutes, plus 2 hours refrigeration time

Cooking Time: 30 minutes

Make Ahead: The salad can be made up to 1 day ahead.
Family Favorite, Buffet Dish

If you are like me, and you can't decide what toppings to put on your baked potato, and end up with a little of each, then make this salad to heap next to grilled steak. The dressing is mainly sour cream thinned with milk. Scallions provide the bulk of the onion flavor because chives are a bit too mild on their own.

3 pounds baking potatoes, such as russets, scrubbed but unpeeled

¼ cup distilled white vinegar, as needed

5 slices bacon, cut into 1-inch pieces

1 cup sour cream

¼ cup whole milk

4 celery ribs, thinly sliced

6 scallions (white and green parts), thinly sliced

1¼ cups shredded Cheddar cheese (5 ounces)

Kosher salt and freshly ground black pepper

3 tablespoons finely sliced fresh chives or green scallion tops, for garnish

1. Put the potatoes in a large saucepan and add enough cold salted water to cover them by 1 inch. Cover the saucepan and bring it to a boil over high heat. Reduce the heat to medium and set the lid ajar. Cook the potatoes at a steady simmer until they are tender when pierced with the tip of a small, sharp knife, 25 to 30 minutes.

2. Drain and rinse them under cold running water. Let them cool slightly. Peel the potatoes and cut them into ½-inch rounds. Place the warm slices in a bowl. Sprinkle and toss them with the vinegar. Let them cool completely.

3. Meanwhile, cook the bacon in a large skillet over medium heat, turning occasionally, until it is crisp and browned, about 8 minutes. Transfer the bacon to paper towels to drain and cool. Coarsely chop the bacon.

4. In a small bowl, whisk the sour cream and milk together. Pour them over the potatoes and add the celery, scallions, 1 cup of the Cheddar, and 4 chopped bacon slices. Mix well and season the salad with salt and pepper. Cover and refrigerate until the salad is chilled, at least 2 hours and up to 1 day.

5. Just before serving, reseason the salad with vinegar, salt, and pepper to taste. Sprinkle the remaining ¼ cup Cheddar and the remaining bacon on top of the salad, followed by the chives. Serve chilled.

WARM GERMAN POTATO AND BACON SALAD

MAKES 8 SERVINGS

Serve with sausages, smoked pork chops, baked ham, or breaded fried chicken.

Prep Time: 15 minutes

Cooking Time: 35 minutes

Weeknight Suppers, Family Favorite, Holiday Feasts, Company Fare, Buffet Dish, Cooking Classic

Most of us think of potato salad as a warm-weather dish. So, when it is cold outside and you need a side dish for smoked meats or breaded chicken, here is a warm version with bacon and a sweet-and-sour dressing. This recipe was created from my memories of my German-speaking great-aunts' cooking. No one wrote down the recipe, so I had to confer with my cousins to come up with this mouthwatering replica.

3 pounds medium boiling potatoes, such as Yukon Gold, scrubbed

4 slices bacon, cut into 1-inch pieces

½ cup finely chopped yellow onion

1 tablespoon all-purpose flour

⅓ cup plus 1 tablespoon cider vinegar

1 teaspoon celery seed

Kosher salt and freshly ground black pepper

3 tablespoons finely chopped fresh flat-leaf parsley

2 tablespoons finely sliced fresh chives

1. Put the potatoes in a large saucepan and add enough cold salted water to cover them by 1 inch. Cover the saucepan and bring it to a boil over high heat. Reduce the heat to medium and set the lid ajar. Cook the potatoes at a steady simmer until they are tender when pierced with the tip of a small, sharp knife, 20 to 25 minutes.

2. Meanwhile, cook the bacon in a large skillet over medium heat, turning it occasionally, until the bacon is crisp and browned, about 8 minutes. Transfer the bacon to paper towels to drain, leaving the fat in the skillet. Coarsely chop the bacon.

3. Add the onion to the fat in the skillet and cook, stirring it occasionally, until it is tender, about 4 minutes. Sprinkle it with the flour and stir well. Stir in ¾ cup water, the vinegar, celery seed, 1 teaspoon salt, and ½ teaspoon pepper. Bring them to a simmer and reduce the heat to medium-low. Simmer until the dressing is lightly thickened, about 2 minutes. Remove it from the heat.

4. Drain the potatoes and let them cool for 5 minutes. Using a clean kitchen towel to protect your hands, and working over a medium bowl, slice the potatoes into ½-inch rounds, letting them fall into the bowl. Add the dressing, bacon, and parsley and toss. Season to taste with salt and pepper. Sprinkle the salad with the chives and serve warm.

Slaws

Coleslaw comes from the Dutch word for cabbage salad, but slaw can be made with other vegetables as well. The term has come to be used for any thinly sliced or shredded vegetables marinated in a tart dressing. Many slaws improve in flavor as they marinate, so because they can be made ahead, this family of salads is very useful for entertaining.

- A food processor makes short work of cutting cabbage into the thin shreds for coleslaw. Use the slicing blade, and not the shredder. The shredder can be used for carrots, apples, and other hard ingredients.

COLESLAW WITH CELERY SEED DRESSING

MAKES 8 TO 10 SERVINGS

Serve as a buffet salad at a picnic with barbecued or grilled meats, poultry, seafood, fried chicken, or burgers.

Prep Time: 15 minutes, plus 2 hours refrigeration time

Make Ahead: The slaw can be made up to 1 day ahead.

Family Favorite, Buffet Dish, Cooking Classic, Vegetarian

I have simple requirements for coleslaw: It should be refreshingly tart, with very little sugar, and the vegetables as the stars. This recipe may be a standard slaw, but it is the gold standard. Try the Old Bay variation when you are serving seafood, for a spicy alternative.

1⅓ cups mayonnaise

3 tablespoons distilled white or cider vinegar

1½ teaspoons sugar

1 teaspoon celery seeds

1 small head green cabbage (2 pounds), cored and
  thinly sliced

3 carrots, shredded

4 scallions (white and green parts), thinly sliced

2 tablespoons chopped fresh flat-leaf parsley

Kosher salt and freshly ground black pepper

1. In a large bowl, whisk together the mayonnaise, vinegar, sugar, and celery seeds.

2. Add the cabbage, carrots, scallions, and parsley and mix well. Season to taste with salt and pepper. Cover and refrigerate the slaw until chilled, at least 2 hours or up to 1 day. Serve it chilled.

Coleslaw with Old Bay Seasoning: Substitute 1 tablespoon Old Bay Seasoning for the celery seeds.

MARINATED SWEET AND TANGY SLAW

MAKES 8 SERVINGS

Serve with burgers or sandwiches (especially corned beef and pastrami), baked ham, or fried chicken.

Prep Time: 15 minutes, plus 4 hours refrigeration time

Make Ahead: The salad can be made up to 3 days ahead.

Family Favorite, Buffet Dish, Cooking Classic, Vegetarian

Where I live in New Jersey, the natives still talk about the coleslaw at the long-gone Claremont Diner in Verona, New Jersey. Luckily, one of my neighbors had the recipe, and it is a keeper. Many delicatessens call this "health salad," probably because it has much less dressing than the typical slaw. A food processor is the best tool for thinly slicing the vegetables. Marinating is key to this slaw's flavor, so be sure to make it at least 4 hours before serving.

1 head green cabbage (2¼ pounds)

1 large cucumber, peeled, halved lengthwise, seeds scooped out with a dessert spoon

1 large green bell pepper, cored and seeded

1 small yellow onion

1 large carrot

¼ cup distilled white vinegar

¼ cup sugar

1 tablespoon kosher salt

½ teaspoon freshly ground black pepper

¼ cup vegetable oil

1. Using a food processor fitted with the slicing blade (not the shredding blade), slice the cabbage and transfer it to a large bowl. Repeat with the cucumber, green pepper, and onion. (Or use a large, sharp knife to cut the vegetables into thin slices.)

2. Fit the food processor with the shredding blade. Shred the carrot and transfer it to the bowl with the other vegetables. (Or shred the carrots on the large holes of a box shredder.)

3. In a medium bowl, whisk together the vinegar, sugar, salt, and pepper to dissolve the sugar and salt. Gradually whisk in the oil. Pour the dressing over the vegetables and toss well. Cover and refrigerate until the slaw is wilted and chilled, at least 4 hours or preferably overnight.

4. Serve chilled, using a slotted spoon to remove the slaw from the brine. (The slaw will keep, covered, refrigerated, and stored in its brine, for up to 3 days.)

COLESLAW WITH APPLES AND POPPY SEEDS

MAKES 4 TO 6 SERVINGS

Serve as a buffet salad at a picnic with barbecued or grilled meats, poultry, seafood, fried chicken, or burgers.

Prep Time: 10 minutes, plus 2 hours refrigeration time

Make Ahead: The slaw can be made up to 1 day ahead.

Family Favorite, Holiday Feasts, Buffet Dish, Vegetarian

This truly delectable slaw has become part of my family heritage, and I have served it at weddings, wakes, and backyard birthdays. The apples and apple juice concentrate give it a natural sweetness that everyone loves. I usually make it with a bag of shredded coleslaw mix so I can mix up a big bowl of salad in just a few minutes.

½ cup mayonnaise

1 tablespoon thawed apple juice concentrate

1 tablespoon cider vinegar

1 tablespoon poppy seeds

One 16-ounce bag coleslaw mix (green cabbage and carrots)

2 scallions (white and green parts), finely chopped

1 Granny Smith apple, unpeeled, shredded on the large holes of a box shredder

Kosher salt and freshly ground black pepper

1. In a medium bowl, whisk together the mayonnaise, apple juice concentrate, vinegar, and poppy seeds. Add the coleslaw mix, scallions, and apple and mix them together. Season to taste with salt and pepper.

2. Cover and refrigerate for at least 2 hours and up to 1 day. Serve chilled.

BARBECUE SHACK CHOPPED SLAW

MAKES 8 SERVINGS

Serve with barbecued or grilled meats or poultry.
Prep Time: 15 minutes, plus 2 hours refrigeration time
Make Ahead: The slaw can be made up to 2 days ahead.
Family Favorite, Holiday Feasts, Buffet Dish, Cooking Classic, Vegetarian

Whenever I go to North Carolina, I will drive out of my way to sample the fare at a recommended barbecue joint. This is the way that many such places serve their slaw—finely chopped, with a ketchup-based sweet and sour dressing.

1 head green cabbage (2¼ pounds), cored and
   coarsely chopped
4 medium carrots (8 ounces), cut into 1-inch
   lengths
1 small sweet onion, such as Vidalia or Maui, cut
   into sixths
¼ cup cider vinegar

3 tablespoons tomato ketchup
2 tablespoons sugar
1 teaspoon hot red pepper sauce
1 teaspoon kosher salt
¼ teaspoon freshly ground black pepper
¾ cup vegetable oil
2 teaspoons poppy seeds (optional)

1. In batches, pulse the cabbage, carrots, and onion together in a food processor until coarsely chopped into pieces about ¼ inch square.

2. In a large bowl, whisk together the vinegar, ketchup, sugar, hot pepper sauce, salt, and pepper to dissolve the sugar. Gradually whisk in the oil. Whisk in the poppy seeds, if using.

3. Add the dressing to the cabbage mixture and mix well. Cover and refrigerate for at least 2 hours and up to 2 days. Serve chilled, using a slotted spoon to serve the slaw.

SLAW WITH RADISHES AND CILANTRO

MAKES 6 TO 8 SERVINGS

Serve with Mexican-style grilled meats, chicken, or seafood.
Prep Time: 15 minutes, plus 4 hours refrigeration time

Make Ahead: The slaw can be made up to 1 day ahead.

Buffet Dish, Vegetarian

*T*his is a salad for cilantro lovers, with a full cup of the herb. When I first enjoyed this slaw with tacos in northern Mexico, I immediately saw its potential as a side dish at a barbecue and as a buffet salad to be served with enchiladas and other tortilla-based main courses. The spicy crispness of the rad-ishes is wonderful with the mellow cabbage.

½ large head green cabbage (1½ pounds), cored
  and thinly sliced

10 to 12 large radishes, shredded on the large holes
  of a box shredder or with a food processor

6 scallions (white and green parts), chopped

½ cup chopped fresh cilantro

2 tablespoons sherry or cider vinegar

1 jalapeño, seeded and coarsely chopped

1 garlic clove, crushed through a garlic press

½ cup olive oil

½ cup sour cream

Kosher salt and freshly ground black pepper

1. In a large bowl, mix together the cabbage, radishes, scallions, and cilantro.

2. Process the vinegar, jalapeño, and garlic in a blender to purée the jalapeño. With the machine run-ning, add the oil through the hole in the lid to make a smooth dressing. Stir it into the slaw. Add the sour cream and mix well. Season to taste with salt and pepper.

3. Cover and refrigerate the slaw until chilled, at least 4 hours and up to 1 day. Serve chilled.

NAPA CABBAGE SLAW WITH HOISIN-GINGER DRESSING

MAKES 6 TO 8 SERVINGS

Serve with steaks or beef kebabs; grilled pork tenderloin or chops; spareribs; or grilled chicken
or duck breast.

Prep Time: 10 minutes, plus 1 hour refrigeration time

Make Ahead: The slaw can be made up to 4 hours ahead.

Weeknight Suppers, Family Favorite, Company Fare, Buffet Dish, Vegetarian

*S*picy ginger juice and sweet-salty hoisin sauce give this napa cabbage slaw an Asian flavor profile. (To my palate, minced fresh ginger is often tough, but I have a trick to solve the problem.) I serve this slaw most often as part of a summer picnic menu—try it with glazed Chinese-style spareribs. The slaw wilts fairly quickly, so don't let it stand for more than a few hours.

½ cup shredded fresh ginger (about 3 ounces;)

¼ cup unseasoned rice vinegar

2 tablespoons hoisin sauce

1 garlic clove, crushed through a garlic press

½ teaspoon hot red pepper flakes

2 tablespoons toasted sesame oil

¾ cup vegetable oil

2 pounds napa cabbage, cored and cut crosswise into ¼-inch strips

6 carrots, shredded

6 scallions (white and green parts), thinly sliced

Kosher salt and freshly ground black pepper

¼ cup finely chopped fresh cilantro (optional)

1 tablespoon sesame seeds, toasted and cooled (see page 33)

1. A handful at a time, squeeze the shredded ginger in your fist over a large bowl to extract the juice. (Or press the shredded ginger in a potato ricer to juice it.) You should have about 3 tablespoons ginger juice.

2. Add the vinegar, hoisin sauce, garlic, and red pepper flakes and whisk them together. Gradually whisk in the sesame oil, then the vegetable oil.

3. Add the napa cabbage, carrots, and scallions and mix well. Season to taste with salt and pepper. Cover and refrigerate until chilled, at least 1 hour and up to 4 hours.

4. Just before serving, stir in the cilantro, if using, sprinkle the slaw with the sesame seeds, and serve it chilled.

Hoisin and Ginger Slaw with Peanuts: Omit the sesame seeds. Just before serving, stir ½ cup coarsely chopped roasted unsalted peanuts into the slaw.

Pasta Salads

MEDITERRANEAN MACARONI SALAD
MAKES 10 TO 12 SERVINGS

Serve as a buffet or picnic salad with grilled beef, pork, lamb, chicken, or seafood.

Prep Time: 15 minutes, plus 2 hours refrigeration time

Cooking Time: 10 minutes

Make Ahead: The salad can be made up to 1 day ahead.

Family Favorite, Buffet Dish, Cooking Classic, Vegetarian

One of my first culinary jobs was at a delicatessen, where I prepared mountains of macaroni salad every day. Now, who doesn't like a good macaroni salad? The original recipe used ripe sliced olives and parsley, but over the years, I've upped the flavor with kalamata olives and basil. The last time I made this, for a big family party, I had to serve it in a turkey roaster because we didn't have a bowl large enough, and there still wasn't a spoonful left over.

1 pound elbow macaroni

2 tablespoons red wine vinegar, as needed

¾ cup mayonnaise

1 cup coarsely chopped pitted kalamata olives

1 red bell pepper, roasted (see page 77), peeled, cored, seeded, and cut into ¼-inch dice

3 celery ribs, cut into ¼-inch dice

3 tablespoons finely chopped fresh basil

Kosher salt and freshly ground black pepper

1. Bring a large pot of salted water to a boil over high heat. Add the macaroni and cook according to the package directions until tender. Drain, rinse it under cold running water, and drain well.

2. Transfer the macaroni to a large bowl. Sprinkle it with the vinegar and toss well. Stir in the mayonnaise, olives, roasted red pepper, celery, and basil. Season to taste with salt and pepper. Cover and refrigerate the salad until chilled, at least 2 hours or up to 1 day.

3. Just before serving, reseason the salad with vinegar, salt, and pepper. Serve it chilled.

Delicatessen Macaroni Salad: When you want the old-fashioned flavor of a great homemade macaroni salad, make this version: Substitute cider vinegar for the red wine vinegar, fresh flat-leaf parsley for the basil, and two 2.25-ounce cans drained sliced ripe olives for the kalamata olives.

SPICY PASTA SALAD WITH PEPPERONCINI

MAKES 8 TO 12 SERVINGS

Serve with Italian-style beef, pork, sausages, chicken, or seafood.

Prep Time: 15 minutes, plus 2 hours refrigeration time

Cooking Time: 10 minutes

Make Ahead: The salad can be made up to 1 day ahead.

Family Favorite, Company Fare, Buffet Dish

The many pleasures of an antipasti platter are combined in this colorful pasta salad. The spiciness is provided by pepperoncini (Mediterranean pickled green peppers)—both the peppers and the zippy brine from the jar. I use my personal choices, but you can feel free to swap or add your favorite morsels— marinated artichoke hearts, roasted red pepper, black olives, or bite-sized mozzarella balls are all excellent. I served this with Italian stuffed beef rolls (braciole), and it was a very complementary pairing.

DRESSING

3 tablespoons brine from pepperoncini

2 tablespoons red wine vinegar, as needed

1 teaspoon dried oregano

1 garlic clove, crushed through a garlic press

½ teaspoon hot red pepper flakes

¾ cup extra-virgin olive oil

1 pound fusilli

3 medium celery ribs, thinly sliced

½ cup coarsely chopped drained pepperoncini

6 ounces sliced provolone cheese, cut into ½-inch strips

6 ounces sliced sopressata or hard salami, cut into ½-inch strips

½ cup coarsely chopped pimiento-stuffed olives

3 tablespoons chopped fresh flat-leaf parsley

Kosher salt and freshly ground black pepper

1. To make the dressing: In a small bowl, whisk together the brine, vinegar, oregano, garlic, and red pepper flakes. Gradually whisk in the oil.

2. Bring a large pot of salted water to a boil over high heat. Add the fusilli and cook according to the package directions until tender. Drain, rinse it under cold running water, and drain well.

3. Transfer the fusilli to a large bowl. Add the dressing and toss well. Add the celery, pepperoncini, provolone, sopressata, olives, and parsley and mix well. Season to taste with salt and pepper. Cover and refrigerate the salad until chilled, at least 2 hours and up to 1 day.

4. Just before serving, reseason the salad with vinegar, salt, and pepper. Serve it chilled or at room temperature.

ORZO AND VEGETABLE SALAD WITH PESTO DRESSING
MAKES 8 SERVINGS

Serve as a buffet salad with beef, pork, lamb, chicken, or seafood.

Prep Time: 15 minutes, plus 2 hours refrigeration time

Cooking Time: 15 minutes

Make Ahead: The salad (without the vegetables and cheese) and dressing can be made
up to 8 hours ahead.

Family Favorite, Buffet Dish, Vegetarian

*T*his pasta salad is an appetizing fresh green, thanks to the profusion of basil in the dressing. Parsley is added because its high chlorophyll content keeps the basil from discoloring. Briefly cooking the zucchini helps tone down its raw flavor and sets its color, too. I find that this salad is best if made not too far ahead of time because the small orzo can get soggy.

DRESSING

1 cup packed fresh basil leaves

2 tablespoons chopped fresh flat-leaf parsley

3 tablespoons red wine vinegar

1 large garlic clove, crushed under the flat side of a
   knife and peeled

½ teaspoon kosher salt

¼ teaspoon hot red pepper flakes

¾ cup extra-virgin olive oil

8 ounces orzo

1 tablespoon extra-virgin olive oil

1 zucchini, scrubbed and cut into ½-inch pieces

1 cup thawed frozen peas

1 pint cherry tomatoes, halved

4 scallions (white and green parts), finely chopped

½ cup freshly grated Parmesan cheese (2 ounces)

½ cup toasted pine nuts (see page 33)

1. To make the dressing: Process the basil, parsley, vinegar, garlic, salt, and red pepper flakes in a blender to purée the basil. With the machine running, gradually add the oil through the hole in the lid.

2. Bring a large pot of salted water to a boil over high heat. Add the orzo and cook according to the package directions, stirring often, until tender. Drain, rinse it under cold running water, and drain well.

Transfer it to a large bowl and toss the orzo with half of the dressing. Cover the salad and remaining dressing separately and refrigerate them until the salad is chilled, at least 2 hours or up to 8 hours.

3. Meanwhile, bring a medium saucepan of salted water to a boil over high heat. Add the zucchini and cook just until it is crisp-tender and the skin turns a brighter shade of green, about 2 minutes. Drain, rinse it under cold running water, and drain again.

4. Just before serving, add the remaining dressing to the orzo with the zucchini, peas, cherry tomatoes, scallions, and Parmesan and mix well. Sprinkle it with the pine nuts and serve it chilled or at room temperature.

FARFALLE AND BROCCOLI SALAD WITH GORGONZOLA DRESSING
MAKES 8 SERVINGS

Serve as a buffet salad with Italian-seasoned grilled meats, especially beef and veal.

Prep Time: 15 minutes, plus 2 hours refrigeration time

Cooking Time: 15 minutes

Make Ahead: The salad can be made up to 8 hours ahead.

Company Fare, Buffet Dish, Vegetarian

This pasta salad is always popular at cookouts with beef entrées, which are complemented by the blue cheese. When I was catering, I'd serve this with everything from beef kebabs to sliced beef tenderloin.

1 pound broccoli	2 cups crumbled Gorgonzola cheese (8 ounces)
1 pound farfalle (bow-tie pasta)	3 celery ribs, cut into ⅛-inch slices
¾ cup mayonnaise	3 scallions (white and green parts), thinly sliced
½ cup sour cream	3 tablespoons chopped fresh flat-leaf parsley
2 tablespoons white wine vinegar, as needed	Kosher salt and freshly ground black pepper

1. Bring a medium saucepan of lightly salted water to a boil over high heat. Trim the broccoli and cut the tops into bite-sized florets. Pare the stalks, then cut them crosswise into ¼-inch slices. Cook the broccoli stems in the salted water for 2 minutes. Add the florets and cook until the broccoli florets are crisp-tender, about 3 minutes. Drain, rinse them under cold water, and let cool.

2. Bring a large pot of lightly salted water to a boil over high heat. Add the pasta and cook according to the package directions, until tender. Drain, rinse it under cold running water, and drain well.

3. In a large bowl, whisk the mayonnaise, sour cream, and vinegar together. Add half of the Gorgonzola and mash it into the mayonnaise mixture with a rubber spatula. Stir in the remaining cheese. Add the pasta, broccoli, scallions, celery, and parsley and mix. Season to taste with salt and pepper.

4. Cover and refrigerate the salad until cold, at least 2 and up to 8 hours. Just before serving, reseason the salad with vinegar, salt, and pepper and serve it chilled.

COUSCOUS SALAD WITH SAFFRON VINAIGRETTE

MAKES 8 TO 10 SERVINGS

Serve with a buffet salad at a picnic with grilled meats (especially lamb), poultry, or seafood.

Prep Time: 15 minutes, plus 2 hours refrigeration time

Cooking Time: 5 minutes

Make Ahead: The salad can be made up to 1 day ahead.

Family Favorite, Holiday Feasts, Buffet Dish, Vegetarian

Two little steps make a big difference with this good-looking salad, rendered golden yellow with the saffron vinaigrette. First, take a minute to rub the clumps of couscous through your fingers before adding the vegetables and dressing. And, because the salad changes flavor as it absorbs the dressing, reserve some of the vinaigrette to add just before serving.

¾ cup plus 1 tablespoon olive oil

Kosher salt

2 cups plain couscous

One 15-ounce can garbanzo beans (chickpeas), drained and rinsed

1 large red bell pepper, cored, seeded, and cut into ¼-inch dice

4 large carrots, peeled and cut into ¼-inch dice

4 scallions (white and green parts), finely chopped

¼ cup fresh lemon juice

1 garlic clove, crushed through a garlic press

½ teaspoon crumbled saffron

Freshly ground black pepper

⅛ teaspoon cayenne pepper

2 tablespoons chopped fresh mint, plus more for garnish

1. Bring 2¼ cups water, 1 tablespoon oil, and ½ teaspoon salt to a boil in a medium saucepan over high heat. Stir in the couscous and remove the pan from the heat. Cover tightly and let it stand until the couscous is tender, about 5 minutes. Transfer the couscous to a large bowl. Fluff the couscous with a fork and let it cool completely, about 15 minutes. Using your fingertips, rub the couscous to break up any clumps.

2. Add the garbanzo beans, bell pepper, carrots, and scallions to the couscous and mix well.

3. Process the remaining ¾ cup oil, lemon juice, garlic, saffron, ½ teaspoon salt, ¼ teaspoon pepper, and cayenne together in a blender. Pour about two-thirds of the dressing over the couscous, add the mint, and mix well. Cover and refrigerate the salad and remaining dressing until chilled, at least 2 hours and up to 1 day.

4. Just before serving, toss the salad with the remaining dressing and adjust the seasoning with salt and pepper. Transfer the salad to a serving bowl and garnish it with additional mint. Serve it chilled or at room temperature.

NOODLE AND VEGETABLE SALAD WITH PEANUT-TEA DRESSING

MAKES 6 TO 8 SERVINGS

Serve with Asian-style grilled meats, poultry, or seafood.

Prep Time: 25 minutes

Cooking Time: 15 minutes

Make Ahead: The salad can be made up to 8 hours ahead.

Holiday Feasts, Buffet Dish, Vegetarian

Serve this substantial salad when the main course has Asian flavors—soy-marinated flank steak, lemongrass chicken, or miso-glazed seafood would all go well with these tangles of noodles in a tea-scented peanut sauce. Be sure to use a black tea without any additional flavorings—Earl Grey would not do here.

DRESSING

½ cup smooth peanut butter (not all-natural)

¼ cup brewed black tea, such as English Breakfast, as needed

2 tablespoons Thai or Vietnamese fish sauce

2 tablespoons fresh lime juice

1 tablespoon honey

1 tablespoon hoisin sauce

1 tablespoon peeled and very finely minced ginger

1 teaspoon Sriracha or other hot sauce

2 garlic cloves, finely chopped

5 ounces green beans, cut into 1-inch pieces

8 ounces spaghetti

¼ seedless (English) cucumber, cut into ½-inch sticks about 2 inches long

4 scallions (white and green parts), thinly sliced

3 tablespoons finely chopped fresh cilantro, plus more for garnish

1 red Fresno or jalapeño chile, seeded and minced

Kosher salt and freshly ground black pepper

⅓ cup finely chopped dry roasted peanuts

Lime wedges, for serving

1. To make the dressing: Purée the peanut butter, ¼ cup black tea, fish sauce, lime juice, honey, hoisin sauce, ginger, Sriracha, and garlic in a blender until smooth, adding more tea, if needed, to make a smooth dressing. Set the dressing aside.

2. Bring a large pot of salted water to a boil over high heat. Add the green beans and cook until they are crisp-tender and have turned a brighter shade of green, about 2 minutes. Using a wire spider or sieve, transfer the green beans to a bowl of cold water. Keep the water boiling.

3. Add the spaghetti to the water and cook according to the package directions, until it is tender. Drain the spaghetti and rinse it under cold running water. Drain well. Transfer the spaghetti to a large bowl.

4. Drain the green beans and pat them dry with paper towels. Add them to the spaghetti, along with the dressing, cucumber, scallions, cilantro, and chile. Mix well and season to taste with salt and pepper. (The salad can be covered and refrigerated for up to 8 hours. Bring it to room temperature and reseason before serving.)

5. Spread the salad on a platter. Sprinkle it with additional cilantro and the peanuts. Garnish with the lime wedges and serve.

Bean Salads

BLACK-EYED PEAS AND KALE SALAD WITH WARM BACON VINAIGRETTE

Makes 6 servings

Serve with ham or sausages as part of a New Year's buffet.

Prep Time: 15 minutes

Cooking Time: 10 minutes

Make Ahead: The various components (black-eyed pea salad, vinaigrette, the cooked bacon, and the kale) can be stored at room temperature for up to 2 hours; finish the vinaigrette and assemble the salad just before serving.

Holiday Feasts, Company Fare, Buffet Dish

Many cultures, not just our Southerners, traditionally eat legumes and greens at New Year's because the food supposedly looks like currency and encourages prosperity. When I don't have a request for Hoppin' John (page 231), this is what I serve at my New Year's party, accompanied with lots of smoked sausages or a ham from my neighborhood Polish butcher. Frozen black-eyed peas make preparing this salad a breeze, but use 2½ cups freshly cooked dried peas if you prefer. I bet that this salad will become a tradition at your house, too.

VINAIGRETTE

4 slices bacon, cut into 1-inch lengths

1 tablespoon vegetable oil

3 tablespoons cider vinegar

1 teaspoon dry mustard powder

½ teaspoon sugar

1 garlic clove, crushed through a garlic press

Kosher salt and freshly ground black pepper

½ cup olive oil

KALE

1 pound curly kale, thick stems discarded

1 tablespoon cider vinegar

1 teaspoon kosher salt

BLACK-EYED PEAS

One 16-ounce bag thawed frozen black-eyed peas

1 cup halved grape tomatoes

2 celery ribs, cut into ¼-inch dice

¼ cup finely chopped red onion

1 Fresno or red jalapeño chile, seeded and minced

Kosher salt and freshly ground black pepper

1. To make the vinaigrette: Cook the bacon in the vegetable oil in a large skillet over medium heat, turning the bacon as needed, until it is crisp and brown, about 8 minutes. Using a slotted spoon, transfer the bacon to paper towels to drain. Remove the skillet with the fat from the heat.

2. In a small bowl, whisk together the vinegar, dry mustard, sugar, garlic, ½ teaspoon salt, and ¼ teaspoon pepper to dissolve the mustard. Gradually whisk in the olive oil. Return the skillet with the fat to medium heat. Gradually whisk the vinaigrette into the skillet and bring it to a simmer. Remove it from the heat. (The vinaigrette and bacon can be stored separately at room temperature for up to 2 hours; reheat the vinaigrette before using.)

3. To prepare the kale: Cut the kale crosswise into thin slices. Wash the kale well and spin it dry in a salad spinner. Put the kale in a large bowl and sprinkle it with the vinegar and salt. Using your fingers and palms, briskly rub the kale until it is wilted and tenderized, about 2 minutes. (The kale can be stored at room temperature for up to 2 hours.)

4. To prepare the black-eyed peas: In a medium bowl, mix together the black-eyed peas, tomatoes, celery, onion, and chile. Toss them with half of the vinaigrette. Season to taste with salt and pepper.

5. Toss the remaining dressing with the kale. Spread the kale on a large platter and top it with the black-eyed pea mixture and season to taste with salt and pepper. Coarsely chop the bacon and sprinkle it all over the salad. Serve at room temperature.

BEAN SALAD WITH AVOCADO, GRILLED CORN, AND RED PEPPER

MAKES 6 SERVINGS

Serve with grilled meats, poultry, or seafood.

Prep Time: 10 minutes, plus 2 hours refrigeration time

Make Ahead: The salad can be made up to 8 hours ahead.

Weeknight Suppers, Holiday Feasts, Buffet Dish, Vegetarian

The black, pink, green, yellow, and red ingredients in this salad make an explosion of colors and flavors. It works both as a salad and as a salsa, served in smaller amounts as a condiment to grilled foods. I have even topped it with grilled shrimp and chicken to create a main course salad.

DRESSING

Finely grated zest of 1 lime

2 tablespoons fresh lime juice, as needed

1 teaspoon pure ground ancho chile

½ teaspoon ground cumin

½ teaspoon sugar

1 garlic clove, crushed through a garlic press

⅓ cup extra-virgin olive oil

One 15-ounce can black beans, drained and rinsed

One 15-ounce can pinto beans, drained and rinsed

1 cup corn kernels, cut from 1 ear Grilled Corn (page 83)

1 ripe Hass avocado, pitted, peeled, and cut into ½-inch dice

1 red bell pepper, roasted (see page 77), cored, seeded, and peeled, cut into ½-inch dice

½ cup finely chopped red onion

Kosher salt and freshly ground pepper

1. To make the dressing: Pulse the lime zest and juice, ground chile, cumin, sugar, and garlic in a blender to combine. With the blender running, gradually add the oil through the hole in the lid.

2. In a large bowl, mix together the black and pinto beans, corn, avocado, bell pepper, and onion with the dressing. Season to taste with salt and pepper. Cover and refrigerate the salad until chilled, at least 2 hours and up to 8 hours. Just before serving, reseason the salad with lime juice, salt, and pepper. Serve it chilled or at room temperature.

MARINATED LENTIL, TOMATO, AND CHÈVRE SALAD

MAKES 6 TO 8 SERVINGS

Serve with grilled meats (especially lamb), sausages, or poultry.

Prep Time: 15 minutes, plus 12 hours refrigeration time

Cooking Time: 45 minutes

Make Ahead: The salad can be made up to 2 days ahead.

Company Fare, Holiday Feasts, Buffet Dish, Vegetarian

The earthiness of lentils is best appreciated when they are paired with sharp-flavored ingredients like ripe tomatoes and goat cheese. I can't get enough of this salad. Let it marinate overnight to soak up the dressing.

LENTILS

1⅓ cups dried lentils, picked over for stones, rinsed, and drained

Two 3-inch sprigs fresh thyme

1 garlic clove, crushed under the flat side of a knife and peeled

1 teaspoon kosher salt

DRESSING

2 tablespoons red wine vinegar, as needed

2 tablespoons finely chopped shallot

1½ teaspoons minced fresh thyme

1 garlic clove, crushed through a garlic press

Kosher salt and freshly ground black pepper

½ cup extra-virgin olive oil

2 large beefsteak tomatoes, seeded and cut into ½-inch dice

½ cup crumbled goat cheese (2 ounces)

1. To cook the lentils: Bring the lentils, 3 cups water, the thyme sprigs, and peeled garlic to a boil in a medium saucepan over high heat. Reduce the heat to medium-low and cover. Cook for 20 minutes. Add the salt and continue cooking until the lentils are tender, about 25 minutes more. Drain them in a wire sieve and let cool. Discard the thyme sprigs and garlic clove.

2. To make the dressing: In a medium bowl, whisk together the vinegar, shallot, minced thyme, crushed garlic, ½ teaspoon salt, and ¼ teaspoon pepper. Gradually whisk in the oil.

3. Add the drained lentils and tomatoes to the dressing and mix well. Cover and refrigerate the salad for at least 12 hours or up to 2 days.

4. Drain the marinated lentils, discarding the liquid, and return the lentil mixture to the bowl. Let it stand at room temperature for 1 hour before serving. Reseason with vinegar, salt, and pepper. Stir in the goat cheese and serve.

Rice and Grain Salads

Each one of these salads features a different grain as its main ingredient. They are best when served at room temperature because the grains can be too firm when chilled. This is especially important with the rice salad.

ITALIAN RICE, CHERRY TOMATO, AND BASIL SALAD
MAKES 8 SERVINGS

Serve as a buffet salad at outdoor meals with seafood.
Prep Time: 15 minutes, plus 2 hours refrigeration time
Cooking Time: 20 minutes
Make Ahead: The salad can be made up to 8 hours ahead.
Holiday Feasts, Buffet Dish, Vegetarian

Italians know that rice makes a wonderful summer salad. It deserves the same popularity here. Try it as a side dish with grilled seafood. Be sure to serve the salad at room temperature, because chilled rice grains are not tasty.

1½ cups long-grain rice

1 pint cherry or grape tomatoes, halved

2 tablespoons fresh lemon juice

Kosher salt

¼ teaspoon hot red pepper flakes

½ cup extra-virgin olive oil

3 tablespoons finely chopped fresh basil, plus more
  for garnish

Lemon wedges, for serving

1. Bring a large saucepan of salted water to a boil over high heat. Add the rice and cook it, uncovered, until the rice is tender, about 20 minutes. Drain it in a large wire sieve and rinse it under cold water; drain again. Transfer the rice to a large bowl and add the cherry tomatoes.

2. In a medium bowl, whisk together the lemon juice, ½ teaspoon salt, and red pepper flakes to dissolve the salt. Gradually whisk in the oil. Pour about two-thirds of the dressing over the rice, add the basil, and mix. Season to taste with salt. Cover and refrigerate the salad until chilled, at least 1 hour and up to 8 hours.

3. Let the salad stand at room temperature for 1 hour before serving. Toss it with the remaining salad dressing, sprinkle with chopped basil, and serve, with the lemon wedges.

BULGUR SALAD WITH BLOOD ORANGES AND MINT

MAKES 6 SERVINGS

Serve on a buffet with grilled meats (especially lamb), poultry, or seafood.

Prep Time: 15 minutes

Cooking Time: 20 minutes, for soaking the bulgur

Make Ahead: The salad can be made up to 8 hours ahead.

Weeknight Suppers, Company Fare, Buffet Dish, Vegetarian

The nutty flavor of bulgur is a natural contrast to sweet citrus and fresh mint. Blood oranges are available in the winter months, and their deep magenta color gives the salad a dramatic look. You can use navel oranges, if you wish.

DRESSING

3 tablespoons fresh lemon juice, as needed

Finely grated zest of 1 blood orange (reserve the orange for the salad)

Kosher salt

¼ teaspoon hot red pepper flakes

⅓ cup extra-virgin olive oil

1 cup bulgur

2 cups boiling water

4 scallions (white and green parts), thinly sliced

¼ cup finely chopped fresh mint

¼ cup finely chopped fresh flat-leaf parsley

4 blood oranges (including the zested orange), peeled, cut between the membranes into segments

1. To make the dressing: In a small bowl, whisk together the lemon juice, orange zest, ½ teaspoon salt, and red pepper flakes to dissolve the salt. Gradually whisk in the oil.

2. Put the bulgur in a medium heatproof bowl. Stir in the boiling water. Let it stand until the bulgur is tender and has absorbed the water, about 20 minutes. Drain it well in a wire sieve to remove any excess water. Transfer the bulgur to a bowl. Add the dressing, scallions, mint, and parsley and mix well. (The salad can be covered and refrigerated for up to 8 hours. Bring it to room temperature before serving.)

3. Add the orange segments to the salad and mix gently. Reseason the salad with lemon juice, salt, and pepper. Transfer it to a serving bowl and serve.

FARRO, CHERRY, AND FETA SALAD

MAKES 6 SERVINGS

Serve as a buffet salad with grilled meats, especially lamb or poultry.

Prep Time: 15 minutes, plus 15 minutes cooling time

Cooking Time: 20 minutes, plus 30 minutes standing time
Make Ahead: The salad can be made up to 6 hours ahead.
Company Fare, Buffet Dish, Vegetarian

I was at a loss for what to serve with an herb and wine–marinated grilled leg of lamb until I saw a bag of Italian farro sitting next to a bowl of cherries on my kitchen counter. Before long, I had a substantial salad with sweet cherries and tart feta playing off the firm grains . . . and a new favorite side salad for serving with lamb.

FARRO

1½ cups semi-pearled farro

1 small onion, halved crosswise

1 small carrot, halved lengthwise

1 small celery rib, halved lengthwise

1 teaspoon kosher salt

2 tablespoons cherry or other fruit-flavored balsamic vinegar, or plain balsamic vinegar, as needed

Kosher salt and freshly ground black pepper

⅓ cup plus 2 tablespoons extra-virgin olive oil

12 ounces sweet cherries, such as Bing, pitted and coarsely chopped

2 scallions (white and green parts), finely chopped

2 tablespoons finely chopped fresh mint

½ cup crumbled feta cheese (2 ounces)

1. To cook the farro: Bring the farro, 4 cups water, the onion, carrot, celery, and salt to a boil in a medium saucepan over high heat. Reduce the heat to medium-low and cover the saucepan. Simmer until the farro is tender and has absorbed most of the liquid, about 20 minutes. Drain it in a colander, rinse under cold running water, and drain well. Let the farro cool for about 15 minutes. Discard the onion, carrot, and celery.

2. In a large bowl, whisk the vinegar with salt and pepper to taste to dissolve the salt. Gradually whisk in the oil. Add the cooled farro, cherries, scallions, and mint and mix well. Cover and let the salad stand at room temperature for 30 minutes to 2 hours. (The salad can be refrigerated for up to 6 hours. Remove it from the refrigerator 30 minutes before serving.)

3. Reseason the salad with vinegar, salt, and pepper. Stir in the feta cheese and serve the salad at room temperature.

QUINOA, RED PEPPER, AND ROMAINE SALAD WITH MOROCCAN SPICES

MAKES 4 TO 6 SERVINGS

Serve with grilled chicken, lamb chops, or salmon.
Prep Time: 10 minutes, plus 30 minutes refrigeration time

Cooking Time: 20 minutes

Make Ahead: The salad components can be made up to 6 hours ahead and tossed together just before serving.

Weeknight Suppers, Holiday Feasts, Company Fare, Buffet Dish

The mix of seasonings in the vinaigrette and the sweet currants gives this substantial side salad a North African flavor. All you'll need is a grilled or broiled main course, such as harissa-rubbed chicken. Refrigerate the quinoa after cooking to speed the cooling, and you can feasibly serve this for a weeknight supper dish.

DRESSING

2 tablespoons fresh lemon juice

1 teaspoon ground ginger

½ teaspoon sweet paprika

½ teaspoon ground coriander (optional)

Kosher salt and freshly ground black pepper

⅛ teaspoon cayenne pepper

½ cup extra-virgin olive oil

1 cup quinoa, preferably rainbow or tri-color quinoa, rinsed well under cold water in a fine wire sieve and drained

1 romaine heart, cut into bite-sized pieces

1 large red bell pepper, roasted (see page 77), cored, seeded, peeled, and cut into ½-inch dice

2 scallions (white and green parts), chopped

½ cup dried currants

1. To make the dressing: In a medium bowl, whisk together the lemon juice, ginger, paprika, coriander, if using, ½ teaspoon salt, ¼ teaspoon pepper, and cayenne. Gradually whisk in the oil. Set the dressing aside.

2. Bring the quinoa, 2 cups water, and 1 teaspoon salt to a boil in a medium saucepan over high heat. Reduce the heat to medium-low and cover the saucepan. Simmer until the quinoa is tender and has absorbed the liquid, about 20 minutes. Remove it from the heat and let it stand for 5 minutes. Using a fork, fluff the quinoa and transfer it to a large bowl. Refrigerate it until it is completely cooled, at least 30 minutes and up to 6 hours.

3. In a large bowl, combine the quinoa, romaine, bell pepper, scallions, and currants. Add the dressing and mix well. Season to taste with salt and pepper and serve.

Cabbage Family Salads

Every cook knows the value of coleslaw as a side dish, but other cruciferous vegetables are also invaluable. Here are delicious salads made with Brussels sprouts, broccoli, and kohlrabi.

BRUSSELS SPROUTS SLAW WITH RICOTTA SALATA, DRIED CRANBERRIES, AND PISTACHIOS

MAKES 6 SERVINGS

Serve with baked ham, roast chicken, or poached salmon.

Prep Time: 10 minutes

Cooking Time: 3 minutes

Make Ahead: The slaw and dressing can be prepared separately up to 1 day ahead and tossed together just before serving.

Weeknight Suppers, Holiday Feasts, Buffet Dish, Vegetarian

Raw Brussels sprouts make a delectable slaw, and I prepare this during the Christmas season for its green and red colors, and to take advantage of the sprouts' ubiquity in the winter months. And it can be made in minutes, which is very helpful during the busy holiday entertaining blitz. To keep the slaw crisp, prepare the components ahead and toss them together just before serving.

CARAMELIZED SHALLOT DRESSING

⅔ cup plus 2 tablespoons olive oil

¼ cup coarsely chopped shallots

Finely grated zest of 1 lemon

¼ cup fresh lemon juice

2 tablespoons honey

Kosher salt and freshly ground black pepper

½ cup dried cranberries

20 ounces Brussels sprouts, trimmed

½ cup toasted and coarsely chopped pistachios (see page 33)

½ cup coarsely crumbled ricotta salata (2 ounces)

1. To make the dressing: Heat 2 tablespoons of the oil in a small skillet over medium heat. Add the shallots and cook, stirring occasionally, until they are golden brown, about 5 minutes.

2. Transfer the shallots to a blender. Add the remaining ⅔ cup oil with the lemon zest and juice and honey and blend until the dressing is thick and smooth. Season to taste with salt and pepper. (The dressing can be covered and refrigerated for up to 1 day.)

3. Put the dried cranberries in a bowl and cover them with hot tap water. Set them aside to plump for 10 minutes. Drain them and pat them dry with paper towels.

4. In a food processor fitted with the slicing blade, drop the Brussels sprouts through the feed tube while the machine is running to thinly slice the sprouts. (Or thinly slice them with a large knife.) Transfer the sliced brussel sprouts to a medium bowl. Add the dressing, drained cranberries, pistachios, and ricotta salata and toss. Season to taste with salt and pepper. Serve immediately.

GRILLED BROCCOLI, RED PEPPER, AND PINE NUT SALAD

MAKES 6 SERVINGS

Serve with grilled meats, poultry, or seafood.

Prep Time: 15 minutes, plus 30 minutes cooling time

Cooking Time: 8 minutes

Make Ahead: The salad can be made up to 4 hours ahead.

Holiday Feasts, Company Fare, Buffet Dish

If you haven't tried grilled broccoli, you are in for a treat. The high heat transforms the spears into something familiar but different. This salad has Mediterranean flavors that are especially good with grilled foods. If you are roasting the bell pepper on the grill, cook, cool, and peel it before cooking the broccoli.

DRESSING

2 tablespoons red wine vinegar

1 teaspoon anchovy paste

1 teaspoon dried oregano

1 garlic clove, crushed through a garlic press

¼ teaspoon kosher salt

¼ teaspoon hot red pepper flakes

½ cup extra-virgin olive oil

1½ pounds broccoli crowns

2 tablespoons olive oil

1 large red bell pepper, roasted (see page 77), peeled, cored, seeded, and cut into ½-inch dice

½ cup coarsely chopped pitted kalamata olives

⅓ cup pine nuts, toasted (see page 33)

Freshly ground black pepper

1. To make the dressing: In a medium bowl, whisk together the vinegar, anchovy paste, oregano, garlic, salt, and red pepper flakes to dissolve the anchovy paste. Gradually whisk in the oil. Set the dressing aside.

2. Prepare an outdoor grill for direct cooking over medium heat (350° to 450°F). For a charcoal grill, let the coals burn until they are covered with white ash and you can hold your hand about 1 inch above the cooking grate for about 3 seconds. For a gas grill, preheat on high and adjust the thermostat to medium (400°F).

3. Using a large knife, cut the broccoli lengthwise into individual spears, with each stalk ½ to ¾ inch wide. Toss the broccoli spears in a large bowl with the oil to coat the broccoli. Place the spears on the grilling grate, running perpendicular to the grate, and cover the grill. Grill with the lid closed until the undersides are lightly charred, about 2½ minutes. Flip the broccoli over and continue grilling with the lid closed until the other sides are lightly charred and the broccoli is crisp-tender, about 2½ minutes more. Transfer the broccoli to a large bowl and let it cool, about 30 minutes.

4. Add the bell pepper, olives, and pine nuts to the broccoli and mix. Add the dressing and mix again. (The salad can be covered and refrigerated for up to 4 hours. Let it stand at room temperature for 1 hour before serving.)

5. To serve, lift the broccoli spears from the bowl and arrange them on a platter. Spoon the bell pepper mixture with any dressing over the broccoli. Season to taste with pepper and serve.

RAW BROCCOLI SALAD WITH BACON, SUNFLOWER SEEDS, AND RAISINS

MAKES 8 SERVINGS

Serve at picnics and buffets with beef, pork, chicken, or seafood.

Prep Time: 20 minutes

Cooking Time: 20 minutes

Make Ahead: Components of the salad can be made up to 4 hours ahead, stored separately, and mixed together just before serving.

Weeknight Suppers, Family Favorite, Holiday Feasts, Company Fare, Buffet Dish, Retro Recipe

I have to include this crowd-pleaser from my cousin Suzanne Kindle, who is virtually required to bring it to every family gathering. She says that she doesn't mind because it is so easy to make. My family loves the combination of crisp broccoli, sunflower seeds, and bacon, topped off with a thick sweet-and-sour dressing. With this much bacon to cook, I think that it is easier to bake it instead of crowding the slices into a skillet, but the choice is yours.

8 slices bacon

⅔ cup mayonnaise

⅓ cup sugar

2 tablespoons red wine vinegar

1½ pounds broccoli crowns, cut into florets

1 cup sunflower seeds

1 cup seedless raisins

1 small yellow onion, finely chopped

1. Position a rack in the center of the oven and preheat the oven to 400°F.

2. Arrange the bacon side-by-side on a large, rimmed baking sheet. Bake until the bacon is crisp and browned, about 20 minutes. Transfer the bacon to paper towels to drain and cool. Coarsely chop the bacon.

3. In a small bowl, whisk the mayonnaise, sugar, and vinegar together. In a large bowl, mix the broccoli, half of the bacon, the sunflower seeds, raisins, and onion together. Add the mayonnaise mixture and toss. Sprinkle the remaining bacon over it and serve. (To make the salad ahead, whisk the mayonnaise and sugar together without the vinegar. Combine the broccoli, sunflower seeds, raisins, and onion without the bacon. Top with the mayonnaise mixture, cover, and refrigerate for up to 4 hours. Just before serving, sprinkle the salad with the vinegar and mix well. Mix in half of the bacon, sprinkle with the remaining bacon, and serve.)

KOHLRABI, APPLE, AND ALMOND SLAW

MAKES 4 TO 6 SERVINGS

Serve as a buffet salad with grilled or barbecued meat or poultry.

Prep Time: 10 minutes, plus 1 hour refrigeration time

Make Ahead: The slaw can be made up to 1 day ahead.
Buffet Dish, Vegetarian

*K*ohlrabi *is the unexpected star of this crisp slaw, which gets its mild sweetness from apple and honey. If you haven't cooked with kohlrabi before, this is a fine way to make its acquaintance. A mandoline or V-slicer does the best job of slicing the kohlrabi.*

3 kohlrabi (about 1½ pounds), peeled
Kosher salt
⅓ cup sour cream
⅓ cup mayonnaise
2 tablespoons honey

2 Granny Smith apples
Freshly ground black pepper
⅓ cup sliced almonds, toasted (see page 33)
Finely chopped fresh parsley, for garnish
 (optional)

1. Using a mandoline, plastic V-slicer, or large, sharp knife, cut the kohlrabi into thin strips about ⅛ inch wide. Toss the kohlrabi with 1 teaspoon salt in a colander. Let it stand in the sink for 1 hour. Do not rinse the kohlrabi.
2. In a large bowl, whisk the sour cream, mayonnaise, and honey together. Add the kohlrabi and mix.
3. Using a mandoline, slicer, or knife, cut the unpeeled apples down to the core into thin strips the same size as the kohlrabi. Add them to the kohlrabi mixture and mix well. Season to taste with salt and pepper. Cover and refrigerate the salad until chilled, at least 1 hour and up to 1 day.
4. Just before serving, mix in the almonds. Sprinkle the salad with the parsley, if using, and serve chilled.

Cucumber Salads

CUCUMBER SALAD WITH YOGURT AND DILL
MAKES 4 SERVINGS

Serve with lamb roasts and chops, chicken, seafood, or Mediterranean sandwiches.
Prep Time: 5 minutes, plus 15 minutes marinating time
Make Ahead: The salad can be made up to 1 day ahead.
Weeknight Suppers, Family Favorite, Buffet Dish, Cooking Classic, Vegetarian

*T*his *super-simple, endlessly versatile salad should be in every cook's repertoire. Serve it at picnics, on a buffet with leg of lamb, or as a side with your favorite sandwich. For years, I made this with drained regular yogurt, but the thick Greek variety makes an improvement because the dressing doesn't thin upon standing. I also like to mix in sliced tomatoes as a variation.*

2 large standard cucumbers

1 tablespoon red wine vinegar

⅓ cup low-fat plain Greek yogurt

1 tablespoon finely chopped fresh dill

1 garlic clove, crushed through a garlic press

Kosher salt and freshly ground black pepper

1. Peel the cucumbers. Cut each in half lengthwise. Using the tip of a dessert spoon, scoop out and discard the seeds. Cut the cucumber halves crosswise into ¼-inch slices.

2. Transfer the cucumber slices to a medium bowl. Toss them with the vinegar. Add the yogurt, dill, and garlic and mix well. Season to taste with salt and pepper. Cover and refrigerate for at least 15 minutes to marinate. (The salad can be made up to 1 day ahead.) Serve chilled.

CHOPPED GREEK SALAD WITH FETA AND OLIVES

MAKES 6 SERVINGS

Serve with grilled meat kebabs, lamb roasts, lamb chops, pork sausages, or grilled seafood.

Prep Time: 15 minutes

Make Ahead: The salad is best served right after making.

Weeknight Suppers, Family Favorite, Buffet Dish, Vegetarian

Instead of a leafy Greek salad, I often make a chunky, chopped version, which is actually more authentic. Serve it immediately after making, as the cucumbers will give off their juices as the salad stands.

1 tablespoon red wine vinegar

1 teaspoon dried oregano

1 garlic clove, crushed through a garlic press

¼ cup extra-virgin olive oil

1 green bell pepper, cored, seeded, and cut into ½-inch dice

2 Kirby cucumbers, scrubbed, seeds discarded, and cut into ½-inch dice or ½ English cucumber (no need to scrub or remove seeds), cut into ½-inch dice

2 large ripe tomatoes, seeds discarded, cut into ½-inch dice

2 scallions (white and green parts), chopped

½ cup crumbled feta cheese (2 ounces)

⅓ cup coarsely chopped pitted kalamata olives

Kosher salt and freshly ground black pepper

1. In a medium bowl, whisk the vinegar, oregano, and garlic together. Gradually whisk in the oil.

2. Add the bell pepper, cucumbers, tomatoes, scallions, feta, and olives and mix well. Season to taste with salt and pepper. Serve immediately.

CLASSIC TABOULLEH

MAKES 6 SERVINGS

Serve with roast lamb, roast chicken, or salmon.

Prep Time: 20 minutes

Cooking Time: 20 minutes, for soaking the bulgur

Make Ahead: The salad can be made up to 4 hours ahead.

Holiday Feasts, Company Fare, Buffet Dish, Vegetarian

At its best, taboulleh is a refreshing mix of herbs and vegetables with a bit of bulgur added for its nutty flavor. Usually, American cooks get it wrong by adding too much bulgur. The bulk of the ingredients should be vegetables and herbs. While a food processor may be the quickest way to chop the herbs, this is a job for a sharp knife, as the processor will crush the herbs and make a heavy salad. I think you'll also enjoy the hints of spice in the dressing. One last note: You can serve the taboulleh spooned onto romaine lettuce leaves, and while this makes a nice presentation, it is easier to serve the salad on a buffet without the leaves.

BULGUR

¼ cup bulgur

DRESSING

2 tablespoons fresh lemon juice

¼ teaspoon ground allspice

¼ teaspoon ground cinnamon

Kosher salt and freshly ground black pepper

½ cup extra-virgin olive oil

1 cup packed fresh flat-leaf parsley leaves

¼ cup packed fresh dill leaves

¼ cup packed fresh mint leaves

2 plum tomatoes, seeded and cut into ½-inch dice

3 Persian cucumbers or ½ seedless (English) cucumber, cut into ¼-inch dice

2 scallions (white and green parts), minced

1. To prepare the bulgur: Bring 1 cup water to a boil in a small saucepan. Remove it from the heat. Stir in the bulgur and let it stand until the bulgur is tender and has absorbed the water, about 20 minutes. Drain it well in a wire sieve to remove any excess water. Fluff the bulgur with a fork, transfer it to a small bowl, and let it cool completely.

2. To make the dressing: In a medium bowl, whisk together the lemon juice, allspice, cinnamon, ¼ teaspoon salt, and ¼ teaspoon pepper. Gradually whisk in the oil.

3. Combine the parsley, dill, and mint leaves on a chopping board. Using a large, sharp knife, finely chop the herbs, taking care to actually chop them without crushing them. Transfer the herbs to a large bowl.

4. Add the tomatoes, cucumbers, scallions, and bulgur. Add the dressing and toss well. Season to taste with salt and pepper. (The salad can be covered and refrigerated for up to 4 hours.) Serve it chilled or at room temperature.

THREE-BEAN SALAD WITH HONEY VINAIGRETTE

MAKES 8 SERVINGS

Serve with sandwiches or burgers, steaks, grilled chicken, fried chicken, or seafood.

Prep Time: 10 minutes, plus 1 hour refrigeration time

Cooking Time: 3 minutes

Make Ahead: The salad can be made up to 4 hours ahead.

Weeknight Suppers, Family Favorite, Holiday Feasts, Company Fare, Buffet Dish, Retro Recipe,

Cooking Classic, Vegetarian

*T*hree-bean salad is on the short list for side salads that are perfect for cookouts. This is my favorite recipe, with just enough honey to keep it from getting too sweet. The salad shines when made with freshly cooked green beans (as it is here), but don't dress the salad too far ahead or they could discolor.

8 ounces green beans, trimmed and cut into 1-inch lengths

2 tablespoons cider vinegar

2 tablespoons honey

Kosher salt and freshly ground black pepper

½ cup vegetable oil

One 15-ounce can garbanzo beans (chickpeas)

One 15-ounce can kidney or red beans

½ cup finely chopped sweet onion, such as Vidalia or Maui

2 tablespoons chopped fresh flat-leaf parsley

1. Bring a large saucepan of salted water to a boil over high heat. Add the green beans and cook until they are crisp-tender, about 3 minutes. Drain, rinse them under cold running water, and drain again. Pat dry with paper towels.

2. In a large bowl, whisk the vinegar, honey, ½ teaspoon salt, and ¼ teaspoon pepper together to dissolve the honey and salt. Gradually whisk in the oil. Add the vinaigrette to the green beans along with the garbanzo beans and kidney beans, onion, and parsley. Mix well. Season to taste with salt and pepper. Cover and refrigerate to blend the flavors for at least 1 hour, and up to 4 hours. Serve it chilled or at room temperature.

YELLOW AND GREEN BEANS WITH OLIVE VINAIGRETTE

MAKES 4 TO 6 SERVINGS

Serve with leg of lamb, lamb chops, grilled chicken, or shrimp.

Prep Time: 15 minutes

Cooking Time: 3 minutes

Make Ahead: The salad can be made up to 4 hours ahead.

Weeknight Suppers, Buffet Dish, Retro Recipe

This multicolored salad sings with Mediterranean flavors. Try to make it with flat Romano beans to play up its Italian roots, and yellow wax beans for added color. (Purple green beans lose their color when cooked, but I still use the raw beans, finely chopped, as a garnish.) If you only have regular green beans, don't let that stop you.

VINAIGRETTE

¼ cup coarsely chopped pitted kalamata olives

2 tablespoons red wine vinegar

½ teaspoon anchovy paste

1 garlic clove, crushed through a garlic press

Finely grated zest of ½ lemon

Pinch of hot red pepper flakes

⅓ cup extra-virgin olive oil

6 ounces green beans, preferably flat Romano, trimmed and cut into 2-inch lengths

6 ounces yellow wax or additional green beans, trimmed and cut into 2-inch lengths

1 pint grape tomatoes, halved

½ small red onion, thinly sliced

Kosher salt and freshly ground black pepper

½ cup crumbled goat cheese (2 ounces)

4 purple green beans, uncooked, finely chopped (optional)

1. To make the vinaigrette: Purée the olives, vinegar, anchovy paste, garlic, lemon zest, and red pepper flakes together in a blender. With the machine running, gradually add the oil through the center vent.

2. Bring a large saucepan of salted water to a boil over high heat. Add the green and yellow beans and cook just until they are crisp-tender, about 3 minutes. Drain and rinse them under cold running water. Pat the beans dry with paper towels (or spin them dry in a salad spinner).

3. In a large bowl, toss the beans, tomatoes, onion, and olive vinaigrette together. Season to taste with salt and pepper. (The salad can be covered and refrigerated for up to 4 hours.) Sprinkle with the goat cheese and purple beans, if using, and serve.

SUGAR SNAP PEAS AND GRAPE TOMATOES IN LEMON-TARRAGON VINAIGRETTE

MAKES 8 SERVINGS

Serve as a buffet or picnic salad with roasts, chops, chicken, or seafood.

Prep Time: 10 minutes

Cooking Time: 3 minutes

Make Ahead: The sugar snap peas and vinaigrette can be prepared up to 1 day ahead.

Holiday Feasts, Company Fare, Buffet Dish, Vegetarian

Sweet and crisp sugar snap peas are an elegant side dish that can be served with a wide assortment of main courses. They are just as at home with roast lamb as they are with poached salmon. Dress them with the vinaigrette just before serving—if they are allowed to stand, their bright green will turn drab. If there isn't any other cheese on the menu, I'll often add ¾ cup crumbled feta cheese to the salad.

1½ pounds sugar snap peas, trimmed

Finely grated zest of 1 lemon

1½ tablespoons fresh lemon juice

½ teaspoon sugar

Kosher salt and freshly ground black pepper

⅓ cup plus 1 tablespoon extra-virgin olive oil

1 pint grape or cherry tomatoes, halved

2 scallions (white and green parts), chopped

1 tablespoon finely chopped fresh tarragon

1. Bring a large pot of salted water to a boil over high heat. Add the sugar snap peas and cook just until they are crisp-tender, about 3 minutes (the water may not come back to a boil). Drain and transfer the peas to a large bowl of iced water. Drain again and pat the peas dry with paper towels. (The sugar snap peas can be prepared up to 1 day ahead, wrapped in paper towels, and refrigerated in plastic bags.)

2. In a medium bowl, whisk the lemon zest and juice, sugar, ½ teaspoon salt, and ¼ teaspoon pepper together to dissolve the salt. Gradually whisk in the oil. (The vinaigrette can be refrigerated in a covered container for up to 1 day. Whisk it well before using.)

3. Just before serving, mix the sugar snap peas, tomatoes, scallions, tarragon, and vinaigrette, in a medium bowl. Season to taste with salt and pepper. Serve immediately.

Green Salads

These salads can be relied on to refresh the palate on a warm day, or to provide a light element on a buffet table with rich food. Some of these are bolstered with bread to give them a bit more heft on buffet menus.

LAYERED WEDGE SALAD WITH BLUE CHEESE AND BACON

MAKES 8 SERVINGS

Serve as a side salad on a buffet.

Prep Time: 15 minutes, plus 1 hour refrigeration time

Cooking Time: 8 minutes, for the bacon

Make Ahead: The salad can be made up to 4 hours ahead.

Family Favorite, Holiday Feasts, Company Fare, Buffet Dish

A chunk of iceberg lettuce slathered with thick dressing is a terrific side salad, but it is only easy to eat when you have a fork and a knife. This version allows you to serve this favorite on a buffet. You can make it ahead, too, because careful layering protects the produce from the dressing.

¾ cup mayonnaise

¾ cup sour cream

1 tablespoon Worcestershire sauce

½ teaspoon freshly ground black pepper

8 slices bacon

1 small red onion, chopped

1 pint cherry or grape tomatoes, halved

½ seedless (English) cucumber, cut into ¼-inch slices

1 head iceberg lettuce, cored and cut into bite-sized pieces

1 cup crumbled blue cheese (4 ounces)

1. In a medium bowl, whisk the mayonnaise, sour cream, Worcestershire, and pepper together. Set the dressing aside.

2. In batches, if necessary, cook the bacon in a large skillet over medium heat, turning occasionally, until it is crisp and browned, about 8 minutes. (Or bake the bacon according to the directions on page 307.) Transfer it to paper towels to drain and cool. Coarsely chop the bacon.

3. Layer the ingredients in a very large bowl in the order given: onion, tomatoes, cucumber, lettuce, and bacon. Sprinkle the blue cheese over the salad, then spread the top with the dressing. Cover the salad tightly with plastic wrap and refrigerate until the salad is well chilled, at least 1 hour and up to 4 hours.

4. When ready to serve, toss well to combine all of the ingredients and serve immediately.

Layered Wedge Salad with Caesar Dressing: Substitute 1½ cups Creamy Caesar Dressing (page 343) for the mayonnaise mixture, and 1 cup freshly grated Parmesan cheese for the blue cheese. After tossing, sprinkle 1 recipe Garlic Croutons (page 317) over the salad.

MRS. CAVIGLIA'S ITALIAN BREAD SALAD

MAKES 6 TO 8 SERVINGS

Serve with beef, pork, sausages, leg of lamb, lamb chops, chicken, or seafood.

Prep Time: 15 minutes

Make Ahead: The salad is best served immediately. If you wish, the vinaigrette, cucumber, tomatoes, onion, and olives can be prepared up to 4 hours ahead, covered, and refrigerated.

Weeknight Suppers, Family Favorite, Buffet Dish, Retro Recipe, Cooking Classic, Vegetarian

When the Italian bread salad, panzanella, first made a splash in the American food world, I had already been eating it since I was a kid, thanks to the cooking of Mrs. Caviglia, my godmother's Sicilian

mother. *The bread must be very stale, almost hard, as it gets a dunk in cold water to soften it. You can vary the vegetables (roasted bell peppers are a nice addition), but this is the way I was taught to make this classic.*

2 tablespoons red wine vinegar

1 garlic clove, crushed through a garlic press

Kosher salt and freshly ground black pepper

½ cup extra-virgin olive oil

12 ounces (about half a large round loaf), stale coarse-grained, crusty bread, torn into 2- to 3-inch chunks

1 large cucumber, peeled, seeds scooped out with a dessert spoon, cut into ½-inch dice

1 pint cherry or grape tomatoes, halved

½ cup finely chopped red onion

⅓ cup chopped pitted kalamata olives

¼ cup packed torn fresh basil leaves or 3 tablespoons coarsely chopped fresh flat-leaf parsley

1. In a medium bowl, whisk together the vinegar, garlic, ½ teaspoon salt, and ½ teaspoon pepper to dissolve the salt. Gradually whisk in the oil.

2. Just before serving, immerse the bread chunks in a large bowl of cold water. Let them stand until softened but not soggy, about 30 seconds (depending, of course, on the hardness of the bread). Drain. A handful at a time, squeeze out the water from the bread and crumble it well into a large bowl.

3. Add the cucumber, tomatoes, onion, olives, and basil and toss well. Gradually mix in the dressing. Season to taste with salt and pepper and serve immediately.

FATTOUSH WITH PERSIAN CUCUMBERS AND POMEGRANATE VINAIGRETTE

MAKES 8 SERVINGS

Serve with grilled meats, especially lamb, poultry, or seafood.

Prep Time: 15 minutes

Cooking Time: 10 minutes

Make Ahead: The salad components can be prepared a few hours ahead, but the salad is best served immediately after making.

Holiday Feasts, Company Fare, Buffet Dish, Retro Recipe, Vegetarian

A Middle Eastern salad with toasted pita, fattoush is in my summer salad rotation. The pomegranate vinaigrette, made from tart pomegranate molasses, has a fascinating flavor. Small seedless Persian cucumbers, now available in supermarkets, are perfect here, but you could substitute half of an English seedless cucumber. The pita must be toasted so it remains crisp in the dressed salad, but if you don't want to turn on the oven, you can do this on the grill (or even in batches in a toaster oven).

PITA CROUTONS

2 pocket-style pitas, split in half crosswise, each
    half cut into 8 wedges

2 tablespoons olive oil

VINAIGRETTE

2 tablespoons pomegranate molasses (see Note)

2 tablespoons fresh lemon juice

2 garlic cloves, crushed through a garlic press

¼ teaspoon kosher salt

⅛ teaspoon freshly ground black pepper

½ cup extra-virgin olive oil

1 romaine heart, cut into bite-sized pieces

1 pint cherry or grape tomatoes, halved

2 Persian cucumbers, quartered lengthwise, and
    cut into ⅛-inch slices

2 scallions (white and green parts), chopped

½ cup finely chopped fresh flat-leaf parsley

¼ cup finely chopped fresh mint

1. To make the croutons: Position a rack in the center of the oven and preheat the oven to 400ºF.

2. In a large bowl, toss the pita wedges with the oil. Spread them on a large, rimmed baking sheet. Bake until the wedges are lightly toasted, about 10 minutes. Let them cool completely.

3. To make the vinaigrette: In a medium bowl, whisk the pomegranate molasses, lemon juice, garlic, salt, and pepper together. Gradually whisk in the oil.

4. In a large bowl, toss the romaine, tomatoes, cucumbers, scallions, parsley, and mint together with the vinaigrette. Add the pita wedges and toss again. Season to taste with salt and pepper and serve immediately.

Note: Thick and tart, pomegranate molasses is available at Middle Eastern grocers. You can also make your own from bottled pomegranate juice. Bring 1 cup pomegranate juice, 1 tablespoon sugar, and 1 tablespoon fresh lemon juice to a boil in a small nonreactive saucepan over high heat. Cook until the mixture has reduced by half, about 5 minutes. Remove it from the heat—it will continue to thicken as it cools. Transfer it to a covered container and refrigerate for up to 2 weeks.

GARLIC LOVER'S ANTIPASTI SALAD

MAKES 10 TO 12 SERVINGS

Serve with Italian-seasoned steaks, chops, roasts, sausages, chicken, pasta, or seafood.

Prep Time: 15 minutes

Cooking Time: 10 minutes, for the croutons

Make Ahead: The vinaigrette can be made up to 1 day ahead.

Family Favorite, Holiday Feasts, Company Fare, Buffet Dish

This has become my side dish of choice when the main course is lasagna, baked ziti, or another iconic Italian pasta dish for a big group. It is chock-full of goodies like marinated artichoke hearts, roasted bell pepper, salami, and provolone. If you wish, substitute 2 cups of store-bought croutons for these Garlic Croutons.

GARLIC CROUTONS

3 tablespoons olive oil

2 garlic cloves, crushed through a garlic press

3 slices firm white sandwich bread, slightly stale, cut into ½-inch dice

VINAIGRETTE

¼ cup red wine vinegar

2 tablespoons balsamic vinegar

1 large garlic clove, crushed through a garlic press

½ teaspoon kosher salt

½ teaspoon freshly ground black pepper

1 cup extra-virgin olive oil

2 large heads Romaine lettuce, rinsed, dried, and cut into bite-sized pieces

Two 6½-ounce jars marinated artichoke hearts, drained and coarsely chopped

1 large red bell pepper, roasted (see page 77), peeled, seeded, and cut into ½-inch dice

8 ounces sliced salami, cut into ½-inch strips

1½ cups shredded provolone cheese (6 ounces)

1. To make the croutons: Position a rack in the center of the oven and preheat the oven to 350°F.

2. In a small bowl, whisk the oil and garlic together. Put the bread pieces in a large bowl, drizzle them with the garlic oil, and toss well. Spread the bread on a large, rimmed baking sheet. Bake, stirring occasionally, until the bread is lightly toasted, about 10 minutes. Let it cool completely.

3. To make the vinaigrette: Pulse the red wine and balsamic vinegars, garlic, salt, and pepper in a blender to combine the ingredients. With the machine running, gradually add the olive oil through the hole in the lid to make a smooth vinaigrette. (The vinaigrette can be transferred to a covered container and refrigerated for up to 1 day. Whisk it well before using.)

4. In a large serving bowl, toss the lettuce, artichoke hearts, bell pepper, and salami together. Add the vinaigrette and toss again. Top the salad with the provolone and croutons and toss a final time. Serve immediately.

GRILLED HEARTS OF ROMAINE WITH GARLIC CRUMBS AND CAESAR-RANCH DRESSING

MAKES 4 SERVINGS

Serve as a buffet salad at a picnic with barbecued or grilled meats, poultry, seafood, fried chicken, or burgers.

Prep Time: 15 minutes

Cooking Time: 10 minutes

Make Ahead: The dressing and garlic crumbs can be made up to 1 day ahead.

Family Favorite, Buffet Dish, Company Fare

Surprise your guests with a grilled Caesar salad. The light grilling brings out the sweetness in the lettuce. This is a salad about contrasts—warm lettuce with cold dressing and crunchy crumbs will make a party in your mouth.

DRESSING

½ cup mayonnaise

⅓ cup buttermilk

½ cup freshly grated Parmesan cheese (2 ounces)

1 small yellow onion, grated on the large holes of a box shredder

2 tablespoons fresh lemon juice

1 teaspoon anchovy paste or Worcestershire sauce

Freshly ground black pepper

GARLIC CRUMBS

2 tablespoons olive oil

1 garlic clove, finely chopped

1 cup coarse bread crumbs, made in a food processor or blender from slightly stale crusty bread

3 romaine hearts, each cut in half lengthwise

Olive oil, for brushing

2 plum (Roma) tomatoes, cut into quarters lengthwise

1 small red onion, cut into thin rings

1. To make the dressing: In a small bowl, whisk the mayonnaise, buttermilk, Parmesan, onion, lemon juice, and anchovy paste together until combined. Season to taste with pepper. Cover and refrigerate the dressing until chilled, at least 1 hour and up to 1 day.

2. To make the garlic crumbs: Heat the oil and garlic together in a medium skillet over medium heat, stirring often, until the garlic softens, 2 to 3 minutes. Do not burn the garlic. Add the crumbs and cook, stirring occasionally, until they are crisp and golden, about 3 minutes. Transfer them to a plate and let cool. (The garlic crumbs can be stored in a plastic zip-tight bag at room temperature for up to 1 day.)

3. Prepare an outdoor grill for direct cooking over medium heat (350º to 450ºF). For a charcoal grill, let the coals burn until they are covered with white ash and you can hold your hand about 1 inch above the cooking grate for about 3 seconds. For a gas grill, preheat on high and adjust the thermostat to medium (400ºF).

4. Lightly brush the lettuce halves all over with the oil. Place them on the grill and cover. Cook, turning once or twice, just until the lettuce is lightly charred around the edges, 3 to 5 minutes. Transfer the lettuce halves to a platter.

5. Spoon the dressing over the lettuce. Top it with the garlic crumbs, tomatoes, and onion. Serve immediately.

BABY SPINACH, FRESH FIG, AND PANCETTA SALAD
MAKES 4 TO 6 SERVINGS

Serve as part of a buffet with grilled pork, veal, or lamb chops; grilled sausages; or grilled salmon.

Prep Time: 15 minutes

Cooking Time: 6 minutes

Make Ahead: The salad components can be prepared up to 8 hours ahead and tossed just before serving.

Holiday Feasts, Company Fare, Buffet Dish

Figs don't have the longest season, so when they are around, I use them as much as possible. Here they show up in an Italian variation on spinach and pancetta salad that I serve in the late summer when figs are at their plumpest and sweetest. The pancetta provides a crisp, salty accent.

3 ounces sliced pancetta

Two 4- to 5-ounce bags baby spinach

6 ripe figs, cut into quarters

1 large shallot, thinly sliced

Maple Balsamic Vinaigrette (page 335)

Kosher salt and freshly ground black pepper

1. In batches, if necessary, cook the pancetta in a large nonstick skillet over medium heat, turning occasionally, until it is crisp and browned, about 6 minutes. Do not overcook the pancetta, or it will turn bitter. Transfer the pancetta to paper towels to drain and cool. Discard the fat in the skillet. Break up the pancetta into bite-sized pieces.

2. In a large bowl, toss the spinach, pancetta, figs, shallot, and vinaigrette together. Season to taste with salt and pepper and serve immediately.

BACON, LETTUCE, AND TOMATO SALAD

MAKES 6 TO 8 SERVINGS

Serve as a buffet salad with seafood, chicken, steaks, or chops.

Prep Time: 20 minutes

Cooking Time: 20 minutes

Make Ahead: The dressing, croutons, and bacon can be prepared up to 2 hours ahead.

Family Favorite, Buffet Dish, Retro Recipe

Here is one of the most popular of all sandwiches—turned around into a wonderful salad. Because it is so hearty, I like it best with light entrées. In fact, the first time I served it was with a seafood mixed grill of salmon, shrimp, and oysters, which matched up beautifully with the bacon. When cooking a large amount of bacon, baking is much more efficient than frying, so if you haven't tried that method, prepare for a pleasant surprise.

8 slices thick-sliced bacon

5 slices firm white sandwich bread, cut into ½-inch
   squares

1 tablespoon olive oil

½ cup mayonnaise

2 tablespoons sherry or cider vinegar

2 tablespoons whole milk

Kosher salt and freshly ground black pepper

2 romaine hearts, cut into bite-sized pieces

1 pint grape tomatoes, halved

1. Position racks in the top third and center of the oven and preheat the oven to 400°F.

2. Arrange the bacon slices side-by-side on a large, rimmed baking sheet. Spread the bread squares on another large, rimmed baking sheet, drizzle them with the oil, and toss the bread and oil together on the sheet.

3. Place the baking sheets in the oven, with the bread squares on the top rack. Bake, occasionally stirring the bread squares, until the bread is toasted, 12 to 15 minutes. Remove the bread squares from the oven and let them cool. Continue baking the bacon until it is crisp and browned, about 5 minutes more. Let the bacon cool on the baking sheet for 5 minutes, then transfer the slices to paper towels to drain and cool completely. (The bread and bacon can be stored at room temperature for up to 2 hours.)

4. In a large bowl, whisk the mayonnaise, vinegar, and milk together. Season to taste with salt and pepper. Add the romaine hearts and tomatoes and toss together. Spread the lettuce mixture on a serving platter. Coarsely chop the bacon. Sprinkle the bacon and bread squares over the salad and serve.

KALE AND ROASTED BUTTERNUT SQUASH SALAD WITH SPICY PEPITAS

MAKES 6 TO 8 SERVINGS

Serve as a buffet salad with roast pork, baked ham, sausages, or roast chicken.
Prep Time: 15 minutes, plus about 30 minutes cooling time
Cooking Time: 45 minutes
Make Ahead: The kale, squash, and dressing can be prepared up to 2 hours ahead;
assemble just before serving.
Holiday Feasts, Company Fare, Buffet Dish, Vegetarian

This handsome salad features autumn's bounty in a way that would have been unthinkable a few years ago. Now it is one of my most-requested dishes, and while it has a few steps, they are all easy, and the various components can be made ahead for a quick last-minute assembly. Buy the pepitas for the crunchy topping, as experience has shown me that it is foolhardy to use the fresh ones from the butternut squash, because they are too thin to bake.

SQUASH
2 pounds butternut squash, peeled, halved
   lengthwise, seeds discarded
2 tablespoons olive oil
Kosher salt and freshly ground black pepper

DRESSING
1½ tablespoons fresh lemon juice
1 teaspoon honey

½ teaspoon kosher salt
½ teaspoon freshly ground black pepper
⅓ cup extra-virgin olive oil

SPICED PEPITAS
½ cup shelled pepitas (pumpkin seeds)
1 teaspoon chili powder
½ teaspoon sugar
¼ teaspoon kosher salt

KALE

1 pound lacinato or curly kale, thick stems
discarded, well washed and dried

1 tablespoon fresh lemon juice

1 teaspoon kosher salt

½ cup finely chopped red onion

1. To roast the squash: Position a rack in the center of the oven and preheat the oven to 425°F.

2. Toss the squash and oil together on a large rimmed baking sheet. Roast, flipping the squash with a metal spatula halfway through roasting, until the squash is tender and browned, 40 to 45 minutes. Season it lightly to taste with salt and pepper. Let it cool to room temperature.

3. To make the dressing: In a medium bowl, whisk the lemon juice, honey, salt, and pepper together to dissolve the honey and salt. Gradually whisk in the oil.

4. To make the spiced pepitas: Cook the pepitas in a medium nonstick skillet (have the lid handy) over medium heat, stirring occasionally, until they begin to brown and pop, covering the pan with the lid if the pepitas jump out of the pan, about 3 minutes. Sprinkle them with the chili powder, sugar, and salt and stir well. Transfer them to a plate and let cool.

5. To prepare the kale: Put the kale in a large bowl and sprinkle it with the lemon juice and salt. Using your fingers and palms, briskly rub the kale until it is wilted and tenderized, about 2 minutes. (The squash, dressing, pepitas, and prepared kale can be stored at room temperature for up to 2 hours.)

6. Toss the kale with the red onion and half of the dressing. Spread the kale mixture on a serving platter. Top it with the squash and drizzle the squash with the remaining dressing. Sprinkle the top with the pepitas. Serve at room temperature.

Summer Vegetable Salads

TOMATO, GRILLED CORN, AND BASIL SALAD
MAKES 6 TO 8 SERVINGS

Serve at summer meals with beef, lamb, pork, chicken, or seafood.
Prep Time: 15 minutes, plus 30 minutes for draining the tomatoes
Make Ahead: The salad is best served within 2 hours of making.
Family Favorite, Holiday Feasts, Company Fare, Buffet Dish, Vegetarian

For a few weeks every summer, corn, tomatoes, and basil are collectively in season in my area. I am lucky enough to have a farm nearby that grows all three, so I stock up on the goodies for this luscious salad. When the corn is that fresh, I do not bother to cook it, but you can boil or grill the ears if you wish. I try to use heirloom tomatoes because their color and old-fashioned flavor are so beautiful, but beef-steaks are great, too. Salting the tomato cubes helps extract some of the juice that would otherwise dilute the salad.

3 large ripe tomatoes, preferably heirloom

Kosher salt

2 tablespoons balsamic vinegar

Freshly ground black pepper

½ cup extra-virgin olive oil

2 cups fresh corn kernels, cut from 3 to 4 ears

3 tablespoons finely chopped fresh basil

1. Using a serrated knife, cut each tomato in half lengthwise. Using your finger, poke out the gel and seeds. Cut the tomatoes into ¾-inch cubes. Toss the tomatoes with ½ teaspoon salt in a large colander. Let them drain in a sink for 30 minutes.

2. In a large bowl, whisk the vinegar, ½ teaspoon salt, and ¼ teaspoon pepper together in a large bowl to dissolve the salt. Gradually whisk in the oil. Add the tomatoes, corn, and basil and toss. Season to taste with salt and pepper. Serve immediately, with a slotted spoon.

GEMELLI SALAD WITH TOY BOX TOMATOES, BABY MOZZARELLA, AND GREEN OLIVADA

MAKES 8 SERVINGS

Serve at picnics and summer cookouts with grilled meats, chicken, or seafood.

Prep Time: 15 minutes

Cooking Time: 10 minutes

Make Ahead: The salad can be made up to 1 day ahead.

Family Favorite, Holiday Feasts, Company Fare, Buffet Dish, Vegetarian

I enjoy insalata Caprese (tomatoes and mozzarella with basil) as much as the next person, but I also like to take it another step with this pasta salad. Toy box tomatoes are small and multicolored—any cherry-sized tomatoes will do. Gemelli ("twins" in Italian) is a short, twisted pasta, but you can also use short fusilli or rotini.

1 pound gemelli pasta

1 tablespoon olive oil

OLIVADA

1 garlic clove, crushed under a knife and peeled

1 cup pitted and coarsely chopped imported green olives (see Note)

2 tablespoons large or nonpareil capers, drained and rinsed

1 tablespoon red wine vinegar

1 teaspoon anchovy paste

1 teaspoon Dijon mustard

¼ teaspoon hot red pepper flakes

½ cup extra-virgin olive oil

1 pint toy box or grape tomatoes, halved

8 ounces fresh cherry-sized mozzarella balls (*ciligiene de mozzarella*), halved

Kosher salt and freshly ground black pepper

2 tablespoons chopped fresh basil

1. Bring a large pot of salted water to a boil over high heat. Add the gemelli and cook, stirring occasionally, according to the package directions, until tender. Drain and rinse the gemelli under cold running water. Transfer it to a large bowl and toss it with the oil.

2. To make the olivada: In a running food processor, drop the garlic through the feed tube to mince the garlic. Stop the food processor and add the olives, capers, vinegar, anchovy paste, mustard, and red pepper flakes. Pulse a few times to coarsely chop the olives. With the machine running, gradually pour the oil through the feed tube to make a coarse purée. (Or combine all of the ingredients in a blender and process them into a coarse purée.)

3. Add the tomatoes, mozzarella, and olivada to the pasta and mix well. Season to taste with salt and pepper. Let it stand for 30 minutes to blend the flavors. (The salad can be covered and refrigerated for up to 1 day.) Stir in the basil and serve.

Note: For the best flavor, buy large, meaty imported green olives with pits. To pit the olives, smash each one on a chopping board under the flat side of a knife, then pick out the pit. Once you get a rhythm going, this job goes quickly.

ALMOST COBB SALAD WITH SUGAR SNAP PEAS AND CORN
MAKES 6 SERVINGS

Serve with grilled meats or poultry.
Prep Time: 15 minutes
Cooking Time: 10 minutes
Make Ahead: The salad components can be prepared up to 8 hours ahead and combined just before serving.
Weeknight Suppers, Holiday Feasts, Company Fare, Buffet Dish

I call this "almost Cobb salad" because of its avocado, blue cheese, and bacon—all ingredients of the classic salad from Hollywood's legendary Brown Derby. (And also because I serve it most often as a partner to grilled chicken, another essential ingredient of the original Cobb.) When the corn is very fresh and sweet, I don't bother to cook it, and just cut it off the cob. Otherwise, grilling the corn is a good option. Rather than make the salad ahead, I prefer to prepare the components separately and toss them together just before serving.

5 slices bacon, cut into 1-inch lengths

12 ounces sugar snap peas, cut on the diagonal into ½-inch lengths

2 tablespoons cider or red wine vinegar

Kosher salt and freshly ground black pepper

½ cup extra-virgin olive oil

1½ cups fresh corn kernels, cut from about 2 ears

2 ripe Hass avocados, halved, peeled, pitted, and cut into 1-inch pieces

½ cup crumbled blue cheese (2 ounces), preferably Gorgonzola

1. Cook the bacon in a large skillet over medium heat, stirring occasionally, until it is crisp and browned, about 8 minutes. Transfer the bacon to paper towels to drain and cool. Coarsely chop the bacon.

2. Meanwhile, bring a medium saucepan of salted water to a boil over high heat. Add the sugar snap peas and cook just until they turn a brighter shade of green, about 2 minutes. Drain and rinse them under cold running water until cooled. Pat the sugar snap peas dry with paper towels.

3. In a small bowl, whisk the vinegar, ½ teaspoon salt, and ¼ teaspoon pepper together. Gradually whisk in the oil. Set the dressing aside. (The bacon, sugar snap peas, and dressing can be covered and refrigerated for up to 8 hours.)

4. In a medium bowl, combine the sugar snap peas, corn, and avocados. Add the dressing and mix gently. Top the vegetables with the blue cheese and bacon and mix again. Season to taste with salt and pepper. Serve at room temperature.

PERUVIAN SALAD WITH CORN AND FRESH SHELL BEANS
MAKES 4 TO 6 SERVINGS

Serve with grilled meats, poultry, or seafood.

Prep Time: 20 minutes, including 1 hour refrigeration time

Cooking Time: about 10 minutes

Make Ahead: The salad can be made up to 8 hours ahead.

Company Fare, Vegetarian

In Peru, this substantial salad is called solterito, *which means "little bachelor" in Spanish, and could refer to a quick supper that a single man might toss together. The essentials are shell beans (frozen beans work well if you don't have fresh) and corn, two summer ingredients that I like to use as much as possible when they are in season. When the corn is really fresh, don't bother to cook it. This is not true of the fava beans, however, which must be cooked to destroy toxins. You'll find this salad on Peruvian menus as an appetizer, but I find it is perfect with grilled main courses.*

1½ cups fresh corn kernels, cut from about 2 ears

1½ cups fresh or thawed frozen lima or fava beans

3 tablespoons fresh lime juice

1 red Fresno or jalapeño chile, seeded and minced

Kosher salt and freshly ground black pepper

½ cup extra-virgin olive oil

1 large tomato, seeded and cut into ½-inch dice

½ cup chopped pitted kalamata olives

⅓ cup finely chopped red onion

2 tablespoons finely chopped fresh flat-leaf parsley

½ cup crumbled ricotta salata or queso fresco cheese (about 2 ounces)

1. Bring a medium saucepan of salted water to a boil over high heat. Add the corn and cook just until it is barely tender, about 2 minutes. Using a wire sieve, transfer the corn to a bowl of iced water.

2. Add the fresh lima beans to the boiling water and cook until they are tender, about 5 minutes. (No need to cook the thawed beans.) Drain and rinse them under cold running water. If using fresh fava beans, peel them. Drain the beans and pat them dry with paper towels.

3. In a medium bowl, use a fork to beat the lime juice and chile with ½ teaspoon salt and a few grinds of black pepper, crushing the chile slightly with the fork. Gradually beat in the oil. Drain the corn and pat it dry with paper towels. Add the corn, beans, tomato, olives, onion, and parsley and mix well. Cover and refrigerate until chilled, at least 1 hour. (The *solterito* can be made up to 8 hours ahead.)

4. Just before serving, sprinkle it with the ricotta salata and serve chilled.

GRILLED SUMMER VEGETABLES WITH HARISSA VINAIGRETTE

MAKES 6 TO 8 SERVINGS

Serve at picnics and summer cookouts with grilled meats, poultry, or seafood.

Prep Time: 15 minutes

Cooking Time: 10 minutes

Make Ahead: The salad can be stored at room temperature for up to 2 hours.

Holiday Feasts, Company Fare, Buffet Dish, Vegetarian

A big salad of grilled vegetables is a spectacular side dish at a summer gathering. This one has zesty North African flavors provided by harissa, a hot spice paste. If you aren't familiar with it, adjust the amount to taste. Be sure to grill the vegetables over medium heat, so they cook to tenderness without burning. Check out my method for grilling the bell pepper flat, which allows it to cook in less time and with less attention than a whole pepper.

VINAIGRETTE

2 tablespoons fresh lemon juice

1½ teaspoons harissa (see Note)

½ teaspoon kosher salt

½ cup extra-virgin olive oil

1 large red bell pepper

1 globe eggplant (1½ pounds), cut into ½-inch rounds

2 zucchini (1 pound total), halved lengthwise, then in half crosswise to make 8 pieces total

4 ripe plum (Roma) tomatoes, halved lengthwise

Olive oil, for brushing

3 tablespoons coarsely chopped fresh cilantro or basil

Lemon wedges, for serving

1. To make the vinaigrette: In a medium bowl, whisk the lemon juice, harissa, and salt together. Gradually whisk in the oil. Set the vinaigrette aside.

2. Prepare an outdoor grill for direct cooking over medium heat (350° to 450°F). For a charcoal grill, let the coals burn until they are covered with white ash and you can hold your hand about 1 inch above the cooking grate for about 3 seconds. For a gas grill, preheat on high and adjust the thermostat to medium (400°F).

3. Cut ½ inch off the top and bottom of the bell pepper to resemble "lids." Discard the stem. Cut down the length of the pepper, and open the pepper up so it lies flat. Remove the ribs and seeds.

4. Brush the bell pepper strip and lids, eggplant, zucchini, and tomatoes all over with oil. Place the bell pepper pieces on the cooking grate, skin-side down. Add the eggplant, zucchini, and tomatoes, cut-sides down. Cover the grill and cook for the following times, removing the vegetables from the grill as they are done:

Tomatoes: Grill for 2 minutes, then flip and grill until the skins begin to split, about 3 minutes more.
Zucchini: Grill until it is crisp-tender and seared on both sides with grill marks, about 6 minutes.
Bell pepper: Grill until the skin is blackened, about 10 minutes.
Eggplant: Grill until it is tender and golden brown on both sides, about 10 minutes.

5. Let the vegetables cool until they are tepid. Remove the skin from the bell pepper. Coarsely chop all of the vegetables and arrange them on a serving platter. Drizzle the vegetables with the dressing. Season to taste with salt. Sprinkle the vegetables with the cilantro and serve, with the lemon wedges.

Note: Harissa is available in jars, cans, or tubes at specialty food stores, spice purveyors, and many natural food supermarkets. (The tube-packed harissa is very convenient to use and store in the refrigerator.) If you can't find it, substitute an equal amount of Chinese chili-garlic paste mixed with ¼ teaspoon ground ginger.

Root Vegetable Salads

CARROT SLAW WITH MISO VINAIGRETTE
MAKES 4 SERVINGS

Serve with Asian-style grilled meats, poultry, or seafood.
Prep Time: 15 minutes
Make Ahead: The slaw can be made up to 8 hours ahead.
Weeknight Suppers, Holiday Feasts, Company Fare, Buffet Dish, Vegetarian

Tablespoon for tablespoon, miso is one of the most flavor-packed ingredients in my kitchen. Because a little goes a long way, I always have a container in the refrigerator (where it keeps indefinitely) to bring its deep umami notes to dishes like this one. With a food processor to shred the carrots, this bright orange slaw is ready in minutes. The only caveat here is not to shred the carrots too fine.

MISO VINAIGRETTE

2 tablespoons rice vinegar

1 tablespoon white miso

½ teaspoon soy sauce

1 garlic clove

½ cup vegetable oil

1 pound carrots, trimmed

1 scallion (white and green parts), finely chopped

Kosher salt and freshly ground black pepper

Sesame seeds, for garnish

1. To make the vinaigrette: Process the vinegar, miso, soy sauce, and garlic in a blender. With the machine running, gradually add the oil through the hole in the lid. (Or crush the garlic through a garlic press into a medium bowl. Add the vinegar, miso, and soy sauce and whisk until combined. Gradually whisk in the oil.)

2. In a food processor fitted with the coarse shredding blade, shred the carrots. (It is important not to shred the carrots too fine. If your food processor only has a fine shredding disk, use a V-slicer to julienne the carrots into strips less than ⅛ inch wide.)

3. In a medium bowl, toss together the carrots, scallion, and vinaigrette. Season to taste with salt and pepper. (The slaw can be covered and refrigerated for up to 8 hours.) Serve it chilled or at room temperature, topping each serving with a sprinkle of sesame seeds.

CARROT RIBBONS WITH POMEGRANATE DRESSING

MAKES 6 TO 8 SERVINGS

Serve with sliced roast beef tenderloin, leg of lamb, lamb chops, roast chicken,

roast duck, fish fillets, or sautéed shrimp.

Prep Time: 10 minutes

Make Ahead: The salad can be refrigerated for up to 8 hours.

Holiday Feasts, Company Fare, Buffet Dish, Vegetarian

This salad of orange curlicues of carrot topped with garnet pomegranate seeds is one of my favorite cold-weather dishes. Inspired by Turkish cuisine, the dressing uses tart pomegranate molasses and paprika-like Aleppo pepper, which can be found at Mediterranean grocers and online. But if you don't feel like going that route, the suggested substitutes also make a lovely salad without any drop in quality.

1½ pounds large carrots (sometimes called chef's carrots), peeled

1 tablespoon sherry vinegar

1 tablespoon pomegranate molasses (see Note page 328)

½ teaspoon Aleppo pepper or sweet paprika

½ teaspoon dry mustard powder

⅓ cup extra-virgin olive oil

Kosher salt and freshly ground black pepper

1 cup pomegranate arils (seeds)

4 large scallions (white and green parts), chopped

3 tablespoons chopped fresh mint or cilantro

1. Place a carrot on a work surface. Using a sturdy vegetable peeler, and pressing hard on the carrot, shave off wide, thick slices and transfer them to a large bowl of iced water. The carrots can stand in the water for up to 1 hour. Drain them well and pat dry with kitchen towels.

2. Process the vinegar, pomegranate molasses, Aleppo pepper, dry mustard, and oil together in a blender until thickened and emulsified. Season to taste with salt and pepper.

3. In a large bowl, toss the carrots, ½ cup of the pomegranate arils, the scallions, and mint together. Add the dressing and toss again. Season to taste with additional salt and pepper. Transfer the slaw to a serving platter. (The salad can be covered loosely with plastic wrap and refrigerated for up to 8 hours.) Just before serving, top it with the remaining pomegranate arils. Serve chilled or at room temperature.

Note: Substitute 2 tablespoons pomegranate-flavored balsamic vinegar for the sherry vinegar and pomegranate molasses, if desired.

CELERY ROOT AND CHIVE RÉMOULADE
MAKES 4 TO 6 SERVINGS

Serve as a buffet salad with roast beef, ham, sausages, chicken, fish fillets, or sautéed shrimp.
Prep Time: 15 minutes, plus 1 hour standing time
Make Ahead: The salad can be made up to 2 days ahead.
Holiday Feasts, Company Fare, Buffet Dish, Cooking Classic, Vegetarian

Celeri rémoulade, *strips of celery root tossed with a mustardy dressing, can be found on the menus of classic French bistros. I am surprised at how long it took to become known here, as it is so crisp and refreshing. The celery root is not cooked, but marinated in lemon and salt to tenderize it. When I am putting together a picnic, nine times out of ten, this is on the menu. This is another recipe that makes good use of a V-slicer or mandoline.*

1½ pounds celery root

1 tablespoon fresh lemon juice

Kosher salt

½ cup Mayonnaise (page 436), or store-bought

1 tablespoon stone-ground prepared mustard

2 tablespoons finely chopped fresh chives, plus more for garnish

Freshly ground black pepper

1. To peel the celery root, use a sturdy vegetable peeler and a small, sharp knife to remove the thick skin. Do not rinse the celery root until after peeling, as the water could turn any dirt in the gnarly nooks into mud.

2. Using a mandoline, plastic V-slicer, or a large, sharp knife, cut the celery root into thin strips about ⅛ inch wide. In a large colander, toss the celery root, lemon juice, and 1 teaspoon salt together. Let them stand on a plate for 1 to 2 hours to drain away excess juices and tenderize the celery root. Do not rinse the celery root.

3. In a medium bowl, whisk the mayonnaise and mustard together. Add the celery root and chives and stir well. Season to taste with salt and pepper. Cover and refrigerate the salad until chilled, at least 2 hours. (The salad can be made up to 2 days ahead.) Sprinkle it with additional chives and serve chilled.

Apple, Pear, and Citrus Salads

MEXICAN CHRISTMAS EVE SALAD
MAKES 8 SERVINGS

Serve with Mexican-style main courses, especially at Christmas Eve;
baked ham; or barbecued meats and poultry.
Prep Time: 20 minutes, plus 1 hour refrigeration time
Make Ahead: The salad components can be refrigerated for up to 4 hours.
Holiday Feasts, Company Fare, Buffet Dish, Cooking Classic, Vegetarian

The traditional Mexican Christmas Eve feast always includes this salad, known as ensalada de noche buena, *a sweet and spicy winter fruit salad. The recipe changes from family to family, and there are versions that include beets (although they bleed), bananas, and jicama, and use vinaigrette instead of this creamy dressing. Don't wait for Christmas to serve it—try it with barbecued spareribs or baked ham.*

CREAMY LIME DRESSING
½ cup mayonnaise
½ cup plain low-fat yogurt (see Note)
Finely grated zest of 1 lime
3 tablespoons fresh lime juice
1 tablespoon honey
Kosher salt and freshly ground black pepper

2 tablespoons fresh lemon juice
2 sweet apples, such as Ginger Gold or Golden Delicious, cored and cut into ½-inch cubes
½ ripe pineapple, pared, cored, and cut into ½-inch cubes
2 navel oranges, cut into suprêmes
1 jalapeño, seeded and minced
2 romaine lettuce hearts, cut into bite-sized pieces
½ cup pomegranate arils (see page 55)
⅓ cup coarsely chopped dry-roasted peanuts

1. To make the dressing: In a medium bowl, whisk the mayonnaise, yogurt, lime zest and juice, and honey together. Season the dressing with salt and pepper to taste.

2. In a medium bowl, toss the lemon juice and apple cubes together. Add the pineapple and orange suprêmes. Add 3 tablespoons of the dressing and mix well. Separately cover and refrigerate the salad and dressing until chilled, at least 1 hour and up to 4 hours.

3. Just before serving, mix the jalapeño into the fruit mixture. Spread the lettuce on a deep serving platter and top it with the fruit salad. Sprinkle it with the pomegranate seeds and peanuts. Serve the salad chilled, with the remaining dressing on the side.

Note: If using Greek yogurt, thin the dressing as needed with a few tablespoons of milk.

CHOPPED SALAD WITH PEARS, PARMESAN, AND WALNUTS

MAKES 6 SERVINGS

Serve with roast chicken or pork chops.

Prep Time: 10 minutes

Make Ahead: The salad can be prepared, without the cheese, up to 2 hours ahead.

Weeknight Suppers, Holiday Feasts, Company Fare, Vegetarian

I am always looking for an excuse to serve this winter salad, and I especially like it next to roast chicken or pan-cooked pork chops, where it can play off the browned pan juices. Pears are always shipped hard, so if you want to make this salad, think ahead and purchase the pears a few days ahead so they have time to ripen. Red Bartlett pears will add an extra bit of color to the salad, but any juicy variety will work.

1 tablespoon sherry vinegar

Kosher salt and freshly ground black pepper

¼ cup extra-virgin olive oil

3 ripe pears, such as Red Bartlett or Anjou, peeled, cored, and cut into ½-inch dice

4 celery ribs, thinly sliced

½ cup toasted and coarsely chopped walnuts (see page 33)

One 4-ounce chunk Parmesan cheese

1. In a medium bowl, whisk the vinegar, ¼ teaspoon salt, and ⅛ teaspoon pepper together. Gradually whisk in the oil.

2. Add the pears, celery, and walnuts and mix well. Season to taste with salt and pepper. (The salad can be covered tightly with plastic wrap and refrigerated for up to 2 hours.)

3. Just before serving, use a vegetable peeler to shave about 2 ounces of curls from the Parmesan chunk over the salad, saving the remaining cheese for another use. Serve immediately.

BABY SPINACH SALAD WITH GRILLED ASIAN PEARS AND GOAT CHEESE

MAKES 6 SERVINGS

Serve as a buffet salad with roasts and chicken.

Prep Time: 15 minutes

Cooking Time: 5 minutes

Holiday Feasts, Company Fare, Buffet Dish, Vegetarian

*A*sian *pears are now available at just about every supermarket, but most of us don't have enough recipes for this juicy and aromatic fruit. Its firm texture is perfect for a quick grilling before serving, but you can broil them or even skip this step.*

VINAIGRETTE

2 tablespoons red wine vinegar

1 tablespoon minced shallot

1 teaspoon Dijon mustard

Kosher salt and freshly ground black pepper

½ cup extra-virgin olive oil

2 firm-ripe Asian pears, cored with a fruit corer from top to bottom, and cut into ¼-inch rings

Vegetable oil, for brushing

8 ounces baby spinach

¾ cup crumbled goat cheese (3 ounces)

½ cup toasted and coarsely chopped walnuts (see page 33)

1. Prepare an outdoor grill for direct cooking over medium heat (350º to 450ºF). For a charcoal grill, let the coals burn until they are covered with white ash and you can hold your hand about 1 inch above the cooking grate for about 3 seconds. For a gas grill, preheat on high and adjust the thermostat to medium (400ºF).

2. Meanwhile, make the vinaigrette: Pulse the vinegar, shallot, mustard, ½ teaspoon salt, and ¼ teaspoon pepper in a blender to combine. With the machine running, gradually pour in the oil through the hole in the lid to make a smooth vinaigrette.

3. Lightly brush the pear rings on both sides with vegetable oil. Place the pears on the grill. Cook, with the lid closed, until the undersides are seared with grill marks, about 2 minutes. Turn and grill the other side about 2 minutes more. Remove the pears from the grill.

4. In a large bowl, toss the spinach and vinaigrette together. Add the pears with the goat cheese and walnuts and toss again. Season to taste with salt and pepper and serve.

FRESH AMBROSIA SALAD WITH BLOOD ORANGES AND PINEAPPLE

MAKES 8 SERVINGS

Serve as a side salad on a buffet.

Prep Time: 20 minutes, plus 1 hour refrigeration time

Make Ahead: The salad can be made up to 8 hours ahead.

Holiday Feasts, Company Fare, Buffet Dish, Cooking Classic, Vegetarian

This has nothing to do with the ambrosia salad with marshmallows and salad dressing. My version is fresh and makes a beautiful addition to a winter buffet, the season when magenta blood oranges are sold. The salad is also excellent made with navel oranges. And while orange liqueur gives the salad a je ne sais quoi, *you can substitute orange juice if you are serving this to kids.*

½ pineapple, peeled, cored, and cut into bite-sized
  pieces

4 blood oranges, cut into suprêmes

½ cup pomegranate arils (see page 55)

⅓ cup desiccated coconut

2 tablespoons orange-flavored liqueur, such as
  Grand Marnier, or fresh orange juice

1. In a serving bowl, toss all of the ingredients together. Cover the salad tightly with plastic wrap and refrigerate until chilled, at least 1 hour or up to 8 hours. Serve chilled.

WATERCRESS, TANGERINE, AND HAZELNUT SALAD

MAKES 6 SERVINGS

Serve as part of a buffet with roast meat or poultry or seafood.

Prep Time: 15 minutes

Make Ahead: The components for the salad can be prepared up to 1 day ahead,

but combine them just before serving.

Holiday Feasts, Company Fare, Buffet Dish, Vegetarian

Watercress is a deliciously spicy salad green, a notch less spicy than arugula, with a nice crisp texture. I have been using a lot more of it now that my supermarket sells it cleaned and in bags with the other salad greens in the refrigerated produce section. Here, sweet tangerines and crunchy hazelnuts play off the watercress for a fine winter salad. Because of their size, tangerines should be segmented by hand, and not with a knife like other oranges and grapefruits.

DRESSING

1 tablespoon red wine vinegar

1 tablespoon balsamic vinegar

Finely grated zest of 1 tangerine (reserve the
tangerine for the salad)

Kosher salt and freshly ground black pepper

⅓ cup olive oil

2 tablespoons hazelnut oil or more olive oil

3 tangerines (including the zested tangerine)

Two 4-ounce bags prewashed watercress or
10 ounces bunched watercress, washed well and
tough stems removed

1 small red onion, cut into thin half-moons

½ cup toasted, peeled, and coarsely chopped
hazelnuts (see page 33)

1. To make the dressing: In a medium bowl, whisk together the wine vinegar, balsamic vinegar, tangerine zest, ½ teaspoon salt, and ¼ teaspoon pepper. Gradually whisk in the olive oil and hazelnut oil.
2. Peel all of the tangerines, separating them into segments, and removing any seeds (just poke the seeds through the membranes). (The tangerines and dressing can be separately covered and refrigerated for up to 1 day. Whisk the dressing well before using.)
3. In a large bowl, toss the watercress, tangerine segments, onion, and dressing together. Sprinkle with the hazelnuts, toss again, and season to taste with salt and pepper. Serve immediately.

ORANGES, DATES, AND SHALLOTS ON BABY ARUGULA

MAKES 4 TO 6 SERVINGS

Serve as part of a buffet with grilled meats, poultry, or seafood.
Prep Time: 15 minutes, plus soaking time for the shallots
Weeknight Suppers, Company Fare, Buffet Dish, Vegetarian

Here is another recipe that is great to have on hand when the party is in the winter and you are searching for an interesting, colorful, and light buffet salad to add to the menu. Dates are very sweet, so the acidic oranges and spicy arugula work to cut their richness. For the best results, use fresh, moist dates that you have chopped yourself, not precut dates.

DRESSING

4½ teaspoons balsamic vinegar

1 tablespoon pitted and coarsely chopped dates

Kosher salt and freshly ground black pepper

⅓ cup extra-virgin olive oil

1 large shallot, cut into thin rounds

3 navel oranges

One 4-ounce bag baby arugula

6 dates, pitted and coarsely chopped (¾ cup)

1. To make the dressing: In a blender, combine the vinegar, dates, ½ teaspoon salt, and ¼ teaspoon pepper until the dates are puréed. With the machine running, gradually add the oil through the hole in the lid.

2. Put the shallot rounds in a small bowl and cover them with cold water. Let them stand for 15 to 30 minutes. (This removes some of the raw onion flavor from them.)

3. Working with one orange at a time, trim off the top and bottom of the fruit so it stands securely on the work counter. Using a serrated knife, cut off the thick peel where it meets the flesh to end up with a skinless sphere. Cut the oranges into ½-inch rounds.

4. Toss the arugula in a large bowl with half of the dressing and season to taste with salt and pepper. Spread the arugula on a serving platter. Drain the shallot. Toss the shallot, orange rounds, and dates with the remaining dressing and season to taste with salt and pepper. Heap the orange mixture on the arugula and serve.

Gelatin Salads

Gelatin salads are divisive: I have friends who wax rhapsodically over their family's Jell-O mold, and others who aren't so enamored. In my family, it is not a holiday without a gelatin salad. I still make them for the retro fun of it—a kind of edible *Mad Men* episode. The recipes that follow have stood the test of time.

- Don't make double batches of these recipes to make large gelatin salads in molds larger then 6 cups or so. If the salad is too tall, it could collapse, no matter how much gelatin it contains.
- The gelatin must be partially set before adding any solid ingredients to keep them suspended. Some recipes call for refrigerating the gelatin mixture at this point, but I find it much easier and quicker to chill it in a large bowl set in another large bowl of iced water. Stir the mixture occasionally until it has the consistency of egg whites. It is now ready for the add-ins.
- To help them keep their shape, gelatin salads contain less water than the amount usually called for in package directions, so don't think that you've made a mistake in the measurements.
- To unmold the gelatin salad, first run a dull knife around the edge of the mold, being sure to go deep enough (about ½ inch) to break the air seal. Fill a sink or a large bowl with warm tap water. Dip the mold up to its lip in the water and hold it there for 5 to 10 seconds. Dry the outside of the mold with a kitchen towel. Put a serving platter on the pan. Holding the pan and platter together, flip them over. Give them both a good shake to dislodge the salad onto the platter. If it is stubborn, repeat the procedure.

RETRO CRANBERRY GELATIN SALAD
MAKES 12 TO 16 SERVINGS

Serve as part of a holiday meal with roast turkey, baked ham, or other all-American entrées.
Prep Time: 15 minutes, plus at least 12 hours refrigeration time
Make Ahead: The salad can be made up to 2 days ahead.
Family Favorite, Holiday Meals, Company Fare, Retro Dish

Here is the gelatin salad that my in-laws served at every Yuletide meal. In fact, its recipe card is titled "Christmas Time Cranberry Salad." You may recognize it from your family's collection, too, perhaps in its Waldorf variation with apples. Because the Fisher clan is from West Virginia, they preferred local black walnuts, but the standard California variety (also called English) is just fine.

Two 3-ounce packages raspberry gelatin dessert

2 cups boiling water

One 14-ounce can cranberry sauce

One 20-ounce can crushed pineapple, very well
  drained (see Note)

1 cup finely chopped celery

1 cup coarsely chopped black or standard
  walnuts

Vegetable oil, for the mold

1. Put the gelatin in a large bowl. Add the boiling water and stir well for at least 1 minute, until it is thoroughly dissolved. Stir in the cranberry sauce and 1 cup cold water. Place the bowl in a larger bowl of iced water. Let it stand, stirring occasionally, until the mixture is partially set and the semi-firm consistency of egg whites, about 10 minutes.

2. Stir the drained crushed pineapple, celery, and walnuts into the gelatin mixture. Oil a 6- to 8-cup fluted tube pan or ring mold and then pour the mixture in. Cover with plastic wrap. Refrigerate until set, at least 12 hours and up to 2 days.

3. To unmold the salad, fill a large bowl with hot tap water. Run a dull dinner knife around the inside of the mold, reaching down to the bottom of the mold to help break the air seal. Dip the mold, up to its lip, in the hot water for 5 seconds. Dry the outside of the pan with a kitchen towel. Put a serving platter over the mold. Holding the mold and platter together, invert them to unmold the salad onto the platter. Serve chilled.

Note: Do not substitute fresh pineapple in this recipe. Raw pineapple contains enzymes that will destroy the setting ability of gelatin. The enzymes are destroyed by heat, so canned pineapple does not have the same effect.

Cranberry Waldorf Gelatin Salad: Substitute ¾ cup peeled, cored, and diced (¼-inch) apples (any variety) for the crushed pineapple.

PROSECCO MIMOSA SALAD

MAKES 12 SERVINGS

Serve with chicken or seafood on a buffet.
Prep Time: 20 minutes, plus 8 hours refrigeration time
Make Ahead: The salad can be made up to 1 day ahead.
Holiday Feasts, Company Fare, Buffet Dish, Retro Recipe

I was asked by a friend to develop an appropriately festive and "girly" recipe for a bridal shower, and the result was this gelatin salad with the flavors and bubbles of a mimosa cocktail. Keep in mind that the alcoholic content makes it adults-only fare. For large parties or nondrinkers, make a second salad (or a half-batch in individual plastic glasses) for the kids, substituting lemon-lime soda or ginger ale for the Prosecco, and a different berry to identify the separate salads. Prosecco is the best sparkling wine for this because it is tasty and more reasonably priced than other options.

3 envelopes unflavored powdered gelatin (about 6¾ teaspoons)

¾ cup sugar

One 750-ml bottle Prosecco, chilled (about 3¼ cups)

1 large navel orange, zest finely grated, rind cut off

with a serrated knife and flesh cut out from membrane

One 6-ounce (half-pint) container fresh raspberries, blueberries, or blackberries (about 1⅓ cups)

Vegetable oil, for the mold

1. Pour 2 cups cold water into a medium saucepan and sprinkle in the gelatin. Let it stand to soften the gelatin, about 5 minutes. Using a rubber spatula, stir the mixture constantly over medium-low heat until the gelatin is completely dissolved, about 3 minutes. Do not simmer. Add the sugar and stir just until it is dissolved, about 1 minute more. Pour the gelatin mixture into a large bowl set in a larger bowl of iced water. Let it stand, stirring occasionally, until the mixture is partially set and the semi-firm consistency of raw egg whites, about 10 minutes.

2. Gradually stir the Prosecco into the partially set gelatin. The mixture will bubble up, but that's what you want. Let it stand, stirring occasionally, until the Prosecco mixture sets again to the egg-white consistency, about 10 minutes more. Stir in the orange zest and segments with the raspberries, which will be suspended in the Prosecco mixture.

3. Lightly oil a 6-cup gelatin salad mold, ring mold, or fluted cake pan. Pour in the Prosecco mixture. (Pour leftover gelatin into a ramekin as the cook's treat.) Cover with plastic wrap. Refrigerate until the salad is chilled and set, at least 8 hours and up to 1 day.

4. To unmold the salad, fill a large bowl with hot tap water. Run a dull dinner knife around the inside of the mold, reaching down to the bottom of the salad to help break the air seal. Dip the mold, up to its lip, in the hot water for 5 seconds. Dry the outside of the pan with a kitchen towel. Put a serving platter over the mold. Holding the mold and platter together, invert them to unmold the salad onto the platter. Serve chilled.

STRAWBERRY AND CREAM CHEESE SALAD
MAKES 8 SERVINGS

Serve as a buffet salad at a picnic or with barbecued meats or chicken, or with baked ham or fried chicken.
Prep Time: 10 minutes, plus 4 hours refrigeration time

Make Ahead: The salad can be made up to 1 day ahead.

Family Favorite, Holiday Feasts, Company Fare, Buffet Dish, Cooking Classic

Old-fashioned in the best sense of the word, this creamy strawberry mold is inspired by nostalgia for the era when a salad was not always that far away from dessert. The salad is ready for refrigeration in a few minutes, and, unlike most recipes of this type, is full of true fruit flavor. Be sure that the strawberry purée and cream cheese are at room temperature when you add the dissolved gelatin, because if they are cold, the gelatin will clump and set too quickly.

2¼ pounds strawberries (3 dry pints), at room temperature

1 tablespoon unflavored powdered gelatin (about 1½ envelopes)

8 ounces cream cheese, cut into chunks, at room temperature

½ cup sugar

Nonstick oil spray for the mold

Fresh mint sprigs, for garnish

1. Reserve seven of the best-looking strawberries for the garnish. Hull the remaining strawberries. Process enough of the hulled strawberries (about two-thirds) in a blender or food processor to measure 2 cups purée. Chop the remaining hulled strawberries into ½-inch pieces.

2. Sprinkle the gelatin over ⅓ cup water in a small heatproof bowl. Let it stand to soften the gelatin, about 5 minutes. Add enough water to come about ½ inch up the sides of a small skillet and bring it to a simmer. Place the bowl of dissolved gelatin in the skillet and stir constantly until the gelatin is completely dissolved, 1 to 2 minutes. Do not simmer. Remove the bowl from the water.

3. Return the strawberry purée to the food processor. Add the dissolved gelatin mixture, cream cheese, and sugar and process until they are smooth and combined. Transfer them to a medium bowl placed in a larger bowl of iced water. Let it stand, stirring occasionally, until the strawberry mixture is beginning to set, about 15 minutes. Fold in the chopped strawberries.

4. Lightly spray the inside of a 5- to 6-cup ring mold with the oil. Pour in the strawberry mixture and cover with plastic wrap. Refrigerate until the salad is chilled and set, at least 4 hours and up to 1 day.

5. To unmold the salad, fill a large bowl with hot tap water. Run a dull dinner knife around the inside of the mold and the inner tube, reaching down to the bottom of the mold to break the air seal. Dip the mold, up to its lip, in the hot water for 5 seconds. Dry the outside of the mold with a kitchen towel. Put a serving platter over the mold. Holding the mold and platter together, invert them to unmold the salad onto the plate. Fill the center hole in the salad with the reserved whole strawberries and mint sprigs. Serve chilled.

Salad Dressings

Here, I offer a curated selection of the most popular dressings for everyday salads. Because they all store well in the refrigerator, you might want to make a double batch to keep in a jar to use for a few meals.

- Match the dressing with the texture of the salad greens. In general, a thick dressing (such as green goddess or Russian) will crush and wilt tender greens and works best with sturdy lettuce varieties, such as romaine and iceberg. Delicate greens, especially the ubiquitous spring mix with baby lettuces, should be dressed with a thin-bodied vinaigrette.
- For a thicker consistency, make vinaigrettes in the blender, as the blades emulsify the ingredients more completely than a whisk.

CLASSIC VINAIGRETTE
MAKES ABOUT I CUP

Serve with tender salad greens.
Prep Time: 5 minutes
Make Ahead: The vinaigrette can be made up to 3 days ahead.
Weeknight Suppers, Family Favorite, Holiday Feasts, Company Fare, Cooking Classic, Vegetarian

The key to a great vinaigrette is a good balance of oil and vinegar. Here is my basic version, for which I offer a few variations. Always taste the salad before serving, and add additional seasonings or vinegar, if you wish.

¼ cup red wine vinegar
½ teaspoon kosher salt

¼ teaspoon freshly ground black pepper
¾ cup extra-virgin olive oil

1. In a medium bowl, whisk the vinegar, salt, and pepper together to dissolve the salt. Gradually whisk in the oil. (The dressing can be refrigerated in a covered container for up to 3 days. Whisk it well before using.)

French Vinaigrette: Add 2 tablespoons finely chopped shallot and 1 teaspoon sweet paprika to the bowl with the vinegar, salt, and pepper.
Mustard Vinaigrette: Substitute white wine vinegar for the red wine vinegar. Add 2 teaspoons Dijon mustard to the bowl with the vinegar, salt, and pepper.
Garlic Vinaigrette: Add 1 garlic clove, crushed through a garlic press, to the bowl with the vinegar, salt, and pepper.
Roasted Garlic Vinaigrette: Add 2 to 3 teaspoons mashed Simple Roasted Garlic Cloves (see page 159) to the bowl with the vinegar, salt, and pepper.

ORANGE-GINGER DRESSING

MAKES ABOUT 1 CUP

Serve with tender salad greens.

Prep Time: 10 minutes

Make Ahead: The vinaigrette can be made up to 3 days ahead.

Weeknight Suppers, Family Favorite, Holiday Feasts, Company Fare, Vegetarian

This is an Asian-inspired dressing with a light consistency, and its spicy flavor is best with mild greens like baby spinach. The fresh ginger and Sriracha give this plenty of zing. I suggest cutting the orange used for the zest into segments to use in the salad.

½ cup peeled and coarsely chopped fresh ginger

2 tablespoons sherry or rice vinegar

1 tablespoon soy sauce

Finely grated zest of ½ navel orange

1 teaspoon sugar

1 teaspoon Sriracha or other hot red pepper sauce

½ teaspoon kosher salt

½ cup vegetable oil

2 tablespoons toasted sesame oil

1. Pulse the ginger, vinegar, soy sauce, orange zest, sugar, Sriracha, and salt, together in a blender to mince the ginger. With the machine running, gradually pour the vegetable and sesame oils through the hole in the lid to make an emulsified dressing. Strain the vinaigrette through a fine-mesh wire sieve into a small bowl. Press hard on the solids, and discard them. (The dressing can be refrigerated in a covered container for up to 3 days. Whisk it well before using.)

MAPLE-BALSAMIC VINAIGRETTE

MAKES ABOUT 1 CUP

Serve with tender salad greens.

Prep Time: 5 minutes

Make Ahead: The vinaigrette can be made up to 1 day ahead.

Weeknight Suppers, Family Favorite, Holiday Feasts, Company Fare, Vegetarian

The birthplaces of maple syrup and balsamic vinegar are thousands of miles apart, but their rich flavors pair well. I use this dressing on wilted bitter greens, such as kale, that would benefit from a bit of sweetness.

2 tablespoons balsamic vinegar

1 tablespoon maple syrup, preferably Grade A Dark

¼ teaspoon pure maple extract (optional)

½ teaspoon kosher salt

¼ teaspoon hot red pepper sauce

⅔ cup olive oil (not extra-virgin)

1. In a medium bowl, whisk together the vinegar, maple syrup, and maple extract, if using, with the salt and hot pepper sauce to dissolve the salt. Gradually whisk in the oil. (The dressing can be refrigerated in a covered container for up to 3 days. Whisk it well before using.)

MUSTARD-HONEY VINAIGRETTE
MAKES 1 CUP

Serve with tender salad greens or as a dressing for cabbage or broccoli salads.
Prep Time: 5 minutes
Make Ahead: The vinaigrette can be made up to 3 days ahead.
Weeknight Suppers, Family Favorite, Holiday Feasts, Company Fare, Vegetarian

This thick vinaigrette is especially delicious with cruciferous vegetables, a group that includes Brussels sprouts, cabbage, broccoli, and cauliflower. Because mustard can absorb many times its weight in liquids, the dressing will have a creamy consistency without any thickeners. Vary the recipe by using other mustards—a German-style stone-ground one would be great.

2 tablespoons cider vinegar
2 tablespoons honey
1 tablespoon minced shallot
2 teaspoons Dijon mustard

¼ teaspoon kosher salt
¼ teaspoon freshly ground black pepper
⅔ cup olive oil (not extra-virgin)

1. In a medium bowl, whisk together the cider vinegar, honey, shallot, mustard, salt, and pepper to dissolve the salt. Gradually whisk in the oil. (The dressing can be refrigerated in a covered container for up to 3 days. Whisk it well before using.)

RETRO RED FRENCH DRESSING
MAKES ABOUT 1¼ CUPS

Serve with crisp and sturdy greens.
Prep Time: 5 minutes
Make Ahead: The dressing can be made up to 3 days ahead.
Weeknight Suppers, Family Fare, Retro Recipe, Vegetarian

I admit nostalgia for red French dressing, but much prefer my homemade version to the commercial stuff. The not-so-secret ingredient is ketchup, an American cooking stalwart that has been shown to contain high amounts of umami. When I have youngsters at the table, I serve this with a classic iceberg lettuce, tomato, and cucumber combo, and everyone eats their salad.

¼ cup tomato ketchup

2 tablespoons balsamic vinegar

2 tablespoons coarsely chopped shallot

1 teaspoon light or dark brown sugar

1 teaspoon Dijon mustard

1 garlic clove, crushed under a knife and peeled

¼ teaspoon kosher salt

⅛ teaspoon freshly ground black pepper

⅔ cup olive oil (not extra-virgin)

1. In a blender, pulse the ketchup, vinegar, shallot, brown sugar, mustard, garlic, salt, and pepper together to combine and finely chop the shallot and garlic. With the machine running, gradually pour in the oil through the hole in the lid. Serve immediately. (The dressing can be refrigerated in a covered container for up to 3 days. Whisk it well before serving.)

JAPANESE CARROT DRESSING

MAKES ABOUT 1 CUP

Serve with baby spinach and other tender greens.

Prep Time: 5 minutes

Make Ahead: The dressing can be made up to 3 days ahead.

Weeknight Suppers, Cooking Classic, Vegetarian

In this deliciously spicy dressing from Japanese cuisine, fresh ginger and miso pack a lot of flavor. I like it best on assertively flavored greens, such as spinach or Romaine lettuce, but then again, it will gussy up iceberg (as you have probably seen in Japanese restaurants). As you use only the white scallion bottom for the dressing, reserve the green top to slice and sprinkle on the salad as a garnish. For the smoothest texture, be sure to shred the carrot before blending.

1 large carrot, shredded on the large holes of a box shredder (about 4½ ounces)

1 scallion (white part only), coarsely chopped

2 tablespoons white miso

2 tablespoons rice vinegar

2 tablespoons toasted sesame oil

1 tablespoon peeled and finely minced ginger

2 teaspoons sugar

1. In a blender, purée the carrot, scallion, white miso, vinegar, sesame oil, ginger, sugar, and ¼ cup water until smooth. (The dressing can be covered and refrigerated for up to 3 days. If it separates, process the dressing in the blender until it emulsifies.)

RASPBERRY, CHIPOTLE, AND POPPY SEED DRESSING

MAKES ¾ CUP

Serve with crisp and sturdy salad greens.

Prep Time: 5 minutes

Make Ahead: The dressing can be made up to 3 days ahead.

Weeknight Suppers, Family Favorite, Holiday Feasts, Company Fare, Vegetarian

A couple of tablespoons of raspberry preserves give this dressing a delicious fruit flavor. You can substitute standard red pepper sauce for the chipotle, but the latter gives the dressing a nice smokiness.

2 tablespoons balsamic vinegar

2 tablespoons raspberry preserves

1 tablespoon finely chopped shallot

½ teaspoon kosher salt

½ teaspoon chipotle hot pepper sauce or adobo
from canned chipotles

½ cup olive oil (not extra-virgin)

1 tablespoon poppy seeds

1. In a blender, pulse the vinegar, preserves, shallot, salt, and hot pepper sauce to combine. With the machine running, gradually pour the oil through the hole in the lid. Add the poppy seeds and pulse a few times to crush the seeds. (The dressing can be refrigerated in a covered container for up to 3 days. Whisk it well before serving.)

AVOCADO GREEN GODDESS DRESSING

MAKES 2 CUPS

Serve with crisp and sturdy salad greens.

Prep Time: 10 minutes, plus 1 hour refrigeration time

Make Ahead: The dressing can be made up to 1 day ahead.

Weeknight Suppers, Family Favorite, Holiday Feasts, Company Fare, Vegetarian

Luscious Green Goddess dressing was invented in San Francisco during the early twentieth century to promote a hit play that was on tour in the city. Avocado is a recent twist, and its fresh flavor makes a good thing better.

1 ripe Hass avocado, pitted, peeled, and cubed

½ cup sour cream

⅓ cup whole milk

2 scallions (white and green parts), coarsely chopped

¼ cup packed fresh flat-leaf parsley leaves

3 tablespoons coarsely chopped fresh tarragon

3 tablespoons fresh lemon juice

1 tablespoon white wine vinegar

2 teaspoons anchovy paste

1 garlic clove, crushed under a knife and peeled

½ cup olive oil (not extra-virgin)

Kosher salt and freshly ground black pepper

1. In a food processor or blender, process the avocado, sour cream, milk, scallions, parsley, tarragon, lemon juice, vinegar, anchovy paste, and garlic together until the scallions are very finely minced. With the machine running, gradually pour the oil through the feed tube (or the hole in the blender lid). Season to taste with salt and pepper. Transfer the dressing to a container, cover, and refrigerate it until chilled, at least 1 hour and for up to 1 day. Serve chilled.

STEAKHOUSE BLUE CHEESE DRESSING
MAKES 2 CUPS

Serve with crisp and sturdy salad greens.
Prep Time: 10 minutes, plus 1 hour refrigeration time
Make Ahead: The dressing can be made up to 3 days ahead.
Weeknight Suppers, Family Favorite, Holiday Feasts, Company Fare, Retro Recipe, Cooking Classic, Vegetarian

This is how I have made this iconic dressing for years, from a recipe from a friend who worked at a steakhouse. Mashing the blue cheese distributes its flavor beautifully throughout the mayonnaise mixture, and extra crumbled cheese provides texture. Use your favorite moderately priced blue cheese here, and save the more expensive varieties (such as Cabrales and Stilton) for enjoying on their own. Make the dressing a couple of hours before serving, to blend the flavors.

1 cup crumbled blue cheese (4 ounces)
⅔ cup mayonnaise
⅔ cup sour cream
¼ cup buttermilk

1 teaspoon Worcestershire sauce
2 scallions (white and green parts), minced
1 garlic clove, crushed through a garlic press
½ teaspoon freshly ground black pepper

1. Using a flexible spatula, mash ½ cup of the blue cheese with the mayonnaise and sour cream in a medium bowl. Add the buttermilk, Worcestershire sauce, scallion, garlic, and pepper and mix well. Stir in the remaining ½ cup blue cheese. Cover and refrigerate the dressing for at least 1 hour before serving. (The dressing can be refrigerated in a covered container for up to 3 days. Stir it well before serving.)

CREAMY CAESAR DRESSING
MAKES ABOUT 1 CUP

Serve with crisp and sturdy salad greens.
Prep Time: 10 minutes, plus 1 hour refrigeration time
Make Ahead: The dressing can be made up to 3 days ahead.
Weeknight Suppers, Family Favorite, Holiday Feasts, Company Fare, Buffet Dish, Cooking Classic

Authentic Caesar salad is made in the salad bowl with a coddled egg, to give the vinaigrette a thicker consistency. Over the years, mayonnaise (which is also egg-based) has become the main ingredient, and it does make a very good dressing.

¾ cup mayonnaise

⅓ cup freshly grated Parmesan cheese (about 1½ ounces)

3 tablespoons fresh lemon juice

1 teaspoon anchovy paste

1 garlic clove, crushed through a garlic press

½ teaspoon freshly ground black pepper

1. In a small bowl, whisk the ingredients together. Cover the bowl with plastic wrap and refrigerate the dressing for at least 1 hour to blend the flavors. (The dressing can be refrigerated in a covered container for up to 3 days. Whisk it well before serving.)

THE BEST RANCH DRESSING
MAKES ABOUT 1½ CUPS

Serve with mixed greens as a side salad, or as a topping for baked potatoes.

Prep Time: 10 minutes

Make Ahead: The dressing can be made up to 3 days ahead.

Weeknight Suppers, Family Favorite, Holiday Feasts, Company Fare, Buffet Dish,

Cooking Classic, Vegetarian

The most popular dressing in America, ranch dressing was first served to the public at Hidden Valley Ranch, a resort near Santa Barbara. Buttermilk is the ingredient that gives the thick dressing its tang, and the combination of onions, garlic, and herbs is truly mouthwatering. Of course it is fantastic with salad greens (especially a big chunk of iceberg), but try it as a dressing for coleslaw and macaroni salads, or as a topping for baked potatoes.

1 cup mayonnaise

⅓ cup buttermilk

½ small yellow onion, shredded on the large holes of a box shredder (1 tablespoon)

1 garlic clove, crushed through a garlic press

1 tablespoon finely chopped fresh dill

1 tablespoon finely chopped fresh flat-leaf parsley

½ teaspoon celery seed

¼ teaspoon freshly ground black pepper

1. In a medium bowl, whisk all of the ingredients together. Cover the bowl with plastic wrap and refrigerate the dressing for at least 1 hour to chill and blend the flavors. (The dressing can be refrigerated in a covered container for up to 3 days. Whisk it well before serving.)

Chipotle Ranch Dressing: In a blender, process the ingredients with 1 canned chipotle chile in adobo plus 1 teaspoon adobo sauce until smooth.

THOUSAND ISLAND DRESSING
MAKES ABOUT 1 ¼ CUPS

Serve with crisp salad greens as a side salad.
Prep Time: 10 minutes, plus 1 hour refrigeration time
Make Ahead: The dressing can be made up to 3 days ahead.
Weeknight Suppers, Family Favorite, Cooking Classic, Vegetarian

Legend has it that Thousand Island dressing originated in the chain of small island in the St. Lawrence River. Essentially a blend of mayonnaise and ketchup with a lot of finely chopped additions, this is my simplified version with chili sauce, capers, and pickle relish to give lots of flavor without lots of chopping. If you are in the mood, you can add minced hard-boiled eggs or black or green olives. Russian dressing is closely related, except the original recipe for that classic included the ultimate Russian ingredient—caviar.

¾ cup mayonnaise

¼ cup ketchup-style chili sauce (not Asian chili sauce)

2 tablespoons sweet or dill pickle relish

2 tablespoons nonpareil capers

1 teaspoon Worcestershire sauce

1 teaspoon hot red pepper sauce

1. In a small bowl, whisk all of the ingredients together. Cover the bowl with plastic wrap and refrigerate the dressing for at least 1 hour to chill and blend the flavors. (The dressing can be refrigerated in a covered container for up to 3 days. Whisk it well before serving.)

YOGURT, TAHINI, AND GARLIC DRESSING
MAKES ABOUT 1 CUP

Serve with crisp salad greens as a side salad.
Prep Time: 10 minutes, plus 1 hour refrigeration time
Make Ahead: The dressing can be made up to 3 days ahead.
Weeknight Suppers, Vegetarian

This Middle Eastern dressing is an interesting alternative to vinaigrette and has fewer calories, too, as yogurt replaces much of the oil. Give it a try when you want a thick dressing (this is great with romaine, cucumber, and tomatoes) that isn't mayonnaise based.

½ cup plain low-fat Greek yogurt

2 tablespoons tahini

2 tablespoons fresh lemon juice

2 tablespoons extra-virgin olive oil

1 garlic clove, crushed through a garlic press

½ teaspoon hot red pepper sauce

½ teaspoon kosher salt

2 tablespoons finely chopped fresh cilantro

1. In a small bowl, whisk together the yogurt, tahini, lemon juice, oil, garlic, hot pepper sauce, and salt with ¼ cup water. Stir in the cilantro. Cover the bowl with plastic wrap and refrigerate the dressing for at least 1 hour to chill and blend the flavors. (The dressing can be refrigerated in a covered container for up to 3 days. Whisk it well before serving.)

PASTA AND FRIENDS

While the word *pasta* is Italian, every country has a similar food that is made from flour and cooked in water. By that definition, couscous and dumplings are very closely related to pasta, as are spaëtzle and Roman-style gnocchi. When it comes to side dishes, the familiar dried shapes and noodles are the most convenient because, with the bulk of the preparation spent on the main course, you won't have extra time on your hands for rolling pasta. However, you may be surprised to find how simple some of these fresh "friends of pasta" are to make. Keep in mind that, like potatoes, rice, and other starchy foods, pasta side dishes are filling, so make them in reasonable serving sizes to allow room for the other items on the menu. That doesn't mean that you can't make a double batch or have seconds.

Macaroni and Cheese

One of the best reasons for eating at a Southern-style restaurant is that you can order macaroni and cheese as a side dish instead of as a main course. It's just enough to satisfy a mac and cheese craving without being a caloric splurge. (And it goes so well with barbecued meats and chicken, not to mention collard greens and coleslaw, my other two faves.) Americans do not have a corner on the combination of pasta and cheese, though, and while our Cheddar-based classic is well represented here, I've included some international recipes, too.

- If the macaroni and cheese will be baked, be sure that the pasta is boiled only until it is al dente, as it will finish cooking in the oven.

MACARONI AND CHEESE WITH CHEDDAR AND GRUYÈRE

MAKES 4 SERVINGS

Serve with baked ham, barbecued meats, or roast chicken.

Prep Time: 15 minutes

Cooking Time: 30 minutes

Weeknight Suppers, Family Favorite, Cooking Classic, Vegetarian

On the surface, this may look like a boilerplate mac and cheese, but it employs a few tricks to make it extraordinary. First, two cheeses, Cheddar and Gruyère, give it a deeper flavor, and a little dry mustard accents the Cheddar's sharp flavor. An egg, not a common ingredient for this dish, enriches the sauce. Finally, the cheese cracker topping is a worthy final fillip. (Or use the crispy topping for the Stovetop Macaroni and Pimiento Cheese opposite.)

2 tablespoons (¼ stick) unsalted butter, plus softened butter for the dish

8 ounces elbow macaroni

2 tablespoons all-purpose flour

2 cups whole milk, heated

1 cup shredded sharp Cheddar cheese (4 ounces)

1 cup shredded Gruyère or Swiss cheese (4 ounces)

¼ teaspoon dry mustard powder

1 large egg, beaten to blend

Freshly grated black pepper

½ cup crushed Cheddar cheese crackers, such as Cheez-Its

1. Position a rack in the center of the oven and preheat the oven to 350°. Lightly butter a 2-quart round baking dish.

2. Bring a large pot of salted water to a boil over high heat. Stir in the macaroni and cook, stirring occasionally to keep the macaroni from sticking, according to the package directions, until it is just al dente. Drain the macaroni.

3. Meanwhile, melt the butter in a medium saucepan over medium heat. Sprinkle in the flour and whisk until smooth. Reduce the heat to low and let it bubble without browning for 1 minute. Whisk in the milk, increase the heat to medium, and bring it to a simmer, whisking often. Return the heat to low and simmer, stirring often, until the sauce is smooth and thickened, about 2 minutes. Remove it from the heat. Add the Cheddar, Gruyère, and dry mustard and stir until the cheeses are completely melted. Briskly stir in the egg. Season with the pepper (you are unlikely to need any salt). Stir the macaroni into the sauce. Spread it in the baking dish. Sprinkle the crackers over the top.

4. Bake until the macaroni is bubbling, about 20 minutes. Let it stand for 5 minutes, then serve.

Macaroni and Cheese with Bacon: Cook 2 slices bacon in a large skillet over medium heat, turning occasionally, until they are crisp and browned, about 8 minutes. Transfer the bacon to paper towels to drain and cool. Coarsely crumble the bacon. Add it to the macaroni with the cheeses and dry mustard.

MAKES 4 TO 6 SERVINGS

Serve with baked ham, barbecued meats, or poultry.

Prep Time: 10 minutes

Cooking Time: 10 minutes

Weeknight Suppers, Family Favorite, Buffet Dish, Retro Recipe, Vegetarian

The goal of this recipe was to make a mild and super-creamy mac and cheese that would be ready for serving in minutes—a dish that kids would love and adults would treasure for its nostalgia value. This unbaked version resembles the one found at many Southern barbecue joints and cafeterias. Even if Velveeta is not your favorite "cheese," it does give the dish an old-fashioned flavor and smooth texture that you can't get from Cheddar. I've provided a baked variation if you want a crispy topping.

8 ounces elbow macaroni

2 tablespoons (¼ stick) unsalted butter

2 tablespoons all-purpose flour

1 cup whole milk, heated

8 ounces pasteurized prepared cheese product,

such as Velveeta, cut into ¾-inch cubes, or coarsely chopped American cheese slices

One 4-ounce jar diced sweet pimiento, drained, rinsed, and patted dry

Freshly grated black pepper

1. Bring a large pot of salted water to a boil over high heat. Stir in the macaroni and cook, stirring occasionally to keep the macaroni from sticking, according to the package directions, until it is just al dente.

2. Meanwhile, melt the butter in a medium saucepan over medium heat. Sprinkle in the flour and whisk until smooth. Reduce the heat to low and let it bubble without browning for 1 minute. Whisk in the milk, increase the heat to medium, and bring it to a simmer, whisking often. Return the heat to low and simmer, stirring often, until the sauce is smooth and thickened, about 2 minutes. Remove it from the heat. Add the cheese product and stir until it is completely melted. Stir in the pimientos. Season with the pepper (you are unlikely to need any salt).

3. Drain the macaroni and return it to its cooking pot. Add the cheese sauce and mix well. Serve hot.

Macaroni and Cheese with Crispy Topping: Position the broiler rack about 6 inches from the source of heat and preheat the broiler. Spread the macaroni mixture in a buttered 8-inch flameproof baking dish. Mix ⅓ cup panko with 2 tablespoons melted, unsalted butter, and sprinkle it evenly over the macaroni. Broil, watching carefully to avoid burning, just until the topping is lightly browned, about 1 minute.

ALMOST ALFREDO ZITI WITH CREAMY PARMESAN SAUCE

MAKES 4 SERVINGS

Serve with simply prepared, cream-free meats, poultry, or seafood.
Prep Time: 5 minutes
Cooking Time: 12 minutes
Weeknight Suppers, Family Favorite, Company Fare, Buffet Dish, Vegetarian

Pasta Alfredo is always a highly indulgent dish. However, when the main course is sauce-free, a little of this creamy pasta goes a long way to elevating the entire meal. And it is the basis for a couple of wonderful variations. (By the way, the original Alfredo sauce omits the egg yolks, but our cream is thinner than the Italian variety, so the yolks are useful as thickeners.)

8 ounces ziti or other tube-shaped pasta
½ cup heavy cream
¾ cup freshly grated Parmesan cheese (3 ounces),
   plus more for serving

2 large egg yolks, beaten
Kosher salt and freshly ground black pepper

1. Bring a medium saucepan of salted water to a boil over high heat. Stir in the ziti and cook, stirring occasionally to keep the ziti from sticking, according to the package directions, until it is just al dente. Drain the ziti in a colander.

2. Add the heavy cream to the saucepan and bring it to a boil over high heat. Return the ziti to the saucepan and reduce the heat to low. Add the Parmesan and stir until smooth. Remove the pan from the heat. Gradually stir in the egg yolks. Return the pan to low heat and stir just until the sauce thickens lightly; do not simmer. Remove the pan from the heat and season the sauce to taste with salt and pepper. Transfer the pasta to a serving dish and serve immediately, with additional Parmesan passed on the side.

Ziti with Creamy Basil Sauce: Stir in 2 tablespoons finely chopped fresh basil just before serving.
Ziti with Creamy Parmesan Sauce and Peas: Cook ½ cup frozen baby peas in a small saucepan of boiling salted water until hot, about 3 minutes. (Or microwave the peas in a small covered microwave-safe bowl with ¼ cup water on high for 1 minute.) Drain well. Add the peas to the saucepan with the heavy cream.

FRENCH MACARONI AND CHEESE WITH LEEKS

MAKES 4 TO 6 SERVINGS

Serve with roast meats and poultry.
Prep Time: 10 minutes

Cooking Time: 30 minutes
Weeknight Suppers, Holiday Feasts, Company Fare, Buffet Dish, Vegetarian

Necessity is often the mother of culinary invention. Once, when teaching some cooking classes in France, I had to use up some groceries in the refrigerator. So this side dish was created with the odds and ends, and a new favorite was born. Cantal is now sold at supermarkets, but if you can't find it, substitute a white sharp Cheddar or Gruyère. The crusty ends of the pasta are the best part. Sometimes I'll add a few sliced and sautéed mushrooms to the pasta before baking.

1 garlic clove

2 tablespoons (¼ stick) unsalted butter, plus more for the dish

8 ounces ziti or other tube-shaped pasta

2 large leeks (white and pale green parts), thinly sliced

¾ cup crème frâiche (see page 154)

¾ cup shredded Cantal cheese (3 ounces)

Kosher salt and freshly ground black pepper

1. Position a rack in the center of the oven and preheat the oven to 400°F. Rub the inside of a 2-quart round baking dish with the garlic clove, and discard the garlic. Slather butter inside the dish.

2. Bring a large pot of salted water to a boil over high heat. Stir the ziti into the boiling water and cook, stirring occasionally to keep the ziti from sticking, according to the package directions, until it is just al dente. Drain the ziti well and return it to the pot.

3. Meanwhile, melt the 2 tablespoons of butter in a large skillet over medium heat. Stir in the leeks and cover the skillet. Cook, stirring occasionally, until the leeks are tender, about 10 minutes. Set the leeks aside.

4. Add the leeks, crème frâiche, and Cantal to the pasta and mix well. Season with salt and pepper. Spread the pasta in the prepared dish.

5. Bake until the pasta is piping hot and the tips are tinged with brown, about 20 minutes. Let it stand for 5 minutes, then serve hot.

BAKED ZITI WITH BROCCOLI AND GORGONZOLA

MAKES 4 SERVINGS

Serve with roast veal or pork; or veal or pork chops.
Prep Time: 15 minutes
Cooking Time: 25 minutes
Weeknight Suppers, Company Fare, Buffet Dish

This creamy side consists of both a green vegetable and a starch, so you'll just have to zero in on a main protein. Because of its rich flavor profile, it is best with a simple dish, such as veal or pork rubbed with herbs and garlic. Domestic Gorgonzola is perfect for this recipe, but if you use the imported kind, choose the piccante *(also called* montagna*) variety, as it is drier and crumbles better than the* dolce *type. Do not overcook either the ziti or the broccoli in the water, as they will finish cooking during baking.*

4 tablespoons (½ stick) unsalted butter, plus
   softened butter for the baking dish
12 ounces broccoli crowns
8 ounces ziti or other tube-shaped pasta
3 tablespoons unbleached all-purpose flour

¾ cup reduced-sodium chicken broth
¾ cup whole milk
1 cup crumbled Gorgonzola (4 ounces)
Kosher salt and freshly ground black pepper
½ cup panko

1. Position a rack in the center of the oven and preheat the oven to 400°F. Lightly butter an 11½ × 8 × 2-inch baking dish.

2. Bring a large saucepan of salted water to a boil over high heat. Meanwhile, cut the broccoli tops from the stems, and cut the tops into bite-sized florets. Peel the stems and cut them into bite-sized pieces.

3. Add the broccoli florets and stems to the boiling water and cook just until they turn a brighter shade of green and are still quite crisp, about 3 minutes. Do not overcook, as they will be cooked more in the oven. Using a wire spider or slotted spoon, transfer the broccoli to a bowl of cold water, leaving the water in the saucepan boiling. Rinse the broccoli.

4. Stir the ziti into the boiling water and cook, stirring occasionally to keep the ziti from sticking, according to the package directions, until it is just al dente. Drain it in a colander and rinse under cold running water.

5. Return the saucepan to medium heat. Add 3 tablespoons of the butter and melt it. Whisk in the flour and reduce the heat to medium-low. Let the mixture bubble without browning for 1 minute. Whisk in the broth and milk and bring them to a boil over medium heat. Return the heat to medium-low and simmer, whisking occasionally, until the sauce has lost any raw flour taste, about 5 minutes. Remove it from the heat. Whisk in ¾ cup of the Gorgonzola, reserving the remaining cheese for the topping. Season to taste with salt and pepper.

6. Stir the pasta and broccoli into the sauce. Spread the pasta mixture in the dish. Sprinkle it with the panko and remaining ¼ cup cheese and dot it with the remaining 1 tablespoon of butter. Bake until the sauce is bubbling and the topping is lightly browned, 15 to 20 minutes. Serve hot.

Noodles

There is something especially comforting about noodles, which get their tender texture from the eggs in the dough. (Pasta is usually just semolina and water, even if the homemade version usually includes eggs.) Half of these noodle recipes use sour cream. If you want to use low-fat sour cream, go ahead, but whole-fat does have superior flavor.

NOODLES ROMANOFF

MAKES 6 SERVINGS

Serve with steaks, chops, or chicken breast.

Prep Time: 10 minutes

Cooking Time: 15 minutes

Weeknight Suppers, Family Favorite, Holiday Feasts, Company Fare, Buffet Dish,

Cooking Classic, Vegetarian

Kids love this dish—at least I know I did when Mom made it for my brothers and me. If you wish, substitute ¾ cup cream-style cottage cheese for an equal amount of the sour cream.

12 ounces medium egg noodles

2 tablespoons (¼ stick) unsalted butter

1 small yellow onion, chopped

1 garlic clove, chopped

1½ cups whole-fat sour cream

⅔ cup whole milk

½ cup freshly grated Parmesan cheese (2 ounces)

Kosher salt and freshly ground black pepper

2 tablespoons finely chopped fresh chives
  (optional)

1. Bring a medium saucepan of salted water to a boil over high heat. Add the noodles and cook according to the package directions, stirring occasionally, until they are al dente.

2. Meanwhile, melt the butter in a large nonstick skillet over medium heat. Add the onion and cook, stirring occasionally, until the onion is tender without browning, about 4 minutes. Stir in the garlic and cook until it is fragrant, about 1 minute more.

3. Drain the noodles and add them to the onion mixture. Stir in the sour cream, milk, and Parmesan. Stir well, until the noodles are coated with the sour cream sauce and the sauce is hot but not boiling, about 1 minute. Season to taste with salt and pepper. Transfer the noodles to a serving bowl, sprinkle them with the chives, if using, and serve.

Noodles Stroganoff: Omit the onion and Parmesan cheese. Melt the butter in a large skillet. Add 8 ounces sliced white button mushrooms and cook, stirring occasionally, until they are lightly browned, about 8 minutes. Stir in 2 tablespoons finely chopped shallots and the garlic and cook until they soften, about 1 minute. Stir in the sour cream and cook, stirring often, until it is hot but not simmering, about 1 minute. Add the drained noodles and the milk and cook until they are hot but not boiling, about 30 seconds. Season to taste with salt and pepper. Sprinkle with 1 tablespoon finely chopped fresh chives and serve.

CRISP EGG NOODLES WITH POPPY SEEDS

MAKES 4 SERVINGS

Serve with beef, pork, or veal sautés or stews; veal or pork chops; or chicken sautés or stews.

Prep Time: 5 minutes

Cooking Time: 15 minutes

Weeknight Suppers, Family Favorite, Buffet Dish, Cooking Classic, Vegetarian

These simple noodles, sautéed in butter to give them irresistibly crisped edges, are one of the most perfect side dishes to serve with sauced main courses. Poppy seeds are a great spice to keep on hand for quickly bringing flavor to plain food. You'll find the best prices for them at Indian grocers. Because of their high oil content, they can go rancid, though, so they will keep best in the freezer or refrigerator.

12 ounces medium egg noodles

1 tablespoon vegetable oil

2 tablespoons (¼ stick) unsalted butter

2 teaspoons poppy seeds

Kosher salt and freshly ground black pepper

1. Bring a large saucepan of salted water to a boil over high heat. Add the noodles and cook according to the package directions, stirring occasionally, until just tender. Drain and rinse them well under cold running water. (The noodles must be cold, if not chilled.) Drain them well. Toss the noodles with the oil.

2. Melt the butter in a large nonstick skillet over medium-high heat until the foam in the skillet starts to subside. Don't worry if the butter begins to brown. Add the noodles and cook, without stirring, until the edges begin to crisp, about 2 minutes. Stir the noodles and continue cooking, stirring occasionally, until they are lightly browned, about 2 minutes more. Sprinkle in the poppy seeds and mix well. Season to taste with salt and pepper. Transfer the noodles to a serving bowl and serve hot.

Crispy Noodles with Scallions: During the last minute of cooking, add 2 scallions (white and green parts), finely chopped, to the skillet.

APPLE AND SOUR CREAM NOODLE KUGEL

MAKES 10 TO 12 SERVINGS

Serve with smoked or baked salmon, especially at Yom Kippur breakfast or as a sweet Rosh Hashanah treat.

Prep Time: 15 minutes

Cooking Time: 1 hour, 10 minutes

Make Ahead: The kugel can be made up to 1 day ahead.

Family Favorite, Holiday Feasts, Company Fare, Vegetarian

My dear friend Diane Kniss and I put our heads together to come up with the ultimate noodle kugel, which is a must at a Yom Kippur break fast. Apples are coming into season at that time of year, so we layered them with our seriously creamy concoction of sour cream, cottage cheese, and cream cheese. If you are tempted to use reduced-fat dairy products for this recipe—don't. When I served it at a Chanukah party, I was told, "This is the best kugel I ever ate, but if you tell my mother that, I'll never speak to you again."

APPLES

2 tablespoons (¼ stick) unsalted butter, plus extra for the dish

3 Golden Delicious apples, peeled, cored, and cut lengthwise into eighths

2 tablespoons sugar

1 tablespoon fresh lemon juice

1 teaspoon ground ginger

⅛ teaspoon ground cloves

12 ounces wide egg noodles

One 16-ounce container cottage cheese

One 16-ounce container sour cream

One 8-ounce package cream cheese, cut into chunks, at room temperature

½ cup (1 stick) unsalted butter, melted

1 cup plus 1 tablespoon sugar

2 teaspoons vanilla extract

5 large eggs, at room temperature, beaten to blend

1 teaspoon ground cinnamon

1. Position a rack in the center of the oven and preheat the oven to 350°F. Lightly butter a 13 × 9 × 2-inch baking dish

2. To prepare the apples: Melt the butter in a large skillet over medium-high heat. Add the apples and cook, stirring occasionally, until they are softened but holding their shape and beginning to brown, 3 to 5 minutes. Sprinkle them with the sugar, lemon juice, ginger, and cloves and stir just until the sugar is melted into a glaze, about 1 minute. Spread the apple mixture in the baking dish.

3. Meanwhile, bring a large pot of salted water to a boil over high heat. Add the noodles and cook according to the package directions, stirring occasionally, until they are al dente. Drain them well. Return the noodles to the cooking pot.

4. Add the cottage cheese, sour cream, cream cheese, and melted butter. Mix until the cream cheese has melted. Stir in 1 cup of the sugar and the vanilla. Gradually stir in the eggs. Pour the mixture over the apples and smooth the top. In a small bowl, mix the remaining 1 tablespoon sugar and the cinnamon and sprinkle them over the noodle mixture.

5. Place the dish on a large, rimmed baking sheet. Bake until the kugel is puffed evenly and golden brown, about 1 hour. (The kugel can be cooled, covered with aluminum, and refrigerated for up to 1 day. Reheat, covered, in a 350°F oven for about 30 minutes.) Let it stand for 15 minutes before serving. Serve it warm or cooled to room temperature.

SWEET NOODLE KUGEL WITH ROSEMARY AND BLACK PEPPER

MAKES 8 TO 12 SERVINGS

Serve as part of a Passover Seder with roast lamb or chicken.

Prep Time: 20 minutes

Cooking Time: 1 hour

Make Ahead: The kugel can be made up to 1 day ahead.

Holiday Feasts, Company Fare, Buffet Dish, Vegetarian

This sweet, savory, and mildly spiced noodle pudding is a simplified variation of Jerusalem kugel, which is made with caramelized sugar. (Supposedly, this kind of kugel was brought from Eastern Europe to Jerusalem by Hasidic Jews, hence the name.) I find brown sugar much easier to use and the results to be the same. I gave the recipe to a friend who wanted to make something different for a Seder with many highly judgmental eaters. She reported back that she was asked to bring it to every Seder from now on.

12 ounces fine egg noodles

¾ cup packed light brown sugar

⅓ cup extra-virgin olive oil, plus more for the baking dish

3 large eggs, beaten to blend

2 teaspoons chopped fresh rosemary

1 teaspoon freshly ground black pepper

½ teaspoon kosher salt

1. Position a rack in the center of the oven and preheat the oven to 350°F. Lightly oil a 13 × 9 × 2-inch baking dish.

2. Meanwhile, bring a large pot of salted water to a boil over high heat. Add the noodles and cook according to the package directions, stirring occasionally, until they are barely tender. Scoop out and reserve ¼ cup of the cooking water. Drain the noodles well.

3. In the same pot, whisk together the brown sugar, oil, and reserved water. Bring them to a boil, whisking often to dissolve the sugar. Remove the pot from the heat and stir in the drained noodles. Let them cool slightly. Gradually stir in the beaten eggs, stirring briskly so the eggs don't set from the heat of the noodles, then add 1 teaspoon of the rosemary and the pepper and salt. Spread the mixture in the baking dish.

4. Bake until the kugel top is golden brown and feels set when pressed in the center, about 45 minutes. (The kugel can be cooled, covered with aluminum, and refrigerated for up to 1 day. Reheat, covered, in a 350° F oven for about 30 minutes.) Let it stand at room temperature for 5 minutes. Sprinkle it with the remaining 1 teaspoon rosemary and serve warm or cooled to room temperature.

Orzo

This rice-shaped pasta can be simply boiled, but it also takes well to being baked into a casserole and toasting for extra flavor.

ORZO WITH LEMON, PARMESAN, AND PEAS
MAKES 4 SERVINGS

Serve with roast beef, pork, or lamb; roast chicken; or seafood.
Prep Time: 5 minutes
Cooking Time: 10 minutes
Weeknight Suppers, Family Favorite, Company Fare, Buffet Dish, Vegetarian

Orzo is one of the most versatile in the entire pasta family—and that's saying a mouthful. I turn to this citrusy side dish time and time again to serve with salmon or shrimp. As the butter melts with the Parmesan, it forms a lovely sauce.

1 cup orzo

½ cup thawed frozen peas

1 tablespoon unsalted butter

⅓ cup freshly grated Parmesan cheese (about
   1½ ounces)

Grated zest of half a lemon

2 tablespoons fresh lemon juice

Kosher salt and freshly ground black pepper

1. Bring a medium saucepan of lightly salted water to a boil over high heat. Add the orzo and cook according to the package directions, stirring occasionally, until it is barely tender. Drain the orzo well and return it to the pot.

2. Add the peas and butter and cook, stirring constantly over low heat, until the peas are heated through, about 1 minute. Remove the pan from the heat and stir in the Parmesan, lemon zest, and juice. Season to taste with salt and pepper.

3. Transfer the mixture to a serving bowl and serve hot.

TOASTED ORZO PILAF WITH CORN AND ROSEMARY
MAKES 4 SERVINGS

Serve with lamb or pork chops; sautéed chicken; fish fillets; or shrimp.
Prep Time: 5 minutes
Cooking Time: 20 minutes
Weeknight Suppers, Family Favorite, Buffet Dish

Here, orzo is browned and cooked with broth and vegetables for a version of pilaf. Because I always have corn kernels on hand in the freezer, this is how I prepare this orzo most often, but I have also used thawed peas or such leftover vegetables as broccoli or roasted carrots.

1 tablespoon olive oil

1 tablespoon unsalted butter

1 cup orzo

2 tablespoons finely chopped shallot

1 garlic clove, finely chopped

3 cups reduced-sodium chicken broth

½ teaspoon kosher salt

¼ teaspoon freshly ground black pepper

½ cup fresh or thawed frozen corn kernels, at
   room temperature

1 teaspoon finely chopped fresh rosemary

2 tablespoons freshly grated Parmesan cheese
   (½ ounce)

1. Heat the oil and butter together in a medium nonstick skillet over medium heat, until the butter melts. Add the orzo, shallot, and garlic and cook, stirring occasionally, until the orzo is lightly browned, about 2 minutes.

2. Stir in the broth, salt, and pepper and bring them to a simmer. Reduce the heat to medium-low and cover. Simmer for 8 minutes. Add the corn and rosemary, but do not stir them in. Cover again and continue to cook until the pilaf is tender and the corn is heated, about 2 minutes more. Remove the pan from the heat and stir.

3. Transfer the pilaf to a serving bowl, sprinkle it with the Parmesan, and serve.

ORZO, SPINACH, AND FETA CASSEROLE

MAKES 6 SERVINGS

Serve with lamb roasts or chops; grilled whole fish or fish fillets; or sautéed shrimp.

Prep Time: 10 minutes

Cooking Time: 30 minutes

Make Ahead: The casserole can be prepared up to 8 hours ahead.

Weeknight Suppers, Family Favorite, Buffet Dish, Vegetarian

This Greek-style pasta casserole is a natural with lamb, but I really like it as a side served with whole grilled fish. It uses one of my favorite tricks—cooking vegetables in the same water as the pasta to save time and cleanup. There is a lot of room for personal expression in this recipe, as the variations suggest. For a large group, double the recipe and bake it in a 13 × 9 × 2-inch baking dish for about 30 minutes.

2 tablespoons olive oil, plus more for
   the baking dish

1 heaping cup orzo

One 10-ounce bag baby spinach

4 scallions (white and green parts), chopped

2 garlic cloves, minced

1 cup halved grape tomatoes

½ cup crumbled feta (2 ounces)

2 tablespoons finely chopped fresh dill or

1 tablespoon finely chopped fresh oregano

Kosher salt and freshly ground black pepper

1. Position a rack in the center of the oven and preheat the oven to 350°F. Lightly oil an 8-inch square baking dish.

2. Bring a large pot of salted water to a boil over high heat. Add the orzo and cook according to the package directions, stirring often to prevent it from sticking together, until it is almost tender. In three or four additions, keeping the water at a boil, stir in the spinach and cook just until it is wilted. Drain the orzo and spinach. Press gently on the mixture with a rubber spatula to remove excess moisture from the spinach. Return the orzo and spinach to the cooking pan.

3. Meanwhile, heat the oil over medium heat in a medium skillet. Add the scallions and cook, stirring occasionally, until they are wilted, about 2 minutes. Stir in the garlic and cook until it is fragrant, about 1 minute. Add the tomatoes and cook, stirring occasionally, until they give off their juices, 2 to 3 minutes. Add to the orzo mixture with the feta and dill. Mix well and season to taste with salt and pepper. Spread the mixture in the baking dish. (The casserole can be cooled, covered, and refrigerated to this point up to 8 hours ahead.)

4. Bake, uncovered, until the top is beginning to brown, about 20 minutes (or 30 minutes if refrigerated). Serve hot.

Orzo, Spinach, and Gorgonzola Casserole: Omit the dill. Substitute ½ cup crumbled Gorgonzola cheese (2 ounces) for the feta.

Orzo, Spinach, and Jalapeño Jack Casserole: Omit the dill and use the oregano. Substitute ½ cup shredded jalapeño Jack cheese (2 ounces) for the feta.

Spaëtzle

A hybrid of dumplings and noodles, spaëtzle are really easy to make and a little too delicious for their own good. A spaëtzle maker looks like a flat metal cheese grater carriage that holds the batter. Sold at well-stocked kitchenware stores and online, it may be a single-purpose gadget, but it is relatively cheap, and I can almost guarantee that you will use it often. My favorite way to eat it is to fry chilled spaëtzle in butter until the edges are crispy.

CLASSIC SPAËTZLE

MAKES 4 SERVINGS

Serve with sauerbraten, roast pork, pork chops, sausages, roast duck, or roast goose.

Prep Time: 5 minutes

Cooking Time: 3 minutes

Make Ahead: The spaëtzle can be refrigerated for up to 1 day.

Weeknight Suppers, Family Favorite, Holiday Feasts, Company Fare, Buffet Dish,

Cooking Classic, Vegetarian

Spaëtzle is a classic German recipe, and I serve it with sauerbraten, sausages, and anything remotely Teutonic. Here is the basic recipe, simply tossed with butter, but there is a lot of room for variations. An inexpensive spaëtzle maker is much easier to use than a colander, and once you have one, you will be looking for reasons to make spaëtzle.

SPAËTZLE

3 large eggs

½ cup whole milk

1½ cups (195 g) unbleached all-purpose flour, as needed

Kosher salt

A few gratings of fresh nutmeg

Freshly ground black pepper

2 tablespoons (¼ stick) unsalted butter

2 teaspoons finely chopped fresh chives (optional)

Special Equipment: A spaëtzle maker or colander with large (¼-inch) holes

1. Bring a large pot of salted water to a boil over high heat.

2. To make the spaëtzle: In a medium bowl, whisk the eggs and milk together. Add the flour, 1 teaspoon salt, nutmeg, and ⅛ teaspoon pepper. Stir with a wooden spoon to make a smooth, thick batter about the consistency of muffin batter. If the batter seems too thick, add more milk, or if it is thin, add flour.

3. Set the spaëtzle maker, with the flat section facing down, on the edges of the saucepan over the boiling water. Spoon the batter into the container. Quickly move the container back and forth, forcing the batter through the holes and into the water. Remove the spaëtzle maker. (Or pour all of the batter into a colander with large holes. Holding the colander over the saucepan, use a rubber spatula to force the batter through the holes and into the water.) Return the water to a boil and cook until all of the spaëtzle have risen to the surface. Drain carefully. (The spaëtzle can be rinsed under cold water and cooled, tossed with 2 teaspoons vegetable oil, and stored in a 1-gallon plastic zip-tight bag in the refrigerator for up to 1 day.)

4. Transfer the spaëtzle to a serving bowl and toss it with the butter. Season to taste with salt and pepper. Top with the chives, if using, and serve.

Spaëtzle with Poppy Seeds: Substitute 1 tablespoon poppy seeds for the chives.

Spaëtzle with Sour Cream: Omit the butter for the sauce. Top the spaëtzle with a large dollop of room-temperature sour cream, and sprinkle it with the chives.

Fried Spaëtzle: This is the way I remember my grandmother making spaëtzle. The golden brown edges are delicious. When draining the spaëtzle, rinse it under cold running water and drain well. Toss the spaëtzle with 2 tablespoons vegetable oil. Transfer it to a 1-gallon plastic zip-tight bag and refrigerate it until chilled, at least 2 hours or up to 1 day. Heat 2 tablepoons unsalted butter in a large nonstick skillet over medium-high heat. Add the spaëtzle and cook, stirring occasionally, until they are lightly browned, about 5 minutes.

Fried Spaëtzle with Caramelized Onions: Top the spaëtzle with caramelized onions (page 207).

Couscous, Moroccan and Israeli

Traditional couscous, a staple of Moroccan cuisine, is made from tiny pellets of dried semolina dough. It cooks to tenderness in 5 minutes, a time that is hard to beat when you have to get a side dish on the table in a hurry. In addition to plain couscous, colored green (spinach) and orange (tomato) varieties are available. They look great, but the vegetable flavors are not pronounced.

Israeli couscous are small, toasted balls of white pasta dough, and they take about 10 minutes to simmer to a deliciously chewy texture.

COUSCOUS WITH GARBANZOS AND HERBS
MAKES 6 SERVINGS

Serve with spicy meat, poultry, or seafood stews.
Prep Time: 5 minutes
Cooking Time: 10 minutes
Weeknight Suppers, Company Fare, Vegetarian

This is a very easy way to bring extra flavor to plain couscous. Use whatever fresh herbs you have handy, although cilantro goes especially well with Moroccan seasonings, and I serve this often with North African tagines.

2 tablespoons olive oil
1 garlic clove, finely chopped
One 15-ounce can garbanzo beans (chickpeas),
 drained and rinsed

1 teaspoon kosher salt
1 cup plain couscous
2 tablespoons finely chopped fresh cilantro,
 oregano, parsley, or mint

1. Heat 1 tablespoon of the oil and the garlic together in a small saucepan over medium heat, stirring often, until the garlic is fragrant, about 1 minute. Stir in the garbanzo beans and cover the saucepan. Cook, stirring occasionally, until the garbanzo beans are heated through, about 5 minutes. Transfer the garbanzo bean mixture to a serving bowl, tent it with aluminum foil to keep warm, and set aside.

2. Add 2¼ cups water and the salt to the saucepan and bring them to a boil over high heat. Stir in the couscous and tightly cover the saucepan. Remove it from the heat and let it stand until the couscous is tender and has absorbed the liquid, about 5 minutes. Add the garbanzo bean mixture, remaining 1 tablespoon of the oil, and the cilantro and stir them into the couscous with a fork, fluffing the couscous as you do so. Transfer the couscous to a serving bowl and serve.

BUTTERED COUSCOUS WITH SCALLIONS AND CUMIN
MAKES 4 SERVINGS

Serve with spicy meat, poultry, or seafood stews.
Prep Time: 5 minutes
Cooking Time: 10 minutes
Weeknight Suppers, Company Fare

Another simple recipe for upgrading couscous, it can be varied by substituting 1 teaspoon coarsely ground coriander seed for the cumin.

1 teaspoon cumin seed	1 cup plain couscous
2¼ cups reduced-sodium chicken broth or water	1 scallion (white and green parts), finely chopped
¾ teaspoon kosher salt	2 tablespoons unsalted butter, thinly sliced

1. Heat a small saucepan over medium heat. Add the cumin and cook, stirring occasionally, until it is toasted, about 2 minutes.
2. Add the broth and salt and bring them to a boil over high heat. Stir in the couscous and tightly cover the saucepan. Remove it from the heat and let it stand until the couscous is tender and has absorbed the liquid, about 5 minutes. Add the scallion and butter and stir them into the couscous with a fork, fluffing the couscous as you do so. Transfer the couscous to a serving bowl and serve.

ISRAELI COUSCOUS WITH RED BELL PEPPER AND SCALLION
MAKES 4 SERVINGS

Serve with pork or lamb chops; sausages; roast chicken or chicken sautés; fish fillets or shrimp.
Prep Time: 5 minutes
Cooking Time: 20 minutes
Weeknight Suppers, Family Favorite, Holiday Feasts, Company Fare, Buffet Dish

Israeli couscous has an interesting pedigree. It was invented in the late 1940s, when the Israeli government needed a sustainable domestic substitute for rice, which had to be imported. This recipe shows off its chewy texture.

1 tablespoon olive oil

¾ cup (½-inch) diced red bell pepper

1 tablespoon unsalted butter

1⅓ cups Israeli couscous

1 cup reduced-sodium chicken broth

¾ teaspoon kosher salt

1 scallion (white and green parts), thinly sliced

1. Heat the oil in a small saucepan over medium heat. Add the bell pepper and cook, stirring occasionally, until it is tender, about 4 minutes. Transfer the bell pepper to a small bowl.

2. Add the butter to the saucepan and melt it over medium heat. Add the couscous and cook, stirring often, until it is lightly browned, about 2 minutes. Add the broth, ¾ cup water, and the salt and bring them to a boil over high heat. Reduce the heat to medium-low and cover the saucepan. Simmer until the couscous is tender and has absorbed the liquid, 8 to 10 minutes.

3. Remove the pan from the heat. Return the bell pepper to the saucepan, along with the scallion, but do not stir the couscous. Cover again and let it stand for 3 minutes to reheat the bell pepper. Fluff the couscous with a fork, transfer it to a serving bowl, and serve hot.

Gnocchi

Potato gnocchi are substantial enough to be served as a pasta main course. By contrast, their cousin, semolina gnocchi, is relatively plain and makes a good side dish. For a German relative to the potato gnocchi, see the dumplings on page 366.

ROMAN-STYLE SEMOLINA GNOCCHI

MAKES 8 SERVINGS

Serve with roast veal or lamb; veal or lamb chops; chicken cacciatore; or shrimp scampi.

Prep Time: 20 minutes, plus 2 hours refrigeration time

Cooking Time: 40 minutes

Make Ahead: The gnocchi can be prepared, without baking, up to 1 day ahead.

Weeknight Suppers, Family Favorite, Holiday Feasts, Company Fare, Buffet Dish, Vegetarian

A specialty of Roman cooks, these gnocchi are usually cut into rounds, but I prefer squares so I don't have to discard any trimmings. Semolina is finely ground durum wheat, the same variety used to make pasta. Not as smooth as flour, it has a somewhat gritty consistency (semolina means "sandy" in Italian).

1 tablespoon cold unsalted butter, cut into ½-inch pieces, plus softened butter for the baking dish

2 cups whole milk

1⅓ cups semolina

1 teaspoon kosher salt

¼ teaspoon freshly ground black pepper

1 cup freshly grated Parmesan cheese (4 ounces)

2 large eggs

1. Lightly butter an 11½ × 8 × 2-inch baking dish.

2. Whisk together 2 cups water with the milk, semolina, salt, and pepper in a medium, heavy-bottomed saucepan. Bring them to a simmer, whisking constantly to avoid scorching on the bottom of the saucepan, over medium heat. Reduce the heat to low and cook, whisking often, until the mixture is very thick and has lost its raw taste, at least 10 minutes. Remove the saucepan from the heat. Add ½ cup of the Parmesan and whisk until smooth.

3. In a medium bowl, whisk the eggs together. Whisk in about 1 cup of the semolina mixture, then whisk the egg mixture back into the saucepan. Spread the semolina evenly into the baking dish. Let the mixture cool until tepid. Cover it loosely with plastic wrap and refrigerate until it is chilled and firm, at least 2 hours and up to 8 hours.

4. Position a rack in the center of the oven and preheat the oven to 400°F.

5. Invert the baking dish and unmold the cold semolina onto a cutting board. Wash and dry the baking dish, then butter the inside. Cut the semolina into thirds lengthwise, and then into sixths crosswise to make 18 equal gnocchi. Arrange the gnocchi, overlapping as needed, in the baking dish. Sprinkle them with the remaining ½ cup Parmesan and dot with the 1 tablespoon cold butter.

6. Bake until the cheese is melted and the tips of the gnocchi are browned, about 30 minutes. Serve hot.

Dumplings

Plump and tender pillows of cooked dough, American dumplings are cooked directly in the main course's gravy (or sauce, if you will). German dumplings are simmered separately in water and served with gravy spooned on top.

OLD-FASHIONED DUMPLINGS
MAKES 8 DUMPLINGS

Serve with meat, poultry, or vegetable stews, including chili.
Prep Time: 5 minutes
Cooking Time: 20 minutes
Weeknight Suppers, Family Favorite, Cooking Classic

Life can be pretty hectic, so it is a real pleasure to slow down and make a delicious stew for dinner with meat and vegetables married together by long simmering. In my opinion, stew is even better when fluffy dumplings are floating on top of the gravy. These are the simple and basic dumplings of my childhood, but I provide less elementary variations.

• The dumpling dough should be added to the stew during the last 20 minutes of cooking, when the sauce has developed flavor and the meat is almost tender. In the case of red meat, you can usually cook the stew until the meat is just tender because these cuts (beef chuck or short ribs, and veal, pork, and lamb shoulder) are pretty forgiving and can stand to take an extra 20 minutes of cooking without drying out. However, poultry, especially chicken breast, can overcook, so don't wait until it is tender before adding the dumpling dough.

• When you are ready to add the dough, evaluate the consistency of the sauce. Remember that it is going to cook for another 20 minutes, so if you think that it is already thick enough at the point that the dough is added, add some water or broth to thin it slightly. Otherwise, the sauce could scorch.

• Dumplings cook best in stews with a generous amount of sauce. There should be enough liquid to completely cover the stew ingredients.

• Dumplings expand quite a bit in the pot, so leave plenty of room between the drops of dough, as they will double in size.

• There is no butter in my dumpling dough. I believe that the stew sauce is rich enough. But if you want to gild the lily, try the Rich Dumplings variation.

1½ cups (195 g) unbleached all-purpose flour

2 teaspoons baking powder

½ teaspoon fine sea or table salt

¾ cup whole milk

1. In a medium bowl, whisk the flour, baking powder, and salt together. Make a well in the center and stir in the milk to make a sticky dough.

2. Using a heaping tablespoon for each dumpling and, working close to the surface of the simmering sauce, drop 8 mounds of dough into the stew. Cover the pot tightly and simmer until the dumplings have doubled in size and cooked through, about 20 minutes. Serve hot.

Herb Dumplings: Add 1 tablespoon finely chopped fresh rosemary, thyme, sage, or parsley (or 1 teaspoon dried rosemary, thyme, or sage) to the dough.

Rich Dumplings: Whisk the flour, baking powder, and salt together. Add 2 tablespoons cold unsalted butter, cut into ½-inch cubes. Cut the butter into the flour mixture until it resembles coarse crumbs. Stir in the milk.

Cornmeal Dumplings: This is especially good with chili. Replace ⅓ cup of the flour with yellow cornmeal, preferably stone-ground.

GERMAN POTATO DUMPLINGS

MAKES 1 DOZEN

Serve with sauce-based German dishes, such as sauerbraten or any stews; or roast goose.

Prep Time: 15 minutes

Cooking Time: 10 minutes

Make Ahead: The dumplings can be prepared for cooking up to 1 hour ahead.

Family Favorite, Holiday Feasts, Company Fare, Vegetarian

If you have German heritage, you have probably eaten your share of these dumplings, made from mashed boiled potatoes and a bread stuffing. On paper, they may look similar to Italian potato gnocchi, but there are a few differences. While gnocchi is served as a first course, these are always a side dish, usually covered with the main course's gravy. And while there are unstuffed potato dumplings, the bread cubes create a space that keeps the ball from becoming too compact and heavy. But you can skip the stuffing and cook the dumplings for an extra few minutes, or until a wooden toothpick inserted into the center comes out clean. I prefer a potato ricer to process the potatoes into a smooth consistency, or you can force them through a wire mesh sieve.

1½ pounds baking potatoes, such as russets, scrubbed

2 tablespoons (¼ stick) unsalted butter

2 slices firm sandwich bread, lightly toasted and cooled, cut into ½-inch squares

⅓ cup (45 g) unbleached all-purpose flour, as needed

⅓ cup (55 g) unbleached farina (see Note)

1 large egg, beaten to blend

1 teaspoon kosher salt

¼ teaspoon freshly ground white or black pepper

A few gratings of fresh nutmeg

1. Put the potatoes in a large saucepan and add enough cold salted water to cover. Cover and bring them to a boil over high heat. Reduce the heat to medium and cook at a brisk simmer until the potatoes are tender when pierced with the tip of a small, sharp knife, 25 to 35 minutes.

2. Meanwhile, melt the butter in a medium skillet over medium heat. Add the bread squares and cook, stirring occasionally, until they are browned, 2 to 3 minutes. Transfer the bread to a plate and let it cool completely.

3. Bring a second pot of salted water to a boil over high heat for cooking the dumplings. It must be large enough to hold the 12 dumplings without crowding.

4. Drain the potatoes well. To peel, spear a hot potato onto a meat fork and use a small knife to remove the skins. Put the potatoes through a potato ricer (or rub them through a medium-mesh wire sieve) into a large bowl. Stir the flour and farina into the potatoes. Beat in the egg, working quickly so it doesn't set. Stir in the salt, pepper, and nutmeg. Shape a few tablespoons of the dough into a ball; if it doesn't hold together, add more flour as needed.

5. Line a baking sheet with waxed paper and sprinkle it with flour. Using floured hands, divide the dough into 12 equal balls. Working with one ball at a time, flatten the dough between your palms into a thick disk. Place 2 or 3 bread pieces in the center of the disk and bring up the sides to enclose the bread. Shape it into a tangerine-sized ball and transfer it to the baking sheet. (The dumplings can be covered with a clean kitchen towel and stored at room temperature for up to 1 hour.)

6. One at a time, add the dumplings to the boiling water, being sure that they have enough room to "swim" without crowding. Reduce the heat to medium so the water maintains a brisk simmer. Partially cover the saucepan. Cook until the dumplings rise to the surface. From that point, continue cooking until the dumplings look slightly puffed and lighter in texture, about 5 minutes more. Using a slotted spoon, transfer the dumplings to a platter and serve immediately.

Note: Farina is a coarsely ground wheat flour with a speckled beige appearance. You will find it in the hot cereal section of the supermarket. Do not confuse it with quick-cooking or instant breakfast cereal, such as Cream of Wheat. If necessary, substitute semolina, which is similar in texture to farina but milled from gold-colored durum wheat.

THE BREAD BASKET

For holiday meals, I always serve a basket of freshly baked rolls, hot from the oven. But you don't really need a special occasion or lots of time to bring freshly baked bread into your everyday cooking. Instant yeast has made bread baking easier than ever (and quicker, too, if you choose to go that route). There are also many quick breads (those leavened with baking powder, baking soda, or eggs) that you can have on the table in less than an hour, including preparation time, and biscuits and cornbread clock in at under thirty minutes. I have concentrated on rolls and other individual baked goods specifically because they cook quickly. You'll also find poultry stuffings in this chapter, because their main ingredient is traditionally bread, although I have a gluten-free wild rice option, too.

- I prefer to bake with fine sea or table salt because I can be sure that it will dissolve in the batter or dough. If you want to substitute kosher salt, use about one-quarter more because the large crystals in the kosher salt fit more loosely in the measuring spoon than the fine salt does.

- These breads are meant to be enjoyed the day you bake them, but of course, leftovers can always be reheated at a later meal. When I have just a few rolls or a slice of cornbread, I use my toaster oven.

- In recent years, many home bakers have come to prefer weighing flour to the volume method of measuring in a cup. Weighing is more accurate because the volume method has too many variables, mainly the issue of how the flour is packed or mounded or leveled in the cup. I have provided both metric and volume measurements for flour (and similar dry ingredients) over 3 tablespoons. I am skipping ounces in favor of grams because the metrics are commonly found on the inexpensive digital scales sold at every kitchenware stop and online. Also, because the main problems in baking usually occur from inaccurate flour measurement, I have stopped short of giving the metric equivalent of every ingredient. All volume measurements are level, not heaped, with 1 cup of flour equaling 130 grams.

Cornbread

Surely the reason that cornbread is such an embodiment of solid country cooking is that it was so easy to make that it could be served at every meal. Preheating the oven is the most difficult part of the recipe. First, you whisk the dry ingredients together, literally dump in the wet ingredients, and stir a few times until the batter comes together. Then all you have to do is pour it into the pan. (Some recipes call for the pan to be heated in the oven first, a step that gives the bottom crust an extra bit of browned flavor.) You'll also find hush puppies, a fried version of cornbread, in this section.

BUTTERMILK CORNBREAD

MAKES 6 TO 8 SERVINGS

Serve with Southern-style foods, especially fried chicken or barbecued ribs; grilled pork chops; or braised greens.
Prep Time: 10 minutes
Baking Time: 25 minutes
Weeknight Suppers, Family Favorite, Holiday Feasts, Company Fare, Buffet Dish, Retro Recipe, Cooking Classic, Vegetarian

Cornbread and biscuits vie for the honor of "most beloved Southern bread," and many barbecue places serve cornbread as a matter of course. This version is not too sweet, which I often prefer when serving cornbread with savory barbecued foods. The variation is a large-batch version (made with sweet milk and baking powder) to use for cornbread stuffing.

Vegetable oil, for the baking pan
1¼ cups (165 g) unbleached all-purpose flour
¾ cup (95 g) yellow cornmeal, preferably stone-ground
2 tablespoons sugar
2 teaspoons baking soda

½ teaspoon fine sea or table salt
1 cup buttermilk
3 tablespoons unsalted butter, melted and slightly cooled
1 large egg

1. Position a rack in the center of the oven and preheat the oven to 400°F. Lightly oil an 8-inch square baking dish.
2. Place the baking dish in the oven and heat until the dish is hot, about 3 minutes. Meanwhile, in a medium bowl, whisk the flour, cornmeal, sugar, baking soda, and salt together. In another bowl, whisk the buttermilk, butter, and egg together. Make a well in the center of the dry ingredients and pour in the buttermilk mixture. Stir just until the flour is moistened.
3. Remove the baking dish from the oven. Pour in the batter and smooth it evenly with a spatula. Return the baking dish to the oven. Bake until the cornbread is golden brown, 20 to 25 minutes. Let it stand at room temperature for 5 minutes. Cut it into squares and serve warm.

Cornbread for Stuffing: Use 2½ cups (325 g) flour, 1½ cup (130 g) yellow cornmeal, 2 tablespoons sugar, 2 tablespoons baking powder (not baking soda), 1½ teaspoons fine sea or table salt, 2 cups whole milk, 6 tablespoons (¾ stick) unsalted butter, melted, and 2 large eggs. Spray a 13 × 9 × 2-inch baking dish with the oil. Bake in a 375ºF oven until golden brown, about 30 minutes. Let it cool in the pan on a wire cake rack. Cut the cornbread into pieces and remove them from the pan. Crumble the cornbread into coarse pieces on a large, rimmed baking sheet. Let them stand, uncovered, at room temperature, for at least 18 hours to become stale. (The cornbread can be packed in plastic zip-tight storage bags and frozen for up to 2 months. Thaw the cornbread at room temperature before using.)

MOIST AND SWEET CORNBREAD

MAKES 6 TO 9 SERVINGS

Serve with ham, sausages, fried chicken, or shrimp.

Prep Time: 10 minutes

Baking Time: 25 minutes

Weeknight Suppers, Family Favorite, Holiday Feasts, Company Fare,

Buffet Dish, Cooking Classic, Vegetarian

While I prefer my cornbread on the savory side, I have to admit that my guests absolutely love this thick version with a soft, muffin-like crumb. The sour cream and sugar make it incredibly tender.

¼ cup (½ stick) unsalted butter, melted and cooled to tepid, plus softened butter for the baking pan

1 cup (130 g) unbleached all-purpose flour

1 cup (130 g) yellow cornmeal, preferably stone-ground

¼ cup sugar

1 teaspoon baking powder

1 teaspoon baking soda

½ teaspoon fine sea or table salt

1 cup sour cream

½ cup whole milk

1 large egg

1. Position a rack in the center of the oven and preheat the oven to 400°F. Butter the inside of an 8-inch square baking pan.

2. In a medium bowl, whisk the flour, cornmeal, sugar, baking powder, baking soda, and salt together. In another bowl, whisk the sour cream, milk, and butter together, then whisk in the egg. Make a well in the center of the flour mixture, pour in the sour cream mixture, and stir just until combined. Do not overmix. Spread the batter evenly in the pan.

3. Bake until the cornbread is golden brown and a wooden toothpick inserted in the center comes out clean, about 25 minutes. Let it cool in the pan for 5 minutes. Serve it hot or warm.

JALAPEÑO, BACON, AND CORN MUFFINS

MAKES 8 MUFFINS

Serve with Southern-style foods, such as fried chicken, barbecued ribs, pork chops, or braised greens.

Prep Time: 10 minutes, plus at least 30 minutes to chill the bacon fat

Baking Time: 30 minutes

Weeknight Suppers, Family Favorite, Holiday Feasts, Company Fare, Buffet Dish, Cooking Classic

With just enough bacon to give them a meaty, smoky accent, but not so much as to make them heavy and porky, these muffins are useful for special celebrations when you want to gussy up cornbread. Because the butter is beaten to a fluffy state, the muffins have a cake-like texture. Be sure to cook the bacon at least 45 minutes ahead so you can collect and cool the fat before making the batter.

• Every professional baker I know uses a food service portioning scoop to transfer batter to muffin cups, giving the batter a nice round top that bakes into an attractive dome. The scoop of choice for common muffin cups is a ¼-cup capacity Number 16 (so-called because it takes sixteen scoops to make a quart), standardized with a blue handle for easy identification. For a few bucks, this utensil could make your muffin baking much easier.

4 slices bacon

¾ cup (95 g) unbleached all-purpose flour

¾ cup (95 g) yellow cornmeal, preferably stone-ground

2 teaspoons baking powder

½ teaspoon fine sea or table salt

4 tablespoons (½ stick) unsalted butter, at room temperature

2 tablespoons sugar

1 large egg, at room temperature

¾ cup whole milk

½ cup fresh or thawed frozen corn kernels

1 jalapeño, seeded and minced

1. At least 45 minutes before baking, cook the bacon in a large skillet over medium heat, turning it halfway through cooking, until it is crisp and browned, about 8 minutes. Transfer the bacon to paper towels to drain and cool. Pour the bacon fat into a custard cup or ramekin. Freeze it until cool and almost solidified, about 30 minutes.

2. Position a rack in the center of the oven and preheat the oven to 400°F. Line 8 standard muffin cups with paper liners.

3. Coarsely chop the bacon. Measure out 2 tablespoons of the bacon fat and discard the remainder. In a medium bowl, whisk the flour, cornmeal, baking powder, and salt together. In another medium bowl, beat the butter and bacon fat together with a handheld electric mixer on medium speed until combined. Add the sugar and beat until the fat is light in color, about 2 minutes. Beat in the egg. Reduce the mixer speed to low. (Or beat the butter, fat, and sugar together with a wooden spoon in a medium bowl until pale, about 4 minutes. Whisk in the egg.) In thirds, mix in the cornmeal mixture, alternating with two equal additions of the milk, mixing just until combined. Using a rubber spatula, fold in the chopped bacon, corn, and jalapeño. Preferably using a ¼-cup spring-loaded scoop, divide the batter evenly among the muffin cups, filling them half full.

4. Bake until the muffins are golden and a wooden toothpick inserted in the center comes out clean, about 20 minutes. Let them cool in the pan for 10 minutes. Remove them from the pan and serve warm.

BUTTERMILK

I always have a carton of buttermilk in the refrigerator—it keeps for weeks—because I use it so often. It is the secret ingredient of my favorite baked goods because its acidic components weaken the gluten in the flour to give a tender crumb. And I love it in ranch dressing, mashed potatoes, and more.

In spite of its name, buttermilk is actually a low-fat product. Shake the container well before using, as buttermilk tends to separate. If you need buttermilk for baking, you can substitute ⅔ cup plain low-fat yogurt (not the thick Greek yogurt) whisked with ⅓ cup whole milk for every cup of buttermilk. Or put 1 tablespoon cider or white distilled vinegar (or fresh lemon juice) in a 1-cup liquid measure and add enough whole or reduced-fat (not skim) milk to reach 1 cup. This substitute does not work for savory recipes, though, where the buttermilk flavor would be a factor.

BUTTERMILK AND SAGE SPOON BREAD
MAKES 6 SERVINGS

Serve with ham, sausages, or barbecued meats or poultry.
Prep Time: 10 minutes
Baking Time: 25 minutes
Weeknight Suppers, Family Favorite, Holiday Feasts, Company Fare,
Buffet Dish, Retro Recipe, Cooking Classic, Vegetarian

Spoon bread is a soft, spoonable cornbread that is almost a pudding. Sometimes I'll add a couple of cooked and chopped slices of bacon or ½ cup shredded Cheddar cheese to the batter with the yolks.

¼ cup (½ stick) unsalted butter, plus softened
  butter for the baking dish
3 cups whole milk
¾ teaspoon fine sea or table salt
1 cup (130 g) yellow cornmeal, preferably stone-
  ground

1 cup buttermilk
1 tablespoon finely chopped fresh sage
3 large eggs, at room temperature, separated

1. Position a rack in the center of the oven and preheat the oven to 375°F. Lightly butter an 8-inch square baking dish.

2. Bring the milk and salt to a simmer in a medium saucepan over medium heat. Gradually whisk in the cornmeal. Reduce the heat to low and simmer, whisking often, until the mixture is thick and smooth, about 5 minutes. Remove the pan from the heat. Add the butter and whisk until it melts. Whisk in the buttermilk and sage. One at a time, whisk in the yolks.

3. In a medium bowl, use a handheld electric mixer at high speed to whip the egg whites until they form soft peaks. Stir about one-quarter of the whites into the cornmeal mixture. Fold in the remaining whites. Spoon the batter into the baking dish.

4. Bake until the spoon bread is puffed and golden brown, about 25 minutes. Serve it hot.

SCALLION AND JALAPEÑO HUSH PUPPIES

MAKES 3 DOZEN

Serve with barbecued meats and poultry, fried chicken, fried fish, or fried shrimp.
Prep Time: 5 minutes
Cooking Time: 3 minutes
Weeknight Suppers, Family Favorite, Company Fare, Cooking Classic, Vegetarian

In the South, wherever there is barbecue (or fried chicken or fried fish, for that matter), hush puppies are usually not far behind. Crunchy on the outside and moist within, these puppies are everything they are supposed to be, and more. My recipe gets a boost from minced scallions and chilies. If you want to make a smaller batch, halve the ingredients, using 1 large egg yolk instead of the whole egg.

Vegetable oil, for deep-frying

1½ cups (195 g) yellow cornmeal, preferably stone-ground

½ cup (65 g) unbleached all-purpose flour

1 teaspoon baking powder

½ teaspoon baking soda

½ teaspoon fine sea or table salt

1 cup buttermilk

1 large egg, beaten to blend

¼ cup minced scallions (white and green parts)

1 jalapeño, seeded and minced

1. Position a rack in the center of the oven and preheat the oven to 200°F. Place a wire cooling rack in a large, rimmed baking sheet.

2. Pour enough oil into a large, deep, heavy skillet to come halfway up the sides and heat it over high heat until the oil is shimmering but not smoking (350°F on an instant-read thermometer).

3. While the oil is heating, in a medium bowl, whisk the cornmeal, flour, baking powder, baking soda, and salt together. Make a well in the center and pour in the buttermilk and egg. Stir with a wooden spoon just until moistened. Add the scallions and jalapeño and stir until combined.

4. In two or three batches, drop heaping teaspoons of the batter into the hot oil and cook, turning the hush puppies as needed, until they are golden brown on both sides, about 3 minutes. Using a wire spider or slotted spoon, transfer the hush puppies to the wire rack and keep warm in the oven while making the rest. Serve hot.

Biscuits

I learned how to bake Southern biscuits from a friend's grandmother, and I have continued to pick up tips from the many bakers I've helped with writing their cookbooks.

- Many cooks prefer low-gluten Southern flour (White Lily is the most popular brand), which is milled from soft wheat and difficult to find north of the Mason-Dixon Line. Yes, it is good, but that doesn't mean you can't bake biscuits with another kind of flour. In some of my biscuit recipes, I approximate Southern flour with a mixture of all-purpose and cake flours. And in others, I use unbleached all-purpose flour.
- Biscuits are not supposed to take long to make. They should be mixed in a few minutes' time and popped into a hot oven. If the dough is handled too much, the gluten in the flour is activated, and you could end up with tough biscuits. So work quickly.
- Most bakers roll out the biscuit dough and cut out rounds. This creates scraps that must be collected and kneaded together for subsequent batches, and this toughens the gluten, so the second batches are tough and misshapen. To solve this problem, I cut the dough into rectangles or squares to bypass making scraps. I highly recommend this technique. It also avoids the cutting-out and rerolling process to reduce the time and fussiness factors.
- If you are a die-hard round biscuit fan, equip yourself with a 2½-inch round biscuit or cookie cutter. Roll or pat out the dough ¾ inch thick. Cutting out rounds as close as possible to each other, stamp out the biscuits without twisting the cutter. Place the biscuits, with the sides touching, on an ungreased, rimmed baking sheet. Gather up the dough scraps and press them together, just enough to eliminate the seams where the scraps meet. Do not knead the dough scraps into a mass. Repeat the rolling and cut out more biscuits until all of the dough has been used.

EVERYDAY BISCUITS
MAKES 8 SQUARE BISCUITS

Serve with fried chicken, creamed chicken or fish dishes, baked ham,
meat stews, braised greens, or fried eggs and bacon.
Prep Time: 10 minutes
Baking Time: 20 minutes
Weeknight Suppers, Family Favorite, Holiday Feasts, Company Fare,
Buffet Dish, Cooking Classic, Vegetarian (if not made with lard)

These are the sure-fire biscuits that I make when I don't happen to have buttermilk in the house. The kind of fat is almost immaterial, but each one is good in its own way. Butter gives its hard-to-beat flavor, and most of us have it on hand. However, shortening makes the fluffiest biscuits. (One Southern baker once said to me, "Why would I want to 'waste' butter in the dough when I am going to put butter on the biscuits anyway?" She had a point.) Lard has the tenderness of shortening while adding its own taste, which can be preferable when you are making a down-home Southern meal.

2 cups (260 g) unbleached all-purpose flour, plus more for rolling out the dough

1 tablespoon baking powder

2 teaspoons sugar

½ teaspoon fine sea or table salt

½ cup (1 stick) cold unsalted butter, shortening, or lard, cut into ½-inch cubes

¾ cup whole milk

1. Position a rack in the center of the oven and preheat the oven to 425°F.

2. In a medium bowl, whisk the flour, baking powder, sugar, and salt together. Add the butter and stir to coat it with the flour mixture. Using a pastry blender or two knives, cut the butter into the flour until the mixture resembles coarse crumbs with some pea-sized pieces of butter. Make a well in the center of the flour mixture and pour in the milk. Stir just until the dough is moistened. Lightly knead the dough in the bowl a few times, just until the dough comes together.

3. Turn the dough out onto a lightly floured work surface and dust the top of the dough with flour. Roll or pat the dough into a 10 × 5-inch rectangle about ¾ inch thick. Cut it into eight 2½-inch squares. Transfer the squares to a large, rimmed baking sheet, placing them close together, almost touching.

4. Bake until the biscuits are risen and golden brown, about 20 minutes. Serve them warm.

EXTRA-TENDER BUTTERMILK BISCUITS
MAKES 12 SQUARE BISCUITS

Serve with fried chicken, creamed chicken or fish dishes, baked ham, meat stews, or braised greens.

Prep Time: 10 minutes

Baking Time: 20 minutes

Weeknight Suppers, Family Favorite, Holiday Feasts, Company Fare, Buffet Dish, Cooking Classic, Vegetarian

These biscuits use a few tricks to ensure their melt-in-your-mouth lightness. The combination of low-gluten cake and unbleached flours reduces the total gluten percentage content, and the acids in the buttermilk tenderize the dough. This makes a slightly larger batch of biscuits than the Everyday Biscuits (above).

1½ cups (195 g) unbleached all-purpose flour, plus more for rolling out the dough

1½ cups (190 g) cake flour

1 tablespoon sugar

2 teaspoons baking powder

1 teaspoon baking soda

¾ teaspoon fine sea or table salt

¾ cup (1½ sticks) cold unsalted butter, cut into
½-inch cubes

1¼ cups buttermilk

1. Position a rack in the center of the oven and preheat the oven to 425ºF.

2. In a medium bowl, whisk the unbleached and cake flours, sugar, baking powder, baking soda, and salt together. Add the butter and stir to coat it with the flour mixture. Using a pastry blender or two knives, cut the butter into the flour until the mixture resembles coarse crumbs with some pea-sized pieces of butter. Make a well in the center of the flour mixture and pour in the buttermilk. Stir just until the dough is moistened. Lightly knead the dough in the bowl a few times, just until the dough comes together.

3. Turn the dough out onto a lightly floured work surface and dust the top of the dough with flour. Roll or pat the dough into a 15 × 5-inch rectangle about ¾ inch thick. Cut it into twelve 2½-inch squares. Transfer the squares to a large, rimmed baking sheet, placing them close together, almost touching.

4. Bake until the biscuits are risen and golden brown, about 20 minutes. Serve them warm.

ANGEL BISCUITS
MAKES ABOUT 15 ROUND BISCUITS

Serve with roast turkey, fried chicken, creamed chicken or fish dishes, baked ham,

meat stews, braised greens, or fried eggs and bacon.

Prep Time: 15 minutes, plus at least 6 hours refrigeration time

Baking Time: 25 minutes

Make Ahead: The dough can be made up to 2 days ahead.

Weeknight Suppers, Family Favorite, Holiday Feasts, Company Fare, Buffet Dish,

Cooking Classic, Vegetarian

These are a hybrid between a biscuit and a dinner roll, with a bit of yeast to add fluffiness to the flakiness. Another advantage is that this dough does not require kneading and can be mixed a couple of days ahead of baking, which is very helpful for a holiday meal. For those of you who like round biscuits, you can roll out the scraps without their toughening. Don't ask me to pick my favorite biscuit, but I am very partial to this recipe, especially for my Thanksgiving menu.

2½ cups (325 g) unbleached all-purpose flour

2 tablespoons sugar

1½ teaspoons baking powder

½ teaspoon baking soda

½ teaspoon instant (also called quick-rise or bread machine) yeast

¾ teaspoon fine sea or table salt

½ cup cold vegetable shortening or unsalted butter, cut into ½-inch chunks

1 cup buttermilk

1. In a large bowl, whisk the flour, sugar, baking powder, baking soda, yeast, and salt together. Add the shortening, and cut it into the flour mixture with a pastry blender or two forks until the mixture resembles coarse crumbs. Stir in the buttermilk to make a shaggy dough. Turn out the dough onto a lightly floured work surface and cut it in half.

2. Place each dough half in a 1-gallon plastic zip-tight bag and close. Refrigerate the dough for at least 6 hours or up to 2 days. If refrigerated for longer than 6 hours, punch down the dough whenever it occurs to you, but no less than twice every 24 hours.

3. Position racks in the top third and lower third of the oven and preheat the oven to 400°F. Turn out the dough onto a lightly floured surface and knead it briefly. On a lightly floured surface, pat out the dough with lightly floured hands (or dust the top of the dough with flour and roll out to ¾ inch thick. Using a 2½-inch round biscuit or cookie cutter, cut out biscuits and place them 1 inch apart on 2 ungreased large, rimmed baking sheets. Gather up the dough scraps and knead them briefly to combine; repeat the procedure until the dough is all cut out.

4. Bake, switching the positions of the baking sheets from top to bottom halfway during baking, until the biscuits are barely golden, 20 to 25 minutes. Serve them warm.

WHOLE WHEAT, CHEDDAR, AND SAGE DROP BISCUITS

MAKES 9 BISCUITS

Serve with roast turkey, fried chicken, creamed chicken or fish dishes, baked ham,
meat stews, braised greens, or fried eggs and bacon.
Prep Time: 10 minutes
Baking Time: 25 minutes
Weeknight Suppers, Family Favorite, Holiday Feasts, Company Fare, Buffet Dish, Vegetarian

*D*on't feel like rolling out biscuit dough? Then drop dollops of this soft, flavor-packed dough onto a baking sheet for a more rustic look. These savory biscuits, redolent of sage, are terrific for sopping up gravy.

1 cup (130 g) unbleached all-purpose flour
1 cup (135 g) whole-wheat flour
1 tablespoon baking powder
1 teaspoon sugar
½ teaspoon fine sea or table salt

6 tablespoons (¾ stick) cold unsalted butter, cut
    into ½-inch cubes
½ cup shredded sharp Cheddar cheese (2 ounces)
1 tablespoon finely chopped fresh sage or
    1½ teaspoons dried
1 cup whole milk, as needed

1. Position a rack in the center of the oven and preheat the oven to 400°F. Line a large, rimmed baking sheet with parchment paper.

2. In a medium bowl, whisk the unbleached and whole-wheat flours, baking powder, sugar, and salt together. Add the butter and stir to coat it with the flour mixture. Using a pastry blender or two knives, cut the butter into the flour until the mixture resembles coarse crumbs with some pea-sized pieces of butter. Add the Cheddar cheese and sage and stir to coat the cheese. Make a well in the center of the flour mixture. Stir in enough of the milk to make a moist, spoonable dough. Using a soup spoon, drop 9 mounds of the dough about 1 inch apart onto the baking sheet.

3. Bake until the biscuits are risen and golden brown, 20 to 25 minutes. Serve them warm.

Yeasted Dinner Breads

I have a soft spot in my heart for freshly baked dinner rolls, and I serve them as often as I can to my guests. That actually turns out to be quite often, because they are not difficult to make at all. Part of this newfound ease is thanks to instant yeast (also called bread machine or quick-rising yeast).

- Old recipes asked the home baker to dissolve the active dry yeast (which is a different yeast strain) in warm water. The water had to be the right temperature to dissolve the yeast granules—water that was too hot would kill the yeast, and if it was too cold, the yeast wouldn't dissolve. Rather than deal with the water temperature issue, many home bakers just threw in the towel.

- With instant yeast, you can use cold or hot (no higher than 140°F) tap water. If you use hot water, the yeast will go into its quick-rising mode, and the dough will rise in about 45 minutes for the first rise and 30 minutes for the second. If you use cold water, the dough will rise at the same rate as the active dry yeast, about 1½ hours for the first rise and 45 minutes for the second.

- Even if you use hot water to decrease the rising time, it may be more convenient to make the dough the night before. Be sure that the dough is well-covered, and refrigerate it for up to 18 hours. Let the covered dough stand at room temperature for about 2 hours to lose its chill before shaping, the second rise, and baking.

- A heavy-duty stand mixer will also change the way you bake bread. Like most people, I learned how to knead bread by hand, and I still enjoy the Zen-like rhythm of this activity. But using a mixer frees my hands to do other things during the 8 minutes or so that the mixer does the work, and in most kitchens, there is usually always something else that needs to be done.

- A high-gluten flour will also improve your bread and give it better texture and flavor. Gluten is the combination of enzymes in wheat flour that strengthens the dough and gives it structure. "All-purpose flour" is not really a useful term, because the standard bleached version has a moderate gluten count that is really only good for cookies, cakes, and some pastry doughs. The amount of gluten in unbleached all-purpose flour changes dramatically from brand to brand. I use bread flour, which has a reliably high gluten content, for most of my yeast doughs.

- All of these dinner rolls can be baked, cooled, and wrapped in aluminum foil up to 8 hours ahead. (Reheat them in the foil in a preheated 350°F oven until hot, about 15 minutes.)

BUTTERMILK CLOVERLEAF ROLLS

MAKES 12 ROLLS

Serve with just about any roast or stew, from beef to chicken.

Prep Time: 10 minutes, plus about 2¼ hours rising time

Baking Time: 25 minutes

Make Ahead: The dough can be refrigerated for up to 18 hours before baking; allow

2 hours standing time before shaping.

Family Favorite, Holiday Feasts, Company Fare, Cooking Classic, Vegetarian

Buttermilk gives these rolls a gentle tang and a tender crumb. The old-fashioned cloverleaf shape is easy to create, and its professional appearance will have your guests thinking that you bought the rolls at the best bakery in town. Cutting the larger balls into marble-sized orbs takes only a few minutes, and kids love to help with this step. You can simply place the large balls in the muffin cups and bake for the same amount of time, but I hope I have convinced you to give the cloverleaf rolls a try.

1 cup buttermilk

¼ cup (½ stick) unsalted butter, softened, plus
   more for the bowl

1 large egg

2 tablespoons sugar

One ¼-ounce package instant (quick-rising or
   bread machine) yeast (2¼ teaspoons)

1½ teaspoons fine sea or table salt

½ teaspoon baking soda

3¼ cups (420 g) bread flour, as needed

2 tablespoons (¼ stick) unsalted butter, melted and
   cooled to tepid

1. To make the dough in a stand mixer: Whisk the buttermilk, softened butter, egg, sugar, yeast, salt, and baking soda together in the bowl of a heavy-duty stand mixer. Fit the bowl on the mixer with the paddle attachment. With the mixer on low speed, gradually beat in enough of the flour to make a dough that cleans the sides of the bowl. Change to the dough hook. Mix on medium-low speed, adding more flour as necessary, until the dough is soft, supple, and elastic, occasionally pulling it down as it climbs up the dough hook, about 8 minutes.

To make the dough by hand: In a large bowl, whisk the buttermilk, softened butter, egg, sugar, yeast, salt, and baking soda together. Add 1 cup of the flour and whisk well to make a thick batter and break up the butter. Gradually stir in enough of the remaining flour to make a dough that is too stiff to stir. Turn out the dough on a floured work surface. Knead, adding more flour as necessary, to make a soft, supple dough, about 10 minutes. The dough will be somewhat tacky, but do not add too much flour. If the dough does not stick excessively to the work surface, then it has enough flour.

2. Butter a medium bowl with softened butter. Shape the dough into a ball, add it to the bowl, turn to coat it with the butter, and leave it smooth-side up. Cover the bowl tightly with plastic wrap. Let it stand in a warm place until doubled in volume, about 1½ hours. (The covered dough can be refrigerated for up to 12 hours. Let stand at room temperature for 2 hours before shaping.)

3. Lightly butter the cups of a 12-cup muffin pan. Turn out the dough onto an unfloured work surface. Cut the dough into 12 equal portions. Shape each dough portion into a taut ball. For each roll, cut the ball into thirds, and shape it into 3 small balls. Place the balls side by side in a muffin cup. Cover the pan loosely with plastic wrap and let it stand in a warm place until the balls have almost doubled in volume, about 45 minutes.

4. Position a rack in the center of the oven and preheat the oven to 350ºF.

5. Generously brush the tops of the balls with the melted butter. Bake until the rolls are golden brown, 20 to 25 minutes. Let them stand for 5 minutes. Serve them warm.

OLD-FASHIONED DINNER ROLLS

MAKES 12 ROLLS

Serve with just about any roast or stew, from beef to chicken.

Prep Time: 10 minutes, plus about 2¼ hours of rising time

Baking Time: 25 minutes

Make Ahead: The dough can be refrigerated for up to 18 hours before baking; allow 2 hours standing time before shaping.

Family Favorite, Holiday Feasts, Company Fare, Vegetarian, Cooking Classic

As much as I recommend mashed potatoes or buttermilk in dough, this wonderful recipe shows that you can make excellent dinner rolls with everyday ingredients. This is the classic formula for pain de mie *("crumb bread" in French), whose fine texture is so renowned that it gives the loaf its name. This dough makes top-notch rolls, too.*

DOUGH

1 cup whole milk

2 large eggs

4 teaspoons sugar

One ¼-ounce package instant (quick-rising or bread machine) yeast (2¼ teaspoons)

1½ teaspoons fine sea or table salt

4 cups (520 grams) bread flour

3 tablespoons unsalted butter, softened, plus more for the bowl

GLAZE

1 large egg yolk

1 tablespoon whole milk

1. To make the dough in a stand mixer: Whisk the milk, eggs, sugar, yeast, and salt in the bowl of a heavy-duty stand mixer. Fit the bowl on the mixer with the paddle attachment. With the mixer on low speed, gradually beat in enough of the flour to make a dough that cleans the sides of the bowl. A tablespoon at a time, beat in the softened butter. Change to the dough hook. Mix on medium-low speed, adding more flour as necessary, until the dough is soft, supple, and elastic, occasionally pulling it down as it climbs up the dough hook, about 8 minutes.

To make the dough by hand: In a large bowl, whisk the milk, eggs, sugar, yeast, and salt together.

Gradually stir in enough of the flour to make a dough that is too stiff to stir. Using floured hands, add the butter 1 tablespoon at a time, and knead and squeeze the butter until it is absorbed into the dough. Turn out the dough on a floured work surface. Knead, adding more flour as necessary, to make a soft, supple dough, about 10 minutes. The dough will be somewhat tacky, but do not add too much flour. If the dough does not stick excessively to the work surface, then it has enough flour.

2. Butter a medium bowl with softened butter. Shape the dough into a ball, add it to the bowl, turn to coat it with the butter, and leave it smooth-side up. Cover the bowl tightly with plastic wrap. Let it stand in a warm place until doubled in volume, about 1½ hours. (The covered dough can be refrigerated for up to 12 hours. Let stand at room temperature for 2 hours before shaping.)

3. Lightly butter the inside of an 11½ × 8 × 2-inch baking pan. Turn out the dough onto an unfloured work surface and knead briefly. Cut the dough into 12 equal portions and shape each into a taut ball. Arrange the balls evenly apart, with the smooth sides up, in the pan. Cover the pan loosely with plastic wrap and let it stand in a warm place until the balls have almost doubled in volume, about 45 minutes.

4. Position a rack in the center of the oven and preheat the oven to 350ºF.

5. To make the glaze: In a small bowl, whisk the yolk and milk together. Lightly brush the tops of the balls with the yolk glaze. Bake until the rolls are golden brown, 20 to 25 minutes. Let them stand for 5 minutes. (The rolls can be baked, cooled, and wrapped in aluminum foil up to 8 hours ahead. Reheat in a preheated 350ºF oven until hot, about 15 minutes.) Serve them warm.

FLUFFY POTATO ROLLS

MAKES 1 DOZEN

Serve with just about any roast or stew, from beef to chicken, as part of a buffet or barbecue.

Prep Time: 15 minutes, plus about 2¼ hours rising time

Cooking Time: 20 minutes (for the potatoes)

Baking Time: 25 minutes

Make Ahead: The dough can be refrigerated for up to 18 hours before baking;

allow 2 hours standing time before shaping.

Family Favorite, Holiday Feasts, Company Fare, Vegetarian

When I tell you that these are the fluffiest, lightest rolls on earth, I mean it. Cooked potatoes replace some of the flour, which reduces the gluten to increase the rolls' tenderness. There are recipes that use leftover or instant (phooey) mashed potatoes, but these big rolls are best made with freshly cooked spuds.

1 medium baking potato, such as russet, peeled
   and cut into 1-inch chunks

¼ cup sugar

7 tablespoons unsalted butter, melted and cooled
   to tepid, plus softened butter for the bowl

1 large egg

One ¼-ounce package instant (quick-rising or
   bread machine) yeast (2¼ teaspoons)

1½ teaspoons fine sea or table salt

3 cups (390 g) bread flour, as needed

1. Put the potato chunks in a small saucepan and add enough cold unsalted water to cover by 1 inch. Bring it to a boil over high heat. Reduce the heat to medium and cook at a brisk simmer until the potatoes are tender when pierced with the tip of a small, sharp knife, 15 to 20 minutes. Strain them in a wire sieve over a bowl, reserving the cooking water. Rub the potatoes through the sieve into a bowl. Measure ½ cup of cooked potatoes and ⅔ cup of cooking water, discarding the remaining potatoes and cooking water. (Or use them in a soup.)

2. To make the dough in a stand mixer: Pour the reserved cooking water and potatoes into the bowl of a heavy-duty stand mixer. Add the sugar, 5 tablespoons of the melted butter, the egg, yeast, and salt. Fit the bowl on the mixer with the paddle attachment. With the mixer on low speed, gradually beat in enough of the flour to make a dough that cleans the sides of the bowl. Change to the dough hook. Mix on medium-low speed, adding more flour as necessary, until the dough is soft, supple, and elastic, occasionally pulling it down as it climbs up the dough hook, about 8 minutes.

To make the dough by hand: Pour the reserved cooking water and potatoes into a large bowl. Stir in the sugar, 5 tablespoons of the melted butter, the egg, yeast, and salt. Gradually stir in enough flour to make a dough that is too stiff to stir. Turn out the dough on a floured work surface. Knead, adding more flour as necessary, to make a soft, supple dough, about 10 minutes. The dough will be somewhat tacky, but do not add too much flour. If the dough does not stick excessively to the work surface, then it has enough flour.

3. Butter a medium bowl with the softened butter. Shape the dough into a ball, add it to the bowl, turn to coat it with the butter, and leave it smooth-side up. Cover the bowl tightly with plastic wrap. Let it stand in a warm place until doubled in volume, about 1½ hours. (The covered dough can be refrigerated for up to 12 hours. Let stand at room temperature for 2 hours before shaping.)

4. Brush the inside of an 11½ × 8 × 2-inch baking pan with a little of the remaining melted butter. Turn out the dough onto an unfloured work surface and knead briefly. Cut the dough into 12 equal portions. Shape each dough portion into a taut ball. Place the balls, spaced evenly apart with the smooth sides up, in the baking pan. Cover the pan loosely with plastic wrap and let it stand in a warm place until the balls have almost doubled in size, about 45 minutes.

5. Position a rack in the center of the oven and preheat the oven to 350°F.

6. Re-melt the and cool the remaining butter, if necessary. Generously brush the tops of the balls with the melted butter. Bake until the rolls are golden brown, 25 to 30 minutes. Let them stand for 5 minutes. Serve them warm.

BRAZILIAN CHEESE ROLLS

MAKES I DOZEN

Serve with stews or sauce-based entrées; or Latino main courses.

Prep Time: 10 minutes

Cooking Time: 25 minutes

Make Ahead: The rolls can be made up to 8 hours ahead.

Weeknight Suppers, Family Favorite, Holiday Feasts, Company Fare, Buffet Dish, Vegetarian

Made from gluten-free tapioca (cassava) flour, these crusty rolls have a moist, chewy interior and are a Brazilian classic. Not only are they delicious, they can be mixed to served in about thirty minutes. Romano stands in for the traditional Brazilian cheese.

Nonstick cooking oil spray, for the muffin pan

½ cup whole milk

½ cup (1 stick) unsalted butter, thinly sliced

½ teaspoon fine sea or table salt

2 cups (240 g) tapioca flour (see Note)

2 large eggs, beaten to blend, at room temperature

1½ cups grated Romano cheese (6 ounces)

1. Position a rack in the center of the oven and preheat the oven to 350°F. Lightly spray a 12-cup muffin pan with the oil.

2. In a medium saucepan over medium heat, bring ½ cup water to a simmer with the milk, butter, and salt, stirring to melt the butter. Transfer the mixture to the bowl of a heavy-duty standing mixer. Add the tapioca flour and fit the mixer with the paddle attachment. Mix on medium-low speed until the mixture is warm and looks like smooth cake icing, about 4 minutes. Gradually mix in the beaten eggs. With the mixer on low speed, mix in the Romano. The batter will be thick and sticky.

3. Using an oiled ¼-cup spring-loaded scoop or two soup spoons (one to scoop up the batter, and another to scrape it from the first spoon into the muffin cup), divide the batter among the muffin cups. Bake until the rolls are crusty and golden brown, 20 to 25 minutes. Run a knife around each roll to loosen it from the pan. Let them cool in the pan for 5 to 10 minutes. Serve them warm. (The rolls are also excellent cooled to room temperature, although the creamy interior will firm up.)

Note: Because of the popularity of gluten-free cooking, tapioca flour (also called tapioca starch) is no longer a specialty item and is found in the baking or natural foods aisle at many supermarkets. Bob's Red Mill is the most popular brand. Tapioca flour is also sold at Latino markets as manioc or cassava flour/starch (also labeled *almidón dulce* in Spanish or *amido doce* in Portuguese).

PUMPERNICKEL ALE ROLLS

MAKES 1 DOZEN

Serve with hearty soups, such as borscht; or stews and other entrées with sauces,

especially those with Eastern European flavors.

Prep Time: 15 minutes, plus about 2¼ hours rising time

Baking Time: 25 minutes

Make Ahead: The dough can be refrigerated for up to 18 hours before baking;

allow 2 hours standing time before shaping.

Family Favorite, Holiday Feasts, Company Fare, Buffet Dish, Cooking Classic, Vegetarian

Now that I can find dark rye flour at my supermarket so easily, I bake these dark brown rolls with the flavor trifecta of onion, dill, and caraway often. Their heartiness makes them very satisfying with soup on a cold day. A few tips for working with this dough: For the best flavor, use a moderately bitter ale, such as amber or pale, but not a hoppy India pale ale. Remember that bread dough with high grains content should be tacky, so don't add more flour to compensate. Dried onion is easiest to use because the fresh onion gives off moisture that changes the dough texture. Finally, don't let the cocoa throw you off, as it is used more as a coloring than a flavoring.

1 cup amber or pale ale, at room temperature

1 tablespoon molasses (not blackstrap)

1 tablespoon vegetable oil

1 tablespoon natural or Dutch-processed cocoa powder

One ¼-ounce package instant (quick-rising or bread machine) yeast (2¼ teaspoons)

2 cups (260 g) unbleached all-purpose flour, as needed

1 cup (120 g) dark rye flour (see Note page 386)

1½ teaspoons fine sea or table salt

1 tablespoon chopped dried onion

2 teaspoons dried dill seed

2 teaspoons dried caraway seed

2 tablespoons (¼ stick) unsalted butter, melted and cooled to tepid, plus softened butter for the bowl

1. To make the dough in a stand mixer: Pour the ale, molasses, oil, cocoa, and yeast into the bowl of a heavy-duty stand mixer. Add 1 cup of the unbleached flour with the rye flour and salt. Fit the bowl on the mixer with the paddle attachment. With the mixer on low speed, gradually beat in enough of the remaining unbleached flour to make a dough that cleans the sides of the bowl. Change to the dough hook. Mix on medium-low speed, adding more flour as necessary, until the dough is soft, supple, and elastic, occasionally pulling it down as it climbs up the dough hook, about 8 minutes. During the last minute or so, add the onion, dill seed, and caraway seed.

To make the dough by hand: In a large bowl, combine the ale, molasses, oil, cocoa, and yeast. Stir in 1 cup of the unbleached flour with the rye flour and salt. Gradually stir in enough of the remaining unbleached flour to make a dough that is too stiff to stir. Turn out the dough on a floured work surface. Knead, adding more flour as necessary, to make a soft, supple dough, about 10 minutes. The dough will be somewhat tacky, but do not add too much flour. If the dough does not stick excessively to the work surface, then it has enough flour. Pat out the dough into a thick rectangle. Sprinkle it with the onion, dill, and caraway and roll it up into a cylinder. Knead it for a minute more to distribute the onion, dill, and caraway.

2. Butter a medium bowl with softened butter. Shape the dough into a ball, add it to the bowl, turn to coat it with the butter, and leave it smooth-side up. Cover the bowl tightly with plastic wrap. Let it stand in a warm place until doubled in volume, about 1½ hours. (The covered dough can be refrigerated for up to 12 hours. Let stand at room temperature for 2 hours before shaping.)

3. Brush the inside of an 11½ × 8 × 2-inch baking pan with some of the melted butter. Turn out the dough onto an unfloured work surface and knead briefly. Cut the dough into 12 equal portions. Shape each dough portion into a taut ball. Place the balls, spaced evenly apart with the smooth sides up, in the baking pan. Cover the pan loosely with plastic wrap and let it stand in a warm place until the balls have almost doubled in volume, about 45 minutes.

4. Position a rack in the center of the oven and preheat the oven to 350°F.

5. Remelt and cool the remaining butter, if necessary. Brush the tops of the balls with the melted butter. Bake until the top of the rolls are browned, 25 to 30 minutes. Let them stand for 5 minutes. Serve them warm.

Pumpernickel Raisin Rolls: This slightly sweet variation is very popular at New York bakeries. Omit the dried onion, dill, and caraway. Knead ½ cup golden raisins into the finished dough.

Note: Dark rye flour, unlike light rye flour, contains the bran and germ, which gives the rolls a darker color and richer flavor. It is sold at natural food stores and most supermarkets. If the flour is just labeled "rye flour," it is usually light rye, which can be used in this recipe, although the rolls will be lighter in color.

SWEET POTATO AND PECAN DINNER ROLLS

MAKES 1 DOZEN

Serve with roast pork, baked ham, roast chicken, or turkey.
Prep Time: 20 minutes, plus 30 minutes cooling time and 2¼ hours rising time
Cooking Time: 8 minutes to 1 hour (for cooking the yam)
Baking Time: 25 minutes
Make Ahead: The dough can be refrigerated for up to 18 hours before baking;
allow 2 hours standing time before shaping.
Family Favorite, Holiday Feasts, Company Fare, Buffet Dish, Retro Recipe, Vegetarian

*R*oasted orange sweet potatoes give these mildly sweet rolls an autumnal orange color, but the yam flavor is subtle. That's actually a plus, so you can serve these for a holiday menu with another sweet potato dish and not worry about repeating flavors. The yams should be microwaved or baked in a conventional oven because they will soak up too much water if boiled and throw off the amount of flour needed to make the dough.

1 large orange-fleshed sweet potato (yam; about
  12 ounces) pierced a few times with a fork
½ cup whole milk
¼ cup (½ stick) unsalted butter, thinly sliced, plus
  softened butter for the bowl and pan
¼ cup packed light brown sugar

1¼ teaspoons fine sea or table salt
One ¼-ounce package instant (quick-rising or
  bread machine) yeast (2¼ teaspoons)
3¼ cups (425 g) bread flour, as needed
½ cup coarsely chopped pecans
1 large egg yolk, beaten

1. Cook the sweet potato in a microwave oven on high until tender, 5 to 8 minutes, depending on the wattage of your oven. (Or bake it on a rimmed baking sheet in a preheated 400ºF oven until tender, about 1 hour.) Let it cool until easy to handle, about 30 minutes. Peel the sweet potato, transfer the flesh to a small bowl, and mash it with a fork. Measure and reserve ½ cup mashed sweet potato and let it cool completely, about 30 minutes. Discard the remaining sweet potato or save it for another use.

2. Bring the milk to a simmer in a small saucepan over medium heat. Remove it from the heat and add the sliced butter. Let it stand until the butter is melted. Add the reserved mashed sweet potatoes, ¼ cup water, the brown sugar, and salt.

3. To make the dough in a stand mixer: Pour the sweet potato mixture into the bowl of a heavy-duty stand mixer. Stir in the yeast. Fit the bowl on the mixer with the paddle attachment. With the mixer on low speed, gradually beat in enough of the flour to make a dough that cleans the sides of the bowl. Change to the dough hook. Mix on medium-low speed, adding more flour as necessary, until the dough is soft, supple, and elastic, occasionally pulling it down as it climbs up the dough hook, about 8 minutes. During the last minute, add the pecans.

To make the dough by hand: Pour the sweet potato mixture into a large bowl. Stir in the yeast. Gradually stir in enough of the flour to make a dough that is too stiff to stir. Turn out the dough on a floured work surface. Knead, adding more flour as necessary, to make a soft, supple dough, about 10 minutes. The dough will be somewhat tacky, but do not add too much flour. If the dough does not stick excessively to the work surface, then it has enough flour. Pat the dough into a thick rectangle. Sprinkle it with the pecans and roll it up into a cylinder. Knead it briefly to distribute the pecans.

4. Gather up the dough into a ball. Generously butter a medium bowl with softened butter. Shape the dough into a ball, add it to the bowl, turn to coat it with the butter, and leave it smooth-side up. Cover the bowl tightly with plastic wrap. Let it stand in a warm place until doubled in volume, about 1½ hours. (The covered dough can be refrigerated for up to 12 hours. Let stand at room temperature for 2 hours before shaping.)

5. Butter the inside of an 11½ × 8 × 2-inch baking pan. Turn out the dough onto an unfloured work surface and knead briefly. Cut the dough into 12 equal portions. Shape each dough portion into a taut ball. Arrange the balls evenly spaced, with the smooth sides up, in the baking pan. Cover the pan loosely with plastic wrap and let it stand in a warm place until the balls have almost doubled in volume, about 45 minutes.

6. Position a rack in the center of the oven and preheat the oven to 350ºF.

7. In a small bowl, beat the egg yolk with 1 tablespoon water. Lightly brush the tops of the balls with the yolk glaze. Bake until the rolls are golden brown, 20 to 25 minutes. Let them stand for 5 minutes. Serve them warm.

SEEDED BREAD STICK TWISTS

MAKES 14 BREAD STICKS

Serve with Italian pasta dishes, salads, or soups.

Prep Time: 15 minutes, plus about 3 hours rising and refrigeration times

Baking Time: 20 minutes

Make Ahead: The dough can be refrigerated for up to 18 hours before baking;
allow 2 hours standing time before shaping.

Family Favorite, Holiday Feasts, Company Fare, Buffet Dish, Vegetarian

These attractive bread sticks, with barber pole–like twists of seeds, can really jazz up a simple meal of lasagna or spaghetti and meatballs. I often use three or four different seeds, applying them on the dough in separate sections, or use a combination for an "everything" version. The dough is easiest to twist if it is chilled, so make room in the refrigerator before you cut it into strips.

DOUGH

1 tablespoon extra-virgin olive oil, plus more for the bowl

One ¼-ounce package instant (quick-rising or bread machine) yeast (2¼ teaspoons)

Fine sea or table salt

1 teaspoon sugar

3¼ cups (425 g) unbleached all-purpose flour, as needed

1 large egg white

Pinch of fine sea or table salt

3 tablespoons sesame, black sesame, poppy, flax, caraway, or nigella (see Note) seeds

1. To make the dough in a stand mixer: Combine 1¼ cups cold water with the oil, yeast, salt, and sugar in the bowl of a heavy-duty stand mixer. Fit the bowl on the mixer with the paddle attachment. With the mixer on low speed, gradually beat in enough of the flour to make a dough that cleans the sides of the bowl. Change to the dough hook. Mix on medium-low speed, adding more flour as necessary, until the dough is soft, supple, and elastic, occasionally pulling it down as it climbs up the dough hook, about 8 minutes.

To make the dough by hand: In a large bowl, whisk 1¼ cups cold water with the oil, yeast, salt, and sugar. Gradually stir in enough of the flour to make a dough that is too stiff to stir. Turn out the dough on a floured work surface. Knead, adding more flour as necessary, to make a soft, supple dough, about 10 minutes. The dough will be somewhat tacky, but do not add too much flour. If the dough does not stick excessively to the work surface, then it has enough flour.

2. Shape the dough into a ball. Oil a medium bowl. Add the dough to the bowl, turn to coat it with the oil, and leave it smooth-side up. Cover the bowl tightly with plastic wrap. Let it stand in a warm place until the dough has almost doubled in volume, about 1½ hours. (The covered dough can be refrigerated for up to 12 hours. Let stand at room temperature for 2 hours before shaping.)

3. Turn out the dough onto an unfloured work surface and shape it into a rough rectangle. Dust the top of the dough with flour. Roll the dough into a 13 × 9-inch rectangle with the long side facing you.

Transfer the dough to a large rimmed baking sheet and cover it with plastic wrap. Refrigerate the dough on the baking sheet until it is chilled, about 30 minutes.

4. Remove the dough on the sheet from the refrigerator and uncover it. In a small bowl, use a fork to beat the egg white and salt together until foamy. Lightly brush the surface of the dough with the egg white mixture. Sprinkle the seeds evenly over the brushed dough and pat them gently to help them adhere.

5. Line 2 large, rimmed baking sheets with parchment paper. Using a pizza wheel or a sharp knife, cut the dough from top to bottom into 14 strips, each a little less than 1 inch wide. One dough strip at a time, lifting it just off the work surface, twist the dough, being sure to occasionally lift it up at the center (any part of the strip that touches the work surface will not twist) into a corkscrew shape about 12 inches long. The dough will be stretchy, but you'll get the hang of it. Arrange the twists 1 inch apart on the baking sheets. Cover the sheets loosely with plastic wrap and let them stand in a warm place until they look somewhat puffy, about 1 hour.

6. Position racks in the top third and center of the oven and preheat the oven to 400ºF. Uncover the bread twists. Bake until they are lightly browned, switching the positions of the pans from front to back and top to bottom halfway through baking, about 20 minutes. Let them cool on the pans. Serve them warm.

Note: Nigella seeds have a distinct onion flavor, and they are sometimes called black onion seeds, even though they are unrelated to the Lilium family. They are easily available at Indian markets, spice stores, and online. Like all seeds, store nigella seeds in an airtight container in the refrigerator or freezer, and they will keep for about a year. Use them in savory baking or sprinkle the oniony seeds on salads or dips.

OVERNIGHT FOCACCIA
MAKES 12 SERVINGS

Serve with Italian-inspired menus, from spaghetti and lasagna to stews or roasts.

Prep Time: 10 minutes, plus 40 minutes resting and 18 to 72 hours refrigeration time

Cooking Time: 20 minutes

Make Ahead: The dough can be made up to 3 days ahead. The focaccia can be baked up to 8 hours ahead.

Family Favorite, Holiday Feasts, Company Fare, Buffet Dish, Cooking Classic, Vegetarian

Why would you want to let focaccia dough rise overnight? Because that is the best way to give it a light, almost fluffy, crumb. I first learned this no-knead method (although the dough is "stretched") from my friend, the very highly regarded baker and cookbook author Peter Reinhardt, and now it is my favorite technique to make this Italian flatbread. The dough is very moist, but that is the consistency required for the gluten in the flour to strengthen over time as it absorbs the water. You can even make the dough up to three days ahead before baking.

5½ cups (715 g) unbleached all-purpose flour

1 tablespoon instant (also called quick-rising or
   bread-machine) yeast

2 tablespoons extra-virgin olive oil, plus more for
   the bowl, baking sheet, and drizzling

2 teaspoons fine sea or table salt

1 tablespoon finely chopped fresh rosemary or
   thyme (optional)

1. In a large bowl, stir the flour, 2⅓ cups cold water, the yeast, oil, and salt together to make a wet, sticky dough. (The bowl should be large enough to contain the dough after it rises and doubles.) Cover the bowl with plastic wrap and let it stand for 10 minutes.

2. Using a hand rinsed in cold water, grab a quarter of the dough and stretch it above the rest of the dough by about 8 inches. Fold the stretched dough over to the center of the remaining dough in the bowl. Repeat three more times, working with a quarter of the dough at a time and rotating the bowl after each stretch. The dough will get slightly firmer after each stretching period. Tightly cover the bowl. (Or transfer the dough to a 6-quart or larger lidded food storage container, which will take up less refrigerator space.) Refrigerate the dough for at least 18 hours and up to 3 days.

3. Lightly oil an 18 × 13 × 1-inch rimmed baking sheet with oil. Line the bottom of the baking sheet with parchment paper, and oil the paper.

4. Scrape the dough into the baking sheet. Pat and stretch the dough to fit the pan. Loosely cover the top of the dough with oiled plastic wrap, oiled-side down. Let it stand in a warm place until the dough doubles in volume to almost reach the top edge of the baking sheet, about 1 hour.

5. Position a rack in the center of the oven and preheat the oven to 400°F.

6. Using your fingertips, press "dimples" all over the top of the dough. Drizzle the dough lightly with oil. Sprinkle it with the rosemary, if using. Bake until the focaccia is golden brown, about 30 minutes. Let it cool for 10 minutes. Remove the focaccia from the pan and discard the parchment paper. (The focaccia can be baked, cooled, and wrapped in aluminum foil up to 8 hours ahead. Reheat in a preheated 350°F oven until hot, about 15 minutes.) Cut the focaccia into large rectangles and serve them warm or cooled to room temperature.

Quick Breads

These delicious breads are considered "quick" because they get their lift from chemical leavenings (such as baking powder or baking soda) or nature (eggs and air). They do not need a rising period before baking, and go right from the mixing bowl to the baking pan. And if you really want to treat your friends and family, make one of these recipes for a weeknight supper. These become stale fairly quickly, and are best served the day of baking, but I don't have any trouble getting rid of leftovers.

BEER AND GOUDA BREAD

MAKES 8 SERVINGS

Serve with just about any stew, pot roast, or oven-roasted meat with gravy.

Prep Time: 10 minutes

Baking Time: 40 minutes, plus 15 minutes cooling time

Weeknight Suppers, Holiday Feasts, Company Fare, Buffet Dish, Cooking Classic, Vegetarian

Here is a crusty loaf fragrant with herbs and cheese that can be ready for baking in minutes. The trick is to use a flavorful dark beer or ale (but not stout) and to avoid light-flavored beer (such as lager). If you can't find aged Gouda, which is firmer and sharper than semi-soft young Gouda, try Asiago or sharp Cheddar.

4 tablespoons (½ stick) unsalted butter, melted

3 cups (390 g) unbleached all-purpose flour

2 tablespoons sugar

1 tablespoon baking powder

1 teaspoon granulated onion

1 teaspoon fine sea or table salt

1 cup (½-inch) diced aged Gouda cheese
 (4 ounces)

2 tablespoons finely chopped fresh thyme or sage
 or 2 teaspoons dried

One 12-ounce bottle dark beer (but not stout)

1. Position a rack in the center of the oven and preheat the oven to 350ºF. Spoon 1 tablespoon of the butter into a 9-inch cake pan or cast-iron skillet and set it aside.

2. In a large bowl, whisk the flour, sugar, baking powder, granulated onion, and salt together. Add the Gouda and thyme and stir to coat. Make a well in the center of the flour mixture and pour in the beer and remaining 3 tablespoons melted butter. Mix just until the dough comes together.

3. Place the cake pan with the butter in the oven and bake to heat the pan without browning the butter, about 2 minutes. Remove the pan from the oven and tilt to coat the bottom with the butter. Pour the batter into the pan and spread it evenly with a metal spatula. Return it to the oven and bake until the loaf is crusty brown and a bamboo skewer inserted in the center of the loaf comes out clean, about 40 minutes. Let the loaf cool for 15 minutes. (This loaf is best if the beer's alcohol flavor is allowed to dissipate before serving.) Remove it from the pan, cut it into wedges, and serve it warm or at room temperature.

SAVORY GREEN OLIVE MUFFINS

MAKES 8 MUFFINS

Serve with roasts, chops, stews, or roast chicken.

Prep Time: 15 minutes

Baking Time: 20 minutes

Weeknight Suppers, Holiday Feasts, Company Fare, Buffet Dish, Vegetarian

These savory muffins flecked with green and red made their first appearance at my house for a Christmas dinner. They were such a hit that I have continued to serve them at summer cookouts and weeknight meals, too.

Nonstick cooking oil spray

1½ cups (195 g) unbleached all-purpose flour

½ cup (65 g) yellow cornmeal, preferably stone-ground

½ cup plus 2 tablespoons freshly grated Parmesan cheese (2½ ounces)

1 tablespoon sugar

1½ teaspoons baking powder

½ teaspoon baking soda

2 teaspoons chopped fresh oregano or 1 teaspoon dried

½ teaspoon granulated garlic

½ teaspoon granulated onion

½ teaspoon fine sea or table salt

½ teaspoon freshly ground black pepper

½ cup drained and coarsely chopped pimiento-stuffed green olives

2 large eggs, beaten to blend

½ cup whole milk

⅓ cup extra-virgin olive oil

¼ cup low-fat plain yogurt (not Greek)

1. Position a rack in the center of the oven and preheat the oven to 350°F. Line 8 standard muffin cups in a muffin pan with paper liners. Spray the liners with cooking spray.

2. In a large bowl, whisk the flour, cornmeal, ½ cup of the Parmesan, the sugar, baking powder, baking soda, oregano, granulated garlic, granulated onion, salt, and pepper together. Add the olives and stir to coat them with the flour mixture. In another bowl, whisk the eggs, milk, oil, and yogurt together until combined. Make a well in the center of the flour mixture and pour in the egg mixture. Stir just until combined.

3. Preferably using a ¼-cup spring-loaded scoop, divide the batter evenly among the muffin cups, filling them half full. Sprinkle the remaining 2 tablespoons Parmesan on the muffin tops. Bake until the muffins are golden brown and a wooden toothpick inserted in the center comes out clean, about 20 minutes. Let them cool in the pan for 10 minutes. (The Parmesan in the muffins may cause them to cling to the paper liners if the muffins are cooled for less than 10 minutes.) Remove them from the pan and serve them warm.

GRUYÈRE AND THYME SCONES
MAKES 8 SCONES

Serve with roast pork, roast chicken, or stews.

Prep Time: 15 minutes

Weeknight Suppers, Family Favorite, Holiday Feasts, Company Fare, Buffet Dish, Vegetarian

The aroma of these thyme-flecked scones wafting through the house will certainly call the troops to dinner. They are no-fuss and do not require a cookie cutter—just pat out the dough and cut it into triangles.

2 cups (260 g) unbleached all-purpose flour, plus more for the pan and the work surface

1 tablespoon sugar

2½ teaspoons baking powder

¼ teaspoon baking soda

1½ teaspoons finely chopped fresh thyme or ¾ teaspoon dried

1 teaspoon fine sea or table salt

¼ teaspoon freshly ground black pepper

6 tablespoons (¾ stick) cold butter, cut into ½-inch cubes

¾ cup shredded Gruyère or Swiss cheese (3 ounces)

¾ cup buttermilk

1. Position a rack in the center of the oven and preheat the oven to 400°F. Line a large, rimmed baking sheet with parchment paper.

2. In a medium bowl, whisk the flour, sugar, baking powder, baking soda, thyme, salt, and pepper together. Add the butter and toss to coat it with the flour mixture. Using a pastry blender or two knives, cut the butter into the flour mixture until the mixture resembles coarse crumbs with some pea-sized pieces of butter. Stir in ½ cup of the Gruyère. Make a well in the center of the flour mixture. Pour in the buttermilk and stir just until the mixture is moistened. Knead the dough briefly in the bowl until the dough holds together.

3. Turn out the dough onto a lightly floured work surface and pat it into an 8-inch disk. Cut the dough into 8 equal triangles. Transfer the triangles to the baking sheet, placing them about 2 inches apart. Sprinkle the remaining ¼ cup Gruyère over the tops of the triangles.

4. Bake until the scones are golden brown, about 20 minutes. Serve them warm.

PARCHMENT PAPER

For years, I fought against parchment paper. Waxed paper was good enough for me. And then I worked on a cookbook with recipes contributed by professional bakers, and not one of them used waxed paper. During the same period, parchment paper became more readily available, so I couldn't use the excuse that it was too difficult to find.

I buy precut parchment paper sheets by the case now, because, unlike the rolled paper at the supermarket, the sheets won't curl. I have virtually a lifetime supply, so I share some of the paper with my friends who are also home bakers. You can also find flat parchment paper online. If rolled parchment paper curls when you are lining the pan, spray the pan with a little cooking oil to help the parchment stick.

In my experience, silicone nonstick baking mats run a far second to parchment paper. The thick mats insulate the baked goods, preventing nicely browned bottoms that translate into flavor. Also the mats eventually absorb butter from the dough or batter, and when it goes rancid, the flavor will transfer to the food.

IRISH SODA BREAD
MAKES 1 LOAF; 6 TO 8 SERVINGS

Serve with corned beef and cabbage, or meat stews.
Prep Time: 10 minutes
Baking Time: 40 minutes, plus 15 minutes cooling time
Weeknight Suppers, Family Favorite, Holiday Feasts, Company Fare,
Buffet Dish, Cooking Classic, Vegetarian

This Irish bread is the real thing, with only four ingredients: flour, baking soda, salt, and buttermilk (standing in for soured milk, which is not easy to come by with today's pasteurized dairy products). Rustic and earthy, with a crisp crust and chewy crumb, this is less sweet than the Americanized version (opposite).

2 cups (260 g) unbleached all-purpose flour, plus
   more for the work surface
1 cup (135 g) whole-wheat flour

1 teaspoon baking soda
1 teaspoon fine sea or salt
1½ cups buttermilk, as needed

1. Position a rack in the center of the oven and preheat the oven to 400ºF. Line a large, rimmed baking sheet with parchment paper.
2. In a large bowl, whisk the flour, whole-wheat flour, baking soda, and salt together. Stir in the buttermilk to form a rough dough. (Add a little more buttermilk if the dough seems too dry.) Knead the dough briefly in the bowl, just until it comes together. Turn out the dough onto a lightly floured work surface and shape it into a ball about 6 inches in diameter. Transfer the ball to the prepared baking sheet. Using a serrated knife, cut a large cross, about ½ inch deep, into the top of the dough. (This cross will open up during baking and help the dough bake more evenly.)
3. Bake until the bread is golden brown and sounds hollow when tapped on the bottom, 35 to 40 minutes. Let it cool on the baking sheet for 15 minutes. Slice and serve it warm.

CURRANT AND CARAWAY SODA BREAD

MAKES 6 TO 8 SERVINGS

Serve with corned beef, lamb or beef stew, or sausages.

Prep Time: 10 minutes

Baking Time: 45 minutes, plus 15 minutes cooling time

Weeknight Suppers, Family Favorite, Holiday Feasts, Company Fare,

Buffet Dish, Cooking Classic, Vegetarian

The beauty of authentic Irish soda bread (opposite) is its simplicity. However, when company is coming, I go for this version, with the added goodness of brown sugar and egg to make a sweeter, richer crumb, and both caraway and currants for extra flavor. No one in Dublin would recognize this, but it sure is delicious.

2½ cups (325 g) unbleached all-purpose flour, plus more for the work surface

1½ teaspoons baking powder

½ teaspoon baking soda

½ teaspoon fine sea or table salt

½ cup dried currants, seedless raisins, or golden raisins

1½ teaspoons caraway seed

1 cup buttermilk

¼ cup (½ stick) unsalted butter, melted and cooled to tepid

2 tablespoons packed light brown sugar, well crumbled

1 large egg, beaten to blend

1. Position a rack in the center of the oven and preheat the oven to 375°F. Line a baking sheet with parchment paper.

2. In a large bowl, whisk the flour, baking powder, baking soda, and salt together. Stir in the currants and caraway seed. In a medium bowl, whisk the buttermilk, butter, brown sugar, and egg together until the sugar is dissolved. Stir them into the flour mixture to form a rough dough. (Add a little more buttermilk if the dough seems too dry.) Knead the dough briefly in the bowl, just until it comes together. Turn out the dough onto a lightly floured work surface and shape it into a ball about 5½ inches in diameter. Transfer the ball to the prepared baking sheet. Using a serrated knife, cut a large cross, about ½ inch deep, into the top of the dough. (This cross will open up during baking and help the dough bake more evenly.)

3. Bake until the bread is golden brown and sounds hollow when tapped on the bottom, 45 to 55 minutes. Let it cool on the baking sheet for 15 minutes. Slice and serve it warm.

BROWN BREAD WITH DRIED CRANBERRIES

MAKES 8 SERVINGS

Serve with baked beans, corned beef, or sausages.

Prep Time: 10 minutes

Steaming Time: 1¼ hours, plus 20 minutes cooling time

Make Ahead: The baked bread can be stored, wrapped in plastic, for up to 1 day.

Family Favorite, Cooking Classic, Vegetarian

A Yankee cooking stalwart, steamed brown bread harkens back to the time when not every home had a reliable oven and yeasted breads were cooked on top of the stove. Today, this quickly assembled whole-grain bread is worth making for its rich, molasses-sweetened flavor. Old recipes steam the batter in a coffee can, which is not a good idea because coffee cars are not guaranteed to be heatproof. The bread cooks much more quickly and efficiently in a tubed pudding mold.

Softened butter and flour, for the pudding mold	¾ cup buttermilk
¾ cup (105 g) plus 1 tablespoon whole-wheat flour	½ cup molasses (not blackstrap)
½ cup (60 g) dark rye or light rye flour	1 large egg, beaten to blend
½ cup (65 g) yellow cornmeal, preferably stone-ground	½ cup dried cranberries
½ teaspoon baking soda	Special Equipment: Collapsible steamer rack;
½ teaspoon fine sea or table salt	2-quart covered steamed pudding mold

1. Place a collapsible steamer in a large pot and add enough water to almost reach the bottom of the steamer. (If you have another kind of steamer, just set it up as needed.) Bring the water to a boil over high heat. Lightly butter a 2-quart tubed pudding mold, dust it with flour, and tap out the excess flour.
2. In a medium bowl, whisk ¾ cup of the whole-wheat flour, the rye flour, cornmeal, baking soda, and salt together. Make a well in the center, and pour in the buttermilk, molasses, and egg. Stir with a wooden spoon just until combined. Toss the cranberries with the remaining 1 tablespoon whole-wheat flour and fold them into the batter. Pour the batter into the mold and cover it with the lid or cover it tightly with aluminum foil.
3. Place the mold on the rack of the steamer. Reduce the heat to medium-low to keep the water at a steady, strong simmer and cover the pot. Steam the bread until a long bamboo skewer inserted into the center of the bread comes out clean, about 1¼ hours. Transfer the mold to a wire cake rack, un-cover it, and let it cool for 10 minutes. Invert the mold onto a plate to unmold the bread. Let it cool for at least 10 minutes more. Serve it warm. (This quick bread stores well because of its moisture. Cool, wrap in plastic, and store at room temperature for up to 1 day. Reheat the bread in a microwave oven or toast slices in a toaster oven.)

POPOVERS

MAKES 6 POPOVERS

Serve with sauced chicken or seafood main courses, meat stews, or egg-based main courses.
Prep Time: 10 minutes
Baking Time: 40 minutes
Weeknight Suppers, Family Favorite, Holiday Feasts, Company Fare, Buffet Dish, Retro Recipe,
Cooking Classic, Vegetarian

Gorgeously puffed and golden, with crispy exteriors and custardy insides, popovers are American classics that unfortunately seem to be slipping into the "culinary endangered species" category. This version is from my grandmother's recipe card, which I have used to create many variations, even though I love the original. While a special pan for baking popovers exists, it is fairly useless outside of its single purpose, and I much prefer to use a muffin pan. Also I find that the popover pan makes huge popovers, and that can be too much of a good thing.

• Popovers rise best when the eggs and milk for the batter are at room temperature. To do this quickly, place the uncracked eggs in a bowl of hot tap water to cover for 5 minutes and microwave the milk at medium (50% power) until it loses its chill, about 1 minute. Also, because the batter is thin, it is best to transfer it to a pitcher or 1-quart liquid measuring cup for easy pouring.

1 cup (130 g) unbleached all-purpose flour	2 large eggs, at room temperature
1 teaspoon sugar	1 tablespoon unsalted butter, melted and cooled
½ teaspoon fine sea or table salt	slightly
1 cup whole milk, at room temperature	Vegetable oil, for the muffin cups

1. In a large pitcher or medium bowl with a pouring lip, whisk the flour, sugar, and salt together. Add the milk, eggs, and butter and whisk just until combined. (The batter should be slightly lumpy.) Set it aside and let it stand while the oven is preheating.

2. Position a rack in the center of the oven and preheat the oven to 400°F. Brush 6 standard muffin cups in a muffin pan with oil.

3. Place the muffin pan in the oven and heat until the pan is very hot, about 2 minutes. Remove the pan from the oven. Pour equal amounts of the batter into the buttered cups. Return the pan to the oven. Bake (without opening the oven door) until the popovers have risen and are a deep golden brown, about 35 minutes. Remove the pan from the oven and pierce the side of each popover with the tip of a small, sharp knife to release the steam. Return the popovers to the oven and bake until they are a bit darker, about 5 minutes. Remove them from the cups and serve warm.

Bacon Popovers: Stir 2 bacon strips, cooked until crisp, cooled, and finely chopped, into the flour. If desired, substitute 1 tablespoon rendered bacon fat from cooking the bacon for the melted butter.

Cheddar or Gruyère Popovers: Add ¼ teaspoon hot red pepper sauce to the liquid ingredients. Sprinkle ⅓ cup shredded sharp Cheddar or Gruyère cheese (about 1½ ounces) evenly over the popover tops before baking.

Dijon Popovers: Add 1 tablespoon Dijon mustard to the liquid ingredients.

Herb Popovers: Add 1 tablespoon finely chopped fresh chives, oregano, rosemary, sage, or thyme to the flour mixture, or use 1½ teaspoons dried versions of any of these herbs, except chives.

Lemon Popovers: Add the freshly grated zest of 1 lemon to the batter with the liquid ingredients.

Nut Popovers: Add ¼ cup finely chopped pecans, walnuts, or skinned hazelnuts.

Parmesan-Pepper Popovers: Add ½ teaspoon freshly grated black pepper to the flour mixture. Sprinkle 3 tablespoons freshly grated Parmesan cheese evenly over the popover tops before baking.

HERBED YORKSHIRE PUDDINGS

MAKES 12 PUDDINGS

Serve with roast beef or pork.
Prep Time: 10 minutes
Baking Time: 30 minutes
Family Favorite, Holiday Feasts, Company Fare, Buffet Dish, Cooking Classic

Yorkshire puddings are popovers made with the rendered fat from a roast beef (and roast pork is good, too). The name reveals their British background, and I have found that they are unfamiliar to many Americans, which is a shame. To be sure that you have enough fat, ask the butcher not to trim the roast too closely, or ask for eight ounces or so of separate beef fat trimmings (you might have to purchase them) to cook in the roasting pan along with the roast. As for timing, bake the puddings while the roast is standing before carving. I always allow at least thirty minutes for this rest period, and believe me, the roast will not cool down too much.

7 tablespoons rendered beef or pork fat from the roasting pan	**1 teaspoon minced fresh rosemary or ½ teaspoon dried**
1½ cups (195 g) all-purpose flour	**¾ teaspoon fine sea or table salt**
1 teaspoon minced fresh thyme or ½ teaspoon dried	**¼ teaspoon freshly ground black pepper**
	1½ cups whole milk
	3 large eggs, beaten to blend

1. Position a rack in the top third of the oven and preheat the oven to 400°F. Measure 3 tablespoons of the beef fat and set it aside. Spoon about 1 teaspoon of the remaining fat into each of 12 standard muffin cups.

2. In a large bowl, whisk the flour, thyme, rosemary, salt, and pepper together. Make a well in the center of the flour mixture and pour in the milk, eggs, and reserved 3 tablespoons beef fat. Whisk the ingredients together just until smooth. Transfer the batter to a 1-quart measuring cup. Pour equal amounts of the batter into the prepared muffin cups.

3. Bake until the puddings are puffed, golden brown, and crisp, 30 to 35 minutes. Serve them immediately.

Stuffings and Dressings

I worked for a turkey processor for many years, and traveled all over the country teaching Thanksgiving cooking classes. Along the way, I wrote books on holiday cooking, so I have learned a thing or two about that classic American side dish, turkey stuffing. (Call it dressing if you wish—they are the same thing.)

- You can stuff turkey without any food safety concerns. The stuffing in the bird should reach at least 160°F after roasting to kill any harmful bacteria. To reach this temperature, always stuff the turkey with a warm, freshly prepared stuffing, not chilled stuffing from the refrigerator. Never make stuffing ahead of time.

- To save some time on Thanksgiving morning, you can cook the stuffing vegetables (and any other ingredient that needs to be cooked, such as sausage or bacon) the night before and refrigerate them in a covered container. The next morning, heat the ingredients in a large skillet in a little vegetable oil or butter over medium heat to warm them up.

- I have nothing against prepared bread stuffing cubes, as they have a firm texture that holds up to the long roasting period. If you are using cubes cut from a loaf, let the cubes stand out overnight, uncovered, at room temperature, to stale slightly. Or bake them on large, rimmed baking sheets in a preheated 350°F oven, stirring occasionally, until dried but not toasted, about 15 minutes. The cubes will continue to crisp as they cool.

- You can only fit so much stuffing into the turkey body cavity and neck area. The stuffing that is left over after filling the bird should be transferred to a buttered baking dish, covered with aluminum foil, and refrigerated until ready to bake and serve. The size of the baking dish and the baking time will depend on the amount of stuffing. The recommended baking temperature and times in the recipes are estimates. At Thanksgiving, there are usually a variety of sides in the oven that need to be baked at the same time, so flexibility is a necessity when it comes to cooking times. Essentially, just bake the stuffing until it is hot, removing the foil about halfway through to crisp the top, if you wish.

CLASSIC HERB STUFFING

MAKES 12 SERVINGS

Serve with roast turkey or goose.

Prep Time: 15 minutes

Cooking Time: 40 minutes

Make Ahead: The vegetable mixture can be prepared up to 1 day ahead.

Family Favorite, Holiday Feasts, Company Fare, Buffet Dish, Cooking Classic

This old-fashioned recipe features all of the flavors that people expect from a traditional dressing. If you wish, use fresh herbs, substituting 2 teaspoons of finely chopped herbs for each of the dried versions.

¼ cup (½ stick) unsalted butter, plus softened butter for the dish

2 medium onions, chopped

6 medium celery ribs with leaves, chopped

1 teaspoon dried thyme

1 teaspoon dried sage

1 teaspoon crumbled dried rosemary

1 teaspoon dried marjoram (optional)

½ teaspoon freshly ground black pepper

One 16-ounce package seasoned bread cubes for stuffing

⅓ cup chopped fresh flat-leaf parsley

2 cups Giblet Turkey Stock (see page 401), as needed

Kosher salt

1. Melt the butter in a large skillet over medium heat. Add the onion and celery. Cover and cook, stirring occasionally, until the vegetables are tender, about 10 minutes. Stir in the thyme, sage, rosemary, marjoram, if using, and pepper. (The vegetable mixture can be prepared up to 1 day ahead. Reheat in a skillet over medium heat.)

2. In a large bowl, mix together the stuffing cubes, vegetable mixture, and parsley. Gradually stir in enough of the stock (about 1½ cups) to evenly moisten the stuffing. Season to taste with salt and pepper. Use it immediately as a turkey stuffing.

3. Transfer any remaining stuffing to a buttered baking dish (the size depends on the amount of leftover stuffing) and drizzle with the remaining ½ cup stock. Cover the dish with aluminum foil, and refrigerate it to bake separately.

4. When ready to serve, preheat the oven to 350°F. Bake the stuffing in the baking dish for 15 minutes. Uncover the baking dish and bake until the stuffing is hot and the top is lightly browned, about 15 minutes more.

Sausage Stuffing: Cook 1 pound bulk pork sausage or sweet turkey sausage, casings removed, in 2 tablespoons vegetable oil in a large nonstick skillet over medium heat, stirring occasionally and breaking up the meat with the side of a spoon, until the sausage is thoroughly cooked and shows no sign of pink, about 10 minutes. Add the sausage with any pan drippings to the stuffing.

Chestnut Stuffing: Add 2 cups coarsely chopped Basic Roasted Chestnuts (see below) to the stuffing.
Giblet Stuffing: Add the cooked and finely chopped giblets, liver, and neck meat from the Giblet Turkey Stock (see below).
Oyster and Sausage Stuffing: I have a couple of friends who like oyster stuffing, so I often add oysters to the Sausage Stuffing for them. Drain ½ pint shucked oysters. Cut the oysters into bite-sized pieces and add them to 4 cups of the Classic Stuffing. Transfer the stuffing to a buttered baking dish, cover it with aluminum foil, and refrigerate it until ready to use.

BASIC ROASTED CHESTNUTS

For chestnut stuffing, you can purchase cooked chestnuts in jars or bags (look for these at Asian grocers), but freshly roasted chestnuts are a seasonal treat that should be savored. Here's how to do it.

Preheat the oven to 400°F. Using a small, sharp knife, cut a deep X in the flatter side of each chestnut. Place them in a single layer on a large rimmed baking sheet. Bake until the outer skin is split and crisp, 30 to 40 minutes. They never seem to be done at the same time, so work with the ones that are ready and continue roasting the others. Place the roasted chestnuts in a kitchen towel to keep them warm. Using a small, sharp knife, peel off both the tough outer and thin inner skins. To loosen the peels on stubborn, hard-to-peel chestnuts, return them to the oven for an additional 5 to 10 minutes, or microwave them on High for 1 minute.

The peeled chestnuts can be refrigerated in a covered container for a few days. One pound of fresh chestnuts equals about 2½ cups roasted and peeled chestnuts.

GIBLET TURKEY STOCK
MAKES 2 QUARTS

Use to make stuffing and gravy for roast turkey.
Prep Time: 10 minutes
Cooking Time: 2 hours
Make Ahead: The stock can be refrigerated for up to 2 days or frozen for up to 3 months.
Holiday Feasts, Company Fare, Cooking Classic

One of the best ways to upgrade your holiday turkey dinner is to use homemade turkey stock for the important side dishes of gravy and stuffing, which should taste like turkey and not plain canned broth. It's an easy job to simmer the turkey giblets and neck with a few vegetables to make a broth worthy of your best bird.

• Reserve the turkey liver for another use; it will make the stock bitter. Give it to your cat or dog as a holiday treat, or sauté it and use it in the Giblet Stuffing on page 401. To use it in the stuffing, melt 1 tablespoon unsalted butter in a small nonstick skillet over medium heat. Trim the liver of any connective tissues and green areas, and season it lightly with salt and pepper. Cook it in the skillet, turning occasionally, until it is browned and barely cooked through when pierced with the tip of a small, sharp knife, 8 to 10 minutes. Let it cool completely before chopping.

• I highly recommend adding the turkey wing to the stock because it really boosts the turkey flavor. However, turkey wings are not always easy to find at the supermarket, even during the holidays. If the butcher can't chop the wing for you, do it at home. But don't attempt to chop the heavy wing bones unless you have a cleaver—cutting the wing apart at the joints is sufficient. I mention this because I chipped a knife this way once.

• The foam that develops on the stock is only the coagulating collagen and gelatin from the bones, and it isn't harmful, but it should be removed to keep the broth clear. Add the seasonings after skimming the stock or you will remove them with the foam.

• For a clear, delicious stock, let it bubble at a gentle simmer. If it boils, the fat will be suspended in the liquid, and the stock will look cloudy and taste greasy.

• A bowl of stock can take up a lot of room in the refrigerator (or freezer). For space-saving storage, transfer the stock to 1-quart delicatessen containers or similar receptacles.

• There will be a layer of solidified fat on the surface of the chilled stock. It should be removed from the stock, but don't discard it. Save the fat to add to the roasting pan to create more drippings for the gravy.

2 tablespoons vegetable oil	1 turkey wing (1¼ pounds), chopped apart at the
Giblets (heart and gizzard, but not the liver) and	joints with a heavy knife (optional)
neck from 1 turkey	4 large sprigs fresh flat-leaf parsley
1 small yellow onion, coarsely chopped	¼ teaspoon dried thyme
1 small carrot, coarsely chopped	⅛ teaspoon black peppercorns
1 small celery rib with leaves, coarsely chopped	1 small bay leaf
1 quart reduced-sodium turkey or chicken broth	Kosher salt

1. Heat the oil in a large saucepan or soup pot over medium-high heat. Using a large heavy knife, chop the neck into 1- to 2-inch chunks. Add the giblets and neck chunks to the saucepan and cook, turning occasionally, until they are browned, about 8 minutes. Add the onion, carrot, and celery and cook, stirring occasionally, until they are softened, about 3 minutes.

2. Add the broth and scrape up the browned bits in the bottom of the saucepan with a wooden spoon. Add the turkey wing, if using. (It is unnecessary to brown the turkey wing.) Add enough cold water (about 1½ quarts) to cover the ingredients in the saucepan by 1 inch. Bring it to a simmer over high heat, skimming off and discarding the foam that rises to the top of the stock. Add the parsley, thyme, peppercorns, and bay leaf.

3. Reduce the heat to low. Simmer until the stock is full-flavored, at least 2 and up to 3 hours. Season the stock lightly with salt, keeping in mind that the finished dish will be seasoned, too. Strain the stock through a wire sieve over a large bowl. Let it cool to room temperature.

4. Transfer the stock to covered containers. Refrigerate it for up to 2 days or freeze it for up to 3 months. Remove the solidified fat from the surface of the stock, reserving the fat, if desired.

HAM, KALE, AND CORNBREAD DRESSING
MAKES 12 TO 14 SERVINGS

Serve as a stuffing for roast turkey.
Prep Time: 30 minutes
Cooking Time: About 1 hour
Make Ahead: The ham mixture can be cooked up to 1 day ahead.
Family Favorite, Holiday Feasts, Company Fare, Buffet Dish

Not a typical dressing (or call it stuffing, if you prefer), but still one that is a crowd-pleaser, especially now that so many people have come around to liking kale. I have also made this with diced andouille sausage instead of ham for a spicier version.

8 tablespoons (1 stick) unsalted butter, plus
   softened butter for the dish
1 ham steak (12 ounces), cut into bite-sized pieces
8 ounces lacinato or curly kale, tough stems
   removed, coarsely chopped and washed well (but
   not dried)
1 large yellow onion, chopped
1 large red bell pepper, cored, seeded, and cut into
   ½-inch dice
4 large celery ribs, cut into ½-inch dice

4 scallions (white and green parts), thinly sliced
2 garlic cloves, minced
2 teaspoons sweet paprika
¼ cup finely chopped fresh flat-leaf parsley
2 tablespoons finely chopped fresh rosemary
1 recipe Cornbread for Stuffing (page 370),
   crumbled into coarse pieces
2 cups Giblet Turkey Stock (page 401) or reduced-
   sodium chicken broth, as needed
Kosher salt and freshly ground black pepper

1. Melt 4 tablespoons of the butter in a large skillet over medium heat. Add the ham and cook, stirring occasionally, until it is lightly browned, about 5 minutes. In two or three additions, stir in the kale with any clinging water, letting the first addition wilt before adding another. Cook, stirring occasionally, until the kale is tender, about 10 minutes. Transfer the ham and kale mixture to a large bowl.
2. Add the remaining 4 tablespoons butter to the skillet and let it melt. Add the onion, bell pepper, and celery. Cover and cook, stirring occasionally, until the vegetables are tender, about 10 minutes. Uncover, stir in the scallions and garlic, and cook, stirring often, until the scallions are tender, about 3 minutes. Stir in the paprika. Transfer the vegetables to the bowl with the ham and kale mixture. Stir in the parsley and rosemary. (The ham and vegetable mixture can be cooled, covered, and refrigerated

for up to 1 day. Reheat it in a large skillet over medium heat, stirring often, for about 5 minutes before using.)

3. Add the cornbread. Stir in enough of the stock (about 1½ cups) to moisten the stuffing. Season to taste with salt and pepper. Use the stuffing immediately to stuff a turkey.

4. Transfer any remaining stuffing to a buttered baking dish (the size depends on the amount of left-over stuffing) and drizzle with the remaining ½ cup stock. Cover it with aluminum foil and refrigerate it to bake separately.

5. When ready to serve, preheat the oven to 350°F. Bake the stuffing in the baking dish for 15 minutes. Uncover the baking dish and bake until the stuffing is hot and the top is lightly browned, about 15 minutes more.

SOURDOUGH AND ROASTED ROOT VEGETABLES STUFFING
MAKES ABOUT 12 SERVINGS

Serve with roast turkey.
Prep Time: 20 minutes
Cooking Time: About 1¼ hours plus 30 minutes cooling time for the vegetables
Make Ahead: The vegetables can be roasted up to 1 day ahead.
Family Favorite, Holiday Feasts, Company Fare, Buffet Dish

Autumn root vegetables, with their firm textures and hint of sweetness, are especially wonderful when roasted, and can be turned into a fabulous stuffing. As a time saver, roast the vegetables the night before, if you wish. Don't be afraid to let the vegetables get nicely browned—the caramelization will only enhance their flavor.

3 large carrots, cut into ½-inch rounds

2 large parsnips, cut into ½-inch rounds

1 large celery root (1¼ pounds), pared and cut into
  ½-inch cubes

1 large yellow onion, cut into sixths

3 tablespoons olive oil

1 loaf crusty sourdough bread (1 pound), cut into
  ½-inch cubes (about 10 cups)

⅓ cup chopped fresh flat-leaf parsley

1 tablespoon finely chopped fresh rosemary

1 tablespoon finely chopped fresh sage

2 cups Giblet Turkey Stock (page 401) or reduced-
  sodium chicken broth, as needed

Kosher salt and freshly ground black pepper

2 large eggs, beaten to blend

1. Position a rack in the center of the oven and preheat the oven to 425°F.

2. Combine the carrots, parsnips, celery root, and onion in a very large roasting pan. Drizzle them with the oil and toss with your hands to coat the vegetables.

3. Roast, stirring the vegetables often, until they are tender and nicely browned, about 45 minutes. Let them cool until tepid, about 30 minutes. On a work surface, coarsely chop the cooled vegetables into pieces about ½ inch square. (The roasted vegetables can be prepared up to 1 day ahead, covered and refrigerated.)

4. Transfer the roasted vegetables to a large bowl. Mix in the bread cubes, parsley, rosemary, and sage. Gradually stir in enough of the stock (about 1½ cups) to make a moist, but not wet, stuffing. Season to taste with salt and pepper. Stir in the eggs. Use it immediately as a turkey stuffing.

5. Transfer any remaining stuffing to a buttered baking dish (the size depends on the amount of left-over stuffing) and drizzle with the remaining ½ cup stock. Cover it with aluminum foil, and refrigerate it to bake separately.

6. Thirty minutes before you are ready to serve, preheat the oven to 350ºF oven. Bake the stuffing in the baking dish for 15 minutes. Uncover the baking dish and bake until the stuffing is hot and the top is lightly browned, about 15 minutes more.

RICE MEDLEY DRESSING WITH BLUEBERRIES AND PISTACHIOS

MAKES 8 TO 10 SERVINGS

Serve with roast turkey or baked ham.

Prep Time: 15 minutes

Cooking Time: 50 minutes

Make Ahead: The wild rice mixture can be cooked up to 8 hours ahead.

Holiday Feasts, Company Fare, Buffet Dish

With the attention being paid to gluten-free diets these days, you may want to have a bread-free dressing with the holiday turkey. This festive-looking dish is best served on the side and not cooked in the bird, so the berries stay whole. Use any wild rice combination with a variety of grains for this—I used a generic brand from my local natural food supermarket—but read the instructions and tweak the recipe as needed if the rice you use calls for a different cooking time.

2 tablespoons (¼ stick) unsalted butter	1 tablespoon finely chopped fresh sage
2 celery ribs, finely chopped	1 teaspoons kosher salt
⅓ cup minced shallots	¼ teaspoon freshly ground black pepper
1 pound wild rice medley	Two 6-ounce containers (about 2⅔ cups) fresh
3 cups Giblet Turkey Stock (page 401) or	blueberries
reduced-sodium chicken broth	½ cup pistachios, toasted (see page 33)

1. Melt the butter in a large saucepan over medium heat. Add the celery and cover. Cook, stirring occasionally, until it is softened, about 5 minutes. Add the shallots and cook uncovered, stirring occasionally, until they are tender, about 3 minutes. Add the wild rice medley and stir well.

2. Add the stock, 2½ cups water, the sage, salt, and pepper and bring them to a boil over high heat. Reduce the heat to low and cover tightly. Simmer until the rice is tender and the liquid is absorbed, about 35 minutes. Remove it from the heat. (The wild rice can be cooled, covered, and refrigerated for up to 8 hours. Reheat in a microwave oven on high in a covered microwave-safe container for about 5 minutes.)

3. Add the blueberries and pistachios to the saucepan, but do not stir. Cover tightly and let them stand for 5 minutes. The retained steam will heat the berries and pistachios. Fluff the rice with a fork, mixing in the berries and nuts. Serve it hot.

Quinoa with Carrot and Mint (page 277)

Slaw with Radishes and Cilantro (page 290)

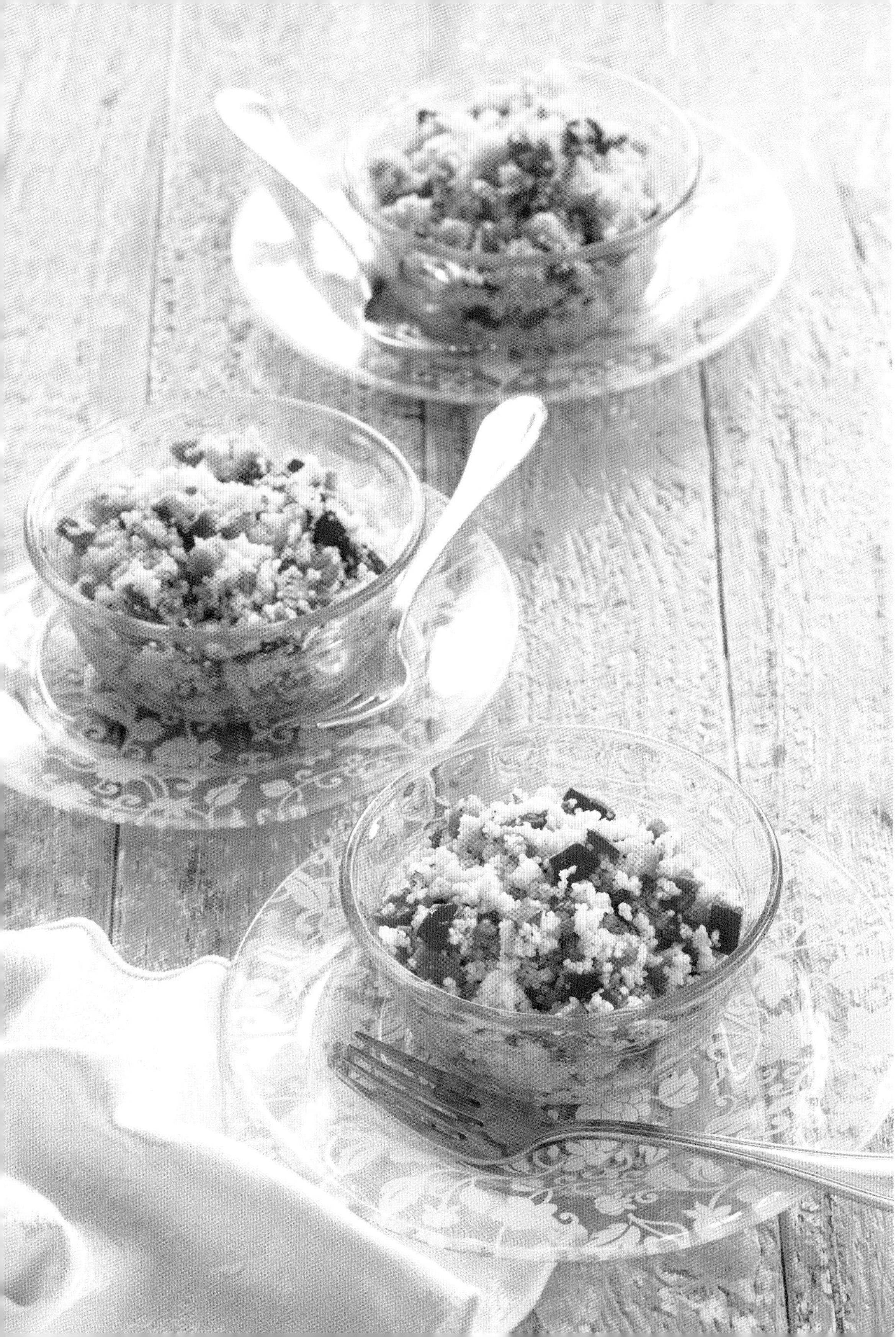

Couscous Salad with Saffron Vinaigrette (page 296)

Grilled Hearts of Romaine with Garlic Crumbs and Caesar-Ranch Dressing (page 317)

Carrot Ribbons with Pomegranate Dressing (page 327)

Prosecco Mimosa Salad (page 335)

Salad dressings (left to right): Thousand Island (page 345), Japanese Carrot (page 341), and Avocado Green Goddess (page 342)

Stovetop Macaroni and Pimiento Cheese (page 349) and Baked Ziti with Broccoli and Gorgonzola (page 351)

Fried Spaëtzle (with farmer's cheese and chives) (page 360)

Fluffy Potato Rolls (page 382)

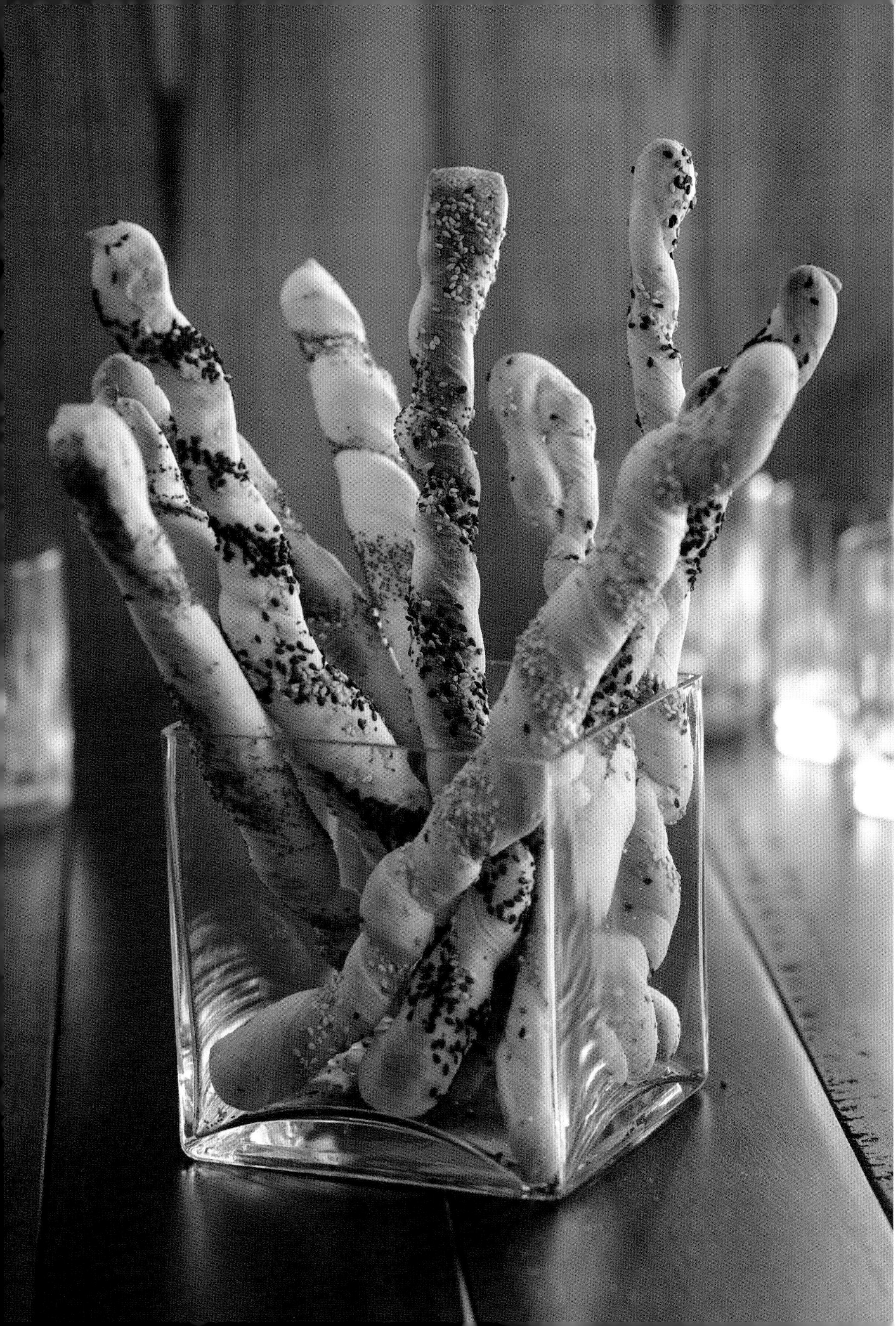

Seeded Bread Stick Twists (page 388)

Ham, Kale, and Cornbread Dressing (page 403)

Quick pickles (left to right): Napa Cabbage Kimchi (page 411), Bread and Butter Pickles (page 408), and Giardiniera (page 410)

Cranberry and Dried Pineapple Mostarda (page 422)

Stuffed Celery with Liptauer Cheese Spread (page 422), Bread and Butter Pickles (page 408), and Deviled Eggs with Horseradish and Bacon (page 423)

Gravy 101 (page 437)

PICKLES, RELISHES, AND SAUCES

Pickles, relishes, and sauces should never be afterthoughts. Especially for a festive menu, these extras can turn a meal into an event. In my family, Mom's cut-glass relish tray only comes out at holidays, where it is filled to the brim with store-bought nibbles. But homemade pickles and relishes are even better. These are very easy to make, especially when prepared in the small batches that I offer here. There is also a concise collection of the most useful sauces to embellish and complement simply prepared main courses.

Pickles

The days are over when I would spend an entire day putting up cases of produce. That doesn't mean I forgo the old-fashioned delights of homemade pickles. Now I make my favorite recipes in small batches, one or two jars at a time, to store in the refrigerator and enjoy over a couple of weeks' time.

- Because the jars will not be stored at room temperature, they do not need to be sterilized or hot-packed in boiling water. Just use freshly washed, rinsed, and dried jars. Out of habit, I use hot jars right out of the dishwasher, but it isn't really necessary if the jars are sparkling clean. If you are filling Mason jars, the rings can be reused, but the tops should be fresh. Of course, this is not an issue with hinged lock-type jars.
- One-quart, widemouthed jars are the most convenient and allow you to make a moderate amount of food—not so much that you won't use it all in a reasonable length of time, and not so much that it will clutter your refrigerator.
- Traditional pickles get their sour taste from the naturally occurring lactic acid created during fermentation. Most of these recipes are quick pickles that use vinegar to supply the acidic flavor. I have included a couple of naturally fermented pickles because they may take a few days to develop, but the actual work is very minimal. In these cases, I do recommend sterilized jars to prevent unwanted bacteria, and I include the simple instructions in the recipes.

- These recipes call for noniodized salt, which you will find at every supermarket labeled as either plain or pickling salt. Regular fine sea or table salt sometimes contains elements that cloud the pickling brine.

BREAD AND BUTTER PICKLES
MAKES 1 QUART

Serve with barbecued meat or poultry, fried chicken, or sandwiches.
Prep Time: 15 minutes, plus 2 to 3 hours draining
Cooking Time: 5 minutes, plus about 14 hours cooling time
Make Ahead: The pickles can be refrigerated for up to 1 month.
Family Favorite, Holiday Feasts, Company Fare, Buffet Dish, Cooking Classic, Vegetarian

These pickles may have gotten their name because they were once as common as bread and butter and often served with sandwiches. On the sweet side, with spicy notes of mustard, celery seed, cloves, and turmeric, these are much less cloying than commercial pickles. Don't leave out the turmeric (available inexpensively at Indian markets), as it gives the pickles their characteristic yellow tint.

4 Kirby cucumbers, scrubbed but not peeled, cut into ½-inch rounds
1 small yellow onion, cut into ½-inch half-moons
1 small red bell pepper, cored, seeded, cut into ½-inch strips
1 tablespoon plain (noniodized) salt

1 cup white distilled vinegar
¾ cup sugar
2 teaspoons yellow mustard seed
1 teaspoon celery seed
½ teaspoon ground turmeric
3 whole cloves

1. Toss the cucumbers, onion, bell pepper, and salt together in a colander. Layer the top with about 1 quart of ice cubes. Place the colander in the sink. Let it stand and drain for 2 to 3 hours to crisp the vegetables. Discard any unmelted ice cubes, but do not rinse the vegetables.

2. Pack the vegetables into a clean 1-quart canning jar. Bring the vinegar, sugar, mustard seed, celery seed, turmeric, and cloves to a boil in a medium nonreactive saucepan over high heat, stirring often to dissolve the sugar. Pour the hot vinegar brine into the jar. Discard any remaining brine. Cover the jar with the lid.

3. Let the jar stand until the pickles reach room temperature, about 2 hours. Refrigerate them for at least 12 hours before serving. (The pickles can be stored in the refrigerator for up to 1 month.)

OVERNIGHT DILL AND GARLIC PICKLES

MAKES 1 QUART

Serve with barbecued meat or poultry, fried chicken, or sandwiches.

Prep Time: 10 minutes

Cooking Time: 5 minutes, plus about 14 hours cooling time

Make Ahead: The pickles can be refrigerated for up to 1 month.

Family Favorite, Holiday Feasts, Company Fare, Buffet Dish, Retro Recipe, Cooking Classic, Vegetarian

A bite of crisp dill pickle cuts through rich food like a garlicky sword. These are not as sour as traditional fermented pickles (see page 407), but many of my friends prefer these for that very reason. If you have dill in your garden (as I always do), use six dried dill seed heads and ¼ cup dill sprigs to replace the dill seeds and sprigs in the recipe.

1 cup distilled white vinegar

1 tablespoon sugar

2 teaspoons plain (noniodized) salt

3 large garlic cloves, crushed under a knife and
   peeled

2 teaspoons dill seeds

½ teaspoon coriander seeds

½ teaspoon black peppercorns

½ cup packed fresh dill sprigs

4 Kirby cucumbers, scrubbed but not peeled, each
   cut lengthwise into 6 spears

1. Bring the vinegar, 1 cup water, the sugar, salt, garlic, dill seed, coriander, and peppercorns to a boil in a nonreactive medium saucepan over high heat, stirring often to dissolve the sugar and salt.

2. Put half of the dill sprigs in the bottom of a clean 1-quart canning jar. Tightly pack the cucumbers side by side in the jar. Pour enough hot vinegar brine into the jar to cover the cucumbers, being sure to add all of the mixed spices and garlic. If any air pockets form, use a long spoon to move the vegetables and disperse the pocket. Top with the remaining dill and add the remaining brine. Discard any remaining brine. Close the jar with its lid and ring.

3. Let the jar stand until the pickles reach room temperature, about 2 hours. Refrigerate them for at least 12 hours before serving. (The pickles can be stored in the refrigerator for up to 1 month.)

SPICY SAKE AND GINGER PICKLES

MAKES 4 SERVINGS

Serve with Asian main courses, grilled chicken, or grilled pork chops.

Prep Time: 5 minutes, plus at least 15 minutes standing time

Make Ahead: The pickles can be refrigerated for up to 3 days.

Weeknight Suppers, Vegetarian

When I need something to round out a meal with Asian flavors, I make these simple pickles. Green beans, red pepper sticks, and cauliflower also can be used. Use an inexpensive brand of sake.

1 Kirby or Persian cucumber, scrubbed

2 carrots

2 tablespoons rice vinegar

2 tablespoons sake, such as Gekkeikan Traditional

One 1-inch piece fresh ginger, peeled and cut into matchsticks

2 teaspoons soy sauce

1 teaspoon light brown sugar

½ teaspoon hot red pepper flakes

1. Cut the cucumber and carrot into strips about 3 inches long and ½ inch wide. Transfer them to a medium nonreactive bowl and toss them with the vinegar, sake, ginger, soy sauce, brown sugar, and red pepper flakes. Refrigerate them for at least 15 minutes and up to 2 hours.

2. Using a slotted spoon, transfer the pickles to a serving bowl and serve chilled.

GIARDINIERA

MAKES 2 QUARTS

Serve with Italian-style meats or poultry, pasta main courses, or sandwiches.

Prep Time: 15 minutes

Cooking Time: 5 minutes, plus about 14 hours cooling time

Make Ahead: The giardiniera can be refrigerated for up to 1 month.

Family Favorite, Holiday Feasts, Company Fare, Buffet Dish, Cooking Classic, Vegetarian

Italian-style pickled vegetables, giardiniera, is one of my very favorite relishes, with puckery brine flavored with oregano and garlic. Individual pepperoncini are often integral to the mix of colorful vegetables. Unless you grow them yourself, fresh ones are hard to find, even at well-supplied farmer's markets. Luckily there are lots of substitutes, which I have listed below. I like white wine vinegar to give the giardiniera an appropriately European profile (I buy an inexpensive brand at my local ethnic market), but regular distilled vinegar works as well.

2 cups white wine or distilled white vinegar

1 tablespoon plain (noniodized) salt

1 tablespoon sugar

1 teaspoon dried oregano

½ teaspoon black peppercorns

1 bay leaf, broken into quarters

2 garlic cloves, crushed under a knife and peeled

½ head cauliflower, broken into small florets

1 red bell pepper, cored, seeded, and cut into 1-inch squares

1 Cubanelle or Italian frying pepper (see Note)

1 long, slender carrot, cut into ½-inch rounds

1 large celery rib, cut into ½-inch slices

½ cup olive oil, as needed

1. Bring the vinegar, 2 cups water, the salt, sugar, oregano, peppercorns, bay leaf, and garlic to a boil in a medium nonreactive saucepan over high heat, stirring to dissolve the salt and sugar.

2. In a large bowl, combine the cauliflower, bell and Cubanelle peppers, carrot, and celery. Divide the vegetables equally between two 1-quart canning jars. Pour enough hot brine into each jar to cover the vegetables, dividing the peppercorns, bay leaf, and garlic between the jars. Discard the remaining brine. Top off each jar with a ¼-inch layer of oil. Close the jars.

3. Let the jars stand until the giardiniera reaches room temperature, about 2 hours. Refrigerate it for at least 12 hours before serving. (The giardinera can be stored in the refrigerator for up to 1 month.)

Note: Cubanelle peppers are pale green, with blunt ends and a mild heat level. Italian frying and Hungarian wax peppers also work well. If you don't have any of these fresh options, add ½ teaspoon hot red pepper flakes (in addition to the black peppercorns in the brine) to each jar with the vegetables. You could also use 4 or 5 small padrón or shishito peppers, often available at specialty or Asian markets, for each large Cubanelle.

BLUE GARLIC?

When garlic comes into contact with vinegar for an extended period of time, a chemical reaction will make it change its color. So don't be surprised if you find a clove of blue-green garlic in your batch of giardiniera.

NAPA CABBAGE KIMCHI

MAKES I QUART

Serve with Asian-style grilled meats or poultry; use to make Kimchi Fried Rice (page 260).

Prep Time: 10 minutes, plus 2 hours salting and 12 to 36 hours fermentation times

Make Ahead: The kimchi can be refrigerated for up to 1 month.

Company Fare, Cooking Classic

I learned how to make this fiery cabbage pickle many years ago, long before it acquired hip status. My teacher was Yang Su, a Korean colleague at my restaurant job, who ran a grassroots kimchi business out of her Manhattan apartment. Yang Su impressed upon me that kimchi can be personalized with additional vegetables (julienned daikon and/or carrots) or extra ginger and garlic. After it starts to bubble at room temperature, indicating that fermentation has taken place, refrigerate it for further storage, where it will ferment at a slower rate. (The warmer the temperature, the quicker the fermentation will occur, and in a hot summer kitchen, I have had kimchi ready for refrigeration after 12 hours.) After a month, the kimchi can be quite sour; I prefer it when it is a week or so old. Beyond its role as a side dish served with Asian food, add it to fried rice (see page 260) or fold it into scrambled eggs. It can even be used as one heck of a hot dog relish.

1 head (2 pounds) napa cabbage

2 tablespoons kosher salt

6 scallions (white and green parts), thinly sliced
   into rounds

¼ cup Thai or Vietnamese fish sauce

¼ cup Korean coarse chile flakes (see Note)

¼ cup peeled and minced ginger

6 large garlic cloves, minced

1 teaspoon sugar

1. Cut the cabbage in quarters lengthwise and cut out the core. Cut the cabbage roughly into pieces about 2 inches square. Transfer them to a bowl, sprinkle them with the salt, and mix well with your hands to separate the leaves. Let them stand for 2 hours. Rinse the cabbage well and drain. Repeat the rinsing and draining twice.

2. A handful at a time, squeeze the excess liquid from the cabbage and transfer the cabbage to a large bowl. Add the scallions, fish sauce, chile flakes, ginger, garlic, and sugar and mix with long tongs. (Do not use your hands, unless you wear latex gloves, or you run the risk of burning your skin with the chiles as well as smelling like garlic for a few days.)

3. Bring a large pot of water to a boil over high heat. Submerge a 1-quart canning jar (and ring, if using) in the water and reduce the heat to medium-low. Simmer for 10 minutes. Using tongs, remove the jar from the water and set it aside. If using Mason jars, soak the lid in a bowl of hot (but not boiling) water. Stand the jar, right-side up, on the work surface.

4. Using the tongs, transfer the cabbage mixture to the hot jar. Using a long wooden spoon, crush the mixture in the jar to release enough juices to barely cover the vegetables. Cover the jar with its lid. Let it stand at room temperature, opening the jar every 8 hours or so to release the building gases, until you see bubbles forming in the juices in the jar, 12 to 36 hours, depending on the ambient temperature.

5. Pack the fermented kimchi into a 1-quart covered container (it doesn't have to be glass at this point). Refrigerate the kimchi, where it will continue to ferment at a slower rate, for up to 1 month. After 1 month, it may be quite sour, although some kimchi aficionados like it that way.

Note: Korean chile flakes (*gochugaru*), essential for making kimchi, are available at Asian markets and online. Korean chile powder is not the same, as it is more finely ground and spicier than the flakes. You can use leftover Korean chile flakes as an all-purpose seasoning, similar to, but milder than, cayenne. If you can't find Korean chile flakes, substitute 2 tablespoons Hungarian paprika and 2 tablespoons hot red pepper flakes.

PICKLED OKRA

MAKES 1 QUART

Serve with barbecued meats or poultry, fried chicken, or meat sandwiches.

Prep Time: 10 minutes

Cooking Time: 5 minutes, plus 2 hours cooling time

Make Ahead: The pickles can be refrigerated for up to 1 month.

Holiday Feasts, Buffet Dish, Cooking Classic, Vegetarian

These crisp, tangy spears make okra lovers out of okra haters. In fact, I have a friend who replaced the olive in his martini with pickled okra. If you have dill in your garden, use 6 dried dill seed heads and ¼ cup dill sprigs to replace the dill seeds and sprigs in the recipe. The green bean variation is equally welcome, especially at a summer barbecue.

2 cups cider vinegar

2 teaspoons plain (noniodized) salt

2 garlic cloves, crushed under a knife and peeled

1 teaspoon yellow mustard seeds

12 ounces okra (about 30 pods)

2 serrano chilies or 1 jalapeño, split lengthwise

1. Bring the vinegar, 1 cup water, the salt, garlic, and mustard seeds to a boil in a medium nonreactive saucepan over high heat, stirring often to dissolve the sugar and salt.

2. Tightly pack the okra side by side into a 1-quart canning jar, using the longest ones first, and laying the smaller ones on top. Add the chilies to the jar. Pour enough hot vinegar brine into the jar to cover the okra, being sure to add all of the mixed spices and garlic. Discard any remaining brine. Close the jar with its lid and ring.

3. Let the jar stand until the pickles reach room temperature, about 2 hours. The pickles are ready to serve. (The pickles can be stored in the refrigerator for up to 1 month.)

Pickled Green Beans: Substitute 14 ounces green beans, stem ends trimmed, for the okra.

Relishes

What is the difference between a relish and a pickle? A pickle is made of relatively whole vegetables, but a relish can be spooned up. A relish also has a more piquant combination of sweet, tart, and savory. A pickle truly stands alone as an accent, while relishes are most often served in combination with a main course—as in a hot dog with cucumber relish. Another example is turkey with cranberry sauce, which I have included here because of its pairing of tart cranberries with a sweet ingredient. The relishes are ready to eat right after they have cooled, but their flavors are fuller if the relish is refrigerated overnight. And because, at least in my experience, a true relish tray always includes stuffed celery or deviled eggs (or both), I am sharing my favorite recipes for these icons.

CLASSIC CUCUMBER AND PEPPER RELISH
MAKES ABOUT 3 CUPS

Serve with hot dogs, sausages, or hamburgers.
Prep Time: 10 minutes, plus 1 hour standing time
Cooking Time: 5 minutes, plus 4 hours refrigeration time
Make Ahead: The relish can be made up to 2 days ahead.
Family Favorite, Holiday Feasts, Company Fare, Buffet Dish, Cooking Classic, Vegetarian

While this hot dog relish is based on the classic ballpark kind, its fresh flavor and crisp texture will knock your frank out of the ballpark. For a spicier version, I have been known to add a seeded and minced jalapeño to the skillet when cooking the bell peppers and onions.

3 tablespoons distilled white vinegar

1 tablespoon sugar

1½ teaspoons yellow mustard seeds

2 Kirby cucumbers, scrubbed, halved lengthwise, seeds scraped out with the tip of a spoon, and cut into ¼- to ½-inch dice

¾ teaspoon kosher salt

1 tablespoon vegetable oil

¾ cup finely chopped yellow onion

¾ cup (¼- to ½-inch dice) red bell pepper

1. In a small bowl, combine the vinegar, sugar, and mustard seeds and let them stand for 1 hour to soften the mustard seeds. Toss the cucumbers and salt in a wire sieve over a medium bowl, and let them drain for 1 hour. Rinse the cucumbers under cold running water. Drain them again and pat the cucumbers dry with paper towels. Transfer the cucumbers to a medium bowl.
2. Heat the oil in a medium skillet over medium heat. Add the onion and bell pepper and cook, stirring occasionally, until they are crisp-tender, about 3 minutes. Stir them into the cucumbers. Add the vinegar mixture and mix well. Cover the bowl with plastic wrap and refrigerate it for at least 4 hours. (The relish can be refrigerated for up to 2 days.)

CHOW-CHOW
MAKES ABOUT 4 CUPS

Serve with hamburgers, hot dogs, or sandwiches.
Prep Time: 15 minutes, plus 1 hour draining
Cooking Time: 5 minutes, plus about 12 hours refrigeration time

Make Ahead: The chow-chow can be refrigerated for up to 3 weeks.

Holiday Feasts, Company Fare, Buffet Dish, Cooking Classic

Chow-chow is a cabbage pickle that is augmented with other vegetables to make a relish that is an outstanding hamburger condiment. If you wish, add a cup of fresh corn kernels or a chopped green tomato or two, to the mix. This makes a fairly large batch, which is good because I also enjoy it on ham sandwiches and hot dogs. This is another one of my battery of "secret ingredients" that takes only a few minutes to prepare but pays off big-time in the flavor department.

4 cups chopped green cabbage (about ½ head)

½ sweet red bell pepper, cored, seeded, and cut into ½-inch dice

2 Kirby cucumbers, scrubbed, seeded, and cut into ½-inch dice

1 large yellow onion, chopped

1 tablespoon kosher salt

1 cup distilled white vinegar

⅔ cup packed light brown sugar

1 teaspoon dry mustard powder

½ teaspoon celery seeds

½ teaspoon hot red pepper flakes

¼ teaspoon ground turmeric

1. In a large colander, mix the cabbage, bell pepper, cucumbers, onion, and salt and place the colander in the sink. Put a plate on top to fit inside the colander, and weigh it down with a few large, heavy cans of food. Let it stand for 1 hour to drain off the excess juices.

2. Bring the vinegar, sugar, mustard, celery seeds, red pepper flakes, and turmeric to a boil over high heat in a nonreactive large saucepan, stirring to dissolve the brown sugar. Add the vegetable mixture (do not rinse it), and return it to a boil. Reduce the heat to medium and simmer, uncovered, until the cabbage is crisp-tender, about 5 minutes.

3. Transfer the chow-chow to a medium bowl and let it cool to room temperature. Cover the bowl with plastic wrap and refrigerate it overnight. (The chow-chow can be refrigerated for up to 3 weeks.)

CORN AND JALAPEÑO RELISH

MAKES 1 QUART

Serve with grilled salmon or chicken, baked ham, or barbecued spareribs.

Prep Time: 10 minutes

Cooking Time: 5 minutes, plus about 12 hours refrigeration time

Make Ahead: The relish can be refrigerated for up to 1 month.

Holiday Feasts, Company Fare, Buffet Dish, Cooking Classic

As colorful as a Fourth of July parade, this relish is a great addition to any summer gathering. It goes with everything from grilled salmon to baked ham.

1½ cups cider vinegar

2 tablespoons sugar

2 teaspoons plain (noniodized) salt

½ teaspoon celery seeds

½ teaspoon yellow mustard seeds

½ teaspoon ground turmeric

1¼ cups corn kernels (from 2 ears corn)

½ sweet onion, cut into ½-inch dice

½ red bell pepper, cored, seeded, and cut into ½-inch dice

1 small rib celery, cut into ½-inch dice

1 jalapeño, seeded and cut into ¼-inch dice

1. Bring the vinegar, sugar, salt, celery seeds, mustard seed, and turmeric to a boil in a medium saucepan over high heat, stirring often to dissolve the sugar and salt.

2. Stir in the corn, onion, bell pepper, celery, and jalapeño and return them to a boil. Reduce the heat to low and simmer until the celery is crisp-tender, about 3 minutes.

3. Using a slotted spoon, pack the vegetable mixture into a 1-quart canning jar. Pour in enough of the cooking liquid to cover the vegetables. Cover the jar with the lid. Let the jar stand until the relish reaches room temperature, about 2 hours. Refrigerate it overnight. (The relish can be refrigerated for up to 1 month.)

BLUEBERRY, LIME, AND ROSEMARY CHUTNEY

MAKES ABOUT 1¾ CUPS

Serve with roast pork, pork chops, baked ham, or roast or grilled chicken.

Prep Time: 10 minutes

Cooking Time: 10 minutes, plus about 2 hours refrigeration time

Make Ahead: The chutney can be refrigerated for up to 1 month.

Holiday Feasts, Company Fare, Buffet Dish, Vegetarian

*B*ecause of the alluring combination of sweet and savory in this deep purple chutney, I am sure to have a container of this in the refrigerator to serve with grilled meats and poultry throughout the summer. Unlike preserves with a high pectin content, it doesn't set on its own and needs a little help from cornstarch.

Two 6-ounce containers (about 2⅔ cups) fresh blueberries

6 tablespoons sugar

⅓ cup finely chopped shallots

¼ cup fruit-flavored (blueberry or pomegranate) or regular balsamic vinegar

1 tablespoon finely chopped fresh rosemary

Finely grated zest of 1 lime

3 tablespoons fresh lime juice

¼ cup hot red pepper flakes

1 teaspoon cornstarch dissolved in 1 tablespoon water

1. Combine the blueberries, sugar, shallots, vinegar, rosemary, lime zest and juice, and red pepper flakes in a medium nonreactive saucepan. Bring them to a simmer, stirring often to dissolve the sugar, over medium heat. Reduce the heat to low and simmer, stirring often, until the berries have burst and the juices are syrupy, about 10 minutes.

2. Stir in the dissolved cornstarch and return the pan to a simmer to lightly thicken the chutney. Let the chutney cool. Transfer it to a covered container and refrigerate until chilled, about 2 hours. (The chutney can be refrigerated for up to 1 month.) Serve it chilled or at room temperature.

FIG, RED WINE, AND HERB JAM
MAKES ABOUT 1¼ CUPS

Serve with pork roast, pork chops, ham, leg of lamb, lamb chops, or roast duck.

Prep Time: 10 minutes

Cooking Time: 10 minutes, plus 2 hours cooling

Make Ahead: The jam can be refrigerated for up to 1 month.

Holiday Feasts, Company Fare, Buffet Dish, Vegetarian

*F*aced with a rapidly ripening box of figs and a half-full bottle of red wine, and needing a side to go with an end-of-summer grill of lamb chops, I simmered up this not-too-sweet, almost savory jam. To say that it did the trick is an understatement. Leftovers are also excellent spooned over goat cheese to serve with crackers as an appetizer.

1 pound ripe figs (any variety), stemmed and coarsely chopped

¼ cup hearty red wine

¼ cup honey

Finely grated zest of ½ lemon

2 tablespoons fresh lemon juice

2 teaspoons finely chopped fresh rosemary

1 teaspoon finely chopped fresh thyme

¼ teaspoon freshly ground black pepper

Pinch of kosher salt

1. Combine the figs, wine, honey, lemon zest and juice, rosemary, thyme, pepper, and salt in a medium nonreactive saucepan. Bring them to a simmer over medium heat. Reduce the heat to low and simmer, stirring often, until the figs are very tender and the juices are syrupy, about 10 minutes.

2. Let the jam cool to room temperature, about 2 hours. (The jam can be refrigerated for up to 1 month.) Serve it at room temperature.

SPICED PEACHES WITH BOURBON
MAKES 1 QUART

Serve with barbecued meats or poultry, grilled pork chops, or baked ham.

Prep Time: 5 minutes

Cooking Time: 10 minutes, plus 8 hours refrigeration time

Make Ahead: The peaches can be refrigerated for up to 1 month.
Holiday Feasts, Company Fare, Buffet Dish, Vegetarian

At my local farmer's market, many vendors sell New Jersey peaches, and I can never buy too many. Needing a little something extra to serve with grilled pork chops, I created this when confronted with leftover peaches from making a pie, and I served them up with grilled smoked pork chops. The usual spice suspects (cinnamon and cloves) are simmered with ginger, star anise, and a bit of hot red pepper flakes to give these pickled peaches an extra kick. And the bourbon doesn't hurt, either.

5 large ripe (but not soft) freestone peaches

⅔ cup cider vinegar

½ cup packed light brown sugar

2 tablespoons bourbon

3 quarter-sized slices fresh ginger (no need to peel)

One 3-inch cinnamon stick

4 whole cloves

1 star anise

¼ teaspoon hot red pepper flakes

1. Have ready a hot, sterilized 1-quart canning jar (see page 412, step 3).

2. Bring a medium saucepan of water to a boil over high heat. In batches, add the peaches and boil until the skins loosen, about 30 seconds. Using a slotted spoon, transfer the peaches to a bowl of iced water. Let them stand until the peaches cool. Using a small, sharp knife, peel the peaches. Cut each peach into 5 wedges, discarding the pit. Put the peach wedges in the jar.

3. Bring 1⅓ cups water, the vinegar, brown sugar, bourbon, ginger, cinnamon stick, cloves, star anise, and red pepper flakes to a boil in a medium nonreactive saucepan over high heat, stirring often to dissolve the sugar. Pour the hot liquid into the jar to cover the peaches, being sure to add all of the solid ingredients to the jar. Close the jar with its lid and ring.

4. Let the jar stand until the peaches reach room temperature, about 2 hours. Refrigerate them overnight. (The peaches can be stored in the refrigerator for up to 1 month.)

Cranberry Sauces

Cranberry sauce is as important to Thanksgiving dinner as the turkey itself, so it is a mystery to me why so many people insist on serving the canned version at such an important meal. Homemade cranberry sauce literally takes a few minutes to make. Do yourself (and your friends and family) a favor, and make one of these wonderful sauces on the next fourth Thursday of November.

• Cranberries contain a high proportion of pectin, and when they are cooked with sugar, the pectin will set the sauce. The thickness of the berry juices during cooking indicate the consistency of the cooled sauce. Thin juices will yield a relatively thin, spoonable sauce, and thick, syrupy juices make a firm sauce.

• The sugar and acid in cranberry sauce make a very inhospitable place for bacteria, so the sauce will keep for at least two weeks in the refrigerator. I have often served Thanksgiving's sauce at New Year's without any problems. But in the Make Ahead section of the following recipes, I use two weeks as an average.

FRESH CRANBERRY SAUCE
MAKES 2¼ CUPS

Serve with roast turkey, roast pork, or baked ham.
Prep Time: 5 minutes
Cooking Time: 10 minutes, plus 2 hours refrigeration time
Make Ahead: The sauce can be refrigerated for up to 2 weeks.
Holiday Feasts, Company Fare, Buffet Dish, Cooking Classic, Vegetarian

As easy as this sauce is to make, it is difficult for me to understand how canned sauce became such an icon. Take a few minutes and make this beautiful sauce for a real treat.

One 12-ounce bag fresh cranberries   1 cup packed light or dark brown sugar

1. Bring the cranberries, brown sugar, and 1 cup water to a boil in a medium saucepan over medium heat. Reduce the heat to medium-low and cook, stirring occasionally, until the cranberries have all popped and the juices have thickened to a light-bodied syrup, about 10 minutes. The sauce will thicken more as it cools. Transfer the sauce to a small bowl and let it cool. Cover it tightly with plastic wrap. Refrigerate the sauce until chilled, at least 2 hours. (The sauce can be refrigerated for up to 2 weeks.) Serve it chilled or at room temperature.

JELLIED CRANBERRY-LEMON SAUCE
MAKES ABOUT 2½ CUPS

Serve with roast turkey, roast pork, or baked ham.
Prep Time: 10 minutes
Cooking Time: 10 minutes, plus 4 hours refrigeration time
Make Ahead: The sauce can be refrigerated for up to 2 days.
Holiday Feasts, Company Fare, Buffet Dish, Vegetarian

This sauce is smooth and jelly-like, without the texture of the berry skins. The lemon adds a nice spark of citrus flavor.

One 12-ounce bag fresh cranberries

1 cup sugar

Finely grated zest of 1 lemon

2 tablespoons fresh lemon juice

1 envelope unflavored powdered gelatin (about 2¼ teaspoons)

Vegetable oil, for the mold

1. Bring the cranberries, 1 cup water, the sugar, lemon zest, and lemon juice to a boil in a medium saucepan over medium heat, stirring to dissolve the sugar. Reduce the heat to medium-low and simmer gently until all of the cranberries have burst, 7 to 10 minutes. The mixture should look juicy and not reduced.

2. Meanwhile, sprinkle the gelatin over ¼ cup cold water in a small bowl. Let it stand until the gelatin swells and softens, about 5 minutes.

3. Remove the cranberry mixture from the stove. Add the softened gelatin and stir it well to completely dissolve the gelatin, about 1 minute. Pour the cranberry mixture into a wire sieve over a medium mixing bowl. Mash the sauce with the back of a flexible spatula, frequently scraping the outside of the strainer, until only the skins remain in the sieve. Stir the sauce well and discard the skins.

4. Lightly oil a 4- to 6-cup ring mold. Pour the sauce into the mold and let it cool to tepid. Cover it tightly with plastic wrap. Refrigerate the mold until it is chilled and set, at least 4 hours. (The sauce can be prepared up to 2 days ahead.)

5. To unmold the sauce, run a knife around the inside of the mold to loosen the sauce. Dip the mold up to the rim in a larger bowl of warm water for 5 to 10 seconds. Dry the outside of the mold and place a serving plate on top. Invert the mold and plate together to unmold the sauce. Serve it chilled.

SOUTHERN CRANBERRY SAUCE

MAKES ABOUT 3 CUPS

Serve with roast turkey, roast pork, or baked ham.

Prep Time: 10 minutes

Cooking Time: 10 minutes, plus 2 hours refrigeration time

Make Ahead: The sauce can be refrigerated for up to 2 weeks.

Holiday Feasts, Company Fare, Buffet Dish, Vegetarian

Bourbon, fresh ginger, and orange give this cranberry sauce a tasty profile that makes it difficult to stop eating. Do not add the bourbon until after the sauce has cooled, though, or much of its flavor will evaporate in the steam. If you wish, add ½ cup seedless raisins to the finished sauce.

One 12-ounce bag fresh cranberries

1 cup packed light brown sugar

Finely grated zest of 1 orange

3 tablespoons fresh orange juice

2 tablespoons peeled and minced fresh ginger

2 tablespoons bourbon

1. Combine the cranberries, brown sugar, orange zest and juice, ginger, and 1 cup water in a medium nonreactive saucepan. Bring them to a boil over medium heat, stirring often to help dissolve the brown sugar.

2. Reduce the heat to medium-low and simmer, stirring often, until all of the cranberries have burst and the juices have thickened to a light syrup, 7 to 10 minutes. Let the sauce cool until tepid. Stir in the bourbon. Transfer the sauce to a covered container and refrigerate it until chilled, at least 2 hours or up to 2 weeks. Serve the sauce chilled or at room temperature.

MULLED CIDER–CRANBERRY SAUCE

MAKES ABOUT 3 CUPS

Serve with roast turkey or baked ham.

Prep Time: 5 minutes

Cook Time: 10 minutes, plus 2 hours refrigeration time

Make Ahead: The sauce can be refrigerated for up to 2 weeks.

Family Favorite, Holiday Feasts, Company Fare, Buffet Dish, Vegetarian

Mulled cider is one of the icons of cold-weather cooking. If you like that aromatic brew, you will love this cranberry sauce with the welcome additions of apple cider and warm spices.

One 3-inch cinnamon stick

1 star anise

6 whole cloves

6 whole allspice

¾ cup apple cider

One 12-ounce bag fresh cranberries

¾ cup packed light brown sugar

1. Rinse and wring a 6-inch square of cheesecloth. Wrap the cinnamon, star anise, cloves, and allspice together in the cheesecloth and tie it with kitchen twine.

2. Bring the spice packet and cider to a simmer in a medium saucepan over low heat. Stir in the cranberries and brown sugar, increase the heat to medium, and bring them to a boil. Cook, stirring often, until all of the cranberries have burst and the juices have thickened to a light syrup, 7 to 10 minutes.

3. Transfer the sauce with the spice packet to a covered container. Let it cool completely. Discard the spice packet. Cover and refrigerate the sauce until chilled, at least 2 hours and up to 2 weeks. Serve the sauce chilled or at room temperature.

CRANBERRY AND DRIED PINEAPPLE MOSTARDA

MAKES ABOUT 4 CUPS

Serve with roast turkey, baked ham, or roast pork.
Prep Time: 10 minutes
Cooking Time: 10 minutes, plus 2 hours refrigeration time
Make Ahead: The sauce can be refrigerated for up to 2 weeks.
Holiday Feasts, Company Fare, Buffet Dish, Vegetarian

Mostarda is an Italian condiment of candied fruits and mustard oil. My version uses mustard seeds and dried mustard, which are much easier to find than mustard oil. I served this with my Christmas ham this year, and many thank-you notes mentioned the cranberry mostarda as "the best cranberry sauce ever." This wasn't empty praise, as the sharp mustard and sweet-tart cranberries did a delicious balancing act. I use dried pineapple because it holds its shape in cooked sauces better than fresh chunks.

One 12-ounce bag fresh cranberries
2 cups diced dried pineapple (9 ounces)
1½ cups sugar

3 tablespoons mustard seeds
2 tablespoons dry mustard powder

1. Combine the cranberries, dried pineapple, sugar, mustard seeds, and ¼ cup water in a medium nonreactive saucepan. Bring them to a boil over medium heat, stirring often to help dissolve the sugar.
2. Reduce the heat to medium-low and simmer, stirring often, until all of the cranberries have burst and the juices have thickened to a light syrup, 7 to 10 minutes.
3. In a small bowl, dissolve the dry mustard in 2 tablespoons water, and stir it into the cranberry sauce. Transfer the sauce to a covered container and refrigerate it until chilled, at least 2 hours or up to 2 weeks. Serve the sauce chilled or at room temperature.

TWO RELISH-TRAY CLASSICS

Here is a pair of relish-tray icons that are beloved by my family and friends. Stuffed celery and deviled eggs may be familiar, but when you make them with care, they are not mundane.

STUFFED CELERY WITH LIPTAUER CHEESE SPREAD

MAKES 8 TO 12 SERVINGS

Serve as part of a relish tray for a holiday meal.
Prep Time: 15 minutes, plus at least 2 hours refrigeration time

Make Ahead: The celery sticks can be made up to 1 day ahead.

Family Favorite, Holiday Feasts, Company Fare, Buffet Dish, Vegetarian

When I wrote a book on Austro-Hungarian desserts, I savored my time in Budapest, where I learned to appreciate that country's beautifully seasoned food. Liptauer cheese is put on the table in almost every restaurant as a spiced (but not spicy) bread topping. I immediately saw its promise as a stuffing for celery. Its provenance is Lipto, a sheep's milk cheese from a northern province in Hungary of the same name. Lipto isn't easy to find, but a combination of goat and cream cheeses makes a good substitute. Any soft cheese will do, and some recipes use farmer's cheese, quark, or even sieved cottage cheese. And while you can add a couple of tablespoons of finely chopped cornichons or capers (or both), I like my Liptauer relatively smooth.

4 ounces rindless goat cheese (chèvre), such as Bucheron, at room temperature

4 ounces cream cheese, at room temperature

¼ cup (½ stick) unsalted butter, at room temperature

2 tablespoons minced yellow onion

2 teaspoons sweet paprika

1 teaspoon caraway seed, toasted in a skillet, cooled, and crushed in a mortar

1 teaspoon stone-ground mustard

1 teaspoon anchovy paste

8 celery ribs

1. Using a rubber spatula, mash the goat cheese, cream cheese, butter, onion, paprika, caraway seed, mustard, and anchovy paste together in a medium bowl.

2. Transfer the cheese to a pastry bag fitted with a ½-inch fluted pastry tip. Pipe the cheese into the celery. Arrange the celery, side by side, on a baking sheet and refrigerate it until the cheese is firm, about 1 hour. Cut the celery into 2- to 3-inch lengths. Return them to the baking sheet, cover loosely with plastic wrap, and refrigerate until ready to serve, at least 1 hour and up to 1 day. Serve the celery chilled or at room temperature.

DEVILED EGGS WITH HORSERADISH AND BACON

MAKES 8 TO 12 SERVINGS

Serve as part of a relish tray for a holiday meal.

Prep Time: 10 minutes

Cooking Time: 25 minutes, plus 20 minutes chilling time

Make Ahead: The prepared eggs can be made up to 1 day ahead.

Family Favorite, Holiday Feasts, Company Fare, Buffet Dish

Deviled eggs are must-haves on most relish trays. This is one of my favorite ways to dress them up, with fresh horseradish and crisp bacon. Interestingly, vinegar acts as a fixative to the

horseradish, preventing it from losing its heat. If you wish, substitute drained prepared horse-radish for the fresh horseradish and vinegar, and skip the shredded horseradish garnish.

• You can always just spoon the filling into the yolks, but the pastry bag gives the filling a nice tailored look. Be sure to mince the scallion and celery very fine so they don't clog the pastry tip.

1 dozen large eggs
1 tablespoon peeled and finely grated fresh horseradish (use the small holes on a box shredder), plus more for garnish
1 teaspoon white distilled vinegar
½ cup mayonnaise

1 scallion (white and pale green parts), minced
1 small celery rib, minced
Kosher salt and freshly ground black pepper
2 slices bacon

1. Place the eggs in a single layer in a large saucepan. Add enough cold water to cover the eggs by ½ inch. Bring them to a simmer (the pot will be filled with small bubbles) over high heat. Remove the pan from the heat and cover. Let it stand for 15 minutes. Using a slotted spoon, transfer the eggs to a bowl of iced water. Let them stand until the eggs are chilled, about 20 minutes.

2. Crack and peel the eggs. Cut each egg in half lengthwise. Remove the egg yolks and reserve the whites.

3. In a medium bowl, mix the horseradish and vinegar together. Rub the egg yolks through a coarse wire sieve with a rubber spatula into the bowl. Stir in the mayonnaise, scallion, and celery. Season to taste with salt and pepper.

4. Transfer the yolk mixture to a pastry bag fitted with a ½-inch fluted pastry tip. Pipe the mixture into the egg whites. (You can also simply spoon the mixture into the whites. Or transfer the yolk mixture into a plastic storage bag, snip off one corner of the bag, and use it as an impromptu pastry bag without the tip.) Arrange the eggs, filled-sides up, in a shallow dish. Cover them loosely with plastic wrap and refrigerate until chilled, at least 1 hour. (The eggs can be made up to 1 day ahead.)

5. Meanwhile, cook the bacon in a medium skillet over medium heat, turning it occasionally, until it is crisp and browned, about 8 minutes. Transfer the bacon to paper towels to drain. Let it cool. Coarsely chop the bacon.

6. Just before serving, top the eggs with the bacon. Grate fresh horseradish over the eggs and serve them chilled.

Sauces

When I was a culinary student, we were taught about the classic five sauces of French cuisine, from which many others are formulated. The quintet (there will not be a quiz later) are béchamel (white sauce), velouté, espagnole (brown sauce), hollandaise (the yolk-emulsified butter sauce), and tomate (a light tomato sauce). Only a couple of these are truly useful to today's cooks. The only time I make a béchamel now is as the base for macaroni and cheese. Instead, my repertoire of sauces is global, with recipes from Italy, the Middle East, Mexico, and elsewhere. I have purposely made this a short list of the sauces and condiments that I personally turn to again and again when the main course (usually a protein) needs a bit of dressing up.

PESTO
MAKES ABOUT 1 CUP

Serve as a condiment to roast and grilled meats, poultry, or seafood.
Prep Time: 10 minutes
Make Ahead: The pesto can be refrigerated for up to 1 month.
Weeknight Suppers, Family Favorite, Holiday Feasts, Cooking Classic, Vegetarian

Pesto is undoubtedly one of the most indispensable ingredients in a good cook's kitchen. And now that basil is available all year, pesto can be made whenever the mood strikes. Use pesto as a condiment for roasts, steaks, and chops, or stir it into sauces or vegetables as a flavoring. Check out the variations for ways to use other full-flavored leafy ingredients (kale or ramps) instead of the basil.

• Basil has a tendency to darken when it comes into contact with hot food, so the additional chlorophyll provided by the parsley is helpful to keep the green color.
• If you wish, substitute walnuts, pistachios, or almonds for the traditional pine nuts.
• Pesto is often tossed with boiled foods, such as pasta or potatoes. A few tablespoons of the cooking water should be added to lightly thin the pesto.
• To freeze pesto, leave out the Parmesan cheese, and transfer the pesto to an airtight container. Just before serving, stir the Parmesan into the thawed pesto.

2 garlic cloves, crushed under a knife and peeled
2 cups packed fresh basil leaves
¼ cup pine nuts or finely chopped walnuts or pecans

½ cup freshly grated Parmesan cheese (2 ounces)
¼ cup coarsely chopped fresh flat-leaf parsley
½ cup extra-virgin olive oil, plus more for storage
Kosher salt and freshly ground black pepper

1. With a food processor running, drop the garlic cloves through the feed tube to finely chop them. Stop the machine, add the basil, pine nuts, Parmesan, and parsley, and pulse a few times to coarsely chop the mixture. With the machine running, gradually pour the oil through the feed tube. (Or process the ingredients in batches in a blender.) Season to taste with salt and pepper.

2. Use the pesto immediately, or transfer it to a container. Pour a thin layer of oil on top of the pesto, cover the container, and refrigerate it until ready to serve. (The pesto can be refrigerated for up to 1 month. After using, smooth the top of the remaining pesto, and cover it with additional oil.)

Kale Pesto: This pesto is excellent tossed with boiled potatoes. Substitute one 8-ounce bunch Tuscan (also called lacinato or dinosaur) kale for the basil. Strip the leaves from the stems, discarding the stems. Coarsely chop the leaves; you should have about 2 packed cups. Substitute walnuts for the pine nuts. Leave out the parsley.

Ramp Pesto: I love this tossed with a sturdy pasta, such as ziti, and bit of the pasta's cooking water. Substitute 1 cup well-washed and coarsely chopped ramps for the basil. Leave out the garlic.

ITALIAN SALSA VERDE
MAKES ABOUT ¾ CUP

Serve with fish fillets, shrimp, steaks, or chops.
Prep Time: 10 minutes, plus 2 hours refrigeration time
Make Ahead: The salsa can be made up to 8 hours ahead.
Weeknight Suppers, Holiday Feasts, Company Fare, Buffet Dish, Cooking Classic

Salsa means "sauce" in Italian, as well as Spanish. This bright green condiment is similar to pesto, but with even more flavor, if that is possible. Mustard, capers, anchovy, garlic, and red pepper flakes all do their stuff to turn parsley into a bold room-temperature sauce. Just a spoonful of salsa verde goes a long way with seafood and meats. It tastes best the day it is made.

1 garlic clove, peeled	Finely grated zest of 1 lemon
2 packed cups fresh flat-leaf parsley	¼ teaspoon hot red pepper flakes
2 tablespoons nonpareil capers, drained	½ cup extra-virgin olive oil
1 teaspoon Dijon mustard	Kosher salt

1. With a food processor running, drop the garlic through the feed tube to finely chop it. Stop the food processor, add the parsley, capers, mustard, lemon zest, and red pepper flakes. Pulse the processor a few times to finely chop the mixture. With the machine running, gradually add the oil through the feed tube. (Or process the ingredients in batches in a blender.) Season to taste with salt.

2. Transfer the salsa to a bowl. Cover it tightly with plastic wrap and refrigerate it for at least 2 hours and up to 8 hours to blend the flavors. Serve the salsa at room temperature.

FIRE-KISSED RANCHERO SALSA

MAKES ABOUT 2½ CUPS

Serve with grilled meats, poultry, or seafood.

Prep Time: 10 minutes

Cooking Time: 10 minutes

Make Ahead: The salsa can be made up to 5 days ahead.

Family Favorite, Holiday Feasts, Company Fare, Buffet Dish, Cooking Classic, Vegetarian

Most salsas are made from raw ingredients, especially when they are served with chips. But for a main course, I prefer a cooked salsa. The cooking heightens the vegetables' flavors and gives them a less firm texture that I think goes well with grilled meats. If you wish, grill the vegetables on a perforated grill grate to the same degrees of doneness indicated for direct medium-high heat (see page 326).

1 small yellow onion, cut into ½-inch rings	1 jalapeño
4 garlic cloves, unpeeled	2 tablespoons fresh lime juice
1 tablespoon vegetable oil	2 tablespoons coarsely chopped fresh cilantro
6 plum (Roma) tomatoes	Kosher salt

1. Position a broiler rack about 6 inches from the source of heat and preheat the broiler on high.

2. In a large bowl, toss the onion rings and garlic with the oil. Put the tomatoes, jalapeño, onion rings, and garlic on the broiler rack. Broil, turning occasionally, until the tomatoes and jalapeño are blistered and blackened, and the onion rings and garlic are charred with brown spots, about 5 minutes. Remove the vegetables from the broiler and let them cool.

3. Remove the skins from the tomatoes. Cut each tomato in half and poke out the gel and seeds with your forefinger. Peel the garlic. Remove the skin from the jalapeño, then cut it in half lengthwise and remove the seeds.

4. In batches, purée the vegetables, lime juice, and cilantro in a blender. Season to taste with salt. Serve immediately. (The salsa can be covered and refrigerated for up to 1 week.)

GREEN TOMATILLO SALSA

MAKES ABOUT 2½ CUPS

Serve with pork chops, salmon, or shrimp.

Prep Time: 15 minutes

Cooking Time: 10 minutes, plus 1 hour refrigeration time

Make Ahead: The salsa can be made up to 1 week ahead.

Holiday Feasts, Company Fare, Buffet Dish, Retro Recipe, Cooking Classic, Vegetarian

I spent my first semester in college at the University of Guadalajara, where I learned more about Mexican cooking than I did Spanish grammar. This pleasantly tart sauce has served me well since then to accompany pork chops, salmon, and shrimp. In fact, I try to keep some in the freezer to have at the ready. Be sure to let the ingredients cool before puréeing because hot vegetables will create a force of steam in the blender that could splash hot salsa all over the kitchen . . . and you.

1½ pounds tomatillos, papery husks removed

2 tablespoons olive oil

½ cup chopped white or yellow onion

2 garlic cloves, finely chopped

1 jalapeño, seeded and finely chopped

3 tablespoons coarsely chopped fresh cilantro

Kosher salt

1. Position a broiler rack about 6 inches from the source of heat and preheat the broiler on high.

2. Put the tomatillos on the broiler rack and broil, turning occasionally, until they are charred in spots and turn olive green, about 10 minutes. Do not cook the tomatillos until they burst. Remove them from the broiler.

3. Heat the oil in a medium skillet over medium heat. Add the onion, garlic, and jalapeño and cook, stirring occasionally, until the onion softens, about 3 minutes. Stir in the tomatillos and cook, breaking them up with the side of a spoon, until the tomatillos are completely tender, about 3 minutes. Remove the pan from the heat and let the vegetables cool.

4. Stir in the cilantro. In batches, purée the tomatillo mixture in a blender. Season to taste with salt. Transfer it to a covered container and refrigerate it until ready to serve, at least 1 hour. (The salsa can be covered and refrigerated for up to 1 week.)

MANGO-HABANERO KETCHUP

MAKES ABOUT I CUP

Serve with beef, pork, or poultry burgers; or grilled meats or poultry.

Prep Time: 10 minutes, plus 1 hour refrigeration time

Make Ahead: The ketchup can be refrigerated for up to 1 week.

Weeknight Suppers, Company Fare, Buffet Dish, Vegetarian

The blazing hot, Caribbean-inspired flavor of this sunset-orange hot sauce gets its zip from Tam o' Shanter–shaped habaneros. It's a good idea to wear rubber gloves when prepping these chilies, as their oils can cling to your skin for hours. Try the ketchup on burgers, especially when the patties are made from ground pork, chicken, or turkey.

2 garlic cloves, crushed under a knife and peeled

2 habanero or Scotch bonnet chilies, seeded and coarsely chopped

1 large ripe mango, peeled, pitted, and coarsely chopped (see Note)

1 scallion (white and green parts), coarsely chopped

Finely grated zest of 1 lime

2 tablespoons fresh lime juice

2 tablespoons coarsely chopped fresh cilantro

½ teaspoon kosher salt

1. With the machine running, drop the garlic and chilies through the hole in the lid of a blender (or the feed tube of a food processor) to mince the garlic. Add the mango, scallion, lime zest and juice, cilantro, and salt and purée. Transfer the ketchup to a covered container and refrigerate it for 1 hour to blend the flavors. (The ketchup can be refrigerated for up to 1 week.) Serve it chilled or at room temperature.

Note: To peel a mango, place the fruit on the work surface, where it will balance itself. As the mango lies on the counter, the pit runs horizontally through the center of the fruit. Don't cut vertically into the fruit, or you'll run into the pit. Use a sharp knife to cut off the top of the fruit just above the pit. Turn the mango over and cut off the other end of the fruit. Using a large metal spoon, scoop the mango flesh from each portion in one piece. The peeled mango can now be cut as the recipe requires. Pare the pit portion with a small knife, and eat the flesh from the pit as your treat.

FRESH HORSERADISH CREAM

MAKES ABOUT 1 ½ CUPS

Serve with roast beef or as part of a Passover Seder menu.
Prep Time: 10 minutes, plus refrigeration time
Make Ahead: The sauce can be made up to 1 month ahead.
Holiday Feasts, Company Fare, Buffet Dish, Cooking Classic

*F*resh *horseradish has a vibrancy that the bottled version lacks. Its flavor dissipates as the flesh is exposed to the air, but vinegar acts as a fixative. This incredible condiment is nothing but horseradish, vinegar, and salt processed to a creamy sauce, so if you aren't sure of the tolerance level of your guests, make the sour cream variation. Remember that horseradish is very spicy, and avoid inhaling the fumes as the cream is grinding in the food processor.*

8 ounces fresh horseradish

Ice water, as needed

2 tablespoons distilled white vinegar

Kosher salt

1. Using a sturdy vegetable peeler, peel the horseradish. Chop the horseradish into 1-inch chunks. Immediately transfer the horseradish to a food processor and add ¼ cup ice water. Process, adding more ice water as needed, to make a rough purée. If you want the cream to be very spicy, add the vinegar now. For a milder cream, let the purée stand for 3 to 5 minutes, then add the vinegar. Pulse the cream to combine, and season with salt.

2. Transfer the cream to a container, cover, and refrigerate it until ready to serve. (The cream can be refrigerated for up to 1 month, or frozen for up to 3 months.)

Sour Cream with Fresh Horseradish and Chives: In a bowl, whisk together 1 cup sour cream, 3 tablespoons Horseradish Cream, and 2 tablespoons finely chopped fresh chives. Use as a sauce for roast beef or roast beef sandwiches.

BACON, ONION, AND BOURBON MARMALADE
MAKES ABOUT 2¼ CUPS

Serve with corned beef, hamburgers or sandwiches; pork roast;
pork chops; ham, sausages, barbecued meats or poultry; or grilled salmon.
Prep Time: 10 minutes
Cooking Time: 45 minutes, plus 1 hour refrigeration time
Make Ahead: The marmalade can be refrigerated for up to 3 weeks.
Holiday Feasts, Company Fare, Buffet Dish

This seriously indulgent amalgamation takes some of the most popular flavors from the collective American palate (caramelized onions, smoky bacon, maple syrup, balsamic vinegar . . . and booze) and melds them together. It makes a holiday spread of pork roast or sliced ham even more festive, and raises a weekend burger or barbecue dinner to new heights. Use the extra-thick bacon (sometimes called butcher-sliced) for this recipe so the pieces retain their character in the marmalade.

8 ounces super-thick sliced hickory- or applewood-
    smoked bacon, cut crosswise into 1-inch pieces
3 pounds yellow onions, cut into thin half-moons
Kosher salt and freshly ground black pepper

¼ cup balsamic vinegar
¼ cup maple syrup, preferably Grade A Dark
¼ cup bourbon
1½ teaspoons finely chopped fresh thyme

1. Cook the bacon in a large, deep skillet over medium heat, stirring occasionally, adjusting the temperature so the bacon cooks evenly but the glaze in the bottom of the skillet does not burn, until the bacon is crisp and browned, about 10 minutes. Transfer the bacon to paper towels to drain, leaving the fat in the skillet.
2. Stir in the onions with 1 teaspoon salt and ½ teaspoon pepper. (You may have to add the onions in two batches, cooking the first batch for a few minutes to shrink and make room for the remaining onions.) Cover the skillet and cook, stirring occasionally, until the onions are softened, about 5 minutes. Reduce the heat to medium-low. Cook, uncovered, stirring occasionally, until the onions are very tender and golden brown, about 25 minutes.
3. Stir in the reserved bacon with the vinegar, maple syrup, bourbon, and thyme and bring them to a simmer over medium heat. Return the heat to medium-low and simmer, stirring often, until the liq-

uids have reduced to a few tablespoons and the mixture is thick and spreadable, about 10 minutes. Transfer it to a bowl and let it cool. (The marmalade can be refrigerated in a covered container for up to 3 weeks. Remove it from the refrigerator 1 hour before serving.) Serve the marmalade at room temperature.

ROMESCO
MAKES ABOUT 1 CUP

Serve with steak; veal, lamb, and pork chops; halibut and other firm, white fish; or shrimp.
Prep Time: 10 minutes
Cooking Time: 15 minutes (for the peppers), plus 2 hours refrigeration time
Make Ahead: The romesco can be made up to 2 weeks ahead.
Holiday Feasts, Company Fare, Buffet Dish, Cooking Classic

A thick Spanish sauce served at room temperature, romesco has many uses in the side dish world. Try it on baked, steamed, or roasted cauliflower or potatoes, or serve it with grilled meats or as a sandwich spread. Romesco keeps very well, so consider making a double batch.

2 garlic cloves, crushed under a knife and peeled
3 red bell peppers, roasted (see page 77), skinned, cored, seeded, and coarsely chopped
½ cup sliced natural almonds
1 tablespoon sherry or red wine vinegar

1½ teaspoons sweet paprika, preferably smoked, such as Pimentón de la Vera
½ teaspoon dried oregano
½ cup extra-virgin olive oil
Kosher salt and freshly ground black pepper

1. With a food processor running, drop the garlic through the feed tube to finely chop it. Stop the food processor and add the bell peppers, almonds, vinegar, paprika, and oregano. Pulse the processor a few times to finely chop the mixture. Scrape down the sides of the work bowl. With the machine running, gradually add the oil through the feed tube to make a coarse purée. Season to taste with salt and pepper.
2. Transfer the romesco to a small bowl. Cover it tightly with plastic wrap and refrigerate it for at least 2 hours to blend the flavors. (The romesco can be refrigerated for up to 2 weeks.)

MUHAMMARA
MAKES ABOUT 1⅓ CUPS

Serve with lamb kebabs, leg of lamb, lamb burgers, hamburgers, or seafood.
Prep Time: 10 minutes
Cooking Time: 15 minutes (for the peppers), plus 2 hours refrigeration time

Make Ahead: The muhammara can be made up to 1 week ahead.

Holiday Feasts, Company Fare, Buffet Dish, Vegetarian

Muhammara resembles a Middle Eastern romesco, with roasted peppers and nuts ground together to make a thick sauce that can also be served as a dip. Of course, the seasonings are entirely different, with the sweet tang of pomegranate molasses and warm Aleppo pepper. Serve this on lamb burgers or even beef burgers

2 garlic cloves, crushed under a knife and peeled

2 red bell peppers, roasted (see page 77), skinned, cored, seeded, and coarsely chopped

½ cup soft bread crumbs, made in a food processor or blender from slightly stale crusty bread

⅓ cup coarsely chopped walnuts

1 tablespoon pomegranate molasses (see Note, page 316) or fresh lemon juice

1 teaspoon Aleppo pepper or ½ teaspoon sweet paprika

¼ teaspoon hot red pepper flakes

½ cup extra-virgin olive oil

Kosher salt

1. With a food processor running, drop the garlic through the feed tube to finely chop it. Stop the food processor and add the bell peppers, bread crumbs, walnuts, pomegranate molasses, Aleppo pepper, and red pepper flakes. Pulse the processor a few times to finely chop the mixture. With the machine running, gradually add the oil through the feed tube and process until the mixture is ground into a rough sauce, about 30 seconds. Season to taste with salt.

2. Transfer the muhammara to a medium bowl. Cover it tightly with plastic wrap and refrigerate it for at least 2 hours to blend the flavors. (The muhammara can be refrigerated for up to 1 week.)

TZATZIKI
MAKES ABOUT 1 ½ CUPS

Serve with grilled fish fillets and shrimp; butterflied leg of lamb; or pork or lamb chops.

Prep Time: 10 minutes, plus 30 minutes standing and 1 hour refrigeration time

Make Ahead: The tzatziki can be made up to 2 days ahead.

Family Favorite, Holiday Feasts, Company Fare, Buffet Dish, Cooking Classic, Vegetarian

Tzatziki can be served as a dip with pita bread, and I often order it that way at my local Greek restaurant. But it is also a fantastic condiment for grilled fish and meats. It is almost, but not quite, a cucumber-yogurt salad, but the cucumber should be finely diced so it has a chunky sauce consistency. As simple as this recipe is, there are a few tricks. To keep the sauce from thinning out, salt the cucumber before chopping to remove excess juices and use thick Greek yogurt. And allow at least one hour to chill the tzatziki to blend the flavors.

2 large standard cucumbers

Kosher salt

1 tablespoon white or red wine vinegar

3 tablespoons extra-virgin olive oil

1 cup plain low-fat or whole-milk Greek yogurt

1 tablespoon finely chopped fresh dill

1 garlic clove, crushed through a garlic press

Freshly ground black pepper

1. Peel the cucumbers. Cut each in half lengthwise. Using the tip of a dessert spoon, scoop out and discard the seeds. Cut the cucumbers into ¼- to ½-inch dice. Transfer them to a colander and toss with 2 teaspoons salt. Let them stand on a plate at room temperature to drain, for at least 30 minutes and up to 1 hour.

2. In a medium bowl, whisk the vinegar and gradually whisk in the oil. Whisk in the yogurt, dill, and garlic.

3. A handful at a time, wrap the diced cucumbers in a clean kitchen towel, wring the towel to squeeze excess liquid from the cucumbers, and add them to the yogurt mixture. Mix well and season to taste with pepper. Cover the bowl tightly with plastic wrap and refrigerate it for at least 1 hour and up to 2 days. Serve chilled.

BEURRE BLANC

MAKES ABOUT ⅔ CUP

Serve with seafood or poultry, or as a sauce for asparagus, artichokes, broccoli, or cauliflower.
Prep Time: 5 minutes
Cooking Time: 10 minutes
Make Ahead: The sauce can be made up to ½ hour ahead.
Weeknight Suppers, Family Favorite, Holiday Feasts, Company Fare, Cooking Classic, Vegetarian

Beurre blanc (which means "white butter" in French, and is an indication of its color) is a butter sauce every bit as luxurious as its cousin, hollandaise. And there are no concerns about raw eggs. Once you learn how to make beurre blanc, you may find yourself whipping it up at a moment's notice, as I do. To create its creamy consistency, the butter must soften and not melt, so keep the heat low.

1 cup dry white wine, such as Sauvignon Blanc or Pinot Grigio

2 tablespoons white wine vinegar

2 tablespoons chopped shallots

1 cup (2 sticks) cold unsalted butter, cut into ½-inch pieces

Kosher salt and freshly ground white or black pepper

1. Bring the wine, vinegar, and shallots to a boil in a small nonreactive saucepan over high heat. Cook until the mixture is reduced to about 2 tablespoons, 5 to 7 minutes.

2. Reduce the heat to its lowest setting. Add the butter pieces to the saucepan a few at a time, whisking constantly until the butter softens into a creamy sauce but does not melt. Continue adding the butter, whisking until each addition softens into a sauce before adding more. Strain the sauce through a wire sieve into a heatproof bowl. Season to taste with salt and pepper. Serve it immediately, or keep the sauce warm by setting the bowl in a small skillet of barely simmering water over very low heat for up to 30 minutes.

Beurre Blanc with Herbs: Add 1½ teaspoons finely chopped fresh tarragon or chives to the sauce.
Beurre Rouge: This sauce is incredible with steak. Substitute hearty red wine, such as Shiraz, for the white wine.

HOMEMADE SWEET AND HOT ALE MUSTARD
MAKES ABOUT 1 ½ CUPS

Serve with roast beef, beef brisket, corned beef; steak, hamburgers; roast veal, veal chops; pork roast, pork chops, sausages, or hot dogs.
Prep Time: 10 minutes, plus 1 to 2 days soaking time
Aging Time: 1 week
Make Ahead: The mustard can be refrigerated for at least 3 months.
Holiday Feasts, Company Fare, Buffet Dish, Retro Recipe

Homemade mustard is so easy to make, it is a wonder that every cook doesn't do so. The most difficult part is the aging period, as the mustard must be exposed to oxygen for its hot flavor to dissipate. When I serve this with sausages or hot dogs, it becomes the subject of conversation, no matter how great the sausages may be. This recipe makes a lot of mustard, but it keeps forever in the refrigerator.

¾ cup pale ale

¾ cup brown mustard seeds (see Note)

½ cup balsamic vinegar (an inexpensive
  supermarket variety)

⅓ cup light brown sugar

1¼ teaspoons kosher salt

½ teaspoon freshly ground black pepper

½ teaspoon Chinese five-spice powder

1. Start the mustard at least 1 week before using. Mix the ingredients together in a non-aluminum bowl. Cover it with plastic wrap and let it stand at room temperature for at least 1 and up to 2 days to soften the mustard seeds and mellow the flavor.
2. Transfer the mixture to a food processor and process it for 2 to 3 minutes to make a thick, coarse purée. Transfer the mustard to a covered container and refrigerate it for at least 1 week to mellow before using. (The mustard can be refrigerated for at least 3 months.)

Note: Be sure to buy brown mustard seeds, as there is a difference between these and the common black seeds that can be purchased at Indian markets. Black mustard seeds are most often used in small quantities in Indian cooking to flavor oil in a sauté. I once had to throw out a very large batch of mustard made from black seeds. You may also want to use half yellow mustard seeds to make a milder condiment. Brown mustard seeds are easy to find in bulk at spice stores and online.

TOMATO AND RED PEPPER KETCHUP

MAKES ABOUT 1¾ CUPS

Serve with meat loaf, hamburgers, hot dogs, sandwiches, or French fries.
Prep Time: 15 minutes
Cooking Time: 1 hour, plus 1 day refrigeration time
Make Ahead: The ketchup can be made up to 2 weeks ahead.
Family Favorite, Holiday Feasts, Company Fare, Buffet Dish

I love seeing my friends' eyes light up when they taste this ketchup for the first time. It is just what they expect . . . only better, with a little extra spice. No one can believe that it is homemade.

One 28-ounce can crushed tomatoes
1 red bell pepper, cored, seeded, and
  chopped
¼ cup honey
3 tablespoons cider vinegar
2 tablespoons finely chopped onion
1 small garlic clove, crushed through a
  garlic press
1 tablespoon light brown sugar

1 teaspoon kosher salt
⅛ teaspoon freshly ground black pepper
⅛ teaspoon hot red pepper flakes
Pinch of ground allspice
Pinch of ground cloves
Pinch of celery seeds
Pinch of yellow mustard seeds
½ bay leaf

1. At least 1 day before serving, bring all of the ingredients to a boil in a medium, heavy-bottomed saucepan over medium heat, stirring often. Reduce the heat to medium-low. Cook at a brisk simmer, stirring often to avoid scorching, until the ketchup has thickened and reduced by half, about 1 hour.
2. Rub the ketchup through a wire mesh strainer into a medium bowl, discarding any solids that do not pass through the sieve. Let it cool completely. Transfer it to a covered container and refrigerate it for at least 18 hours to blend the flavors. (The ketchup can be stored, refrigerated in an airtight container, for up to 2 weeks.)

MAYONNAISE

MAKES ABOUT 1 CUP

Serve with cold meat and fish main courses; sandwiches or burgers; or as a salad ingredient.

Prep Time: 10 minutes

Make Ahead: The mayonnaise can be made up to 3 days ahead.

Family Favorite, Holiday Feasts, Company Fare, Buffet Dish

I promise: Making your own mayonnaise is easy. And it is a simple way to ramp up your cooking, especially with salads. I learned to whip up mayo with a whisk, but now modern appliances speed the job and cut down on the fear of curdling and poor emulsification from lazy whisking. An electric hand mixer is my favorite tool because a bowl is easier to clean than a food processor or blender. Master mayonnaise, and then expand your repertoire with one of the many variations.

• If you are concerned with the risks of raw eggs, use a pasteurized egg (available at natural food stores and many supermarkets). At the very least, use an uncracked egg from organically raised hens.

• The egg must be warm to accept the oil, so don't use cold eggs. I actually warm the egg (in the shell) in hot water to ensure the right temperature.

• The mustard is not optional because it has a double purpose as a flavoring and a thickening agent.

• Don't use extra-virgin olive oil because its acidity can cause curdling—and it makes a heavy sauce, too. A blend of regular olive oil and vegetable oil works best.

• And even though you will be using a whiz-fast mixer of some kind, add the oil slowly to the egg mixture so it can emulsify properly.

1 large egg, preferably pasteurized	½ cup olive oil (not extra-virgin)
1 teaspoon fresh lemon juice	¼ cup canola or vegetable oil
1 teaspoon Dijon mustard	Kosher salt and freshly ground black pepper

1. Put the egg in a small bowl and add enough hot tap water to cover. Let it stand for 2 to 3 minutes to warm the egg.

2. To make the mayonnaise with a handheld electric mixer: Crack the egg into a medium bowl. Add the lemon juice and mustard. Mix the olive and canola oils together in a liquid measuring cup. Beat the egg mixture with an electric hand mixer on high speed. (Do not use a standing mixer, as there is not enough volume in the ingredients to mix properly.) Gradually drizzle in the oil mixture—it should take at least a minute to do this—to make a thick mayonnaise.

To make the mayonnaise with a blender or food processor: Crack the egg into the blender (or bowl). Add the lemon juice and mustard. Mix the olive and canola oils together in a liquid measuring cup. With the machine running, occasionally stopping it to scrape down the jar (or bowl), gradually drizzle in the oil mixture through the hole in the lid (or the feed tube)—it should take at least a minute to do this—to make a thick mayonnaise.

3. Season the mayonnaise to taste with salt and pepper. Use it immediately. (The mayonnaise can be stored in a covered container and refrigerated for up to 3 days.)

Aïoli: This garlic mayonnaise has gone from being an esoteric Provençal condiment to an American favorite. Stir 2 garlic cloves, crushed through a garlic press, into the finished mayonnaise.

Chipotle Mayonnaise: Put this on a burger and you can skip the ketchup. Stir 1 or 2 minced canned chipotle chilies in adobo and 1 garlic clove, crushed through a garlic press, into the finished mayonnaise.

Herbed Mayonnaise: You can experiment with other herbs, but the ones listed are my favorites. Stir 1 tablespoon finely chopped fresh basil, chives, oregano, parsley, rosemary, or tarragon into the finished mayonnaise.

Pesto Mayonnaise: An especially good condiment for sliced meats and sandwiches. Stir 1 tablespoon finely chopped fresh basil, 1 tablespoon freshly grated Parmesan cheese, and 1 garlic clove, crushed through a garlic press, into the finished mayonnaise.

Rouille: Serve this with fish stews, especially bouillabaisse, or as a dip for artichokes or asparagus. Whisk 2 teaspoons fresh lemon juice and 1 teaspoon tomato paste together in a medium bowl to dissolve the tomato paste. Add 1 cup mayonnaise, 2 garlic cloves, crushed through a garlic press, the finely grated zest of 1 lemon, 1 teaspoon sweet paprika (or smoked sweet paprika), and a pinch of cayenne pepper and mix well.

Sauce Ravigote: A New Orleans classic, this zesty sauce pairs beautifully with seafood. Add 1 finely chopped scallion (white and pale green parts only), 2 tablespoons finely chopped celery, 1 tablespoon spicy brown mustard (preferably Creole-style, such as Zatarain's), 1 tablespoon fresh lemon juice, 1 tablespoon minced fresh flat-leaf parsley, ½ teaspoon hot red pepper sauce, and 1 garlic clove, crushed through a garlic press, to the finished mayonnaise and mix well.

Sauce Verte: I rarely serve poached salmon without this sauce. Mix ¾ cup mayonnaise, ¼ cup plain Greek-style yogurt, 1 tablespoon each finely chopped chives, parsley, and tarragon, the finely grated zest of 1 lemon, 1 tablespoon fresh lemon juice, and an additional 1 teaspoon of Dijon mustard into the finished mayonnaise.

Tartar Sauce: Fried seafood dishes are even better with homemade tartar sauce, and this is much less sweet than the commercial versions. Mix 2 tablespoons dill pickle relish (or sweet pickle relish for a sweeter sauce) or finely chopped cornichons, 1 tablespoon finely chopped fresh flat-leaf parsley, 1 tablespoon drained nonpareil capers, 1 teaspoon Worcestershire sauce, and ¼ teaspoon hot red pepper sauce into the finished mayonnaise.

GRAVY 101
MAKES 2 CUPS GRAVY; 6 TO 8 SERVINGS

Serve with roast poultry, roast beef, or roast pork.
Prep Time: 10 minutes

Cooking Time: 10 minutes

Weeknight Suppers, Family Favorite, Holiday Feasts, Company Fare, Buffet Dish, Cooking Classic

Any time you have pan drippings from a roast, be it red meat or fowl, you have the beginnings of gravy. Just think of gravy as any roux-based sauce: Make a roux from fat and flour, add a liquid, and simmer. That's it. Make the gravy directly in the roasting pan so you are sure to get every last bit of the browned meat juices, as these provide flavor and color.

• The secret to great gravy is measuring. My grandmother would simply stir flour into whatever was in the roasting pan (fat, juices, and browned bits) to make a paste, then add enough broth to thicken the mixture. She was a great lady, but her gravy was unreliable to say the least, because the amount of fat varies with every roast. Separate the fat from the juices and go from there.

• For every cup of gravy, use 1 cup of liquid (the degreased pan juices combined with an appropriate chicken or beef broth), with a roux made from 1½ tablespoons each flour and the fat from the pan. Just multiply this amount as needed. You may only want 1 cup of gravy for a roast chicken, but 2 quarts for a roast turkey. If you run out of fat from the pan, use melted butter.

• Allow ⅓ cup of gravy per person—some people will want more, and some less, so know the appetites of your audience. It's better to make too much gravy and have leftovers than to run out.

• A gravy separator is a great utensil, and even if you use it rarely, it is worth the investment. The 2-cup size is fine for chicken and duck, but for larger birds, use the 4-cup model.

• A flat whisk (also called a roux whisk) is another useful utensil, as it allows you to get into the corners of the pan, and whisks in a wider swath than a narrow whisk. If you have a nonstick roasting pan, use a silicone-coated whisk.

• During roasting, let the drippings evaporate so they brown to a deep mahogany color, as dark drippings will flavor and color the gravy. To stop them from browning too deeply and burning, add broth or water to the pan. I never need to use gravy coloring.

Pan drippings from roast chicken, turkey, goose, beef, or pork

2 cups reduced-sodium chicken or beef broth (see Note), as needed

3 tablespoons all-purpose flour

Kosher salt and freshly ground black pepper

1. Pour the pan drippings into a 2-cup gravy separator (or glass bowl), leaving any browned bits in the bottom of the pan. Let the pan drippings stand for 3 to 5 minutes. Pour off the dark juices from the separator into a liquid measuring cup, leaving the clear fat in the separator. (Or spoon off the fat from the top of the pan drippings in the bowl, and transfer them to a smaller bowl. Pour the degreased juices into a liquid measuring cup.)

2. Evaluate the color of the pan juices, as these will give the gravy its color. If the juices are not a rich, dark brown, pour half of the juices back into the roasting pan. Bring the juices to a boil over high heat and cook until they reduce and darken, about 1 minute. Stir in the remaining juices and return the darkened juices to the measuring cup. (The amount of drippings will decrease, but the finished gravy will be darker and taste better and you don't have to resort to bottled gravy coloring.) Add enough stock to the drippings to measure 2 cups total cooking liquid.

3. Place the roasting pan on top of the stove over medium-low heat. Add 3 tablespoons of the reserved fat to the pan. Whisk the flour into the pan. Let the mixture bubble, whisking constantly, until it turns beige, 1 to 2 minutes. Add the broth mixture and whisk well. (This is your chance to eliminate any lumps, so put some elbow grease into it!) Bring it to a simmer, whisking up the browned bits on the bottom of the pan. Cook, whisking occasionally, until the gravy has thickened and lost any taste of raw flour, 2 to 3 minutes. If the gravy seems too thin, increase the heat to medium and boil until it is as thick as you wish. If the gravy seems too thick, thin it with additional stock. Season to taste with salt and pepper. If desired, strain the gravy through a wire sieve to remove any extraneous bits of drippings. Serve it immediately. (Leftover gravy can be cooled, covered, and refrigerated for up to 3 days.)

Note: If making turkey gravy, use the Giblet Turkey Stock (page 401).

Cream Gravy: For every cup of liquid, use ¾ cup of the stock mixture and ¼ cup heavy cream.
Giblet Gravy: If you have made Giblet Turkey Stock (page 401), finely chop the cooked giblets and neck meat. Add the giblets and neck meat to the finished gravy.
Roast Garlic Gravy: For every 2 cups finished gravy, stir in 1 head Simple Roasted Garlic Cloves (page 159), hulled and mashed.
Wine Gravy: Substitute up to one-fourth of the cooking liquid with dry white wine. For example, for about 2 cups gravy, use 1½ cups of the broth mixture and ½ cup white wine. I do not recommend red wine, though, because it gives the gravy a murky color.
Spiked Gravy: A judicious amount of alcohol heightens the overall flavor of the gravy, but don't add more than the recommended amount or the taste will be overpowering. For every 1 cup of cooking liquid, add 2 tablespoons bourbon, brandy, Cognac, dry sherry, Madeira, dry Marsala, or port.
Herbed Gravy: For every 2 cups gravy, stir in 1 tablespoon minced fresh herbs, such as thyme, sage, rosemary, parsley, chives, or tarragon, or a combination.

CLASSIC PAN SAUCE
MAKES ABOUT ⅔ CUP; 4 SERVINGS

Serve with sautéed steaks, chops, or chicken.
Prep Time: 5 minutes
Cooking Time: 5 minutes
Weeknight Suppers, Family Favorite, Holiday Feasts, Company Fare, Cooking Classic

Whenever you sauté meat or chicken in a skillet, there is a treasure trove of browned pan drippings clinging to the bottom of the pan. It is a crime not to turn these juices (known as a fond *in classic French cuisine terminology) into a quick pan sauce. Because it is so intensely flavored, you only need a couple of tablespoons per serving. The technique is the same for either meat or chicken (just change the broth accordingly) and makes for a few simple variations.*

Pan drippings from sautéed beef, pork, lamb, or
   chicken
2 tablespoons (¼ stick) cold unsalted butter

1 tablespoon finely chopped shallot
1 cup reduced-sodium chicken or beef broth
Kosher salt and freshly ground pepper

1. After the meat or poultry has cooked, transfer it to a large plate and tent it with aluminum foil to keep warm while making the sauce.

2. Remove the skillet from the heat. Tilt the skillet so the pan juices gather in a pool in the corner of the skillet. Skim off and discard the clear fat from the pan juices.

3. Return the skillet to the stove. Add 1 tablespoon of the butter and the shallot. Cook over medium heat, stirring often, until the butter is melted and the shallot is tender, about 1 minute. Pour in the broth and increase the heat to high. Bring the broth to a boil, scraping up the browned bits in the skillet with a wooden spoon. Cook until the liquid has reduced by about one-third, about 1 minute. Remove it from the heat and add the remaining 1 tablespoon butter. Whisk until the sauce has absorbed the butter. Season to taste with salt and pepper.

4. Transfer each serving of the meat or poultry to a dinner plate. Drizzle each with the sauce and serve.

Herb Pan Sauce: Just before serving, add 1 to 2 teaspoons finely chopped fresh flat-leaf parsley, thyme, rosemary, tarragon, or sage to the sauce.

Dijon Pan Sauce: Whisk 1 tablespoon Dijon mustard into the sauce with the broth.

Cream Pan Sauce: Substitute ¼ cup heavy cream for an equal amount of the chicken or beef broth.

Wine Pan Sauce: Before adding the broth, stir ¼ cup dry white wine or vermouth into the skillet and cook until it is reduced to 1 tablespoon, about 30 seconds.

ACKNOWLEDGMENTS

When a writer creates a cookbook, it is always a labor of love. With a book as large as this one, truer words were never spoken. In addition, it was a group effort, with many good friends and colleagues contributing their family favorites. Thanks to Joan Authenrieth, David Bonom, Mary Cleaver, Annie Denver, Norene Gilletz, Barbara Scott Goodman, Beth Hensperger, Dana Jacobi, Katy Keck, Suzanne Kindle, Julie Mitenberger, Michael Northern, Yvonne Ortiz, and Michael Tyrell for their recipes. Thanks also to Laura Baddish for marketing support.

On the business end of my life as a cook and a writer, my agent, Susan Ginsburg, has given me the kind of support that you would possibly expect from a family member, which, after all of the years we've worked together, she has become. Her assistant, Stacy Testa, is an invaluable member of our trio.

I am very grateful to my editor at Ballantine, Pamela Cannon, for her priceless help and support from the first day of this book's conception, and to her assistant, Betsy Wilson, whose efficiency kept us all on track. Alison Masciovecchio and Quinne Rogers helped get the word out. Nancy Delia dealt with the various passes of the book as the massive manuscript went through the editing process. Ann Rolke Smith was my hard-working copy editor. Proofreaders Barbara Greenberg, Maggie Carr, and Muriel Jorgensen did a thorough job. Jacket designer Anna Bauer and book designer Diane Hobbing were responsible for the book's graphics. And Ben Fink created the beautiful images of the food.

Many of the recipes in this book required a Dutch oven, and Le Creuset sent over some wonderful pots for me to use in testing. *Merci.*

My readers see two names over and over again in my books. My (now) husband, Patrick Fisher, has cleaned up after me and lent his palate to tasting over twenty-five years of recipe testing. For the same period (which is impossible for me to believe, but true), Diane Kniss has tirelessly worked by my side in the kitchen and been the best friend one could every hope for. Writing a book is never easy, but these two can make it fun.

INDEX

ABOUT THE AUTHOR

Rick Rodgers is an award-winning cookbook author and cooking teacher and the writer of more than forty cookbooks on subjects from baking to grilling and more. Rodgers often works behind the scenes as a recipe tester, co-author, and consultant on cookbooks by other authors, including Lilly Pulitzer and Sarabeth Levine of Sarabeth's Bakery. He has also written corporate cookbooks for clients such as Kingsford Charcoal and Sur La Table, as well as many titles for Williams-Sonoma. Rodgers's recipes have appeared in *Bon Appétit, Cooking Light, Men's Health, Food and Wine,* and *Fine Cooking,* among other magazines. He has received *Bon Appétit* Magazine's Food and Entertaining Award as Outstanding Cooking Teacher and an IACP Cookbook Award for *The Chelsea Market Cookbook*. Rick Rodgers has been guest chef on all of the national morning shows.

ABOUT THE TYPE

This book was set in Minion, a 1990 Adobe Originals typeface by Robert Slimbach (b. 1956). Minion is inspired by classical, old-style typefaces of the late Renaissance, a period of elegant, beautiful, and highly readable type designs. Created primarily for text setting, Minion combines the aesthetic and functional qualities that make text type highly readable with the versatility of digital technology.